THE
AMERICAN
PRESIDENCY

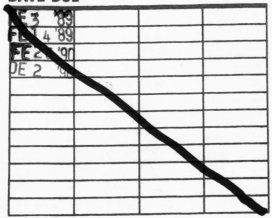

THE
AMERICAN
PRESIDENCY

A New Perspective

JAMES W. DAVIS
Western Washington University

HARPER & ROW, PUBLISHERS, New York
Cambridge, Philadelphia, San Francisco, Washington,
London, Mexico City, São Paulo, Singapore, Sydney

1817

Sponsoring Editor: Robert Miller
Project Editors: Bonnie Biller/Carla Kay
Cover Design: 20/20 Services Inc.
Text Art: Fineline Illustrations
Production Manager: Willie Lane
Compositor: ComCom Division of Haddon Craftsmen
Printer and Binder: R. R. Donnelley and Sons

THE AMERICAN PRESIDENCY: A New Perspective

Library of Congress Cataloging in Publication Data

Davis, James W., 1920–
  The American presidency.

  Includes index.
  1. Presidents—United States. I. Title.
JK516.D38 1987   321.8'042   86–22803
ISBN 0–06–041558–4

86 87 88 89 9 8 7 6 5 4 3 2 1

Contents

PREFACE

The American presidency, James MacGregor Burns reminds us, is "our most indispensable and dangerous governmental institution." Plainly, our constitutional system of shared powers cannot function effectively—indeed, it is rudderless—without a strong chief executive, especially in times of national crisis. Still, there is the danger that the imperial presidency of the 1960s and early 1970s will reappear. (Some critics insist that President Reagan's actions in Lebanon, Grenada, Nicaragua, and Libya signal the return of the imperial presidency.)

Recently, Theodore J. Lowi has warned against the emergence of the plebiscitarian president, a chief executive who develops a popular mass base, relies on his personal appeal rather than political bargaining to achieve his goals, and seeks to govern with minimal support from Congress.[1] Even more frightening, the possibility exists that an erratic, power-driven president might unilaterally order the Pentagon to launch an all-out nuclear attack against the Soviet Union.

Another presidential scholar, Thomas E. Cronin, has noted: "The ultimate paradox of the modern presidency is that it is always too powerful and yet always inadequate."[2] Although there continues to be disagreement over whether the president is too powerful or inadequate to cope with the nation's endless problems, we should remember that the presidency is always a composite of the office and the occupant. Indeed, the dimensions of presidential power at any given moment will be the sum of the incumbent's conception of this high office and the level of energy he devotes to carrying out his constitutional responsibilities. History shows us that presidential power varies considerably with each president's capacity to influence and shape the course of domestic and international events.

Presidential power, it seems clear, is dependent at any given time upon

[1]Theodore J. Lowi, *The Personal President* (Ithaca, NY: Cornell University Press, 1985), esp. Chap. 6.
[2]Thomas E. Cronin, *The State of the Presidency,* 2nd ed. (Boston: Little, Brown, 1980), p. 22.

several factors: (1) the formal constitutional sources of executive authority; (2) the current power balance between president and Congress; (3) the personal attributes and governing style of the chief executive; (4) the particular set of economic conditions or international crises confronting the nation; (5) the level of the president's popularity and the degree to which he enjoys the public's trust and confidence.

Because these factors constantly change, the dimensions of presidential power never remain static for long. It is this unpredictable shifting tide of presidential power that never ceases to fascinate presidential watchers. A single national election, for example, can produce a remarkable shift in national leadership. The reader need not search far for confirmation of this observation. Compared to the Herbert Hoover presidency, the Franklin D. Roosevelt presidency is scarcely recognizable. Similarly, the Ronald Reagan presidency bears little resemblance to that of his predecessor, Jimmy Carter. But no matter who occupies the White House these days, the demands placed on the presidency by the American public continue to escalate.

The central theme of this text is that the public's high expectations of the president—maintenance of full employment, low inflation, reduced taxes, increased retirement benefits for senior citizens, averting nuclear war, halting international terrorism, avoidance of military entanglements—continue to grow. At the same time the president, in face of a resurgent Congress, the ever-growing number of special interest groups seeking to maximize their power and influence, the growing threat of foreign economic competition, and huge national deficits, finds himself unable to fulfill these exaggerated expectations. And failure to satisfy these public expectations has in recent years led to such disenchantment with the White House occupant that until Ronald Reagan's reelection, we have had a series of revolving-door, one-term presidencies.

Another major underlying theme of this text is the central role that network television plays as an instrument of presidential leadership. Unlike nineteenth-century presidents, who lacked access to mass communications, modern presidents regularly appear before national audiences numbering 50 million or more to deliver the State of the Union address, the annual budget message, or the annual economic report. To help promote and maintain their dominant leadership role, presidents frequently hold televised press conferences during prime-time evening hours, or the president may decide to announce a major foreign policy initiative via network television.

"Going public" on television does not end here. Foreign travel to China, visiting the cemetery near the Normandy beaches to honor America's fallen heroes, greeting visiting foreign heads of state, congratulating the Olympic gold medal winners on the White House lawn—all these events enhance the president's standing with the American public. Furthermore, such popularity gives him added leverage in pushing his programs through Congress. Indeed, the president's ultimate goal in going public is not the American voter, but the members of Congress—often reluctant partners in some of the president's top-priority legislative projects. More than anything else, except the power to wage nuclear war, the growth of the "public presidency" and the widespread use of mass communication differentiates the presidential leadership of recent chief executives from that of their nineteenth-century predecessors.

My decision to write this text stems from thirty-five years of president watching. Much of my scholarly activity during this period has been devoted to monitoring and writing about the presidential nominating process. Over the past quarter-century I have also had the privilege of observing first-hand more than two dozen presidential hopefuls campaigning for the nation's highest nomination, including all four successful convention nominees—Kennedy, Nixon, Carter, and Reagan. But concentrating on presidential nominations has meant neglecting a far more important subject—the performance of these national leaders once they reached the White House. From my viewpoint, the next logical step therefore seemed to call for a study of the White House occupants and the institutionalized presidency. Though this text concentrates primarily on the twentieth-century presidency, the constitutional growth of the presidency since its inception also receives careful scrutiny.

OVERVIEW OF THE BOOK

We begin with overview chapters to set the context. Chapter 1 sketches the major thesis of the text—namely, the rising level of public expectations of the American president versus the declining ability of our presidents to meet or satisfy these escalating demands. Chapter 2 provides an overview of the presidency from our first chief executive, George Washington, to Ronald Reagan, the fortieth president of the United States. Chapters 3 and 4 explore the growth of popular participation in the nominating process and winning strategies in presidential elections. Chapter 5 analyzes the powerful impact television has had upon the presidency over the past three decades.

Then we turn to the functions of the office. In Chapter 6 we deal with the president's role as chief legislator. Chapter 7 discusses the president's constitutional responsibility as commander in chief, and Chapter 8 covers the president's closely related responsibilities as chief diplomat. Chapter 9 analyzes the president's duties as chief executive, and Chapter 10 discusses the declining influence of the president as party leader in an era of party "decomposition" and potential party realignment. Chapter 11 explores the relations between the president and the judiciary and the Court's role in legitimating and sometimes constraining the nation's leaders. Chapter 12 examines the rise of the rhetorical presidency. Chapter 13 explores the president's role as overseer of the economy.

The last few chapters are devoted to proposals for reform and some institutional changes. In Chapter 14, the growing importance of the vice-presidency is analyzed and assessed. Chapter 15 reviews the leading proposals advanced by presidential critics over the years to reform the presidency, but all—except repeal of the Twenty-second Amendment—are rejected as offering only false hopes of improvement over the existing presidential office. Finally, in Chapter 16 we take a look at the reciprocal relationship between presidential power and popular support and conclude that the country need not be inevitably saddled with a succession of one-term presidencies in the future.

ACKNOWLEDGMENTS

During the preparation of this book I have benefitted tremendously from the advice and counsel of Professor William C. Spragens, Bowling Green State University; Michael Baruch Grossman, Towson State University; Tom Patterson, Syracuse University; Herbert E. Alexander, Citizens' Research Foundation; Roger G. Brown, University of North Carolina at Charlotte; and Robert L. Dudley, George Mason University. Several anonymous reviewers for Harper & Row have been invaluable in providing suggestions for structural changes and chapter revisions. Over the years I have also received encouragement from the late Theodore H. White, whose classic *The Making of the President* series blazed the trail for all students of the presidential nominating process.

Publication of this book would not have been possible without the solid editorial support of Executive Editor Marianne J. Russell; Sponsoring Editor Robert Miller; my project editors, Bonnie Biller and Carla Kay; my copy editor, Jeannine Ciliotta; and my proofreader, Genevieve Coyne. Nor would this study have been completed on schedule without the permission of Barron's Education Series, publisher of my jointly authored (with Delbert Ringquist) *The President and Congress: Toward a New Power Balance,* to quote from this early post-Watergate paperback.

My special thanks go to Dean Peter J. Elich, College of Arts and Sciences, and Dean of Graduate Studies Sam Kelly, Western Washington University, who both provided needed secretarial and financial assistance to complete this study. I wish to express my special personal appreciation to Mrs. Patricia Houtchens, secretary, College of Arts and Sciences, who has now efficiently typed three book manuscripts for me. I would also like to thank Mrs. Gail Fox, Bureau of Faculty Research, who helped prepare the final draft.

Finally, this study would not have been undertaken without the encouragement and support of my wife, Nanette, and my six children (now grown)—Katherine, Susan, Elizabeth, Timothy, Michael, and Patricia. It is to them that I dedicate this book.

James W. Davis

chapter 1

Introduction

Since the advent of the New Deal in the 1930s, the image of the president as the nation's chief domestic problem solver has grown along with the expansion of the federal government's power and influence. Prior to 1933, domestic public policy was handled almost exclusively at the state and local level. The federal government rarely impinged on the daily lives of most Americans. But with the nation reeling from the Great Depression, the citizenry turned to President Franklin D. Roosevelt to lead the country out of economic chaos. Congress responded to FDR's leadership and passed a host of reform measures covering unemployment insurance, social security, agriculture, banking, the stock market, and collective bargaining for unions, to mention only part of the list. Henceforth, the White House assumed the chief responsibility for the nation's welfare. The Great Society legislation of the Kennedy-Johnson years extended federal involvement in education, civil rights, health care, urban renewal, and transportation. Popular expectations for federal assistance, no matter what the need, led directly to the White House steps. If a solution was to be found, the president and his staff were expected to find it. From FDR's administration onward, the White House, like it or not, came to assume the chief responsibility for setting the domestic agenda.

As long as the American economy continued to expand after World War II, presidents were able to deliver on most of their promises. But the 1970s marked an end of the era of unlimited growth and the seemingly inexhaustible supply of natural resources, especially oil. Above all else, the war in Vietnam brought a sudden awakening that maintaining many federal programs, particularly in light of rampant inflation and foreign competition, could not be continued indefinitely. Public demands on and expectations of the federal government,

1

especially the president, continued to grow, even in the face of chronic economic dislocation. By the mid-1970s, public frustration and disappointment with the nation's leadership surfaced at a steadily rising tempo, as more and more interest groups sought to gain new benefits or carefully protect those won during earlier struggles. No longer did presidents have the luxury of developing new comprehensive federal programs to win over voters or major interest groups. For the White House, the era of open-ended federal assistance had truly come to a halt. Paul C. Light, a specialist on presidential domestic policy, has put it more bluntly: The nation now has a "no-win" presidency in domestic affairs.[1]

As we move ever closer to the 200th anniversary of the founding of the Republic, the public's expectations of the president's public and private conduct, his style of leadership, and his policy performance remain high and show no signs of abating. The reasons for these high expectations are not hard to find. Presidential scholar George C. Edwards III has explained it this way: "Promises made on the campaign trail and once in office, the president's prominence, political socialization focused on greater former presidents, faulty memories of past chief executives, the public's penchant for personalizing complex issues, and its lack of understanding of the president's power all serve to maintain and increase public expectations of the president."[2] According to one survey in 1980, approximately 75 percent of the American people, when questioned, admitted that their expectations of the president were unfairly high.[3] It is the difference between what some Americans imagine the president to be and what he is that often leads to disappointment and disenchantment with the incumbent.

EXAGGERATED PUBLIC EXPECTATIONS

Typically, the public expects the president to anticipate problems. Failing that, the public expects the president to provide imaginative solutions. In truth, as the respected British commentator Godfrey Hodgson has put it: "The American people expect too much of their presidents. They demand more from them than any man or woman is going to be able to give."[4] It is this gap between limited presidential power and the all-encompassing responsibilities of the American chief executive—indeed, the impossibility of presidents meeting these exaggerated expectations—that constitutes the central theme of this text.

To narrow the gap between public expectations of the president and his ability to meet public goals, Thomas E. Cronin has urged that we scale down our presidential expectations: "When Americans realize that the presidency is incapable of dealing with everything well, and that politics in general is not suited to provide answers to every social and economic malaise, then there may be less savaging of the president."[5]

Part of the explanation for the public's lofty expectations of the president stems from a lack of understanding of the context in which presidential decision making takes place, especially with respect to his chief rival power base—Congress. As Richard E. Neustadt pointed out in his celebrated study, *Presidential Power,* first published in 1960, a president can rarely command; he must devote most of his time persuading people to join, help, and vote with him.[6]

The phenomenon of rising public expectations for our president, it should be emphasized, is a twentieth-century development. Clearly, it is an outgrowth of the United States' emergence as a world power, the rapid industrialization and urbanization of the nation, the rise of the welfare state, and the remarkable growth of mass communications. Starting with Theodore Roosevelt and Woodrow Wilson, the American public turned increasingly toward the White House to find answers to pressing national problems and to respond to recurring international crises. Most nineteenth-century presidents, by contrast, encountered few public demands.

In the area of policymaking, public expectations of the president center on his ensuring peace, prosperity, and security. Table 1.1 shows the results of polls conducted in December 1976 and 1980, following the elections of Presidents Carter and Reagan. Performance expectations of each president, it can be seen, are high and cover a wide range of policy areas.

Over the past two centuries, we have vastly multiplied the requirements for presidential leadership, but we have not matched this expansion by giving the president sufficient tools to do the job. Frequently, it appears public expectations are too high to be fulfilled by one person alone. In the words of Thomas E. Cronin: "We overestimate the powers of the office and underestimate the economic, social and cultural factors that so often shape presidential performance and so greatly shape the people we place in the presidency."[7] Still, we are demanding more, not less, of our presidents. "It would take a political superman to do all the things Americans want their presidents to do," is the way Godfrey Hodgson, the British observer, has assessed the president's responsibilities. Hodgson, who has watched five American presidents over a period of nearly two decades, has elaborated further on the overloading of the presidency:

> He must simultaneously conduct the diplomacy of a superpower, put together separate coalitions to enact every piece of legislation required by a vast and complex society, manage the economy, command the armed forces, serve as a spiritual example and inspiration, respond to every emergency.[8]

Table 1.1 EARLY EXPECTATIONS OF PRESIDENTS CARTER AND REAGAN

Response to the question: "Here are some things various people have said are likely to happen once Governor Carter (Governor Reagan) becomes President. (Card shown respondent.) Would you read down that list and for each one will you tell me whether you think it is something that can be expected of him during the next four years or something that cannot be expected of him?"

Expectation	Percent of public holding expectation	
	Carter	Reagan
Reduce unemployment	72%	69%
Reduce inflation	*	66
Reduce cost of government	59	70
Reorganize government for more efficiency	81	76
Deal effectively with foreign policy	79	77
Make our national defense strong**	81	89

*Not available.
**In December, 1976, "Keep our national defense strong."
Source: "Early Expectations: Comparing Chief Executives," *Public Opinion,* February–March 1981, p. 39, as cited in George C. Edwards III, *The Public Presidency* (New York: St. Martin's Press, 1983), p. 189. Surveys by the Roper Organization, December 1976 and December 6–13, 1980.

The concept of exaggerated public expectations was never put better than by one of President Franklin D. Roosevelt's advisors, Louis Brownlow, more than thirty years ago: ". . . the nation expects more of the President than he can possibly do; more than we give him either the authority or the means to do. Thus, expecting from him the impossible, inevitably we shall be disappointed in his performance."[9]

LIMITED PRESIDENTIAL POWER

Even though the president is the most prominent figure in American politics and the focal point of our expectations for public policymaking, he is not in a position to satisfy many of the needs of the electorate. Indeed, in recent years there has been a "substantial enlargement of presidential responsibilities, explicit and implied, but without a corresponding increase in presidential power."[10] Less than a month before he was assassinated, President John F. Kennedy remarked: "The powers of the presidency are often described. Its limitations should be occasionally remembered."[11] Americans nevertheless want presidents to solve problems. But some foreign issues—for example, international terrorism, the pricing policies of the international oil cartel—are either beyond presidential influence or control, or involve such drastic responses that the high cost of undertaking them would not be commensurate with the risks wagered. On the domestic front, the president's ability to implement policy is circumscribed by the separation of powers, a recently decentralized power structure in Congress, the declining number of cross-issue coalitions needed to pass legislation, a slow-moving federal bureaucracy, and the potent influence of special interest groups opposed to the redistribution of power. Also, the mass media, preoccupied with results, do not discuss how complicated the processes of governmental change are; nor do they convey the difficult tradeoffs often involved in important decisions.

Because some demands on the presidency are becoming more insistent at the same time as they are getting harder to meet, presidential nominees and recently elected presidents may sometimes overpromise and overextend themselves. Persistent expectations that a president can direct sweeping changes encourage presidents to attempt more than they can accomplish in any single term. In some cases, the negative impact of the public's high expectations of the president can be of his own making—and sometimes his undoing. Jimmy Carter, for example, was his own worst enemy in this matter. Of all the twentieth-century presidents, Carter made the most campaign pledges.[12] Repeatedly, he became the victim of his own excessive promises. Both before and after entering the White House, he set extremely high goals that probably no president could have fulfilled, certainly not in his first year in office. Yet Carter pledged during his election campaign to present a complete reform of the welfare system by the first of May of his first year in office. He promised to balance the budget and reduce unemployment to 3 percent by 1980, and to keep his administration free of scandal.[13] But when the federal books did not balance by 1980 and unemployment stood at 7.5 percent and when his director of the Office of Management and Budget Bert

Lance had to step down to defend himself in a Georgia trial involving questionable banking activities (he was acquitted), Carter's stock fell sharply in the public's eyes (see Table 1.2).

Although President Reagan too promised to balance the budget during his 1980 election campaign and subsequently failed to do so, the public did not seem to hold him up to the same high standards as President Carter because he had fulfilled two other campaign promises—to cut taxes and to step up military preparedness. Moreover, the economic recovery, which began in early 1983, and the continued reduction in the inflation rate (down to less than 4 percent in late 1984) also helped the Reagan administration shift public attention away from the continued unbalanced budgets and the record-breaking deficits.

President Reagan, unlike Carter, developed a sophisticated strategy to avoid much of the political fallout from unfulfilled campaign promises. As Jeff Fishel has pointed out: "Reagan permitted some of his controversial proposals, the social issues, for example, to slide on and off the agenda, without seeming to alter the rhetoric of his conservative principles in supporting them. The White House packaged this stance as proof that he is still a 'strong' leader, undercut by a willful Congress that is dominated by irresponsible Democrats."[14] Furthermore, the Reagan administration did not openly and completely reverse itself on very many of its campaign promises, partly because Reagan made fewer concrete promises than many predecessors, and partly because "the administration opted for a strategy of deferring or not acting rather than clearly repudiating their commitments."[15]

CONTRADICTORY EXPECTATIONS

Paradoxically, public expectations of the president are not only high, but also frequently contradictory. Presidents, faced with contradictory expectations, find it difficult to escape criticism and loss of approval—no matter what course of action they take. Most voters want better education and improved health services but are against increased taxes; they favor economic development but without damage to the environment; they favor a strong defense but are against another Vietnam—and so on. Despite the contradictions inherent in these expectations, the public nevertheless holds the president accountable for meeting them. That

Table 1.2 POLITICAL FALLOUT FROM PRESIDENT CARTER'S JOB PERFORMANCE

President Carter is partly, largely, or primarily to blame:	Percent agree
Continued inflation	78%
High energy prices	68
Gasoline shortage	61

Source: NBC—AP Poll, July 16–17, 1979, cited in Thomas E. Cronin, "Looking for Leadership, 1980," *Public Opinion,* February/March 1980, p. 15, as cited in George C. Edwards III, *The Public Presidency* (New York: St. Martin's Press, 1983), p. 189.

the public's expectations of the president are not only high but also contradictory does not seem to matter; the public holds the expectations anyway. Moreover, the greater the expectations of the chief executive, the more the potential for disappointment. While some presidents may succeed in educating the public to alter their expectations, George C. Edwards III has noted: "The public's views change slowly and usually the changes that take place only create additional burdens for the president."[16]

Lack of programmatic success usually translates into declining approval ratings in the opinion polls. Except for Eisenhower and Reagan, all post-World War II presidents have suffered a notable decline in approval ratings as their terms have drawn to a close (see Table 1.3).

In the age of television, presidents are portrayed and perceived as successful chief executives less frequently than in the pre-TV era. Television has raised people's expectations of what the president can and should do, and it has made it more difficult for the president to measure up to these expectations. Moreover, as Austin Ranney has observed, television "has made most government achievements seem transitory, unimportant, and even illusionary."[17] Ranney continues, "presidents seem to be more vulnerable in the television age than they were before, and it may be that in the future it will be just as unusual for an incumbent president to be reelected as it used to be for one to be defeated."[18]

Table 1.3   AVERAGE YEARLY PRESIDENTIAL APPROVAL, 1953–1985 (GALLUP POLL)

Year	Percent approval	Year	Percent approval
1953	68%	1970	58%
1954	66	1971	51
1955	71	1972	58
1956	73	1973	43
1957	64	1974	36
1958	54	1975	44
1959	64	1976	49
1960	61	1977	63
1961	76	1978	45
1962	71	1979	38
1963	65	1980	42
1964	75	1981	58
1965	66	1982	44
1966	50	1983	44
1967	44	1984	56
1968	43	1985	61
1969	63		

Sources: Data for the period 1953–1980 are from Gallup polls cited in George C. Edwards III, *The Public Presidency* (New York: St. Martin's Press, 1983), p. 22; for the period 1981–1984, the percentages are from the *Gallup Report,* December 1981, 1982, 1983, and 1984. The 1985 percentage is from *The New York Times,* June 15, 1986.

FEWER CURTAIN CALLS IN THE SECOND TERM

While President Reagan, unlike several of his recent predecessors, defied recent history by winning reelection, the first year of his second term has seen his influence erode perceptibly. Whereas he was able to proclaim a number of symbolic victories during his first term, such as the invasion of Grenada in October 1983, his overall record of problem solving has fallen somewhat short of public expectations. In the first year of his second term, for example, the annual national deficit remained at nearly $200 billion; moreover, the total national debt had more than doubled during President Reagan's first term (from $600 billion to $1.3 trillion). The foreign trade deficit also hit a record-breaking $150 billion in 1985.

After dominating Congress in his first term and honoring his 1980 campaign pledges for a tax cut, a sharp military buildup, and slashes in social welfare spending, President Reagan and his staff found themselves early in the second term compromising on foreign policy and adjusting their posture on several domestic issues. In 1985, despite his overwhelming victory in the 1984 election, Reagan was also forced within four months after his second inauguration to compromise with Congress on nonmilitary aid to Nicaraguan Contra rebels, accept a limit of 50 MX missiles (instead of the 100 requested by the White House) to be deployed in existing silos, and agree to a trim in the stepped-up military budget—all a major departure from relations with Congress during his first four years in the White House.

How much of this decline in presidential influence could be attributed to the fact that President Reagan became a lame duck president the day after his reelection in November 1984? It is clearly too early to answer this question. But White House insiders reportedly conceded that, despite Mr. Reagan's 65 percent approval rating in the September 1985 Gallup poll, the fact that he is in his final term has affected his relations with an increasingly independent Congress.[19]

Major domestic and international problems that Mr. Reagan shunted aside or dismissed as unimportant during his reelection campaign, such as the huge annual deficit, the skyrocketing international trade balance, and the flood of cheap imported goods, refused to go away. President Reagan's "sunny, not a care in the world style" of leadership no longer seemed to fit the mood of the country as the mounting problems both at home and abroad demanded greater attention than Mr. Reagan was prepared to give them. During the summer of 1985 Mr. Reagan obtained a reprieve for dealing with these seemingly intractable problems when he was hospitalized for colon cancer surgery. But the growing inability of the president to deflate the mounting national pressure on the White House to come up with solutions, coupled with the growing determination of Congress to deal with such matters as protectionism, deficit reduction, and limitations on military spending, underscores the major thesis of this text: The gap between the public expectations of presidents and their inability to resolve major domestic and international problems remains wide and may be getting wider.

Even his own Republican party's congressional leadership, concerned that the White House was neglecting or mishandling many of the key issues likely to be at the center of the 1986 midterm elections, was by the summer of 1985 in open conflict with President Reagan on a wide range of foreign policy and domestic questions. Heavy pressure from Capitol Hill, much of it from GOP members, forced Reagan to reassess, and in some cases modify, his position on military spending, sanctions against the Union of South Africa to protest its *apartheid* (segregation) policy, protectionist trade policies, and a number of other issues. President Reagan's top priority—tax reform—had been pushed far down the ladder of the congressional agenda. Even the President's 1985 "fall offensive" campaign, which included almost a dozen weekly speeches around the country, failed to persuade congressional leaders, even from his own party, to give tax reform high billing.

Longtime national party observers recognize that it is not unusual for members of the congressional wing of the president's party to assert its independence from their president before a midterm election. In Reagan's case, his successful reelection practically invited this rupture. In that campaign the main themes were a rebirth in the nation, "American standing tall," and "four more years." Virtually no effort was made to outline a second-term agenda. In a sense, President Reagan may have become a victim of his own electoral success. Indeed, once the euphoria of his reelection victory wore off, Reagan had to respond to a number of issues that had lurked in the background during his race against former Vice President Mondale.

Reagan's inability to pull off a repeat performance of his first-term assault on federal social programs demonstrated that even a newly reelected president with a big popular mandate will be hard-pressed to overcome the built-in checks and balances of the American political system. Reagan soon learned that putting together a winning electoral coalition for a second time is not the same as constructing a successful governing coalition. Faced with divided control of Congress, especially a restless GOP majority in the Senate (one-third of whom faced reelection in 1986), President Reagan was forced, less than nine months into his second term, to make further "preemptive compromises" with Congress that would have been unheard of during his first term.

Reluctantly, Reagan bowed to congressional pressure in early September 1985 and announced the imposition of limited sanctions against the government of South Africa. A few days earlier, he had responded to aggressive bipartisan congressional pressure to limit foreign imports by announcing moves against several major American allies for "unfair trading practices."[20] In any event, President Reagan's inability to maintain the momentum of the early months of his first term should come as no great surprise. Indeed, presidential scholar Thomas E. Cronin has commented: "The more we learn about the workings of the presidency, the more it appears that the president cannot act as serious initiator of reforms in more than a few areas at a time."[21] The built-in constraints of the American constitutional system will frequently prevent most presidents— unless there is a national emergency—from measuring up to the high expectations the American public establishes for its chief executives. Throughout the text, we will return again and again to this underlying theme in our study of the presidency.

NOTES

1. Paul C. Light, *The President's Agenda* (Baltimore: Johns Hopkins University Press, 1982), 11–12, 202–233.
2. George C. Edwards III, *The Public Presidency* (New York: St. Martin's Press, 1983), 188.
3. *Every Four Years: A Study of the Presidency,* Public Broadcasting Service, 1980, p. 17, as cited by Robert E. Denton, Jr., "On 'Becoming' President of the United States: The Interaction of the Office with the Office Holder," *Presidential Studies Quarterly,* 13 (Summer 1983), 371.
4. Godfrey Hodgson, *All Things to All Men* (New York: Simon and Schuster, 1980), 238–239.
5. Thomas E. Cronin, *The State of the Presidency,* 2nd ed. (Boston: Little, Brown, 1980), 24.
6. Richard E. Neustadt, *Presidential Power* (New York: Wiley, 1960).
7. Cronin, *The State of the Presidency,* 2.
8. Hodgson, *All Things to All Men,* 239.
9. Louis Brownlow, "What We Expect the President to Do," excerpted from his *The President and the Presidency* (Chicago: University of Chicago Press, 1949), 52–56, 62–76, reprinted in Aaron Wilddavsky, ed., *The Presidency* (Boston: Little, Brown, 1969), 35.
10. Robert Shogan, *None of the Above* (New York: New American Library, 1982), 13.
11. As cited in Ben W. Heineman, Jr., and Curtiss A. Hessler, *Memorandum for the President* (New York: Random House, 1980), 9.
12. Michael G. Krukones, "The Campaign Promises of Jimmy Carter: Accomplishments and Failures," *Presidential Studies Quarterly,* 15 (Winter 1985), p. 143; for further discussion, see Jeff Fishel, *Presidents and Promises* (Washington, DC: Congressional Quarterly Press, 1985), 57–120.
13. Krukones found that President Carter fulfilled nearly 60 percent of his campaign pledges, but his failure to fulfill major campaign pledges such as curbing unemployment and inflation created a strong negative public reaction. Krukones concluded that fulfilling a respectable percentage of campaign pledges may not be as important for presidential success as making good on pledges which are most important to the electorate. Ibid., 130, 143.
14. Fishel, *Presidents and Promises,* 170.
15. Ibid., 173
16. Edwards, *The Public Presidency,* 187.
17. Austin Ranney, *Channels of Power* (Washington, DC: American Enterprise Institute, 1984), 174.
18. Ibid., 147–148.
19. Bernard Weinraub, *The New York Times,* September 9, 1985.
20. Ibid.
21. Cronin, *The State of the Presidency,* 375.

chapter *2*

The Presidency: From Washington to Reagan

Since World War II, the president of the United States has become the most powerful leader in the free world. His military powers are so vast that they rival those of any modern dictator. By comparison, the Caesars of ancient Rome would rank as mere provincial governors. Indeed, with the single push of a button, the modern American president could launch an intercontinental missile attack that would, in all probability, lead to a world holocaust. Contrast the magnitude of power exercised by the modern president with the limited authority wielded by the nation's first president, George Washington, in the newly established republic of 3 million people.

How the presidency of this infant American republic evolved over two centuries, despite periods of contraction, into an office of awesome power will be the main theme of this chapter. Our survey will also reveal that, for long periods in the nineteenth century, Congress clearly overshadowed a series of weak presidents. We will examine several factors that account for the rise of the powerful presidency in the twentieth century, as well as the impact of two world wars and the development of nuclear weaponry on the nation's highest office. We need to look closely at the "heroic" presidency of the 1950s and early 1960s and the growth of the "imperial presidency" in the Johnson-Nixon years. Congressional reaction to an expanding presidency and Watergate led to the post-imperial presidency—some called it the "imperiled presidency." In a final section we look at the resurgence of presidential power under Ronald Reagan and reconfirm a thesis developed early in the chapter—that the presidency is a composite of the office, and the occupant and the dimensions of executive power at any given time in our history are mainly the interrelated consequences of the incumbent's personality and energy, plus his conception of the office.

ABSENCE OF EXECUTIVE LEADERSHIP: BEFORE 1787

The evolution of the American presidency began during the 1780s as the thirteen former colonies floundered in economic stagnation and interstate rivalries under the Articles of Confederation. Within the states, the former colonists insisted that power be centered in the legislature. In most states the American governor, or the president as he was called in several states, became a figurehead. His term was for one year, except in South Carolina (where it was two) and in Delaware (where it was three).

Governors were chosen by the legislature and were therefore creatures of a popularly elected body. State constitution writers left the executive branch purposely fragmented. In all states except Pennsylvania, the governor shared power with a council chosen by the legislature. Most of the enumerated powers and functions were subject to council veto. If any question over the division of power arose, the legislature generally settled it in its own favor. In Massachusetts the governor was slightly less circumscribed—he possessed the veto power, subject to an override by two-thirds of the legislature.[1] Only in New York could the governor be termed a strong executive. Significantly, the New York governorship served as the chief model used by the Founding Fathers in outlining many of the powers and functions assigned to the future president of the United States.[2]

The Articles of Confederation provided for no chief executive; all decision making was handled by a five-member committee of representatives. Routine decisions on foreign policy, the levying of assessments against each of the thirteen states (since the Confederation had no power to tax), and the maintenance of the small armed force and navy were left to the committee.[3] But since any major decision required the agreement of nine out of thirteen states, decision making by the committee was, more often than not, hamstrung or postponed. The simmering feuds between states over the imposition of tariffs, the nearly worthless currency, and the threat to private property posed by the Shays's Rebellion in western Massachusetts all generated concern over the viability of the newly established Confederation. To the more thoughtful state leaders, the weakest link in the Confederation was the absence of an independent executive. State leaders were increasingly concerned about the inability of the Confederation to carry out the governmental responsibilities of the young nation. The general impotence of the Confederation government, the badly battered economy, and the threat of possible foreign intervention all pointed toward the compelling need for strong leadership within the young nation. It was this chaotic state of affairs that faced the Philadelphia convention when the Founding Fathers met in the late spring of 1787.

ESTABLISHING A CHIEF EXECUTIVE

While deploring the absence of leadership within the Articles of Confederation, several members of the convention expressed considerable misgivings about the excesses of the state legislatures during the American Revolution and afterward. Drawing from his observations of state legislatures during the period, James Madison stated: "Experience had proved a tendency in our government to throw all power into the legislative vortex. The executives of the states are in general little more than Cyphers."⁴ Madison, who had been won over by the "presidentialists" during the course of the convention, viewed an independent executive as an essential counterpoise to an all-powerful legislature.

Most of the delegates to the Philadelphia convention, however, were "congressionalists," suspicious of executive power—a carryover from the days of the hated colonial governors. Several convention leaders—Gouverneur Morris, James Wilson, George Washington, and Alexander Hamilton—favored a strong and forceful executive. The ability of this minority of "presidentialists" to outmaneuver the dominant "congressionalist" majority and establish a greatly strengthened executive was undoubtedly the paramount achievement of the convention. But this goal was not easily reached. No problem was thornier or consumed more drafting time than the office of president.

The men of 1787 had several alternatives. One choice was to create a Council of States as a plural executive to run the new government. This type of weak executive would have assured a system of legislative supremacy. Another choice was to establish a president to be chosen by Congress. A third choice was to establish a strong executive with independent grants of power who might assume the functions, if not the form, of the British Crown. At least four major proposals for president were introduced at the constitutional convention, and "no fewer than eight methods for choosing a president were first and last suggested in the Convention."⁵

One of the major contributions of the constitutional craftsmen at Philadelphia was the blending of two fundamental structural concepts: separation of powers and checks and balances. By establishing the president as an independent executive, the Framers prevented the president from being a mere tool of the legislative branch. Yet the Framers, with their fear of executive tyranny, imposed checks on the president to prevent him from overwhelming the legislative branch.

Although the presidency has become the keystone of the American governmental system, a careful reading of the Constitution would not reveal this central fact. The Founding Fathers, most historians agree, went to considerable lengths to avoid delineating the specific powers and duties of the president in order to calm the widespread fear of monarchy. They seemed to want a president of somewhat limited powers. They wanted a chief executive who would remain above parties and factions, enforce the laws Congress passed, negotiate with foreign governments, and help the states in times of civil disorder.

In a sense, the Framers sought to have it both ways: to create a president strong enough to match Congress, but not so powerful as to overshadow Congress. Gouverneur Morris put the problem this way: "Make him too weak; the Legislature will usurp his power; make him too strong; he will usurp on the Legislature."⁶ In the final draft, the Framers empowered the president to make treaties, provided two-thirds of the Senate concurred, and to nominate, with the advice and consent of the Senate, ambassadors, other public ministers and consuls, and justices of the Supreme Court. The president's term was set at four years, with no limits on reelection. He was given the veto power, but Congress could override his veto by a two-thirds majority. The president was also made commander in chief of the armed forces.

It seems doubtful, however, if the Framers fully perceived in their deliberations in Philadelphia how much authority they had actually granted to the new chief executive. Article II contains only a hint of the potential power of this office. Does this cryptic statement merely serve as an introduction to the executive branch article, or does it confer a broad grant of inherent power to act in any way the president deems appropriate to protect the public interest? For two hundred years, this constitutional ambiguity has allowed presidents wide latitude in defining their executive duties. If they prefer, they can remain largely a ceremonial caretaker of the federal government, performing minimal duties and allowing Congress to determine the national agenda. But if they choose a bold course, they can grasp the reins of leadership, chart a course of action to lead the country out of a severe depression, ward off a totalitarian threat from abroad, or establish a new set of national priorities to deal with pressing domestic problems.

The constitutional flexibility of the office, in the words of one commentator, "has made the Presidency both the most dynamic and most dangerous of our political institutions."[7] Still, the record of the past two centuries shows that in no other nation has so much power been invested in one individual, nor have the constitutional restraints imposed on this office worked so effectively as in the United States.

A UNIQUE OFFICE

If two factors stand out above all others in the study of the presidency, they are that the presidency is a composite of the office and the incumbent, and that the "dimensions of the executive power at any given moment are largely consequences of the incumbent's character and energy."[8] As a result, history shows that the development of the presidency is a discontinuous one, marked by periods of expansion, stasis, and contraction of executive power. All presidents, it should be emphasized, enter office with the same constitutional grants of authority, but the similarity usually ends there. Some presidents have employed the war power and the role of commander in chief to expand executive power. Others have used the "take care that laws be faithfully executed" clause to broaden the concept of executive authority. Still others have relied heavily on the position of party leader to exert strong executive leadership.

At the other end of the leadership continuum, a majority of presidents have taken a relatively passive view of executive power and been satisfied to carry out the purely administrative and ceremonial duties of the office. E. S. Corwin, for example, estimated in the 1950s that only one out of three chief executives contributed to the development of presidential power.[9]

How different the nation's history might have been if, say, the first president had been Martin Van Buren rather than George Washington, or if Andrew

Johnson had been president when the first shots were fired at Fort Sumter in 1861. How different the history of the country would have been if Warren G. Harding had moved into the White House on March 4, 1933, instead of Franklin D. Roosevelt.

As indicated earlier, the Founding Fathers, in outlining the broad, open-ended grants of authority in Article II, left it to future presidents and history to determine how the office would evolve. Thus, in the words of E. S. Corwin's editors: "An undefined office on paper has become enlarged with accumulated traditions and with the cumulate legacy of brilliant presidential achievements."[10]

EARLY PRESIDENTS

Historically, Washington's conception of the presidency could be best described as a benevolent protector or a "quasi-monarchical" leader. Some Federalists viewed the president as an elected king without the trappings of monarchy. Washington's successor, John Adams, also adhered to a quasi-monarchical conception of the presidency. But "the Revolution of 1800," which swept Thomas Jefferson into the White House on a democratic tide, rapidly submerged this view of the presidency.

A strong president, Jefferson derived his power chiefly from his role as party leader and only secondarily as chief executive.[11] Through his control of the party caucus, Jefferson compiled a formidable legislative record. But his successors, James Madison and James Monroe, were both selected by the congressional caucus—a plan that had, in effect, been rejected by the Framers. The sixth president, John Quincy Adams, though not nominated by a congressional caucus, was nonetheless selected by Congress, since the election was thrown into the House of Representatives when no candidate received a majority of electoral votes in 1824.

The Jacksonian Legacy   Jackson's accession to the presidency four years later, however, checked any further enfeebling of the chief executive. As E. S. Corwin interpreted the shift, "Jackson's presidency was, in truth, no mere revival of the office; it was a remaking of it."[12] As a surrogate of the people, Jackson was clearly a stronger party leader than Jefferson. Also, by frequent use of the veto Jackson developed this constitutional instrument into a powerful executive weapon in dealing with Congress. Furthermore, his claim that the presidency was one of three co-equal branches implied further claims that *all* his powers were autonomous, even his purely executive power.[13]

Though Jackson's critics could do little to thwart his exercise of power while he remained in office, once he retired they mounted an all-out attack on executive autocracy. "The President," thundered Daniel Webster, "carries on the government; all the rest are subcontractors." Another of Jackson's opponents, Henry Clay, declared the country was in the midst of a revolution "hitherto bloodless, but tending rapidly towards a total change of the pure republican character of the Government, and to the concentration of all power in the hands of one man."[14]

Presidential Decline   Even more responsible than these anti-Jackson critics for curbing executive power was the rise of the slavery question in the 1840s—an issue that seemed to call more for legislative compromise than executive direction. Moreover, the leaders of the two major parties—Democrats and Whigs (Democrats and Republicans after 1856)—selected a series of undistinguished nominees who could easily be dominated by Congress. The historic "two-thirds" rule in the Democratic party, which required that a nominee receive a two-thirds majority vote of the convention delegates, helped ensure selection of pliable presidential candidates.

The rise of the committee system in Congress also weakened the president's influence within the legislative branch. Except for the shrewd James K. Polk (1845–1849), the decline of the presidency continued without interruption until the election of the first Republican president, Abraham Lincoln, in 1860. But in the first eleven weeks after the fall of Fort Sumter, Lincoln pushed the inherent powers of the presidency to their constitutional limits and beyond.

Lincoln's Constitutional Dictatorship   To meet the challenge of secession, he called up and amalgamated the state militias into a ninety-day volunteer force, called 40,000 volunteers for three years' service, added 23,000 men to the regular army and 18,000 to the navy, purchased the needed supplies, and paid out $2 million from unappropriated funds in the Treasury to persons not authorized to receive it, without even bothering to convene Congress for authorization until midsummer.[15] Throughout this critical period, Lincoln alone constituted the government of the United States. No president before or since has ever stretched the authority of the office to the degree that the Civil War president did during the country's darkest hours. Called a dictator by his critics, Lincoln nevertheless became the greatest defender of the Constitution in the nation's history. His legacy endowed the presidency with sufficient authority and power to meet any future challenge to national survival.

After Lincoln's "constitutional dictatorship," the presidency quickly contracted. Lincoln's successor, Andrew Johnson, came to the presidency destined to confront a Congress angered by the excesses of the Lincoln administration and determined to reassert its dominance. Radical Republican hostility to Johnson's moderate Reconstruction policies toward the South eventually led to his impeachment trial. Though Johnson escaped impeachment by a single vote, the entire proceeding signaled the beginning of an era of congressional dominance of the United States government that would not be seriously challenged until the turn of the century.

POST-CIVIL WAR PRESIDENTS

After the Civil War, congressional aggressiveness seemingly placed the presidency in permanent eclipse. Woodrow Wilson's classic, *Congressional Government* (1885), described the focus of power in the national government as follows:

> . . . our present government is simply a scheme of congressional supremacy.
> . . . It is said that there is no single or central force in our federal scheme

. . . but only a balance of powers and a nice adjustment of interactive checks, as all the books say. How is it, however, in the practical conduct of the federal government? In that, unquestionably, the predominant and controlling force, the center and source of all motive and all regulative power, is Congress. . . . Congress (is) the dominant, nay, the irresistible, power of the federal system . . . that high office (the presidency) has fallen from its first estate of dignity because its power has waned; and its power has waned because the power of Congress has become predominant.[16]

This passage indicates that the presidency had become completely subordinate to Congress under presidents such as Grant, Hayes, Arthur, and Benjamin Harrison. In the 1880s, the noted British political scientist James Bryce observed that "The expression of his [the President's] wishes conveyed to Congress in messages has not necessarily any more effect on Congress than an article in a prominent party newspaper."[17]

Three major reasons can be put forth to explain congressional dominance of the executive branch during this period. Congress, from the passage of the Tenure of Office Act (1867), which preceded the Johnson impeachment trial, through the next thirty years, regularly challenged the chief executive over appointment and control of personnel in the executive branch. Congress insisted upon the advice and consent of the Senate in the selection of high officials as well as subordinates. Controllers and auditors in the Treasury, as well as coiners and even melters in local mints, were subject to Senate confirmation.[18]

A second major reason for congressional dominance during this period was its control of the purse and its careful specificity in legislation. Congress forbade the transfer of funds from one year to another. One observer of the period notes: "On the major legislation of the era—reconstruction, currency, tariffs, veterans' affairs, interstate commerce—Congress left a heavy imprint."[19] Congress intruded into day-to-day operations by attaching substantive legislation to appropriations bills which the president dared not veto. In addition, Congress enacted legislative details ordinarily delegated to administrators, such as renaming the steam yacht *Fanny* and repairing the fence around the cemetery at Harpers Ferry.[20] So assertive was Congress that Grover Cleveland used 414 vetoes in his first term.

Another major factor explaining congressional dominance during this era was the absence of emergencies and crises requiring presidential action. Depressions, urban and rural poverty, and the strikes and riots of the period were viewed as within the jurisdiction of state and local governments. Congress and the courts had excluded the national government from oversight of the industrial giants.

As a matter of fact, attempts were made during the post-Civil War period to cripple the presidency permanently. Horace Greeley championed a constitutional amendment to restrict presidents to one term in office. The Pendleton Committee proposed that cabinet members be authorized to sit in the House and Senate and be required to attend sessions twice a week for the purpose of supplying information. Had these proposals been successful, Congress would have upset the balance of power in the federal government and, as Leonard White concluded, "would have weakened the President's effective participation in departmental business by increasing the authority of Congress and its committees."[21]

In light of presidential domination of the American government during most of the twentieth century, it is difficult to envisage a period when the president of the United States played second fiddle to the legislative branch. But in post-Civil War America, Congress clearly set the national agenda. The office of the president, as one eminent historian has put it:

> . . . remained small in scale and limited in power, caught up more in the vicissitudes of party politics and patronage than in the formulation and conduct of public policy. Late nineteenth century Presidents had little to say over the estimates, appropriations, expenditures, and policies of government bureaus and departments. These agencies were much more responsive to the House Appropriations Committee and other organs of Congress than to the White House.[22]

Let's take a moment to look more closely at the post-Civil War presidency.

THE ERA OF POSTAGE-STAMP PRESIDENTS

Despite being overshadowed by Congress, late nineteenth-century presidents had one of the better jobs available in the country. The hours were good, and the salary was not too bad ($50,000 annually in an era of low inflation and before the federal income tax). Nor were the demands of the job oppressive. With an annual national budget of approximately $400 million (not billion), the president had no trouble balancing the books. Indeed, throughout the period 1866 to 1893, the protective tariff provided a surplus every year. During the 1880s, for example, the annual surplus was $100 million.[23] Unlike the $300 billion military budgets of the present era, the post-Civil War budgets for the army and navy seldom exceeded $100 million. Just prior to the outbreak of the Spanish-American War, the standing army consisted of less than 29,000 officers and men.[24]

Unlike the heavily involved twentieth-century chief executives, most of the nineteenth-century presidents, other than meeting frequently with congressional leaders to talk over patronage matters, usually sat back and reacted to congressional initiatives. Congress seldom overloaded the president's agenda. The lawmakers stayed in session only a few months a year, adjourning well before the summer's heat descended along the Potomac. The White House press corps was limited to reporters from the metropolitan papers and a handful of foreign correspondents. Since presidential press conferences had not yet been invented, White House news was handed out in periodic press announcements.

Foreign affairs were left to the secretary of state to manage, with only an occasional consultation with the president. Other members of the cabinet conducted their business routinely, with no huge White House staff looking over their shoulder, second-guessing their every move or preempting any newsworthy action reflecting favorably upon the president. Generally, the president spent most of the year right in the nation's capital, with an occasional train trip for a speech in Boston, New York, or a major Midwest city. Foreign junkets were unheard of. If one were to select the standard model of the "postage stamp" or figurehead presidency, it would be Benjamin Harrison, whose single term (1889–1893) has all but been forgotten, even by most historians.

The post-Civil War era, called "the Gilded Age" by Mark Twain, is best remembered as an era of economic individualism and laissez-faire economics, in which the prevailing view of government was to serve business by erecting high tariffs and to help the railroads with huge federal land grants to settle the West.[25] Toward the end of the century, however, the first signs of a more dynamic and assertive presidential style appeared during Grover Cleveland's first administration. His major weapon for displaying his independence from Congress was the veto. During his first term (1885–1889), he brandished his veto pen three times more frequently than all his predecessors combined. But this "government by veto" was essentially negative in nature and did not reflect broad policy initiatives from the White House.

Similarly, the office of the president was still viewed essentially as a ceremonial headquarters, lacking virtually all the trappings of power and influence that have characterized the post-World War II White House executive office. In 1901, for example, the White House staff consisted of a secretary, two assistant secretaries, two executive clerks, four lesser clerks or telegraphers, and a few doorkeepers and messengers.[26]

THE PRESIDENCY COMES OF AGE: TR TO FDR

Several factors account for the rise of the modern presidency and the establishment of a new congressional-presidential relationship in the twentieth century: (1) growing federal regulation of the modern industrial state, (2) the emergence of the United States as a world power, (3) the concentration of authority in the executive branch during World War I, (4) the establishment of an executive-controlled budget in 1921, (5) White House occupancy by two dynamic chief executives—Theodore Roosevelt and Woodrow Wilson, and (6) several Supreme Court decisions that strengthened the hand of the president.

Before 1885, few statutes had been passed to protect the public from the giant economic combinations that increasingly dominated national life. After the passage of the Interstate Commerce Act in 1887 and the Sherman Anti-Trust Act of 1890, however, no fewer than 37 laws were passed to give the national government regulatory power, albeit limited, over industry.[27] Congress attempted to put most of this regulatory power in the hands of independent commissions, yet much of it ultimately ended up in the executive branch.

Another major factor altering presidential and congressional relationships and adding to the power of the presidency was the emergence of the United States as a world power. Presidential responsibilities in the field of foreign affairs took a quantum leap at the turn of the twentieth century. By the end of the Spanish-American War (1898–1899), the United States had suddenly become a world— and imperial—power. Though the country had always espoused a staunch anti-imperial bias, the acquisition of the Philippines and the establishment of an American protectorate over Cuba marked the beginning of a new era in American history.

From 1900 to the outbreak of World War I, Congress generally chose to watch quietly as United States military forces were used for numerous "expeditions" and "interventions" in such places as China, Haiti, Cuba, Nicaragua, Mexico, Honduras, and Panama. Public opinion seemed to favor military activity, and Congress did not choose to intrude into this area of executive prerogative. At the turn of the century, for example, President McKinley sent American troops to China during the Boxer Rebellion, without congressional approval. In one instance when Congress balked at an executive action, Commander in Chief Theodore Roosevelt sent the fleet halfway around the world and left it up to Congress to buy enough coal to bring it back home. In 1916, President Wilson did not hesitate to send American troops deep into Mexico without congressional approval in a vain attempt to capture Pancho Villa, a Mexican insurgent leader who had attacked several border towns in New Mexico.

World War I added greatly to the president's authority. Woodrow Wilson resorted to powers that had not been exercised since the Civil War—and to other powers that had never been exercised. Congress delegated to the president the authority to take over and operate the railroads, regulate and prohibit exports, commandeer factories, withhold fuel, and fix transportation priorities. Unlike Lincoln, Wilson sought and received from Congress express legislative authority for almost every unusual step he undertook. "The source of Lincoln's power was the Constitution, and he operated in spite of Congress," writes one presidential authority, "[while] the source of Wilson's power . . . was a batch of statutes, and he cooperated with Congress."[28] Even so, Wilson relied on his authority as commander in chief to create such agencies as the War Industries Board, the Committee on Public Information, and the War Labor Board. International events of the twentieth century and the enormous military strength of the United States, especially since World War II, have added greatly to the powers exercised by modern presidents.

Revised public expectations of the need for an expanded presidential role in directing the nation's domestic affairs and institutional changes within the federal government itself also help account for the president emerging as the chief architect of public policy. Theodore Roosevelt is remembered as the first great reformer of the modern industrial era. He revealed in his autobiography that in the anthracite coal strike of 1902, he had planned to use army troops to run the mines if a settlement had not occurred. Taft, while less flamboyant than Roosevelt, was no less vigorous in his campaign against the giant industrial trusts and proposed the Sixteenth Amendment, which made a graduated income tax possible in 1913. This amendment opened a huge reservoir of funds for the federal government, which could be employed by future presidents to underwrite social and economic programs for the benefit of the entire nation.

The inability of Congress, through its numerous appropriations and revenue committees, to coordinate a comprehensive budget led eventually to an executive-controlled budget. President Taft's Commission on Economy and Efficiency first suggested a national budget system in 1912. Seven years later, a select committee of the House of Representatives proposed a national budget under presidential control, vested in a bureau of the Treasury. Finally, in 1921 the passage of the Budget and Accounting Act eliminated the freedom the departments had enjoyed to submit requests for money directly to Congress. Henceforth, budget requests would come from the president. The major impact of this centralization of budget making was to strengthen the president's hand in dealing with Congress and with the departments, agencies, and bureaus under his jurisdiction. By the New Deal era, the president's budget message had become a basis for presidential leadership. The institutionalized presidency was coming of age.

Woodrow Wilson firmly believed that the president's constitutional duty "to give the Congress information on the State of the Union and recommend to their consideration such measures as he shall judge necessary and expedient" could be used as a source of power. Unlike all presidents since Washington, Wilson delivered his State of the Union address in person, rather than merely dispatching it to Congress in written form. Wilson often went to Congress personally to deliver special messages. After his address on the tariff bill, he lobbied with senators in the Senate President's Room and returned often to discuss legislative strategy with party leaders.

Two Supreme Court decisions in the 1890s also significantly enhanced presidential power. In the case of *In re Neagle,*[29] the Supreme Court set forth a doctrine of inherent presidential power to defend the "peace of the United States." The *Neagle* case arose out of a bizarre set of circumstances. The attorney general of the United States had assigned a U.S. marshal to protect Supreme Court Justice Stephen Field after the jurist had been threatened by a disappointed litigant named Terry in California. While Justice Field was touring the circuit court district in that state, Terry approached him at a railroad station and appeared ready to make a physical attack on the Justice. Neagle, the U.S. marshal, reacted quickly and killed Terry.

When local authorities arrested Neagle for murder, the United States district attorney sought a writ of habeas corpus under federal statutes making the writ available to one "in custody for an act done or omitted in pursuance of a law of the United States." In a unanimous opinion, the Supreme Court upheld the president's duty to take action, even though Congress had enacted no law authorizing the president or attorney general to assign federal marshals as bodyguards. The president's duty to see that the laws are faithfully executed, the Court said, is not "limited to the enforcement of acts of Congress . . . according to their *express terms,*" but includes also "the rights, duties and obligations growing out of the Constitution itself, our international relations, and all the protection implied by the nature of the government under the Constitution."[30]

Five years later, the Supreme Court upheld presidential intervention and the use of federal troops in a labor dispute in *In re Debs.*[31] In 1894, a strike by the railwaymen's union against the Pullman Company spread to trains using Pullman equipment, causing almost a complete stoppage on the railroads operating out of Chicago. When the union leader, Eugene V. Debs, and other union officers disobeyed a federal injunction forbidding them to hinder the mails or interstate commerce, President Grover Cleveland ordered federal troops into Chicago to restore order and get the trains running again. Debs and the other union officials were arrested for contempt of court in disobeying the injunction; they all received sentences of from three to six months. Debs' attorneys appealed for a writ of habeas corpus, but the Supreme Court rejected the request, upholding the presidential action in a unanimous opinion.

For a twelve-year interim (1921–1933), Presidents Harding, Coolidge, and Hoover served in the White House with a general pledge not to be executive autocrats in their dealings with Congress. Herbert Hoover summed up his own belief and those of his two immediate predecessors about the misfortune of aggressive executive leadership by declaring: "The militant safeguard to liberty . . . [is] . . . legislative independence . . . the weakening of the legislative arm leads to encroachment by the executive upon individual liberty."[32] Faced with economic collapse during Hoover's administration, the nation demanded a president who would not be timid in leading Congress and the nation.

The unwillingness of President Hoover to respond to a national crisis mirrors the contrasting leadership roles perceived by different American presidents. A historical review of national leadership roles shows that the presidents generally fall into two major categories—weak and strong. Some presidents, such as Gerald Ford and Jimmy Carter, do not conveniently fit into either of these categories, since some of their actions have typified the "strong" president model, while their general inability to provide effective leadership or to project the image of a "take charge" chief executive more closely fit the model of the "weak" or Whig president. For our purposes, these chief executives have been consigned, for want of a better term, to the "intermediate" category. Another category that almost defies classification includes two presidents—Washington and Eisenhower —who, for convenience' sake, we have labeled "benevolent protectors." Let us take a brief look at each of these major categories.

WHITE HOUSE LEADERSHIP MODELS

The Whig Model   Described as the weak executive or Buchanan-type of presidential leadership, the Whig conception prevailed in the White House throughout the nineteenth century. The Buchanan-type president also includes James Madison and Calvin Coolidge. These presidents all adhered to the strict construction of the Constitution. Indeed, President Buchanan viewed his office merely as executor or administrator of acts of Congress. "My duty," he said, "is to execute the laws . . . and not my individual opinions."[33] He shrank from initiating any positive action, even in the face of threatened southern secession, and did nothing to prod Congress into national preparedness. In fact, he believed he lacked the legal power to use force against the southern rebels.

The Whig view of the presidency includes subordination to the Congress and cautious use of those inherent prerogatives of the commander in chief and the executive powers. As one scholar observed: "In the Buchanan concept, the President has no undefined or residual powers of protecting the public welfare or dealing with national emergencies; he is limited to the powers expressly given him in the Constitution."[34] The result of this concept of a weak executive finding shelter in the status quo translated into minimal social change or political innovation and a president with little influence on Capitol Hill. The Buchanan-type of president rejects the idea that the presidency is a political office; instead, it is viewed as the administrative arm of Congress. President Taft spelled out the operative belief of the Whig president:

> The true view of the Executive function is . . . that the President can exercise no power which cannot be fairly and reasonably traced to some specific grant of power as proper and necessary to its exercise. Such specific grant must be either in the Federal Constitution or in an act of Congress passed in pursuance thereof. There is no undefined residium of power which he can exercise because it seems to him to be in the public interest.[35]

Briefly, then, Whig presidents will be reluctant to advocate or enforce policies that enlarge national power or that impinge on state or local authority.

The Stewardship Model   The second category of presidents is the strong executive, such as Lincoln, Jackson, Wilson, the two Roosevelts, Truman, Kennedy, Johnson, and Reagan. Frequently identified as the "Lincoln-type," most of the strong presidents have served in times of crisis—a war or a depression—and so have had the opportunity for the exceptional leadership that marked their administrations. Some have also served during periods of reform, such as the Progressive era and the New Deal. This too accentuated confident leadership. All were liberal in construing the Constitution; none hesitated to fill in the gaps with his own interpretation when the occasion arose. Supporters of the strong executive have often been labeled "presidentialists."

Theodore Roosevelt viewed the president as the "steward of the people." He believed that a president was obliged to act when circumstances demanded it, even if he could not find "some specific authorization to do it." As the Rough Rider president explained:

> My belief was that it was not only his right but his duty to do anything that the needs of the Nation demanded unless such action was forbidden by the Constitution or by the laws. Under this interpretation of executive power, I did and caused to be done many things not previously done by the President and the heads of departments. I did not usurp power, but I greatly broadened the use of executive power.[36]

Confident of their leadership ability, the strong executives have been precedent-setters—sometimes stretching their powers to such an extent that the legality of their acts is questioned and even challenged in the courts. As described by one commentator: ". . . the strong president advocates the extension of national authority and is untroubled by the decline of localism. He attempts to bridge the separation of powers, to join the political branches of government, and to direct the legislative process."[37]

The strong president must inspire confidence even in times of adversity, as FDR did during the banking crisis of the Great Depression. His warm voice came over the radio to say: "We have nothing to fear but fear itself," and a nation on the verge of panic moved forward.

A strong president must use public techniques, such as all modes of communication, to shape public opinion. Every message to Congress, every speech made around the country, and even his veto messages must be intended to influence people. Even modern conservatives, it should be emphasized, have been influenced by the concept of an activist president developed by the two Roosevelts and Wilson. Ronald Reagan's foreign policy, for example, reflects his firm belief that the president should pursue an aggressive course in dealing with Communist threats in the Western Hemisphere and elsewhere.

Not all presidents, as we explained earlier, conveniently fit entirely in either major category. While the gradations of strength and weakness among presidents could probably be stretched into the two broad classifications outlined above, we have added another category to provide greater clarity.

The Benevolent Protector Model   Chief executives in this third category seek for the most part to remain above politics and to be "president of all the people." Two popular presidents—George Washington and Dwight D. Eisenhower—personify this type of presidential leadership.

Following General Washington's example, the benevolent protector president endeavors to rise above political divisions to build a national consensus. Author Sidney Hyman, writing with President Eisenhower in mind, has characterized the benevolent protector model as follows:

> All men are by nature good. Government alone corrupts them. Therefore to the extent that governments can be reduced in importance, the natural goodness of men will assert itself in social cooperation voluntarily given. However irreconcilable rival interests may seem to be, once their representative men sit down and talk things over without intervention of government, natural goodness will resolve all difficulties. His own presidential function, then, was to be "the President to all the people."[38]

Both benevolent protector presidents were former generals. Unless either major party decides to turn to the military again for another nominee, it seems unlikely that we will see a president of this category in the foreseeable future.

Some presidential scholars mark the beginning of the modern presidency with Franklin D. Roosevelt, who will be found on all historians' lists of great presidents.

THE NEW DEAL: THE WHITE HOUSE TAKES OVER

When Franklin Delano Roosevelt won the election in 1932, the nation was in such desperate straits that the day after the president's inauguration Will Rogers, the renowned humorist, observed: "The whole country is with him just so he does something. If he burned down the Capitol, we would cheer and say 'Well, we at least got a fire started.' "[39] The massiveness of the economic collapse of the 1930s can hardly be exaggerated. With a population only half the size of the nation in the 1980s, between 12 and 15 million persons were unemployed; 25 percent of the blue-collar workers were out on the streets competing for jobs that did not exist; one family out of seven was receiving public relief; 4,600 banks throughout the nation had shut their doors; auto plants in Michigan and textile factories in New England were closed; farmers let crops rot in the fields because it cost more to harvest them than they could be sold for at the market. The economic chaos of the Great Depression and the desperate mood of the nation demanded action and vigorous leadership. Both were not long in coming under Roosevelt's administration.

On March 4, 1933, Roosevelt laid the challenge facing the nation before Congress in his inaugural address:

> It is to be hoped that the normal balance of executive and legislative authority may be wholly adequate to meet the unprecedented task before us . . . I am prepared under my constitutional duty to recommend the measures that a stricken nation in the midst of a stricken world may require. . . . But in the event that the Congress shall fail to take these courses and in the event that the national emergency is still critical I shall not evade the clear course of duty that will then confront me. I shall ask the Congress for the one remaining instrument to meet the crisis—broad executive power to wage a war against the emergency as great as the power that would be given to me if we were invaded by a foreign foe.[40]

The president moved with breathtaking swiftness to deal with the crisis by calling for a special session of Congress to convene five days after his inaugural address. Then followed the famous Hundred Days during which more legislation was passed by Congress than at any other time in the history of the Republic. This feverish activity went beyond any normal "honeymoon" period between a newly elected president and Congress. The tense political climate in the nation and in Congress fostered experimentation and change. Relief, recovery, and reform were the goals, and quick, decisive action was the method used to achieve them.

Throughout the 1930s Roosevelt refined leadership techniques which had been employed less effectively by his predecessors. The first was the presidential message. His cousin, Theodore, had indicated to a critic the inadvisability of proposing details of a bill when a message was sent to Congress. Franklin Roosevelt, however, not only sent a flurry of messages to Congress, but also sent along carefully drafted bills (NRA, AAA, Lend-Lease) to accomplish the purpose of the message. From 1933 to 1938, he sent over 120 special messages to Congress.

A second device employed by FDR to control legislation was the veto. At the close of his second term in 1941, FDR had vetoed 505 measures—over 30 percent of all measures disapproved by presidents since 1792. That the veto is an effective device in the legislative process can be seen by the fact that from 1792 to 1941, only 49 of 1,645 vetoes were overridden by Congress. (Presidential vetoes are discussed further in Chapter 6.)

A third device of which Roosevelt made extensive use was patronage. Not since Woodrow Wilson, twelve years before, had a Democrat occupied the White House. In addition to the federal marshals, judges, postmasters, and high-level cabinet posts that were normally available, President Roosevelt was also able to appoint thousands to new offices in the relief and recovery agencies—all outside the merit system.

Undoubtedly, the outstanding reason for FDR's early success with Congress and his legislative achievements was the unprecedented support given him by the American people. He would scan both critical and friendly newspapers each morning to take the pulse of people in Chicago, Philadelphia, Boston, and St. Louis. In dealing with the press corps, he would trade wisecracks with them, call them by their first names, and meet with them twice a week, year after year, to give them lead stories for their papers. FDR abolished the written question format and let the reporters interrogate him orally.

By such activity, he dominated the front page in a way that no president has—until Presidents Kennedy and Reagan arrived in the White House. Mr. Roosevelt was the first president to master the techniques of modern communication. He talked directly with the people via radio. One observer notes: "In his fireside chats, he talked like a father discussing public affairs with his family in the living room."[41] He had occasional setbacks, such as when he tried to pack the Supreme Court in 1937; yet he knew how to rally people behind his legislative programs.

To mount his New Deal programs, Roosevelt obtained authority from Congress by specific statutes. But the growing defense buildup after the fall of France in 1940 changed Roosevelt's approach to presidential power. To marshal the manpower and weapons needed to defeat Hitler, Mussolini, and the Japanese militarists, Roosevelt turned instead to his warmaking and commander in chief authority—based upon sweeping emergency authority granted him by Congress —to mobilize a huge military machine of 12 million men and women, the total industrial plant capacity of the nation, and almost the entire civilian work force.

As Arthur M. Schlesinger, Jr., has commented: "War again nourished the Presidency. The towering figure of Franklin Roosevelt, the generally-accepted wisdom of his initiatives of 1940 and 1941, his undisputed authority as Commander in Chief after Pearl Harbor, the thundering international pronouncements emanating from wartime summits of the Big Two or the Big Three—all these gave Americans in the postwar years an exalted conception of presidential power."[42]

THE HEROIC PRESIDENCY

After World War II, the United States, the first country to develop the atomic bomb, emerged as the most powerful nation in the world. Other nations, especially Britain and France, which had been bled white by two world wars in a generation, turned to the United States for international leadership. President Truman responded to the challenge by obtaining passage of the Marshall Plan to fund the huge reconstruction task in Western Europe. Meanwhile, the United States, under strong presidential leadership, became a powerful member of the United Nations and by the mid-fifties had pledged this nation in treaties to defend 43 nations around the world. With the onset of the Cold War between the United States and the Soviet Union shortly after the end of World War II, the president became, in one commentator's words, the "permanent commander in chief of the free world's militia."[43]

The first two decades after World War II have been depicted by some writers as the era of the heroic presidency, which might be described as an updated version of the stewardship concept. The heroic models—Washington, Jackson, Lincoln, Wilson, both Theodore and Franklin Roosevelt, and Truman —all boldly used the powers of the presidential office to meet the challenges and crises of their times. During the 1950s and 1960s, leading writers on the presidency extolled the dominant role of the American chief executive. The late Clinton Rossiter, for example, lauded the American presidency as "one of the truly successful institutions created by men in their endless quest for the blessings of free government."[44]

Adherents of the heroic presidency insisted that a strong president was needed to overcome Congress's innate conservatism and inability to respond to sudden crisis. The widespread use of executive authority has often been justified by defenders of the heroic presidency on the basis that the president more directly "represents" all the people, since members of Congress must be more responsive to the parochial interests of their districts and states. In reaffirming the heroic concept of the presidency, political scientist Richard E. Neustadt vividly contrasted how far the heroic presidency had expanded in the twentieth century from the earlier years in the century:

> Once TR daringly assumed the "steward's" role in the emergency created by the great coal strike of 1902; the Railway Labor Act and the Taft-Hartley Act now make such interventions mandatory upon Presidents. Once, FDR dramatically asserted personal responsibility for gauging and guiding the American economy; now the Employment Act binds his successors to that task. Wilson and FDR became chief spokesmen, leading actors on the world stage at the height of war; now UN membership, far-flung alliances, the facts of power prescribe the role continuously in terms termed "peace." Through both wars, our presidents grappled experimentally with an emergency-created need to "integrate" foreign and military and domestic policies; the National Security Act takes that need for granted as a constant of our times. FDR and Truman made themselves responsible for the development and first use of atomic weapons; the Atomic Energy Act now puts a comparable burden on the back of every President.[45]

Beyond doubt, the Cold War reinforced the growth and superordinate status of the presidency. Arthur M. Schlesinger, Jr., later to become the foremost critic of the "imperial presidency," conceded at the time that:

> The uncertainty and danger of the early cold war, with the chronic threat of unanticipated emergency always held to require immediate response, with,

above all, the overhanging possibility of nuclear catastrophe, seemed to argue all the more strongly for the centralization of control over foreign policy, including the use of armed forces, in the presidency.[46]

When North Korea invaded South Korea in 1950, Truman immediately used his powers as commander in chief and ordered U.S. armed forces to come to the aid of the South Koreans. His successor, President Eisenhower, relied more on traditional methods when faced with the task of aiding friendly governments overseas—he asked Congress to pass joint resolutions granting him broad authority to use the armed forces as he saw fit in the Middle East and in the Formosa Straits. Congress responded promptly, confident that Ike would take care of any crisis in the same manner as he had handled the victorious Allied Forces in World War II.

Since 1950, presidents have ordered U.S. armed forces into Korea, Lebanon, the Dominican Republic, Vietnam, Cambodia, Laos, and Grenada. They have ordered a naval quarantine around Cuba, approved undercover plots directed by the CIA against several foreign governments, dispatched military advisors to friendly countries and even ordered aerial overflights of countries behind the Iron Curtain—all actions undertaken without obtaining advance congressional assent. Public trust in the president during the New Deal and post-New Deal eras remained high, even though presidents placed more demands on the citizenry in World War II than at any time since the Civil War.

During America's involvement in Vietnam, however, public confidence in presidential leadership began to wane, reaching an all-time low during the Watergate hearings and the impending impeachment proceedings against President Nixon, who resigned from office before the impeachment trial could be started. While the seeds were planted earlier, the excesses of presidential power became evident soon after the President Lyndon B. Johnson's landslide victory in the 1964 election. Complaints about President Johnson's "credibility gap" began to surface in 1965–1966 over his handling of the American intervention in Vietnam. Charges that he had lied, or at least misrepresented the facts surrounding the initial North Vietnamese attack on American ships in the Tonkin Gulf in order to obtain a blank-check authorization to deal with future attacks, echoed through the halls of Congress and across the land. Johnson's decision not to seek reelection in 1968, instead of halting the growth of the imperial presidency, accelerated a great concentration of authority in the White House during the Nixon years.

President Nixon's unilateral decision to invade Cambodia in 1970, his secret orders for stepped up bombing of Laos without telling Congress, as well as his impoundment of congressionally approved appropriations for programs he wished to see cut back or terminated, all helped reinforce the belief of many Americans that the President was moving the country ever closer to an "imperial presidency," a term coined by historian Arthur M. Schlesinger, Jr.[47]

THE IMPERIAL PRESIDENCY

While President Johnson invariably pointed to the Gulf of Tonkin Resolution whenever his congressional critics alluded to his unilateral actions, such as expanding American troop deployment to 525,000 troops in Vietnam in 1965, not until President Nixon mounted secret bombing attacks in Laos and Cambodia did congressional patience with the conduct of the Vietnam war wear thin. Finally, in 1973, Congress voted to rein in the "imperial presidency" by passing the War Powers Resolution, a subject we discuss in greater detail in Chapter 7.

More than anything else, the undeclared war in Vietnam had alerted Congress and the public to the danger that the open-ended powers and prerogatives of presidents had expanded to such a degree that our constitutional system of balanced government was in serious jeopardy. The emergence of the "imperial presidency," however, did not occur overnight. The twentieth century, marked by two world wars, the Great Depression, the threat of nuclear war, two undeclared wars in Korea and Vietnam, and numerous "brushfire" wars, has been fertile ground for the growth of executive power—and eventually an imperial presidency.

Arthur M. Schlesinger, Jr., in his book *The Imperial Presidency,* published in 1973, the same year as the Watergate hearings, contended that presidential power had been so expanded and abused by the early 1970s that it endangered our constitutional system. Two critical instruments—the commander in chief's role and presidential secrecy—were, according to Schlesinger, primarily responsible for the rise of presidential autocracy. The president's power as commander in chief, because it is an undefined office, not a function, is sufficiently ambiguous to allow him to stretch its meaning far beyond what the Founding Fathers intended. While the Framers expected that a president would respond to sudden attacks and act to protect the rights and property of American citizens, they did not envisage the president's resorting to undeclared wars. The ambiguous constitutional authority, Schlesinger argued, especially in the field of foreign policy, enabled presidents to arrogate to themselves the right to wage an undeclared war unilaterally, a power the Framers expected the president to share with Congress.

Schlesinger made a crucial distinction between the *abuse* and the *usurpation* of power. In his view, Lincoln, FDR, and Truman temporarily usurped power in wartime, but recognized that they had no intention of retaining this power in peacetime. By contrast, Presidents Johnson and Nixon abused power, even in peacetime, and saw this near-absolute power as a permanent prerogative of the presidency.

In reviewing the president's role in waging war from Washington's administration to Nixon's, Schlesinger perceived this power culminating in an imperial presidency of the Johnson-Nixon type. Furthermore, this "plebiscitary" conception of the office, as propounded by President Nixon, justified his actions beyond foreign affairs into domestic policy matters as well.

Members of the Democratic majority in both houses of Congress also objected strenuously to Nixon's practice of impounding (refusing to spend) appropriated funds for water pollution control, urban aid, and the emergency loan program of the Farm Home Administration. Lawmakers complained that by refusing to spend appropriated money, the chief executive was, in effect, exercising an *item veto* and thereby avoiding the use of a regular veto and the risk of a congressional override.[48]

Other practices of the imperial presidency included excessive secrecy and heavy reliance on the presidential prerogative known as executive privilege, a claim based on the constitutional separation of powers, to the effect that the president or his designated officials may withhold information from Congress. While constitutional scholars, the courts, and Congress all concede that a president has the right to withhold certain diplomatic and military information when it is essential to national security—such as the Normandy invasion plans in World War II—the critics objected to the studied practice of Mr. Nixon withholding information on matters relating to military assistance and five-year plans and foreign aid for Cambodia—data that could scarcely be vital to national security.

WATERGATE

The imperial presidency continued to expand until it was finally halted by the emerging Watergate scandals in early 1973. Watergate is the name given to the constitutional crisis precipitated by a string of unlawful Nixon White House-sponsored acts ranging from illegal entry into the Democratic National Committee headquarters in the Watergate office-hotel complex to burglary, perjury, misuse of the FBI and CIA to cover up illegal activity, the destruction of evidence, the creation of a White House secret police unit (the so-called plumbers group), illegal wiretapping, questionable White House intervention in two antitrust cases, and the illegal solicitation of corporate contributions for President Nixon's 1972 reelection campaign. These actions, many of them first reported in the *Washington Post* and widely publicized by the special Senate Watergate Investigation Committee, led to the prosecution and conviction of more than a dozen top-level White House aides, including Attorney General John Mitchell. The Watergate scandals cast the darkest shadow over the presidency since the impeachment of President Andrew Johnson after the Civil War. Even in Johnson's case, no charges of criminal activity were made against him or his aides. By the summer of 1974, President Nixon, facing an impeachment trial in the Senate, resigned the presidency—the first chief executive in American history to be driven from office.[49]

Watergate had a profound effect on our view of the presidency. Some contemporary observers declared that the presidency, discredited by abuses of power unparalleled in American history, had been irreparably wounded. But these observers underestimated the resilience and durability of the chief executive office. Once Mr. Nixon left Washington, the greatest constitutional crisis since the Civil War subsided. Congressional opposition to the imperial presidency had hastened the "deroyalization" of the presidency, as evidenced by the passage of the Case Act (to curb the wholesale use of secret executive agreements by imperial presidents), enactment of the War Powers Act of 1973, and approval of the Budget and Impoundment Control Act of 1974. Congress thus reclaimed some of the powers its members had too easily and sometimes casually ceded to the White House over several decades. The emergency powers exercised by several presidents also came under scrutiny during the Watergate era.

THE PRESIDENT AND EMERGENCY POWERS

No emergency powers are granted to the president under the Constitution, but neither does the Constitution forbid the president to take appropriate action in times of national emergencies. If the Framers were seriously concerned with which branch of the government should deal with national emergencies, a review of the Constitutional Convention debates, the *Federalist* papers, or the ratification debates in the states does not show it. Except for Article I, section 9, of the U.S. Constitution, which states: "The Privilege of Writ of Habeas Corpus shall not be suspended unless when in Cases of Rebellion of Invasion the Public Safety may require it," the Founding Fathers seemed satisfied that the provisions they had written into the fundamental document were sufficient to deal with any national emergency.

Except for Lincoln's drastic actions during the Civil War, the concept of national emergency is almost exclusively a twentieth-century phenomenon. During World War I, President Wilson exercised wartime powers nearly equal to those of a Roman proconsul. Indeed, during America's eighteen-month involvement in the European conflict, Congress was more than willing to pass measures giving President Wilson dictatorial powers over the American industrial system. But until President Franklin D. Roosevelt declared a national emergency the day after he assumed office on March 1933 to forestall the collapse of the American banking system, the use of national emergency power had always been confined to wartime. Actually, Roosevelt's measures were pleasing to the banking community, and within a week the major banks reopened their doors. Both the Federal Reserve Board and the Reconstruction Finance Corporation came to the aid of the banking industry. When Congress convened four days later, the lawmakers passed Roosevelt's bank aid bill in a record four hours.

Shortly after the outbreak of World War II in Europe (more than two years before Pearl Harbor), FDR announced a "limited" national emergency. In May 1941, President Roosevelt announced an "unlimited" national emergency in the face of Hitler's conquest of France. President Truman, following in the footsteps of FDR a decade later, put the nation on an emergency basis soon after our entry into the Korean conflict. No further national emergencies were proclaimed until President Nixon announced one at the time of the postal strike in March 1970. So impressed was Mr. Nixon with the dynamic effect of this national emergency declaration that he proclaimed another one in August 1971 in response to the perilously high deficit in the U.S. balance of payments. Fourteen years later, however, President Ronald Reagan saw no need to declare a national emergency, even though the record-breaking international trade deficit for 1984 hit $101.6 billion—more than twice the previous record of $41.6 billion set in 1983.[51]

It is noteworthy that in none of these national emergencies has the president requested Congress to authorize a formal declaration of a national emergency—even though the circumstances seemed to allow Congress sufficient time for legislative action.

Looking back in history, Roman proconsuls were granted dictatorial powers for a maximum of six months. But at no time in the six emergency declarations proclaimed by American presidents since the Great Depression has the American president ever specified the duration of his emergency declaration.[52] Of these six national emergencies, only two were rescinded by the president—Mr. Truman in 1952 issued a proclamation terminating Roosevelt's national emergency declarations of 1939 and 1941.[53] The other four national emergency statutes (1933, 1950, 1970, and 1971) remained on the books until 1976.

In the aftermath of the U.S. invasion of Cambodia, a Senate Special Committee on the Termination of the National Emergency, chaired jointly by Senators Frank Church (D.-Idaho) and Charles Mathias (R.-Md.), unearthed some 470 emergency statutes dating back to March 5, 1933, and ranging from suspending the writ of habeas corpus to placing the entire nation under martial law. Committee members discovered that since the early 1930s President Roosevelt and his successors had declared four separate national emergencies, but none had ever been rescinded. By passing the National Emergencies Act of 1976, Congress trimmed much of the presidents' historic freedom to declare national emergencies and simultaneously invoke sweeping powers.

The 1976 Act repealed all the previous emergency acts; it also stipulated that future presidentially declared emergencies can be terminated by Congress by concurrent resolution (which is not subject to a presidential veto), or by a presidential proclamation. Furthermore, if the president declares a national emergency, he must inform Congress of the provisions of the law under which he acts. The president and the designated federal agencies must report to Congress all rules and regulations issued during an emergency, as well as expenditures. Congress, in turn, must at six-month intervals determine whether or not the emergency should be terminated.[54]

Significantly, the new law states that a majority vote in both the Senate and House can terminate the emergency at any time. President Ford termed this action unconstitutional and indicated that future presidents might turn to the courts to challenge this provision if Congress chose to invoke it.

THE POST-IMPERIAL PRESIDENCY

In retrospect, passage of the War Powers Resolution of 1973, the Watergate hearings, and the forced resignation of President Nixon in August 1974 represented the high-water mark of congressional constraints against the imperial presidency. The congressional and public backlash against overreaching presidential actions temporarily halted further expansion of presidential power and prerogatives. Congressional resurgence was marked by increased skepticism of claims for presidential prerogative, careful scrutiny of presidential proposals, demands for more extensive consultation of congressional leaders by the White House, and more exacting confirmation of presidential appointments.

The elevation of the first appointed vice president, Gerald Ford, to the White House gave the country a short breathing spell from the repeated clashes between President Nixon and Congress. President Ford signaled that a *rapprochement* between the two branches would be the highest priority on his agenda. In his first address to Congress, delivered three days after taking office,

Mr. Ford declared: "I do not want a honeymoon with you. I want a good marriage. As President, I intend to listen. . . ." Ford stated that his relations with Congress would be characterized not by confrontation, but by "communication, conciliation, compromise, and cooperation."[55] The honeymoon lasted slightly over thirty days. It came to an abrupt halt the day President Ford pardoned former President Nixon for his complicity in the Watergate coverup. Still, President Ford went a long way toward deemphasizing the pomp and ceremony surrounding White House activities.

Though President Ford vetoed 69 measures during his twenty-nine months in office, he nevertheless maintained personal rapport with many of his former colleagues on Capitol Hill. Indeed, the country heard little about the "crisis" in the presidency and the "imperial presidency" after the resignation of Richard Nixon. Congress, now working with an appointed president, quickly reasserted some of its lost authority. Furthermore, by the establishment of the Congressional Budget Office in 1974 and the addition of a sizable professional staff of policy analysts, computer specialists, and economists, Congress gained an increased institutional capacity to participate to a greater degree in the "codetermination" of public policy and the maintenance of its legislative oversight function. Presidential power was also vitiated by the fact that Mr. Ford was an appointed, not an elected, president.

President Jimmy Carter, though he enjoyed solid Democratic majorities in both houses of Congress during his single term, did not fare much better than Ford with his legislative program. Insensitive to the need to curry the favor of his fellow Democrats on Capitol Hill, Carter failed to win approval of his energy package, welfare reform, election reforms, a proposed consumer protection agency, and other White House-sponsored measures. Even so, Ford and Carter "bent over backward in an effort to restore as much integrity and openness to the office as possible."[56] In the words of one presidential scholar, "Perhaps more than anything else the appointment of Gerald Ford and election of Jimmy Carter ended the fears about the imperial presidency."[57]

By the time President Carter reached the halfway point in his term, however, critics began complaining about his inability to work effectively with Congress, his failure to consult adequately with party leaders, and his lack of strong leadership. Thomas E. Cronin summarized his performance as follows: "Carter seemed often to prefer a government by surprise. He also had a penchant for bypassing Congress and going to the country. Of course, most presidents do this, but his style of doing it coupled with his reputation as an 'outsider,' came back to weaken his ties with Congress."[58] Before long, concern about the imperial presidency was replaced by apprehension about presidential inadequacy.

By 1980—six years after Nixon's resignation—some political leaders and analysts began expressing concern that Congress had overreacted to Vietnam, the Watergate scandals, and President Nixon. While they conceded that some rebalancing was needed to restore the equilibrium between the two branches, "presidential" supporters argued that Congress was carried away with its reform zeal. Passage of the War Powers Act, the Case Act (regulating executive agreements), the Budget Control and Impoundment Act, and other legislative constraints on the president, these critics claim, so hobbled the president that he became a helpless giant.

When Ronald Reagan moved into the White House in 1981, many Washington observers were lamenting that we had entered an era of one-term presidencies. In the previous two decades they had seen John Kennedy assassinated, Lyndon Johnson pushed into political exile, Nixon forced to resign under the threat of impeachment, and both Gerald Ford and Jimmy Carter rejected by the voters in their first races as incumbents.

Presidential watchers commented, not implausibly, that the pressures of the presidency were so intense and public expectations so much higher than its limited institutional authority that no incumbent could hope to be returned for a second term. Critics could see nothing but revolving-door presidencies in the years ahead. But with President Reagan's reelection in 1984, most naysayers agreed that Mr. Reagan had restored the presidency to its central role in our governmental system. One respected national columnist concluded: "It is no exaggeration to say he has rescued the office."[59] In his first eight months in office, Mr. Reagan obtained congressional passage of major reductions in government spending, corporate and individual tax cuts, and won bipartisan support for a massive national defense buildup. Within this brief time span President Reagan's policies had provided the basis for a fundamental redirection in American government. Though his "supply-side" tax cuts—despite his optimistic predictions—had generated the largest deficits in the nation's history, the national electorate found little fault with Mr. Reagan's handling of economic affairs. In foreign policy the president's strident rhetoric against the Soviet Union generated widespread popular support throughout his first term, and the United States' allies in Europe and Asia, following the leadership of the American president, found renewed reasons to maintain a solid front against Soviet expansionism.

Though the oldest man in history to occupy the nation's highest office, President Reagan entered his second term with a 49-state mandate, and the vigor of a man fifteen years his junior. The nation seemed to thrive on his jaunty approach toward an office that had broken his four immediate predecessors. Polls showed, for example, after his reelection, that even though many citizens disagreed with the president's position on a number of issues, they still voted to give him a second term.[60] Whether voters agreed or disagreed with Mr. Reagan's policies, most Washington pundits conceded after his first four years in the White House that Mr. Reagan had already left a more profound imprint on American domestic and foreign policy than any other chief executive since Franklin D. Roosevelt.

SUMMARY

If one thing is certain about the study of the presidency, it is clear that the tides of presidential influence and power ebb and flow as the occupants of the White House change. Louis W. Koenig, a longtime student of the presidency, has observed:

> In the American system, more than the systems of other nations, the chief executive is unable to stabilize his political influence. Potent forces in American society and culture and in its politics cause fluctuations and discontinuities in the President's role. . . . Partly the volatility of power results from the circumstance that it is shared between the executive and Congress, but the precise patterns of sharing are unclear and tentative, and even after nearly two centuries of constitutional practice, they remain largely unpredictable.[61]

As we near the two hundredth anniversary of the Republic's founding, the constitutional prerogatives of the presidency continue to offer unmatched opportunities to provide the country with dynamic leadership and vision. Indeed, as one constitutional scholar has observed: "The successful operation of the American constitutional system requires that this power be used."[62] Furthermore, presidents who fail to exercise their broad powers and prerogatives vigorously "are condemned as weak leaders and failures in office." On the domestic front, however, presidential leadership and initiatives are often neutralized by the countervailing forces inherent in a separation of powers system. In normal times the president frequently finds himself hamstrung by congressional refusal to support many of his domestic programs.

But in the conduct of foreign affairs and the handling of national security matters, the powers of the president are expansive, and the constitutional restraints upon a president's actions are fewer and less effective. Even the Supreme Court, the final adjudicator of disputes between the different branches of the government, has been reluctant to impose restraints on the presidential actions in these areas. Except for the Court's ruling limiting the inherent powers of the president in the famous steel company seizure case of 1952, the justices have shown a disposition to support broad presidential authority in foreign affairs and national security matters by reliance on long-standing precedent, executive authority as the "sole organ in foreign relations," the constitutional directive to the president to "take care that the laws be faithfully executed," and the president's responsibilities as commander in chief.

Throughout our history the power of the presidency has to a large extent been what the president has made of it. Presidential conceptions of the power of his office have varied widely. Indeed, as John F. Kennedy pointed out in 1960, "The history of this nation—its brightest and bleakest pages—has been written largely in terms of the different views our presidents have had of the Presidency itself." Our fifteenth president, James Buchanan, for example, lacked the Jacksonian conception of the president's powers. Confronted with an agonizing decision of threatened secession of the South, Buchanan considered issuing a presidential proclamation condemning secession. But then he backed away from this forceful move. Instead, he sent a message to Congress adopting the equivocal position that while no state had the right to leave the Union, the president was powerless to block this action. As the war clouds moved ever closer, Buchanan retreated to his White House quarters to wait out his remaining weeks in office until the newly elected president, Abraham Lincoln, could assume the reins of government.

By contrast, Lincoln held a radically different view of the president's power in time of crisis. Initially conciliatory toward the South, Lincoln nevertheless made it abundantly clear that he viewed secession as rebellion and that as president and commander in chief, he had the responsibility and authority to use whatever measures needed to preserve the Union. At no time during the bloody four-year conflict did Lincoln permit the constitutional limits on his office to thwart him from achieving this single-minded goal. It is no surprise that the Lincolnian conception of presidential power became the model for his successors in times of national crisis; indeed, they have all turned to the Civil War president's record as justification for their actions.

History shows that presidents and their administrations generally reflect the dominant mood of the times. Weak and strong presidents have generally been associated with different historical circumstances. During periods of normalcy, consolidation or national reconciliation presidents have usually been content to live with the status quo and not mount national crusades. But in times of rising tension and crisis the nation craves leadership, and presidents have usually been quick to respond to the cries for action.

The nation's willingness to support the president and his perception of the need for action usually go hand in hand. Conversely, no extraordinary presidential actions can succeed without the existence of conditions that justify and legitimize his use of decisive measures. Thus, President Truman could, under his own broad view of inherent executive authority, unilaterally decide to send U.S. armed forces to South Korea in 1950 to halt the North Korean invasion of this divided country and be widely applauded for his decisive action. Less than two years later, however, when the crisis atmosphere faded and public support of the extended Korean military action turned sour, Truman discovered that the Supreme Court would not sustain his concept of inherent power when he seized the steel mills to avert a threatened strike.

Under somewhat different circumstances President Kennedy, in his first eighteen months in office, found that the southern Democratic-Republican coalition in Congress thwarted nearly all his legislative initiatives. But when he imposed a naval blockade—it was called a "quarantine"—around Castro's Cuba to block the shipment of Soviet Union missiles to the island in 1962 and risked a possible nuclear war, Congress and the country immediately rallied behind him. His successor, Lyndon B. Johnson, pushed his Great Society domestic programs through Congress in 1964–1965 with relative ease, but by 1968, his costly Vietnam policies so deeply divided the country and eroded his popularity that he decided not to seek reelection.

Clearly, when the nation's fate is at stake or the public perceives that social change is long overdue, extraordinary power seems to flow to the president. In times of national emergency the president's authority expands, as if regulated by an invisible thermostat, to meet the crisis. Lincoln's "constitutional dictatorship" during the Civil War, Woodrow Wilson's full-scale mobilization during World War I, and Franklin D. Roosevelt's sweeping use of emergency power to combat the Great Depression and his all-out mobilization of the nation's human and material resources during World War II are all cases in point. As one presidential scholar has described these actions: "National peril creates conditions—psycho-logical as well as constitutional and political—for the use of power by a power-oriented President."[63] Partisanship and special interest lobbying subsides, and the nation turns to its president for direction in meeting the crisis. It is no wonder that all of our "great" presidents have served in office during crisis periods in our history.

Every modern president is under intense pressure to succeed, but relatively few do. Why? Part of the reason is that in a time of declining economic resources and recognized national limitations that became painfully evident in the 1970s, it is the president who becomes the chief target for public frustrations. With the decline of political parties, recent presidents have become increasingly dependent on an electoral coalition consisting of numerous single-issue and interest groups who expect specific rewards for their campaign support. New pressure groups—women, blacks, senior citizens, Hispanic Americans and other minority groups—have been added to the list of constituencies demanding to be heard and served. Most of these insistent demands have come to rest on the White House doorsteps. As a result, recent presidents often find the gap between public expectations and their ability to solve the nation's top-priority problems is unbridgeable. For most presidents this chronic disparity between hope and reality first arises during the nominating race for president—the subject of the next chapter.

NOTES

1. This section draws heavily upon Everts G. Greene, *The Provincial Governor in the English Colonies of North America* (New York: Longmans, Green and Company, Vol. VII, Harvard Historical Series, 1898).
2. Edward S. Corwin, *The President: Office and Powers, 1787–1957* (New York: New York University Press, 1957), 7.
3. Merrill Jensen, *The Articles of Confederation* (Madison: University of Wisconsin Press, 1940).
4. Corwin, *The President: Office and Powers,* 11.
5. Ibid., 317, footnote 25.
6. As cited by Louis W. Koenig, *The Chief Executive* (New York: Harcourt, Brace and Jovanovich, 1961), 30.
7. Robert R. Hirschfield, ed., *The Power of the Presidency,* 3rd ed. (New York: Aldine, 1982), 3.
8. "Postscript," in Corwin, *The President: Office and Powers, 1787–1984,* eds. Randall W. Bland, Theodore H. Hindson, and Jack W. Peltason, 5th ed. (New York: New York University Press, 1985), 31.
9. Ibid., 30.
10. Ibid.
11. Corwin, *The President: Office and Powers,* 18.
12. Ibid., 20.
13. Ibid., 21.
14. Ibid., 22.
15. Ibid., 264.
16. Woodrow Wilson, *Congressional Government* (1885) (New York: Meridian Edition 1908), Vol. 1, 230.

17. James Bryce, *American Commonwealth* (New York: Commonwealth Edition, 1908), 230.
18. Leonard D. White, *The Republican Era: 1869–1901* (New York: Macmillan, 1948), 113.
19. James MacGregor Burns, *Presidential Government: The Crucible of Leadership* (New York: Avon Books Edition, 1967), 50.
20. Ibid., 51.
21. Leonard D. White, *The Republican Era: 1869–1901,* 109.
22. Morton Keller, *Affairs of State* (Cambridge, MA: The Belknap Press of Harvard University, 1977), 297.
23. Ibid., 310.
24. Russell F. Weigley, *History of the United States Army* (New York: Macmillan, 1967), 295.
25. Ray Ginger, *The Nationalizing of American Life, 1877–1900* (New York: Free Press, 1965), 1–27; Robert Wiebe, *The Search for Order, 1877–1920* (New York: Hill and Wang, 1967), 1–163.
26. James Bryce, *The American Commonwealth,* 3rd ed. (New York: Macmillan, 1888), Vol. 1, 54 and 64.
27. F. D. G. Riddle, *State and National Power Over Commerce* (New York: Columbia University Press, 1937), 117–119.
28. Clinton Rossiter, *The American Presidency,* rev. ed. (New York: Mentor Books, 1960), 100.
29. 135 U.S. 1 (1890).
30. Ibid.
31. 158 U.S. 564 (1895).
32. Wilfred E. Binkley, *President and Congress,* 3rd ed. (New York: Vintage Books, 1962), 281.
33. Ibid., 142.
34. Ibid., 151.
35. William Howard Taft, *Our Chief Magistrate and his Powers* (New York: Columbia University Press, 1916), 139.
36. Theodore Roosevelt, *An Autobiography* (New York: Scribner's, 1924), 357.
37. "Introduction," in Hirschfield, *The Power of the Presidency,* 10.
38. Sidney Hyman, "What Is the President's True Role?" *New York Times Magazine,* September 7, 1958, 17, 108–109.
39. Arthur M. Schlesinger, Jr., *The Coming of the New Deal* (Boston: Houghton Mifflin, 1958), 13.
40. As cited in Wilfred E. Binkley, *President and Congress,* 294.
41. William E. Leuchtenberg, *Franklin D. Roosevelt and the New Deal* (New York: Harper & Row, 1963), chap. 14.
42. Schlesinger, *The Imperial Presidency* (Boston: Houghton Mifflin, 1973), 122–123.
43. Thomas E. Cronin, *The State of the Presidency,* 2nd ed. (Boston: Little, Brown, 1980), 85.
44. Rossiter, *The American Presidency,* 13.
45. Richard E. Neustadt, "The Presidency at Mid-Century," in Aaron Wildavsky, ed., *The Presidency* (Boston: Little, Brown, 1969), 195.
46. Arthur M. Schlesinger, Jr., "Congress and the Making of American Foreign Policy," *Foreign Affairs,* (1972), 94–95.
47. Schlesinger, *The Imperial Presidency.*
48. Cronin, *The State of the Presidency,* 195.

49. For a fascinating account of the Watergate story, consult Bob Woodward and Carl Bernstein, *All the President's Men* (New York: Simon and Schuster, 1974); see also Theodore H. White, *Breach of Faith: The Fall of Richard Nixon* (New York: Atheneum, 1975).

50. Under this act, executive agreements with sensitive national security agreements may be submitted to the Senate Foreign Relations Committee and the House Foreign Affairs Committee on a classified basis.

51. *The New York Times,* March 19, 1985.

52. Robert C. DiClerico, *The American President,* 2nd ed. (Englewood Cliffs, NJ: Prentice-Hall, 1983), 266.

53. Ibid., 267.

54. Public Law 94-412 National Emergencies Act, 94th Congress, September 14, 1976.

55. *The New York Times,* August 13, 1974.

56. Cronin, *The State of the Presidency,* 210.

57. Ibid., 218.

58. Ibid., 216.

59. David Broder, *Washington Post,* January 21, 1985.

60. *New York Times*/CBS Poll, *The New York Times,* November 8, 1984.

61. Louis W. Koenig, *The Chief Executive,* 4th ed. (New York: Harcourt, Brace, and Jovanovich, 1981), 6.

62. C. Herman Pritchett, "The President's Constitutional Position," in Thomas E. Cronin, ed., *Rethinking the Presidency* (Boston: Little, Brown, 1982), 135.

63. Hirschfield, *The Power of the Presidency,* 11.

chapter 3

Presidential Nominations: The Great American Steeplechase

If the Founding Fathers were to return to earth and view the presidential nominating system of the 1980s in operation, they would blink their eyes in amazement at its complexity—the long selection process, the incredibly high cost, and the dominant role of presidential primaries and television in singling out the eventual nominee. That the process should involve the participation of millions of rank-and-file voters and party members and be officially spread over half a year and unofficially over most of the four-year term would astound them, as would the huge expenditures of the two major parties ($104 million for the 1980 nominating races). Equally startling would be the discovery that an electronic device, found in nearly every living room in America, has largely replaced the political party as the major decision-making agent in presidential nominations.

After a brief historical overview, we will survey the remarkable changes in the nominating process over the past two decades that have revolutionized the way we select presidential nominees: the rapid spread of primaries to more than 30 states; new delegate selection rules (especially in the Democratic party) that tie delegates to a presidential candidate; wholesale revisions in federal campaign finance legislation that now limit the size of individual contributions as well as provide matching subsidies to all candidates who meet minimal fundraising requirements; and the powerful impact of the mass media on the selection process.

We will look at the proliferation of presidential primaries and how the selection of national convention delegates by rank-and-file voters, not state party leaders, has taken away the decision-making power of state delegation leaders. As a result of this power shift, presidential nominees are now, in effect, chosen in the primaries, and the national convention has become chiefly a ratifying body that anoints the popular favorite of the primaries. We will look closely at the role of the mass media in "handicapping" the various contenders in the preprimary period and their *de facto* role as chief arbitrators of the "winners" and "losers" during the primary season.

Public opinion polls now single out the frontrunner early in the race and in turn help him or her generate more publicity and campaign dollars. Candidates also make extensive use of private polls to map strategy and tactics. We now have candidate-centered campaign organizations that recruit delegates pledged to the presidential candidate, not the state party organization. The result is a decline in party influence in the nominating process. The national nominating convention, though less important today than in years gone by, still plays a unique role in maintaining the independent status of the president in the American political system. We will look at all these factors and how the changes are affecting the system.

PRESIDENTIAL NOMINATIONS: A UNIQUE SYSTEM

Beyond all doubt, the process by which American parties select their nominees for president is the longest, most convoluted, and most expensive in the Western world. The U.S. presidential nominating process is unique in another sense; it permits a degree of popular control and participation not found elsewhere in the free world, except in Canada.[1] In 1984, approximately 25 million Americans participated in the presidential primaries, more than double the number of participants in the 1968 primaries. That rank-and-file voters should have a voice in the selection of a national party leader seems bizarre to a foreign observer; in European democracies, there is a clear distinction between the nominating and electing processes. To be sure, the final choice of a national leader is left to the electorate, but the preliminary decision—the nomination that determines which candidate is to be selected as the party standard-bearer—belongs to the party.

In the United States, the presidential nominating race has become a gigantic enterprise in which as many as a dozen candidates in the out-of-power party will campaign for months and spend upward of $70 million before the field is ultimately narrowed to one at the national convention. The nomination preliminaries consist of thirty-plus individual state election contests, or a three- or four-tier caucus-convention system for selecting delegates in states that do not wish to use a popular election system. At the national convention, the delegates (nearly 4,000 at the Democratic convention and more than 2,000 at the GOP gathering) will make the final decision on the candidate who may within four months occupy the most powerful office in the free world.

The transformation of the nominating process over the past 190 years has profoundly affected the evolution of the modern presidency, enhancing the strength and grandeur of the office. The nominating process also has a profound effect on the type of presidential candidate. It seems doubtful, for example, that Abraham Lincoln, an ungainly and unphotogenic country lawyer, would have been able to create a favorable "image" on TV and attract enough voters in the primaries to make a serious bid for the nomination. Nor would a George McGovern or a Jimmy Carter have fared very well at an old-fashioned convention in which the big state delegation leaders sat around the table in a "smoke-filled" room and negotiated political bargains before agreeing on an experienced, "safe" nominee.

THE IMPORTANCE OF THE NOMINATING PROCESS

Nineteenth-century political boss William Marcy Tweed once observed, "I don't care who does the electing just so I can do the nominating." His sage observation underscores a basic political fact of life: Nominations are the decisive stage in the whole process of presidential selection.

Put simply, the presidential nominating process narrows the alternatives from a theoretical potential candidate pool of millions who meet the constitutional requirements to only two candidates, one Republican and one Democrat, with a realistic chance of winning the White House. Political scientist Donald R. Matthews has also noted: "The nominating decision is one of the major determinants of who wins in November."[2] Indeed, because electoral considerations usually take on greater importance in nominating decision making than calculations on probable performance in the White House, the presidential nominating process has as much effect, if not more, as the election itself in shaping the future of the country. The choice of Franklin Delano Roosevelt over Alfred E. Smith in the 1932 Democratic race, the Republican preference for Dwight D. Eisenhower over Senator Robert A. Taft in the 1952 contest, the selection of John F. Kennedy over Adlai E. Stevenson and Lyndon Johnson in 1960, and the Republicans' choice of Ronald Reagan over Howard Baker, George Bush, or John Connally in the 1980 race are all cases in point.

The presidential nominating process has evolved through three basic systems. We have borrowed Thomas R. Marshall's classification: the congressional caucus system, 1800–1824, the brokered convention system, 1832–1968, and the system of popular appeal, 1972–present.[3] Each of these systems differs from the others in several respects: the type of candidate favored, the focus of the nomination, the role of party leaders and rank-and-file members, and the role of campaign funds and the media. In the course of our brief review of these systems, we will also seek an explanation of why the first two ultimately collapsed.

The Constitution says nothing about presidential nominations, even though more than a quarter of the Constitution's article on the presidency (Article II) is devoted to spelling out the complex method by which he is chosen. Why? The Framers seemed to assume that the choice would be made by a council of notables and limited to a small number of obviously well-qualified men, with the best one being selected. Parties, it should not be forgotten, did not exist at the time. Nor did the Framers foresee that the method of picking presidents would soon evolve into a two-stage process: first, the nomination of candidates, and second, an election between candidates from different parties.

It was assumed that after George Washington stepped down, electoral votes would be so widely distributed (because each state would probably vote for its favorite son) that rarely would a candidate receive a majority; most presidents would therefore ultimately be chosen by the House of Representatives. In other words, the electors would "screen" (nominate) the candidates, and the House of Representatives would make the final choice. This arrangement was a package of compromises. To placate large states, the Framers gave them an elector for each congressional seat, so that in the initial vote of the Electoral College the large states would have an advantage. But since it was assumed that most presidents would be finally chosen in the House of Representatives, with each state having one vote, the small states would have a greater voice in the final choice.

TWO CENTURIES OF PRESIDENTIAL NOMINATIONS

The first presidential nomination presented no problem, since George Washington was the unanimous choice of his countrymen. Eight years later, however, Washington's announcement that he would not seek a third term signaled the opening of the first presidential nominating contest. But his belated announcement in his Farewell Address left little time for potential contenders to organize campaigns. Rival factions in Congress—the Federalists and Democratic-Republicans—convened into newly formed congressional caucuses to select their nominee. The Federalists, aware that Washington was planning to step down, actually had already held caucuses during the summer of 1796 and chosen Vice-President John Adams to be their nominee and Thomas Pinckney as his running mate. Thomas Jefferson was the choice of the Democratic-Republican (later to be called Democrats) caucus to head the ticket, and Aaron Burr was picked as his running mate. In neither case did the parties make formal nominations; they merely decided among themselves, counting upon their political influence to keep the presidential electors in line. But as Neal Peirce, a leading authority on the electoral college, has noted: "The rise of the caucus system destroyed forever any lingering pretense that the Presidential electors, chosen later in the election year in each state, would be dispassionate searchers for men of 'continental character' who were fit to be Chief Magistrate of the republic."[4]

Congressional Caucus System: 1800–1824. From 1800 to 1820, the Democratic-Republicans relied exclusively on their congressional caucus to pick the party standard-bearers—Jefferson, Madison, and Monroe. The congressional caucus (known as King Caucus) had quickly become a centralized or national mechanism that contained some representatives from all or nearly all the states. For almost a quarter of a century the congressional caucus gave its official stamp of approval to each Democratic-Republican nominee and thereby suppressed any serious challenge to his candidacy.

The rival Federalists, their numbers dwindling in the face of widespread Democratic-Republican popularity, turned to other means to pick their nominees. In 1808 and 1812, the Federalists resorted to an informal nominating convention. Unlike the national conventions that subsequently emerged in the Jacksonian era, the Federalist conventions consisted of small groups, designated in a variety of ways, meeting in secret. These small conclaves furnished a measure of legitimacy to the presidential candidates they nominated, even though some states were not represented. But the Federalists, no match for the Democratic-Republican nominees, were overwhelmed in the presidential contests. By 1816, the Federalists had faded into history. The superficial unity of the congressional caucus disintegrated in 1824 because there was no opposition party to force the reigning Democratic-Republicans, faced with a multicandidate field, to unite and make a binding nomination.

The dominant Democratic party (the leaders had dropped the hyphenated name) had splintered into warring factions. William Crawford, former secretary of the treasury in Madison's cabinet, was the caucus choice, but he won only 64 votes out of the 240 eligible among members of Congress. Almost three-quarters of the congressmen boycotted the caucus. Ten states were not represented at the meeting, and five others had only one member present.[5] The anti-Crawford forces wanted to scuttle King Caucus once and for all, but they had no alternate system available. Three candidates—Henry Clay of Kentucky, Andrew Jackson of Tennessee, and John C. Calhoun—were nominated by their home state legislatures; John Quincy Adams was endorsed by several New England legislatures. All these candidates were subsequently endorsed by the legislatures in other states.

The election of 1824 marked the end of an era—the demise of the congressional caucus and the short-lived one-party system. The system was abandoned because it smacked of aristocratic privilege; it violated the great touchstone of Jacksonian democracy, popular sovereignty. Another charge against the caucus, an argument that came to a head in 1824, was that it violated the separation of powers, a basic principle of the Constitution. Contemporary critics pointed out that the congressional caucus amounted, in effect, to the selection of the chief executive by the legislative branch. This could lead, they said, to domination of the president by Congress or the corruption of Congress by presidents or would-be presidents.

Spokesmen for the expanding sectional interests complained that the Virginia dynasty (Jefferson, Madison, and Monroe) and their congressional caucus system of presidential nominations had transformed the selection process into an oligarchical scheme to perpetuate control of the national government. Moreover, interested and informed citizens who participated in politics at the grassroots level, especially during campaigns, were totally excluded from the presidential nominating process.[6]

The demise of the congressional caucus, it has been pointed out, not only altered the character of the young political parties, but changed the constitutional system as well. From 1800 to the 1820s, "the main impact of caucus nominations was to convert the formal separation of powers between the President and Congress into a *de facto* 'fusion of powers' not unlike such parliamentary systems as the British."[7] But the collapse of the congressional caucus, the rise of the popular favorite Andrew Jackson, and the emergence of presidential nominations by national conventions consisting of delegations chosen by state parties gave "him and succeeding Presidents a base of power independent of Congress . . . totally split Congress off from the presidential succession and established for the first time an institutionalized, *real* separation of powers."[8] State and local parties, though their leaders may not have recognized it at the time, had won a great victory.

Brokered Convention Systems: 1832–1968. Presidential nominations shifted totally to the state level in 1828. State legislatures and party conventions selected "favorite sons," such as Andrew Jackson and President Adams, as their nominees. But state leaders were dissatisfied with this decentralized form of nomination, since it lacked a national mandate. Three years later, a small splinter group, the Anti-Masonic party, decided to experiment with a unique nominating mechanism—a national convention. Almost by accident, the Anti-Masons discovered that a national party convention, consisting of delegates chosen in most of the states, could serve as a forum to assess and discuss prospective presidential candidates before choosing a party standard-bearer. Though the Anti-Masons, caught in the Jacksonian electoral tide, did not survive to hold another national convention, this minor party will forever be credited with developing the unique American nominating system.

Following the trail blazed by the Anti-Masonic party, the newly formed National Republicans, consisting of former Federalists and disgruntled Democrats, decided to call a national convention in 1832. They chose Henry Clay to carry the party banner. President Jackson, borrowing a page from the Anti-Masons and National Republicans, instructed his managers to convene a national convention in 1832 in order to ensure that his hand-picked vice-presidential running mate, Martin Van Buren, would be nominated, rather than trusting to endorsement of Van Buren by various state legislatures. Jackson agreed too that a national convention would emphasize his great popular support.

By 1840, the newly emergent Whig party (formed from the elements of the defunct National Republican party and anti-Jackson Democrats) had also adopted the national convention to pick its nominee. Sixteen years later, the new Republican party also borrowed the convention idea. Since then, the national nominating conventions of the two major parties have been a regular part of the American scene. The national convention was clearly an idea well suited for the young nation:

> The national convention system has concentrated the electorate behind the two major party nominees, thus keeping the final selection away from Congress and giving the President a base of support independent of the legislative branch. Clearly, the national convention has strengthened the nominee's ability not only to lead his party but—if successful at the polls—to lead the nation as well. Thus, it can be said that the national convention, though it has escaped constitutional regulation, has profoundly shaped the nature of the Presidency as much as the party system itself has.[9]

Within a short time, the national conventions and the party system underwent a major transformation. State party leaders took control of the conventions and forced the various aspirants to bargain with them over patronage matters—cabinet posts, judgeships, and other federal appointments—before gaining their stamp of approval. The rapid shift of power from the candidates to the state party leaders operating in convention must have surprised some leading presidential contenders. Three-time nominee Henry Clay suddenly discovered this fact of political life in 1840 when the Whig party managers at their convention passed him over in favor of the veteran Indian fighter General William Henry Harrison because the aging general and his running mate, John Tyler of Virginia, appeared to have more chance of success.

By the mid-1840s, the national nominating convention had reached maturity. The caucus-convention system remained the only method of nominating candidates—both presidential and state and local candidates—until about 1910. Defenders of the convention system insisted that it reflected the "popular will" because delegates had been chosen by other delegates selected from county and precinct caucuses. Unlike present-day conventions, most of the political bargaining took place at the convention itself, rather than before. National conventions were often protracted multiballot conclaves, because the party choice usually did not bubble to the surface until after state party leaders had reached a consensus or at least discarded most of the unacceptable candidates. Within the Democratic party, conventions were also prolonged by the two-thirds rule (repealed in 1936), which required that the eventual nominee receive a two-thirds and not a simple majority to claim the nomination.[10]

Late in the nineteenth century, critics began protesting that political rings were manipulating state nominating conventions and that the delegates attending these conventions and those chosen to represent the state at the national nominating conventions were often unsavory characters affiliated with the moneyed interests and the underworld. By the turn of the century, the reformers' charges against the party bosses and the vested interests who worked with them reverberated across the land. It was this rising discontent among the middle class—the small businessman, members of the professions, and independent farmers—that spawned the Progressive movement.[11] From this protest movement was to emerge the direct primary system and the first major reform of the national nominating convention in almost a century—the presidential primary.

Emergence of Presidential Primaries. The Progressives demanded that the state party "kingmakers" and political machines be replaced by popularly elected national convention delegates chosen in state presidential primaries. To sidetrack boss control of the presidential nominating process, the Progressives proposed giving rank-and-file voters the opportunity to elect national convention delegates and to express their personal preferences for the candidate for president. Indeed, some of these reformers believed that the national party convention eventually should merely ratify the choice of president made in primaries held throughout the United States.

By 1912, a dozen states had adopted presidential primaries to pick delegates and, in some instances, to register their personal choice for president. Structurally, the Progressives' institutional plan called for shifting the locus of decision making in the nominating process from the national convention itself to the preconvention stage—the primary. By 1916, more than two dozen states had experimented with some form of popular selection of delegates,[12] but at no time were a majority of delegates chosen in the primaries. Indeed, the Progressive dream for a popularly selected nominee fell far short of the mark. The conservative reaction after World War I took the momentum out of the Progressive movement. By 1935, eight states had repealed their presidential primary laws, and the party regulars had moved back into the driver's seat. More than two-thirds of the states again used the caucus-convention system to pick national convention delegates, and most of the primary state delegates were unpledged.

Until the 1960s, presidential candidates depended mostly on informal contacts with state party leaders in the various states. While primary victories were sometimes a necessary condition for winning party support, they never played a decisive role in obtaining the nomination. Traditionally, the leading contenders dispatched "drummers"—usually personal confidants—to various sections of the country to contact state leaders and prospective delegates to seek pledges of support and to reach "understandings" on possible second ballot support, in the event the state wished to put forth a "favorite son" on the first ballot. During this period most primaries were "advisory"—that is, elected delegates were not pledged, and the presidential preference vote was not binding on the state delegation.[13]

Demands for Reform within the Democratic Party.   Since the tumultuous 1968 Democratic convention in Chicago, however, the loosely drawn delegate selection rules have been thoroughly overhauled. In politics the old adage, "Knowing the rules is half the game," has more relevance to presidential nominating races than almost any other aspect of the political process. Insurgent presidential contender and senator Eugene McCarthy of Minnesota and his supporters discovered this fact repeatedly in the spring of 1968, as he sought to wrest the Democratic nomination from Vice-President Hubert H. Humphrey, who replaced Lyndon Johnson as the party insiders' choice for the nomination after Johnson announced his intention not to seek another term. At almost every turn the McCarthyites found the rules stacked against a challenger. Closed caucuses, unpledged delegates who refused to support the winner of the presidential preference primary, and iron-clad control over the selection of at-large delegates by the state party organization were typical barriers the McCarthy backers encountered in most of the caucus-convention and primary states.[14]

In 1968, 26 states and 3 territories selected their entire delegation to the national convention at state conventions. As further evidence of "boss rule," the McGovern Commission discovered that in 1968 four state Democratic parties— Arizona, Arkansas, Maryland, and Rhode Island—and the territory of Puerto Rico selected their entire delegations to the national convention by party committees. In 2 other states, Georgia and Louisiana, the chairman of the State Democratic Executive Committee chose the entire state delegation, with the advice and consent of the governor—in effect, the governor made the choice. A few states used a "mixed" system. Illinois, for example, chose two-thirds of its delegates by convention and one-third by primary.[15]

Sixteen states and the District of Columbia used primaries, but only in four states were the delegates officially bound by the presidential preference vote for one or two ballots; most of the primaries were "advisory." Thus, Senator McCarthy won 78.5 percent of the Pennsylvania presidential preference vote, but collected only 18 percent of the delegates. Clearly, the cards were stacked against an "outsider" candidate like McCarthy. For the McCarthy supporters, the ultimate miscarriage of justice occurred at the Chicago convention when Vice-President Humphrey, the 1968 Democratic nominee, who did not enter a single primary, received 1,760 delegate votes to McCarthy's 601.

It was this type of leadership control of the presidential nomination process that generated widespread demands within the Democratic party for reform of the delegate selection process. Charges by McCarthy's anti-Vietnam-war supporters that party rules were "rigged" against his insurgent candidacy fell mostly on deaf ears, but the Humphrey-controlled 1968 Democratic convention delegates agreed to the repeal of the *unit rule* (the requirement that all members of a state delegation must vote with the majority) at future conventions. The minority report of the Convention Rules Committee, subsequently passed by the convention, also decreed that "All feasible efforts [be] made to assure that delegates are selected through party primary conventions, or committee procedures open to public participation within the calendar year of the national convention."[16] (The McCarthy reformers claimed that more than a third of the convention delegates —over 600 delegates—had, in effect, already been selected prior to 1968, before either the issues or possible candidates were known.)

As a result of these protests, the convention directed the Democratic National Committee to establish a commission to implement the convention resolutions. In accordance with this directive, Senator Fred Harris, chairman of the Democratic National Committee, appointed a Commission on Party Structure and Delegate Selection, chaired by Senator George McGovern of South Dakota, in early 1969. Little did the Democrats realize that with the appointment of the McGovern Commission, the party—in fact, American politics—would never be the same again. (The task force name was later changed to McGovern-Fraser Commission when McGovern resigned the chairmanship to run for president in 1971, and was replaced by Congressman Donald Fraser of Minnesota.)

McGovern-Fraser Commission Reforms.   To avoid a repeat of the 1968 convention, the McGovern-Fraser Commission recommended that all state parties adopt and make readily available rules on how delegates are to be picked. Furthermore, the task force recommended that all delegates be given the opportunity to list their presidential preference on the ballot (including the designation "uncommitted"). To correct other serious abuses in the delegate selection process, the commission adopted a series of rules changes that (a) required delegates to be chosen during the calendar year of the election; (b) banned proxy voting by an *ex officio* delegate; (c) banned secret caucuses, closed slatemaking, and other procedural irregularities; (d) established quorum requirements at 40 percent; and (e) restricted the number of appointed delegates to 10 percent of the national delegation.[17]

Though the McGovern-Fraser Commission expressed no preference be-

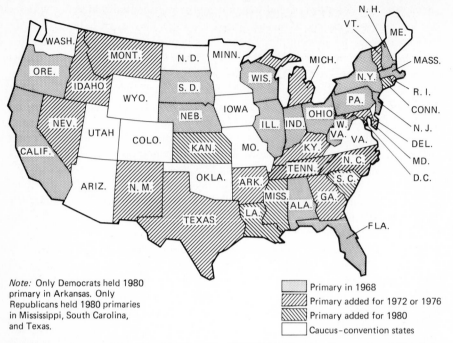

Note: Only Democrats held 1980 primary in Arkansas. Only Republicans held 1980 primaries in Mississippi, South Carolina, and Texas.

▨ Primary in 1968
▧ Primary added for 1972 or 1976
▨ Primary added for 1980
☐ Caucus-convention states

Figure 3.1 Growth of Presidential Primaries, 1968–1980 (*Source: Congressional Quarterly Weekly Report,* February 2, 1980, p. 283.)

tween the caucus-convention and primary systems for selecting delegates to future national conventions, one of the unintended consequences of the commission's report was to spawn a proliferation of presidential primaries. By 1980, the number of presidential primary states had risen to 35 (see Figure 3.1). Thus, nearly 75 percent of the convention delegates attending the 1980 Democratic convention (the figure was slightly lower at the GOP convention) were chosen by rank-and-file voters, and most of these delegates were pledged to specific candidates. In a number of states the Republican party, which had not been overly enthusiastic about party reform, was swept along by the Democratic reform tide, since state primary laws usually covered both parties.

Between 1980 and 1984, however, six states shifted from a primary to a caucus system (see Table 3.1). The proportion of delegates chosen in the caucus-convention states rose from 28 percent in 1980 to 32 percent in 1984. Within the Democratic party, officeholders and party officials—the so-called superdelegates—accounted for another 14 percent. As a result, only 54 percent of the 1984 Democratic delegates were chosen in primaries.[18] Within the GOP, approximately 71 percent of the delegates were selected in primaries.

With the rapid proliferation of primaries, presidential candidates now have no choice but to campaign in the primaries. For most presidential aspirants, the march toward the nomination begins long before the presidential primary season opens.[19] Indeed, in some respects, the quest for the presidency has become a continuous four-year campaign.

Table 3.1 **NUMBER OF PRESIDENTIAL PRIMARIES AND PERCENTAGE OF CONVENTION DELEGATES FROM PRIMARY STATES, BY PARTY, SINCE 1912**

	Democratic		Republican	
Year	Number of primaries	Percentage of delegates	Number of primaries	Percentage of delegates
1912	12	32.9	13	41.7
1916	20	53.5	20	58.9
1920	16	44.6	20	57.8
1924	14	35.5	17	45.3
1928	17	42.2	16	44.9
1932	16	40.0	14	37.7
1936	14	36.5	12	37.5
1940	13	35.8	13	38.8
1944	14	36.7	13	38.7
1948	14	36.3	12	36.0
1952	15	38.7	13	39.0
1956	19	42.7	19	44.8
1960	16	38.3	15	38.6
1964	17	45.7	17	45.6
1968	17	37.5	16	34.3
1972	23	60.5	22	52.7
1976	29*	72.6	28*	67.9
1980	31*	71.8	35*	76.0
1984	26	62.1	30	71.0

*Does not include Vermont, which held nonbinding presidential preference votes but chose delegates in state caucuses and conventions.

Sources: 1912–1976, James W. Davis, *Presidential Primaries: Road to the White House,* 2nd ed. (Westport, CT: Greenwood Press, 1980), pp. 279–357, copyright © 1980 by James W. Davis, used by permission of the publisher; Richard C. Bain and Judith H. Parris, *Convention Decisions and Voting Records,* 2nd ed. (Washington, DC: The Brookings Institution, 1973); William Crotty and John S. Jackson III, *Presidential Primaries and Nominations* (Washington, DC: Congressional Quarterly Press, 1985), pp. 62–63; figures for 1980 and 1984 were supplied by the Democratic and Republican national committees.

System of Popular Appeal: 1972 to Present. Today, presidential nominations have become a vast national popularity contest and a delegate-hunting sweepstakes. No longer can a candidate hope to strike deals with state delegation leaders at the national convention and nail down the nomination. The recently expanded primaries, with their pledged-delegate requirements, have taken power away from the party leaders and put it in the hands of rank-and-file voters. Participatory democracy has become the watchword, and the number of Americans involved in the nominating process has risen steadily. Between 1968 and 1984, the number of participants in the Democratic primaries increased from 12 to nearly 18 million.[20] Almost 6.5 million votes were cast in the uncontested 1984 GOP primaries, with President Reagan collecting 98.6 percent of the vote.[21]

Because primaries have become the main battleground for the nomination and because the early primaries have such a decisive impact on the amount of media coverage received and the outcome of subsequent primaries, some of the bigger states have moved up their primary dates to the first six weeks of the season. With their far larger delegations, they wish to exercise influence commensurate with their size. *Frontloading* is the term given to this shifting to the earlier dates.

For those who question the devastating impact that the first primary, that of New Hampshire, has on sorting out the winners and losers in recent nominating races, it might be noted that within ten days following the 1976 Democratic primary in New Hampshire, Senator Birch Bayh (D–Ind.) dropped out of the race, along with three other lesser-known candidates. In the 1980 GOP nominating race, Senators Howard Baker (R–Tenn.) and Robert Dole (R–Kan.) were so badly wounded politically by their poor showings in New Hampshire that they soon pulled out of the Republican contest. Within two days after the 1984 New Hampshire primary, Senators Alan Cranston (D–Calif.) and Ernest Hollings (D–S.C.) and former Florida governor Reubin Askew all folded their campaigns, even though in Cranston's case he had invested over $3 million in a year-long national bid for the nomination.

The rapid spread of primaries also enticed more candidates to enter primary contests, since candidates could not hope to win the nomination without capturing a major share of the primary state delegates. Other factors also contributed to the growing crop of contenders in presidential nominating races of the out-of-power party. Adoption of proportional representation primaries in more than a dozen states encouraged more candidates to enter the race because any reasonably attractive candidate could expect to collect a portion of the delegates in these states. With only a modest effort, it was unlikely that candidates would be shut out from receiving some pledged delegates.[22] James Lengle and Byron Shafer have also noted: "By 1972, the linkage between candidate preference and delegate selection had been tightened so much that the free agents of past primaries—'favorite sons,' 'bosses,' and 'uncommitted'—had almost disappeared."[23]

The overall effect of the Democratic party reforms was to tie the popular vote more closely to the allocation of convention delegates. As a result of the McGovern-Fraser reforms, most delegates began running as pledged to a specific candidate. Presidential candidates, operating under the new rules, began actively recruiting pledged delegate candidates to run on their slates. For these delegates, loyalty to a candidate became far more important than loyalty to the state delegation.

STAGES OF THE NOMINATING RACE

Within the out-of-power party, the nominating process, according to political scientist John Kessel, proceeds through four stages: the early days between the midterm congressional elections and the selection of the first delegates (this period has been called "the invisible primary" by Arther T. Hadley); the opening round contests when the long-awaited caucuses and primaries signal the beginning of the presidential steeplechase; the "mist clearing" stage in which doubts about the outcome are cleared away by the crucial contests, especially in the big-delegate states; and finally the national convention, which ratifies the nomination of the popular favorite of the primaries and caucuses and marks the beginning of the general election campaign.[24]

Nominating races, Kessel agrees, do not always follow this precise pattern, but his time frames for the nominating process are a convenient outline for these marathon contests. Certainly the 1984 Democratic nominating race evolved through Kessel's four-stage process, with former Vice-President Walter F. Mondale eventually clinching the nomination in the final week of the primary season. Within the Republican party, the 1976 nominating battle between President Ford and Ronald Reagan unfolded through the same four-stage process. However, some other recent nominating races have ended, unofficially at least, somewhat earlier. In 1968, for example, former Vice-President Nixon almost won the GOP nomination by default when his leading competitor, Michigan governor George Romney, withdrew from the primaries a week before the first-round New Hampshire contest. In 1976, Jimmy Carter effectively locked up the Democratic nomination by driving his last major opponent, Senator Henry M. Jackson, from the race after the Pennsylvania primary in late April. Four years later, the GOP frontrunner Ronald Reagan virtually had the field to himself after his big Illinois primary victory in mid-March, though George Bush, his chief rival, persisted against hopeless odds until late May. Looking ahead, it seems reasonable to expect that most nominating races will unfold through the four-stage process outlined by Kessel.

Most candidates in the out-of-power party will spend upward of two years gearing up for the big race, establishing fundraising operations and lining up support throughout the country, with special attention focused on the early primary and caucus states. To win, they know they will have to score well in the early contests and collect a major share of the big state primaries. To achieve these dual objectives, however, they will first need to develop a strategic plan for their nominating campaign.

CANDIDATES' STRATEGIC PLANNING

Candidate game plans will depend upon a number of factors: their name recognition, their standing in the polls, and the availability of money and trained staff. Furthermore, as Crotty and Jackson point out: "Candidates face the complex task of appealing not only to the party's electorate but to the potential delegates and to the influential party elites (who can attract and provide money and endorsements); the general election voter is continually in the background."[25] Generally, candidate strategies fall into two major categories: frontrunner and outsider.

The Frontrunner Strategy. Leading contenders within the out-of-power party, relying on their superior resources, hope to score an early knockout victory. With their high name identification, strong campaign organizations in the early primary and caucus states, skilled pollsters, media experts, and efficient fundraising operation, the frontrunners try to drive their intraparty rivals out of the race early by demonstrating widespread popular appeal and a big delegate lead—big enough, they hope, to persuade their opponents of the futility of continuing the race. If this tactic fails, they can switch, as Mondale did in 1984, to waging a political battle of attrition, wearing down their less-equipped opponents by fighting each primary and caucus battle until they accumulate enough pledged delegates to claim victory.

To be rated a frontrunner in the presidential nominating race is both a blessing and curse. The chief advantages in the out-of-power party (frontrunner defined here as the leader of the Gallup poll before the primary season begins) are widespread name recognition and a broader political base, plus favorable ratings in the early polls. The frontrunner finds it easier to raise money, to set up campaign organizations in the major primary states, and to obtain endorsements from national and state party figures. But the frontrunner's position creates expectations that he is a winner and should perform accordingly. Although a frontrunner can overcome a limited number of defeats, he will find it difficult to survive a series of setbacks.

The track record of frontrunning candidates in the out-of-power party is mixed. Frontrunners John F. Kennedy in 1960, Richard Nixon in 1968, and Ronald Reagan all used the frontrunner strategy effectively to nail down the nomination on the first ballot by impressive victories in the primaries and caucus-convention states. Ronald Reagan's preconvention campaign in 1980 is a good model of the frontrunner candidate. Though he suffered an initial defeat in the first-round Iowa precinct caucuses, he quickly regained momentum by a solid victory in the New Hampshire primary and a string of triumphs in several southern primaries and caucuses. By the time Reagan had won the Wisconsin primary in early April, he had driven all of his competitors except George Bush from the field.[26] His early-round victories also persuaded former President Gerald Ford, who had been considering a late entry into the race, to stay out. By heavy expenditures in the early primary and caucus states, Reagan was able to build an in-depth organization and a delegate lead that generated the momentum—"Big Mo," as it has been called—that soon made him look like a winner.

In 1984, former Vice-President Walter F. Mondale soon learned that the frontrunner position can be a mixed blessing. After three years of continuous campaigning for the nomination, Mondale had gained endorsements from the AFL-CIO, numerous lawmakers on Capitol Hill, and support from ethnic and women's groups as well as educators. But as the primary season opened, he found that he had become identified as the candidate of the "special interests"—a label that dogged him throughout the primaries and the general election. Mondale jumped out of the starting gate quickly with a victory in the first-round Iowa caucuses. Although upset by Senator Gary Hart in early-round contests in New Hampshire, Vermont, Maine, Massachusetts, and Florida, Mondale's organization and strength, coupled with victories in two southern primary states, Alabama and Georgia, and then followed by key big-state primary wins in Illinois, Michigan, New York, and Pennsylvania, enabled him to recover from his defeats and go on to claim the nomination.

The Outsider Strategy.   Over the past three decades, the road to the nomination has been littered with the bones of many defeated challengers and outsider candidates—Kefauver, McCarthy, Bayh, Shapp, and Crane, to mention only a few victims. But two outsiders—George McGovern and Jimmy Carter—captured the nomination, and Carter, of course, made it to the White House for one term.

For political unknowns, an outsider strategy is the only course open to them. They must first become recognized by the voters and then prove their vote-getting strength in the early primaries, or face political oblivion. Senator George McGovern, although he was the choice of less than 4 percent of the voters in a January 1972 Gallup poll, soon discovered in New Hampshire and Wisconsin that he had the popular appeal and campaign organization to gain the party nomination.[27]

Underfinanced and forced to live off the land until some early victories attract more financial supporters, the outsider candidate is often much like a financially strapped debtor who must stay one jump ahead of the creditors until more money flows into his bank account. Four years later, former Georgia governor Jimmy Carter proved with a carefully mapped campaign plan and nearly 275 days of preprimary campaigning in the early primary and caucus states the year before the 1976 race that an outsider candidate could follow this campaign route all the way to the White House. The Carter game plan, drafted more than a year before the 1976 primary season by Hamilton Jordan, his manager, rested on four assumptions which, if they proved correct, might open the road to the nomination—and possibly the White House:

1. That the nomination would be won in the parade of over 30 primary elections and in the early-round caucus-convention states, not in the smoke-filled back rooms at the Democratic convention.
2. That fellow southerner Governor George Wallace, despite his spectacular primary campaign in 1972 before he was gunned down by a would-be assassin, could be knocked out of the race in 1976 and his influence as a national political figure reduced to a token level.
3. That Carter's own southern origins and his image as an unknown newcomer without ties to the Washington establishment could be turned into formidable assets, not crippling liabilities.
4. That most voters would be more favorably disposed toward a candidate stressing personal qualities—trust and integrity—than toward a candidate emphasizing his ideological stand on the issues.[28]

By concentrating on the first-round Iowa precinct caucuses and the first-in-the-nation New Hampshire primary—and winning plurality (not majority) victories in both states—Carter reaped a publicity bonanza. Television networks suddenly gave him four times the coverage of all his defeated opponents combined, and his face quickly appeared on the covers of *Time* and *Newsweek.* His name recognition jumped from 20 to 80 percent in the polls—the fastest rise in the history of the Gallup poll. When he defeated Alabama governor George Wallace in the Florida primary, Carter became the undisputed frontrunner. By then, most of the other outsider candidates had dropped out of the race—Birch Bayh, Fred Harris, Sargent Shriver, Terry Sanford, Milton Shapp, and Lloyd Bentsen. When Senator Henry M. Jackson, the early frontrunner, withdrew from the race after his loss to Carter in the late April Pennsylvania primary, Carter had a clear road to the nomination.

One of Carter's aides readily conceded in a postconvention interview: "We organized only three states in depth—Iowa, Florida, and New Hampshire."[29] But winning the early contests to become known nationally and pyramiding these victories into triumphs in the big-delegate states, Carter used his outsider strategy to carry him all the way to the White House.[30]

The frontrunner/outsider strategies, it should be noted, are not mutually exclusive. Ronald Reagan, for example, pursued an outsider strategy against President Ford in 1976. Four years later, with the GOP no longer in control of the White House, Reagan and his campaign advisers successfully used the frontrunner strategy to capture the nomination.

In 1984, six Democratic aspirants—Reubin Askew, Alan Cranston, Gary Hart, Ernest Hollings, George McGovern, and Jesse Jackson—pursued the outsider strategy. Only Gary Hart emerged from this field to become a serious contender. Gary Hart's surprise showing in Iowa, and his primary victories in New Hampshire, Massachusetts, and Florida, catapulted him into a temporary lead. But the bane of most outsider candidates—shortage of professional staff, especially skilled field organizers and inadequate funds—prevented him from organizing sufficiently in the big primary states of Illinois, Michigan, New York, and Pennsylvania and knocking Mondale out of the race.

Jesse Jackson, the first serious black candidate for president in American history, demonstrated that an outsider candidate with minimal funding and a small, inexperienced staff can sometimes be a formidable challenger to the leading contenders. Dismissed as a mere publicity-seeker early in the 1984 race, Jackson soon developed a grassroots movement among younger blacks—the black political establishment supported Mondale—that carried him all the way to the Democratic national convention in San Francisco. Jackson, leading his "rainbow coalition" of blacks, Hispanics, native and Asian Americans, low-income whites, and liberal activists, proved his vote-getting power by winning Louisiana and the District of Columbia—and capturing 18 percent of the Democratic vote. As a result of the reformed Democratic rules, however, Jackson received only 7 percent of the convention delegates. Jackson complained repeatedly right down to convention time that the party rules shortchanged him, but his protests fell mostly on deaf ears. In the televised debates with his Democratic rivals, Jackson more than held his own. Throughout the primary season the national news media—especially the TV networks—accorded him near-celebrity status. At no time, however, did Jackson come close to winning the Democratic nomination. Still, this eloquent Baptist preacher—the product of the militant civil rights movement of the 1960s—altered presidential nominating politics by injecting the racial factor directly into the already fragmented Democratic party. The full impact of Jackson's entry into Democratic presidential politics, it seems fair to say, may not be known for years to come.

RENOMINATION STRATEGY

If a president wishes to seek reelection, the old cliché still applies: "The presidency is the best place to campaign for President." In 1980, Jimmy Carter used his incumbency effectively, as Gerald Pomper has noted:

> He emphasized the experience he had gained as the nation's chief executive, an asset unavailable to any Democratic contender. Without any special effort,

he could be assured of daily news coverage and could request network time for "non-political" events at any time. Every visit of a foreign dignitary, every signing of legislation, and every speech to the Congress or news conference was a reminder that Jimmy Carter was president, while others only hoped for the job.[31]

Throughout the nominating season, Carter pursued this Rose Garden strategy, which permitted him to remain in the nation's capital, thus removing himself as a target of criticism. Also, Carter did not hesitate to use the traditional benefits of incumbency: the release of federal funds for state and local improvement projects and federal appointments to achieve maximum electoral impact. As the campaign unfolded, Carter also utilized other prerogatives of the office to generate popular support, such as inviting the U.S. Olympic hockey champions, who had just defeated the Russians in the finals, to the White House on the eve of the New Hampshire primary. Still, Carter faced a strong challenge for the Democratic nomination from Senator Edward Kennedy, the youngest brother of the fallen president.

Challenging an incumbent president seeking a second term, however, has never been an easy task. In fact, no sitting president has been denied renomination —not even Herbert Hoover in 1932—in the twentieth century.

Who are the presidential nominees? What route have they followed to reach a point only one step removed from the White House? Let's take a moment to examine how an aspirant becomes a "presidential possibility" and assess what the prospects are of this person becoming the party nominee.

THE SERIOUS PRESIDENTIAL POSSIBILITIES

Political scientists Keech and Matthews found that between 1936 and 1972 only slightly more than 100 men (and one woman) emerged as "presidential possibilities"—serious candidates. Using the criterion of 1 percent or more public support in the Gallup poll, Keech and Matthews calculated that 62 Democrats and 47 Republicans met this "presidential possibility" criterion during this period.[32] The recent plethora of candidates in the 1976 Democratic and 1980 Republican races (using the same Gallup criterion) would expand this number of presidential possibilities by only a handful. Other similar criteria probably would not enlarge this entire list of presidential possibilities by more than a dozen or so. Indeed, this working list probably errs on the side of including too many potential candidates rather than too few. It is also noteworthy that no one between 1936 and 1972 was nominated for the presidency who was not on this list. Moreover, with the exception of Wendell Willkie, no one has been nominated who had not been on this list for a substantial period of time. Undoubtedly, a more realistic rule of thumb for developing a short list of presidential possibilities would be to exclude all candidates who fail to become the choice of at least 15 percent of their partisans in the Gallup poll sometime during the preconvention campaign.

During the 1928–1984 period, over 85 percent of all nominees were elected officeholders—the only exceptions being Herbert Hoover (1928), a cabinet member in the Harding and Coolidge administrations; Wendell Willkie (1940), a businessman-lawyer; and retired General Dwight D. Eisenhower (1952). The record during this period also shows that all presidential nominees who have held public office have been either vice-presidents, governors, or U.S. senators at the time of their nomination or formerly held one of these offices (see Table 3.2). The exact route followed by each of the nominees for the period 1928–1984 is depicted in Figure 3.2.

One of the most significant trends in the twentieth-century nominating politics has been the electoral success of vice-presidents winning the White House outright after moving to the presidency upon the death of the incumbent. This represents a complete reversal from the nineteenth century pattern.[33] Four twentieth-century vice-presidents—Theodore Roosevelt, Calvin Coolidge, Harry Truman, and Lyndon Johnson—have all been subsequently nominated and elected president on their own. Only Gerald Ford, who won nomination to a full term after taking over the presidential duties from the deposed President Nixon (who had also previously served two terms as vice-president), failed to retain his office. Of the four nineteenth-century presidents who succeeded automatically to the presidency—Tyler, Fillmore, Johnson, and Arthur—all sought renomination and none achieved it. This complete reversal of the nineteenth-century experience can

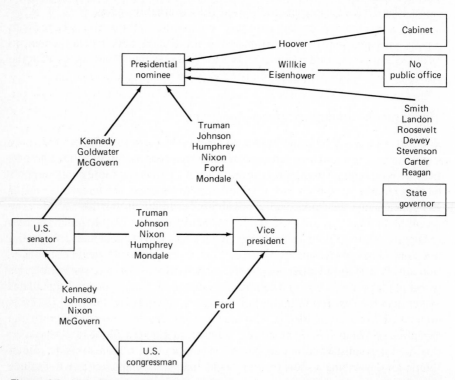

Figure 3.2 High Public Offices Held by Major Party Presidential Nominees, 1928–1984 (*Source:* John A. Crittenden, *Parties and Elections in the United States* [Englewood Cliffs, N J: Prentice-Hall, 1982], p. 213. Adapted from William R. Keech and Donald R. Matthews, *The Party's Choice* [Washington, DC: The Brookings Institution, 1976], p. 20. Reprinted by permission of The Brookings Institution.)

probably be explained by the twentieth-century presidents' ability to capitalize on the expanded role of presidents as world leaders, the persistence of international crises, and continuing domestic problems. The power and expanded prestige of the White House has also helped the incumbents keep potential challengers at a distance—at least for one term. It might also be noted that all four incumbents won office before the recent age of party reform and the rapid spread of presidential primaries.

More recently, the vice-presidency has become an important steppingstone to the nomination for president in yet another way. Since 1956, each time an incumbent president has stepped down, the incumbent vice-president—Nixon in 1960 and Humphrey in 1968—has received the nomination of the party in power. In 1984, former Vice-President Mondale, who had left office in 1981, won the Democratic nomination. Even serving as the party nominee for vice-president in an unsuccessful venture or seeking the number two spot can sometimes have future payoffs. Franklin D. Roosevelt was the Democratic vice-presidential nominee in 1920, twelve years before he won the presidency. In 1956, John F. Kennedy narrowly missed being selected the Democratic vice-presidential nominee, and four years later he moved into the White House.

In recent years, the U.S. Senate has been depicted as the "incubator" of presidential candidates.[34] But this recent emergence of the Senate as a major source of presidential candidates should not hide the fact that from 1878 to 1960 only two members of the U.S. Senate—Benjamin Harrison and Warren G. Harding—were nominated and elected. Several reasons have been advanced to explain the senatorial failure to win nomination contests. First, presidential duties were considered largely administrative and, unlike that of governors, the legislative experience of senators was not seen as directly relevant to the skills required of the president. Second, governors frequently controlled state party delegations at national conventions and so were usually in a better position to launch their own candidacies. Third, senators were not popularly elected until 1914 (after passage of the Seventeenth Amendment in 1913).

Consequently, senators usually lacked firsthand campaign experience and popularity testing in their own states. Without established political track records in an era of closely contested national elections, especially when special importance was attached to carrying one's own state, senators were viewed as riskier candidates than governors fresh from one or more recent election victories. More recently, however, the reasons formerly advanced for picking governors as presidential nominees have come to be regarded in some instances as liabilities, and the former liabilities of senators have been transformed into political assets.

As a result of the nationalization of American politics and the growth of the mass media centered in Washington, senators have found that they can become nationally known as experts on foreign affairs, energy, and military affairs, even in a first term, by appearing frequently on national television news and the regular news interview panels, such as "Meet the Press" and "Face the Nation." Indeed, the rise of the mass media has made it possible for relatively junior senators to use subcommittee chairmanships to build up their standing in the national opinion polls. Meanwhile, the purely administrative aspects of the president's job have been overshadowed by global diplomacy and pressing domestic issues. Moreover, the longer six-year senatorial term means that those members infected with the presidential virus have more free time to advance their presidential ambitions than, say, governors, who often face almost insoluble fiscal problems and inadequate sources of revenue.

In the century between 1868 and 1968, more governors were selected as presidential nominees than any other category of nominees listed in Table 3.2. Before the era of the mass media and jet aircraft, support of state and local party organizations and the ability to carry a large doubtful state were often more important for winning the presidency than personal candidate appeal. As a result, the criteria for ability to win dictated that national convention delegates find a candidate acceptable to most, if not all, party factions who would help carry the state and local tickets.

Typically, the candidates who most closely met the criteria were governors of a large swing state—for example, New York or Ohio. Governors also enjoyed the luxury of evading difficult decisions on national policy. More important, governors from the big states controlled large blocs of delegates. In the days when state parties dominated the selection of delegates, the governor of a big state such as New York could be assured upon arrival at the convention of at least 15 percent of the delegates needed to win the nomination. Small wonder, then, that governors from New York, whether Democratic or Republican, were frequently nominated. But as political scientists Peabody and Lubalin have observed, "The patterns in the nominating process, patterns that obtained as recently as forty years ago, seem almost quaint in light of contemporary preconvention campaigns."[35] Clearly, the rapid expansion of the mass media, especially television, the decline of sectionalism, the proliferation of two-party competitive politics to a relatively large number of pivotal states, and the spread of presidential primaries to two-thirds of the states have all drastically changed the political landscape and the conditions under which candidates for the highest office have sought the nomination.

Table 3.2   LAST OFFICE HELD BEFORE PRESIDENTIAL NOMINATION IN TWO MAJOR PARTIES, 1868–1984

	1868–1892		1896–1924		1928–1956		1960–1984	
	%	(N)	%	(N)	%	(N)	%	(N)
Vice-president succeeded to presidency			18.1	(2)	11.1	(1)	50.0	(5)
Senate	10.0	(1)	9.1	(1)			30.0	(3)
House of Representatives	10.0	(1)	9.1	(1)				
Governor	40.0	(4)	27.3	(3)	55.6	(5)	20.0	(2)
Federal appointive	20.0	(2)	27.3	(3)	11.1	(1)		
Statewide elective			9.1	(1)				
None	20.0	(2)			22.2	(2)		
	100	(10)	100	(11)	100	(9)	100	(10)

Source: Robert L. Peabody and Eve Lubalin, "The Making of Presidential Candidates," in James I. Lengle and Byron E. Shafer, eds., *Presidential Politics* (New York: St. Martin's Press, 1980), p. 55, for the period 1868–1956. The more recent calculations have been made by the present author.

National convention delegates are now looking for candidates with national appeal who have successfully campaigned in the presidential primaries, enjoy a high standing in the opinion polls, and have a favorable television image. As a result of this transformation of the nominating process, governors have been passed by in favor of vice-presidents and U.S. senators. Asking state legislatures to increase taxes became the chief preoccupation of many state chief executives, and so incumbent governors found themselves increasingly vulnerable politically. They often failed to win reelection. Another set of liabilities that have plagued contemporary governors is "their relative anonymity and the public's image of them as parochial figures."[36] Network television producers rarely find reason to cover state politics or to invite governors to appear on "Meet the Press" and the other news panel programs. What happens in Springfield, Columbus, Lansing, or Madison is of minimal concern to network decision makers. No wonder state chief executives have been perceived, at best, as marginal presidential candidates.

However, another category of state executives—former governors—should also be added to our list of presidential possibilities. Indeed, the two most recent White House occupants—Jimmy Carter and Ronald Reagan—both received their political apprenticeship in the state executive mansions, though they had stepped down from the governorship before launching successful presidential drives. It remains an open question, of course, as to whether this recent phenome-

**Table 3.3 REPUBLICAN AND DEMOCRATIC
CANDIDATE EXPENDITURES IN
NOMINATING RACES, 1952–1980
($ MILLIONS)**

Year	Republicans	Democrats
1952	$ 5.8	$ 0.8
1956	0.5	2.5
1960	0.5	2.1
1964	10.0	1.0
1968	20.0	25.0
1972	5.7	32.7
1976	26.2	40.7
1980	71.5	35.7
1984	27.1	79.6

Sources: Figures for 1952 and 1956 are from Alexander Heard, *The Costs of Democracy* (Chapel Hill: University of North Carolina Press, 1960), pp. 334–338; the data for 1960–72 are from Herbert E. Alexander's studies: *Financing the 1960 Election* (Princeton, NJ: Citizens Research Foundation, 1962), *Financing the 1964 Election* (Princeton, NJ: Citizens Research Council, 1966), and reprinted by permission of the publisher from Herbert E. Alexander, *Financing the 1968 Election* and *Financing the 1972 Election* (Lexington, MA: Lexington Books, Copyright 1971 and 1976, D. C. Heath and Company); figures for 1976 are from FEC Disclosure Series No. 7: *1976 Presidential Campaign Receipts and Expenditures* (Washington, DC: Federal Election Commission), p. 9. Figures for 1980 are from a FEC news release dated November 15, 1981. Figures for 1984 are from FEC data supplied to author by Herbert F. Alexander, Director, Citizens Research Foundation, University of Southern California, Los Angeles.

non represents the emergence of a new category of nominees, or is merely an aberration.

All presidential contenders, winners and losers alike, share one problem in common—the need for campaign cash. Let us now turn to this vitally important aspect of the nominating race.

NOMINATING FINANCES

Financing presidential nominations has become a big business (see Table 3.3). Twenty-five years ago, a presidential contender could mount a respectable nominating campaign for $1 million. This is no longer true, as most presidential aspirants have learned. Campaign finance, it should be emphasized, has a much greater influence on presidential nominations than general election campaigns, especially since passage of the Federal Election Campaign Act of 1974. Under this legislation, presidential nominating campaigns are now financed partially by matching funds from the U.S. Treasury. Even so, costs have skyrocketed over the past two decades.

The new delegate selection rules, for example, make it imperative that candidates campaign actively in nearly all 50 states, particularly in the presidential primary states. Indeed, the assignment of delegates in proportion to the popular vote in about half of the primary states means that candidates must try to pick up some delegates in nearly every primary in order to stay competitive. To be sure, the 1974 law provides matching subsidies of up to $10 million for candidates, but since the money must be raised in amounts no larger than $1,000 from individuals, $5,000 from a group, and only the first $250 of each individual contribution is matched by the federal government, candidates must establish sophisticated fundraising operations early, long before the primary season opens. No longer can candidates rely on "fat cat" contributors, such as several individual contributors who gave approximately $400,000 each to outsider candidates Eugene McCarthy in 1968 and George McGovern in 1972.[37]

Plainly, the drive for funds has been another factor contributing to longer nominating campaigns. For most candidates, it starts at least two years before the presidential election. Unemployed candidates (those who hold no public office with its heavy time demands) enjoy a special advantage. It is noteworthy that the three most recently nominated candidates in the out-of-power party—Carter (1976), Reagan (1980), and Mondale (1984)—were politically unemployed at the time of nomination. Incumbent governors and United States senators who take their official duties seriously are at a severe disadvantage. In 1980, for example, GOP Senate minority leader Howard Baker, a loser in that year's GOP presidential nominating race, lamented afterward that running for president "requires you to be unemployed to be a successful candidate."[38] Vice-President George Bush's 1980 general counsel readily conceded that the campaign finance law discriminates in favor of those who can spend two and a half years before the election organizing and fundraising.[39]

Does money make a difference in nominating campaigns? Early in the

Table 3.4   PRENOMINATION RECEIPTS AND EXPENDITURES OF MAJOR DEMOCRATIC CONTENDERS, 1980 ($ MILLIONS)

Candidate	Adjusted receipts	Individual contributions	PAC contributions	Matching funds	Adjusted disbursements
Brown	$ 2.7	$ 1.7	$.04	$ .9	$ 2.7
Carter	18.6	12.9	.46	5.0	18.5
Kennedy*	12.3	7.8	.23	4.1	12.3
LaRouche	2.1	1.6	.01	.5	2.2
Total	$35.7	$24.0	$.74	$10.5	$35.7

*Draft-Kennedy totals of $538,454 were in addition to the authorized committees noted in table, expended prior to Kennedy's announcement of candidacy.

Source: FEC news release, November 15, 1981, includes contributions and expenditures reported from January 1, 1978, through December 31, 1980. Matching funds and adjusted disbursements revised through March 1982.

Table 3.5 PRENOMINATION RECEIPTS AND EXPENDITURES OF MAJOR REPUBLICAN CONTENDERS, 1980 ($ MILLIONS)

Candidate	Adjusted receipts	Individual contributions	PAC contributions	Matching funds	Adjusted disbursements
Anderson*	$ 6.6	$ 3.9	$.02	$ 2.3	$ 6.5
Baker	7.1	4.2	.13	2.5	7.0
Bush	16.7	10.9	.13	5.7	16.7
Connally	12.7	11.6	.20	—	12.7
Crane	5.2	3.5	.00	1.9	5.2
Dole	1.4	.9	.05	.4	1.4
Fernandez	.3	.2	.00	—	.3
Reagan	21.4	13.8	.29	6.3	20.7
Stassen	.1	.0	.00	—	.1
Total	$71.5	$49.0	$.82	$19.1	$70.6

*The Anderson Republican prenomination campaign transferred $713,000 of this amount to his independent campaign.
Source: FEC news release, November 15, 1981, includes contributions and expenditures reported from January 1, 1978, through December 31, 1980. Matching funds and adjusted disbursements revised through March 1982.

Table 3.6 PRENOMINATION RECEIPTS AND EXPENDITURES OF MAJOR DEMOCRATIC CONTENTERS, 1984 ($ MILLIONS)

Candidate	Individual contributions minus refunds	Federal matching funds	Adjusted campaign total	Expenditures subject to FEC limit
Askew	1,684,918	975,898	2,671,533	1,936,086
Cranston	3,360,565	2,113,731	5,978,179	4,613,316
Glenn	6,562,226	3,325,377	12,264,013	8,102,321
Hart	8,870,598	5,328,463	14,990,615	12,028,453
Hollings	1,347,925	821,598	2,466,430	2,117,416
Hubbard	180,596	-0-	235,671	-0-
Jackson	5,125,192	3,061,394	8,228,937	6,795,630
LaRouche	2,055,761	494,142	4,327,932	3,838,680
McGovern	828,267	612,732	1,447,326	827,458
Mondale	17,210,910	9,494,915	26,844,119	19,927,545
Willis	114,847	-0-	146,049	-0-
Totals	$47,241,805	$26,228,250	$79,600,804	$60,186,905

Note: Former Vice-President Mondale's adjusted nominating campaign expenditures exceeded the Federal Election Commission's $20,117,335 limit, but since a candidate is permitted to charge off fundraising and accounting costs, Mondale's net expenditures were under the FEC ceiling.

Source: FEC Reports on Financial Activity 1983-1984. Final Report Presidential Pre-Nomination Campaigns (Washington, DC: Federal Election Commission, April 1986), Tables A-1, A-2, and A-6.

campaign a shortage of funds can be crippling, especially to outsider candidates struggling to gain name recognition. But once the early primary shakeout or winnowing out of the weak candidates has taken place and the nominating race boils down to two or three leading candidates, the impact of money does not appear to be a decisive factor. In the 1984 primaries and caucuses, for example, Gary R. Orren reports that in the Mondale-Hart duel, there were 26 events in which the winner outspent the loser and 26 events in which the loser outspent the winner.[40] Another study in 1976 found that in 25 primaries the winner outspent the loser in 15 of the GOP contests, but in only 6 of the Democratic primaries.[41]

Table 3.7 PRENOMINATION RECEIPTS AND EXPENDITURES IN REPUBLICAN PARTY, 1984 (IN MILLIONS)

	Individual contributions minus refunds	Federal matching funds	Other receipts	Adjusted campaign total	Expenditures subject to FEC limit
Reagan	$16,358,345	$10,099,998	$682,664	$27,141,007	$20,117,535

Note: President Ronald Reagan's adjusted nominating campaign expenditures exceeded the Federal Election Commission's $20,117,335 limit, but since a candidate is permitted to charge off fundraising and accounting costs, Reagan's net expenditures were under the FEC ceiling.

Source: FEC Reports on Financial Activity 1983-1984. Final Report Presidential Pre-Nomination Campaigns (Washington, DC: Federal Election Commission, April 1986) Tables A-1 and A-2.

Paradoxically, one result of the 1974 campaign reform law was to increase dependence on the mass media, although the original intent of the legislation appeared to be just the opposite. Since candidates must reach millions of voters in the 30-plus primary states in a short period of time, they have no choice but to spend most of their campaign funds on television advertising.

Passage of the 1974 Federal Election Campaign Finance Act has also altered the way candidates conduct their nominating campaigns. Matching federal subsidies to candidates in the presidential primaries has fostered far greater candidate self-sufficiency than ever before. The availability of matching federal subsidies of up to $10 million and the $1,000 limitation on individual contributions has forced candidates to set up huge fundraising operations, based heavily on direct mail solicitation. With more than a quarter of the campaign funds now supplied by Uncle Sam (see Tables 3.4, 3.5, 3.6, and 3.7) presidential candidates can now build their own independent campaign organizations, hire their own media specialists, direct mail experts, fundraisers, and accountants.[42]

Important as candidate-centered organizations are to winning the nomination, nothing matches the importance candidates place on national and local television coverage for helping to win the nomination.

THE POWERFUL IMPACT OF TELEVISION

Television has revolutionized the presidential nominating campaigns. Over the past two decades, presidential contenders and their managers have all concluded that presidential nominating races simply cannot be conducted successfully without using the national media, especially television, to communicate with voters in the primary states. The rapid growth of primaries has complicated the presidential contenders' task of trying to reach large numbers of voters in the primary states. Television enables the candidates to meet the voters face-to-face via the television set. No longer are state and local party footsoldiers needed in the fast-moving nominating races that shift from state to state nearly every week. Before the 1976 nominating campaign opened, Gerald Rafshoon, Jimmy Carter's media advisor, summed up the situation this way: "The media is an extension of the campaign." One campaign manager has gone even further: "The media is the campaign."[43] Richard Rubin, a perceptive observer of contemporary political parties, has noted:

> The development of television, for example, has provided lesser-known challengers, shunned by established party leaders, with a quick and effective way to gain recognition among the party's mass electorate. And as a result, the rapid development of modern communications techniques together with the decline of patronage-supported organization workers have shattered the near monopoly over campaign resources once maintained by local machines in primary competition.[44]

To win the attention of the national media's opinion makers and become better known has become the top priority of presidential aspirants. As Christopher

Arterton has put it: "Name recognition has become a critical ingredient in the calculus of electability."[45]

Consequently, campaign operatives concentrate on media strategies to build candidate visibility and needed press coverage. Christopher Arterton reports: "Campaigners take the view that the press corps constitutes an alternative electorate within which they must campaign simultaneously with their efforts to gather votes."[46] Federal limitations on overall campaign spending in individual primaries have made it more imperative than ever that the candidate turn to the national and local media as early as possible to reach—hopefully without cost to the candidate's treasury—the voting public and uncommitted delegates. This frantic concern to obtain early media coverage is understandable because of the overwhelming attention given to winners and losers in the early primaries and caucuses. Candidates know they must build a quick record of success or risk political oblivion.

Similarly, television has become so dominant, especially in the early primary and caucus states, that the TV reporters have become the chief handicappers of the candidates. How the network reporters and national press rate a candidate's performance, or even his chances, in the early races, for example, can affect not only the amount of television coverage he receives, but also his standing in the opinion polls and the amount of financial support he can attract. Because the national media overemphasized the significance of the early primaries (especially the New Hampshire primary, whose voters number less than one-half of 1 percent of the American electorate), failure to run well in the early races spells disaster.[47] Presidential contenders know they will no longer receive attention from the television networks, whose reporters now label him a "loser." This negative labeling quickly undermines the candidate's chances of gaining heavy TV coverage in subsequent primaries and dries up his campaign fundraising. Clearly, winning is everything in the early contests.

In many respects, the mass media have a far more pervasive influence on the presidential nominating process than on the general election. First of all, the official nominating race is nearly three times longer (6.5 months versus 2.5 months) than the general election campaign. Because of the highly competitive field, frequently involving as many as a half-dozen candidates, the four television networks devote far more coverage and money to the primary and key caucus states than they do to the main election campaign. With primaries scheduled almost every Tuesday from late February to early June, the networks give extensive news coverage to these individual nominating contests each Tuesday, plus daily reportage on the status of the race. Because there is usually a multicandidate field at the start of the race, the ability of individual candidates to attract the early attention of the television networks and local stations can be a decisive factor in winning or losing these individual elections—and possibly the nomination. Additionally, the primary race is far more complicated and ambiguous than the general election: Several state contests (both primaries and caucuses) occur on the same day; the early primary field is usually crowded; the delegate selection rules vary in the different states—winner-take-all, proportionality, presidential "beauty contests," separate caucus selection of the delegates in open primary states, and so on. The mass media, with their extensive coverage of these contests, can help the voters "make sense" out of these complicated matters.

Furthermore, early in the preconvention campaign the voters' knowledge of the candidates is often meager; consequently they tend to rely far more heavily on the media in the primary season to assess the candidates and interpret the primary and caucus results. Voters are more susceptible than in the fall campaign to media stories on the nominating race and to the candidates' paid spot ads. Prospective voters are also more likely to be influenced by the "horserace" or game aspects of the nominating contests, as the television networks identify the real "winners" and "losers." The media also report on the national opinion poll standings of the various candidates, who is ahead and who is behind in the delegate count, how the contenders compare in "trial heat" matchups with the president or leading candidates in the opposition party.[48] With a crowded field of contenders and faced with sharp time constraints, the media focus most of their attention on candidates and their images. Indeed, many analysts believe that the candidates' personal qualities and image are becoming the dominant factor in determining who will be the party nominee and, more often than not, the next president.

Sometimes the media establish a level of expectation that the frontrunner must meet in a specific primary. In the 1972 New Hampshire Democratic primary, the national media declared that Senator Edmund Muskie, from neighboring Maine, would have to collect 50 percent of the vote to be labeled the true winner. When Muskie received only 46 percent of the New Hampshire vote he was perceived as the "loser," even though he had outpolled second-place finisher George McGovern by 9 percentage points. Generally, the media give the frontrunner more coverage, but treat him more harshly than the long-shot candidates.

Some observers see the media taking over the function formerly performed by the party organization, such as informing voters about policy issues, structuring the decisions of voters and conventions, and in effect delineating both the nature and the limits of the nominating contest.[49] Significantly, the media's influence seems to be the greatest during the period before the primary season opens and during the early primaries, a time when the public has relatively little information about the various contenders. Christopher Arterton notes: "The latitude of journalistic interpretation is also greatest at this time, when the indicators of growing or declining political support are at their poorest in predictive validity."[50] Nor would most observers dispute political scientist Thomas E. Patterson's assessment that "Today's presidential campaign is essentially a mass media campaign."[51]

To win a presidential nomination, candidates must also run well in the public opinion polls. Let's take time for a moment to explore the growing role of pollsters in presidential nominations.

POLITICAL BAROMETERS: THE OPINION POLLS

Public opinion polls, still in their infancy when World War II began, have become sensitive barometers in presidential nominating races. Except for a brief loss of confidence after the polls incorrectly predicted that Governor Thomas E. Dewey would defeat President Truman in the 1948 general election, the polls have become a pervasive force in the selection of presidential candidates. Long before convention time, polls single out the frontrunner, show nip-and-tuck races between leading contenders, and expose the poor vote getters.[52]

In this section we will be talking about two kinds of polls: public and private. Public opinion polls, such as Gallup, Harris, and the the *New York Times*/CBS News, are published periodically to reveal the latest sounding of the public's view toward various candidates or other political phenomena. The distinguishing feature of the published polls is that they are conducted as a form of journalism to inform the public about the political world, and not for political intelligence. Private polls are those commissioned for the personal use of candidate and staff in charting campaign strategy and tactics.

Over the years, the Gallup polls have shown considerable evidence that a relationship exists between the candidate's standing in the polls, success in the primaries, and capture of the nomination. Since 1936, over two-thirds of the time (69 percent) the leader in the Gallup polls after the first major primary has gone on to win the nomination (see Table 3.8). No wonder high ratings in the early Gallup polls are so coveted by presidential contenders.

In the age of primaries, private polls and the political intelligence they contain can be as valuable to a presidential candidate as a campaign manager. Senator John F. Kennedy first popularized the use of private polls in the primaries. His pollster, Louis Harris, made a political reputation for his client and himself during the 1960 Democratic primaries. Surveys by Harris showed that Kennedy's chief opponent, Senator Hubert H. Humphrey, was vulnerable in Wisconsin and West Virginia, two important primary states. With this valuable data, Kennedy boldly entered the Wisconsin primary, thought to be Humphrey country since he lived in neighboring Minnesota, and won a decisive victory. Similarly, with poll data available from West Virginia, Kennedy decided to enter the primary of this overwhelmingly Protestant state and prove that his Roman Catholicism was not a political handicap.

When Kennedy again defeated Humphrey and drove him out of the race, he demonstrated clearly that he had the vote-getting ability needed to win the White House. His West Virginia triumph persuaded many fence-sitting state leaders and national convention delegates that his religion was not a political liability.[53] Since then, leading presidential candidates in both parties have regularly used private polls to identify voter attitudes on key issues, suggest the kinds of appeals to be made to targeted demographic groups, and help design a campaign to maximize campaign time and money. Frequent polling during the campaign allows the candidate to make adjustments in strategy and tactics.

Presidential contenders, it seems fairly clear, have come to depend far more on private polls than on the widely circulated public polls, such as the Gallup and Harris polls. Indeed, it is unlikely that a presidential candidate will ever venture into a campaign again without a trusted private pollster at his side.

Because the Gallup and Harris polls have come to be considered reliable barometers of candidate popularity, all presidential contenders make it one of

Table 3.8 PUBLIC OPINION AND THE NOMINATION

Year and party		Gallup poll after first primary	Final Gallup poll before convention	Party nominee
1940	D	Roosevelt	Roosevelt	Roosevelt*
	R	Dewey	Willkie	Willkie
1944	D	Roosevelt	Roosevelt	Roosevelt*
	R	Dewey	Dewey	Dewey
1948	D	Truman	Truman	Truman*
	R	Stassen	Dewey	Dewey
1952	D	Kefauver	Kefauver	Stevenson
	R	Eisenhower	Eisenhower	Eisenhower*
1956	D	Stevenson	Stevenson	Stevenson
	R	Eisenhower	Eisenhower	Eisenhower*
1960	D	J. Kennedy	Kennedy	Kennedy*
	R	Nixon	Nixon	Nixon
1964	D	—	Johnson	Johnson*
	R	Lodge	Goldwater and Nixon (tie)	Goldwater
1968	D	R. Kennedy	Humphrey	Humphrey
	R	Nixon	Nixon	Nixon*
1972	D	Humphrey	McGovern	McGovern
	R	—	Nixon	Nixon*
1976	D	Humphrey	Carter	Carter*
	R	Ford	Ford	Ford
1980	D	Carter	Carter	Carter
	R	Reagan	Reagan	Reagan*
1984	D	Mondale†	Mondale†	Mondale
	R	Reagan	Reagan	Reagan*

D = Democrat; R = Republican.
*Indicates general election winner.
†Mondale was the choice of Democrats; he trailed Hart among self-identified Independents.
Source: The Gallup Poll, Public Opinion 1933–1971, vols. 1–3 (New York: Random House, 1972; *Gallup Opinion Index* (Princeton, NJ: Gallup International, 1971–1980). Reprinted with permission.

their top preconvention objectives to gain the top spot in the opinion poll ratings. Favorable ratings can be used to build momentum, raise campaign funds, and generate additional media coverage. By pinpointing the probable winners in the primaries, public opinion polls affect the amount of attention the media will give each candidate. Especially during the early weeks of the primary season, this added media coverage for the frontrunner helps attract more financial support and campaign volunteers. If a candidate is doing well in the polls, it is a foregone conclusion that he is doing well in the primaries. If, conversely, the candidate cannot break out of the "also-ran" category in the Gallup polls after the first few weeks of the primary season, his candidacy is destined to fail.

PRIMARIES OVERSHADOW NATIONAL CONVENTIONS

Officially, presidential nominees of the two major parties continue to be nominated by delegates to national party conventions, just as they have been for the past 150 years. But over the past three decades presidential primaries have, in effect, taken over the latent functions of convention balloting. In the traditional national nominating convention, multiple ballots served the function of informing delegates about the relative strengths of the various contenders and of pointing to the likely nominee. In recent years, however, this balloting or informing function has been usurped by the presidential primaries.[54] Each primary, or set of primaries, serves, in effect, as a convention ballot, with the consequent shift in delegate strength among the candidates after each primary calculated and assessed by the national media, especially the three television networks. Unlike the typical four-day national convention, presidential primaries are held over a four-month period. Winning a single primary is not enough to sweep the nomination. Instead, candidates usually acquire only a portion of delegates from each state, since the proportional vote rule applies in most states. Building a majority of national delegates to win the nomination is a slow, incremental process. But it is imperative that a candidate demonstrate powerful voter appeal in the early primaries, or he will be ignored by the national media and the voters in the other primary and caucus-convention states.

If the primary returns do not point to a clear-cut winner, the delegates always have the option to use the convention as a "brokering" agency for arriving at a compromise choice. But in point of fact the national convention over the past three decades has been transformed from a decision-making body into a ceremonial institution that merely serves as a mechanism to legitimize the popular favorite of the primaries. Still, the national convention remains an important political institution, as will be explained in the next section.

NATIONAL NOMINATING CONVENTIONS

Though the presidential primaries, the television networks, and national opinion polls have pinpointed several weeks before the convention the eventual nominee of the out-of-power party in each nominating race since 1956, with the possible exception of 1964, the final choice must still be made by the party's national nominating convention. Incumbent presidents seeking another term must also be formally renominated and voted by the convention delegates before they are officially authorized to carry the party banner again. Indeed, if a majority of convention delegates wish, they can jettison an incumbent president in favor of a new face, though this has not occurred in the twentieth century. However, since 1968 three incumbent presidents—Johnson, Ford, and Carter—have all faced major intraparty challenges to renomination.

History shows that for over 150 years national conventions have nominated or renominated presidential and vice-presidential candidates acceptable to most factions within each major party, except in 1860, 1912, and 1964 for the GOP, and 1924, 1968, and 1972 for the Democrats. Especially in a close race, the convention has almost always served to break the deadlock and "broker" a compromise candidate behind whom a majority of the delegates can unite.

Another convention function that appears to be emerging, or reemerging in new form, is the shaping of the vice-presidential choice. Custom has long dictated that the presidential nominee has the prerogative of naming his own running mate. The trend in recent years has been to use the vice-presidential nomination as a consolation prize to a defeated faction at the convention or to give representation to a growing constituency within the party. Thus, in 1980 Ronald Reagan decided to recommend to the GOP convention that it select his chief rival in the primaries, George Bush, as his running mate. Four years later, Democratic nominee Walter F. Mondale boldly charted new ground when he asked the national convention to nominate Representative Geraldine Ferraro of New York as the first woman vice-presidential nominee. National conventions have also hammered out party platforms each quadrennium for 140 years.

National conventions serve too as a campaign rallying mechanism for the national party. This function of arousing party faithful to unite behind the ticket has long been recognized as a valuable attribute of the national conclaves. Television coverage of the conventions has also helped arouse the enthusiasm of the millions of home viewers for their candidate. Indeed, some critics argue that free television coverage of these conventions "poses an almost irresistible temptation to convention managers to concentrate on the mass rally aspect of the conventions at the expense of platform-writing, rules changes, and even bargaining over the vice presidential nomination."[55]

In the years ahead, convention managers will undoubtedly continue to deemphasize the conduct of party business and endeavor instead to capitalize on the rally functions (as exemplified by the nominee's acceptance speech) to persuade the national electorate—via the free network coverage of the convention —to vote for their party nominee in November. By 1972, an estimated 115 million people watched some part of the two nominating conventions on one of the three major networks. By 1984, the television viewing audience, at least for some part of the two conventions, exceeded 150 million people.

National conventions also perform a number of latent (unintended) functions that are sometimes overlooked. First, over the years the quadrennial gatherings have performed a valuable legitimizing function for the nonconsensus candidate. Clearly, the conventions furnish a stamp of legitimacy for the nominee that tells all party members and the nation as a whole that the party stands behind the nominee as its standard-bearer. It has sometimes been overlooked, for example, that in 1976 Democratic nominee Jimmy Carter was the choice of only 39 percent of the primary voters nationwide before the national convention; yet once nominated, he was accepted by almost all party groups as the legitimate nominee.

Early national conventions performed another latent function of nullifying the intent of the Founding Fathers, as prescribed in the Constitution, to have members of the Electoral College exercise independent judgment in voting for president and vice-president. Indeed, the national convention was the key device through which nineteenth-century political parties democratized the choice for president. The national convention succeeded far better than the congressional party caucus in transforming the Electoral College into a recording instrument for registering the popular choice for president. Once access to presidential power was freed from screening by a highly centralized group of national party leaders in the congressional caucus, the presidency became more rooted in the support of the voting masses. Moreover, the evolution of the national convention as a nominating device is closely intertwined with the development of the president's independent power base. Indeed, these quadrennial party grand councils fulfill an indispensable role in helping to build and maintain the independent stature of the president in the American system of government.[56]

Finally, we might ask about the overall record of national conventions in picking well-qualified presidents. By and large, the record of these conclaves is well above average in selecting outstanding leaders—Lincoln, Theodore Roosevelt, Wilson, Franklin D. Roosevelt, and John F. Kennedy. Attention should also be called to some of the highly qualified nominees who, though nominated, failed to reach the White House—Stephen Douglas, Samuel Tilden, Charles Evans Hughes, Alfred E. Smith, Wendell Willkie, Thomas E. Dewey, Adlai E. Stevenson, and Hubert H. Humphrey. (The critics argue, of course, that outstanding nominees were selected despite the system, rather than because of the national convention.) To be sure, the national convention has occasionally come up with some inept, uninspiring, or corrupt nominees who became president—James Buchanan, Ulysses S. Grant, Warren G. Harding, and Richard M. Nixon. But the critics should be reminded that the convention record, on the whole, has been far above average.[57]

In other words, judge the convention by the overall quality of the product —the number of outstanding presidents it has produced—not the mediocrities it has chosen from time to time. As James MacGregor Burns has evaluated the national convention: "It has had many triumphs and few failures."[58] Another thoughtful commentator has also observed: ". . . in the eighteen presidential elections between 1900 and 1968, only ten nominations went to candidates who are even arguably second-rate. Twenty-six major party nominations went to evidently first-rate people."[59]

Over the past century the national convention has profoundly influenced the evolution of the modern presidency. Had the congressional caucus by some quirk of fate survived as the method for nominating presidential candidates, the odds are high that the presidency would have but a faint resemblance to the powerful institutional chief executive that has emerged in the twentieth century.

CONCLUSION

Several factors stand out prominently in the modern presidential nominating system, especially since the post-1968 Democratic party reforms. With the rapid proliferation of presidential primaries after 1968, rank-and-file voters, not party professionals, have gained the dominant voice in the selection of candidates. Approximately 30 states, including 9 of the 10 largest, use presidential primaries to select national convention delegates. As a result, state party leaders, especially in the populous states, have lost most of their former bargaining and decision-making power. Before 1968, state delegation leaders dominated the caucus-convention system used to choose national convention delegates. National conventions served as forums for these leaders to forge agreement on a single candidate and to rally the state delegations behind the proposed nominee.

Party rules governing presidential nominations, particularly in the Democratic party, have drastically changed the selection process. Delegate selection rules, adopted by three Democratic reform commissions between 1968 and 1980, have had a twofold goal: to broaden the base of public participation in the nominating process, thereby making it more representative of the rank-and-file views, and to make candidates and delegates more directly accountable to the voters. In 1980, for example, over 25 million Americans participated in the presidential nominating process.

Presidential nominees in the challenging party are now, in effect, chosen in the presidential primary sweepstakes. Though they are not officially anointed until the national convention ratifies and legitimizes the popular choice, the winner of the primary race has been chosen the nominee of the out-of-power party in every nominating race since 1968. Unlike earlier times, national conventions are no longer brokering agencies for picking candidates acceptable to most factions within the party. Instead, they have become televised mass rally events that launch the general election campaign.

National conventions also nominate vice-presidential candidates (usually the president's hand-picked choice) and thus help legitimize the number two member of the ticket in the event that death or disability of the president requires that he assume the reins of national leadership. Platform building still remains an important function of these quadrennial national conclaves. National conventions also serve as an indispensable rallying mechanism for encouraging the party faithful and the electorate to unite behind the party ticket. Above all, the national conventions reinforce the independent position of the presidency in the American government system.

Winning the presidential nomination, however, is only half the battle. The party standard-bearer cannot, of course, lay claim to the White House until he or she defeats the nominee of the rival major party in the fall presidential election —the subject of the next chapter.

NOTES

1. For more background on the Canadian leadership conventions, see John Courtney, *The Selection of National Party Leaders in Canada* (Hamden, CT: Shoe String Press, 1973).

2. Donald R. Matthews, "Presidential Nominations: Process and Outcomes," in James David Barber, ed., *Choosing the President* (Englewood Cliffs, NJ: Prentice-Hall, 1974), 36.

3. Thomas R. Marshall, *Presidential Nominations in a Reform Age* (New York: Praeger, 1981), 17–64.

4. Neal Peirce, *The People's President* (New York: Simon & Schuster, 1968), 63.

5. James S. Chase, *Emergence of the Presidential Nominating Convention, 1789–1832* (Urbana: University of Illinois Press, 1973), 60.

6. James W. Davis, *National Conventions in an Age of Party Reform* (Westport, CT: Greenwood Press, 1983), 25.

7. Theodore J. Lowi, "Party, Policy and Constitution in America," in William Nisbet Chambers and Walter Dean Burnham, eds., *The American Party System* (New York: Oxford University Press, 1967), 248, as cited by Austin Ranney, *Curing the Mischiefs of Faction* (Berkeley: The University of California Press, 1975), 173.

8. Ibid, 173-174.

9. Davis, *National Conventions in an Age of Party Reform,* 31.

10. Paul T. David, Ralph M. Goldman, and Richard C. Bain, *The Politics of National Party Conventions* (Washington, DC: The Brookings Institution, 1960), 208–212.

11. For an excellent discussion of the Progressive reforms, see James W. Ceaser, *Presidential Selection: Theory and Development* (Princeton, NJ: Princeton University Press, 1979), Chapter 5; see also Ranney, *Curing the Mischiefs of Faction.*

12. James W. Davis, *Presidential Primaries: Road to the White House,* 2nd ed. (Westport, CT: Greenwood Press, 1980), 43–44.

13. Ibid., 44–47.

14. For an excellent account of McCarthy's travels during the 1968 preconvention campaign, see Lewis Chester, Godfrey Hodgson, and Bruce Page, *An American Melodrama: The Presidential Campaign of 1968* (New York: Viking Press, 1969), 547–558.

15. *Mandate for Reform,* a report of the Commission on Party Structure and Delegate Selection to the Democratic National Committee (the McGovern–Fraser Commission) (Washington, DC: Democratic National Committee, 1970), 18–19.

16. Ibid., 15.

17. Ibid., 34–35.

18. Gary R. Orren, "The Nomination Process: Vicissitudes of Candidate Selection," in Michael Nelson, ed., *The Election of 1984* (Washington, DC: Congressional Quarterly Press, 1985), 35.

19. Robert E. DiClerico and Eric M. Uslaner, *Few Are Chosen: Problems of Presidential Selection* (New York: McGraw-Hill, 1984), 21.

20. Although these figures reflect a greater turnout since 1968, this turnout rate (approximately 30 percent) is actually lower than what it was between 1948 and 1968. Austin Ranney, in a study of eleven states holding competitive primaries for the earlier period, found an average of 39 percent voting in the primaries and 69 percent in the general election. Austin Ranney, "Turnout and Representation in Presidential Primary Elections," *American Political Science Review,* 66 (March 1972), 21–37.

21. Stephen J. Wayne and George Edwards III, *Presidential Leadership* (New York: St. Martin's Press, 1985), 22.

22. Nelson W. Polsby, *Consequences of Party Reform* (New York: Oxford University Press, 1983), 61–62.

23. James Lengle and Byron Shafer, "Primary Rules, Political Power and Social Change," *American Political Science Review* 70 (March 1976), pp. 25–40.

24. John Kessel, *Presidential Campaign Politics* (Homewood, IL: Dorsey Press, 1984), 3–12.

25. William Crotty and John S. Jackson III, *Presidential Primaries and Nominations* (Washington, DC: Congressional Quarterly Press, 1985), 149.

26. Jack W. Germond and Jules Witcover, *Blue Smoke & Mirrors: How Reagan Won and Why Carter Lost the Election of 1980* (New York: Viking Press, 1981), 116–140.

27. Davis, *Presidential Primaries,* 78–110.

28. *The New York Times,* June 10, 1976.

29. "People Don't Know Who I Am," *Time,* August 2, 1976, 14; see also Richard Reeves, *Convention* (New York: Harcourt, Brace Jovanovich, 1977), 180.

30. For an in-depth analysis of strategic planning and candidate choices in both parties during the 1976 nominating races, see John H. Aldrich, *Before the Convention* (Chicago: University of Chicago Press, 1980).

31. Gerald Pomper, ed., *The Election of 1980: Reports and Interpretations* (Chatham, NJ: Chatham House, 1981), 20-21.

32. William R. Keech and Donald R. Matthews, *The Party's Choice* (Washington, DC: The Brookings Institution, 1976), 15.

33. The discussion in this section relies heavily on Robert L. Peabody and Eve Lubalin,

"The Making of Presidential Candidates," in James I. Lengle and Byron E. Shafer, eds., *Presidential Politics* (New York: St. Martin's Press, 1980), 50–68.

34. Ibid.
35. Ibid., p. 59.
36. Ibid., p. 61.
37. Davis, *Presidential Primaries,* 203–242.
38. *The New York Times,* August 30, 1980.
39. Gary R. Orren, "Presidential Campaign Finance: Its Impact and Future," *Commonsense* (1983), 55.
40. Gary R. Orren, "The Nomination Process," 50.
41. Joel H. Goldstein, "The Influence of Money on the Prenomination Stage of the Presidential Selection Process: The Case of the 1976 Election," *Presidential Studies Quarterly* (Spring 1978), 164–179.
42. Jeane J. Kirkpatrick, "Dismantling the Parties: Reflections on the Role of Policy in the Process of Party Decomposition." Paper delivered at the American Political Science Association annual meeting, Washington, DC, September 1–4, 1977, p. 21.
43. F. Christopher Arterton, "Campaign Organizations Face the Mass Media in the 1976 Presidential Nominating Process." Paper delivered at the American Political Science Association annual meeting, Washington, DC, September 1–4, 1977.
44. Richard L. Rubin, *Party Dynamics: The Democratic Coalition and the Politics of Change* (New York: Oxford University Press, 1976), 153.
45. F. Christopher Arterton, "Campaign Organizations Face the Mass Media," 6.
46. Ibid., 1–4.
47. Davis, *Presidential Primaries,* 78–110.
48. Thomas E. Patterson, *The Mass Media Election: How Americans Choose Their President* (New York: Praeger, 1980), 21–30.
49. Crotty and Jackson, *Presidential Primaries and Nominations,* 77; see also Ronald Berkman and Laura W. Kitch, *Politics in the Media Age* (New York: McGraw-Hill, 1986), chap. 5.
50. F. Christopher Arterton, "Campaign Organizations Confront the Media Environment," in James David Barber, ed., *Race for the Presidency* (Englewood Cliffs, NJ: Prentice-Hall, 1978), 4.
51. Patterson, *The Mass Media Election,* 3.
52. James R. Beniger, "Polls and Primaries," in James W. Davis, *Presidential Primaries,* 111–133.
53. Theodore H. White, *The Making of the President 1960* (New York: Atheneum, 1961), 78–114.
54. Davis, *National Conventions in an Age of Party Reform,* 5–12.
55. Ibid., p. 273.
56. Ibid., p. 31.
57. Ibid., p. 275.
58. James MacGregor Burns, "The Case for the Smoke-Filled Room," *New York Times Magazine,* June 15, 1952, p. 26.
59. Wilson Carey McWilliams, "The Meaning of the Election," in Pomper, ed., *The Election of 1980,* 171.

chapter 4

Presidential Elections

Winning the presidential nomination means the candidate is only halfway to the finish line. Although the party nominee will have campaigned in most of the 30 presidential primaries and in nearly a score of caucus-convention states, delivered dozens of speeches, shaken thousands of hands, and spent upward of $20 million to become the party standard-bearer, he still faces a relentless ten-week general election campaign before he can hopefully lay claim to the grand prize. Especially for the challenger, the general election campaign, which begins on or about Labor Day, will entail a string of nearly 70 continuous, 16-hour working days, with time out to prepare for one or more presidential debates and an occasional home visit on Sunday.

Presidential elections, it should be remembered, are not primarily gigantic public opinion polls on the issues. To be sure, a presidential election involves issues, but it is, to borrow Gerald Pomper's phrase, "more simply a choice of leadership to deal with recognized societal needs by acceptable means."[1] Basically, voters are concerned with the candidate's (or incumbent's) competence, trustworthiness, and managerial abilities. Put another way, the electorate is concerned more with the candidate's character, his leadership qualities, and his vision than his stand on the issues.

General election campaigns differ from nominating campaigns in a number of crucial aspects. Nominating campaigns are aimed at winning delegates; general election campaigns are aimed at winning votes. Most important, the general election contest is a battle between rival party contenders, not an intramural contest between competitors within the same party. Whereas in the primaries the presidential aspirants in the same party have had to guard against flailing their party rivals too harshly because they will need the support of these defeated adversaries to help wage all-out political war against the opposition party in the fall campaign, the two major party candidates will now take off the gloves and start verbally pummeling each other. Party identification and issue differences soon come into play. Moreover, the incumbent's record (if he is running), party ideology, personal qualifications, and "image" will all be weighed by the voters. While a majority of voters usually make up their minds soon after the party conventions (see Table 4.1), a sizable portion of the electorate will remain undecided. During the general election campaign it is on this large bloc of voters that the two major party nominees will concentrate their attention, while also seeking to reassure their own partisans that their votes too are needed in November.

In this chapter special attention will be focused on Electoral College politics, a widely misunderstood aspect of presidential elections. Equally important, the strategic environment in which presidential campaigns operate will be assessed, as well as the strategies for building a winning coalition. The prominent role that the televised presidential debates have come to play in presidential campaigns is also discussed. Additionally, the powerful impact television has had on the way presidential campaigns are conducted and how preoccupation with the "horserace" aspects of the campaign often leads the media to downgrade coverage of the major issues of the campaign receive detailed treatment. Also, we evaluate the pervasive influence of political polls in predicting presidential elections and especially the extensive use of "exit" polls to provide more detailed information on demographic voting patterns. Finally, we explore briefly the meaning of the election to the voters and to the newly elected or reelected president. Does the quadrennial election give the president a broad mandate, or is it to be considered an instructional message from the people?

HISTORICAL BACKGROUND

During the nineteenth century, presidential election campaigns were usually marked by torchlight parades, mass rallies, and plenty of hard cider—but presi-

Table 4.1 REPORTED TIME OF VOTE DECISION ON PRESIDENT, 1960–1984

	1960	1964	1968	1972	1976	1980	1984
Knew all along, always vote same party, preconvention	31%	41%	35%	44%	33%	41%	52%
At time of conventions	31	25	24	18	21	18	18
After conventions	26	21	19	22	22	15	17
Within two weeks of election, on election day	12	13	21	13	24	26	13

Note: The responses above were made to the standard question asked quadrennially by interviewers from the University of Michigan's Institute for Social Research: "How long before the election did you decide that you were going to vote the way you did?"

Sources: "Opinion Roundup," *Public Opinion* (December–January 1981), 26. Reprinted by permission of American Enterprise Institute for Public Policy Research. Data for 1980 and 1984 supplied by Institute for Social Research, University of Michigan, and reprinted by permission.

dential candidates rarely appeared on the scene. Abraham Lincoln, for example, was elected president without leaving the state capital in Springfield, Illinois. Presidential campaigns were decentralized. Candidates depended almost exclusively on party leaders in each state to manage and conduct their campaigns while they issued an occasional lofty statement from their office or home on the major issues of the day—usually the tariff or a currency problem. Candidates devoted themselves largely to "front porch" campaigns. Biographer Margaret Leech has described a typical William McKinley front-porch performance in 1896 at his home in Canton, Ohio:

> He bade them welcome to his home and thanked them for the honor of their call. He said a few words on the campaign issues, adapting the discussion to suit the special interests of his audience. In conclusion, he expressed a desire to shake the hand of each and every one, and held an informal reception on the porch steps.[2]

In the same year, however, the first modern campaigner burst on the scene in the midst of the free silver controversy—William Jennings Bryan, the Democratic nominee. Known as the Boy Orator of the Platte—Bryan was only thirty-six years old when he received the first of his three nominations—he had been nominated largely on the basis of his famous Cross of Gold speech to the 1896 Democratic convention. Unlike his predecessors, Bryan decided to take his case directly to the people with a nationwide campaign tour. By his own account, Bryan journeyed more than 18,000 miles on a whirlwind whistlestop campaign, delivering more than 600 speeches to an estimated grand total of almost 5 million listeners.[3] In 1912, the flamboyant Teddy Roosevelt also took his Bull Moose third-party campaign directly to the people; in fact, he was wounded by a would-be assassin during one of his speeches.[4] His Democratic rival, Woodrow Wilson, an accomplished orator, also engaged in extensive nationwide political stumping. Full-time campaigning, however, did not become standard practice until Democratic challenger Franklin D. Roosevelt mounted a full-scale whistlestop campaign against President Hoover in 1932. FDR used his nationwide rail tour not only to castigate Hoover, but also to squelch a whispering campaign about his health. Roosevelt had suffered a serious polio attack in the early 1920s that had incapacitated him for more than two years. His relentless attacks against the Republican incumbent forced President Hoover onto the campaign trail. As the first incumbent president to campaign actively, Hoover logged over 10,000 miles, speaking to audiences across the land.[5]

With the advent of radio in the late 1920s, candidates for the first time could also reach large audiences heretofore denied them. Whistlestop campaigning reached its zenith in 1948 when President Truman, a political underdog, launched the famous speaking tour that carried him over 32,000 miles across the length and breadth of the land—and back to the White House for another four years. By 1952, however, the age of television had arrived, and with the availability of this new communications medium, presidential campaigns entered the electronic era.

ELECTORAL POLITICS

Most political bystanders view the presidential election as one gigantic swirling battle between opposing political forces. But in fact the presidential contests are really 50 separate, state winner-take-all elections for the electoral vote in each of the 50 states. The prime goal of a candidate and his staff is not to capture a majority of the popular vote, but to collect 270 out of the 538 votes in the Electoral College—a simple majority in this ancient electoral institution. Then, and only then, can the party nominee claim the presidency. It is therefore understandable that when candidates and their staffs map out an electoral strategy, they talk in terms of carrying state electoral votes, not the national popular vote.

Generally, both major candidates concentrate their heavy firepower on the "battleground" states—California, New York, Illinois, Pennsylvania, Ohio, Michigan, New Jersey, Texas, and most recently, Florida—since winning these nine states will ensure 241 electoral votes, just 29 short of the needed majority. During the fall campaign, the presidential and vice-presidential candidates of both major parties cross and recross these states, stopping each time in one or more of the major media markets to obtain valuable television coverage.[6] The Electoral College also affects campaign strategy in another way: Candidates seldom campaign in states in which they have little chance of winning; nor do they waste time in those states in which they are viewed as sure-fire winners.

Electoral College politics is often confusing to many Americans. It is a commonly held belief that if a presidential candidate receives a majority of the popular vote—or even a plurality (more than any other candidate)—he will automatically be elected president of the United States. Not so. The Founding Fathers, with their innate distrust of popular democracy, set up an indirect system of presidential election called the Electoral College. Under this system, each state is allocated a sum of electors equal to its total number of U.S. representatives and senators. Thus California, which has 45 U.S. representatives and two U.S. senators, is allocated 47 electoral votes (see Table 4.2); Alaska, which has one U.S. representative and two senators, is allocated 3 electoral votes; New York has 34 U.S. representatives and two U.S. senators, or 36 electoral votes. Under the Electoral College ground rules that have prevailed since the beginning of the nineteenth century, the candidate who wins a plurality of votes within the state wins all the state's electoral votes.[7] In other words, when President Reagan in 1984 won California, Alaska, and New York—as well as forty-six other states— he collected the 86 electoral votes from these three states and the 439 electoral votes from the other forty-six states. His grand total was 525 electoral votes to 13 for Walter F. Mondale, who carried only his home state of Minnesota (10 votes) and the District of Columbia (3 votes).

Most presidential elections, of course, have been much closer than the 1984 contest. Indeed, the outcome of presidential elections in 1960, 1968, and 1976 would have been reversed or shifted to the House of Representatives with the switch of only a few thousand popular votes in two, three, or a handful of states. In 1960, a shift of a total of 11,424 votes in the five states of Illinois, Missouri, New Mexico, Nevada, and Hawaii would have made Nixon the president. In 1968, the shift of only 42,000 votes in three states would have sent the election

Table 4.2   NUMBER OF ELECTORS FOR EACH STATE, 1984*

Alabama	9	Montana	4
Alaska	3	Nebraska	5
Arizona	7	Nevada	4
Arkansas	6	New Hampshire	4
California	47	New Jersey	16
Colorado	8	New Mexico	5
Connecticut	8	New York	36
Delaware	3	North Carolina	13
Florida	21	North Dakota	3
Georgia	12	Ohio	23
Hawaii	4	Oklahoma	8
Idaho	4	Oregon	7
Illinois	24	Pennsylvania	25
Indiana	12	Rhode Island	4
Iowa	8	South Carolina	8
Kansas	7	South Dakota	3
Kentucky	9	Tennessee	11
Louisiana	10	Texas	29
Maine	4	Utah	5
Maryland	10	Vermont	3
Massachusetts	13	Virginia	12
Michigan	20	Washington	10
Minnesota	10	West Virginia	6
Mississippi	7	Wisconsin	11
Missouri	11	Wyoming	3

*The District of Columbia, which has no voting delegation in Congress, receives 3 votes.

to the House. In 1976, a shift of less that 4,000 votes in Hawaii and less than 6,000 in Ohio would have given the election to Gerald Ford, despite his trailing Carter by 1.7 million votes in the popular vote figures.[8] Actually, under the Electoral College system, a presidential candidate can win the popular vote and yet fail to win a majority of the electoral vote and the presidency, as was the case with Grover Cleveland in 1888. Cleveland won a plurality of approximately 95,000 popular votes but only 168 electoral votes, compared to 233 electoral votes for the Republican Benjamin Harrison. Cleveland's loss of New York, his home state, by about 15,000 votes and Indiana, Harrison's home state, by about 3,000 votes cost him reelection. Four years later, however, former President Cleveland won a second term with a convincing 279 to 145 electoral-vote victory over President Harrison in their rematch. No winning presidential candidate since 1888, it should be noted, has failed to win at least a plurality of the popular vote.

What happens if no candidate wins a majority of the electoral college vote? According to the U.S. Constitution, Article II, section 2, if no person shall have a majority, then the House of Representatives shall choose the president from the five highest persons (later changed to three by the Twelfth Amendment) on the list with each state having one vote. To become president when an electoral impasse shifts the election to the House of Representatives, a candidate must win a majority of the states (26 votes) in the House. Only once since the passage of the Twelfth Amendment in 1804 has the House selected the president. In 1824, the House picked John Quincy Adams over Andrew Jackson, Henry Clay, and

William Crawford. In the presidential election Jackson had collected 99 electoral votes to 84 for Adams, 41 for Crawford, and 37 for Clay. In 1876, Democratic candidate Samuel Tilden, who led by 250,000 popular votes was denied the presidency when a special congressionally appointed commission, consisting of eight Republicans and seven Democrats, was established to settle the question of disputed electoral votes. By upholding the Republican claims in all three states —all under questionable circumstances—the GOP candidate, Rutherford B. Hayes, emerged victorious by a single electoral vote, 185 to 184.[9]

THE STRATEGIC ENVIRONMENT

No two presidential elections are exactly alike, and only infrequently do the same candidates square off against each other more than once, such as the Eisenhower-Stevenson matchups in 1952 and 1956. The Electoral College provides the legal framework and dictates the electoral strategy each candidate is likely to follow. Public attitudes, demographics, and group loyalties all affect the political climate.

While the Electoral College makes the state the critical unit over which elections are fought, candidate managers do not view the state as a single entity, but rather divide it into distinct areas—metropolitan areas, suburbs, congressional districts—that have been characterized by different patterns of support in the past. Consequently, one may hear a strategist insist that in order to carry Illinois, the candidate must come out of Chicago with a certain lead. Or to carry California, he must build up a certain margin in Los Angeles and Orange counties. In short, the candidate must run well in his strongest areas of support. Assertions about carrying Chicago must be further refined to identify the specific demographic groups (blacks, unionized workers, Catholics) and the level of support needed for victory. Campaign managers naturally focus on groups that collectively add up to a majority. By dealing with demographic groups, campaign managers have found an economical way to target their campaign, rather than trying to focus on individuals.[10] To maximize their advantage within the strategic environment, candidates and their managers concentrate on the elements that determine voter choice. Past research on voting behavior has shown that three major factors (which vary from election to election) have the greatest impact on voter decision making: party identification, issues, and the candidate's image.[11] No serious contender can entertain hopes of victory unless he includes all three factors in his campaign planning.

Party Identification.   For more than two decades, party identification has been viewed as the most stable indicator of voter intentions. Party identification is the psychological attachment voters feel toward one party or the other. Generally, it is based upon family influence during childhood and later contact with issues and candidates. When voters are undecided about issues and candidates, they usually make their choice on the basis of party identification. Consequently, one major decision presidential candidates and their managers must make is whether to try to reinforce or dilute party identification in order to improve its importance in the vote.

Because Democratic party identifiers have outnumbered Republican identifiers since the New Deal era, Republicans tend to downplay their candidate's party affiliation. Thus, in 1984 President Reagan concentrated on such nonpartisan themes as patriotism, "America's back," a strong economy, and low inflation. So frequently did he identify with Democratic presidents such as Franklin D. Roosevelt, Truman, and Kennedy that challenger Mondale repeatedly complained the president was trying to steal the Democratic heroes while never mentioning former GOP presidents such as Hoover and Nixon. President Reagan also invited Democrats to defect to the GOP ranks, pointing out that he was once a Democrat who left the party only after it lost its moorings.

By contrast, Mondale sought to reinforce Democratic party identification in the hope of capitalizing on the larger number of Democratic identifiers. But Mondale also tried to avoid overplaying party identification for fear of driving away the political independents, who now make up about one-quarter of the electorate. In other words, Mondale had to walk a public tightrope that would persuade Democrats to support him as the candidate of his party while he asked independents to support him as the best candidate on issues and leadership. Mondale also made a special effort to attract those voters who in 1980 had supported third-party candidate John Anderson, a former Republican. During the fall campaign Anderson, in fact, endorsed Mondale.

Issues. Generally, issues surface in every presidential campaign in three forms. The first involves specific policy questions of the moment. For example, in 1984, the leading questions were how to deal with the insurgency in Central America, whether income taxes should be indexed, how should the annual deficit be reduced, and whether the MX missile should be built. The second form of issue concerns how the country is doing—political scientists call these *valence issues.* If the country is prospering or is better off than during a previous administration, the valence issues will generally help a president win reelection. If the valence issues are unfavorable, the incumbent will probably be rejected by the voters. The third form of issue relates to the public's verdict on the overall direction of the president's policy leadership or that offered by the challenger. Thus, it was not necessary for Franklin D. Roosevelt to have lifted the country out of the Great Depression by reelection time in 1936. Because a majority of Americans felt he was trying hard, moving in the right direction, and that his policies were preferable to those of his GOP predecessor, they returned him to the White House again.

In 1984, the opinion polls showed that the voters felt President Reagan was moving the country in the right direction, especially on matters of inflation and foreign affairs, even though they did not always agree with him on specific issues. Plainly, these favorable circumstances were tailor-made for a successful reelection drive. President Reagan outlined early the issues on which he planned to campaign—peace, prosperity, and a strong national defense—and challenged Mondale to meet him on this ground. Reagan could claim that inflation was down from the double-digit levels of 1980 to just over 4 percent in 1984. He also pointed with pride to the fact that interest rates were down substantially from 1980, and that America was "standing tall" in the world.

Challenger Mondale was forced to focus on more complicated issues—the national deficit, the trade balance deficit, Reagan's Star Wars satellite defense system, and the nuclear freeze issue. Mondale, in accepting his party's nomination, warned the American public that he endorsed a tax increase to reduce the soaring national deficit. Most of these issues were difficult to understand. Consequently, voters made their election day decisions on the issues that affected them personally—inflation, interest rates, employment rates, and the absence of war.

According to the *Washington Post*/ABC News exit polls, voters who went for Reagan most often mentioned the strong economy and national defense as the issues that motivated their vote. Mondale voters expressed greatest concern about the threat of nuclear war and the fairness issue. Military spending was the issue that most disposed them to vote *against* Reagan, and Mondale's proposed tax increase was the issue that most influenced members of the electorate to vote against the former vice-president. Leadership, the exit polls showed, clearly emerged as the dominant concern, and on this point Reagan clearly was the favorite. What about voters' view of the future? Sixty-three percent of the Reagan voters thought it would be a good one for the next generation. Approximately 70 percent of Mondale voters thought that future generations would be heavily bogged down by the unsolved problems left behind by the current generation.[12]

Candidate Image.   Favorable public perception of the incumbent president or his challenger will often tip the scales on election day. President Reagan was the chief beneficiary of candidate image in 1984, especially the image of leadership. According to *Washington Post*/ABC News Polls, 72 percent of the respondents said the president has "strong leadership qualities." Only 49 percent held this view for Walter F. Mondale.[13] Reagan's strong leadership ratings helped him effectively neutralize Mondale's effort to make the future direction of the country a major issue in the campaign. Thus, if voters were worried about the threat of tax increases and nuclear war, why drop a proven leader in favor of the unknown? Past research suggests that the more uncertain the public feels about the future, the greater their potential support for a strong president.

Throughout the entire campaign, Mondale was unable to shake the image that he lacked presidential qualities, particularly strong leadership. By mid-September 41 percent of the respondents of a *Washington Post*/ABC News poll had an unfavorable view of Mondale, with 27 percent favorable. Even more disconcerting to Mondale strategists, less than half the Democratic respondents felt favorably toward Mondale, thus seriously undermining his plans to build a solid electoral base on party identification. Among independents, only 19 percent felt favorably toward Mondale.[14] By contrast, 56 percent of the across-the-board voters felt favorably toward Reagan. Nearly the same number of independents —55 percent—viewed Reagan favorably.

OTHER KEY FACTORS

Financial resources and mass media, two topics discussed later in the chapter, constitute the principal instruments through which campaign objectives may be reached.[15] But time is another important factor that is sometimes overlooked. To have any serious hope of contacting a major segment of the potential 170 million voters, directly or most likely via television, requires more than a weekend planning session. Since the out-of-power party holds its national convention in mid-July, the party's nominee and his staff have at most 110 days to map a campaign strategy, allocate resources (especially the $40.4 million federal campaign grant), put key state managers in place, purchase TV time, and produce the commercials for an arduous 50-state campaign.[16] For the in-power party, whether it renominates the incumbent or chooses a new standard-bearer, the time frame is considerably shorter. Incumbent party conventions are generally not held until the third week in August. Consequently, the head of the ticket and his managers have at most 85 days to mount and execute their strategic plan. No wonder presidential campaign plans are often like the battle plans of rival field commanders.

All elements of the master plan must be carefully weighed and integrated into a grand strategy for the general election campaign. Failure to develop this plan early in the campaign can be fatal to a candidate's chances, as several defeated contenders have learned. Vice-President Hubert H. Humphrey, for example, emerged from the strife-torn 1968 Democratic convention with the nomination in hand, but his campaign organization in disarray. No general election campaign plan had been drafted; no television film was ready for commercials; and no money was available to purchase critical television time near election day. It took his campaign manager Larry O'Brien and the staff until the end of September to get back on track.[17] In the final five weeks Humphrey closed Richard Nixon's 43 percent to 25 percent Gallup poll lead to less than a point, but failed by a whisker to win the presidency. Several veteran Washington observers contended afterward that if the election campaign had lasted a week longer Humphrey would have won, since he appeared to be picking up nearly 500,000 supporters a day in the final ten days of the campaign. Failure to deal adequately and early enough with the strategic environment contributed heavily to his electoral loss.

Above all, the candidates must assess the strategic climate prevailing nationally during the year of the presidential election. Will an incumbent be running for reelection? What is the state of the economy? What is the rate of unemployment? Has the inflation rate risen or dropped sharply in the past 12 months? What is the current status of relations with the Soviet Union? Are any American hostages being held abroad? All these questions will have a direct bearing on the presidential campaign and its outcome.

ADVANTAGES OF INCUMBENCY

Until President Reagan won reelection in 1984, recent incumbents had not fared too well. Three out of four of the most recent incumbents failed to gain a second term. Lyndon B. Johnson decided not to make another try in 1968 because he faced impending defeats in several upcoming primaries, and his Vietnam policies had badly divided the nation. Gerald Ford barely won his party's nomination in 1976 and then lost to Jimmy Carter on economic issues, his party's role in the Watergate scandals, and his decision to pardon former president Nixon. Four years later, Jimmy Carter lost his reelection bid to Ronald Reagan on economic issues and the public's dissatisfaction with his presidential leadership.

Still, the advantages of incumbency cannot be easily dismissed in a general election campaign. First, the incumbent holds the highest office in the land, and can capitalize on all the respect and prestige that attaches to the office. As president, he enjoys instant recognition, dominates the news, and sets the national agenda. Generally, incumbents are viewed as experienced and knowledgeable. The incumbent chief executive, for example, can assume the Rose Garden strategy—almost too busy with the affairs of state to participate in a partisan campaign. As head of state, greeting foreign dignitaries and participating in White House ceremonies, he can remain "presidential" throughout the fall campaign. Through his decision-making power, he can influence events both at home and abroad. Also, he has a huge, trained staff and numerous surrogates who can campaign for him around the clock. Federal "spoils" in the form of grant money for urban transit, sewage treatment plants, and other pressing local projects can be released in the weeks before election to help influence the outcome. And, as Stephen J. Wayne has observed: "Since security is one of the major psychological needs which the Presidency serves, the certainty of four more years with a known quantity is likely to be more appealing than the uncertainty of the next four years with an unknown one, provided the initial four years were viewed as acceptable."[18] Understandably, presidential incumbents point with pride to their accomplishments, note the unfinished work, and sound a "let us continue," "stay the course" theme.

On paper, at least, the incumbent president possesses so many advantages over a challenger that it seems a wonder that he should ever be defeated. And until the advent of instant mass communication, only two twentieth-century incumbents—Taft and Hoover—were turned out of office after a single term. But in the age of television the gap between expectations and performance has widened. Presidents are expected to solve the problems of inflation, high interest rates, and unemployment, and to extricate the country from foreign quagmires. Failure to halt inflation or the rise of unemployment, even though there is relatively little that a president can do alone on these issues, can wreck his chances for a second term. Failure to impress the public that he is a decisive leader who is on top of his job can be equally fatal. The excessively high expectations placed on the president, especially in the economic sector, make the campaign task of the challenger much easier. Nevertheless, the challenger must demonstrate leadership potential and also appear "presidential."

Since the public knows less about the challenger and his personal life, he must rely on the mass media to display his openness, decisiveness, and leadership potential for all America to see. Television and its exposure of any presidential shortcomings, however, has narrowed the margins an incumbent enjoys over the challenger. Most media specialists believe, for example, that presidential debates usually help the challenger more than the incumbent. In the case of Kennedy (1960), Carter (1976), and Reagan (1980), most observers certainly held this view. Since challengers are less well known and their leadership a question mark, the debates help them demonstrate competence to a 100-million-person audience and remove some of the voter doubt that hangs over their candidacies. And as Stephen J. Wayne has commented: "By appearing to be at least the equal of their incumbent opponents, the presidential images of the challengers are enhanced."[19] Other things being equal, however, the incumbent should generally be favored to win reelection. After all, in the twentieth century, 14 incumbent presidents have run for reelection and 10 of them have won. Franklin D. Roosevelt was reelected three times.

What kind of strategy is generally preferred by the candidates? For our purposes, the 1980 race between President Jimmy Carter and challenger Ronald Reagan, and the 1984 contest between President Reagan and former Vice-President Walter F. Mondale, make two excellent case studies. In the first instance, the challenger won; in the second case, the incumbent retained the White House.

RECENT CAMPAIGN STRATEGY

In 1980, both candidates—President Carter and Ronald Reagan—perceived their opponents as vulnerable, and each made these vulnerabilities the focus of his campaign. President Carter waged an offensive against Reagan's competence from the day the former California governor was nominated. Since Reagan was not the incumbent and did not have a specific record (other than two terms as governor of California), Carter often resorted to a more personal type of campaign. Sometimes, in the eyes of reporters, he hit too hard or unfairly and had to spend time defending his campaign tactics rather than attacking his opponent. In the end, Carter failed to make the extremist/incompetent image stick to Reagan.

Challenger Reagan's strategy was to attack Carter's performance but not to attack the president personally. From the campaign kickoff to election day, Reagan and his campaign team painted Carter as an ineffective, error-prone leader whose vacillating foreign policy had created a climate of crisis. Repeatedly, the GOP contender contrasted Carter's promises with his performance. As an alternative, Reagan outlined his economic and national defense positions, and claimed that he would return the country to prosperous times. Reagan held Carter personally responsible for the double-digit inflation and skyrocketing interest rates that approached 19 percent by election time. Throughout the 1980 campaign, Reagan's chief pollster, Richard Wirthlin, centered his strategy on converting several key groups into Reagan supporters: southern white Protestants, blue-collar workers in the industrial states, urban ethnics, and rural voters, especially in the big electoral vote states of New York, Ohio, and Pennsylvania. Convinced that Reagan could count on virtually all states west of the Mississippi, Wirthlin concluded that the key to success was to capture the ethnic blue-collar vote of the Northeast while seeking to deny Carter his southern base.[20]

The Reagan campaign plan was divided into three periods, each of which had a major objective. The first phase, from the end of the Democratic convention until shortly after Labor Day, was to be used to solidify the Republican base of support, anchored by California's 45 electoral votes. The second phase, from about the second week of September until mid-October, was designed to deepen public perception of Governor Reagan as an effective leader and to broaden his political base, especially among political independents. The third phase, from October 20 to November 4, was viewed as the decisive period in which the election could be won by maximum use of candidate appearances and a media blitz to achieve a big turnout. Sufficient flexibility was also built into the plan to permit needed shifts if political conditions dictated a change.[21]

The 1980 Carter campaign plan, as designed by pollster-strategist Patrick Caddell, consisted of four key components:

1. Hold the South.
2. Concentrate on the larger industrial states (Ohio, Pennsylvania, Illinois, Texas, Michigan, New Jersey, Missouri, and Wisconsin).
3. Take New York or California.
4. Add small state targets of opportunity to the same base states.[22]

Obviously, the Reagan strategy produced the better result on election day, but few critics would fault the soundness of Carter's strategic plan. It was well conceived, but it simply could not be implemented.

Unlike most presidential elections, the 1980 campaign had a strong third-party entrant, John Anderson, a former GOP contender who withdrew from the Republican race in late April to mount his independent campaign. During the early summer Anderson was listed as the choice of 25 percent of the Gallup poll respondents—only a short distance behind Reagan and Carter. But as soon as the general election campaign began, he started to fade. Handicapped by a shortage of funds—he was not eligible to receive federal funding until after he qualified for 5 percent of the vote in the general election—Anderson failed to carry a single state or become a serious competitor in more than a handful of states. Forced to borrow funds, Anderson spent $2 million of the $12.1 million raised just in organizing a signature petition drive and legal assistance in getting on the ballots in all 50 states.[23] Clearly, the 1980 campaign demonstrated once again how high the odds are against making a serious run for the presidency under a third-party banner.

For the 1984 race, most observers and pollsters agreed that the strong economy, the low inflation rate, and the successful invasion of Grenada to topple the Marxist government in October 1983 placed Reagan in an enviable position to win reelection. The Grenada "victory," more than any other event of his presidency, laid the foundation for Reagan's basic campaign theme—namely that his brand of leadership had made America strong and proud again, in stark contrast with the condition it was in when he assumed office. Reagan sidestepped discussing issues and, in particular, avoided becoming embroiled with Mondale in specific disputes over public policy. Theodore J. Lowi has neatly summarized the Reagan strategy: "Mondale was permitted to raise all the issues he wanted, but the response of the Reagan camp was to treat them as if they were simply prophecies of doom and gloom."[24] And by mobilizing all the advantages of incumbency, Reagan maintained his formidable lead throughout the entire campaign.

Repeating his "retrospective" strategy of 1980, Reagan asked the voters if they were better off now than they were four years ago. The president wanted the voters to look back over four years of declining inflation and vote retrospectively. In short, he endeavored to turn the election into a referendum on his presidency. Incumbents seeking reelection in a year of economic prosperity can, as Jeff Fishel reminds us, "push a personalized version of retrospective accountability to the extreme, emphasizing an upbeat of the present and *recent* past, ignoring with impunity past mistakes, policy reversals and specific future commitments."[25] Challenger Walter F. Mondale's chief hope of winning rested on a "prospective" strategy. Mondale tried to get the voters to look ahead, to cast their ballots on the basis of their fears of another deep recession, gigantic deficits, an endangered environment, and the threat of nuclear war provoked by a trigger-happy president.[26]

To try and break free from his identity with the Democratic party's past, Mondale chose Representative Geraldine Ferraro of New York as his running-mate—the first woman ever to be nominated on a major party ticket. Still, Mondale indirectly accepted a number of Reagan achievements—increased defense spending (but at a slower rate), preservation of the 1981 tax cut and the plan to start indexing in 1985, except for those in the upper tax brackets, and a qualified endorsement of the Grenada invasion. As president he said he would make Reagan's policies fairer and complete the agenda of the 1980 campaign and balance the budget. But Mondale soon discovered that running against a popular incumbent president who had brought peace, prosperity, and renewed feelings of national pride to most Americans was a losing cause. None of the issues he raised seemed to sway many voters, men or women, young or old. As one congressman put it: "Mondale learned the hard way that people don't care about the deficit."[27]

What does the future hold for presidential campaign strategies of the late 1980s and early 1990s? Clearly, the Sunbelt states of the South and Southwest will take on increased importance as the population shifts away from the Northeast and the Midwest Rustbelt states boost their electoral vote.[28] By the 1980s Texas ranked third in the Electoral College, and Florida was not far behind. By the 1990s, Florida is expected, if present projections are accurate, to be at least the fifth most populous state (Florida gained four electoral votes after the 1980 reapportionment). Based upon voting patterns of the past three decades, the Republicans can view states west of the Mississippi almost as the Solid West and use this base as the start for continuing to build their winning coalition.

Undoubtedly, the Democrats will look to the northeastern, midwestern, and border states as the starting point for constructing a winning coalition. But they can no longer count on the Solid South as the foundation of a winning combination of states in the Electoral College. Since the 1960s, more southern states have gone Republican than Democratic, and the polling data suggest that this trend will probably continue. In 1984, for example, President Reagan captured 71 percent of the white vote in winning all eleven states of the old Confederacy.[29] However, despite two recent Reagan landslides, polling data reveal no strong evidence that a major party realignment has occurred or is likely to happen in the immediate years ahead.[30] More likely, the result will be continued two-party competition in presidential campaigns for the remainder of the century.

One wild card in recent presidential campaign strategy has been the candidates' performance in the revived televised presidential debates.

THE DEBATES

Presidential debates have come to represent the most important single campaign event of the presidential race, especially for the challenger. The debates provide a forum where the two contenders are placed on a relatively equal footing. Thus the challenger, though less experienced than the incumbent, is in an excellent position to counter charges that he lacks experience and presidential qualities. Even if neither candidate is an incumbent, these confrontations can sometimes make or break candidacies in a single roll of the dice.

In the first series of nationally televised debates, held between Senator John F. Kennedy and Vice-President Nixon in 1960, Kennedy was considered by those watching as the winner of the opening round in four-debate series. More than anything else, Kennedy's outstanding forensics performance—his crisp answers, his cool-headed demeanor, and his "presidential" qualities of decisiveness and conviction—was also thought to have turned him into the frontrunner overnight. Curiously, most people listening to the first debate on radio rated the candidates about even or Nixon slightly ahead. But this reaction was almost completely ignored by the commentators, and many of the estimated 60 million viewers who lauded Kennedy's brilliant presentation. The results of the other three debates were judged to be nearly standoffs, but it did not matter, because Kennedy won the laurels on the opening night.[31]

No debates were held in the next three presidential elections because President Johnson refused to debate Senator Barry Goldwater in 1964, and Nixon declined to debate Vice-President Humphrey in 1968 and Senator George McGovern in 1972.[32] But in 1976 challenger Jimmy Carter, according to most pollsters, benefitted in the second debate from President Ford's misstatement (and his subsequent refusal for several days to correct his remark) that Poland was not under the domination of the Soviet Union. This gaffe was thought by most observers to have halted Ford's remarkable fourth-quarter comeback (Ford had been listed nearly 30 percentage points behind Carter in the late August polls), which fell just short on election day.

Four years later, challenger Ronald Reagan came up the victor against President Jimmy Carter, according to most pollsters, in the single, winner-take-all encounter just one week before the election. (Previously, Carter had refused to debate both Reagan and third-party candidate John Anderson on the same platform.) Compared to the 1976 series, the Carter-Reagan confrontation was relatively low-keyed. There were no major rhetorical blunders like Ford's gaffe in 1976. Even though he was the incumbent, Carter was on the attack more than Reagan, the challenger. Reagan, however, had the last word with his famous summation: "Ask yourself, are you better off than you were four years ago?" Most press observers at the debate rated it as fairly even.

But the public scored it differently. A *New York Times*/CBS News poll taken the next day indicated that 44 percent of the viewers thought Reagan had won, while 36 percent picked Carter. Approximately 6 percent said they had changed their vote after watching the debate; these respondents went for Reagan by a 2 to 1 margin.[33] Data from the University of Michigan's Survey Research Center postelection poll showed Reagan's performance to be impressive. Among Democratic respondents who said they were more impressed with Carter, only 1 percent chose Reagan, but if they were more impressed with Reagan, 71 percent chose the GOP nominee.[34]

Subsequent events revealed that Reagan may have enjoyed a hidden advantage over Carter in the 1980 debate. A Reagan "mole" working on the Carter campaign staff apparently purloined a copy of President Carter's debate briefing book and turned it over to the Reagan team. For a time reporters talked about a "Debategate" emerging from the congressional subcommittee investigation, but failure to uncover sufficient evidence of illegal activity led to a termination of the probe.

Reagan's strong debate performance, high inflation and high interest rates, and Carter's inability to win freedom for the 50-odd American hostages held for almost a year by the Iranian government before election day were critical factors in sending Carter down to defeat. Significantly, the *New York Times*/CBS News poll reported in its final survey of the 1980 election campaign that about one voter in five changed his or her mind about for whom to vote, or whether to vote at all, in the last four days, and that about three-fifths made a change that hurt President Carter.[35] The economic issue, for example, received new prominence after Reagan asked the national television debate audience if they were better off today than four years ago. According to the *New York Times*/CBS News exit poll of 10,000 voters leaving the polling booths across the nation, two-thirds cited economic problems such as unemployment, taxes, and inflation as the key factors for their vote.[36] The Iranian hostage crisis, which had been relatively dormant, suddenly erupted in the closing days; 23 percent of the vote changers who went against Carter cited the hostage crisis as the reason for their vote shift.[37]

In 1984, most observers agreed that challenger Mondale would have to score a political knockout in the two debates with President Reagan in order to have a serious chance of defeating the president. Most presidential watchers agreed that Mondale clearly won the first debate. The president appeared tired and poorly prepared. But Reagan bounced back surprisingly well in the second debate. He looked refreshed, and his presentation was convincing. Once again, the president's humor appeared to rescue him, especially on the age issue, which had suddenly become front-page news after his weak performance in the first debate. Asked if he would be able to function during a crisis, the seventy-three-year-old Reagan quipped: "I will not make age an issue of this campaign. I am not going to exploit, for political purposes, my opponent's youth and inexperience." With this one humorous rejoinder, Reagan seemed to regain the initiative, reassure the voters, and hold off Mondale's strong thrusts.

Mondale's failure to clearly outpoint Reagan in the second debate in effect ended his hopes of capturing the presidency. Although Mondale responded with some of the best speeches of his campaign after the second debate, he failed to dent Reagan's heavy support among major demographic groups.

For a Republican candidate to win the presidency, he must do well not only among his own partisans, but also among college-educated male voters, those with incomes over $25,000 per year, WASPs (White Anglo-Saxon Protestants), middle-aged voters, white-collar workers, and independents. For a Democratic candidate to win he must do well among union members, Catholics, blacks, and Hispanics, those with incomes below $25,000, the less educated, young voters, senior citizens, and women. In 1984, according to the *Washington Post*/ABC News exit poll, Reagan ran well for a Republican with every demographic group except blacks, voters with incomes below $10,000, and liberals. Independents voted for Reagan by a 2 to 1 margin, up 10 percentage points from 1980. One-quarter of all Democrats defected to Reagan, but only 6 percent of GOP voters went over to Mondale. Reagan also made significant inroads among Catholics, high-income blue-collar workers, and southern whites.[38]

Mondale and his staff entertained hopes that the "senior gap" and the "gender gap" would help them win the presidency. But the exit polls showed that, although the senior gap existed early in the year, it closed during the fall campaign. Senior citizens gave Reagan heavy support on election day. With the first woman vice-presidential nominee ever on a national ticket, Geraldine Ferraro, Democrats hoped to cash in heavily on election day. Although an 8 percent "gender gap" between men and women existed on that day, both men and women supported Reagan over Mondale. So-called Yuppies (young urban professionals) supported Reagan heavily, reflecting their affluence and lack of party identification. One-third of Senator Gary Hart's supporters, according to a *Washington Post*/ABC News exit poll, voted for Reagan, even though Hart campaigned extensively for Mondale.[39]

No presidential campaign can operate without money for more than a few hours. The funding of presidential campaigns has changed remarkably in the past decade, and it is to this subject that we now turn.

CAMPAIGN FINANCE

Presidential campaign finance has become a big business. In 1972, President Richard M. Nixon spent $61.4 million—an all-time record—to retain his White House residence. A century earlier, President Ulysses S. Grant spent $250,000. In 1932, Franklin D. Roosevelt's financial outlay was approximately $2.3 million in his winning campaign.

History shows that the greatest increases in presidential campaign spending occurred in the 1960s and early 1970s (see Table 4.3). Skyrocketing costs of television advertising, the growing "professionalization" of campaign staffs, communications specialists, high-priced chartered jet air travel, and the inflated costs of phone banks, office space, computerized mailing lists, and campaign polling all contributed to the zooming costs of running for the White House. Until Congress intervened in the 1970s, an ever greater reliance on fat cat contributors had become an integral part of presidential campaigns. The number of individuals contributing $10,000 or more rose dramatically during this period. In 1972, for example, W. Clement Stone, the Chicago insurance magnate, contributed more

Table 4.3 **COSTS OF PRESIDENTIAL GENERAL ELECTIONS, 1860–1984,**
MAJOR PARTY CANDIDATES

Year	Republican		Democratic	
1860	$100,000	Lincoln*	$50,000	Douglas
1864	125,000	Lincoln*	50,000	McClellan
1868	150,000	Grant*	75,000	Seymour
1872	250,000	Grant*	50,000	Greeley
1876	950,000	Hayes*	900,000	Tilden
1880	1,100,000	Garfield*	335,000	Hancock
1884	1,300,000	Blaine	1,400,000	Cleveland*
1888	1,350,000	Harrison*	855,000	Cleveland
1892	1,700,000	Harrison	2,350,000	Cleveland*
1896	3,350,000	McKinley*	675,000	Bryan
1900	3,000,000	McKinley*	425,000	Bryan
1904	2,096,000	T. Roosevelt*	700,000	Parker
1908	1,655,518	Taft*	629,341	Bryan
1912	1,071,549	Taft	1,134,848	Wilson*
1916	2,441,565	Hughes	2,284,590	Wilson*
1920	5,417,501	Harding*	1,470,371	Cox
1924	4,020,478	Coolidge*	1,108,836	Davis
1928	6,256,111	Hoover*	5,342,350	Smith
1932	2,900,052	Hoover	2,245,975	F. Roosevelt*
1936	8,892,972	Landon	5,194,741	F. Roosevelt*
1940	3,451,310	Willkie	2,783,654	F. Roosevelt*
1944	2,828,652	Dewey	2,169,077	F. Roosevelt*
1948	2,127,296	Dewey	2,736,334	Truman*
1952	6,608,623	Eisenhower*	5,032,926	Stevenson
1956	7,778,702	Eisenhower*	5,106,651	Stevenson
1960	10,128,000	Nixon	9,797,000	Kennedy*
1964	16,026,000	Goldwater	8,757,000	Johnson*
1968†	25,402,000	Nixon*	11,594,000	Humphrey
1972	61,400,000	Nixon*	30,000,000	McGovern
1976	21,800,000‡	Ford	21,800,000‡	Carter*
1980	29,200,000‡	Reagan*	29,200,000‡	Carter
1984	40,400,000‡	Reagan*	40,400,000‡	Mondale

*Indicates winner.

†George Wallace spent an estimated $7 million as the candidate of the American Independent party in 1968.

‡Candidates opted to accept full federal funding of campaign as provided for in the Federal Election Campaign Act of 1974.

Sources: Herbert E. Alexander, *Financing Politics* (Washington, DC: Congressional Quarterly Press, 1980), 5; Federal Election Commission, Washington, DC, supplied data for 1976–1984.

than $2 million to the Republicans, mostly to Nixon. Richard Mellon Scaife, heir to the Pittsburgh-based Mellon fortune, donated more than $1 million to the GOP. Among the big Democratic contributors Stewart R. Mott, heir to a General Motors fortune, headed the list in 1972, with contributions of more than $715,000.[40]

During the pre-Watergate era, there were no limitations on the size of individual contributions, but the Hatch Act of 1940 put a ceiling of $3 million on the amount a single national committee could spend on a presidential election. However, this limit contained a huge loophole, because no limit was placed on the number of national committees that could be formed to aid a candidate. In

1952, General Eisenhower's supporters established a Citizens for Eisenhower and Nixon, along with the regular Eisenhower-Nixon Committee, to help underwrite the heavy campaign bills. Democratic candidates such as Adlai Stevenson, John F. Kennedy, and Lyndon B. Johnson all resorted to this same loophole in their campaigns. However, the excessive expenditures of President Nixon's Committee to Re-Elect the President (better known by the acronym CREEP) marked the end of the laissez-faire era of presidential campaign finance.

The Watergate investigation revelations that the Nixon White House had collected huge illegal campaign contributions from corporations (banned since 1907) and had exerted heavy pressure on big individual contributors led to the passage of the Federal Election Campaign Act of 1974 (FECA). This legislation, among other things, restricted individual contributions to $1,000 for presidential candidates and provided for the option of full public funding of presidential elections and matching federal subsidies in the nominating race.[41] When the funding provision for presidential elections first went into effect in 1976, the federal contribution ceiling for major party candidates was $21.8 million. If candidates agreed to accept Uncle Sam's money for the general election campaign, they were prohibited from soliciting any private funds. Since then, both major party candidates have accepted federal money rather than go it alone, though in 1980 candidate Reagan toyed with the idea of raising his own campaign funds. But he finally decided to put aside his personal bias against government intervention in the election process and accepted the federal funds. In 1984, President Reagan and former Vice-President Walter F. Mondale each received $40.4 million in federal funds for their campaigns.

This federal funding provision clearly discriminates against third-party candidates. Nominees for the two major parties, if they foreswear private funding, automatically qualify for the general election campaign funds. Third-party candidates, however, do not qualify until after they have collected 5 percent of the presidential vote. In that event, they are entitled to federal funds equal to the proportion of the popular vote until that vote falls below 5 percent. Thus, in 1980 third-party candidate John Anderson had to borrow heavily from private sources and rely on loyal contributors to underwrite his campaign. Since he received 6.6 percent of the popular vote, he collected $4.2 million from the Federal Election Commission after the election, enough to pay off his debts, but scarcely enough to have mounted a vigorous campaign. Anderson, having retroactively qualified for federal funds in 1980, was eligible to receive Uncle Sam's funds in 1984, but he chose not to run. Additionally, the 1974 law permits the major national committees to spend 2 cents per citizen of voting age in support of their presidential nominees. In 1984, this figure amounted to $6.9 million each for the GOP and Democratic national committees.

Among the "unanticipated consequences" of the 1974 law was the drying up of local campaign activity on behalf of presidential candidates two years later. Since both the Ford and Carter campaigns earmarked most of their federal funds for TV advertising and national campaign expenses, there were virtually no funds left for campaign buttons, bumper stickers, and yard signs—favorite campaign weapons at the local level. To revive and encourage local grassroots campaign activity, Congress amended the Federal Election Campaign Act in 1979 to permit state and local parties to spend an unlimited amount of funds on voluntary efforts to turn out the vote, distribute campaign literature, operate phone banks, and coordinate registration and get-out-the-vote drives.

Beyond question, the 1974 Federal Election Campaign Act marked the beginning of a new era in presidential election politics. First of all, the legislation equalized spending between the major party candidates, eliminating the traditional funding advantage the GOP had almost always enjoyed. By granting the money directly to the presidential candidates instead of the national party committees, however, the 1974 law has further weakened the political parties and fostered the growing trend toward a plebiscite president. With the $40.4 million federal stipend (for the 1984 election), the presidential candidate can continue to expand his personal campaign committee staff, the team that carried him through the primary nominating campaign; no longer are state and local party organizations needed.

To reach the maximum number of prospective voters and achieve maximum utilization of federal dollars, the presidential candidates now spend the bulk of their campaign dollars on media advertising. In 1984, for example, President Reagan's staff spent over $21 million on TV advertising—over one-half of their entire federal campaign fund. Challenger Mondale and his staff paid out approximately $17 million—over two-fifths of their federally supported budget.[42] Four years earlier, more than half of the federal campaign grant money (approximately $29 million for each party nominee) was spent on mass media advertising. President Carter's campaign in 1980 spent $20.5 million on mass media advertising, $15.8 million of it on television. Radio advertising consumed $2.6 million, with the remainder spent on print media and production costs. The 1980 Reagan campaign spent $16.8 million on mass media advertising and production costs, including approximately $10.8 million on TV, $1.5 million on radio, $2.2 million for newspapers, and $2.3 million on production.[43] Significantly, during the final ten days of the 1980 campaign, the Reagan strategists poured some $6 million into media advertising in states and communities chosen on the basis of extensive surveys and computer simulations.[44]

In the past decade the growth of *political action committees* (*PACs*) has added a new dimension to presidential campaign spending. Though political action committees have existed for more than four decades—the first and best known has been the AFL-CIO Committee on Political Education (COPE)—the Federal Election Campaign Act of 1971 and amendments to it in 1974 and 1976 signaled the beginning of the modern era for PACs. This new legislation specifically authorized corporations and unions to spend their funds on the establishment and administration of "separate segregated funds" for political activities.

Upheld by the Supreme Court in *Buckley* v. *Valeo* in 1976, political action committees came under the protection of the First Amendment.[45] Though PACs could not make direct contributions to presidential candidates in 1976, 1980, or 1984 (because the candidates all chose public funding with its attendant limits on contributions and expenditures), several PACs—the Congressional Club, NCPAC, Americans for Change and Americans for an Effective Presidency, and several others—independently spent $12.2 million in support of the Reagan candidacy in 1980.[46] In the same campaign, PACs independently spent only $45,000 on Jimmy Carter's reelection effort. To a seasoned observer, these figures of PAC spending on behalf of Ronald Reagan are not, however, as one-sided as they appear at first glance. Herbert E. Alexander, the leading authority on campaign finance, has estimated that labor union spending on behalf of President Carter through its political action committees, especially the AFL-CIO Committee on Political Education (COPE), approached $15 million.[47]

Most likely, the disparity between PAC independent spending on behalf of Republican and Democratic presidential candidates will widen in 1988 and thereafter, since the U.S. Supreme Court in early 1985 struck down the $1,000 legal limit on spending by political action committees on behalf of presidential candidates in general elections. The Court held that the spending limit imposed by the Federal Election Campaign Act—the legislation that underwrites public funding of presidential elections—violates the rights of free speech and association protected by the First Amendment.[48]

The campaign finance legislation of the 1970s which banned private contributions in presidential elections if the candidate accepted public funds has enlarged the impact and influence of PACs in presidential elections, further weakening the national parties' influence over both presidential candidates and their parties.

Federal underwriting of presidential election campaigns means increased financial accountability. To avoid exceeding the Federal Election Commission spending limits, and the unwanted publicity and fines this entails, campaign staffs must hire a corps of accountants to aid the campaign finance director. In 1980, for example, the Carter-Mondale campaign closely controlled expenditures by computer. Even with this much control, the Carter-Mondale camp still had a difficult time staying under the prescribed limit. Aside from big media expenditures in 1980, the campaign had the following big ticket items:

Payroll	$ 955,755
Consultants	1,191,299
Contracted services	1,985,124
Telephone	1,826,916
Travel	2,089,725[49]

Small wonder that accountants have become almost as important as campaign managers, especially in the final stretch of the drive to win the White House.

President Reagan's 1985 tax reform plan proposed that Congress end the current system of public financing for presidential elections by repealing the $1 checkoff allowed on individual tax returns. If adopted by Congress, the step would radically alter the way presidential campaigns have been funded since 1976. As a result of the post-Watergate reforms, the public financing system has achieved a rough parity in financial resources between the two major parties' nominees.

President Reagan's opposition to federal campaign finance laws has been a matter of record for several years: "I would like to see us return to the candidates raising their own campaign funds and not have the Government tax funds in it," he told reporters in December 1979.[50] Although President Reagan does not use the $1 checkoff on his own tax return, it is noteworthy that he has accepted more federal money than any presidential candidate since passage of the federal legislation—a grand total of $90.5 million in 1976, 1980, and 1984, according to federal records.[51] "Repeal of the checkoff would eliminate public funds for Presidential campaigns unless direct appropriations were provided" by Congress, the administration said in a book explaining the Reagan tax plan. But Herbert E. Alexander, a leading authority on campaign finance, comments: "With a divided Congress and with the potential of a veto by the President, the possibility of Congress appropriating the money independently is very problematic."[52]

If the federal financing legislation were repealed, presidential campaign finance would probably revert to the pre-Watergate era of private fundraising. Repeal of the checkoff would probably intensify the pressure on Congress to raise the limit of individual contributions. The present limit, unchanged since 1975, is $1,000 to any candidate for federal office in a given election.

Ample funding is, of course, indispensable to a winning campaign. But presidential candidates also need to utilize the latest political technology, a topic that deserves brief discussion.

POLITICAL TECHNOLOGY

Traditionally, the central task of a presidential campaign has been to put together a coalition of support among groups already predisposed toward one's candidacy and to add to this coalition until victory appears within reach. However, the emphasis on specific groups may not be the main strategy of the future as the proportion of citizens within groups identifying with a political party shrinks and the number of independent voters grows. Instead of group appeals, it will be necessary to focus more intensely on individual voters. Clearly, this means that candidate strategists will have to rely more and more on televised appeals to the individual voter.

To reach a potential electorate of 170 million individual voters, modern political campaigns require the latest political technology. Private polling, huge direct mail advertising campaigns, and massive television advertising have all become key elements in the final drive for the White House. Polling too has become a major weapon in the campaign arsenal. Campaign consultants and advisers use their private polls to evaluate the strengths and weaknesses of their candidate and the opposition. They will seek to learn how the voters feel about the key issues and try to judge where the candidate should focus his main effort. They will try to stage campaign activities for maximum impact on the mass media and to help build a favorable "image" of a candidate. Targeting messages to selective audiences has become a highly professional business.

As the late Theodore H. White, presidential chronicler, explains: "The working maps of national politicians now divide the country into sixty-odd ADI's —Areas of Dominant Influence—in which the major television centers control public attention."[53] Campaign experts will further divide these areas into some two hundred DMAs (designated marketing areas), within which smaller television and radio stations provide audiences at lower cost per thousand rates. With computers, audiences can be broken down further by age, sex, occupation, and ethnic loyalty. Trained professionals specialize in time buying to reach black audiences, the Hispanic audience, the evangelical audience, the easy-listening audience, the senior citizen audience, and the rock-and-roll audience. Other specialists mount, cut, and rearrange the short taped commercials.[54]

Campaign media experts and consultants have, in the minds of many observers, taken over many of the functions once performed by political parties. Indeed, a few critics even allege that the campaign consultants and pollsters have become a new "political elite" that can select candidates by determining in advance which contenders have the most attractive image—or the type of image that can be restyled for the widest appeal.

ROLE OF THE MASS MEDIA

Calvin Coolidge, one of the most colorless and uninspiring men ever to hold the presidential office, originated mass media campaigning. In 1924, Coolidge decided that it was unbecoming for a president to go whistlestopping around the country in search of votes for an office he already occupied. Instead, he stayed in the nation's capital throughout most of the campaign and turned to the newly expanding radio stations to reach part of the mass public with his campaign message. Coolidge, in winning reelection, outspent his Democratic opponent, John W. Davis, in the media by a 3 to 1 margin ($120,000 to $40,000).[55] Since then, outlays for mass media advertising have continued to spiral upward to multimillion-dollar figures. But the goal remains the same: how to reach the most voters effectively with the campaign message for the least cost. As the role of the political party has declined in recent decades, the importance of the media, especially television, has understandably multiplied.

With the advent of television and the proliferation of presidential primaries, the nature of the entire presidential election campaign has also changed. Much of this change can be traced to the role of the mass media itself. As Thomas E. Patterson and Richard Davis have pointed out: "Most election coverage is devoted to the campaign contest itself rather than to what the choice of one candidate or the other may mean to the nation."[56] Patterson's studies of recent presidential elections have documented the media's concentration on the "horserace" or game aspects of the campaign—who's ahead? who's behind?—rather than the issues.[57] In the 1976 campaign, for example, approximately twice as much news coverage was devoted to the candidate competition as to the substance of the issues. To be sure, a presidential campaign is as much a game of strategy and confrontation as it is a choice about national policy and leadership. But recent elections show beyond doubt that issues and voters' choice have taken a back seat to the horserace aspects of the election. This has not always been the case.

In the 1940s, Paul Lazersfeld and Bernard Berelson found that about 35 percent of the election news dealt with the battle to win the presidency, and 50 percent dealt with subjects related to policy and leadership.[58] Thirty years later, the prospective voter would have to monitor the media closely to pick out the main issues of the campaign. Although the candidates spend much of their time discussing national problems, policy goals, issues, and government performance, the media prefer to concentrate on the horserace aspects of the presidential contest. Under these circumstances it is understandable why candidates now discuss national issues primarily as they relate to electoral strategy.

Several causes underlie this shift in emphasis by the media. Candidates now organize much earlier—usually at least eighteen months before convention time—and far more intensively. The proliferation of presidential primaries to 30 or more state contests, and the extension of the official preconvention campaign to nearly six months, is partly responsible. With a different state contest virtually every week—and sometimes several on the same day—the horserace or game aspect of politics dominates the primary season, and then carries over to the general election campaign. Because the campaign is so long, the candidate's position on the issues will be reported early on. But once reported, it appears to lose news value. Television reporters and even members of the "pencil press" would much rather update the players' strategies and their standings in the latest polls than reruns of the candidates' policy statements and qualifications. Occasionally, the candidate will come up with a fresh proposal, a new issue—but once covered by the media, it will usually be relegated to the reporters' notebooks.

The steady growth of syndicated public opinion polls has helped tilt the mass media's emphasis on the game aspects of the presidential contest even more. As Patterson and Davis have noted: "The increasing availability of polls—many of them conducted by news organizations themselves—has elevated the probable outcome of the election to an everyday news subject, and thus this speculation has become a constant competitor with the election's substance for space in newspapers and time on television."[59] The same authors found, for example, that in the last week of the 1984 election (October 31–November 6, 1984) *The New York Times* ran fifteen stories—nearly a third of its election coverage stories—based wholly or in significant part on polls, mostly its own jointly operated with CBS News. Another quarter of its election stories made at least some mention of poll results.[60] No longer can there be much doubt that the election agenda centers on the "game," not the issues.

Does this mean that one or the other major candidate suffers unfairly from this emphasis on the horserace aspect of the presidential contest? Not necessarily. Both major party nominees received $40.4 million to conduct their 1984 general election campaigns. Candidates can spend as much of that total as they wish on educating the public via TV and radio advertising on their stand on the issues. Furthermore, presidential debates have almost become an integral part of the general election campaign format, and this offers an additional avenue for the candidates to present their views on the issues. But once again, reportage of these media events concentrates heavily on who won, who lost, who committed a major gaffe, how each candidate reacted to the questions, and so on. With this type of heavy play from the mass media, it is not strange that public reaction has focused on the performance of the candidates and not on their stands on issues.

DECISION TIME

How much influence does the 10-week general election campaign by the major party candidates have on voter choice for president? Data collected over the past quarter century show that although over half the voters have decided on their candidate by convention time, more voters appear to be delaying their choice until the last two weeks of the campaign (see Table 4.1). In 1980, for example, approximately 26 percent of the voters made their decision in the last two weeks of the campaign or on election day. In 1960, only 12 percent decided in the final two weeks of the campaign.

While we can only speculate about the time sequence of voter decision making, it may be that the reestablishment of presidential debates in 1976 (the only previous debates were held between Kennedy and Nixon in 1960) offer prospective voters two or three additional opportunities to size up the presidential nominees before making a final choice. Furthermore, weak party loyalties characteristic of the contemporary electorate leave it inherently more volatile than electorates of yesteryear. This does not mean, however, that large numbers of voters will be in a state of flux every four years. In 1984, for example, an election day poll taken by the *Los Angeles Times* found that an extraordinary 47 percent of the voters stated they had made up their minds on how they would vote before the first presidential primaries in February.[61] Another 21 percent said they had decided on their choice before September. In any event, it is impossible to state precisely how many voters are persuaded by the general election campaign to change their choice of candidates, or decide whether or not to vote at all. But there can be no doubt that campaigns do make a difference and that no presidential candidate, even the most popular incumbent, can afford to stay on the sidelines throughout the entire campaign. Over the past two decades, a shift of even 11.5 percent of the voters nationwide would in all likelihood have reversed the outcome of all recent landslide elections—1964, 1972, 1980, and 1984—and the names of Goldwater, McGovern, and Mondale would have been added to the list of U.S. presidents.[62]

VOTER TURNOUT

Although approximately 174 million Americans over the age of eighteen were eligible to vote in 1984, only 92 million Americans went to the polls—a 52.9 percent turnout. The 1984 turnout, however, was up three-tenths of 1 percent—reversing a 20-year trend of declining participation in presidential elections.[63]

Ironically, as more and more citizens have acquired the right to vote in recent years, voter turnout has declined. As Table 4.4 indicates, the estimated number of those eligible to vote has more than doubled in the past 50 years, but after reaching a peak in 1960—62.8 percent—the percentage of citizens who actually cast ballots has dropped. In the past six presidential elections, voter turnout has fallen almost 10 percentage points. Between 1968 and 1972—the height of the Vietnam war—it fell over 5 percent.

What accounts for the drop in turnout? Political experts are still scratching

Table 4.4 PARTICIPATION IN PRESIDENTIAL ELECTIONS

Year	Total adult population*	Total presidential vote	Percentage of adult population voting
1824	3,964,000	363,017	9 %
1840	7,381,000	2,412,698	33
1860	14,676,000	4,692,710	32
1880	25,012,000	9,219,467	37
1900	40,753,000	13,974,188	35
1920	60,581,000	26,768,613	44
1932	75,768,000	39,732,000	52.4
1940	84,728,000	49,900,000	58.9
1952	99,929,000	61,551,000	61.6
1960	109,674,000	68,838,000	62.8
1964	114,085,000	70,645,000	61.9
1968	120,285,000	73,212,000	60.9
1972	140,068,000	77,719,000	55.2
1976	150,127,000	81,556,000	53.5
1980	162,761,000	86,515,000	52.6
1984	173,936,000	92,032,260	52.9

*Restrictions based on sex, age, race, religion, and property ownership prevented a significant portion of the adult population from voting in the nineteenth and early twentieth centuries.

Source: Population figures for 1824 to 1920 are based on estimates and early census figures that appear in Neal R. Pierce, *The People's President* (New York: Simon and Schuster, 1968), 206. Copyright © 1968 by Neal R. Pierce. Reprinted by permission of Simon & Schuster, Inc. Population figures from 1932 to 1980 are from the U.S. Department of Commerce, Bureau of the Census, *Statistical Abstract of the United States* (Washington, D.C., 1984), 262. Figures for 1984 are from *World Almanac and Book of Facts 1986* (New York: Newspaper Enterprise Association, 1985), 229–230.

their heads on this question because some of the most serious restrictions— stringent registration and residence requirements—have been relaxed. A low education level has always been equated with low voter turnout, but the level of education of American citizens was considerably higher in 1980 than in 1960. Lack of political information is another factor that research has shown reduces turnout; yet the availability of political information, especially via television, which can be found in over 98 percent of America's 84.5 million households, has never been higher. The presidential debates in 1976, 1980, and 1984 attracted from 90 to 120 million viewers. Close political races are thought to generate higher voter turnout, but the turnout in the Johnson landslide of 1964 was 61.9 percent, while the tight Carter-Ford contest 12 years later was only 53.5 percent.

Extension of the right to vote to eighteen-year-olds by the Twenty-sixth Amendment in 1971 is another explanation given for the decline in voting, since young voter turnout has been found to be lower than for those over twenty-one. However, this factor does not explain the drop-off between 1964 and 1968 and again after 1972. Some experts attribute the lower turnout to the decline in party identification, which seems to suggest less psychological involvement in politics. Another explanation is a decline in the sense of political efficacy—that is, over recent decades fewer people have thought public officials care about their views, or that as citizens they have less and less voice in what the government does. Vietnam and the Watergate scandals are thought to have contributed heavily to this voter disaffection.

Both major parties mounted voter registration drives in 1984 to improve voter turnout, especially in the presidential election. But despite their heroic efforts, the rate of turnout remained essentially unchanged.

PREDICTING THE OUTCOME

As the clock ticks on to election day, public interest rises, much as it does before the World Series or the NFL Super Bowl. Who is going to win? How big will the margin be? Will the victor win or retain control of Congress? Since the 1930s, public opinion polls have attempted to predict the outcome before the voters march to the polls. The poor track record of the early opinion polls in predicting the winner, however, still haunts some pollsters. In 1936, the *Literary Digest,* the leading newsmagazine of this era, predicted that Kansas governor Alfred M. Landon would defeat President Franklin D. Roosevelt in his bid for a second term. The result: Roosevelt, 523 electoral votes; Landon, 8 electoral votes. Though its straw poll included a million respondents, the *Literary Digest* missed the mark because it failed to select its sample randomly. By confining itself to automobile owners and telephone subscribers—hardly a representative sample in the midst of the Great Depression—the newsmagazine obtained a defective sample. Its reputation badly tarnished by its 1936 poll, the magazine folded within two years.

In 1948, the Gallup poll received a political black eye for miscalling the famous Truman-Dewey race. Gallup's chief mistake, which needless to say he did not repeat, was to discontinue polling three weeks before the election because the race appeared to be a landslide for Dewey. To compound his problem, Gallup also divided the undecided vote sample equally, though on election day the "undecideds" went for Truman by a 2 to 1 margin.[64] Since then, the Gallup poll has kept its prediction well within the sample's margin of error. Between 1952 and 1980, it averaged close to 1.6 percent from the actual vote. Even so, it predicted President Ford the winner over Jimmy Carter in 1976, which of course was possible, since the closeness of the race kept the voting margin between winner and loser within the poll's margin of sampling error. But in the Reagan landslide of 1980 the Gallup organization missed by 3.8 percent. In 1984, it was right on the mark at 59 percent. While the Gallup poll dominated the field in 1948, it now shares the national stage with nearly a half dozen major polls—the Harris poll, the *New York Times/*CBS News poll, the *Washington Post/*ABC News poll, and so on.

Since 1976, election day excitement has become even more intense as the three television networks, using sophisticated exit polls, have raced to beat one another in making a "call" on the winner before the balloting closes in the Pacific Time zone. In 1980, by 8:15 P.M. (Eastern Standard Time), 15 minutes after the polls closed in many eastern states, NBC News projected Ronald Reagan to be the winner, even though less than 5 percent of the national vote had been counted.[65] The other two major networks—ABC and CBS—were more cautious. ABC News called Reagan the winner at 9:52 P.M. and CBS projected Reagan the victor at 10:32 P.M.—while the polls were still open in Alaska, California, Hawaii,

Idaho, Oregon, and the state of Washington. But even before the latter two networks had made their call, Carter appeared on all three networks to concede defeat.

The country was treated to the spectacle of President Carter conceding the election to challenger Ronald Reagan at 9:45 P.M., Eastern Standard Time, more than an hour before the polls closed on the West Coast. So incensed were many western politicians with the networks' early projections and Carter's actions that several states have passed laws banning network exit polling. In 1985, a federal district court in the state of Washington invalidated the state ban, but the final outcome may have to await a decision from the Supreme Court. Early in 1985, however, the three major networks informally agreed with members of a congressional subcommittee not to announce any national network projections in 1988 until the polls have closed in the Pacific Coast states. But the networks still reserve the right to project New York's winner as soon as polls close in New York.[66]

PRESIDENTIAL MANDATES

Despite the uncertainty about why the voters choose a particular presidential candidate, skilled presidents quickly construct their own mandates. The vague guidance elections provide reelected presidents or the nation's new leader offer broad latitude in initiating public policies. Consequently, the victors frequently interpret the electoral mandate as a broad grant from the people to pursue the policies they personally favor. George Reedy, President Johnson's former press secretary, put it this way: "President Johnson and most of his close advisors interpreted the election result [the 1964 landslide victory of Johnson over Goldwater] as a mandate from the people not only to carry out the policies of the Johnson administration but any other policies that might come to mind."[67]

Similarly, President-elect Ronald Reagan, after his resounding victory in 1980, promptly proclaimed that he was elected to implement his "supply side" economic program of tax cuts and a reduced federal budget, as well as his plan to rebuild national defense and to reverse nearly a half-century of governmental centralization. With this "mandate" in hand, he persuaded Congress to approve the major part of his program in record time, much to the surprise of veteran Washington observers, who watched in amazement. Few would have predicted on November 5, 1980, that Ronald Reagan's victory would have led in less than seven months after his inauguration to the greatest social policy changes since the New Deal reforms of the early 1930s.

Did Ronald Reagan's victory in 1980 constitute a conservative mandate from the voters? It is doubtful. In a nationwide poll conducted by the *New York Times*/CBS News after the 1980 election, respondents were asked whether Reagan's victory was a mandate for more conservative policies or a rejection of President Carter and his presidency. Approximately 63 percent of the respondents saw it as a rejection of Carter, and only 24 percent viewed the election as a conservative victory.[68] Similarly, the National Election Survey polls, conducted at the University of Michigan, revealed that the "key to Carter's defeat was widespread dissatisfaction with his performance in office coupled with doubts about his competence as a political leader."[69] Reagan won, then, not primarily because of his conservative ideology, his policy positions, or his personal appeal, but because he was an acceptable alternative to Jimmy Carter.

Reagan's 1984 reelection victory was described as a "lonely landslide" by some commentators because, though he won 49 out of 50 states, he carried only 14 GOP congressmen on his coattails and lost two U.S. Senate seats. Pollsters, however, have had a difficult time measuring the depth of Mr. Reagan's second-term mandate because his campaign managers chose to have him avoid specific campaign promises. Indeed, Reagan paid scant attention to future policy directions. Instead, he left the electorate to wonder what would follow, other than "four more years" in the same direction, and the vague assurance "You ain't seen nothing yet!"[70] It was impossible for the pollsters to ask the voters if they supported Mr. Reagan on specific issues. According to an election day exit poll questionnaire of 8,671 voters by the *New York Times*/CBS News, the five key factors that most influenced voters (who were asked to check two factors) were: strong leadership, 32 percent; vision of the future, 29 percent; experience, 27 percent; traditional values, 19 percent; and dislike of the other candidate, 17 percent.[71] Significantly, party affiliation was listed by only 9 percent of the respondents as the reason for selecting a candidate.

For a second-term chief executive, a presidential mandate means, it seems fair to say, what the president chooses to make of it. However, a first-term president will soon learn that his electoral mandate is not a blank check, cashable at any time in his term. Jimmy Carter discovered this. A president's mandate remains viable currency only so long as he can prevail upon a majority in both houses of Congress to support his programs and policies. Without strong legislative backing, a presidential mandate will suffer the same erosion of support that an elderly tribal leader who no longer possesses the power to carry out his edict experiences. First-term presidents who wish to retain their tenure for another four years would do well to adhere to the late V. O. Key's advice: "Governments must worry, not about the meaning of past elections, but about their fate at future elections."[72]

CONCLUSION

Presidential elections involve mainly choices in leadership, not profound discussions of the issues. Moreover, each presidential election consists, in reality, of 50 separate winner-take-all elections for the electoral votes in each of the 50 states. The prime goal is not to capture a majority of the popular vote, but to collect the 270 electoral votes needed to claim victory. Because electoral votes are allocated to each state chiefly on the basis of population, the most populous states —California, New York, Texas, Pennsylvania, Illinois, Ohio, Florida, and Michigan—continue to be the major battleground states in which the Republican and Democratic candidates spend most of their time and money, since victories in these states alone will yield 225 electoral votes.

With the advent of television, the electronic screen has largely displaced political parties as the communications link between candidate and voter. Indeed, the nearly universal television use—over 98 percent of all American households have at least one TV set—permits presidential candidates to communicate directly with almost all of the country's potential electorate of 173 million voters. Similarly, the experts in modern political technology—pollsters, media specialists, direct mail experts, and accountants—have replaced state, county, and precinct workers as the backbone of a presidential campaign team.

Television advertising now constitutes between one-half and two-thirds of the entire campaign budget of each major party candidate. Since passage of the 1974 Federal Election Campaign Act (FECA), the method of financing presidential campaigns has been drastically changed. Both major candidates now have their entire general election campaign bill picked up by the federal government —$40.4 million for each candidate in 1984—unless the candidate prefers to fund his own campaign and spend an unlimited amount. Since 1976, the televised presidential debates have become the highlight of the fall campaign. Most party experts believe that political challengers benefit more from the televised debates than incumbents. Television, with its emphasis on "image" and personality, encourages viewers to assess the personal qualities of the candidates—trustworthiness, sincerity, and leadership potential—at the expense of a discussion of the issues. Television coverage of the presidential campaigns has widened the gap between expectations and performance. As a result, the electorate's inflated expectations of what a president can achieve collides with the reality of our system of divided powers. Newly elected presidents proclaim broad mandates, but survey experts often experience great difficulty in discerning what a presidential mandate really means in terms of programs and policies, other than that the public expects a president to maintain a strong economy and to avoid war.

NOTES

1. Gerald Pomper, "The Presidential Election," in Gerald Pomper, ed., *The Election of 1984* (Chatham, NJ: Chatham House Publishers, 1985), 74.
2. Margaret Leech, *In the Days of McKinley* (New York: Harper & Brothers, 1959), 88.
3. William Jennings Bryan, *The First Battle* (Port Washington, NY: Kennikat Press, 1971), 168, as cited by Stephen J. Wayne, *The Road to the White House,* 168; see also Louis W. Koenig, *Bryan* (New York: G. P. Putnam's Sons, 1971), 247–250.
4. George E. Mowry, *Theodore Roosevelt and the Progressive Movement* (Madison: University of Wisconsin Press, 1947), 276.
5. Wayne, *The Road to the White House,* 2d ed. (New York: St. Martin's Press, 1984), 168.
6. For a discussion of the big-state effect of the Electoral College in recent presidential campaigns, see Herbert Asher, *Presidential Elections and American Politics,* 3rd ed. (Homewood, IL: Dorsey Press, 1984), 271–277.
7. The state of Maine is the sole exception. The electoral vote in this New England state is cast on the basis of the popular vote in each of its two congressional districts.
8. Asher, *Presidential Elections and American Politics,* 272.
9. Neal R. Peirce, *The People's President* (New York: Simon and Schuster, 1968), 86–92.
10. Asher, *Presidential Elections and American Politics,* 277.
11. Angus Campbell, Philip Converse, Warren Miller, and Donald Stokes, *The American Voter* (New York: Wiley, 1960).
12. Paul C. Light and Celinda Lake, "The Election: Candidates, Strategies, and Deci-

sions," in Michael Nelson, ed., *The Elections of 1984* (Washington, DC: Congressional Quarterly Press, 1985), 107.

13. Ibid., p. 91.
14. Ibid., pp. 98–99.
15. George C. Edwards III and Stephen J. Wayne, *Presidential Leadership* (New York: St. Martin's Press, 1985), 53.
16. In discussing the differences between nominating politics and a general election campaign, George McGovern's 1972 campaign director, Gary Hart (later a presidential aspirant himself in 1984), listed the abbreviated time frame of the fall campaign as the chief difference. Gary W. Hart, *Right From the Start* (New York: Quadrangle/*New York Times,* 1973), 249.
17. Theodore H. White, *The Making of the President, 1968* (New York: Atheneum, 1969), 334–342.
18. Wayne, *The Road to the White House,* 190.
19. Ibid., 228.
20. See Richard Wirthlin, Vincent Breglio, and Richard Beal, "Campaign Chronicle," *Public Opinion,* 4 (1981), 43–49. Another excellent analysis of the Reagan campaign will be found in John H. Kessel, *Presidential Campaign Politics* (Homewood, IL: Dorsey Press, 1984), 200–214.
21. Ibid.
22. Patrick H. Caddell, "Memorandum on General Election Strategy," in Elizabeth Drew, *Portrait of an Election* (New York: Simon and Schuster, 1981), 394–395.
23. Herbert E. Alexander, "Making Sense About Dollars in the 1980 Presidential Campaigns," in Michael J. Malbin, ed., *Money and Politics in the United States* (Chatham, NJ: Chatham House Publishers, 1984), 29.
24. Theodore J. Lowi, "An Aligning Election, A Presidential Plebiscite," in Michael Nelson, ed., *The Election of 1984* (Washington, DC: Congressional Quarterly Press, 1985), 291.
25. Jeff Fishel, *Presidents and Promises* (Washington, DC: CQ Press, 1985), 206.
26. Light and Lake, "The Election: Candidates, Strategies, and Decisions," 83.
27. As cited in Martha Joynt Kumar, "News Notes," *Presidential Studies Quarterly,* XV (Spring 1985), 454.
28. An early analysis by the Library of Congress of prospective reapportionment in Congress after the 1990 census estimated that 19 more congressional seats (translate as electoral votes) will probably be shifted from the northern industrial and farm states to the Sunbelt states. *The New York Times,* April 1, 1985.
29. Summary of *New York Times*/CBS News election day exit polls, Ibid.
30. See Lowi, "An Aligning Election, A Presidential Plebiscite," 290–296.
31. Elihu Katz and Jacob J. Feldman, "The Debates in the Light of Research: A Survey of Surveys," in Sidney Kraus, ed., *The Great Debate* (Bloomington: Indiana University Press, 1962), 195-200.
32. Another stumbling block to holding debates was the "equal time" rule of the Federal Communications Commission requiring the networks to provide equal time to all presidential candidates, including minor party candidates. Rather than grant equal time to all the candidates, the networks refused to sponsor any presidential debates. In 1960, Congress had temporarily suspended the equal time rule to allow the Nixon-Kennedy debates. To avoid the equal time barrier in 1976 and subsequent elections, the League of Women Voters agreed to "sponsor" the debates. Then the networks could cover them as "news events" without running afoul of the equal time rule.

33. *The New York Times,* October 30, 1980.
34. Paul R. Abrahamson, John H. Aldrich, and David W. Rhode, *Change and Continuity in the 1980 Elections* (Washington, DC: Congressional Quarterly Press, 1982), 46.
35. *The New York Times,* November 16, 1980.
36. Ibid., November 5, 1980.
37. Ibid., November 16, 1980.
38. Light and Lake, "The Election: Candidates, Strategies, and Decisions," 105.
39. Ibid., 105–106.
40. Herbert E. Alexander, *Financing the 1972 Election* (Lexington, MA: D. C. Heath, 1976), 279 and 362.
41. Herbert E. Alexander, *Financing the 1976 Election* (Washington, DC: Congressional Quarterly Press, 1979), 11–58.
42. Herbert E. Alexander, Director, Citizens' Research Foundation, personal communication with the author, October 22, 1985.
43. Alexander, "Making Sense About Dollars in the 1980 Presidential Campaigns," 26.
44. Ibid.
45. 424 U.S. 1.
46. *What Price PAC's?* Report of the Twentieth Century Fund Task Force on Political Action Committees (New York: Twentieth Century Fund, 1984), 53, Table 3-7.
47. Alexander, "Making Sense About Dollars in the 1980 Presidential Campaigns," 22.
48. *The New York Times,* March 19, 1985.
49. Alexander, "Making Sense About Dollars in the 1980 Presidential Campaigns," 29.
50. *The New York Times,* May 31, 1985.
51. Ibid. According to the U.S. Treasury, approximately a fourth of all taxpayers use the checkoff. In 1984, the checkoff system generated $35 million, but the money builds up over the four years preceding a presidential election. During 1984 the Treasury paid out $120 million to eligible presidential candidates and to the Republican and Democratic national committees, which received $8 million each for their nominating conventions.
52. Ibid.
53. Theodore H. White, *America in Search of Itself: The Making of the President, 1956–1980* (New York: Harper & Row, 1982), 166.
54. Ibid.
55. Robert MacNeil, *The People Machine: The Influence of Television on American Politics* (New York: Harper & Row, 1968), 126–127.
56. Thomas E. Patterson and Richard Davis, "The Media Campaign: Struggle for the Agenda," in Michael Nelson, ed., *The Election of 1984* (Washington, DC: Congressional Quarterly Press, 1985), 122.
57. Thomas E. Patterson, *The Mass Media Election* (New York: Praeger, 1980), 22–25.
58. Paul Lazersfeld, Bernard Berelson, and Hazel Gaudet, *The People's Choice,* 3rd ed. (New York: Columbia University Press, 1968), 115–119; Bernard Berelson, Paul Lazersfeld, and William McPhee, *Voting* (Chicago: University of Chicago Press, 1954), 248, as cited by Patterson and Davis in "The Media Campaign: Struggle for the Agenda," 122.
59. Patterson and Davis, "The Media Campaign: Struggle for the Agenda," 124.
60. Ibid.
61. As cited by Everett Carll Ladd, *The American Polity* (New York: Norton, 1985), 454, note 20.
62. The percentage were Johnson 61.1 percent and Goldwater 38.5 percent (1964); Nixon

60.6 percent and McGovern 37.5 percent (1972); Reagan 51 percent and Carter 42.3 percent, Anderson 6.6 percent (1980); Reagan 59 percent and Mondale 41 percent (1984).

63. Curtis Gans, Director, Committee for the Study of the American Electorate, as cited in *The New York Times,* November 8, 1984.

64. See Harold Mendelsohn and Irving Crespi, *Polls, Television, and the New Politics* (Scranton, PA: Chandler, 1970), chap. 2.

65. White, *America in Search of Itself,* 411.

66. *Seattle Post-Intelligencer,* May 2, 1985. In an additional move to thwart early projections of winners by the television networks, the U.S. House of Representatives passed a bill in late January 1986 to establish a simultaneous closing time for polls across the nation. Ibid., January 30, 1986. As of late June 1986, however, the Senate had taken no action on this bill.

67. George Reedy, *The Twilight of the Presidency* (New York: New American Library, 1970), 66.

68. Adam Clymer, *The New York Times,* November 9, 1980. The *New York Times/*CBS exit poll on election day covered 12,782 voters.

69. Gregory B. Markus, "Political Attitudes During an Election Year: A Report of the 1980 NES Study," *American Political Science Review,* 76 (September 1982), 538–560.

70. Pomper, "The Presidential Election," 81.

71. *The New York Times,* November 11, 1984.

72. V. O. Key, with the assistance of Milton Cummings, *The Responsible Electorate: Rationality in Presidential Voting* (Cambridge, MA: Belnap Press of Harvard University, 1966), 77.

chapter 5

The Presidency in the Age of Television

More than anything else, the ability to communicate instantly with millions of American constituents via television differentiates twentieth-century presidents from their nineteenth-century counterparts. Television magnifies the person and institution of the presidency. Indeed, no invention in the past 30 years has had a more profound effect on the American political environment than network television. Presidential chronicler Theodore H. White describes TV's influence in far stronger terms: "Television in modern politics has been as revolutionary as the development of printing in the time of Gutenberg."[1] The truly revolutionary importance of television for a president is that it enables him to communicate directly with the huge American public without any of his words and appeals being filtered through editing or an intermediary process.

TELEVISION'S PERVASIVE REACH

Census data show that television now reaches into almost every home in America—approximately 98 percent of all American households now have at least one television set, and nearly half have two or more sets. According to the 1982 edition of the *Television Factbook,* the United States had approximately 170.8 million TV sets in operation—far more than any other nation.[2] On a typical evening, the three television network news programs attract more than 43 million viewers.[3] Also, the Public Broadcasting Corporation's MacNeil-Lehrer Report, an hour-long news analysis program, now has an audience of more than 2 million viewers. Over and above this huge audience, the recently established

Cable News Network (CNN) offers 24-hour news service to more than 32 million cable television subscribers. Though there may be some question about the amount of overlap between viewers of the three major network news programs and CNN, there can be little doubt that television has become the foremost source of information and entertainment throughout the nation. Moreover, the launching of the first communication satellites in the early 1960s has made possible instantaneous television transmission across oceans and continents. Thus, presidents traveling in Europe or Asia can be covered just as easily as if they were in Philadelphia. The full impact of intercontinental television communication was probably not fully appreciated until an Ethiopian famine relief fundraising show —"Live Aid"—in July 1985 attracted an estimated 1.5 billion viewers and radio listeners around the world.[4]

Modern presidents command the attention of television networks. The network news executives seem to need the president as much as he needs them —a "reciprocal relationship of mutual exploitation"—for they often devote nearly a third of their half-hour evening news programs to presidential activity. In the words of one team of commentators: "The President represents the single most important story that the networks follow on a continuing basis."[5] Indeed, the White House has become a major studio for all three television networks. Each of the networks maintains virtual round-the-clock vigilance at the White House with a full staff of reporters and camera crews. The networks find it easy to focus on the president as domestic policy leader because his office is the only constituency that represents the entire country. As a result, the public expects far more from the president because he symbolizes national leadership and because they see him far more frequently on network television than individual lawmakers, who continue to remain strangers to most of the American electorate.

In this chapter the powerful impact of television on the American presidency will be the main focus of our discussion. The president's ability to exploit this new channel of communication, we will argue, has substantially enlarged his influence over Congress and the entire political system. Television has become the dominant factor in winning both the presidential nomination and the election. Successful nominees have all counted heavily on their performances in the televised debates. Recent presidents have made extensive use of television to carry their legislative messages to the American public. We discuss presidential foreign travel to generate heavy and favorable publicity, as well as White House efforts to utilize televised press conferences to tell the administration's story to the American public.

Another goal will be to show that while television appears to be the chief weapon of a president in winning public support and demonstrating his leadership qualities, the electronic medium also makes him more vulnerable than ever to scrutiny by millions of citizens. If his policies began to turn sour, or if he is unable to deliver on his promises and policies, whether they are to terminate American military involvement abroad, to obtain the release of American hostages from foreign terrorists, or to control inflation, he may discover that network television can become a two-edged weapon—a weapon that can destroy an incumbent as easily as it helped elect him.

PRESIDENTIAL TELEVISION

No political figure in America has benefitted more from television than the president of the United States. As media specialist Michael J. Robinson has noted: "The presidency has a unique mix of media attractiveness and clearly defined institutional authority that virtually insures an advantage for the office itself."[6]

Television brings the president in direct contact with millions of Americans. Their attachment to the president is not like their attachment to any other elected official or symbol of government. Some years ago, Fred I. Greenstein classified the "psychological functions" of the presidency. The president of the United States:

1. "Simplifies perception of government and politics" by serving as "the main cognitive 'handle' for providing busy citizens with some sense of what their government is doing"
2. Provides "an outlet for emotional expression" through public interest in his and his family's public and private life
3. Is a "symbol of unity" and of nationhood (as the national concern over a president's surgery or the death of a president clearly reveals)
4. Furnishes the public with a "vicarious means of taking political action" in that the chief executive can act decisively and effectively whereas they are unable to do so
5. Is a "symbol of social stability" in providing the American public with a feeling of security and direction[7]

Since one of the most important roles of the president is symbolic, television allows presidents to personalize government. Congress, with its 535 separate lawmakers, is hard to personalize; the Supreme Court is remote; and the federal bureaucracy is impersonal. Like a strong father figure, the president can provide reassurance to the American public in times of crisis.

The electronic means of reaching millions of citizens via television explains only half the story of the president's preeminent position in the American political spectrum: "Presidential monopolization of public space" has been equally important.[8] As explained by one team of scholars more than a decade ago, the president's ability to dominate the national media has been relatively easy: "By virtue of his office the president of the United States—its constitutional leader, supreme military commander, chief diplomat and administrator, and preeminent social host—obviously ranks higher in the scale of newsworthiness than anyone else. . . ."[9]

Unlike his nineteenth-century predecessors, the modern twentieth-century president generally receives far more coverage in the mass media than all other political competitors combined. Virtually no aspect of the president's daily life is omitted from television coverage: press conferences, special addresses to the nation and Congress, bill-signing ceremonies (even President Ford's signing of the pardon papers for former President Richard Nixon), welcoming ceremonies for foreign dignitaries in the Rose Garden, and foreign travels—all are carried "live" on the networks. Even when the president goes on vacation, whether it be at a California ranch; Plains, Georgia; or Hyannisport, Massachusetts, the television cameras and the pencil press are seldom far behind.

No president ever remains out of sight of the TV cameras for more than a few days, and even then his press secretary will be in daily contact with the national media at the temporary White House vacation headquarters. Nor have presidents and their closest advisers discouraged this near-saturation coverage. White House staffs now include a host of media specialists whose sole task is to promote as much favorable coverage of the president on television networks as the news executives and producers are willing to carry. As political scientist Bruce Miroff has commented: "Portrayal of national politics as a drama of presidential character has become such a commonplace that the media appear reluctant to depart from it."[10] Furthermore, Miroff continues, the president's "role in the public space is so prominent that it is sometimes hard for others simply to be seen on any large scale."[11]

Television is the chief link between the president and the American people. Unlike previous chief executives, the president can use network television as a powerful vehicle through which he can reach out to the electorate. Modern presidents set the agenda for public policy. Though this power existed before the age of television, TV has enabled modern presidents to frame the issues far more clearly and communicate them far more readily than any pretelevision era presidents could ever hope to do.

Though the Founding Fathers did not intend the president to become the personal symbol of national government, network television—more than any other factor—has expanded presidential influence far beyond anything the authors of the Constitution could have envisaged. Aided by the great reverence Americans have for the office of president, television furnishes the president with an unparalleled opportunity to lead a nation of more than 238 million people.

Television, by personalizing and dramatizing the presidency, has helped enlarge the formal powers of the president. As a matter of fact, the formal powers granted in the Constitution are, despite popular belief to the contrary, rather modest. Through the use of nationally televised messages, however, presidents have been able to expand their role as chief legislator and policymaker.

Presidential television really began with John F. Kennedy. Though Truman was the first president to address the nation on television, his stiff, unsmiling face and his flat Missouri accent left viewers unimpressed. President Eisenhower, one of the most popular presidents in the twentieth century, never pretended to have mastered the electronic medium. After all, he already had won a worldwide reputation as supreme commander of the Allied forces in Europe during World War II, so viewers did not expect him to be a star performer before the cameras.

But President John F. Kennedy's performance on TV, as described by Richard E. Neustadt, "had become by 1963 a masterful affair of 'star' quality, unfailingly of interest, hence always entertaining on an entertainment medium."[12] Moreover, it was during the Kennedy presidency that television news not only became a major influence in American politics, but also reached a new level of maturity. In the fall of 1963, two of the three networks decided, thanks partly to the arrival of intercontinental satellite communication, to extend their evening televised news shows from radio's traditional 15 minutes to the present half-hour.[13] Then, when tragedy struck the nation only weeks later, the television networks devoted almost constant coverage for four days to the Kennedy assassination story, his funeral, and the aftermath, including "live" coverage of the murder of his alleged assassin, as a stunned nation watched. Many thoughtful observers felt that the networks' solemn coverage of this tragic series of events conferred on TV unrivaled status as a news source and enhanced credibility in the public mind.

Each network is more than willing to focus its cameras on the nerve center of American government, since coverage of the president of the United States can help build the network's rating as a top news-gathering agency while enhancing its reputation for public service to the nation. Recent presidents, in turn, have been only too happy to avail themselves of the electronic medium as their primary means of influencing the American electorate—and Congress—to support their policies.

Television as a medium of communication is ideally suited for covering the president of the United States, who is not only the symbolic chief of state but also the personification of traditional American values: openness, fairmindedness, devotion to family, and consideration for the underprivileged. Television's visual orientation puts a premium on style and manner; as the transmitted picture appears in the viewer's living room, its instantaneousness, and its "personal" feeling creates a sense of intimacy with the viewer. Moreover, its feeling—sometimes misleading—of giving a true glimpse of "reality," and its vulnerability to "pseudo-events" and stage-managed activities explain why television's relation to the presidency has become such a dominant aspect of public life in America.

Presidents and their advisers now recognize that television has become a massive national forum, offering far more opportunities to dominate national politics and shape public policy than all other means of communication combined. Indeed, nothing in Western history, not even Gutenberg's invention of the printing press, matches television's capability of reaching and influencing millions of viewers at the same time, indeed, at the flick of a switch. Recently, for example, national observers concluded—and several national polls soon confirmed the judgment—that a single nationally televised speech by President Reagan after the Grenada invasion in late October 1983 halted a rising tide of public criticism against the invasion. Before President Reagan's October 27 TV address to the nation, the *Washington Post*/ABC News poll found a 52 to 37 percent majority in favor of the assault on Grenada. After the speech, that majority had increased to 65 percent in favor and 27 percent opposed.[14]

The impact of television on the presidency begins even before the president-elect reaches the White House. With the advent of presidential television, as Michael Robinson has noted, the electoral system shifted "toward a more plebiscitary process of electing leaders—in which television journalism provided a more direct link between the public and the candidates than had ever existed."[15] Beyond doubt, television has made the quadrennial presidential selection process, in all its various phases, one of the greatest continuing stories in the nation's political experience.

TELEVISION: SPRINGBOARD TO THE WHITE HOUSE

Candidate reliance on television begins early in the nominating race. Indeed, all post-Eisenhower presidents owe a heavy debt of gratitude to the electronic medium for winning the nomination.

John F. Kennedy's understanding of television as a pervasive force in American politics was clearly evident before he announced his candidacy for the 1960 Democratic nomination. Shortly before he threw his hat in the ring, he wrote an article in the November 14, 1959, issue of *TV Guide* the biggest circulation weekly magazine in the United States, entitled "A Force That Changed the Political Scene." The force was television.[16] Kennedy's central thesis was that TV would emphasize a presidential candidate's image above all else. Kennedy's drive for the presidency seldom deviated from this salient theme. After his victorious campaign in 1960, Kennedy commented: "We wouldn't have had a prayer without that gadget." In office, he observed: "We couldn't survive without television."[17]

President Reagan's effective use of television dates back many years before his successful 1980 campaign to his frequent appearances and commentary on the General Electric Hour and especially to his TV speeches on behalf of GOP nominee Barry Goldwater in 1964. Reagan's heavy use of television in the 1976 GOP nominating race helped him stay within hailing distance of the nomination and almost unseated incumbent Republican President Gerald Ford. Four years later, Reagan's remarkable performance in the famous Nashua, New Hampshire, locally televised debate against fellow Republican George Bush catapulted the Californian to victory in the 1980 primary and virtually demolished Bush as a serious rival for the GOP nomination.

Heavy dependence on television not only characterized these contenders' successful drives for the nomination, but also became the dominant factor in their general election campaigns. None of the recent presidents has failed to devote at least half of his funds to television and other mass media advertising. In 1980, more than half of the $29.4 million that the Carter and Reagan campaigns each received from the Federal Election Commission was spent on mass media advertising. Of the $20.5 million the Carter campaign spent on mass media advertising, $15.8 was earmarked for television, and $2.6 million for radio. The remainder was spent on print media and production costs (see Table. 5.1). The 1980 Reagan campaign, according to Herbert E. Alexander, spent $16.8 million on mass media advertising, including about $10.8 million on television, $1.5 million for radio, $2.2 million for newspapers, and $2.3 million on production (see Table 5.2).

**Table 5.1   CARTER-MONDALE MEDIA
           EXPENDITURES IN 1980
           PRESIDENTIAL ELECTION RACE
           ($ MILLIONS)**

TV	$15.8
Radio	2.6
Print media and production costs	2.1

Source: Herbert E. Alexander, "Making Sense About Dollars in the 1980 Presidential Campaigns," in Michael J. Malbin, ed., *Money and Politics in the United States* (Chatham, NJ: Chatham House Publishers, 1984), 24.

During the final ten days of the campaign, Reagan's managers poured some $6 million into media advertising in targeted states and communities.[18] Independent candidate John Anderson spent approximately $2.3 million on media advertising.[19]

Of the $40.4 million in federal funds that the Reagan-Bush and Mondale-Ferraro organizations received to conduct their 1984 general election campaigns, the Reagan-Bush team spent $21,336,000 on TV advertising—93.2 percent of all media expenditures.[20] The Mondale-Ferraro organization spent slightly less on TV advertising—$17.1 million (see Table 5.3).

It is also noteworthy that three of the victorious nominees—Kennedy, Carter, and Reagan—all counted heavily on their performances in the televised debates to win the presidency.

TELEVISED PRESIDENTIAL DEBATES

Presidential campaign debates, most party professionals agree, are more likely to be measured in terms of their effectiveness, not their substance. Success or failure will be measured by the impression a candidate has left with the electorate. As put by two veteran newsmen: "The central question is whether a candidate comes away from a debate having, in the politician's phrase, 'helped himself' or 'hurt himself' with the voters."[21]

Despite all these barriers to measuring the impact of televised debates on voter attitudes in 1960, 1976, 1980, and 1984, polls show the following results. In a poll for CBS in 1960, Elmo Roper estimated that 57 percent of those who voted believed that the debates influenced their decision. Another 6 percent (equivalent to 4 million voters) ascribed their final decision to the debates alone. Of these respondents, 72 percent voted for Kennedy, and 26 percent voted for Nixon.[22]

Another study, conducted by R. H. Bruskin, revealed that 39 percent of the respondents indicated that the debates were the most important thing that led to the Kennedy victory.[23] Data from the Opinion Research Center, Cambridge, Massachusetts, indicated that individual commitment was strengthened for the person who "won" and weakened for the "loser." By and large, it seems fair to say that the 1960 debates—again, particularly the first—were instrumental in increasing Democratic support for Kennedy.

Table 5.2 REAGAN-BUSH COMMITTEE MEDIA EXPENDITURES, 1980 ($ THOUSANDS)

	Total expenditures*			Creative tactics	Target universe
	Gross	Net	Percent		
Television					
Network	$ 7,581	$ 6,444	44.3	70%—30's/25% "Fives"/5%—30 Min	National†
Spot	5,158	4,384	30.2	90%—30's/ 5% "Fives"/5%—30 Min	Twenty-five key states‡
Subtotal	12,739	10,828	74.5		
Radio					
Network	344	292	2.0	98%—60's/ 2% "Fives"	National
Spot	1,417	1,204	8.3	100%—60's	Twenty-five key states‡
Subtotal	1,761	1,496	10.3		
Subtotal broadcast	14,500	12,324	84.8		
Print					
National magazines	265	225	1.5	Spread, black and white (fast-close newsweeklies)	National
Local newspapers	2,345	1,992	13.7	Full-page black and white	Fifteen key states‡
Subtotal print	2,610	2,217	15.2		
Grand total	$17,110	$14,541	100.0		

Note: Does not include $2.25 million in production costs.
*Net figures, which represent those actually paid by the committee, exclude the customary 15 percent advertising agency fee.
†Includes national cable systems and superstations.
‡Includes special-interest and ethnic activity (Black, Spanish, major European voter blocs, as well as campaigns targeted at senior citizens, farmers, and various professional and trade groups).

Source: Information provided by Campaign '80. Reprinted by permission of the publisher from Herbert E. Alexander, *Financing the 1980 Election* (Lexington, Mass., Lexington Books, D.C. Heath and Company, Copyright 1983 D.C. Heath and Company).

**Table 5.3   TV ADVERTISING COSTS
             IN 1984 PRESIDENTIAL
             ELECTION**

	Net cost
Reagan-Bush	$21,336,000
Mondale-Ferraro	$17,100,000
Total	$38,436,000

Source: Herbert E. Alexander, Citizens Research Foundation. For more details, see Herbert E. Alexander, *Financing the 1984 Election* (forthcoming).

Sixteen years later, the two party nominees—President Ford and Democratic challenger Jimmy Carter—squared off for a series of three debates. Unlike the 1960 debates, the vice-presidential nominees—Republican Senator Robert Dole and Democratic Senator Walter F. Mondale—also held a single debate. More than 100 million watched the first debate. According to A. C. Nielsen surveys, approximately 90 percent of the nation's households viewed the debates in 1960 and 1976. In 1960, 90 percent represented 40.6 million households; in 1976, that percentage represented 64.1 million households.[24]

Although most viewers described the 1976 debates as dull and uninformative, viewing rates remained high during the four debates. President Ford may have lost the election to Carter during the second debate when he claimed that Eastern Europe was free of Soviet domination. Voters interviewed less than 12 hours after the debate felt that President Ford had won (53 percent to 35 percent), but once Ford's gaffe had been publicized by the networks and press, those interviewed felt Carter had won (58 percent to 35 percent).[25]

In 1980, only one presidential debate between President Carter and challenger Ronald Reagan was held, just a week before the general election. According to a nationwide *New York Times*/CBS News poll released one day before the general election, Reagan scored a more favorable general impression and gained a larger share of the vote among respondents who watched the debate and said it was important in deciding how to vote than he did among those who either had not watched the debate, or had but said it was not important. The overall Reagan edge in the debate was 38 to 25 percent.[26] Among the 15 percent of the 2,264 registered voters in the sample who contended that they had decided whom to support after the debate in Cleveland, Reagan had the support of 49 percent, to 38 percent for Carter, and 13 percent for Anderson, the independent candidate.[27] In a separate survey, Gallup pollsters reported that 18 percent of their 3,500 sample made up their minds on presidential choice after the Reagan-Carter debate on October 28, 1980.[28] Four years earlier, Gallup polls revealed that approximately 8 percent of the voters in their sample made up their minds during the course of the three presidential debates or just after the last debate.[29]

In 1984, the two presidential debates between President Reagan and former Vice-President Mondale had less impact on the electoral outcome than any of the presidential debates held over the past quarter-century. Although Mondale

Table 5.4   RATINGS AFTER
THE FIRST DEBATE

Q: Which candidate do you think did the best job—or won—Sunday night's debate, Ronald Reagan or Walter Mondale?

Reagan	17%
Mondale	68
A tie/both/neither	10
Don't know/no answer	7

Source: The New York Times/CBS News Post Debate Poll, October 9, 1984 (N = 515). Responses from registered voters. Copyright © 1984 by The New York Times Company. Reprinted by permission.

clearly outpointed Reagan in the first debate, Reagan bounced back strongly to gain the edge in the second debate, held two weeks later. The *New York Times*/CBS News polls in Tables 5.4 and 5.5 showed the results of the two debates.

Some surveys, however, rated the second confrontation more as a draw. But since the networks and the national press reporters agreed beforehand that Mondale had to win a decisive victory in the second debate to stay in serious contention, his failure to score a knockout effectively ended his hopes of winning the election. Most national polls revealed after the second debate that Reagan's big lead ranging between 16 and 23 percentage points was virtually unaffected by the debates.[30] President Reagan's winning margin over Mondale on election night was 59 to 41 percent.

What lies ahead for presidential debates? In November 1983, the Federal Communications Commission (FCC) ruled that television and radio stations may stage political debates between Republican and Democratic nominees without giving equal time to all minor party candidates. By characterizing political debates as "on-the-spot coverage of bona fide news events" and thus exempt from the equal-time provision of the law, the FCC has opened the door to network sponsorship of the political debates.[31] Will this mean more presidential debates in 1988 and beyond? It's too early to say. But it is noteworthy that in late

Table 5.5   RATINGS AFTER
THE SECOND DEBATE

Q: Which candidate do you think did the best job—or won—Sunday night's debate, Ronald Reagan or Walter Mondale?

Reagan	39%
Mondale	26
A tie/both/neither	21
Don't know/no answer	13

Source: The New York Times/CBS News Post Debate Poll, October 24–25, 1984 (N = 546). Responses from registered voters. Copyright © 1984 by the New York Times Company. Reprinted by permission.

November 1985 both the Republican and the Democratic national chairmen signed an agreement to make the two political parties the principal sponsors of presidential debates in general election campaigns in the future. Both chairmen, however, acknowledged that the two candidates would ultimately decide whether or not to participate in debates.[32]

Incumbent presidents would be well advised to review the recent history of the debates. In each of the three sets of debates (1960, 1976, and 1980), the challenger was generally thought to have won the televised confrontations. In each of the three cases, the incumbent or incumbent's party lost the election. And in each election the challenger's perceived victory in the debates was viewed as a major factor, sometimes the most important factor, in winning the election. Robert Strauss, the former Democratic national chairman and a high-level Carter adviser, once observed: "When you're an 'inner,' don't debate an 'outer'." In light of the recent history of presidential debates, incumbents may well consider taking this advice.

Finally, it should be noted that television's impact on presidential primary and general election campaigns has made it increasingly difficult for a presidential contender who does not have a favorable TV "image" to be nominated and elected. Regretfully, there is no direct correlation between the qualities that make people effective on television and the qualities needed to be an outstanding president. The case of Jimmy Carter immediately comes to mind. Carter used network television with consummate skill in 1976 to win the Democratic nomination and the presidency. But the telegenic qualities that enabled him to rise from the position of an ex-governor of Georgia to president of the United States in less than two years were found wanting once he reached the White House. Clearly, the art of governing required quite different skills than the talent needed for winning a presidential election. Carter's inability during his four years in the White House to work effectively with party leaders in Congress, even though his party held sizable majorities in both houses, his refusal to bargain and compromise on pork barrel legislation dear to the hearts of lawmakers, and his general lack of experience in foreign affairs all contributed to limiting his presidential tenure to one term.

Former vice-president Walter F. Mondale, in his 1984 postelection press conference announcing his retirement from politics, noted mournfully that his most serious failure as a campaigner was his inability to master television: "Modern politics requires television. I've never really warmed up to television. And, in fairness to television, it never warmed up to me." Mondale added: "I don't believe it's possible any more to run for president without the capacity to build confidence and communications every night. It's got to be done that way."[33] Most experts agreed.

The mass media must shoulder more than their fair share of the blame for saddling the country in the past decade with television presidents. Throughout the primary and general election campaign, the media—especially television—are so busy with the horserace aspects of the campaign that they ignore, for the most part, comparative evaluations of the candidates on their merits.[34] Indeed, the media are so preoccupied with stories about who is winning and who is losing that they report comparatively little about the qualifications of the various contenders or their positions on the major issues. In 1976, for example, one team of scholars reported that 65 percent of all issues mentioned in election-relevant stories during the presidential primaries focused on campaign events rather than policy issues facing the nation. Approximately 70 percent of the information about candidates during the primary campaign concerned Ford, Reagan, and Carter; seven other Democratic aspirants had to share the remainder of the coverage, which rarely produced headline attention on the networks.[35] Even during the final month of the general election campaign, events constituted 63 percent of the themes in television news.[36]

Once the popular verdict is in, the president-elect does not have to wait until he takes the oath of office before capitalizing on television to win symbolic allegiance as the next chief of state. Throughout the transition period between presidencies, the networks outdo themselves covering the president-elect, his wife and family, and his prospective cabinet officers. Every aspect of the new president's background and career is treated as prime-time news. Inauguration Day ceremonies rate coverage equal to the coronation of royalty. Millions of Americans who do not follow politics closely suddenly feel that television enables them to become, in a sense, "personally" acquainted with the new man in the White House.

Inauguration Day also sets the tone for the new administration. Probably no recent president, except John F. Kennedy, more effectively used the network cameras than did President Jimmy Carter when he and his wife Rosalyn strolled hand-in-hand from the inauguration ceremony at the Capitol down Pennsylvania Avenue to the White House as millions watched on television. Carter, however, was unable to maintain the initial momentum that this egalitarian theme gave to his administration.

PRESIDENTIAL USE OF NETWORK TELEVISION

Thanks to the electronic media, the eyes of the nation are always on the president of the United States. He is front-page news every day of the year. Even a stroll in the Rose Garden makes news. More than 1,700 accredited White House correspondents and corps of newsmen from the three major television networks and the new Cable News Network see to it that a huge daily quota of stories emanate from the White House. Clearly, the television networks devote far more coverage to the president than to all 535 members of Congress. To illustrate how extensively the television networks cover presidential activities, one research team made a content analysis of CBS Evening News for the period 1968–1978 and found that the network devoted on the average 8.5 out of 23 minutes of news time to the presidency—almost 37 percent of each broadcast. On the average, four stories an evening were devoted to the White House, of which approximately 23 percent appeared before the first commercial break—television's equivalent to the front page.[37]

With the arrival of jet travel, presidents have been able to appear virtually anywhere in the country while also maintaining the appearance, if not always the reality, of continuous operations in the nation's capital. Network television coverage of all these trips also fosters the perception that the president is "on top of the job," as he visits various sections of the country while simultaneously conducting the business of government as he moves from one city to the next. Swift air travel also enables a president to visit major countries in Europe and Asia and enlarge his range of options in far less time than nationwide presidential rail trips formerly consumed. Similarly, the jet age has made it possible in recent years to provide a seemingly never-ending flow of visits from foreign heads of state to the White House. In addition to the foreign policy dialogue, their visits generate numerous televised "photo opportunities" showing the president discussing important foreign policy questions with his guests or entertaining them at the White House. Much of this coverage, of course, will appear on the evening network news shows, reinforcing the president's reputation as a world statesman.

No political competitors can rival his power to dominate television and the other media. So important did the television networks view the coverage of the president in the 1960s that they arranged to convert a small theater in the White House into a presidential television studio. They even arranged to have "hot" cameras manned daily so that a president could go on national television on a moment's notice.

Presidents turn to television to speak to the American people whenever they face a crisis or feel they need to defend their policies. As one British commentator has observed: "Television has become more than one of the techniques of American politics; it has become the main forum in which American politics (and also, increasingly, the politics of other democracies) are conducted."[38] No president, it seems, can survive without television.

Each televised presidential address has, of course, the goal of convincing the public that the president's policies are superior to those of the opposition party. With full control over the format and unimpeded by questions from the press, the president can carefully develop and argue policy decisions already undertaken or planned in the future. In the words of one team of writers: "The televised address determines which issues will appear on the national agenda—issues chosen by the president, not the opposition." Television, the opposition party once charged, "is at the call of the President . . . to lay the groundwork for his reelection in hour after hour of prime time."[39] With the Oval Office as his podium, the president can initiate popular legislation. If the proposed legislation fails to pass, the public—generally unaware of the complexities involved in its passage —usually blames Congress. If the president finds the legislation passed to be objectionable, he may go on television to veto a bill and often win public support to sustain his veto. (Only slightly over 3 percent of presidential vetoes during the past 150 years have been overriden.)

Presidential addresses often elicit an avalanche of mail or thousands of phone calls to the nation's capital supporting his position and even quoting his words. No wonder congressmen complain that "network television has become a prime instrument of presidential power."[40] Pollster Louis Harris, having examined the data from surveys taken both before and after presidential speeches, has concluded: "The pattern is so consistent, with few exceptions, that it is probably fair to conclude that Presidential use of television almost automatically gives . . . an important advantage."[41]

White House staff officials of recent presidents, according to Tom Brokaw of NBC, have generally shared "an inclination to think of television as an extension of the President."[42] The president does not have to compete on even terms with such popular programs as "60 Minutes" or "Dallas" because his "reports to the nation" preempt network programming. While the networks are not required to carry these speeches, they invariably do because a network does not want to risk the possibility of missing a headline-producing story. In 1965, for example, two of the networks chose not to carry one of President Johnson's numerous speeches. On that telecast he announced a major decision on the temporary U.S. occupation of the Dominican Republic.

Plainly, the presidency occupies the commanding heights on viewership ratings. When President Nixon, for example, shared the audience for man's first step on the moon by placing a televised "phone call" to the astronauts on the moon, approximately 125 million viewers were watching—the most people ever to see and hear a political leader at one time.[43] Later, when President Nixon made his historic trip to Communist China to reopen the door and pave the way for the resumption of diplomatic relations between the two countries, an estimated 100 million television viewers watched some portion of his seven-day trip. Further, it seems doubtful if any president in the immediate years ahead will exceed the 41 hours of coverage the three TV networks devoted to Mr. Nixon's China visit. During one phase of the trip to the mainland, one major network devoted sixteen straight hours (6 P.M. to 10 A.M.) of coverage with only minor interruptions.[44] Nixon's precedent-breaking China trip, it might be noted, was deliberately scheduled well in advance to coincide with the 1972 New Hampshire presidential primary, where Democratic contenders were battling to gain an early lead in the nominating race. What better way for a president to manage the news?

MANAGING THE NEWS VIA TELEVISION

Recent presidents have never been modest about their intentions to generate greater public acceptance of their policies through the use of network television to address the American people. Presidents Johnson, Nixon, and Ford, for example, sought to obtain television network time on 45 identifiable occasions during the course of their administrations and received it cost-free 44 of those times from all three networks. Most of these "addresses to the nation" were held during prime time, reaching audiences ranging between 40 and 80 million viewers. Not only did these presidents obtain this broad access to the American public, but the opposition party rarely enjoyed an equal opportunity to respond. More often than not, the opposition party was denied cost-free time. Contrasted to easy presidential access to television, Democratic congressional leadership requested access to the air 11 times in seven years (1968–1975) during a Republican administration, but received it only 3 times.[45] If the networks agreed to offer equal time, it was usually at a less desirable hour, particularly on weekends.[46] Generally, the opposition party speaker also lacked the status, prestige, and name recognition of the president. Sometimes the opposition party received free time from only one network, in contrast to the president's monopoly of all three.

While almost all modern presidents early in their administrations have proclaimed their allegiance to an open presidency and to the free flow of information emanating from the White House, the honeymoon between president and national media is usually short-lived. News management follows on the heels of the so-called open presidency as the fall follows summer. Management of the news involves manipulation by the president and the White House press staff of the kinds of information that will be made available to correspondents. One standard technique for managing news and molding public opinion is the manipulation of access. This can be done by arranging special contacts with reporters adjudged friendly to the administration. The president and his top aides can feed policy information privately to selected reporters as part of a coordinated effort to build support. Virtually all this leaked information eventually shows up on network news programs.

During the Nixon years, White House officials, including Vice-President Spiro Agnew, who served as a "pointman" in these attacks, frequently and publicly castigated the television networks for allegedly distorting the news. Nor did this type of manipulation of the media disappear with the Watergate hearings. Recently, Dan Rather, anchorman of the "CBS Evening News," reported that his network news division has been subject to "unrelenting" criticism from the Reagan administration.[47] Responding to Mr. Rather's statement, David R. Gergen, White House communications director, denied that pressure had been exerted but confirmed that more conversations on network fairness have taken place with CBS than with other networks: "This Administration has felt that of the networks, CBS has more frequently than the others written stories that were thought to be slanted and unfair."[48]

Since the president is the chief newsmaking source in the nation's capital, he is most in demand. Consequently, his press secretary will ration his media contacts in ways that maximize favorable news coverage. Managing the news can also involve attempts to manipulate the settings in which information is disseminated—press conferences, briefings, backgrounders, and exclusive interviews. Manipulation can also involve less frequent opportunities, changing the ground rules, or providing less information. President Johnson, for example, avoided a press conference for more than three months as he escalated the United States commitment in Vietnam in 1965. By contrast, President Franklin D. Roosevelt continued with regularly scheduled press conferences even in wake of such disastrous events as Pearl Harbor and heavy American setbacks in the Western Pacific, including the loss of the Philippines.[49]

Midway in Reagan's first term, one top aide candidly described the White House television news management issue this way: "There is a certain sense in which the White House is theater and we put on our show. Particularly with the advent of TV, the White House has become more and more theater, and it is not unnatural that White House staffs over the years have become more and more the station managers. They want to run the show."[50]

Michael K. Deaver, President Reagan's first-term deputy chief of staff, proudly defended the administration's efforts to manage the news "because you know the press is constantly looking for the negative. This is a professional relationship that I understand and the media understand. So we spend a great deal of time trying to show the positive aspects of this administration. You have to, otherwise you would end up like all the rest of the presidents have ended up."[51] He meant, of course, that no American president had finished a second term since President Eisenhower.

So sensitive were President Reagan's staff aides to the importance of obtaining favorable stories on television and in the newspapers that, according to one source, they met almost daily during his first term to draft a master media strategy. Throughout the week the White House senior staff went over the day's forthcoming news events and the president's schedule and discussed opportunities for television evening news and still cameras to photograph the president for next day's newspapers. Every Wednesday a media relations session was held, chaired by the White House deputy chief of staff. Participants included an ad hoc media team, the president's schedulers, and the chief of the White House political office. Each Thursday a public relations group met to review the foreign coverage the president was getting and to plan stories that were to appear not only in the United States, but also abroad. On Friday, Reagan's public relations advisers met again for lunch at Blair House to "brainstorm" future strategy.[52] Commenting on Reagan's White House advisers, journalist Sidney Blumenthal has written: "At the end of the day, they become spectators seeing their performance tested by the contents of the television news programs. For the Reagan White House every night is election night on television."[53]

Another way presidents have sought to manage the news is through nationally televised news conferences.

PRESIDENTIAL PRESS CONFERENCES

Admirers of the presidential press conferences view these periodic sessions between the chief executive and the media as a valuable democratic institution, "The American equivalent of the question period in the English Parliament."[54] Outwardly, the press conference appears to allow representatives of the media to obtain unrehearsed responses to their questions, probe the justifications a president offers for his policies, and inquire about his future plans.

Most features of the televised presidential press conferences were formed during the Eisenhower years (1953–1961).[55] President Truman did not perform well before the cameras; he much preferred informal chats with the press while on his traditional early morning walk around the streets of the nation's capital. Furthermore, the plain-spoken man from Independence complained: "The television producers always put make-up powder all over your face, and they don't even let you comb your own hair."[56]

While presidential press conferences have been held in a number of settings and operated under a variety of ground rules, control of the agenda has seldom slipped from the hands of the White House. Generally, the correspondents receive only the information the White House wants to give them. Furthermore, correspondents frequently lack the opportunity to ask follow-up questions to obtain a better explanation, since at least a dozen other impatient correspondents are always popping up from their seats trying to gain the president's attention and an opportunity to ask their own carefully honed questions.

Presidents have used a variety of approaches (or tactics) to orchestrate their press conferences. They can open the conference with a prepared statement. In the words of one observer: "This mini-speech formally and uninterruptedly presents a presidential initiative, accomplishment, or concern; transforms a partially mediated into an unmediated forum; restructures the reporters' agenda; and reduces the time available for questions."[57] President Kennedy frequently used these statements to get across his foreign policy goals, according to one White House insider.[58] When the president opens the question period, he can answer with some well-rehearsed statistics, giving the illusion of mastery of detail; or he can restate a standard answer in different words, respond to a planted question, decline to answer sensitive questions for reasons of state or national security, ignore hostile reporters, and dismiss tricky questions with a quip or "non answer."

Historically, the roots of the modern press conference date back to the pre-TV decades of the twentieth century. Franklin Roosevelt's crowded press conferences, often held twice weekly, were always lively and full of news and Washington gossip. Since the end of World War II, heavy American involvement in international affairs, repeated foreign policy crises, and the televised press conference have all influenced the shift toward less frequent and less regular meetings with the media (see Table 5.6). Although presidents in the age of television seem more visible, the record shows that they are less accessible. Franklin D. Roosevelt averaged 6.9 press conferences a month, Truman 3.4, Eisenhower 2, Kennedy 1.9, Johnson 2.2, Nixon 0.5, Ford 1.3, Carter 1.2, and Reagan 0.5.[59]

The advent of televised press conferences in 1955 during the first Eisenhower administration marked the end of the traditional and less formal news conference. Eisenhower's televised sessions, crowded with cameras, radio micro-

Table 5.6 **PRESIDENTIAL PRESS CONFERENCES**
(1933–1984)

President	Number	Years in office	Average per year
Roosevelt	998	12	83
Truman	322	8	40
Eisenhower	193	8	24
Kennedy	64	3	21
Johnson	126	5	25
Nixon	37	5½	7
Ford	39	2½	16
Carter	59	4	15
Reagan	26	4	7

Source: From *American Government: Institutions and Policies,* 3rd edition by James Q. Wilson. Copyright © 1986 by D. C. Heath and Company. Reprinted by permission of the publisher.

phones, and several hundred correspondents, no longer lent themselves to the easy give-and-take of the earlier years. Further, as one authority has noted: "The change in the nature of the presidential press conferences from semi-private to public events has diminished their utility in transmitting information from the president to the press."[60] Eisenhower, more familiar with the formal military briefings from his days as the commander of the Allied forces in Europe, treated the press in a far more official manner. While the exchanges were pleasant, the president often rambled on in his ambiguous fashion, frequently fracturing his syntax. Eisenhower held press conferences fairly frequently, but they were not as informative as those of his predecessors. Furthermore, Eisenhower's press conferences were not live telecasts. Eisenhower's astute press secretary James Hagerty, a former newsman, insisted that all press conference transcripts be carefully edited before release to the networks.

The televised presidential press conference reached new heights during John F. Kennedy's administration—in 34 months in the White House, he held 64 formal televised news conferences. The youthful, articulate president was clearly the star of every show. With a ready wit and a remarkable memory for details on almost every question asked, Kennedy invariably held the correspondents in the palm of his hand. For the first time, presidential press conferences were telecast live by the networks. Kennedy was especially adept at his press conferences because he prepared so well. Two or three days before a scheduled press conference, he would have his top aides draft over a hundred questions he was likely to be asked, rehearse them at breakfast meetings with his staff, and order them to get more information if he didn't know an answer well.[61]

Kennedy has been accurately described as the first television president. As one veteran British commentator, long stationed in Washington, put it: Kennedy "knew exactly what television could do for him and why it was so valuable."[62] The young president was also aware of what it could do *to* him. Kennedy, for example, understood the danger of overexposure. Consequently, he did not call a presidential conference at the sight of a television camera, as his successors Johnson and Nixon were prone to do. Kennedy asked his media-wise secretary, Pierre Salinger, to look up how many radio "fireside chats" President Roosevelt had made every year and then indicated that FDR's practice would be a guide to the right number of his own appearances.[63] (Actually, Kennedy appeared on TV far more than FDR had spoken over the radio.)

Sixteen years before Richard Nixon reached the White House, he was quoted as saying that there was "a very early point of diminishing returns in using television" and that people "probably got tired of seeing their favorite programs thrown off" in favor of presidential or political speeches.[64] Nevertheless, Nixon became the most televised president in history. During his first three years and three months in office, one network computed that he made 31 special appearances in prime time, compared with 24 appearances by President Johnson in five years and 10 by President Kennedy.[65] Though Nixon recognized the almost unlimited potential of television, he preferred controlled scenarios rather than televised press conferences (in his first four years in office, Nixon held only 30 press conferences). After his reelection in 1972, he held even fewer sessions with the press corps. To double the size of his national audience (to 50 million and up), however, President Nixon shifted his press conferences to the prime-time evening hours (7 P.M. to 11 P.M.), winning far greater exposure than Kennedy's intrinsically more exciting early afternoon meetings with the press.

Both Presidents Ford and Carter relied heavily on press conferences to publicize their policies and defend them against hostile comment. But neither of them were masters of the media. Nor, despite their frequent appearances on television, were they successful in using this priceless resource to win another term in the White House.

President Ronald Reagan, labeled the Great Communicator by many political professionals, is the most telegenic president since Kennedy. Reagan's press conference performances have not matched Kennedy's, but his skilled use of the formal presidential speech compares favorably with Kennedy's flawless style. Though Reagan sometimes has given evidence that he had not done his homework for his press conferences, he nevertheless exudes confidence in his policies, and this impression seems to carry to the viewing public. Reagan and his staff, it seems fair to say, have scheduled just enough press conferences to be able to assert that they have maintained an open avenue to the White House press corps. In his first two and a half years, he held 19 press conferences.[66] But during the late summer months of 1983, he went over twelve weeks without meeting formally with the White House correspondents. Instead, Reagan preferred to drop by the White House pressroom for an impromptu 10- to 15-minute question-and-answer period with the network correspondents. These "mini" press conferences, the Washington press corps felt, enabled Reagan to get his story across to the public without running the risk of facing thorny or hostile questions at the regular televised conferences.

When the senior White House correspondent from the wire services says "Thank you, Mr. President," the conference abruptly ends. However, as the president steps down from the podium, the television cameras follow him as he moves slowly toward the door, pausing to chat with a reporter, "a part of yet apart from the crowd."[67] What scene could better symbolize the majesty and common touch of the American chief executive? Some eager reporters try to slip in a new question over the din of the crowd, but the president usually brushes them aside with a smile or offhand remark. Recently, however, Reagan and his advisers have eliminated these informal exchanges by having him enter and leave the auditorium via a long hallway in back of the podium, thereby denying the reporters any further access to the president.

It would appear that presidents who feel lukewarm toward press conferences in this age of television should reassess their views. Indeed, when twenty leading Washington correspondents and columnists were asked a few years ago whether the conference benefits the president or the press, they "overwhelmingly felt that it is the president's show."[68] Furthermore, the president who dominates the press conference creates the impression of similar mastery of his office and the country's problems. But the president's unlimited access to television is not always an unmixed blessing.

TELEVISION: A TWO-EDGED WEAPON FOR PRESIDENTS?

Television can be both a blessing and a curse to presidents.[69] Television coverage of the president-elect and the first few months of an administration—the so-called honeymoon period—tends to be exceedingly favorable. The networks emphasize the unique personal qualities of the new chief executive; they provide closeups of the president's family and friends. In short, they lean over backward to give the president every benefit of the doubt. But then, as in real life, the honeymoon ends. Network news stories become more critical.

Before the arrival of satellite transmission, the public was largely insulated from global news and disinterested in foreign affairs. But in this age of television major events such as the Vietnam war, the 1973 Middle Eastern war, the Iranian seizure of the U.S. embassy in Teheran, and the more recent TWA airplane hijacking and the hostage crisis in Beirut have become instant news. As a result, the president of the United States is often expected to find quick solutions to extremely complicated or nearly intractable problems. In this sense, the mass media undermine the president's ability to pursue quiet diplomacy to work out a compromise or solution to recurring crises.

On the domestic front, network television indirectly undermines the president's authority by exaggerating his power and influence. As one presidential scholar has put it: "Paradoxically, the media magnify the president's domestic role at the same time they undermine him with constant revelations of his inadequacy and failures while minimizing the part that members of Congress play in the domestic policy process."[70]

Television puts the president under a powerful magnifying glass. The camera shows every wrinkle and blemish, every hesitation, every frown. Furthermore, as one team of researchers has noted: "The large financial resources commanded by the broadcasting industry have permitted the networks to cover the presidency with an immediacy and intensity that have magnified the faults in the institution and its occupant."[71] Thus, when presidents resort to the electronic medium, they are dealing with a two-edged weapon. But the stakes are high. While the president seeks to use the TV networks to justify his policies or to capitalize on a new diplomatic initiative, he is sometimes risking as much as he may hope to gain. The president's paramount position in the mass media may allow him to set the issue agenda, but this is no guarantee that he can obtain public approval for his program or his performance. Commentator Eric Sevareid observed some years ago to a White House aide that television "not only exposes what a man wants to say, but it also exposes a man. It would seem," he concluded, "that there were some things about Lyndon Johnson and Richard Nixon that television made all too clear—and not to their advantage."[72]

Attempts by the president and his aides to foster the image of an open administration can sometimes backfire. Openness is an image-enhancing concept that does not necessarily ensure more effective government. Sometimes secrecy, access control management, and information control are tools presidents can use to their advantage. President Carter's efforts to demonstrate an open administration soon turned out to be counterproductive. When White House aides and cabinet officers began arguing their policy differences in public, for example, the press immediately publicized these disagreements. As political scientists Paletz and Entman have commented: "The result was an exaggerated impression of the chief executive as indecisive, stubborn, unable to control events or command obedience—a failure."[73]

Presidents are especially vulnerable to what might be called the "set 'em up, knock 'em down" syndrome, in which the television and print media temporarily withhold serious criticism and give the newly elected president every benefit of the doubt during his first year in office. During the second year the correspondents begin focusing on his warts and weaknesses. David L. Paletz and Robert M. Entman have described President Carter's experience with this media treatment: "After the honeymoon, Carter was increasingly treated as guilty unless he proved himself innocent. More than ever, White House reporters interpreted presidential actions as politically motivated. The media events undertaken by the president were described by reporters as attempts to manipulate press and public rather than taken at face value as efforts by a conscientious president to communicate with the American public."[74] Under these circumstances, the president becomes just another politician attempting to retain and enhance his power, not a leader of all the people. In President Carter's case, the television journalists, having helped build great expectations for the president's performance, were among the first to "contrive the chorus of dismay and disillusion when Carter's effectiveness was found wanting against standards of action and achievement propounded by presidents and the press."[75]

In the case of President Lyndon Johnson, however, it was not just media overexposure that destroyed his presidency. It was the loss of public support for his Vietnam policies that eventually did him in. Television's on-the-spot coverage of the Southeast Asian war, the bloody battle scenes, the torching of Vietnamese huts in search of Vietcong guerrillas, and the rising American casualty lists carried night after night on the networks gradually turned out to be a major factor in the nation's growing disenchantment with a seemingly endless and futile conflict.

Reportedly, CBS anchorman Walter Cronkite played an unpublicized major role in persuading President Johnson to reverse his course and start deescalating America's involvement in the Vietnam war. Despite growing public disillusion, President Johnson still felt in early 1968 that the war in Vietnam could and must be won. Walter Cronkite, LBJ's favorite television newsman, became increasingly skeptical about the American "success" stories emanating from the Pentagon and Saigon, especially during the Vietcong Tet offensive. The veteran newsman, who had covered the European theater during World War II, decided to go to Vietnam to see for himself and then make a firsthand report. Upon his return, he broadcast a special half-hour report, which President Johnson watched. In Cronkite's view, the war had turned into a bloody stalemate and a military victory was probably beyond reach.

Johnson, upon hearing Cronkite's verdict, reportedly turned to his press secretary George Christian and said: "It's all over."[76] Johnson, who respected Cronkite more than any other newsman, also knew that a recent national poll had shown that Americans trusted Walter Cronkite more than any other American to "tell it the way it is."[77] According to Bill Moyers, one of Johnson's top aides, Johnson felt that if Walter Cronkite thought the war was a lost cause, the average American citizen soon would think so too. Consequently, the only statesmanlike thing for Johnson to do was to start winding down the American war effort. Just a few weeks later, the president went on national television and announced that the air and sea attacks in most of Vietnam would end—and also that he would not seek reelection. This action prompted David Halberstam, the Pulitzer-prize-winning reporter in Vietnam, to remark: "It's the first time in history a war has been declared over by an anchorman."[78] While this somewhat flippant observation is clearly an overstatement, Halberstam's comment underscores once again the remarkable influence that the electronic medium, especially its top-level commentators, have on the American public—and its leaders.

Overexposure to television also weakened, rather than strengthened, President Ford's and Carter's standing with the American public. Though Ford was a Big Ten football player at the University of Michigan, network television's excessive coverage of his vacations in Colorado frequently showed his ski spills on the slopes at Vail, reinforcing the theme that he was a decent man, but clumsy. Similarly, one commentator, speaking of President Carter's overexposure on television, observed: "The more Jimmy Carter, coached by his television advisers, attempted to project himself as tough and decisive, the more people wondered whether he was strong enough to be an effective president; only after his spontaneous outrage at the taking of U.S. hostages in Iran did he come across as strong without affectation."[79]

Televised presidential messages also contain another potential threat to the president's credibility and performance. To demonstrate his leadership, the president must go on television to describe a special problem or crisis and then outline or spell out what he proposes to do about it. But many of the national and international problems are far more complex or intractable than they seem at first glance. Perhaps Congress views the costs as too high or too threatening to key interest groups. Time passes, and nothing is done to alleviate the problem. Once again, the president's standing with the public falls.

Occasionally the president may achieve a short-term gain in popularity by more frequent appearances, but the long-term effect can undermine his credibility as an effective leader. By going on television more and more frequently—in 1964, President Johnson made 36 speeches on TV—presidents are using up one of their most valuable assets at an accelerated rate. Eventually the public tires of these presidential addresses, cynicism sets in, and then a majority of the electorate turns against the president at the next election. President Johnson's blatant attempts to manipulate the mass media were so crass and transparent that they backfired, creating a serious "credibility gap" for this president. In the case of the Vietnam war, people simply stopped believing a word the White House said about the progress of the war to save South Vietnam.

Johnson's credibility problems actually began earlier. In April 1964, after a revolt in the Dominican Republic, Johnson went on television to announce that he was sending 400 marines to this small Caribbean country to protect American lives. Within days, Johnson dispatched 24,000 U.S. troops to the Dominican Republic "to protect the regime from a Communist takeover." The president spent hours personally trying to convince American newsmen that his military action was justified because "fifteen hundred innocent people were murdered and shot and their heads cut off."[80] This report subsequently turned out to be totally unfounded. During this Caribbean crisis Johnson more than once personally interrupted the network evening news to give the White House version of developments in the Caribbean.

Plainly, these heavyhanded efforts marked the beginning of President Johnson's credibility gap, and they were all self-inflicted.[81] Nor was Richard Nixon, despite frequent network speeches, able to convince his nationwide television audiences that he was not culpable in the Watergate coverup. Indeed, the more he tried to appear sincere, the more people suspected that he was merely more devious than ever.[82] Even Nixon's 1974 trip to the Middle East, which included a stopover in Moscow to visit with Soviet leader Leonid Brezhnev, failed to divert the persistent network and press reporters' questions about Watergate and his involvement in the scandal.

Presidential televised speeches often give, at best, only a temporary boost in the ratings: "Four decades of Gallup Poll measurements of presidential popularity," writes George Gallup, summing up the shot-in-the-arm effect of presidential television speeches, "show that these sudden gains are rarely sustained over a long period of time."[83] The evidence to document Gallup's contention is not hard to find. In 1973, after President Nixon's announcement of the Vietnam peace agreement, his standing in the Gallup poll rose sharply from 51 to 67 percent in a few days; but within three months, before the Ervin Committee's televised Watergate hearings had driven Mr. Nixon into a fortified defensive position behind the White House walls, his Gallup rating dropped to 54 percent. Gerald Ford's rating in the Gallup poll rose from 40 percent approval to 51 percent after the *Mayaguez* incident off Cambodia in 1975, but within three months it had slipped again to 45 percent.[84]

President Jimmy Carter's Gallup poll ratings were a similar story. In July 1978, his popularity languished at 39 percent, but after Carter negotiated the Camp David agreement ending hostilities between Egypt and Israel, an event that received heavy television coverage, it climbed to 56 percent—the highest short-term jump ever recorded by the Gallup organization. But then his ratings began drifting downward. By July 1979, at the time of his ill-fated national malaise speech, the public had seemingly forgotten about Carter's diplomatic coup; his Gallup ratings had plummeted to the middle 20s—the same disaster level at which Truman found himself during the waning days of his administration, and comparable to Nixon's bleak ratings shortly before he was forced to resign.[85]

Discussing the relentless impact that the nightly televised coverage of bad international news has on the political fortunes of an incumbent president, Theodore H. White has described it with brutal frankness: "He who comes to power by television must be prepared to be destroyed by television."[86] White was speaking of the Iranian hostage crisis that began in December 1979, with the Iranian militants' occupation of the American embassy in Teheran, and did not end until the final negotiations led to the release of the 52 American hostages on Ronald Reagan's inauguration day, January 20, 1981. Carter's adroit use of television to capture the Democratic nomination and the subsequent presidential election failed him when he needed it most. Indeed, many national political reporters concluded that President Carter's inability to resolve the Iranian hostage crisis and obtain the release of the Americans before the 1980 general election contributed significantly to his defeat at the hands of Ronald Reagan.

In assessing the influence of television on the presidency, another team of writers put it this way: "The media's obsession with the presidency can victimize the president, making him an easy target."[87] Television finds it much easier to focus on the president, rather than Congress. In the case of Carter, Congress's failure to pass a number of his programs was blamed on him. Although journals of opinion might explain that part of the failure could be attributed to the changes in the congressional committee system, notably the proliferation of subcommittees, and the general decentralization of power on Capitol Hill, the overwhelming media coverage of the presidency made it appear that Carter's incapacity was the chief cause of legislative inaction. And reports of Carter's ineptitude only decreased his influence with Congress. As Paletz and Entman have explained: "Through no fault or plan of their own, the media's routine and limitations, which lead them to converge on the presidency, contribute to the fragmentation of the policy process." In the case of President Nixon in 1974 and President Carter in 1978, "Critical coverage of those very actions can further reduce a president's ability to control events; the coverage portrays his behavior as a series of cynical and doomed ploys to recover the public's trust by manipulation."[88] Unless there is a redeeming international or domestic crisis, the negative media coverage of the president can be expected to have a further debilitating effect.

TELEVISION: A NEW CHECK AND BALANCE
ON THE PRESIDENT

Television's insatiable need for excitement, conflict, action, and compelling drama often drive it toward a negative treatment of presidents. Initially, the national media coverage generates expectations of quick results from a newly elected president. During the postinaugural honeymoon, the president is invariably pictured as about to embark on a new era, aided by an energetic new cabinet and staff. But then reality sets in. Innovation in our system of limited government and checks and balances is never easy, especially if it involves domestic legislation. As Paletz and Entman explain: "Because the media cannot deal effectively with such structural complexity but love a colorful fight between personalities, the stalemate is portrayed as a conflict of political will, influence, and savvy of the president and his opponents. If the innovation fails (as most do) the media's framework allows but one explanation: a personal failure of the president."[89]

Presidents, as we all know, are not always masters of their own fate. The seizure of American embassy employees as hostages, a damaging strike by the steelworkers or coal miners, an uncooperative Federal Reserve Board whose policies push interest rates to an all-time high—all these factors can form the basis of continuing network news coverage strongly negative in tone toward the president and his administration.

Television's intense daily coverage of the president also has the subtle effect of squeezing time sequences and inflating the public's expectations about how much a president can accomplish in one term. The president has less time to put his programs in place and get results. Failure to deliver on his promises soon fosters disenchantment among political commentators and the public alike. One commentator, William C. Adams, has observed: "Accounts of unresolved problems, of policies gone wrong, of politicians wrangling, of impending crises, often coupled with 'worst case' scenarios, absorb a consistently higher share of network news than newspaper news."[90]

This "bad news" agenda can only add up to trouble for the president. As described by Adams: "Without necessarily explicitly blaming the party in power, the implicit linkage builds up night after night; government power and societal problems are all at the national level; the president is the pinnacle of national leadership and power; yet grave problems foreign and domestic persist and swell with hopelessly ineffectual responses from the citadel in Washington."[91] Walter Cronkite's memorable closing lines on the CBS-TV Evening News, "And this is the 347th day of captivity of the American hostages in Iran," repeated each succeeding night for over 400 newscasts, could not help but have a negative impact on the public's view of President Carter's handling of the crisis—as well as other national problems. Under these circumstances, the president is virtually powerless in countering the unrelenting approach of television news.

Though the incumbent president may think, by skillful management, that he can determine the agenda for the next election, more often than not network coverage of major news developments will set the agenda for him. One former press secretary has argued that the desire to keep the public interested and the need for continuous coverage produces a subconscious bias in the press against the presidency that leads to critical stories.[92]

Michael J. Robinson has commented: "While television, through its compulsive predilection for the Presidency, has probably made the office powerful, it may also have rendered the authority of the President less legitimate." Consequently, Robinson continues: "The result may be a new sort of equilibrium in Presidential power, in which *television helps move power toward the office but detracts from the legitimacy of the officeholder* (author's italics)."[93] No wonder we have been seeing fewer two-term presidents.

LIMITS ON PRESIDENTIAL OPTIONS

Television has complicated the president's job of conducting foreign policy and developing his own domestic programs. The nation's revulsion against the on-the-spot battle scenes from Vietnam, carried almost nightly on the three television networks, eventually persuaded most Americans that the Southeast Asian war was immoral, or if not immoral, a war the United States was not winning. The end result was to create a climate of public opinion in which the Johnson and Nixon administrations finally concluded that the war was not "winnable," or at least not without an all-out mobilization, and that such a price was too high. Speaking of the powerful impact of television's coverage of the Vietnam war and its effect upon the American public, one leading commentator, Austin Ranney, has said: "It seems unlikely that any future American administration can sustain very long or perhaps even seriously consider launching a war fought on foreign soil for objectives more limited than our country's survival."[94]

If some critics argue that television's graphic accounts of the Vietnam war will prevent this country from sinking into more bloody quagmires like Vietnam and Korea, others will argue that elimination of limited wars leaves no viable military option except all-out nuclear war. As a result, Ranney has concluded: "Television's effective elimination of the limited war option seems undeniable, and that in itself will make the conduct of foreign policy significantly different in the age of television than it was in the 1960's and before."[95] This judgment, however, may be premature. Ronald Reagan and his military advisers, faced with a limited police action in Grenada during October 1983, chose to follow the censorship path established by British Prime Minister Margaret Thatcher and her government in fighting a limited-objective war against Argentina in the Falkland Islands in 1982. Just as Mrs. Thatcher's government prohibited on-the-spot filming of the action in the Falkland Islands by BBC and other British television news services, President Reagan and his U.S. military commanders banned American television and press correspondents from accompanying U.S. landing forces in Grenada. Despite vociferous protests from the television networks and editors of the nation's leading newspapers, the censorship lid was not lifted for nearly five days—not until U.S. marines and paratroopers had secured the island and the captured armed Cuban construction workers, who were building a long airport landing strip, were behind prison camp barbed wire.

During the same period in the Middle East, the frequent sniper attacks and shelling of the U.S. peacekeeping force at the Beirut airport, carried almost nightly on the American television networks, created the same type of negative reaction among the American public as the filmed reports of the Vietnam war had less than two decades ago. The death of 241 U.S. Marines by a lone terrorist truck-bomb attack on the Marine barracks near the Beirut airport in late October 1983 did indeed revive memories of the same type of serious doubt about the reasons for maintaining an American presence in Lebanon that this country experienced in the late 1960s, especially during the 1968 Vietcong Tet offensive. Questions of why U.S. forces were in Lebanon in the first place or why the Marine security wasn't higher around the barracks were temporarily submerged two days later by the successful U.S. intervention in Grenada. However, in the face of mounting congressional criticism of his Lebanese policy, President Reagan suddenly announced the withdrawal of the U.S. peacekeeping contingent four months later in February 1984.

PRESIDENTIAL TELEVISION: A THREAT TO DEMOCRACY?

The president's ability to communicate instantly with 75 million or more Americans during a single address on any issue of his choosing is thought by some critics to pose a potential threat to our democratic institutions because it gives too much influence and power to a single person. One team of analysts has expressed the fear that "Television's impact . . . threatens to tilt the delicately balanced system in the direction of the president."[96] In the words of the same analysts: "It is a nationally-viewed justification of war, invocation of peace, praise for political allies, damnation of opponents, veto of legislation, scolding of Congress by a chief executive, commander-in-chief, party leader, and candidate."[97] But if these fears are true, why is it that four of the most recent presidents, excluding Mr. Reagan, have not been able to win reelection, or in the case of Mr. Nixon, been able to complete their second term?

Despite the enormous advantages an incumbent president has with his instantaneous access to national television, it would appear, in the words of Austin Ranney, that "Television has become a potent new force helping to keep government and the elected politicians who are supposed to run it from becoming too powerful."[98] Certainly any president who seeks to disregard a congressional mandate or an unfavorable Supreme Court decision would immediately trigger a flurry of network reports of these actions. By focusing on any alleged wrongdoing or scandals, the network reportage would furnish millions of Americans with vital information about the president's attempts to exceed or violate the powers of his office. The case of the Watergate scandals and President Nixon's involvement in the political coverup that followed are still fresh in the minds of most Americans.

Television's live coverage of the House Judiciary Committee's debate on the articles of impeachment against President Nixon in 1974 lent an aura of legitimacy to the hearings that could never have been provided solely by the print press. Austin Ranney has summarized the impact of television on the congressional proceedings:

> Whatever the millions of viewers may have thought of the committee's ultimate decisions, few doubted the evidence of their own eyes and ears that this divisive and dangerous issue was being decided by conscientious, intelligent, hardworking, and fairminded congressmen from both parties and both sides of the issue. And surely the resulting public confidence in the legitimacy of the decision-making process played a major role in the nation's calm acceptance of a decision that under other circumstances might have left disfiguring scars.[99]

Clearly, the television networks' adversarial role toward political leaders is a new check and balance that has been added to the American system in the past three decades. The public has come to regard the television networks as a public watchdog. Political leaders who seek to exclude network cameras from important public or semi-public meetings can expect to generate a hornet's nest of complaints from outraged citizens. "Open politics" is the order of the day, and few political leaders wish to find themselves coming down on the wrong side of this issue. With television cameras now serving as the new people's tribunes, no major aspect of political life is off limits for the television cameramen. As a result of this ever-expanding flow of information into the homes of millions of Americans every day of the year, network television has become an additional bulwark against abusive governmental action.

CONCLUSION

Television has expanded presidential influence far beyond anything envisaged by the framers of the Constitution. Indeed, television has become the chief link between the president and the American people. By personalizing and dramatizing the presidency, network television has helped enlarge the formal powers of the president, especially his role as chief legislator and policymaker. Presidents now deliver their State of the Union and budget messages directly not only to Congress, but to national television audiences that sometimes exceed 75 million viewers. Presidential press conferences, special TV messages to the American people, and presidential foreign travel all enable the president to dominate the public agenda throughout most of the year.

The impact of television on the presidency begins even before the president-elect reaches the White House. With the spread of presidential primaries making this form of national convention delegate selection the dominant force in the presidential nominating process, televised communications via public appearances and 30-second spot advertising has become an indispensable campaign tool for winning nomination. In the general election campaign presidential candidates now place so much reliance on network television that they devote more than half of their federally funded campaign budgets to televised advertising.

Recent presidents, however, have discovered that network television can be both a blessing and a curse. More than any other phenomenon, television has helped build up excessive public expectations of the president. The television networks' compulsion to focus on the president's personality reinforces the public image that he is responsible or should be responsible for almost everything that happens in the executive branch. When he fails to deliver on his campaign promises or when he alienates one group after another because his policies do not satisfy their demands, his popularity and public opinion ratings invariably begin to sag. Some critics hold the television networks primarily responsible for the recent spate of "revolving door" presidencies (before President Reagan's two successive elections) and the resultant inflated expectations and subsequent disappointments over presidential performance. Plainly, to be successful in the age of television a president must rely heavily on the electronic medium to communicate with the electorate. But he must be careful not to build up public hopes and expectations beyond a reasonable chance of fulfillment.

NOTES

1. Theodore H. White, *America in Search of Itself* (New York: Harper & Row, 1982), 165.
2. *Seattle Post-Intelligencer,* September 2, 1982.

3. Each of the three major networks annually spends approximately $250 million on news gathering, and each employs anywhere from 1,200 to 1,400 people. Sally Bedell Smith, *The New York Times,* August 12, 1985.

4. *The New York Times,* July 15, 1985.

5. Michael J. Robinson and Margaret A. Sheehan, *Over the Wire: CBS and UPI in Campaign '80* (New York: Russell Sage Foundation, 1983), 192.

6. Michael J. Robinson, "Television and American Politics, 1956–1976," *The Public Interest,* 48 (Summer 1977), 22.

7. Fred I. Greenstein, "The Psychological Functions of the Presidency for Citizens," in Elmer C. Cornwall, ed., *The American Presidency* (Chicago: Scott, Foresman, 1966), 30–36.

8. Bruce Miroff, "Monopolizing the Public Space: The President as a Problem for Democratic Politics," in Thomas E. Cronin, ed., *Rethinking the Presidency* (Boston: Little, Brown, 1982), 218–232.

9. Newton N. Minow, John Bartlow Martin, and Lee M. Mitchell, *Presidential Television* (New York: Basic Books, 1973), 21.

10. Miroff, "Monopolizing the Public Space," 222.

11. Ibid., 228.

12. Richard E. Neustadt, *Presidential Power* (New York: Wiley, 1980), 211.

13. Edward Jay Epstein, *News from Nowhere* (New York: Random House, 1973), chap. 3; see also Erik Barnouw, *Tube of Plenty: The Evolution of American Television* (New York: Oxford University Press, 1975), 308–314.

14. The *New York Times*/CBS News poll, however, charted a smaller increase in Grenada policy support following the president's address. Before President Reagan went on television, only a 46 to 42 percent plurality approved sending U.S. troops to Grenada; after the speech, a 55 to 31 percent plurality approved. *The New York Times,* October 29, 1983.

15. Robinson, "Television and American Politics, 1956–1976," 14.

16. Godfrey Hodgson, *All Things to All Men* (New York: Simon & Schuster, 1980), 186.

17. Ibid., 183; Theodore C. Sorenson, *Kennedy* (New York: Bantam, 1966), 364.

18. Herbert E. Alexander, "Making Sense About Dollars in the 1980 Presidential Campaigns," in Michael J. Malbin, ed., *Money and Politics in the United States* (Chatham, NJ: Chatham House Publishers, Inc., 1984), 26–28.

19. The total cost of the Anderson campaign was about $14.4 million. But because Anderson received no federal funds during the general election campaign, he was forced to adopt a different spending format. He spent approximately $3 million on direct mail costs; another $2.3 million was spent on organizing signature drives, legal assistance in getting on state ballots, and other legal fees. Candidate travel cost $2 million, and $1.7 million was spent on personnel. See Herbert E. Alexander, "Making Sense About Dollars in the 1980 Presidential Campaigns," in Michael J. Malbin, ed., *Money and Politics in the United States* (Chatham, NJ: Chatham House Publishers, Inc., 1984), 29.

20. The Reagan-Bush TV outlays in 1984 were divided as follows: network—$11,463,000 (50.1 percent); spot announcements—$9,592,000 (41.1 percent); cable—$281,000 (1.2 percent). No breakdown of the Mondale-Ferraro figures is yet available. Data supplied to author by Herbert E. Alexander, director, Citizens' Research Foundation.

21. Jack W. Germond and Jules Witcover, "Presidential Debates: An Overview," in Austin Ranney, ed., *The Past and Future of Presidential Debates* (Washington, DC: American Enterprise Institute, 1979), 195.

22. See Elihu Katz and Jacob J. Feldman, "The Debates in Light of Research: A Survey

of Surveys," in Sidney Kraus, ed., *The Great Debates: Ford vs. Carter, 1976* (Blooming-ton: Indiana University Press, 1979), 264.

23. Ibid., p. 213.
24. Sidney Kraus, "Presidential Debates: Political Option or Public Decree," Ibid., 10, note 11.
25. Thomas E. Patterson, *The Mass Media Election: How Americans Choose Their President* (New York: Praeger, 1980), 123–125.
26. *The New York Times,* November 3, 1980.
27. Ibid.
28. *Gallup Opinion Index,* No. 183 (December 1980), 29.
29. *Gallup Opinion Index,* No. 137 (December 1976), 8. Steven H. Chaffee and Jack Dennis, in a special panel poll (a series of polls in which the same respondents are reinterviewed several times) in Wisconsin, found that on the eve of the first debate only 55 percent of their sample had made up their minds how to vote. Approximately 63 percent had decided after the first debate and 70 percent by the time the debates were completed. See Steven H. Chaffee and Jack Dennis, "Presidential Debates: An Empiri-cal Assessment," in Austin Ranney, ed., *The Past and Future of Presidential Debates* (Washington, DC: American Enterprise Institute, 1979), 93.
30. *The New York Times,* October 23, 1984; see also "Reagan Wins a Draw," *Newsweek,* October 29, 1984, 26–29.
31. In 1976 and 1980 the League of Women voters hosted the debates, since the networks could not sponsor debates between the two major party candidates without granting equal time to all the minor-party candidates. The networks were unwilling to do this, so if debates were to be held it was necessary to find a private sponsor. Under this arrangement the networks could cover the debates as "legitimate" news events and ignore the minor-party candidates.
32. *The New York Times,* November 27, 1985.
33. Ibid., November 9, 1984.
34. Patterson, *The Mass Media Election,* esp. chap. 3.
35. Doris A. Graber and Young Y. Kim, "Media Coverage and Voter Learning During the Presidential Primary Season," *Georgia Journal of Political Science,* 7 (Spring 1979), 26.
36. Doris A. Graber, *Mass Media and American Politics* (Washington, DC: Congressional Quarterly Press, 1980), p. 179.
37. Martha Kumar and Michael Grossman, "Images of the White House in the Media," in Doris A. Graber, ed., *The President and the Public* (Philadelphia: Institute for the Study of the Human Issues, 1982), 94–95.
38. Hodgson, *All Things to All Men,* 184.
39. Letter from Democratic National Committee to Federal Communications Commis-sion, quoted in Minow, Martin, and Mitchell, *Presidential Television,* 19.
40. Ibid., 19–20.
41. Anne Rawley Saldich, *Electronic Democracy* (New York: Praeger, 1979), 83.
42. Interview between Brokaw and Martha Joynt Kumar, quoted in Michael Baruch Grossman and Martha Joynt Kumar, *Portraying the President* (Baltimore: The Johns Hopkins University Press, 1981), 45.
43. Minow, Martin, and Mitchell, *Presidential Television,* 65.
44. Ibid., 66–67.
45. Saldich, *Electronic Democracy,* 82.
46. In early 1981, the networks offered the Democrats a half-hour to respond to President

Reagan's presentation of his economic program to Congress. But two of the networks offered free time opposite "Dallas," one of the top-rated shows on television. George C. Edwards III, *The Public Presidency* (New York: St. Martin's Press, 1983), 82.

47. *The New York Times,* November 14, 1983.

48. Ibid.

49. William W. Lammers, "Presidential Press Conference: Who Hides, and When?" *Political Science Quarterly,* 96 (Summer 1981), 271.

50. Juan Williams, *Washington Post,* February 13, 1983.

51. Ibid.

52. Ibid. According to one syndicated columnist, "The White House public relations budget is effectively bigger than the combined operating budgets of the wire services, the news departments of the television networks, and the largest newspapers and magazines in the country." Richard Reeves, *Bellingham* [Washington] *Herald,* December 26, 1983.

53. Sidney Blumenthal, "Marketing the President," *The New York Times Magazine,* September 13, 1981, 118.

54. Grossman and Kumar, *Portraying the President,* 241.

55. Originally, TV cameras were restricted to filming the press conference, and the networks were allowed to broadcast it only after the Eisenhower White House staff had reviewed it. This restriction was lifted by the Kennedy administration, which permitted live telecasts. Grossman and Kumar, *Portraying the President,* 243.

56. Robert Trout, "ABC Weekend Report," November 6, 1983. Mr. Trout covered the White House for CBS radio for many years before switching to ABC.

57. David L. Paletz and Robert M. Entman, *Media Power Politics* (New York: Free Press, 1981), 60.

58. McGeorge Bundy, as quoted by Grossman and Kumar, 244.

59. William W. Lammers, "Presidential Press Conference Schedules: Who Hides, and When?" *The New York Times,* January 25, 1986.

60. Edwards, *The Public Presidency,* 115.

61. Sorenson, *Kennedy,* 361–365.

62. Hodgson, *All Things to All Men,* 188.

63. Ibid.

64. Ibid., 189.

65. Minow, Martin, and Mitchell, *Presidential Television,* 56.

66. In 1983, President Reagan set a modern record for distance from the press, holding only six full-scale news conferences—fewer in a single year than any president since the advent of television. Reagan's record amounted to less than a third of the yearly average of his six predecessors. White House staffers contend that Reagan's use of alternative formats—"mini" press conferences, television addresses, weekly radio addresses—compensates for the cutbacks in full-dress news conferences. Reagan conducted seven 10-minute mini conferences during the first four months of 1983; since then he has held only six. The innovative "six on one" small gatherings, where a half-dozen White House reporters spent 30 minutes with the President, were allowed to expire after four sessions in late spring. White House aides conceded that they have cut back on press conferences in favor of prime-time TV addresses because Reagan does better reading his lines than speaking extemporaneously. "Periscope," *Newsweek,* December 19, 1983, 25. In fairness to President Reagan, it should be noted that during President Nixon's first term gaps of 132, 91, and 90 days occurred between some press conferences. Lammers, "Presidential Press Conferences: Who Hides, and When?" 267.

67. Paletz and Entman, *Media Power Politics,* 61.

68. Lewis W. Wolfson, as quoted by Paletz and Entman, 61.

69. William C. Spragens, *The Presidency and the Mass Media in the Age of Television* (Washington, DC: University Press of America, 1978), 398.

70. Harold M. Barger, *The Impossible Presidency* (Glenview, IL: Scott, Foresman, 1984), 390.

71. Grossman and Kumar, *Portraying the President,* 315.

72. Hodgson, *All Things to All Men,* 200.

73. Paletz and Entman, *Media Power Politics,* 73.

74. Ibid., 74.

75. Ibid., 72. Another student of the presidency argues that "The networks, seeking to realize their own goals, set in motion a dynamic pattern that can unravel the career of individual presidents and the public's support for the Office of the Presidency." Fred Smoller, "The Six O'Clock Presidency: Patterns of Network News Coverage of the President," *Presidential Studies Quarterly,* XVI (Winter 1986), 31–49. In his study of the Nixon, Ford, Carter, and Reagan presidencies over a seventeen-year period (1968–1985), Smoller found that no president since the end of Nixon's first term has received a net positive portrayal on the CBS Evening News after his first three months in office. In Smoller's words: "Negative coverage on the evening news appears to be the norm for the televised presidency." Even President Reagan received more negative than positive coverage on the CBS program. President Reagan, however, has been able to neutralize this negative impact and maintain public support by effectively using the "controlled media"—presidential addresses, weekly radio broadcasts, the recently established White House news service. Ibid.

76. Quoted in Robert Metz, *CBS: Reflections in a Bloodshot Eye* (New York: Signet Books, 1975), 352, as cited by Austin Ranney, *Channels of Power* (Washington, DC: American Enterprise Institute, 1983), 4–5.

77. Ranney, *Channels of Power,* 5.

78. David Halberstam, *The Powers That Be* (New York: Knopf, 1979), 514.

79. Hodgson, *All Things to All Men,* 201.

80. Ibid., 188–189.

81. Ibid.

82. Cited in ibid., 201.

83. Ibid.

84. Ibid.

85. Ibid.

86. White, *America in Search of Itself,* 195.

87. Paletz and Entman, *Media Power Politics,* 77.

88. Ibid., 78.

89. Ibid., 76.

90. William C. Adams, "Media Power in Presidential Elections: An Exploratory Analysis, 1960–1980," in Doris A. Graber, ed., *The President and the Public* (Philadelphia: Institute for the Study of Human Issues, 1982), 116. See also Dennis T. Lowry, "Gresham's Law and Network TV News Selections," *Journal of Broadcasting,* 15 (Fall 1971), 397–408; Michael J. Robinson and Margaret Sheehan, *Over the Wire and on TV: CBS and UPI in Campaign '80* (New York: Basic Books, 1982).

91. Ibid.

92. Grossman and Kumar, *Portraying the President,* 12–13.

93. Robinson, "Television and American Politics, 1956–1976," 22.

94. Ranney, *Channels of Power,* 136.
95. Ibid.
96. Minow, Martin, and Mitchell, *Presidential Television,* 10.
97. Ibid., 11.
98. Ranney, *Channels of Power,* 174.
99. Ibid., 167.

chapter 6

Legislator in Chief

During the spring of 1981, a Republican president and a Democratic House of Representatives were locked in a bitter struggle over the size and shape of the federal budget. Ronald Reagan and his GOP allies on Capitol Hill, determined to make deep cuts in domestic social programs, were also supported by a bloc of southern Democrats. Dissatisfied with the Democratic-controlled House budget committee's efforts to meet his proposed spending cuts, President Reagan decided to offer some last-minute changes of his own. "I want a chance to send some substitute language up there on the budget," the president told the Speaker Thomas P. O'Neill, Jr. (D–Mass.) on the phone. "The House has done a good job, but it hasn't gone far enough, and I . . ." "Did you ever hear of the separation of powers?" O'Neill interrupted. "The Congress of the United States will be responsible for spending. You're not supposed to be writing legislation." "I know the Constitution," Reagan interjected testily.[1]

Once again, the two branches were engaged in a classic faceoff. The president was exerting pressure on members of the House to bend to his wishes on the size of the federal budget. Leaders of the House, on the other hand, were equally determined to maintain its power of the purse and to mold legislation in conformity with the wishes of the majority party in the House.

By late April 1981, President Reagan and his Capitol Hill allies persuaded enough southern Democrats—"boll weevils"—to join the GOP House Republicans to pass the president's budget reduction package—the biggest single cut in the federal budget in half a century. By and large, however, presidents lose almost as many rounds as they win with Congress.

Unlike most of the nineteenth century, when Congress dominated the federal government, the twentieth has seen the emergence of the president as chief legislator and agenda setter. In this chapter, we examine and assess the growth of the president's legislative influence. Although the formal powers conferred upon the president are few compared to the explicit grant of powers to Congress, presidential legislative influence and powers have been greatly expanded through custom and practice—and television.

Strong presidents, such as Theodore and Franklin Delano Roosevelt and Woodrow Wilson, are primarily responsible for the growth of presidential legislative influence. Relations between the president and Congress, as the chapter points out, have often been marked by frequent clashes over national priorities, the direction of the domestic economy, and in recent years, foreign policy. Indeed, given the nature of their constitutional relationship, conflict between president and Congress is almost inevitable.

While the strong presidents of the twentieth century have usually received the lion's share of the credit for legislative accomplishments—Wilson's New Freedom domestic reforms, Franklin D. Roosevelt's New Deal, and Lyndon Johnson's Great Society—our discussion will show that Congress has often played a co-equal role in many of these enterprises. Since the Constitution established a government of separate institutions sharing power, presidents and Congress must of necessity cooperate if the federal system is to function effectively. The chapter concludes on the general note that the concept of shared power remains as viable today as was for the Founding Fathers during that hot, humid summer of 1787 in Philadelphia when they hammered out the final draft of the Constitution.

CONSTITUTIONAL GRANTS OF POWER

Despite the enormous influence the president wields over the legislative agenda on Capitol Hill, the formal legislative powers conferred on the president by the Constitution are few compared to the broad and explicit grants of powers to Congress. Indeed, a close reading of the Constitution will reveal that the nation's fundamental document confers minimal legislative authority on the president.

Although the Founding Fathers did stipulate that the president "shall from time to time give the Congress information on the State of the Union, and recommend to their Consideration such Measures as he shall judge necessary and expedient" (Article II, Section 3), the men of 1787 believed that the primary function of the president was to execute the legislation proposed and passed by Congress. To be sure, the Founding Fathers assigned the president a veto power, but they intended this constitutional power, which subsequently became a powerful weapon in the hands of strong presidents, as a mechanism to protect the president against legislation that threatened the constitutional rights of his office.[2]

WHITE HOUSE–CAPITOL HILL POLICYMAKING PATTERNS

The eighteenth-century constitutional framework established by the Founding Fathers requires an unusual degree of cooperation between president and Congress to formulate national policy. One congressional scholar, Randall B. Ripley, has categorized presidential-congressional relationships into four major patterns: executive domination, congressional domination, cooperation, and stalemate.[3]

Except for stalemate, all patterns result in some form of legislative action. Except for the cooperative relationship, all forms of interaction involve varying levels of conflict. The pattern of presidential domination describes conditions under which the president serves as the chief initiator of legislative proposals. Congressional domination refers to the process by which the lawmakers, not the president, serve as the chief initiator of policy proposals. Under the cooperation model, both president and Congress share the burden of initiating and refining legislation. Under the stalemate model, either branch may initiate proposals and both president and Congress may play a role in shaping the proposed legislation, but deadlock is the final result because neither branch is willing to make enough concessions to reach agreement.

Policymaking patterns will, of course, vary according to presidential leadership styles and the issues involved. Generally, presidential domination prevails in the areas of foreign policy and national security, especially when the president places high priority on specific proposals—for example, President Truman's plan for European reconstruction after World War II, President Reagan's plan for a massive buildup of military forces in 1981, or his persistent efforts in 1984–85 to obtain financial support for the anti-Sandinista Contra forces trying to overthrow the leftist government of Nicaragua. Congressional domination has frequently prevailed on legislation affecting environmental protection, consumer protection, and expanded social security benefits.

Presidents and Congress, at least until recently, have tended to cooperate effectively on economic development and agricultural policy. Stalemate, however, has characterized much recent presidential-congressional relations. Compared to the Kennedy-Johnson years, marked by stable prices, sustained economic growth, and low inflation, recent presidents have had to face economic scarcity, especially high energy prices, and an aroused Congress. Vietnam, Watergate, and a sluggish economy have not created a climate conducive to presidential leadership. Widespread concern and anxiety over nuclear weapons, high energy costs, and soaring national deficits have undermined the president's ability to press for legislation. Over and above these factors, a resurgent Congress unimpressed with White House influence has thwarted some presidential goals. Most recently, President Reagan and the GOP senators have had one set of top priorities—reduced domestic programs and increased defense budgets—and the Democrat-controlled House has had another set—protection of many domestic programs dating back to Johnson's Great Society and a scaled-down defense budget. The inevitable result: more presidential-congressional stalemate.

Over the past half-century the country has at different times seen all four policymaking patterns in operation. Activist chief executives—Roosevelt, Johnson, and Reagan—have found presidential domination most conducive to their style of leadership. Because Congress is essentially a reactive institution, some analysts believe that it is better suited for following strong executive initiatives than for shaping its own policy framework. Consequently, periods of congressional domination have not usually been marked by major legislative accomplishments. A recent example would be the post-Watergate 94th Congress (1975–76), which convened amid high hopes that the heavy Democratic majorities in both houses and a weakened presidency offered promise for major legislative initiatives. Six months later, Speaker Carl Albert (D–Okla.) and Senate Majority Leader Mike Mansfield (D–Mont.) both conceded that Congress had failed to get off dead center.[4]

No president, of course, has deliberately made stalemate the centerpiece of his national policy. But the wonder is that stalemate has been avoided most of the time and that the country has functioned reasonably well, though faced with divided government (the president and at least one house of Congress controlled by opposite parties) for twenty out of the last thirty-four years. During the Nixon and Ford administrations, presidential-congressional relations were frequently at an impasse over budgetary and spending priorities and the dismantling of certain federal programs, as well as different interpretations of presidential prerogatives that even included use of the pocket veto. Since President Reagan's major legislative successes in 1981 in obtaining tax cuts, major budget reductions in domestic programs, and huge increases in national defense expenditures, Reagan and Congress have frequently been at odds over the means of reducing the huge national deficit and decisions on the continuation or elimination of a number of domestic programs, such as the Job Corps, Amtrak, and urban transit grants.

Although relations between President Reagan and the Democratic-controlled House of Representatives have frequently been strained, it should be noted that both sides have generally avoided the type of showdown that marked President Nixon's relations with Congress: passage of the War Powers Act of 1973 over Nixon's veto and adoption of the Budget Impoundment and Control Act of 1974. Before reaching a point of no return, Reagan and the Democratic opposition in the House have almost always managed to negotiate some form of face-saving compromise or agreed to do battle again at a later date.

Some observers have suggested that recent controversies between president and Congress may not be too far from how the Founding Fathers expected the federal government to operate—as a government not of separate structures performing separate functions, but of separate structures sharing functions. This may be so, but experience over the past century shows that the federal government is most effective during periods of presidential domination, with Congress willing to be led, yet insistent upon its prerogatives of reviewing policy implementation, molding a national consensus on issues, and checking unwarranted assertions of presidential authority. As legislative specialists Davidson and Oleszek have commented: "Lawmakers expect sure-handed leadership and grumble when it is not forthcoming; yet they chafe under vigorous leadership, sensing a threat to legislative powers."[5]

SOURCES OF CONFLICT BETWEEN WHITE HOUSE AND CAPITOL HILL

The reasons why president and Congress are often on a collision course are not difficult to uncover. First and foremost, one great division of power in the national government remains unbridged—"the division of national government authority between the president, the Senate and the House—three competing institutions that have the power to checkmate one another on most matters if they choose to press their authority to the limits."[6]

The U.S. Constitution is silent on the precise roles of Congress and the president in policymaking, and the manner in which they are to share power. The Founding Fathers mingled presidential and congressional authority, and then left it to future presidents and members of Congress to develop satisfactory working relationships. Almost two centuries ago, one of the Founding Fathers, James Madison, pointed out one of the chief sources of conflict between the president and Congress: different constituencies.[7]

Different Constituencies.   While the president is chosen in a nationwide election, each member of Congress is elected within a congressional district or state-wide election and represents a different geographical interest. To win the presidency, a nominee must appeal to a far more diverse electorate and put together an electoral coalition representing a far wider variety of constituencies than any member of Congress. Furthermore, the staggered election structure in the U.S. Senate means that two-thirds of all U.S. senators are not elected at the same time as the president. One-third of the senators are picked two years before the president and another third two years after. Consequently, they are often responsive to somewhat different moods and points of view. Many senators also believe that their state electorates send them to Washington more to look after the state's business in the nation's capital than to devote themselves to solving national and international problems. Equal representation in the Senate also means that the thinly populated rural states are substantially overrepresented (12 states in the Union have a population of less than 1 million persons; 8 of these states are west of the Mississippi).

Because the two branches represent such diverse constituencies, their different perspectives surface at many stages of policymaking. Members of Congress often subscribe to the view that "What's good for Seattle is good for the nation"; presidents are more likely to say, "What's good for the nation is good for Seattle."[8] Congress is frequently responsive to the desires or pressures of narrow constituencies. Key congressional committee chairpersons, who may represent oil-producing or tobacco-growing states, can exert tremendous pressure on tax legislation or agricultural policy far in excess of their numbers. On more than one occasion in recent years, the Greek and Israeli lobbies in the United States have influenced major foreign policy decisions.

Decentralization in Congress.   While the president can utilize his White House staff and the Office of Management and Budget (OMB) to scrutinize, coordinate, and review comprehensive policies and programs to determine their overall impact on the nation, weighing and balancing various policies is not Congress's strong suit. Each house of Congress is decentralized, and members, especially the chairs and subcommittee chairs, jealously guard their prerogatives and power bases. Committee memberships are often unrepresentative of each chamber, and members of each committee tend to defer to members of other committees and engage in frequent tradeoffs and "logrolling" to protect their district and state interests.

Other factors may also affect the presidential-congressional tug of war. Typically, the opposition party in Congress offers its own programs. Whenever possible, it will try to defeat the president's policy initiatives and substitute its own proposals. Or the opposition party may be satisfied merely to torpedo the president's initiatives. This can be especially annoying to a president if Congress is controlled by a majority of the opposition party. As indicated earlier, the executive branch and Congress have been controlled by different parties for almost half of the post-World War II period, whereas during the preceding half-century there was divided rule for just six years. Since 1980, President Reagan has faced split control of Congress, the GOP controlling the Senate and the Democrats controlling the House.

Institutional Changes in Congress.   In recent years the challenge to the president's legislative leadership ability has been complicated further by institutional changes within Congress, especially in the House of Representatives. Seniority is no longer an automatic guarantee to a committee or subcommittee chairmanship. And a chairman can no longer maintain iron-clad control of his committee; he must now be responsive to the wishes of the members. An aged chairman who has lost his effectiveness may be replaced. For example, in late 1984, a 21-term eighty-year-old Democratic congressman who chaired the House Armed Services Committee was replaced by a more vigorous junior member.

Congressional reforms in the 1970s led to the establishment of a host of subcommittees and subcommittee chairs. As a result, these subcommittees now have a far more important role in handling legislation than formerly. Individual legislators have larger personal, committee, and subcommittee staffs available for assistance. All these additional resources, as Edwards and Wayne and others have pointed out, make it easier for members of Congress to challenge the White House and the congressional leadership.[9] The late Speaker Sam Rayburn's advice to freshman legislators, "to get along, go along," is no longer followed by many new members.

To add to the president's burdens, split and joint committee referrals on many bills make it far more difficult to influence members of Congress because it is not that easy to lobby several committees simultaneously with only a limited White House staff. Davidson and Oleszek, for example, point out that "President Carter's 1977 energy package embracing more than 100 separate legislative initiatives was referred to five different House committees, plus one ad hoc body."[10] Indeed, nearly every House and Senate committee is sooner or later involved in some phase of energy policy. The same is true of other broad topics such as health care, welfare, and international economics.

Other factors have further complicated Capitol Hill lobbying. The steadily increasing number of roll call votes (double the number of the pre-1970 era), the widespread opening of committee and subcommittee hearings, and the heavy turnover of senior House members (partly induced by a very attractive pension system) have all created a new sense of independence among members of Congress. The decline of party loyalty has further hampered party leaders' ability to maintain party discipline on crucial votes. As one former Johnson assistant recently described the changes:

> In 1965, there were maybe ten or twelve people who you needed to corral in the House and Senate. Without those people you were in for a tough time. Now I'd put that figure upwards to one hundred. Believe it, there are so many people who have a shot at derailing a bill that the President has to double his effort for even routine decisions.[11]

Partly an outgrowth of the Vietnam war and partly a result of the White House–Watergate abuses of power, Congress is now less trusting of the president. Consequently, the president's potential influence over legislation is less than in the early days of the Roosevelt, Eisenhower, and Johnson administrations. Congressional and media surveillance of the president also add to the president's leadership problems with Congress.

Different Timetables.   The president and Congress live on different timetables. The president, according to the Constitution, is limited to two terms, or a maximum of ten years if he completes the unfinished term of a predecessor. Members of the House, once reelected, can usually expect to retain their seats for a long time. Senate terms are six years, and the odds are better than even that the incumbent will win reelection.

Modern presidents have discovered that if they are to make a mark in history, they must get their programs off the ground in a hurry, usually during their first year in office. Lyndon Johnson, who knew the inner workings of Congress better than almost any president in history, understood the need to get moving early in his term, for he believed that a president's impact is short-lived. This is how he put it in his memoirs:

> The President and the Congress run on separate clocks. The occupant of the White House has a strict tenancy. . . . A President must always reckon that this mandate will prove short-lived. . . . For me, as for most active Presidents, popularity proved elusive.[12]

Johnson's legislative record was made during his first eighteen months in office. Then Vietnam preempted most of his time and interest. As a result, most domestic policy activity nearly dried up. President Reagan, profiting from the experience of his predecessors, wasted no time in pushing his tax and spending cuts programs through Congress in the weeks following his inauguration. But after this legislation was signed into law in August 1981, Reagan had much less to show for his efforts. For the remainder of his first term, he encountered one long obstacle course in dealing with the Democrat-controlled House of Representatives.

By contrast, Congress has a much slower timetable. Most members view their congressional service, if they continue to be successful at the polls, as a lifetime career; hence they lack the compulsion to push proposed legislation through the congressional machinery quickly. Reluctant legislators, hesitant to follow the president's lead, recognize that if they resist or delay long enough, someone else will be sitting in the White House.

Congress is not organized to deal with major policy options. Under the time-honored committee system, legislative bills are distributed among various committees with limited jurisdictions. This system does not permit the committee to consider comprehensive proposals in areas such as national security, welfare, or management of the economy. Furthermore, House and Senate committees duplicate one another; that is, the House and the Senate both have appropriations committees; the House has a Ways and Means Committee and the Senate a Finance Committee; both chambers have a committee to deal with foreign relations, and so on. Consequently, it is not enough for a bill to receive approval in one chamber; it must receive an affirmative vote in both houses. More often than not, each chamber will have a different version of a bill on the same subject, thus necessitating a conference committee to iron out differences—differences that may sometimes prove insurmountable. Under these circumstances, a presidential proposal may be dropped or indefinitely postponed until the next session. No wonder presidents often feel frustrated in their dealings with Congress.

GROWTH OF THE PRESIDENT'S LEGISLATIVE INFLUENCE

Despite the explicit assignment of most legislative powers to Congress, it has become customary in the twentieth century to speak of the president as the chief legislator. A combination of circumstances after the turn of the century spurred the growth of presidential legislative leadership. Rapid industrialization and the steady urbanization of America, as well as the rise of mass communication, created demands for greater federal government regulation of the transportation system, and of banking and commerce, for passage of antitrust legislation, and for aid to the agricultural sector. The election of two dynamic presidents, Teddy Roosevelt and Woodrow Wilson, who both viewed the presidential office as a source of national leadership, greatly expanded the president's legislative role. Passage of the Budget and Accounting Act of 1921, which required the president to develop a full government budget, also helped hasten the growth of presidential legislative leadership.

Woodrow Wilson, even before he reached the White House, observed, the "President is the only national voice in affairs." In contrast, Wilson noted, "There is no one in Congress to speak for the nation. Congress is a conglomeration of unharmonious elements."[13] Speaking of the president's role as legislative leader, Wilson asserted: "He is the representative of no constituency, but of the whole of the people."

Indeed, by skillfully using the power to request measures for congressional consideration, presidents through the years have built a ready forum to outline the goals of their administrations. Franklin D. Roosevelt's New Deal, John Kennedy's New Frontier, and Lyndon Johnson's Great Society programs were all placed before Congress in State of the Union addresses and special messages.

In each case these recommendations served as the agenda for congressional lawmaking activities. As early as Teddy Roosevelt's administration, Congress began devoting more time to disposing of presidential legislative proposals than to serving as the legislative initiator.

A staunch advocate of executive leadership, Theodore Roosevelt began sending legislative drafts to Capitol Hill fairly regularly, though he did it rather quietly so as not to ruffle the feathers of Congressional leaders. Wilson soon outpaced Roosevelt in using the power and influence of his office to lead Congress. Riding the tide of Progressive movement's demand for reform, Wilson arrived on the scene at a propitious moment. Wilson's New Freedom program led to the passage of several landmark pieces of legislation during his first term—the Adamson Act (which established the eight-hour day for railroad workers), the Federal Reserve Act of 1913, the Underwood Tariff, the Clayton Anti-Trust Act of 1914, and legislation establishing the Federal Trade Commission. Wilson was not content merely to send proposals to Congress; he frequently traveled to Capitol Hill to address Congress in person and also to confer privately with his party leadership in the President's Room. Wilson promoted the use of the party caucus on Capitol Hill to commit party members to a common position on priority legislation. Nor did Wilson hesitate to employ his patronage power, which was far more substantial in those days, to reward his supporters.

President Franklin D. Roosevelt, who had been assistant secretary of the navy in Wilson's two administrations, soon outdid his mentor in the volume and breadth of the legislative proposals he sent to Congress. Elected in the midst of the nation's worst depression—one-quarter of the nation's workers were unemployed and factories were almost at a standstill—Roosevelt was presented with challenges similar to those faced by Lincoln during the Civil War. During the famous Hundred Days at the beginning of his first term, FDR and his overworked staff submitted major bills to Congress at the rate of nearly one a day. Though loosely drafted, these bills encountered little resistance from an overwhelmingly Democratic Congress anxious to do almost anything to help the country fight its way out of the Great Depression.

To some observers, it appeared in the early New Deal days that a reversal of constitutional roles had occurred, with the president acting as legislator and Congress merely exercising a veto power. But this presidential domination did not last. Indeed, early in his second term, soon after the rejection of his court packing plan (which would have authorized the president to appoint up to six additional Supreme Court Justices, if sitting justices did not retire at the age of seventy), Congress regained much of its former power. It refused to endorse most of Roosevelt's second-term legislative proposals. By the time Roosevelt was elected to an unprecedented third term in 1940, however, Hitler's threat of world domination and America's military buildup occupied the top slots on President Roosevelt's national agenda.

Roosevelt's successor, Harry S Truman, a former two-term member of the U.S. Senate, quickly demonstrated that he understood the role of president as chief legislator, even if he was not as adept as FDR. Truman established the presidential practice of submitting an entire package of legislative programs at the beginning of each session of Congress. Earlier Mr. Truman had discovered that when he asked for anti-inflation legislation from Congress in 1947, he was up-braided for not including a draft bill to carry out his recommendation. "If the President wants to tell the people that he stands for a certain thing," complained Senator Homer Ferguson (R.-Mich.), "he ought to come out with his proposal. He ought to come to the House and Senate with a message. And he ought to provide a bill if that is exactly what he wants."[14]

The Eisenhower administration encountered a similar complaint a few years later when the Republican chairman of a House committee reportedly chided an administration witness before his committee for failure to offer a specific proposal: "Don't expect us to start from scratch on what you people want. That's not the way we do things here—*you* draft the bills, and *we* work them over."[15]

President Eisenhower, a strict constructionist of the president's duties under the Constitution, soon ordered his staff to prepare detailed legislative proposals for Congress on a variety of issues. Often labeled a passive chief executive, President Eisenhower could lay claim during his two terms to several landmark pieces of legislation that have had a remarkable impact on the country: The Federal Highway Act of 1956 transformed the face of America, with its 70,000 mile interstate highway system; the St. Lawrence Seaway Project opened mid-America to ocean-going traffic (the project had been bottled up in Congress for nearly half a century); and after the Soviet launching of Sputnik, came the establishment of the National Aeronautics and Space Administration (NASA).

Next to Franklin D. Roosevelt, Lyndon Johnson performed the role of chief legislator with more flair and positive results than any twentieth-century president. Johnson's prior experience as Senate majority leader undoubtedly enabled him to push the levers of power in Congress more effectively than any of his predecessors to obtain passage of his Great Society programs. But President Johnson too discovered that his string of Great Society triumphs came to an abrupt end once he became deeply embroiled in the Vietnam war.

The record also shows that the most successful chief legislators have been presidents who have had large working party majorities in both houses. Wilson, Roosevelt, and Johnson, especially in their first terms, were blessed with huge majorities looking to the White House for leadership. But large party majorities, it should be observed, do not automatically guarantee legislative success. Jimmy Carter, though blessed with large majorities in both houses, lacked the needed leadership skills to persuade his party to adopt his domestic legislative proposals. If there is one iron rule in presidential-congressional relationships in this country, it is that congressional support of presidential initiatives does not follow automatically. Clearly, the record in the twentieth century shows long periods of stalemate or inaction on presidential proposals.

Still, the president has a number of factors working in his favor. Most legislative issues selected for serious attention and consideration in any session of Congress have usually been placed on the agenda by the president. While individual members of Congress retain the prerogative to introduce as many bills as they see fit, they know that it is the president's legislative program, not theirs, that will occupy the center of congressional attention throughout the session.

Television has become a powerful legislative tool for modern presidents; ready access to network television, for example, means that the president can, if he wishes, easily go over the heads of Congress to carry his message to the American people. Even before the advent of television, Franklin D. Roosevelt relied on his radio fireside chats to persuade his "fellow Americans" to support his programs and to urge their senators and congressmen to back New Deal measures.

If necessary, the president can signal his willingness to compromise with congressional leaders, or if he remains firm on his position, he can use the televised sessions to go back to the American people for support. If a close vote is pending, the president's special address can sometimes tip the balance to win passage.

Unlike Congress, which reflects the individual voices of 535 lawmakers often speaking at cross-purposes, presidents speak with one voice. Moreover, the nation now expects the president to exercise strong legislative leadership, to outline proposals and offer sensible solutions to major national problems. Clearly, the complexity of the problems that we face in an advanced industrial society has enhanced presidential dominance of the legislative agenda. National defense, energy conservation, agricultural surpluses, foreign trade, and space stations all require extensive analysis and data that until recently only the executive branch could supply to congressional leaders. In a typical year the president will send between one and four hundred messages and letters to Capitol Hill as part of his legislative program.

PRESIDENTIAL MESSAGES

One of the legislative trump cards the president holds in dealing with Congress is the State of the Union message. To be sure, the constitutional requirement that the president report to Congress on the state of the Union has always provided a forum for the president to point the way on proposed legislation. But from Jefferson's time to Taft's—a span of more than a century—this message was merely transmitted to Capitol Hill by courier. Not until Woodrow Wilson resurrected George Washington's practice of addressing a joint session of both Houses of Congress in person was the potentially powerful impact of the State of the Union message upon the general public as well as Congress again fully recognized.

Though the State of the Union address often includes a laundry list of presidential requests, it is widely viewed as the president's working agenda. Since Woodrow Wilson's day, the annual message has been followed by special messages on specific proposals—a revamped tax program, the Peace Corps, a separate Department of Education, a space station, proposed constitutional amendments to balance the budget and provide the president with the item veto, and so on. Wilson's innovation underscored another important aspect of the message—it was a visible milestone marking more direct presidential participation in the legislative process. Further, the State of the Union message was directed at the public at large as much, if not more, than the members of Congress. In the Wilsonian tradition, the purpose of the message is to inform, persuade, and arouse the force of public opinion to bring pressure upon the lawmakers to support the president's program. Now televised during prime-time evening hours, the president's message receives top billing on all three major networks and the Cable News Network (CNN) and reaches an audience of more than 90 million viewers.

The president's legislative responsibilities have also sometimes been expanded by Congress itself. Passage of the Budget and Accounting Act of 1921 was a landmark in the expanding role of the president in the legislative process. Congress imposed upon the president the duty of presenting to the lawmakers a comprehensive budgetary plan of proposed expenditures for the executive agencies, together with recommendations for financing the government's operations. Since most major policy programs require financial underwriting, the concession and transfer of fiscal planning responsibility to the executive has, in fact, signified legislative acquiescence to presidential legislative leadership. Equally important, the budget message to Congress gives the president an unparalleled opportunity to lay out his fiscal agenda for the lawmakers—and for the public via the mass media.

Shortly after World War II, the rapid growth of the economy and the lingering fear of another traumatic Great Depression also prompted Congress to pass the Employment Act of 1946, requiring the president to report annually to Congress on the state of the economy.[16] This law affords the president an open agenda in his economic report to Congress to discuss employment, inflation, taxes, national deficits, and to offer his proposals for dealing with these formidable issues. The Employment Act of 1946, which imposed on the president the responsibility for a coordinated plan to keep the nation's economy on an even keel, demonstrated further congressional agreement that the president should play a major role in proposing legislative measures in the economic field.

By and large, most presidential messages to Congress are positive in nature, spelling out the president's wishes and goals. But strong presidents have never hesitated "to send a message" through their trusted lieutenants on Capitol Hill and via the press that they are prepared to veto bills in the legislative hopper if a measure reaches the White House with the unacceptable provisions still intact.

THE VETO POWER

One of the most potent weapons in the president's legislative arsenal is his power to withhold his assent to measures passed by the legislative branch. Indeed, as James L. Sundquist has observed: "It is the possession of the veto that makes the executive branch a full partner in the legislative process."[17] If a hostile Congress passes bills the chief executive finds objectionable, the president still possesses the authority to exercise his veto to try and block legislation. Within ten days of passage (excluding Sundays), he can return a bill to Congress detailing his objections. Unless both houses of Congress can muster a two-thirds majority, the president's veto is sustained. If ten days pass and the president has neither signed or vetoed the bill, the measure automatically becomes law (U.S. Constitution Article I, Section 7). If a president receives a bill within ten days of congressional adjournment, he need not sign or return it to Congress. Instead, he can pocket veto the objectionable measure.

The veto power has often been underestimated. Because vetoes are so difficult to override, the veto power makes the president a "third branch of the legislature," declared an observant Woodrow Wilson almost three decades before he reached the White House.[18] The potency of the veto power can be quickly measured by the small percentage of vetoes overridden—approximately 4 percent, or 96 out of 2,425 overridden between 1789 and 1984 (see Table 6.1).

Table 6.1   PRESIDENTIAL VETOES, 1789–1984

	Regular vetoes	Pocket vetoes	Total vetoes	Vetoes overridden
Washington	2	—	2	—
Madison	5	2	7	—
Monroe	1	—	1	—
Jackson	5	7	12	—
Tyler	6	3	9	1
Polk	2	1	3	—
Pierce	9	—	9	5
Buchanan	4	3	7	—
Lincoln	2	4	6	—
A. Johnson	21	8	29	15
Grant	45	49	94	4
Hayes	12	1	13	1
Arthur	4	8	12	1
Cleveland	304	109	413	2
Harrison	19	25	44	1
Cleveland	43	127	170	5
McKinley	6	36	42	—
T. Roosevelt	42	40	82	1
Taft	30	9	39	1
Wilson	33	11	44	6
Harding	5	1	6	—
Coolidge	20	30	50	4
Hoover	21	16	37	3
F. Roosevelt	372	261	633	9
Truman	180	70	250	12
Eisenhower	73	108	181	2
Kennedy	12	9	21	—
L. Johnson	16	14	30	—
Nixon	24	19	43	5
Ford	44	22	66	12
Carter	13	18	31	2
Reagan*	18	21	39	4
Total	1,393	1,032	2,425	96

*For 1981–1984.
  Source: Presidential Vetoes, 1789–1976, compiled by the Senate Library (Washington, DC: U.S. Government Printing Office, 1978), ix; *Congressional Quarterly Almanac* (Washington, DC: Congressional Quarterly, 1981), 7; "Reagan Comparatively Frugal in Exercise of His Veto Power," *Congressional Quarterly Weekly Report,* 42 (November 17, 1984), 2956–2957.

Although primarily a defensive weapon of the president, the mere threat of the veto is so formidable that presidents can often win legislative compromise simply by spreading the word on Capitol Hill that they are considering a veto. On more than one occasion FDR was heard to tell his aides, "Give me a bill that I can veto," as an admonition to keep Congress in line on his main legislative goals. Kennedy brandished the veto 21 times during his brief 1,000 days in the White House; none were overridden.

President Reagan, despite his frequent criticism of Congress for exceeding his spending targets, has been comparatively frugal in his use of the presidential veto. In his first term he vetoed 39 bills—8 more than President Carter in his only term, but far fewer than the 66 bills President Ford vetoed in his 2½ years in the White House. Of Reagan's 39 vetoes, Congress overrode only 4 (see Table 6.1).

So formidable is the constitutional requirement of a two-thirds majority vote to override a veto that frequently no attempt is made in Congress to override.[19] Actually, no presidential veto was overridden until a beleaguered President Tyler saw Congress repass a relatively minor measure to fund the construction of two patrol vessels over his objections. The first six presidents used the veto very sparingly. President Washington rejected only two bills, Madison seven, and Monroe one. The two Adams and Jefferson did not resort to the veto. In the minds of early presidents, the veto was an instrument to be used to protect the executive branch against constitutional infringement, rather than a means to impose the president's policy on Congress.

Andrew Jackson, however, soon gave a different interpretation of the veto power. Believing that the veto should be actively used to establish public policy, Jackson vetoed 12 bills in eight years—more than all six predecessors combined. Moreover, Jackson buttressed his objections with strong arguments based not only upon "constitutional principles," but also upon reasons of what he considered sound public policy. Unlike his predecessors, he maintained that the veto power gave the president a right and duty to push his own judgment against that of Congress. In his famous Bank Veto Message of 1832, Jackson emphasized alleged constitutional grounds for his disapproval. But he also spelled out considerations of social and economic justice in defense of his action. Aimed more directly at the citizens of the country than Congress, Jackson's forceful message also served as a valuable campaign document for the approaching presidential election.

Most presidents since Jackson's time have, it should be emphasized, adhered to Jackson's view.[20] President James K. Polk, in the face of a series of congressional challenges to adopt a constitutional amendment to weaken the presidential veto or eliminate it entirely, devoted a major portion of his last annual message to a defense of the Jacksonian concept of the veto as an integral element in the checks and balance system. It might be noted, however, that President Lincoln, who exercised more extraconstitutional authority than any president in American history, followed the more restrictive Washingtonian–Jeffersonian view on the veto power.[21] Lincoln vetoed only six measures in his White House years. The two Whig presidents—Taylor and Fillmore—did not use the veto power at all. President Grover Cleveland, on the other hand, was the champion in the nineteenth century, compiling a record of 347 regular vetoes and 236 pocket vetoes for a grand total of 583 vetoes during his two separate terms in the White House. Many of Cleveland's vetoes, however, were imposed upon "private" pension bills. Even so, only two were overridden.

Most twentieth-century presidents, with the exception of Harding, have used the veto pen frequently, as Table 6.1 shows. Presidents Franklin D. Roosevelt (633), Truman (250), and Eisenhower (181) have accounted for almost half of the total number since 1789. They rank first, third, and fourth in the frequency of use of the presidential veto, with only Cleveland approaching or surpassing them.

While the rise in the use of the veto in the twentieth century can be partially accounted for by the greater amount of legislation reaching the president's desk, the chief explanation is to be found in the presidential attitude that the chief executive can use the veto as an effective legislative (and campaign) weapon, just as President Jackson did more than 150 years ago. It is worth noting that President Eisenhower, who has often been portrayed as having a more limited "Whig" view of executive authority than his two most immediate predecessors, had no qualms about using his veto to promote public policy he advocated—he vetoed 73 measures and pocket vetoed another 108 bills.

Since the president must send back a message accompanying the veto to Congress stating the reasons for his disapproval, this message can point the way (if the veto is sustained) for Congress to pass a new bill with the objectionable features altered or eliminated to win the president's approval. Sometimes the veto message produces legislation the president will accept. More frequently, however, presidents prefer to take a hard line in their veto messages, ruling out compromise, and in effect addressing their message to the country at large. By this type of bold action presidents aim to draw the line on some basic issue of public policy. Clearly, President Jackson's veto of the bank bill belonged in the category of "hard line" vetoes. President Truman's veto of the 1946 Price Control bill and the Taft-Hartley Labor Relations bill of 1947 would be classified in this category.

The president, however, does not always carry the day with his vetoes. Indeed, several major bills have been enacted over the president's objections: the Volstead (National Prohibition) Act of 1919, the Soldiers' Bonus Payment Act of 1931, the Taft-Hartley Labor Relations Act of 1947, the McCarran-Wood Internal Security Act of 1950, the McCarran-Walter Immigration-Naturalization Act of 1952, and the War Powers Act of 1973. President Andrew Johnson had the dubious distinction of having more vetoes overridden (15) than any other chief executive. During his stormy post-Civil War term, a series of acts dealing with Reconstruction in the South, the admission of Nebraska as a state, the president's removal power, and the size and jurisdiction of the Supreme Court were all enacted over his vetoes.[22]

Line Item Veto. Lack of a "line item" veto—the authority to reject individual sections of a bill—is an important limitation on the president's veto power. Unlike most state governors, who have this power in appropriations bills, the president must accept or reject an entire bill without modification. As a result, Congress sometimes tacks on "riders" (which may be only distantly related to the main subject of the bill) to legislation the president wants. Unless the chief executive wants "to throw the baby out with the bath water," he must sign the legislation despite his misgivings about what he considers to be obnoxious riders.

To counter the use of riders and to strengthen the hand of the president in fiscal matters, most presidents, including Reagan, have advocated that the president be granted a line item veto—that is, the power to strike out individual clauses or sections a president finds objectionable in a bill that has reached his desk. Advocates of the item veto or line item veto argue that it would help the president focus attention on items he considers wasteful or inappropriate, without holding hostage portions of an appropriation he approves. This authority, supporters insist, would tend to discourage inclusion of projects—pork barrel bills—that benefit only particular localities. Some advocates insist that such authority would also redress a hobbling of the president's fiscal powers that they say has occurred over the years. When our Constitution was written, bills generally covered only a single subject and were less complicated. Today spending bills cover dozens of subjects. Thus, according to some advocates, the item veto would restore to the president a constitutional prerogative.[23]

The item veto has achieved a degree of popular support greater than its record warrants in those states using it, as we will explain below. Interestingly, the idea for a line item veto in appropriations bills was first included in the temporary plan of government drawn up in 1861 for the Confederacy.[24] After the Civil War, it reappeared in the amended Georgia constitution, and it soon found favor in states across the land. In 1873, President Grant unsuccessfully urged submission of a constitutional amendment granting an item veto authority to the president. Since then, every president has urged Congress to adopt a constitutional amendment on the item veto, but the lawmakers have never responded positively. President Eisenhower, for example, repeatedly extolled the virtues of the line item veto, calling it "one of the most important corrections that could be made in our annual expenditure program, because it would save tax dollars."[25]

In 1983, nine bills proposing line-item vetoes were introduced by lawmakers as politically diverse as Senator Alan J. Dixon, a liberal Democrat of Illinois, and Representative Jack F. Kemp, a conservative Republican from upstate New York. None came close to passage.[26] Most senators and representatives consider the line item veto to be an unwarranted intrusion into congressional prerogatives. The lawmakers feel, understandably, that the veto would give the president the upper hand over Congress. Presidents and White House aides, for example, could easily use the item veto authority to control the votes of a member of Congress by holding hostage a federal project within a member's district or state in return for the member's support of another of the president's legislative proposals. "The line-item veto would be an abrogation of Congress' jurisdiction and power," declared Representative Silvo O. Conte, the ranking Republican on the House Appropriations Committee in late 1983. "We are three separate branches and ought to keep it that way."[27] Senator Charles McC. Mathias, Jr., Republican of Maryland, has echoed this view:

For example, if President Reagan does not like my position on the issue of school prayer, and if he acquires the power to kill funds for the program that I have long supported to save the Chesapeake Bay without affecting his Pentagon program or any other administration request, then the President, whoever he may be, has a hostage. He can hold the Chesapeake for the ransom of my support for a major change, for my support for State-sponsored school prayer in school, or any other subject that he might want my support on. And it would be a major change in the relationship between the executive and the legislative branches.[28]

President Reagan, in his 1984 State of the Union message, called for the adoption of a constitutional amendment granting the president the power of the item veto as a means of curbing Congressional spending. In asking for support for the amendment from Republican congressional leaders, Mr. Reagan has frequently been heard to say, "Give me the line-item veto up there. I can take the heat." James L. Sundquist, in his recent study of the line item veto, has concluded that "the advocates of the item veto would effect a considerable shift in power from the legislative to the executive branch, with ramifications felt in areas of executive-legislative relations far removed from budget policy."[29]

Even though the item veto is found in some form in 43 state constitutions, it is not a panacea. Many governors are reluctant to use it because it can backfire. The item veto, especially where it may be used to reduce as well as strike out appropriations for specific purposes, is an open invitation for legislators to pass appropriations in excess of projected revenues in the expectation that the governor will have to bear the onus of disallowing them. Also, state legislators have displayed considerable ingenuity in frustrating governors by manipulating the language of items in appropriations measures in such a way as to blend objectionable and unobjectionable funding into the same sentence. Former Senate Majority Leader Howard H. Baker, Jr., (R–Tenn.) undoubtedly had this legislative ingenuity in mind when he recently observed: "I really am afraid if we had line-item vetoes Congress would start sending [the President] appropriation bills with [just] one line."[30] As an alternative, Baker suggested that Congress consider strengthening the president's power to rescind or impound appropriations. (A decade ago Congress sharply curtailed the president's power to rescind or halt expenditure of appropriations after its impoundment battles with President Nixon.) Looking to the future, prospects for the passage of a constitutional amendment on the item veto are, most experts agree, not bright.

PRESIDENTIAL LEGISLATIVE STRATEGY

Most major legislation is enacted in the early part of the president's first term. Unless a president can capitalize quickly on his electoral mandate during the first legislative session, he is unlikely to prevail over the numerous competing special interests in Congress and the committee chair power structure. Lyndon Johnson, like his hero President Franklin D. Roosevelt, understood the need for quick action better than most chief executives. According to Harry McPherson, one of his closest aides, Johnson told his staff on the eve of his inauguration:

> You've got to give it all you can that first year. Doesn't matter what kind of a majority you come in with. You've got just one year when they treat you right and before they start worrying about themselves. The third year, you lose votes . . . the fourth year's all politics. You can't put anything through when half of Congress is thinking about how to beat you. So you've got one year.[31]

Successful presidents monitor their legislative agendas closely. Lyndon Johnson, despite his large electoral majority in 1964, was careful to send only one legislative message at a time to Capitol Hill. Instead of loading up congressional circuits, he wanted Congress to concentrate on one bill at a time. Once a bill passed both houses, Johnson served up another of his priority proposals. This strategy enabled Johnson to compile, within an 18-month period, a legislative record second only to that of Franklin D. Roosevelt.

By contrast, Jimmy Carter, anxious to "hit the ground running" in his first six months in office, sent an impressive collection of complex legislative proposals to Capitol Hill: a major tax cut package, a substantial budget revision, executive reorganization authority, election law reforms, a new Department of Energy, an anti-inflation package, food stamp policy revision, hospital cost containment, an ethics-in-government bill, social security reform, labor law reform, and welfare reform, not to mention a sweeping energy conservation plan.[32] Except for the energy plan, which Carter extolled on national television, there were no clear-cut presidential priorities—all seemed to be top-priority items. Many of these proposals were referred at practically the same time to the House Ways and Means Committee where, in Norman Ornstein's words, "a kind of 'gridlock' resulted." Several—including the widely publicized $50 individual tax rebate—were later withdrawn, abruptly and without advance notice, by President Carter. Paul C. Light critiqued the Carter performance as follows: "The lesson from the Carter administration is simple; presidents ought to target their scarce resources on a limited number of critical topics."[33]

Reagan, also determined to "hit the ground running," benefitted from Carter's early policy actions—and failures. Unlike Carter, Reagan and his staff decided to concentrate their attention on a short list of top priorities centering on the economy. As one of Reagan's top staff aides put it: "The president was determined not to clutter up the landscape with extraneous legislation."[34] From the start, Reagan focused his attention on two basic legislative initiatives: budget and tax reform. Two other issues—the AWACs sale (specially fitted jet aircraft with electronic surveillance equipment) to Saudi Arabia and the farm bill—were, in effect, forced on the administration. These four issues, along with a sharp military buildup, constituted the administration's entire agenda for Congress in 1981.

By focusing first on the budget cutbacks, then on tax cuts, then on the AWACs sale, and finally on the farm bill, the Reagan administration used its "honeymoon" period with Congress to great advantage to reach its goals: The budget and tax cut legislation passed before the Labor Day recess; the other legislative items before the Christmas holidays. With a combination of nonpartisan rhetoric, two nationally televised addresses to promote the tax and budget cuts, and a sophisticated grassroots campaign in districts of wavering congressmen aimed at generating pressure from campaign contributors and prominent citizens, the Reagan team obtained the most comprehensive cutback in federal government spending and tax cuts in half a century. Once again, sound legislative strategy and tactics paid off handsomely for a new president.

In commenting on presidential timing, Paul C. Light has observed: "Presidents are expected to recognize the moment of greatest impact; to hold the agenda like a poker hand, revealing the cards at the moment of maximum impact."[35] The importance of timing by the president has been colorfully described in the Southwest vernacular by Lyndon Baines Johnson:

> Congress is like a dangerous animal that you're trying to make work for you. You push a little bit and he may go just as you want but you push him too much and he may balk and turn on you. You've got to sense just how much he'll take and what kind of mood he's in every day. For if you don't have a feel for him, he's liable to turn around and go wild. And it all depends on your sense of timing.[36]

While presidents are expected to possess that sixth sense of timing in exerting legislative leadership, relatively few in the twentieth century have had it—Teddy Roosevelt, Wilson, FDR, Johnson, Reagan. And all these chief executives achieved most of their programmatic objectives in Congress during their first or second year in the White House. Why is the first year so important? Paul C. Light has put it well:

> The answer rests on the cycle of decreasing influence. Presidents and staffs are painfully aware that their most valuable resources dwindle over the term. They understand that the essential resource, capital, evaporates over time, that the first year offers the greatest opportunity for establishing the domestic program. Though information and expertise are rarely at a peak in the first year, capital does not keep, and Presidents must take advantage of whatever momentum they have; to wait is to squander the most important advantage.[37]

In recent years, the growth of congressional independence has heightened the pressure on executive leadership during the president's first year in office. Furthermore, the growing complexity of legislation on such matters as the environment, energy, social security financing, missile weaponry, communications, consumer protection, and medical care has meant that the president must strike quickly on his legislative program, for he will face delays enough in the labyrinth of the congressional committee apparatus as he seeks to move proposed legislation through both houses. Clearly, the longer a program must wait to be put in the legislative hopper, the greater potential for organized opposition. As one former Nixon aide reflected on one occasion: "We gave our opponents a great deal of time to fight the Family Assistance Plan. They had at least six months to prepare for the initial announcement. Then, because we were late, the program bogged down in committee. We gave them too many chances to hit us."[38]

WHITE HOUSE–CONGRESSIONAL LIAISON

Presidents, since Washington's first administration, have always maintained informal contacts with Congress. Washington dispatched Treasury Secretary Alexander Hamilton to consult with lawmakers. Jefferson met frequently with his congressional allies.

Woodrow Wilson, the first modern president to be an active lobbyist on Capitol Hill, was regularly found in the President's Room near the Senate chamber discussing legislative matters with members of Congress. Franklin D. Roosevelt often dispatched top-level aides such as Tom Corcoran and James Rowe to Capitol Hill to lobby for his New Deal measures. But it was not until the Truman administration in 1949 that any president established an office to maintain ties with Congress. Truman's Capitol Hill liaison unit consisted of two persons inexperienced in legislative politics. Since then, White House liaison with Congress had become far more formalized. President Eisenhower institutionalized the president's legislative role by establishing a formal structure to help carry out this responsibility—the White House congressional liaison office. Modeled after General George Marshall's liaison office during World War II, the office staff, working through congressional leadership, endeavored to explain the president's programs to the GOP-controlled Congress.[39] General Wilton B. Persons, an Eisenhower aide, was the first White House assistant formally assigned to Capitol Hill.

Lawrence (Larry) O'Brien, Special Assistant to the President for Congressional Affairs under John Kennedy and Lyndon Johnson from 1961 until late 1965, perfected the bridge-building activities first formalized by Persons. O'Brien and his staff spent half of their time prowling the corridors of the Capitol. O'Brien centralized the liaison activities of the agencies and departments. He required them to give Monday morning reports of the previous week's legislative lobbying and to make projections on the forthcoming week's activities. O'Brien's staff analyzed and condensed these reports on Monday afternoons and presented them to the president for review on Monday evenings. These reports provided agenda items for the Tuesday morning meetings between congressional leaders and the president.

Lobbying on Capitol Hill during the Carter administration was generally rated below average. First of all, Carter selected an untutored fellow Georgian to be his congressional liaison chief. Most of the other members of the Carter liaison staff also lacked a basic knowledge of the legislative process. Poor coordination between the White House staff and congressional leaders frequently led to a breakdown in communication. Among the early errors committed by the Carter administration was structuring the congressional liaison office along issue lines, instead of regional blocs in each chamber. As one observer noted: "Instead of having specialists for the Senate and for various blocs within the House, there would be specialists for energy issues, foreign policy issues, health issues, environmental issues and so on."[40] By the time this error had been corrected, precious time was lost, and because the general caliber of the Carter lobbyists on Capitol Hill was below average, President Carter's effectiveness with Congress remained low throughout his single term in the White House.

President Reagan's lobbying staff, on the other hand, received excellent grades from the start. Unlike President-elect Carter, whose problems with Congress began during the transition period, President-elect Reagan's transition period was smooth and efficient. Mr. Reagan appointed Max Friedersdorf, who managed the entire Capitol Hill operation for the Ford administration in 1975–76, to head the Reagan congressional office. During the transition Mr. Reagan took an active interest in building bridges with members of Congress and spent considerable time on Capitol Hill stroking Republicans and Democrats alike. In fact, one Reagan transition leader reported in an interview, "We had to lasso him to keep him off the Hill."[41]

Even before the inauguration, the White House congressional liaison staff began making visits to Capitol Hill, working closely with members of Congress. Phone calls from members of Congress were returned promptly, and all correspondence was to be acknowledged in short order. All these actions created a favorable climate for Reagan's program in Congress. President Reagan held bipartisan breakfasts at the White House, met with key Senate Republicans, and even invited Democratic Speaker Thomas P. (Tip) O'Neill, Jr., to two private dinners in the White House—a marked contrast to the treatment the Speaker had received at the beginning of the Carter presidency. (Carter had been panned in January 1977 for allegedly, according to Washington gossips, denying Speaker O'Neill tickets to the inauguration. Reagan gave the Democratic Speaker an ample supply—and let it be known to everyone in the Washington press corps.)

WINNING CONGRESSIONAL SUPPORT: INFORMAL METHODS

The formal legislative powers of the president reveal little about his real powers in securing passage of important legislation. The president does not command senators and members of Congress; he attempts to persuade them. In the words of former presidential advisor Richard Neustadt:

> The essence of a president's persuasive task with Congressmen and everybody else is to induce them to believe that what he wants of them is what their own appraisal of their own responsibilities requires them to do in their interest, not his.[42]

Presidents also rely on a number of other informal methods to achieve most of their legislative objectives.

Party Leadership. All strong presidents have depended upon their role as party leader to achieve most of their legislative goals. Early in our history Thomas Jefferson set the pattern of party leadership. While outwardly deferential to

Congress—Jefferson discontinued the practice of delivering the State of the Union address in person because he thought it too monarchical in nature—he nevertheless worked closely with party leaders to shape his programs. Party leaders were frequently invited to dinner at the White House to discuss legislative matters. During his years in the White House the foundations for party control of the House legislative machinery were built with the establishment of standing committees, and the emergence of the party caucus and the floor leadership post. With close ties to the party caucus and the committee chairs, Jefferson exerted a powerful influence on all legislative proposals.[43]

Other strong presidents have followed the Jeffersonian model. President Theodore Roosevelt, for example, held frequent evening meetings with Speaker Joe Cannon to work out agreements with the autocratic leader of the House of Representatives. President Wilson, a warm admirer of the British parliamentary system, preferred to meet with the chairmen of committees who were in charge of legislation he favored. His successors—especially Franklin D. Roosevelt, Truman, and Lyndon Johnson—have relied heavily on the Speaker of the House and the Senate majority leader to push their programs through Congress. Presidents Eisenhower, Nixon, and Ford (despite the fact that they faced a Congress dominated by the opposition party, except for the first two years of Eisenhower's first term) nevertheless were able, with the help of their minority leaders, to negotiate and achieve limited legislative programs.

In Eisenhower's case, Democratic Senate Majority Leader Lyndon Johnson and Democratic Speaker Sam Rayburn leaned over backward to cooperate with the popular retired field commander whose two-term presidency has earned increased respect in recent years from revisionist commentators.[44] President Reagan, though faced with split party control in Congress, was nevertheless able to use the Senate Republican majority to offset the Democratically controlled House and, by winning the support of almost two dozen southern boll weevil (conservative) Democrats in the House, succeeded in winning congressional approval of his favorite budget and tax cut proposals during his first year in office. (This Reagan success story is discussed further in Chapter 13.)

Since the emergence of the president as legislator in chief, however, no chief executive has assumed that members of his own party in Congress will automatically follow his leadership. Presidents must frequently court and persuade lawmakers, whose constituency interests may conflict with those of the president, to go along with him. Sometimes the president succeeds, sometimes not. President Kennedy, for example, found most of his legislative proposals stalled by conservative southern Democrats, especially in the House of Representatives, during his first two years in the White House. All the Kennedy charm could not transform these southern Democrats into New Frontiersmen, and it was not until Speaker Sam Rayburn won a crucial vote on the membership of the powerful House Rules Committee that the Kennedy legislative programs began to show movement—only to be cut short by the assassination of the young president.

Patronage and Personal Persuasion.   The president has additional tools to help achieve his legislative objectives. His appointment power is one of the most useful. Although the president's power of patronage is now limited by civil service regulations, several thousand presidential appointments—most of them high level and well-paid—can still be made with the view of currying favor among influential lawmakers and ultimately winning congressional approval.

Few presidents have matched Reagan's skill in using personal relationships with congressional leaders to win support for his proposals. During his first hundred days in office, for example, Reagan held 69 meetings with congressmen in which 467 members participated.[45] Unlike Carter, who did not understand the personal equation in winning congressional support for his legislative proposals, Reagan built up a reservoir of goodwill through his personal consultations to help him win bipartisan support for his tax and budget cuts as well as congressional backing for his huge military buildup.

Personal accessibility to congressional leaders of both parties is especially beneficial to a president if he is to be an effective leader. Despite the major constraints on their time, Presidents Kennedy, Johnson, Ford, and Reagan all maintained an "open presidency," even with members of the opposition party. While cordial personal relationships are no guarantee that the lawmakers will automatically rally around the president, presidential popularity helps keep the lines of communication open.

Presidents, knowing that some issues become so polarized that they almost defy a legislative solution, are always on the alert for a new approach to overcome congressional divisions or stalemates. One such approach is the presidentially appointed bipartisan study committee.

LEGISLATING BY BIPARTISAN PRESIDENTIAL COMMISSIONS

President Reagan, faced with Democratic-Republican congressional deadlock on several major issues, discovered that presidentially appointed bipartisan commissions are remarkably effective mechanisms for finding legislative solutions to some seemingly intractable problems.

Unlike Presidents Johnson and Nixon, who sometimes took issue with the findings of special presidential commission task forces they appointed, Reagan found the presidential commission to be one of his most effective legislative weapons. In 1982, for example, congressional Democrats and Republicans were at loggerheads over the means to be used to keep the social security system from becoming bankrupt (without direct appropriations) before the end of the twentieth century. Faced with the prospect of insolvency within 15 years (since benefit payments continued to be made in excess of contributions and anticipated income), Reagan appointed a bipartisan commission on social security headed by Alan Greenspan, former President Ford's chief economic adviser, to come up with an acceptable compromise approach.

To the surprise of many Capitol Hill watchers, Greenspan's task force put together, after considerable sparring among members, a package of recommendations acceptable to both Democratic and Republican lawmakers. The final version of the 1983 Social Security bill, as recommended by the bipartisan commission, moved through Congress with only a few minor hitches. President Reagan's ready acceptance of the bipartisan commission's major recommendations won him plaudits throughout the land. Reagan was far less concerned about examining the fine points of the problem than in helping to end a stalemate between himself and Congress. When the commission accomplished its goals, Mr. Reagan could proudly claim that he had resolved a politically charged issue.

Why have presidential commissions emerged as new legislative catalysts? According to one veteran Washington correspondent: "Commissions may . . . theoretically be viewed as the byproduct of a collective failure of political leadership in Washington. Fear of compromise or of losing political advantage seems to have robbed Congress and the President of the ability to act even when the problem is urgent."[46]

In any case, President Reagan and his top staffers have rediscovered historic uses of presidential commissions. First, a commission task force can be used to defuse the public clamor over an issue and give the president time to decide what to do about the problem. Second, the presidential commission's report can help shape or provoke public debate in a manner that builds political support for the president's own views. Thus, the report of the Reagan-appointed National Commission on Excellence in Teaching was used as a pretext for a highly publicized campaign to upgrade education without spending more money. Sometimes leaks from presidential commission reports help educate the public on a change of policy, or "signal in advance a behind-the-scenes compromise between an administration and its opponents in Congress."[47]

PUBLIC APPROVAL: A KEY LEGISLATIVE TOOL

Sooner or later, presidents recognize that the basis of their success is the amount of public support their policies generate. More than 125 years ago, Abraham Lincoln wisely observed: "Public sentiment is everything. With public sentiment nothing can fail, without it nothing can succeed."[48] More recently, presidential scholar Richard Neustadt concluded that presidents are rarely in a position to command others to comply with their wishes. Rather, they must rely on persuasion.[49] Public approval is the best source of the president's persuasive power. Emmet John Hughes, a former Eisenhower aide and authority on the White House, put it this way: "Beyond all the tricks of history and all quirks of Presidents, there would appear to be one unchallengeable truth: the dependence of presidential authority on popular support."[50] Lyndon Johnson, who experienced both highs and lows in his years in the White House, recounted in his memoirs: "Presidential popularity is a major source of strength in gaining cooperation from Congress."[51]

Former President Richard Nixon also believed that popularity polls affected the president's ability to lead the nation because members of Congress paid close attention to them.[52] Nixon, of course, was speaking from personal experience, for he discovered that even though he scored a landslide reelection victory in 1972 (winning 49 states and approximately 61 percent of the popular vote), his connection with the evolving Watergate scandal steadily eroded his public support. In December 1972, his overall approval stood at 62 percent. Twelve months later, his poll rating plummeted to 29 percent—a drop of 33 points. As public support dropped, so did his influence on Capitol Hill. Action on his legislative proposals, especially his plan to establish a "super cabinet," came to a virtual standstill after the October 1973 Saturday Massacre, in which Nixon fired Special Prosecutor Archibald Cox, the Watergate investigator.

Gerald Ford, who entered office on a high note of public approval, saw the bottom drop out of his approval ratings within a month of his swearing in when he unconditionally pardoned Nixon—a decision made less than ten days after the new president had publicly announced that he would make no decision on a pardon until the "legal processes" of the indictment and the trial had been completed.[53] Ford's approval rating dropped from 71 to 49 percent within a three-week period,[54] and he spent the rest of his term unsuccessfully trying to regain public approval. Insofar as Ford's legislative proposals were concerned, the remainder of his 17 months in the White House amounted to little more than a holding operation.

Reagan, flushed with his tax cut and budget reduction victories in the summer of 1981, soon learned the fickleness of public and congressional support. When he sought a second round of budget cuts a few months later, many of the Republican congressmen who had supported him during the honeymoon phase of his administration deserted him. Without their support, no second round budget cuts were possible. As a matter of fact, Reagan reluctantly signed a huge $95 billion tax increase (mainly to repair the federal interstate highway system) in late 1982.

Public approval alone, however, does not automatically translate into presidential influence on Capitol Hill. Without a majority of congressional seats—or at least a working majority across party lines—no amount of public approval or support in the last election will make an impact on Congress. As one Nixon assistant remarked about the lack of GOP congressional strength after Nixon's first presidential election victory in 1968:

> Any President's basic influence rests on his congressional strength—the actual votes in Congress. With only 190 Republicans in 1968 [218 votes are needed for a majority in the House], we were hamstrung. The President's electoral margin can give some extra juice. With only 44 percent of the vote in the 1968 election [third party candidate George Wallace collected 13 percent of the popular vote], we were in serious trouble. Finally, the President's public approval will help—that was one area where we were strong. But one out of three just wasn't enough.[55]

THE PRESIDENTIAL-CONGRESSIONAL BOX SCORE

Does the president's agenda-setting influence really determine the legislative outcome? Presidential effectiveness as the initiator of legislation since the turn of the century has varied from period to period. One study made in the 1940s showed that Congress had exhibited more leadership in policy making than had the president. In a detailed study of 90 major laws in ten categories spanning the period 1890 to 1940, Lawrence Chamberlain concluded:

The President could be given credit for approximately 20 percent, the Congress for about 40 percent; 30 percent were the products of both the President and Congress, and less than 10 percent of external pressure groups.[56]

During the New Deal era, the legislative ball was clearly in President Roosevelt's court. By the 1950s and 1960s many commentators simply concluded that the president had become the legislator in chief, setting the legislative agenda for Congress. But Moe and Teel, in a study similar to Chamberlain's for the period 1940–1967, found a high level of congressional participation in such areas as the economy, transportation, agriculture, urban policy, and technology. Since 1945, Moe and Teel point out, Congress passed three major acts to deal with technological breakthroughs in atomic energy, space technology, and satellite communications. In all three cases, Congress was an equal or dominant partner in the establishment of new agencies.[57] Similarly, in 1958 Congress reacted quickly to the Soviet-launched Sputnik by passing legislation to establish an organization to conduct a national program in space—the National Aeronautics and Space Act. As Moe and Teel comment: "Congress continues to be an active innovator and very much in the legislative business."[58]

Despite the important contributions of Congress in incubating new programs, presidents often receive the lion's share of the credit. James Sundquist, among others, has pointed out that President Lyndon Johnson's Great Society programs, supposedly initiated in the White House, were frequently remodeled proposals developed by liberal Democratic lawmakers (especially Senators Joe Clark of Pennsylvania and Hubert H. Humphrey of Minnesota and members of the Democratic Study Group in the House) during the Eisenhower years.[59] The truth of the matter is that it is often difficult—indeed almost impossible—to assign exact credit for initiation of a measure.

For several decades the *Congressional Quarterly* research service sought to determine how much legislation the president proposed ultimately became law (see Table 6.2). The record for the period 1954 to 1975 shows that the president never got all he asked for, but presidential accomplishments are fairly substantial —approximately 45 percent, on the average. Presidents also have different success rates, ranging from Johnson's 69 percent in 1965 and Eisenhower's 65 percent in 1954 on the high side and Kennedy's 27 percent in 1963 and Nixon's 20 percent in 1971 on the low side. Clearly, presidents score much higher when their party controls Congress by heavy majorities. Between 1965 and 1967, for example, the Democrats held more than 2 to 1 margins in each chamber.

Presidential batting averages have also been calculated separately for different policy areas. Aaron Wildavsky developed a two presidencies thesis in the 1960s, contending that presidents have been far more successful in foreign policy and defense matters than in domestic policy.[60] Wildavsky attributed the president's high success rate in defense and foreign policy issues to the emergence of a large number of Third World nations, the existence of nuclear weapons, and the threat of global destruction and the Cold War.

In developing this theory about the two presidencies, Wildavsky relied chiefly on the *Congressional Quarterly* Service's "presidential boxscore," an an-

Table 6.2   PRESIDENTIAL BOX SCORE ON PROPOSALS SUBMITTED TO CONGRESS, 1954–1975

Year	No. submitted	No. approved	Percent approved
1954	232	150	65%
1955	207	96	46
1956	225	103	46
1957	206	76	37
1958	234	110	47
1959	228	93	41
1960	183	56	31
1961	355	172	48
1962	298	132	44
1963	401	109	27
1964	217	125	58
1965	469	323	69
1966	371	207	56
1967	431	205	48
1968	414	231	56
1969	171	55	32
1970	210	97	46
1971	202	40	20
1972	116	51	44
1973	183	57	31
1974 (Nixon)	97	33	34
1974 (Ford)	64	23	36
1975	156	45	29

Source: From *Presidential Influence in Congress* by George C. Edwards III. W. H. Freeman Company. Copyright © 1980, 14.

nual compilation of congressional actions on presidential proposals. According to the data collected for the period 1948–1964, Congress passed 73.3 percent of the president's defense policy proposals, supported 58.5 percent of his foreign policy proposals, and backed 70.8 percent of what he requested concerning "treaties, general foreign relations, the State Department, and foreign aid." Over the same 17-year period, however, Congress supported only 40.2 percent of the president's domestic policy proposals.

In another essay published almost a decade later, Wildavsky reaffirmed the main thesis of his now classic essay, although he did express some second thoughts about some aspects of his thesis.[61] But since Wildavsky first expounded his two presidencies theory, two presidents, both elected in landslides, have been driven from office; a third, elevated to the presidency, failed in an election bid; and a fourth has lost the presidency after a single term. How valid is the two presidencies concept in light of developments since the mid-1960s—the Vietnam war, Watergate, and a congressional resurgence typified by passage of the War Powers Resolution, the Case Act (requiring publication of executive agreements), and the Budget Control and Impoundment Act of 1974?

More recently, LeLoup and Shull found that this difference between foreign and domestic policy had narrowed. For the decade 1965–1975, presidents were successful about 55.5 percent of the time in foreign and defense policy, and their success rate on domestic issues rose to 46 percent of the time.[62] Success rates vary too in different domestic policy areas. LeLoup and Shull found, for example, that between 1953 and 1975 approximately 50 percent of social welfare proposals were approved, compared with 35 percent for natural resources and 26 percent for civil rights. However, Professor Lee Sigelman has concluded that the batting average scores compiled by Wildavsky and LeLoup-Shull are skewed because they do not differentiate between major and minor proposals.[63] Thus, President Nixon did not advocate 67 major foreign and domestic proposals and 116 major domestic items, but the presidential box score figures were based on all 183 proposals.

To clarify this question, Sigelman, in a study of key votes (see Table 6.3), found that between 1957 and 1972 the president's batting average on domestic policy rose to 73 percent; between 1973 and 1978, the president's success rate was 56 percent.[64] (On foreign policy and defense issues, the president's success in all three studies was similar.) Sigelman's findings, as Table 6.3 shows, reveal a significant decline in the president's success rate on domestic proposals for the

Table 6.3 PRESIDENTIAL VICTORIES ON KEY VOTES, 1957–1978

President	Years	Domestic issues N	% Victories		Foreign and defense issues N	% Victories	
Eisenhower	1957–60	51	.608		17	.824	
Kennedy	1961–63	47	.702		16	.688	
				.732			.736
Johnson	1964–66	95	.853		17	.647	
Nixon	1969–72	46	.652		18	.778	
Nixon	1973–74	20	.500		7	.429	
Ford	1974–76	27	.593	.565	13	.385	.600
Carter	1977–78	22	.591		10	1.000	
President's party only							
Eisenhower	1957–60	51	.863		17	.882	
Kennedy	1961–63	47	.830		16	.983	
				.879			.853
Johnson	1964–68	95	.926		17	.824	
Nixon	1969–72	46	.848		18	.833	
Nixon	1973–74	20	.950		7	1.000	
Ford	1974–76	27	.852	.884	13	.692	.767
Carter	1977–78	22	.864		10	.700	
Opposition party only							
Eisenhower	1957–60	51	.412		17	.588	
Kennedy	1961–63	47	.128		16	.250	
				.293			.382
Johnson	1964–68	95	.337		17	.412	
Nixon	1969–72	46	.239		18	.278	
Nixon	1973–74	20	.300		7	.000	
Ford	1974–76	27	.185	.217	13	.154	.167
Carter	1977–78	22	.182		10	.300	

Source: Lee Sigelman, "A Reassessment of the Two Presidencies Thesis," *Journal of Politics,* 41 (November 1979), 1201.

1973–1978 period, compared with the earlier 1957–1972 period. Moreover, the difference in presidential success rates for foreign and domestic policies for these two time periods narrowed.

Indeed, in Sigelman's words: ". . . there has been only a slight differential in congressional support on domestic as opposed to foreign and defense issues."[65] Since 1957, Sigelman found that "all presidents, Republican and Democrat alike, have been treated quite well on key votes by members of their own party in Congress."[66] On domestic issues presidents have averaged better than 88 percent support; on foreign and domestic issues, presidential party support has been similar, though it declined somewhat for Presidents Ford and Carter.

The real change in the level of support for the president has occurred, according to Sigelman, in the opposition party. There has been a dramatic erosion of support of presidents among opposition members in Congress since 1973, especially in foreign policy positions. Sigelman found that the opposition party supported the president only 21.7 percent of the time on domestic policy and only 16.7 percent of the time on foreign and defense issues. Sigelman's data also show that "whereas between 1957 and 1972 the opposition party was more supportive of the President in foreign policy and defense than in domestic policy, opposition support for the President's foreign and defense position has now dwindled to a point even lower than support for his domestic position."[67] Overall, Sigelman concludes: "In direct opposition to the two presidencies thesis, in votes on key issues since 1957 most presidents have not enjoyed a freer hand in the foreign and defense arenas than in domestic policy-making."

TOWARD A NEW LEGISLATIVE POWER BALANCE

Future legislation, it seems safe to predict, will continue to bear the strong imprint of both president and Congress—to be shared legislation. While the president can focus national attention on his legislative initiatives, he cannot hope to enjoy many triumphs unless he can carry Congress along with him. For example, President Carter's inability to win congressional approval of his energy conservation measures, even though Democrats controlled both houses, is a case in point.

Congress will continue to enjoy co-equal status in domestic legislative matters, even though the president dominates the public forums, because its recently enlarged professional staff, especially the Congressional Budget Office, the Office of Technology and its corps of computer analysts, technicians, and scientists, now provide invaluable information and expertise.[68] As a result of this improved staffing, the lawmakers are in a position to understand the potential impact of the president's proposals and meet the president's spokesmen head-to-head on virtually all controversial issues. No longer will the lawmakers have to rely exclusively on the president's facts and figures and thus operate at a severe disadvantage at congressional hearings. With the growth in institutional resources, especially computer staff, Congress has become more competitive in challenging presidential initiatives and substituting its own version of bills before they reach the floor of each chamber.

Clearly, the Budget and Impoundment Control Act of 1974, the War

Powers Resolution, and the growth of congressional oversight all signal congressional determination to exercise a greater share of political power. Indeed, it seems highly doubtful that the executive branch will ever again be accorded the special open-arms treatment that Franklin D. Roosevelt's New Deal measures or Lyndon B. Johnson's Great Society proposals received on Capitol Hill.

In recent years Congress has also frequently imposed statutory constraints on the president's domestic discretion. Between 1973 and 1979 there was a threefold increase in the number of bills containing some form of the legislative veto.[69] (The legislative veto permitted one or both houses to veto or rescind a specific piece of legislation, if it found that the president failed to carry out the legislative intent of Congress.) But in 1983 the Supreme Court declared the legislative veto invalid in *Chadha* v. *Immigration and Naturalization Service.*[70] Justice Byron R. White, in a dissent, said that the Supreme Court's decision overturning the legislative veto "strikes in one fell swoop provisions in more laws enacted by Congress than the Court has cumulatively invalidated in its history."[71] Justice Department lawyers gloated over their judicial victory in protecting executive prerogative in *Chadha,* but Louis Fisher of the Congressional Research Service reported that 30 new legislative veto provisions were included in laws enacted the first year after *Chadha.*[72] In light of these actions, one veteran Washington observer, James L. Sundquist, has concluded: "Congress can continue to enact legislative vetoes, in the full knowledge that they are unconstitutional but in the equally full expectation they will be adhered to anyway."[73] At this point, however, it is still too early to pass judgment on the long-term effects of the *Chadha* decision on executive-congressional relations.

While presidents seek to capitalize on their party leadership role to win approval of their legislative programs, they frequently discover that the power structure in Congress, especially in the House, is so fragmented that only by a prodigious effort can the president hope to get even part of his legislative programs approved. Stable political coalitions have, for the most part, disappeared; a new coalition usually has to be constructed for each new major legislative proposal.

Surprisingly, even though numerous obstacles face a president as he attempts to win support for his programs, the executive and legislative branches manage to achieve a notable level of accommodation on proposed legislation.

Despite occasional confrontations between president and Congress over proposed foreign initiatives and domestic legislation, collaboration on a co-equal basis has generally characterized executive-legislative relations since the Watergate era—at least until a major deadlock developed in 1985 between President Reagan and the Democratic-controlled House of Representatives over a deficit reduction package and domestic spending programs.

As one presidential scholar has noted: "Mechanisms that require collaboration, yet permit each branch to innovate and initiate proposals autonomously, seem far more in tune with established constitutional principles of separation of powers and checks and balances than do proposals that invite the legislature to subordinate itself to the president, give up its constitutional responsibilities, and become a handmaiden of the executive branch."[74] Undoubtedly the president will continue to occupy the center of the political stage, but Congress will also play a leading role in the legislative process, not that of an understudy or bit player.

NOTES

1. Hedrick Smith, "Taking Charge of Congress," *The New York Times Magazine,* August 9, 1981, 16.
2. *The Federalist,* No. 73.
3. Randall B. Ripley, *Congress: Process and Policy,* 3rd ed. (New York: Norton, 1983), 28–31.
4. Roger H. Davidson and Walter J. Oleszek, *Congress and Its Members* (Washington, DC: Congressional Quarterly Press, 1981), 429.
5. Ibid., 435.
6. James L. Sundquist, "Congress and the President: Enemies or Partners?" in Lawrence C. Dodd and Bruce I. Openheimer, eds., *Congress Reconsidered* (New York: Praeger, 1977), 223.
7. *The Federalist,* No. 46.
8. Davidson and Oleszek, *Congress and Its Members,* 302.
9. George C. Edwards and Stephen J. Wayne, *Presidential Leadership* (New York: St. Martin's Press, 1985), 323; Davidson and Oleszek, *Congress and Its Members,* especially Chapters 6 and 7.
10. Davidson and Oleszek, *Congress and Its Members,* 435–436.
11. As cited in Paul Light, *The President's Agenda: Domestic Policy Choice from Kennedy to Carter* (Baltimore: Johns Hopkins University Press, 1982), 211.
12. Lyndon B. Johnson, *The Vantage Point* (New York: Holt, Rinehart, and Winston, 1971), 441 and 443.
13. Woodrow Wilson, *Constitutional Government in the United States* (New York: Columbia University Press, 1908), 68.
14. Joseph E. Kallenbach, *The American Chief Executive* (New York: Harper & Row, 1966), 340.
15. Richard E. Neustadt, "Presidency and Legislation: Planning the President's Program," *American Political Science Review,* 49 (December 1955), 1015.
16. The Employment Act of 1946, which created the Council of Economic Advisers, states that the council's job is "to assist and advise" the president in preparing his economic report, to gather "timely and authoritative information, to appraise the various programs of the federal government, and develop and recommend national economic policies to the President." The council, it might be noted, is not subordinate to any other agency. The act placed the council in the Executive Office of the President, and its chairman reports directly to the president. However, in practice to get the ear of the president, he usually has to go through members of the White House staff.
17. James L. Sundquist, *Constitutional Reform and Effective Government* (Washington, DC: The Brookings Institution, 1986), 208.
18. Woodrow Wilson, *Congressional Government* (Boston: Houghton Mifflin, 1885), 52.
19. The president's veto power is, in simple arithmetic, the equivalent to one-sixth of the votes in Congress (three-sixths plus one equals a simple majority, but four-sixths or two-thirds is required to override). For an excellent discussion of the veto power, see Louis Fisher, *Constitutional Conflicts Between Congress and the President* (Princeton, NJ: Princeton University Press, 1985), 140–183.
20. Kallenbach, *The American Chief Executive,* 354.
21. John G. Nicolay and John Hay, *Complete Works of Abraham Lincoln* (New York: F.

D. Tandy Company, 12 vols., 1905), Vol. I, 697, as quoted by Kallenbach, 355, note 13.

22. Kallenbach, *The American Chief Executive,* 350.

23. Richard A. Watson and Norman C. Thomas, *The Politics of the Presidency* (New York: Wiley, 1983), 258.

24. Kallenbach, *The American Chief Executive,* 364.

25. *Congressional Record,* 87th Congress, 1st Session, p. 9184.

26. The Senate, for example, shelved the Dixon proposals by a vote of 53 to 25, *The New York Times,* January 4, 1984. Also, the Republican-controlled Senate in 1973 rejected two variations of a line-item veto. One bill would have required the president to stay within a quarterly debt limit by, if necessary, holding back on the spending of funds Congress had appropriated. This proposal for impounding funds was defeated 49 to 46. Another bill would have required the president to propose reductions of up to 2.5 percent in the discretionary spending programs in the current budget. The Senate turned down this proposal by a vote of 65 to 35. Ibid.

27. *The New York Times,* January 4, 1984. For a summary of the major arguments against the line item veto, see Fisher, *Constitutional Conflicts Between Congress and the President,* 154–162, Sundquist, *Constitutional Reform and Effective Government,* 209–215.

28. James L. Sundquist, *Constitutional Reform and Effective Government,* p. 213. In early 1985, Senator Mack Mattingly (R–GA.) introduced a watered-down version of the line item veto. Responding to President Reagan's request and with one eye toward his own reelection campaign in 1986, Senator Mattingly drafted his plan in statute form, instead of a proposed constitutional amendment. He chose this route because a constitutional amendment requires a two-thirds vote, and he admitted that he lacked that degree of support. Moreover, the Mattingly plan would be put into effect only for a two-year trial experiment. The Georgia lawmaker said this was done to answer the criticism that a constitutional amendment was too drastic and permanent a step. In late July 1985, the Mattingly plan was dropped from further consideration after a bipartisan group of primarily liberal lawmakers filibustered the bill, and Senate by a 57 to 42 vote refused for the third time in a week to invoke closure to halt debate. *The New York Times,* July 25, 1985.

29. Sundquist, *Constitutional Reform and Effective Government,* p. 212.

30. *Washington Post,* January 31, 1984.

31. Harry McPherson, *A Political Education* (Boston: Little Brown, 1972), 268.

32. Norman J. Ornstein, "Assessing Reagan's First Year," in Norman J. Ornstein, ed., *President and Congress* (Washington, DC: American Enterprise Institute, 1982), 94.

33. Light, *The President's Agenda: Domestic Policy Choice from Kennedy to Carter,* 231.

34. Max Friedersdorf, as cited by Stephen J. Wayne, "Congressional Liaison in the Reagan White House: A Preliminary Assessment of the First Year," in Ornstein, *President and Congress,* 56.

35. Light, *The President's Agenda,* 40.

36. Doris Kearns, *Lyndon Johnson and the American Dream* (New York: Harper & Row, 1976), 227.

37. Light, *The President's Agenda,* 41–42.

38. Ibid., 43.

39. Wayne, "Congressional Liaison in the Reagan White House: A Preliminary Assessment of the First Year," 45.

40. Eric L. Davis, "Legislative Liaison in the Carter Administration," *Political Science Quarterly,* 95 (March 1979), 289.

41. Wayne, "Congressional Liaison in the Reagan White House," 50.

42. Richard Neustadt, *Presidential Power* (New York: Wiley, 1960), 53.
43. Kallenbach, *The American Chief Executive,* 289.
44. See Fred Greenstein, *The Hidden Hand Presidency* (New York: Basic Books, 1982).
45. Lou Cannon, *Reagan* (New York: Putnam Publishing Group, 1982), 333.
46. Steven R. Weisman, *The New York Times,* January 16, 1984.
47. Hedrick Smith, *The New York Times,* January 11, 1984.
48. As quoted in George C. Edwards III, *The Public Presidency* (New York: St. Martin's Press, 1983), 1.
49. Neustadt, *Presidential Power.*
50. Emmet John Hughes, *The Living Presidency* (Baltimore: Penguin, 1974), 68, as cited by Edwards, *The Public Presidency,* 1.
51. Johnson, *The Vantage Point,* 443.
52. Richard M. Nixon, *RN: The Memoirs of Richard Nixon* (New York: Grosset and Dunlap, 1977), 753.
53. James W. Davis and Delbert Ringquist, *The President and Congress: Toward a New Power Balance* (Woodbury, NY: Barron's Educational Series, 1975), 170.
54. *The New York Times,* September 12, 1974. Mr. Ford was the first president since the founding of the Gallup organization in 1935 who failed to retain majority support of those polled during his first month in the White House.
55. Light, *The President's Agenda,* 31.
56. See Lawrence Chamberlain, *The President, Congress and Legislation* (New York: Columbia University Press, 1946).
57. Ronald C. Moe and Steven C. Teel, "Congress as Policy-Maker: A Necessary Reappraisal," in Ronald C. Moe, ed., *Congress and the President* (Pacific Palisades, CA: Goodyear, 1971), 34.
58. Moe and Teel, "Congress as Policy-Maker: A Necessary Reappraisal," *Political Science Quarterly* 85 (September 1970), 468.
59. James Sundquist, *Politics and Policy* (Washington, DC: The Brookings Institution, 1968), 471–505.
60. Aaron Wildavsky, "The Two Presidencies," *Trans-Action,* IV (December 1966), 7.
61. Aaron Wildavsky, "The Presidency in the Political System," in Aaron Wildavsky, ed. *Perspectives on the Presidency* (Boston: Little Brown, 1975), 17.
62. Lance LeLoup and Steven A. Shull, "Congress Versus the Executive: The 'Two Presidencies' Reconsidered," *Social Science Quarterly,* 59 (March 1979), 704–719.
63. Lee Sigelman, "A Reassessment of the Two Presidencies Thesis," *Journal of Politics,* 41 (November 1979), 1195–1205.
64. Ibid., 1201.
65. Ibid., 1202.
66. Ibid.
67. Ibid., 1203.
68. As recently as 1965, the total staff for the nineteen standing committees in the House was slightly over 5,000 and for the fifteen standing committees in the Senate, only 3,218. This small, totally outnumbered Capitol Hill staff had to face on uneven terms the tremendous firepower of the executive branch, which could draw upon hundreds of analysts and specialists from various departments and agencies to focus on specific legislative problems. *Congressional Quarterly Weekly Report,* November 24, 1979, 2638.
69. Sundquist, *Constitutional Reform and Effective Government,* 216–217.
70. 103 U. S. 2764.
71. Ibid.

72. Louis Fisher, "One Year After *INS v. Chadha:* Congressional and Judicial Development" (Congressional Research Service, Library of Congress, June 23, 1984), as cited by Sundquist, *Constitutional Reform and Effective Government,* 221–222.

73. Sundquist, *Constitutional Reform and Effective Government,* 221; see also Stephen Labaton, "Wrong Again, Supreme Court: Congress' Veto Power Is Flourishing Despite the Justices' 1983 Ruling and Prediction of Doom," *The Washington Post National Weekly Edition,* August 19, 1985, 10; Joseph Cooper, "The Legislative Veto in the 1980s," in Lawrence C. Dodd and Bruce I. Oppenheimer, eds., *Congress Reconsidered,* 3rd ed. (Washington, D.C.: Congressional Quarterly Press, 1985), 364–389.

74. Pious, *The American Presidency* (New York: Basic Books, 1979), 175.

chapter 7

Commander in Chief

More than 40 million Americans, mostly in the eastern and central time zones, had settled down in their homes on a mid-April 1986 evening to enjoy their favorite evening entertainment—television watching—when regular network scheduling was suddenly interrupted by the appearance of President Ronald Reagan. The commander in chief of the United States armed forces, who had held a nationally televised press conference only five days earlier, obviously had a serious message to relay to the American people:

> My fellow Americans. At 7 o'clock this evening Eastern time, air and naval forces of the United States launched a series of strikes against the headquarters, terrorist facilities and military assets that support Moammar Khadafy's subversive activities. The attacks were concentrated and carefully targeted to minimize casualties among the Libyan people with whom we have no quarrel. From initial reports, our forces have succeeded in their mission. . . .[1]

Clearly, the president of the United States had decided to take stern countermeasures against the Libyan leader, Moammar Khadafy. This action once again underscored the decisive importance that the president's constitutional role as commander in chief has had in our system of government over the past two centuries. Indeed, if the Founding Fathers were to return to earth briefly to review their work on the U.S. Constitution, it seems unlikely that they would be displeased with the military authority they had invested in the nation's chief executive.

INTRODUCTION

Though the men of 1787 devoted more time and energy to drafting Article II on the presidency than any other section of the Constitution, their decision to associate the function of commander in chief of the nation's military forces with the office of president was reached with minimal controversy. Reflecting in depth on their experience during the War for Independence, the Framers revamped the post of commander in chief of the Continental Armies that George Washington had occupied during the Revolutionary War, made it permanent, and added to it a number of civil functions. The statement that the president shall be commander in chief of the nation's armed forces is unique among the clauses delineating the powers and duties of the president in that it confers an *office,* rather than merely a function, upon the chief executive. Special significance has been attached to this clause by one constitutional authority who has stated: "The implication is that whatever powers and duties are necessarily associated with the exercise of supreme military command belong to the president by constitutional prescription and cannot be constitutionally diminished or controlled by statute."[2]

Except for the executive power clause, no part of Article II has been more broadly interpreted and shaped by presidential actions than the commander in chief clause. Indeed, ever since the Civil War, when President Lincoln cited the commander in chief clause as the constitutional source of his authority to undertake a broad range of acts far beyond purely military matters, the commander in chief clause has been stretched repeatedly by other strong presidents to such a point that the Founding Fathers might not recognize their original craftsmanship.

In this chapter we examine the president's duties as commander in chief— one of the Constitution's least defined roles. Members of Congress can point to the specific language in the Constitution for their authority to declare war and appropriate funds for the armed forces, but the Framers clouded the legal sources of the president's authority. Because the president can order troops abroad to counter aggression, the commander in chief can, as we take note, undertake military action before Congress can meet to act on any war declaration or measures short of war. Thus, the lawmakers may face a presidential *fait accompli.* Indeed, as the chapter shows, the history of the past two centuries has often seen the executive and legislative branches attempting to reconcile two fundamental powers: war declaring by Congress and warmaking by the president. The Framers intended that the two activities would operate in tandem, but more often than not the president has taken action unilaterally and only later turned to Congress for financial and retroactive approval.

Our discussion will show that since World War II (1941–1945) the constitutional position of the commander in chief has been strengthened by the creation of a massive, permanent military establishment and the ratification of a network of European and Asian mutual security treaties—pacts that call upon the United States to protect smaller, friendly nations throughout the free world from outside attack. Our discussion then turns to the "High Noon" confrontation between president and Congress over the bombing of Cambodia in 1973 that led finally to the passage of the War Powers Act limiting unilateral presidential warmaking actions. However, since this legislation has been on the books, the act has been only marginally effective in curbing presidential military actions. We conclude with the observation that the uneasy tension that has frequently characterized relations between president and Congress will probably continue indefinitely. This should be no surprise, for the Founding Fathers wanted the best of both worlds—a forceful commander in chief to repel sudden attack against the country and a strong-willed Congress determined to keep the president within constitutional limits.

Even a cursory reading of the Constitution will reveal how defense and security-minded the Framers were.[3] Indeed, there are numerous references to military affairs and warmaking in the nation's charter. Approximately half the clauses in Article I, Section 8, listing the delegated powers of Congress are concerned with military matters and the conduct of war. But the Framers deliberately chose generalities over specifics in drafting the president's duties.

INTENT OF THE FRAMERS

Does the president as commander in chief have the final authority to commit U.S. troops abroad? Does this authority rest with Congress? Is this power shared? To try and answer these questions we must first turn to the Founding Fathers at the Philadelphia convention for their interpretation and understanding of the warmaking power. Then we must review our military history and presidential actions over the past two centuries for further clarification. Even then, the answers will most likely be inconclusive. The men of 1787, however, had no doubt in their minds over which branch of the government should exercise the war power—it should reside in the legislative branch. For evidence we turn to James Madison, whose reports of the proceedings are still our best source:

> The Constitution supposes what the History of all Govts. demonstrates that the Ex is the branch of power most interested in war and most prone to it. It has accordingly with studied care vested the question in the Legist.[4]

This action of placing supreme authority over the military in the hands of the chief civilian official was of course clearly in accord with the development of English constitutional history.

The Founders did, however, qualify this grant of power during the constitutional convention. The first draft of the new fundamental document stated that Congress would have the power to "make war." A later draft was changed to read "declare war," in recognition of the need for an immediate response to a sudden attack on the United States.[5] Clearly, the Founders understood that the president would be in a much better position to take immediate action; indeed, they expected him to repel sudden attacks without seeking prior approval of Congress. Beyond doubt, the men of 1787 recognized that the command of the military is an executive function. Further, they knew that the military must be centralized and capable of secrecy and swift action.

Aware that a president might become a military despot, yet conscious of the need for immediate action in case of national emergency, the Framers decided to divide the power of the United States to wage war between the legislative and executive branches. First of all, the authority to decide if and when the country would go to war was granted to Congress. But Article II of the Constitution states: "The President shall be commander in chief of the United States and of the militia of the several States, when called into actual service of the United States." Though the Framers had the same goal in mind—the means of making war—when they drafted the two separate sections of the Constitution, they could not foresee how the two branches might someday hold widely divergent views in interpreting their constitutional authority. Indeed, the content of the commander in chief clause has been shaped and expanded, far more than the Framers could have envisaged, by strong-minded presidents. And as one recent observer has commented: "The war powers issue has been complicated by the need for snap decisions created by nuclear weapons, by the increase in civil conflicts worldwide, by the growing popularity of 'peacekeeping' operations, and by the Orwellian euphemisms of modern politics, 'preemptive strike,' 'incursion,' 'cross-border operation.' "[6]

Although the Constitution states that the president is to act as the commander in chief of the armed forces, it seems reasonably clear that the Founders did not intend this role to confer special authority upon him to wage war. As Alexander Hamilton commented in the *Federalist* papers: "It would amount to nothing more than the supreme command and direction of the military and naval forces, as first general and admiral of the Confederacy."[7] In other words, the president was to be commander in chief of the armed forces once the nation was committed to battle, but the decision on whether or not to make war was to reside solely with Congress.

PRESIDENTS AND THEIR COMMANDER IN CHIEF RESPONSIBILITIES

Early presidents adhered scrupulously to the constitutional mandate that Congress should make the final decision on war or peace. When George Washington, for example, announced that the United States would remain neutral in the renewed war between Great Britain and France, some critics argued that his action, in effect, prevented Congress from exercising its prerogative to side with France in the conflict and to declare war against Great Britain. After some hesitation, Washington agreed, stating: "it rested with the wisdom of Congress to correct, improve, or enforce the neutrality."[8] Members of Congress, however, subsequently concurred with Washington's view that the country would be better served by maintaining a neutral posture between the two warring European powers. During John Adams's administration, however, the United States became involved in a limited maritime war with France.

Thomas Jefferson deferred to congressional prerogative after an American schooner was attacked by pirates from the Barbary States of North Africa. Despite the fact that the American warship disabled an enemy ship and captured its crew, Jefferson ordered the American commander to release the vessel and crew because the president believed that the commander "was unauthorized by the Constitution, without the sanction of Congress, to go beyond the line of defense." Subsequently, Jefferson asked Congress if it would authorize measures to permit American vessels to take action against ships from the Barbary States. Hamilton, among others, felt that Jefferson may have bent over backward to acknowledge the right of Congress to declare war.

In another instance, however, Jefferson was less concerned about observing the letter of the Constitution. In 1807, after Congress had recessed, a British ship fired on an American vessel, the *Chesapeake.* Jefferson quickly ordered military supplies for the emergency. He did not report his actions until Congress reconvened. His message was directly to the point: "To have awaited a previous and second sanction by law," he wrote, "would have lost occasions which might not be retrieved."[9] While observance of the written law is a high duty of a public official, Jefferson insisted that it was not the highest. Self-preservation and national security rated higher.

Monroe was far less cautious than Jefferson in repelling outside aggressors. In 1817, when Seminole Indians conducted raiding parties against American settlers in Georgia, he ordered General Andrew Jackson to drive them back into Spanish Florida. Jackson wasted little time in carrying out this presidential order. Unlike Jefferson, Monroe issued his orders to send American troops into foreign territory without consulting Congress. This action, known as the doctrine of hot pursuit, was subsequently invoked by several twentieth-century presidents—Wilson, Truman, and Nixon—to justify military actions in Mexico, Korea, and Laos. Surprisingly, Andrew Jackson acted much more cautiously as president. While in the White House, Jackson ordered an American naval vessel to South America to protect American ships there from Argentine raiders without first consulting with Congress, but he nevertheless promptly went before Congress and asked for "authority and means to protect our fellow citizens fishing and trading in these seas."[10]

In this early case and in several twentieth-century incidents, Congress exhibited little hesitancy in allowing presidents to commit American forces in dangerous situations that could lead to armed hostilities, provided that the protection of American lives and property was the justification. This course of action, as we know, came to be abused by several recent White House incumbents.

NUCLEAR WEAPONS

Toward the end of World War II, the commander in chief's military responsibilities suddenly took a quantum jump with the development of the atomic bomb. President Truman was the first chief executive to assume the awesome responsibility of deciding when, if ever, to use the vast destructive power of this new weapon.

Only the president, it should be emphasized, can give the order to launch nuclear weapons. This has been done only once in history—near the end of World War II when Truman ordered atomic bombs dropped on Hiroshima and Nagasaki, Japan. Later presidents have threatened to use nuclear weapons.

Shortly after taking office, Eisenhower threatened Communist China with a nuclear attack unless it supported a truce in the Korean conflict.[11] During the Cuban missile crisis in 1962, Kennedy, to demonstrate to the Soviet Union that the United States would not tolerate the placement of offensive missiles in Cuba, put the Strategic Air Command and its Air Force missile crews on maximum alert. During the 1973 Middle Eastern War, when there were signs that the Soviet Union might intervene to rescue entrapped Egyptian army units, Nixon approved an order to put U.S. armed forces—including the North American Air Defense Command (custodians of the nuclear arsenal)—on a general standby alert.

With the arrival of the nuclear age, presidents faced two momentous concerns. First, they wanted to avoid the possibility of an "accidental" nuclear war, triggered by false alarms—that is, erroneous reports of enemy missiles racing toward the United States, or malfunctioning computers at the defense command. Second, presidents wanted at all costs to prevent some hotheaded or mentally unstable field commander from giving an order to launch a nuclear attack against the Soviet Union, without clearance directly from the president of the United States. "I don't want some young Colonel to decide when to drop an atomic bomb," President Truman was known to have said on more than one occasion.[12]

To be sure, nuclear technology has advanced light years beyond the year 1945 when the first two atomic bombs were dropped from B-29 bombers. Intercontinental ballistic missiles can now deliver these frightful weapons in a fraction of the time the World War II delivery systems required. Nonetheless, the final decision to push the nuclear button still rests squarely on the president's shoulders. Fortunately, numerous fail-safe mechanisms to prevent an accidental nuclear war have been developed since World War II. Indeed, elaborate codes and instantaneous communication circuitry have been established between the president, the secretary of defense, the Joint Chiefs of Staff, and the North American Air Defense Command to provide for instant consultative decision making. The system also contains checks upon a president who, for reasons known only to himself, might decide to mount a preventive nuclear war singlehandedly. Still, all these intricate arrangements are subject to human error and failings—both on our side and that of the Soviet Union.

Since World War II, eight presidents—four Democrats and four Republicans—have had it within their power to order the nuclear strikes that could well lead to all-out nuclear war and the end of Western civilization. All eight, to their everlasting credit, have measured up to their responsibilities as commander in chief without resorting to nuclear weaponry.

DEFENDER OF THE FREE WORLD

Since the Korean war (1950–1953), the United States has also maintained at least 2.4 million men and women on active duty. United States forces are stationed in Western Europe, Japan, South Korea, the Philippines, and smaller jointly operated naval and air bases are maintained in at least three dozen countries around the world. The U.S. Navy's aircraft carrier task forces and nuclear submarines are available for immediate deployment, wherever the president directs them.

Special surveillance aircraft (AWACs) can be sent to the Middle East or else-where overnight, if the president deems it necessary to monitor the actions of unfriendly powers.

With the decline and virtual disappearance of the British empire and the end of French, Dutch, and Italian and Portuguese colonial territories in the post-World War II era, the responsibility for the security of noncommunist nations fell largely upon the United States. Ratification of the North Atlantic Treaty Organization (NATO) in 1949, which committed the United States to the defense of Western Europe and Canada, was followed by the signing of a series of regional and bilateral treaties pledging the United States to meet common external threats side by side with its treaty partners. Thus, the ANZAC Pact (1951) linking Australia, New Zealand, and the United States declared that "an armed attack in the Pacific area or any of the parties would be dangerous to its own peace and security," and each party promised to act "to meet the common danger in accordance with its constitutional processes." Bilateral treaties between the United States and the Philippines (1951), South Korea (1953), and Japan (1960) contained similar language and the same type of commitment to meet external aggression.

In reviewing these pacts—treaties, executive agreements, and congressional resolutions—the reader will search in vain for a definitive interpretation of the "constitutional processes" under which this country is to fulfill its military com-mitments. But in any action requiring military force it is the president as com-mander in chief who possesses the sole power of decision and execution.

CHECKS ON THE PRESIDENT

What, if any, are the limits of the war power of the commander in chief? Four decades ago, the late historian, Charles A. Beard, commented that "the war powers of the President are in fact so great and so indefinite that their nature will not be fully known until our Republic has passed through all its trials and ceased to be. The President's war power is the unexplored and dark continent of Ameri-can Government."[13] While this statement is somewhat wide of the mark, the constitutional definition of the president's warmaking power did not receive a specific interpretation until Congress passed the War Powers Resolution of 1973. More will be said about this legislation later in the chapter.

Other constitutional and extraconstitutional checks on the president as commander in chief also exist. The Constitution, for example, requires that the commander in chief must ask Congress for military appropriations every two years. Congress, if it wishes, has the authority to cut off or eliminate military appropriations. The lawmakers, however, have always been extremely reluctant to use the power of the purse whenever American troops abroad have been involved in hostilities. Also, investigative power, for example, the Pearl Harbor attack hearings and the U.S. Senate's Truman investigating committee on exces-sive war profiteering during World War II, made it patently clear that President Roosevelt's conduct of the war would not escape congressional monitoring and oversight.

In rare instances, the Supreme Court may be a check on the president. But in the historic Civil War case of *Ex parte Milligan* (1866),[14] which involved President Lincoln's suspension of the writ of habeas corpus, the Supreme Court did not rule against the president until a year after the end of the conflict and more than a year after Lincoln's assassination. During the Korean war the Supreme Court invalidated President Truman's action of taking over the steel industry to avert a nationwide strike. The power of public opinion to curb presidential warmaking when the country has become heavily involved in an unpopular conflict abroad should not be underestimated, as the American experience in Vietnam so vividly demonstrated less than two decades ago.

Looking back in history, the wisdom of the Founding Fathers was never more evident than in their decision to place supreme authority over the military in the hands of the chief civilian officer of the nation. But should this much authority be vested in the hands of one official in a democracy? The late Clinton Rossiter, one of the nation's most astute presidential watchers, offered a perceptive response to this question with another query: "We have placed a shocking amount of military power in the President's keeping, but where else, we may ask, could it possibly have been placed?"[15]

MILITARY ACTION ABROAD SINCE 1776

Protecting American citizens and property abroad has been an important function of the president as commander in chief since the beginning of the Republic. Between 1798 and 1945, the United States, according to one authority, was involved in 149 separate military incidents.[16] Between 1945 and 1975, according to another source, the United States was involved in another 215 military incidents, police actions, or "shows of force," including two threats of nuclear action, with other countries.[17] In all these confrontations the president as commander in chief has been the chief decision maker, sending warnings to potential aggressors, deploying troops, or dispatching naval vessels to troubled areas. Members of Congress simply acknowledged that hostilities existed.

Congress, on the other hand, has authorized declarations of war only five times in our history—1812, 1846, 1898, 1917, and 1941. To be sure, in the more than 200 cases that the president has committed the armed forces abroad, most have been minor incidents. Still, in 93 cases hostilities have lasted more than 30 days, even though the president did not ask for a declaration of war.[18] Since passage of the War Powers Resolution in 1973, the president has used the armed forces to undertake a variety of military actions abroad on nearly a dozen separate occasions.

Since the founding of our nation, the constitutional prerogative of the president to serve as commander in chief has never been an empty title in times of crisis. President John Adams, faced with imminent war against France in 1798, recalled George Washington to service, appointing him lieutenant general and commander in chief of the army being raised. During the Civil War President Lincoln picked one commander after another for the Army of the Potomac and not until he fortunately discovered General U. S. Grant did he settle on a general in chief of the Union armies. Earlier in 1862, Lincoln personally issued an order to General George McClellan to make a general advance against Richmond—but the cautious McClellan dithered until he missed a priceless opportunity to deliver a decisive blow against the Confederacy.

Once the United States entered World War I, President Wilson decided, as commander in chief, against merging American armed forces in France with those of the Allies on the Western Front. Instead, Wilson maintained an independent American command. A generation later, President Roosevelt, in his grand strategy meetings with Churchill and Stalin, agreed to pursue the war against Hitler to a successful conclusion before mounting the final all-out attack against Japan. When Vice-President Truman succeeded to the presidency in April 1945, one of his first actions was to order the dropping of atomic bombs on Hiroshima and Nagasaki. With the first eye-blinding blast, the world moved suddenly into the nuclear age, and the commander in chief's military responsibilities became even more awesome.

PRESIDENTIAL WARMAKING

President James K. Polk, one of our lesser known presidents, was the first White House occupant seriously to undermine the warmaking authority of Congress. Determined to add Texas to the Union, Polk ordered General Zachary Taylor to proceed across the Nueces River into disputed territory and station his forces there—an obvious provocation to Mexico, which regarded all of Texas as its own territory. Mexico, however, showed remarkable restraint and declined to challenge the American action. Polk, thwarted by the Mexican government's coolheadedness, then decided to goad the Mexicans further. In January 1846, he instructed General Taylor to move to the banks of the Rio Grande.

Within a matter of days, the Mexicans attacked the American troops, whose presence they viewed as an invasion of their territory. The wily Polk, given the pretext he needed, immediately asked Congress to recognize that a state of war now existed between the United States and Mexico. For the first time, an American president had precipitated a military incident and presented Congress with a *fait accompli* that made war virtually unavoidable. Thus, even though Congress had exclusive power to declare war, Polk had maneuvered events so that Congress had little choice but to go along with the president and declare war against the Mexicans. Several members of Congress, including a young Whig Congressman from Illinois, Abraham Lincoln, challenged the constitutionality of Polk's actions.[19] Two years later, the House voted to censure Polk; the Senate, apparently satisfied with the fruits of a victorious war, declined to support this move.

The outbreak of the Civil War in 1861 erased forever this narrow interpretation of the president's power as commander in chief. In the words of the leading authority on the presidency: "The sudden emergence of the 'Commander in Chief' clause as one of the most highly charged provisions of the Constitution occurred almost overnight in consequence of Lincoln's wedding it to the clause that makes it the duty of the President 'to take care that the laws be faithfully executed.'"[20]

In his resolve to save the Union, Lincoln cited the commander in chief clause as the constitutional source of his authority to undertake numerous actions going far beyond purely military matters. Lincoln held the firm belief that the commander in chief clause underlay the war power and authorized the president to prosecute the war against the secessionists with minimal congressional oversight. In his post as commander in chief, he carried out measures that would have been shockingly unconstitutional in peacetime.

Following the outbreak of hostilities, Lincoln ordered a naval blockade of the Confederacy—without calling Congress into session. Lincoln's authority to impose a blockade was ultimately challenged in the federal courts in a series of suits known as the Prize Cases.[21] The litigants argued that the naval blockade constituted an act of war under international law and because Congress had not declared war, the president had no right to impose a blockade. But the Supreme Court upheld Lincoln's action, ruling that an "invasion or insurrection created a state of war as legal fact." Consequently, the president did not have to wait for Congress to declare war before taking action against the southern states.

Lincoln, it might be noted, never claimed that the authority to take the nation into a war was a prerogative of the president. His sole justification, he repeatedly maintained, was that the very survival of the nation was at stake; hence he had no choice. To be sure, most of these acts were retroactively approved by Congress, but this assertion of presidential prerogative put an indelible imprint upon the commander in chief role that has made it, in the minds of many constitutional lawyers, the most powerful section of the Constitution.

The warmaking power of Congress suffered further erosion at the turn of the twentieth century when President William McKinley, often considered a weak president by some critics, ordered 5,000 American soldiers to China to help other Western powers put down the Boxer Rebellion, directed against foreign nationals. To justify his actions, McKinley insisted that he was sending troops merely to protect American lives and property, even though his motives were apparently more political than military. McKinley did not see fit to ask Congress for authority, and congressional leaders raised no objection to the dispatch of troops to foreign territory. Significantly, the Boxer Rebellion marked the first time that an American president unilaterally committed troops to combat against another country outside the Western Hemisphere.

Lincoln's virtually unlimited use of his power as commander in chief in the Civil War also became the prototype for presidential actions in World War I and II. President Woodrow Wilson, unlike Lincoln who acted boldly on his own initiative, called upon Congress soon after the United States declared war against Germany in 1917 to grant him broad authority to wage total war. Congress quickly obliged by delegating vast powers to the president to mobilize the nation's resources for an all-out war against the Central Powers. The Lever Food and Fuel Act of 1917, for example, authorized the president as commander in chief to regulate by license the importation, manufacture, storage, mining, or distribution of essential items; the power to requisition foods, fuels, and feeds; the power to purchase, store, and sell certain foods; the power to take over factories, packing houses, pipelines, mines, and other plants, and operate them; the power to fix the minimum price for wheat; the power to limit, regulate, or prohibit the use of food materials in the production of alcoholic beverages; the power to fix the price of coal and coke and to regulate their production, sale, and distribution.[22]

By quickly passing the Selective Service Act, Congress vested President Wilson with the authority to raise an army by conscription. The Trading with the Enemy Act gave him power to license trade with the enemy and his allies and to censor all communications by mail, cable, radio, or otherwise. Other statutes empowered the president to take over and operate the rail and water transportation systems of the country, to take over and operate the telegraph and telephone systems, and to redistribute functions among the executive agencies of the national government.[23] Nor did President Wilson ignore his own constitutional prerogatives as commander in chief. His formation of the Committee on Public Information, the War Industries Board, and a War Labor Board all rested exclusively on this power.

Because the United States involvement in World War I lasted slightly more than 18 months (April 1917–November 1918), and the armistice came before the American war machine had reached high gear, the full impact of total war and Wilson's role as commander in chief was not felt by many Americans. In assessing Wilson's role as commander in chief, World War I served, as Edward S. Corwin has commented, as a "prologue and rehearsal" for World War II.[24]

EROSION OF CONGRESSIONAL WARMAKING POWER

Congressional warmaking power was further undermined during the crisis-ridden presidency of Franklin D. Roosevelt. Before America's entry into World War II, Roosevelt engaged in several naval actions of doubtful constitutionality as he sought to aid the Allied Powers in Europe.[25] In early September 1941, for example, Roosevelt ordered American naval forces in the Atlantic to "shoot at sight" any Nazi submarines interfering with American vessels convoying military supplies to a beleaguered Great Britain. At no time did the president seek prior authorization from Congress to undertake these provocative, unfriendly actions, though some isolationist members of Congress complained vociferously that FDR was leading the country into war.

Six months before Pearl Harbor, FDR proclaimed an "unlimited national emergency" and with this edict cloaked a variety of forceful actions under his commander in chief authority. On June 7, 1941, for example, Roosevelt issued an executive order seizing the North American aviation plant in Inglewood, California, where P-51 Mustang fighter planes were being produced, because a strike had halted production. Two other strike-bound plants were also taken over under presidential orders before Pearl Harbor, and four other strike-bound concerns were put under federal control after America's entry into World War II by virtue of authority from the commander in chief. Two years later, Congress authorized presidential seizures of strike-bound manufacturing and production facilities and banned wartime strikes by passing the Smith-Connally Act of 1943.[26]

To maintain the most effective mobilization of the nation's work force,

Roosevelt issued an executive order in December 1942 transferring the Selective Service system to the War Manpower Commission and thereby vesting this agency with complete control over the manpower of the country not yet enrolled in the armed services. Although Roosevelt, acting as commander in chief, never imposed a labor draft, the War Manpower Commission by late 1943 controlled 85 percent of the work force of the country. Through a system of employment ceilings and priority labor referrals, workers were shifted to labor-short plants, unless they preferred to enlist in the military. When labor disputes threatened to interrupt production as the United States approached final victory, Roosevelt directed the seizure of many of the nation's industries.

According to one source, "The total number of facilities taken over is significant: two railroad systems, one public utility, nine industrial companies, the transportation system of two cities, . . . In addition, thereto the President on April 10 [1945] seized 218 bituminous coal mines belonging to 162 companies and on May 7, thirty-three more bituminous mines of twenty-four additional companies. The anthracite coal industry fared no better; on May 3 and May 7, all the mines of 365 companies and operators were taken away from the owners and on October 6 [nearly two months after the end of the war] President Truman ordered the seizure of fifty-four plants and pipelines of twenty-nine petroleum companies."[27] Once again, all these actions were undertaken under the president's authority as commander in chief.

Rationing was imposed to conserve adequate petroleum and rubber tires for the military forces in World War II, especially since all rubber supplies from Southeast Asia were cut off by the Japanese armed forces. When one offender challenged the penalties levied for his violation of rationing rules because they were imposed by the presidentially established Office of Price Administration (OPA) rather than Congress, the Supreme Court refused to overrule the Federal District Court's decision upholding the penalties.[28]

Are there limits to the president's power as commander in chief in wartime? Undoubtedly there are, but the reader will search in vain to find them among the Supreme Court's decisions handed down while a war is in progress. And not until passage of the War Powers Act of 1973 had Congress ever adopted "any legislation that would seriously cramp the style of a President attempting to break the resistance of an enemy or seeking to assure the safety of the national forces."[29] However, during World War II the president and Congress were on a collision course over price controls at one point when President Roosevelt sent a message on September 7, 1942, requesting repeal of a certain provision of the Emergency Price Control Act, which he said threatened "economic chaos." The president indicated that if Congress failed to take action by the first of October, he himself would act, under his powers, "to take measures necessary to avert a disaster which would interfere with the winning of the war." In the words of the foremost authority on the presidency: "Mr. Roosevelt was proposing to set aside, not a particular clause of the Constitution, but its most fundamental characteristic, its division of powers between Congress and the President, and thereby to gather into his own hands the combined power of both. He was suggesting, if not threatening, a virtually complete suspension of the Constitution."[30] The impending collision, it can be reported, was averted when Congress made the satisfactory change in the statute.

THE COMMANDER IN CHIEF'S SORRIEST CHAPTER

One of the most unfortunate episodes involving the president's authority as commander in chief, however, occurred in World War II when more than 100,000 persons of Japanese ancestry (mostly American citizens) were forcibly evacuated from the West Coast in early 1942. The deep-seated animosity toward Orientals in the Far West, coupled with the post-Pearl Harbor jitters that the Japanese might try landing troops on the West Coast, built up heavy public pressure to take action against all persons of Japanese descent, whether citizens or not, in California, Oregon, and Washington.

In response to this public clamor, President Roosevelt two months later issued an executive order in his capacity as commander in chief empowering the secretary of war to designate military areas from which any and all inhabitants might be excluded in order to prevent espionage and sabotage. As a result of this order, all persons of Japanese ancestry, U.S. citizens and aliens alike, were quickly uprooted from their homes in the three West Coast states and a part of Arizona and herded into relocation centers, described by some critics as American-style concentration camps. Congress, less than a month later, gave its approval to this regrettable action by ratifying legislation confirming the executive order. For the moment, the aftershock of the Pearl Harbor attack and subsequent loss of the Philippines and most of Southeast Asia to the Japanese invaders overshadowed the inevitable constitutional tests of these draconian measures that ultimately reached the Supreme Court.

First and foremost was the central question: Does the president, acting in his capacity as commander in chief, have the authority summarily to remove American citizens and aliens lawfully resident in the United States from their homes, their jobs, their property—sometimes with only forty-eight hours notice —to detention centers in the name of military necessity? As a result of the usual delays in getting the Supreme Court to rule on a highly charged issue, the tribunal did not hand down a decision on the first case, *Hirabayashi* v. *United States,* [31] until June 1943—more than 18 months after Pearl Harbor. Furthermore, the circumstances of the case afforded the justices the opportunity to avoid ruling for a time on the most emotionally charged issue—the forced evacuation of the Japanese-Americans and aliens.

The Supreme Court ingeniously narrowed the issue to the special curfew order and avoided ruling on the evacuation for another 18 months. In the *Hirabayashi* case, the Supreme Court held that it was not unreasonable for military officials charged with national defense to believe that the Japanese residents constituted a special danger to national security, since many of them resided near military bases. The Court ruled unanimously that "in time of war residents having ethnic affiliations with an invading enemy may be a greater source of danger than those of a different ancestry."

In the second case, *Korematsu* v. *United States,*[32] the Supreme Court repeated the tactics of delaying the decision and paring down the issue—from an order for detention in a particular area to one of exclusion from another. Decided in December 1944, three years after Pearl Harbor and with the tide of battle shifting heavily in favor of the United States and its allies, the Court concluded on a divided vote that the evacuation program was constitutional. The majority opinion followed the reasoning of its earlier decision, holding that the military order was not unjustified and that the Japanese residents of the coastal area constituted a potentially grave danger to the public safety, a danger so great that there was no time to establish procedures for determining the loyalty or disloyalty of each Japanese inhabitant. (The justices completely ignored the fact that thousands of German and Italian enemy aliens throughout the country had already been investigated on a case by case basis, and the potentially dangerous persons had been put under detention.) Rather than challenge a military order issued in the name of the commander in chief, the Court deferred to the president and gave its imprimatur to a forced evacuation policy that was described in 1947 by President Truman's Commission on Civil Rights as "the most striking mass interference since slavery with the right of physical freedom."[33]

Another Japanese-American case, *Ex Parte Endo,*[34] decided the same day as *Korematsu,* helped the Court recoup part of its reputation as the defender of individual liberties. In this companion case, the Supreme Court upheld the right of a Japanese-American girl, Mitsuye Endo, whose loyalty to the United States had been established beyond any doubt, to a writ of habeas corpus freeing her from the Tule Lake War Relocation Camp in northern California. President Roosevelt and his military officers did not question the Court's ruling. Significantly, the weekend before the Endo ruling, and apparently in anticipation of the Court's decision, the Department of the Army ordered the release of all loyal Japanese-Americans from the relocation centers.[35]

For the record, no evidence was ever uncovered to prove that a single Japanese-American citizen had engaged in acts of sabotage, espionage, or other treasonable activity on the West Coast during the entire course of World War II. In retrospect, the Court's performance in the *Hirabayashi* and *Korematsu* cases suggests that the tribunal is unlikely to blow the whistle on the commander in chief in the midst of an all-out war, even when the basic rights of American citizens are trampled.

PRESIDENTIAL WARMAKING AUTHORITY AFTER WORLD WAR II

Roosevelt's bold actions as commander in chief before America's entry into World War II established a precedent that his successor, Harry S Truman, found easy to follow. United States intervention in the Korean conflict and Vietnam civil war raised a host of new questions about the breadth of the president's powers as commander in chief.

The skirmishing between president and Congress over the president's authority to send American troops abroad without congressional consent actually began in 1948, when President Truman claimed the power to send troops to Palestine as part of a United Nations peacekeeping force. Although no troops were actually dispatched to the Middle East, the issue became a burning question in June 1950 when North Korean troops invaded South Korea. To counter this Soviet-inspired attack, President Truman decided suddenly on June 25, 1950, to send U.S. troops to Korea to repel the invaders.

Truman, it might be noted, issued his order to American commanders to come to the aid of the South Korean government even before the South Korean government had requested any military assistance. Further, Truman decided to aid South Korea even though the United States was not bound by any mutual defense treaty to come to its aid. Truman's actions seemed even more forceful, considering that only six months earlier the American Secretary of State, Dean Acheson, in a public statement did not even include South Korea among those countries on the Pacific Rim that were regarded as vital to our national security.[36] Although the United Nations General Assembly did pass a resolution recommending that armed force be used to repel the North Korean attack, the resolution was passed the day *after* Truman issued his military order.

Significantly, for the first time in American history a president of the United States was asserting that his duties as commander in chief gave him sufficient constitutional authority, without consulting Congress, to take the country into a major war against another foreign state thousands of miles from American shores. Senate critics, led by Senator Robert A. Taft (son of former President William Howard Taft), argued that the president "had simply usurped authority in violation of the laws and the Constitution, when he sent troops to Korea to carry out the resolution of the United Nations in an undeclared war."[37] Taft questioned Truman's authority to commit troops on foreign soil without congressional authorization. But he and his small band of critics were vastly outnumbered by lawmakers who supported the president's actions.

Nor did Truman feel it was necessary to secure congressional approval to send additional American troops to Europe to bolster NATO's defenses. In early 1951 he told members of a press conference that "under the President's constitutional powers as Commander-in-Chief of the Armed Forces" he had the authority to send troops anywhere in the world and that this power had been "repeatedly recognized by Congress and the Courts," and that his administration would "continue to send troops wherever it is necessary to uphold" its obligations to the United Nations.

The so-called great debate of 1951 concerning presidential versus congressional control over the dispatch of troops abroad ended inconclusively. A "sense of the Senate" resolution approved Truman's sending four divisions to Western Europe, but the lawmakers said that no additional troops should be sent "without further congressional approval." Interestingly, Senator Richard M. Nixon of California was among the majority voting against inherent presidential authority and for the principle of congressional control of troop deployment.[38]

President Eisenhower, after a long career as a military officer, nevertheless viewed his authority as more limited than did his predecessor. On several occasions he showed hesitancy in requesting congressional approval for committing

American troops to combat. But he asked and received joint resolutions from Congress authorizing him to use armed forces in defense of Formosa (Taiwan) and the Pescadores Islands in 1955 and to repel a possible Communist takeover in Lebanon in 1958. To illustrate how low Congress's concern over the warmaking power had fallen during this period, leading members of the Senate and House denied that Eisenhower even needed to seek congressional authorization for his actions. Senate Democratic Majority Leader Lyndon B. Johnson, for example, stated: "We are not going to take responsibility out of the hands of the constitutional leader and try to arrogate it to ourselves."[39]

President Kennedy, despite his brief tenure in the White House, faced the gravest crises of any president in the post-World War II era when he learned in the summer of 1962 that the Soviet Union was in the process of installing offensive missile bases in Castro's Cuba. Despite repeated Soviet denials that missile base construction was under way, U.S. Air Force reconnaissance photos showed that the missile bases were nearing completion. With this evidence in hand and after several days of consultations with his advisers, President Kennedy ordered American naval vessels to set up a blockade—the more euphemistic term quarantine was used—around the Caribbean island to prevent Soviet vessels laden with missile warheads from reaching Cuba.

Though Kennedy's action could have led to a nuclear confrontation, he gave the order without any advice or consent from Congress. In this instance, the need for a swift response and the utmost secrecy in planning this decisive move dictated that the president act with both dispatch and surprise. To have consulted Congress prior to this action might well have led to a crucial delay and denied the Soviets the opportunity for a face-saving withdrawal of their vessels from the scene. Congressional leaders subsequently agreed, but some legislators complained that Kennedy had not acted forcefully enough to meet the Soviet challenge!

Clearly, in this nuclear age the scales have tipped heavily in the president's direction whenever the United States has faced military threats from abroad. Indeed, critics of presidential warmaking concede that the declaration of war is in most instances an outmoded method of resolving disputes between sovereign states. If this is true and if most of the formidable questions of war or peace in this country quickly find their way to the Oval Office, the more recent warmaking activities of the president deserve even closer scrutiny.

THE VIETNAM QUAGMIRE

Further expansion of presidential prerogative power occurred within a year after President Johnson moved into the White House. The Tonkin Gulf Resolution, rushed through Congress in August 1964 at Johnson's request (after alleged attacks on American destroyers off the coast of North Vietnam), opened the door to further aggrandizement of the president's powers as commander in chief. Approved in the House unanimously and with only two dissenting votes in the Senate, the resolution stated: "Congress approves and supports the determination of the President, as Commander-in-Chief, to take all necessary measures to repel any armed attack against the forces of the United States and to prevent further aggression."[40]

In his haste to win approval of the Tonkin Gulf Resolution, Johnson may not have been entirely truthful in dealing with Congress. The full story of the president's deception, however, unfolded slowly. In 1968, the Senate Foreign Relations Committee hearings, conducted by Senator J. William Fulbright (D–Ark.), reached the following conclusions: (1) That President Johnson failed to mention that the two American destroyers fired upon the North Vietnam P.T. boats were, in fact, on a snooper mission to obtain electronic intelligence on radar stations along the North Vietnamese coast; (2) that the *U. S. S. Maddox* was between 8 and 9 miles from the coast, well within the 12-mile limit claimed by North Vietnam as its territorial waters; (3) that a South Vietnamese naval operation near the North Vietnamese coast was taking place at the same time; (4) that American naval vessels had been deployed in the Gulf of Tonkin to reinforce the *Maddox* prior to the incident, indicating that the U.S. Navy officers expected that the North Vietnamese might respond with force.[41]

Johnson originally presented a case to congressional leaders in August 1964 that the North Vietnamese had engaged in unprovoked aggression against U.S. naval forces. According to President Johnson, the U.S. vessels were in international waters, 65 miles from the coast, when five North Vietnamese P.T. boats approached in a threatening manner. The *Maddox* fired warning shots, then fired directly at the fast-moving boats. The North Vietnamese fired torpedoes, which the *Maddox* evaded. Subsequently, planes from a U.S. aircraft carrier damaged two of the P.T. boats. The following day U.S. planes attacked the North Vietnamese P.T. boat base, destroying or damaging at least 25 boats and the petroleum storage facilities.

After hurried, closed-door hearings in the Senate Foreign Relations and Armed Services committees and the House Foreign Affairs Committee and nine hours of debate in Congress, the members voted overwhelmingly in August 1964 to support the president. The Tonkin Gulf Resolution, however, did not distinguish between powers the president already possessed and any newly delegated authority.

Did Congress delegate *its* warmaking authority to the president, or was it acknowledging *his* preexisting authority to do whatever he found necessary? Another section of the Tonkin Gulf Resolution stated that the United States government was "prepared, as the President determines, to take all necessary steps, including the use of armed force, to assist any member or protocol state of the Southeast Asia Collective Defense Treaty requesting assistance in defense of its freedom." President Johnson, however, insisted that he did not need the Tonkin Gulf Resolution to justify his action in Vietnam, since he already possessed this authority as commander in chief. Instead, he argued that the resolution merely placed Congress on record in support of his actions as commander in chief.

As Arthur M. Schlesinger, Jr., has commented: "The role of Congress under the Johnson theory of the war-making power was not to sanction but to support the war—a role that nearly all of Congress, except for the indomitable

Senator [Wayne] Morse and Senator [Ernest] Gruening, accepted until 1966, and that most accepted for a long time afterward."[42] Significantly, the federal judiciary refused to intervene when President Johnson relied on his authority as commander in chief to justify sending additional troops to Vietnam.

Lyndon Johnson's interpretation of his role as commander in chief and the dispatch of over 500,000 American troops to South Vietnam, without formal authorization from Congress, eventually produced a strong backlash throughout the country. Although Congress did not pass a resolution limiting the president's authority in South Vietnam until 1973, more than four years after Johnson left office (and indeed not until after he had died), the legislation halted blank-check warmaking authority grants from Congress. This legislation signaled the end of congressional patience and reflected the ultimate disillusion over America's tragic involvement in the Southeast Asian war. In retrospect, many lawmakers felt that they had been tricked by Johnson into passing the 1964 Gulf of Tonkin Resolution authorizing the president "to take all necessary measures to repel any armed attack against the forces of the United States and to prevent further aggression." In any event, Johnson later indicated that he sought congressional approval of his actions for political, not constitutional, reasons.[43]

Johnson insisted that sufficient precedents set by previous presidents existed for him to take action in South Vietnam. Further, he claimed that any president had the right to repel a sudden attack. The Johnson administration's view was that in this modern age of jet aircraft and instant communication, the security of the United States could be endangered by military action thousands of miles from our coastlines. Under this open-ended doctrine, the president could order our armed forces into combat anywhere and anytime that he believed the security of the United States to be threatened. Arthur Schlesinger, Jr., a leading student of the presidency, has observed: "Under this theory it is hard to see why any future President would ever see any legal need to go to Congress before leading the nation into war."[44]

If the Johnson theory of the presidency continued to expand the powers of the president as commander in chief, Nixon's concept of exclusive presidential authority to carry on the Vietnam war pushed it to new highs. By 1970, the Nixon administration had disowned the Tonkin Gulf Resolution.[45] Henceforth, in the words of Schlesinger, "The claim of exclusive presidential authority now rested squarely on the powers of the Commander-in-Chief, especially his power to do whatever he thought necessary to protect American troops."[46] "I shall meet my responsibility as Commander-in-Chief of our Armed Forces," Nixon said in his announcement of the invasion of Cambodia in 1970, "to take the action necessary to defend the security of our American men."

To justify his failure to consult with Congress before he ordered the invasion of Cambodia in 1970, Nixon commented afterwards:

I trust we don't have another situation like Cambodia, but I do know that in the modern world there are times when the Commander-in-Chief . . . will have to act quickly. I can assure the American people that the President is going to bend over backward to consult the Senate and consult the House whenever he feels that it can be done without jeopardizing the lives of American men. But when it is a question of the lives of American men or the attitudes of people in the Senate, I am coming down hard on the side of defending the lives of American men.[47]

According to *The New York Times,* Nixon did not even ask the State Department lawyers to prepare the legal case for the invasion of Cambodia until four days after it began.[48]

As the Vietnam war continued on with no end in sight, Congress became increasingly restless. Despite claims by Presidents Johnson and Nixon that significant progress was being made—they "could see the light at the end of the tunnel" —anti-war critics in Congress sought to force the administration to extricate the United States from the quagmire in Indochina. Between 1966 and July 1973, Congress had 113 roll-call or teller votes on measures to limit or end combat activities, with 94 votes taking place during the Nixon administration.[49] Virtually all these resolutions failed to pass, since a coalition of Democratic hawks and minority Republicans invariably prevailed.

Throughout the entire Vietnam war, Congress chose not to exercise its own war powers, especially its power over appropriations, to check the president in his role as commander in chief. At no time did Congress approve a particular date for withdrawal of Americans from Indochina. Nor did the lawmakers ever use their appropriation power to require evacuation of American forces. Furthermore, through all this legislative skirmishing, the members of Congress made clear that the president's duties as commander in chief elsewhere in the world remained unfettered.

By mid-1973, however, Congress finally became so disenchanted with the Vietnam war that the majority decided to resort to a funding cutoff, even in face of a presidential veto. But Nixon, aware that Congress was preparing to consider a general resolution that would affect presidential war powers, decided to accept a compromise funding cutoff bill. By accepting specific restrictions on the Indochina war, Nixon believed he had headed off a general resolution. And so he had —but only for four months.

THE WAR POWERS RESOLUTION: CURBING PRESIDENTIAL WARMAKING

Antiwar forces in Congress, after repeated failures, finally voted to put a legislative curb on presidential warmaking power in the fall of 1973. At long last Congress finally decided it was time to do something about the imperial presidency—or, more accurately, the president's discretionary use of his commander in chief authority to order American troops into combat situations almost anywhere in the free world.

Passage of the act, called the War Powers Resolution (or War Powers Act), came in the midst of the Middle Eastern crisis with the Soviet Union over hostilities between Israel and Egypt (the Yom Kippur War) and at the very moment President Nixon was embroiled in the Saturday Night massacre firing of the Watergate Special Prosecutor Archibald Cox. This action had prompted Attorney General Elliot Richardson and Deputy Attorney General William Ruckelshaus to resign in protest. Ten days before the Saturday night firestorm, Vice-President Spiro Agnew resigned rather than face possible impeachment over income tax fraud and acceptance of political kickbacks while he was governor of Maryland.

Nixon vetoed the War Powers Resolution, declaring: "The restrictions which this resolution would impose upon the authority of the President are both unconstitutional and dangerous to the best interests of the Nation." In his veto message President Nixon also warned that the resolution would "seriously undermine this nation's ability to act decisively and convincingly in times of international crises," and he asserted that it would "attempt to take away, by a mere legislative act, authorities which the president has properly exercised under the Constitution for almost 200 years."[50] But the vast majority of lawmakers, unimpressed with the president's reasoning, quickly overrode the veto.[51]

Proponents of the War Powers Resolution—perhaps too optimistically— saw it as a means of restoring the original intent of the Founding Fathers to place the basic decisions about war and peace in the hands of Congress. Recognizing that formal declarations of war were outmoded and that the refusal of Congress to approve them would probably not inhibit future presidents from undertaking military action when they deemed it necessary, proponents nonetheless felt that the War Powers Resolution was a reasonable compromise in this nuclear age. Presidents would have sufficient latitude to operate in times of national emergency, but the legislation would encourage Congress to reassert its constitutional authority rather than stand by passively year after year as it had done during the Korean conflict, or until the very end of the decade-long Vietnam war. In any event, Congress was endeavoring to go on record as opposed to the granting of a blank check to an American president, as was given to Lyndon Johnson in the Gulf of Tonkin Resolution in 1964.

The War Powers Resolution stipulated that the president may commit the armed forces to combat only in the event of declarations of war, specific statutory authorization, or a national emergency created by an attack on the United States or its armed forces. Furthermore, the legislation urged the president to consult with Congress in "every possible instance" prior to committing forces to combat abroad, and it required consultation after such a commitment.

Specifically, the resolution required a written report to Congress within 48 hours of a commitment of American forces and required ending of the commitment within 60 days, unless further authorized by Congress. Moreover, the commitment could be extended for 30 additional days if the president certified to Congress that military conditions required continued use of the forces in order to ensure their safety. Finally, the resolution stated that Congress may by concurrent resolution, not subject to presidential veto, order the withdrawal of U.S. forces prior to the end of the first 60 days.

The role of commander in chief versus Congress on matters of undeclared wars and police actions, however, remains ambiguous. In one sense, the resolution was a symbolic victory for Congress, for it reinforced its constitutional voice on matters of undeclared wars and served notice that the dispatch of combat troops to trouble spots outside the country can no longer be made exclusively by presidential order. The War Powers Resolution, designed to permit Congress to overturn unilateral presidential decisions to commit American armed forces abroad and provide more adequate mechanisms of reporting and consulting by the executive branch of Congress, represents—on paper, at least—the most forthright reassertion of congressional prerogative on the war power since the ratification of the Constitution.

Opponents of the War Powers Resolution were divided between those who thought it allowed the president too little or too much discretionary authority. Those who thought the resolution kept the president on too short a leash pointed out that President Roosevelt's naval action in the Atlantic in 1941 and John F. Kennedy's naval quarantine or blockade of Cuba in 1962 would not have been permitted under the 1973 legislation.

The language of the resolution indicates that Congress has not delegated its warmaking power to declare war to the president, but in line with the Constitution simply reaffirms the authority of the president to exercise his own prerogatives as commander in chief. In other words, warmaking is a presidential power that Congress cannot interfere with once the hostilities are under way. Furthermore, the resolution recognizes that the president has authority to repel invasions on his own authority, and it also permits him to use force if the armed forces of the United States are attacked, without specifying what type of attack or restricting the location to United States territory or possessions. Additionally, the resolution sanctions presidential warmaking to defend armed forces based in a foreign country during a revolution or civil war. Conceivably, it might have applied during the Gulf of Tonkin incident in 1964.

Critics have noted that the resolution does not distinguish between a major attack and a minor incident.[52] The resolution has enough leeway to permit the president to deploy forces in such a manner as to create an incident and then lead the country into war. Thus, if American troops were attacked by hostile forces operating from sanctuaries, the president could order the invasion of a neutral country without obtaining a declaration of war—in other words, a repeat performance of Nixon's decision to invade Cambodia in 1970.

Presidents Nixon and Ford argued that the resolution was unconstitutional, and Presidents Carter and Reagan have had serious reservations about its impingement on the president's authority as commander in chief. Others, notably Senator Thomas Eagleton (D–Mo.), asserted that it gave the president virtually a blank check to conduct military action around the globe. In Eagleton's words, "By failing to define the president's powers in legally binding language, the bill provided a legal loophole for the President's broad claims of inherent power to initiate a war."[53]

Several commentators have noted that a number of gaps and ambiguities in the War Powers Resolution have never been clarified. Thus, for example, while the president must submit a written report to Congress within 48 hours after the armed forces are ordered into combat or where imminent hostilities are threatened, and although he must report any substantial enlargement of the armed forces equipped for combat in any foreign country, the reporting requirements are nonetheless incomplete. The resolution, as one close student of the presidency has pointed out, does not cover the following: "military alerts; naval quarantines or blockades in international waters; the use of naval vessels for convoys; the training, equipping, or transporting of mercenaries or guerrillas for combat on foreign territory; or the supply, financing, training, or transporting of forces of another nation into combat in a foreign territory."[54] Nor does the imprecision end here. The resolution, as presently written, does not specify the designated committees or congressional officers with whom the president must consult. Although the resolution requires him to consult "regularly," the wording does not specify whether continuous consultation is required.[55]

THE WAR POWERS RESOLUTION IN OPERATION

During the first decade since passage of the War Powers Resolution, the legislation was not fully tested as a method for controlling presidentially initiated military action.

In his veto of the resolution, Nixon insisted that it would deny the president "a wide range of important peacekeeping tools by eliminating his ability to exercise quiet diplomacy backed by subtle shifts in our military deployment."[56] Each subsequent president since Nixon has upheld his constitutional position on the president's role as commander in chief under the War Powers Act. Presidents Ford, Carter, and Reagan have all given lip service to the reporting provisions of the resolution, but without acknowledging any constitutional obligation to do so. Their reports have been forwarded to Capitol Hill not "pursuant to" the terms of the statute, but "consistent with" or "taking note of" the resolution.[57]

Despite passage of the War Powers Act, White House officials insisted that the president's power extended beyond protecting American territory and armed forces. The Ford administration, according to Louis Fisher, argued that in at least six other situations the president has constitutional authority to introduce armed forces into hostilities: "to rescue American citizens abroad; to rescue foreign nationals where such action directly facilitates the rescue of American citizens abroad; to protect U.S. embassies and legations abroad; to suppress civil insurrection; to implement and administer the terms of an armistice or cease-fire designed to terminate hostilities involving the United States; and to carry out the terms of security commitments contained in treaties."[58] Nor did the Ford spokesperson believe that any listing would be a complete one.

Since passage of the War Powers Resolution in 1973, there have been more than a half-dozen occasions on which the president has committed American combat forces abroad: to evacuate more than 400 Americans from Cyprus in 1974 during the Greek-Cypriot conflict; to evacuate several thousand Americans and refugees from South Vietnam and Cambodia in 1975; to rescue the crew of the merchant ship *Mayaguez* in May 1975; to airlift European troops to Zaire (formerly Belgian Congo) in 1976; to evacuate some 1,400 Americans from strife-torn Lebanon in 1976; to attempt unsuccessfully to rescue 52 American hostages held captive in Iran in April 1980; and to land 1,600 U.S. Marines as part of a multinational peacekeeping force in Lebanon in September 1982. The most recent use of U.S. troops was the lightning invasion of the Caribbean island of Grenada in October 1983, under the pretext of preventing the island from becoming a Cuban military base and to "rescue" 800 American students attending a local university.

Until the 1982 Lebanon crisis, none of the previous crises had consumed more than a few days; consequently, the 60-day deadline provision in the resolution had not been at issue. With respect to the reporting provisions of the resolution, in only three cases did the president fail to report to Congress. But in two of these cases, an argument could be made that the War Powers Resolution was inapplicable. The American military aircraft transporting European troops to Zaire landed more than a hundred miles from the combat zone, and the military personnel evacuating American citizens from Lebanon in 1976 (but not in 1982) were unarmed. The naval forces sent to Cyprus to evacuate stranded Americans *were* heavily armed and entered a hostile region where fighting had already broken out between the Greeks and Turks, a case which seemingly required that the War Powers Resolution be invoked. Still, President Nixon did not submit a report to Congress. While most lawmakers did not make a loud outcry, several critics, led by Senator Thomas Eagleton (D–Mo.), criticized Nixon for his failure to comply with the newly passed resolution.

Shortly after the evacuation of the last American troops from Vietnam in April 1975, the War Powers Act was put to a severe test. The U.S. merchant ship *Mayaguez,* plying between Hong Kong and Sattahip, Thailand, was seized by the Cambodian navy. Two days later, the United States recovered the seized vessel and its crew, but only after U.S. Marines stormed Koh Tang Island, suffering the loss of 41 marines under the erroneous impression that the 39 crewmen were detained there. Moreover, the military action took place even though the Cambodian government had indicated its intention to release the captured crewmen.

President Ford paid only lip service to the War Powers Resolution.[59] Even though there was every reason to believe that military force would be used to free the crewmen, President Ford chose beforehand merely to inform 21 members of Congress that he intended to use some type of force. After the military operation began, the president also briefed a group of congressional leaders. Senate Majority Leader Mike Mansfield (D–Mont.) expressed the views of many lawmakers on Capitol Hill when he observed: "I was notified after the fact about what the administration had already decided to do."[60] At no time did President Ford formally comply with the War Powers Resolution. In light of the national euphoria that followed the quick release of the American crewmen, members of Congress decided not to press the issue.

Jimmy Carter chose not to inform Congress in the spring of 1980 about the administration's plan to attempt the rescue of the 52 American hostages held in Tehran by the Iranian government. Only Senate Democratic Majority Leader Robert Byrd was informed beforehand that some type of covert action would take place, and he was advised less than 24 hours before the mission began. Though Secretary of State Cyrus Vance resigned over the aborted rescue mission, Carter's unilateral action drew only mild criticism from members of Congress. However, the chairman of the Senate Foreign Relations Committee expressed "regret that the President failed to consult congressional leaders prior to making a final decision"; and the chairman of the House Foreign Affairs Committee remarked that "It was stupid on the part of the President not to consult with us."[61]

In flaunting the War Powers Resolution, both Presidents Ford and Carter contended that the need for absolute secrecy precluded any prior consultation with Congress. The Carter White House staff also resorted to a unique argument that the Iranian hostage operation was a "humanitarian," not a military mission. This argument caused more than a few lifted eyebrows on Capitol Hill, especially in light of reports that had the mission succeeded, the second and third stages of the rescue plan called for taking military action against selected targets in Iran.[62] After the aborted mission, *The New York Times* asked: "Why not an ounce of genuine consultation before the raid to avoid a ton of contention and second-guessing afterward?"[63] In the aftermath of the abortive mission the White House retreated from the specious humanitarian justification by filing a report to Congress, as the law required.

President Reagan has gone several rounds with Congress over the scope and authority of the War Powers Resolution. In 1981, however, Reagan did not even bother to report to Congress under any provision of the War Powers Resolution when he sent military advisers to El Salvador. The State Department declared that no report was necessary because the American servicemen were not being introduced into hostilities or imminent hostilities. Subsequently, several members of Congress filed suit that President Reagan had violated the War Powers Resolution. Another group challenged this action and urged that the case be dismissed. Confronted by two congressional factions, a federal district judge in the District of Columbia refused to make a determination on whether or not hostilities or imminent hostilities existed. He pointed out that Congress had failed to use any legislative measures to restrain the president.[64]

President Reagan's order to land American troops in Lebanon in September 1982 subsequently led to a heated war of words between Congress and president over whether the president had complied with the provisions of the War Powers Resolution. The long-standing debate simmered during the first year after the American troop landing in Lebanon. But with the killing of four United States Marines in late August 1983, the first real confrontation between president and Congress over the application and scope of the War Powers Resolution erupted a decade after passage of the landmark legislation.

President Reagan, instead of acting under the procedures of the resolution, had originally deployed the U.S. peacekeeping force, pursuant to the president's "constitutional authority with respect to the conduct of foreign relations and as Commander in Chief of the United States Armed Forces."[65] Hostilities were not merely "imminent" in Lebanon; they had broken out. Nonetheless, President Reagan chose to send in troops without reporting under Section 4(a) (1) of the War Powers Resolution. By merely reporting "consistent" with the resolution, Reagan avoided starting the clock that would limit military action to 60 or 90 days, unless Congress specifically authorized an extension. Congress quickly demanded that the 1973 War Powers Resolution be invoked. The central issue was whether the fighting involving the Marines in Lebanon constituted "hostilities" and, if so, whether Congress had the power to call the troops home. Reagan insisted that since no hostilities had existed, he had fulfilled the requirements of the legislation by informing Congress in September 1982 that "I have authorized the armed forces of the United States to participate" in a multinational peacekeeping force in Lebanon, "to assure the safety of persons in the area and to bring an end to the violence which has tragically recurred."[66]

A year later, President Reagan again sent a status report to the Speaker of the House and the president pro tem of the Senate. Congressional critics, however, argued that with the death of the four marines, the president was required to more than inform Congress. The critics said that the 60-day clock should be running, because the U.S. troops were in a combat situation, as defined by the War Powers Resolution. The White House spokesperson, Larry Speakes, told reporters that President Reagan was opposed to invoking the War Powers Resolution because the fighting was "an isolated incident." "If we were conducting combat operations then it would be different," Mr. Speakes continued. "But we're not. The role there is as a peacekeeping force."[67] But congressional leaders were not dissuaded. President Reagan's refusal to set the War Powers Resolution clock in motion meant that Congress had to pass legislation to invoke Section 4(a) (1).

As the constitutional crisis approached, congressional leaders on both sides of the aisle and the White House worked feverishly to hammer out a compromise resolution that conceded a major point to each side: Reagan continued to express reservations about the War Powers Resolution; congressional leaders said he had recognized its authority. A key to the compromise was that Congress would, on its own, determine that the War Powers Resolution is in effect. This meant that the White House would not have to send Congress formal notification under the act and as a result President Reagan would directly avoid acknowledging the validity of the act in the current situation.

By promising to sign the resolution, Mr. Reagan was to become the first president to acknowledge the validity of the war powers legislation. Essential elements of the compromise consisted of the following: (1) American marines would continue to be deployed for an additional 18 months under the War Powers Resolution; the 18-month authority would begin the day the resolution is signed into law; either the president or Congress could move to bring the troops at an earlier date; if the president wanted to extend their stay in the war zone, he must seek congressional permission; (2) the president would be required to report to Congress at least every 6 months and describe the activities performed by American troops and the continuing search for "national political reconciliation" of Lebanon's warring factions; (3) American air and sea forces based outside Lebanon would be allowed to take "protective measures" that might be necessary to insure the safety of the American troops, but would not be allowed to take offensive measures; (4) the size of the marine contingent would be limited to the current force of 1,200 men, as stipulated in the original agreement of September 1982, when the Americans joined the multinational force; in addition, the marines would be limited to their current positions in the Beirut area.

Clearly, the most important provision was the 18-month time limit. Supporters of the compromise argued if it were limited to 6 months, the Syrians and other hostile forces would simply wait for the Americans to withdraw. And if the date set were one year later, it would fall in the middle of the 1984 presidential election.

Two weeks later, President Reagan signed the compromise legislation, after the House had approved the bill by a vote of 270 to 161, and the Senate by a 54 to 46 margin. In signing the legislation, however, President Reagan insisted obliquely that he already possessed the authority to keep the marines in Lebanon, even without congressional approval. He took issue with parts of the legislation, adding: "I do not and cannot cede any of the authority vested in me by the Constitution as President and Commander-in-Chief of the United States Armed Forces." Citing the congressional determination that the 90-day requirement began August 29, Reagan insisted that the "initiation of isolated or infrequent acts of violence" did not necessarily constitute "actual or imminent involvement in hostilities, even if casualties to those forces result."[68] The president said he also disagreed with the imposition of "arbitrary and inflexible deadlines" on the use of troops in Lebanon. He asserted that such deadlines create "unwise limitations on Presidential authority to deploy United States forces in the interest of United States national security." Furthermore, Mr. Reagan warned that his signing the legislation should not be viewed as "any acknowledgement that the President's constitutional authority can be impermissibly infringed by statute." Congressional leaders, however, hailed passage of the legislation as signaling exactly what the president had renounced.

Members of Congress endorsed this long-term authorization by reasoning that the president, upon signing the bill, would acknowledge the legitimacy of the consulting process established by the War Powers Resolution. Instead, the White House made it clear that the president might continue to keep U.S. troops in Lebanon beyond the 18-month limit without reauthorization from Congress. But following the terrorist truck bombing of the U.S. Marine barracks near the Beirut airport which took the lives of 241 U.S. servicemen, many members of Congress became convinced that the authorization was too long. President Reagan also began to have second thoughts about the continued stationing of U.S. troops near the weakly protected airport and its potentially dangerous impact on American public opinion during the 1984 presidential election. Suddenly, in February 1984, the White House announced that the marines would be withdrawn, and with their removal from Lebanon, the controversy over the War Powers Resolution ceased to be front-page news.

PRESIDENT REAGAN AS COMMANDER IN CHIEF

Congressional muscle-flexing resumed in late October 1983 after U.S. Rangers invaded the Caribbean island of Grenada, which the Reagan administration asserted was being turned into a Cuban-Soviet military bastion. Five days after U.S. forces landed on Grenada, the Senate voted 64 to 20 to adopt an amendment (a "rider" to a bill raising the national debt ceiling), declaring that the War Powers Act now applied to the fighting in Grenada. The House followed up this

Senate action by passing overwhelmingly 403 to 23 a resolution that would apply the War Powers Act to the troops on the island and require that they be withdrawn in 60 days unless Congress granted a specific extension. Since President Reagan had previously announced the same week that the withdrawal had already started, the vote was motivated chiefly by the desire to assert Congress's disputed authority under the War Powers Resolution rather than to actually direct administration policy.

Because the Reagan's Grenada venture was generally hailed as a major military-diplomatic success in blunting a possible future Cuban takeover of the island, further congressional criticism soon dissipated, especially after a congressional study group, appointed by Speaker Thomas P. O'Neill, Jr., announced after a three-day trip to Grenada that Reagan's move was justified.[69]

Few observers would quarrel with the postmortem issued by E. S. Corwin's editors: "The successful 'invasion' of Grenada by the United States without reference to the War Powers Act or 'formal' congressional approval clearly demonstrated the power of the president to both act unilaterally in his role as commander-in-chief and to disregard congressional limitations on his authority in matters of foreign policy concerning war and peace."[70] Most Washington observers concluded that Reagan's role as commander in chief was enhanced by the Grenada operation, just as earlier presidents have capitalized on special military actions to reinforce their authority in commanding the nation's armed forces.

Near the end of Reagan's third year in office, one veteran Washington reporter commented: "Over the last eighteen months, President Reagan has clearly stepped into the front ranks of those American Presidents who, since World War II, have been willing to employ military force as an instrument of national policy."[71] During his first 32 months in office, Mr. Reagan in his post as commander in chief had sent marines and warships to Lebanon, mounted an aerial and naval show of force against Libya, dispatched warships and paramilitary personnel to Central America, and ordered the invasion of Grenada. President Reagan has been described as "bolder in the use of military power than his own generals," with whom he reportedly confers more often than any other president in recent memory.[72] Reagan's policies, according to numerous Washington observers, represented a return to a traditional reliance on military force to achieve political objectives. In February 1983, for example, American and Egyptian intelligence reports indicated that Libya might attack its neighbor, Sudan, located astride American communication lines to the Middle East. Reagan responded by deploying the nuclear-powered aircraft carrier *Nimitz,* with 100 combat planes, off the coast of Libya and dispatched four AWACs (radar warning and control planes) to Egypt. Additionally, the president let it be known that he was prepared to destroy the Libyan air force if the coup were attempted. Libyan dictator Moammar Khadafy made no move, and American forces were withdrawn from the area.

While successive presidents have committed forces to emergency operations on nearly a dozen occasions over the past decade without real consultation, as seemingly required by the War Powers Resolution, it should not be inferred that the 1973 legislation is an empty letter. The War Powers Resolution has stiffened congressional resolve to monitor presidential military overseas ventures closely. Congressional oversight may be "more bark than bite," but in the recent case of Lebanon, congressional critics of President Reagan's use of U.S. Marines as part of the multinational peacekeeping force kept up such a constant drumbeat of criticism against continued U.S. Marine occupation of the Beirut International Airport that the president finally ordered their withdrawal. Reagan indicated in a subsequent press conference that he might order the marines to land in Lebanon again, but the Washington press corps discounted this threat as a mere face-saving gesture by the president in the aftermath of a major diplomatic setback in the Middle East.

Following the withdrawal of U.S. Marines from Beirut to ships offshore, Secretary of State George P. Shultz testified that debate over the War Powers Resolution had made it impossible for the administration to conduct a "sensible" policy in Lebanon. In an appearance before the Senate appropriations subcommittee on foreign relations, Shultz called on Congress to review the law, enacted in 1973, to limit the president's authority to commit forces without congressional approval. "Our own debate here totally took the rug out from under our diplomatic effort," declared Mr. Shultz.[73] "I think it ought to be reviewed by Congress. I think there is a question as to whether that piece of legislation is the most desirable way to structure the interaction between the legislative and executive branches for dealing with issues involving force," he told the lawmakers.[74]

Senator Patrick J. Leahy (D–Vt.), however, told Mr. Shultz that Congress voted for the 18-month extension to avoid facing the crucial issue. Shultz, in seeming to blame Congress and the War Powers Resolution for imposing too many constraints on the president's freedom to use military forces abroad, did not mention the fact that there were also deep divisions within the executive branch over whether the marines should remain in Lebanon. Secretary of Defense Casper Weinberger and the Joint Chiefs of Staff, for example, were known to be opposed to having the marines remain on Lebanese soil.

Some critics have argued that the War Powers Resolution, passed originally to restrain the imperial presidency, has unconstitutionally given the executive more warmaking powers than did the Founding Fathers. But the recent experience in Lebanon suggests that the resolution can serve as a major constraint upon a president who has a propensity to use military force in an effort to achieve diplomatic objectives. Congress originally adopted the War Powers Resolution to remind presidents of their accountability for the use of U.S. troops abroad. After a decade of presidential flaunting of the War Powers Resolution—or at least open indifference to its impact—Congress in the most recent Lebanese crisis finally made its case: Congress must be consulted and listened to in overseas military ventures that involve continued land occupation by U.S. forces for more than a few weeks.

The frequent presidential-congressional clashes over military policy underscore the persistent need for the president to reach an accommodation with Congress. Unilateral actions, in the long run, are seldom successful enterprises. Generally, the president's power is at its lowest ebb when he undertakes actions that lack the support of Congress. Successful policy requires, at some point, that the president secure the support and cooperation of Congress. Indeed, as Justice Robert Jackson noted in the steel seizure case in 1952, presidential authority reaches its highest level when the president's actions are based upon congressional authorization.[75] Franklin D. Roosevelt's counterattack against the Great Depression during the early days of his first administration and Eisenhower's adroit handling of the Formosa Strait and Lebanese crises during the 1950s immediately come to mind as examples of successful executive-congressional consultation.

From midway in his first term, President Reagan was involved in a two-front battle with Congress over warmaking activities—his military-diplomatic policy in Central America was his second front. Reagan's dispatch of military advisers to El Salvador in the first year of his administration made many members of Congress extremely nervous. Indeed, after their bitter experience with Johnson and Nixon in the Vietnam war, these lawmakers were determined that the United States should not make a similar mistake in Central America. Also, during this same period, Reagan's open and covert support of the anti-Sandinista Contra forces seeking to overthrow the leftist regime in Nicaragua produced more than a dozen, often contradictory, votes in Congress over the amount and type of American military aid to be given to these guerrillas.

Advance consultation with Congress, as required by the War Powers Resolution, has not been a high-priority item for the Reagan administration. When President Reagan summoned congressional leaders to the White House for a late afternoon top-level meeting on April 14, 1986, to announce the impending air strikes against the Moammar Khadafy regime, the American F-111 bombers had already left their bases in Great Britain and were on their way to Libya. The air strikes were scheduled to begin at 7 P. M. Washington time. Vice Admiral John M. Poindexter, the president's national security adviser, reportedly told the lawmakers at about 6:20 P. M. that "this is a consultation," and that the mission could be aborted if Congress demanded![76]

Following the air strikes in Libya, the most frequent complaint heard on Capitol Hill was that the administration had not given the lawmakers sufficient notice of the raid. Senator Sam Nunn of Georgia, ranking Democrat on the Armed Service Committee, recommended that in the future the president call in a small group of congressional leaders at an early stage in the decision-making process. Senator Nunn said: "When the President is examining some of the options, it would be helpful for Congressional leaders to look at some of those options. That's consultation."[77]

Under the War Powers Resolution, the president, as indicated earlier, is required to consult with Congress "in every possible instance" before sending planes or troops into battle, but how this consultation should be carried out is left vague. "This needs to be thought through very carefully," declared Senator Richard Lugar (R–Ind.), chairman, Foreign Relations Committee.[78]

Senator Nunn added further that the war powers measure itself should be reexamined. "It leaves a lot to be desired; it's not adhered to by the executive branch."[79] Senator Lowell Weicker, a liberal Republican from Connecticut, put it in stronger terms, insisting that the problem lies not with formal procedures, but with the attitude of the administration: "There's a feeling on the part of the White House to say 'to hell with consultation and deliberation,' " he maintained.[80]

As a result of the War Powers Resolution, more than anything else, this uneasy tension between the President and Congress over American military and paramilitary activities abroad will probably continue indefinitely, or at least until the president takes congressional leaders into his full confidence—or perhaps it will never end. That this executive-legislative conflict persists should be no surprise. For as former Undersecretary of State George Ball testified at a congressional hearing more than a decade ago, the War Powers Resolution represented an attempt by Congress to do something which the Founding Fathers thought they could not do—namely, draw the dividing line between the constitutional power of Congress to declare war and the constitutional power of the president as commander in chief.[81]

Plainly, the Framers wanted the best of both worlds—a forceful commander in chief able to move quickly to repel attacks against the United States and a strong-willed Congress determined to keep the president within constitutional bounds. Almost two centuries later, maintaining a delicate balance between these twin goals still remains at the top of the American public's agenda.

CONCLUSION

The war power of the United States, according to the late dean of presidential scholars, Edward S. Corwin, has undergone a threefold transformation since the early days of the Republic. First, the constitutional basis of the war power has been shifted from the doctrine of delegated to the doctrine of inherent powers, thus guaranteeing that all necessary power is available to the president for conducting the war to a successful conclusion. Second, the president's power as commander in chief has been "transformed from a simple military command to a vast reservoir of indeterminate powers in times of emergency—'an aggregate of powers,'" in the words of one former attorney general.[82] Third, in wartime the sweeping legislative powers claimable by Congress may in fact be delegated by Congress to the president to the extent needed; indeed, they may be merged with the indefinite powers of the commander in chief to create an awesome combination of powers that are "illimitably expansible."

Congressional attempts to rein in the president under the War Powers Act of 1973 have been marked with limited success. Thus far, the power of Congress to impose the resolution's 60-day time limit on the president's authority to commit U.S. troops in hostilities abroad has not been tested. Consequently, this basic constitutional question remains as unsettled as it was at the time of the Vietnam war, or the Korean war, or for that matter, as long ago as President Polk's actions in precipitating the Mexican War more than 140 years ago.[83]

Presidents Nixon, Ford, Carter, and Reagan have all undertaken unilateral military-peacekeeping actions or rescue missions in Southeast Asia, the Middle East, and the Caribbean without prior consultation or communication with Congress. Indeed, all four presidents have acted on the international scene almost as if the War Powers Act did not exist. The one possible exception—President

Reagan's dispatch of a U.S. Marine contingent to Lebanon to serve as part of an international peacekeeping force in 1982—ended inconclusively when the president decided to withdraw the marines from Lebanon in February 1984, less than four months after the loss of 241 marines in a terrorist truck bombing of their barracks and more than a year ahead of a joint executive-congressional agreed-upon timetable. Although this agreement was hammered out under the War Powers Act procedures, President Reagan insisted that as commander in chief, he still had the inherent right to reintroduce troops in Lebanon if, in his judgment, they were needed. In brief, the dividing line between the constitutional power of Congress to declare war and the constitutional power of the president as commander in chief remains as imprecise as a boundary line drawn in the sands of the Sahara.

NOTES

1. *The New York Times,* April 15, 1986.
2. Joseph E. Kallenbach, *The American Chief Executive* (New York: Harper & Row, 1966), 526.
3. Ibid., 524–525.
4. Madison to Jefferson, April 2, 1798, Madison *Writings,* Gaillard Hunt, ed. (New York, 1906), VI, 312–313, as cited by Arthur M. Schlesinger, Jr., *The Imperial Presidency* (Boston: Houghton Mifflin, 1973), 5.
5. Max Farrand, ed., *The Records of the Federal Convention, 1787,* rev. ed. (New Haven, CT: Yale University Press, 1966), 2:318.
6. Alan Tonelson, Christian Science Monitor News Service, as quoted in the *Seattle Times,* March 11, 1984.
7. *The Federalist,* No. 69. In an early case the Supreme Court too ruled that the president's duty and powers as commander in chief were "purely military." *Fleming* v. *Page,* 9 Howard 603, 615 (1815).
8. Schlesinger, *The Imperial Presidency,* 20.
9. The writings of Thomas Jefferson, V, pp. 542–555, as cited by Louis Fisher, *Constitutional Conflicts Between Congress and the President* (Princeton, NJ: Princeton University Press, 1985), 288.
10. Schlesinger, *The Imperial Presidency,* 28.
11. Louis W. Koenig, *The Chief Executive,* 4th ed. (New York: Harcourt, Brace and Jovanovich, 1981), 257; Dwight D. Eisenhower, *Mandate for Change* (Garden City, NY: Doubleday, 1963), 181.
12. Koenig, *The Chief Executive,* 257.
13. Charles A. Beard, *The Republic* (New York: Viking Press, 1943), 103.
14. 4 Wallace 2.
15. Clinton Rossiter, *The American Presidency* (New York: Harcourt, Brace and World, 1956), 23.
16. James Grafton Rogers, *World Policy and the Constitution* (Boston: World Peace Foundation, 1945), 92–123.
17. Information collected by Barry M. Blechman and Steven S. Kaplan, *Force Without War* (Washington, DC: The Brookings Institution, 1978), as quoted in Richard M. Pious, *The American Presidency* (New York: Basic Books, 1979), 373.
18. Ibid, 374.

19. It is worth noting that during the Mexican War Lincoln, who was one of President Polk's severest critics, voted for the Ashmun resolution, which declared the president had "unconstitutionally" begun the war with Mexico. Edward S. Corwin, *The President: Office and Powers,* 5th ed., revised by Randall W. Bland, Theodore T. Hindson, and Jack W. Peltason (New York: New York University Press, 1984), 496–497, note 7.

20. Ibid., 264.

21. 2 Black 635 (1863).

22. Corwin, *The President: Office and Powers,* 270.

23. Ibid., 235.

24. Ibid., 272.

25. Roosevelt, who served as President Wilson's assistant secretary of the navy, may have been influenced by Wilson's course of action before America's entry into World War I in shaping his own policies during this period. After severance of diplomatic relations with Germany in early 1917, Wilson requested Congress to authorize him to arm U.S. merchant ships for defense, but at the same time insisted that he had the authority to do so "without special warrant of law, by the plain implication of my constitutional duties and powers." When Congress rejected his requested authorization, he proceeded to arm the merchant ships on his own initiative as commander in chief. J. M. Matthews, *The American Constitutional System,* 2nd ed. (New York: McGraw-Hill, 1940), 316.

26. Corwin, *The President: Office and Powers,* 280–281.

27. Arthur T. Vanderbilt, "War Powers and Their Administration," *1945 Annual Survey of American Law* (New York University School of Law), as quoted by Corwin, 461–462, note 62.

28. *Steuart and Bro., Inc.* v. *Bowles,* 322 U.S. 598 (1944).

29. Corwin, *The President: Office and Powers,* 4th ed., 259.

30. Ibid., 252.

31. 320 U.S. 81 (1943).

32. 323 U.S. 214 (1944).

33. Cited in C. Herman Pritchett, *The American Constitution,* 2nd ed. (New York: McGraw-Hill, 1968), 391.

34. 323 U.S. 283 (1944).

35. Pritchett, *The American Constitution,* 391.

36. Robert J. Donovan, *Tumultuous Years: The Presidency of Harry S. Truman, 1949–1953* (New York: Norton, 1982), 220–221.

37. Schlesinger, *The Imperial Presidency,* 138.

38. Ibid., 140.

39. Ibid., 160.

40. Ibid., 179.

41. Pious, *The American Presidency,* 387.

42. Schlesinger, *The Imperial Presidency,* 181.

43. Ibid., 180–181.

44. Ibid., 184.

45. Congress revoked the Tonkin Gulf Resolution in January 1971; however, the repeal of the resolution did not direct the president to end hostilities.

46. Schlesinger, *The Imperial Presidency,* 187.

47. Ibid., 189.

48. *The New York Times,* June 30, 1970.

49. *Congressional Quarterly Weekly Reports,* August 11, 1973, 2205.

50. Quoted in Pious, *The American Presidency,* 403.

51. The House voted to override President Nixon's veto 284–135 (four votes more than the needed two-thirds majority) on November 7, 1973; the Senate voted to override a few hours later, 75–18. The full text of the War Powers Resolution (Public Law 93–148, 93rd Congress, H.J. Res 542, November 7, 1973) is available in Pat. M. Holt, *The War Powers Resolution* (Washington, DC: American Enterprise Institute), 43–48.

52. Pious, *The American Presidency,* 404.

53. Thomas Eagleton, *War and Presidential Power* (New York: Liveright, 1974), 203.

54. Pious, *The American Presidency,* 405.

55. Ibid.

56. Cited in Holt, *The War Powers Resolution: The Role of Congress in U.S. Armed Intervention,* 8.

57. James L. Sundquist, *Constitutional Reform and Effective Government* (Washington, DC: The Brookings Institution, 1986), 227.

58. Fisher, *Constitutional Conflicts Between Congress and the President,* 313.

59. Ibid., 314–316.

60. *Congressional Quarterly Weekly Report,* April 26, 1980, 1068.

61. Robert E. DiClerico, *The American President,* 2nd ed. (Englewood Cliffs, NJ: Prentice Hall, 1983), 45.

62. *Washington Post,* August 24, 1980.

63. *The New York Times,* May 2, 1980.

64. *Crockett* v. *Reagan,* 558 F. Supp. 893 (D. D. C. 1982), as cited by Fisher, *Constitutional Conflicts Between Congress and the President,* 318, note 97.

65. Wkly Comp. Pres. Doc., XVIII, 1232 (September 29, 1982), as cited by Fisher, *Constitutional Conflicts Between Congress and the President,* 317.

66. *The New York Times,* September 3, 1983.

67. Ibid.

68. Ibid., *The New York Times,* October 13, 1983.

69. "Getting Back to Normal," *Time,* November 21, 1983, 16–17.

70. Corwin, *The President: Office and Powers,* 301.

71. Richard Halloran, "Reagan as Military Commander," *The New York Times Magazine,* January 15, 1984, 25.

72. Ibid.

73. *The New York Times,* March 2, 1984.

74. Ibid.

75. The discussion in this section relies heavily on Fisher, *Constitutional Conflicts Between Congress and the President,* 323–325.

76. *The New York Times,* April 15, 1986.

77. Ibid., April 16, 1986.

78. Ibid.

79. Ibid.

80. Ibid.

81. Holt, *The War Powers Resolution,* 1.

82. Corwin, *The President: Office and Powers,* 296–297.

83. Sundquist, *Constitutional Reform and Effective Government,* 228. In the case of Grenada, a resolution limiting to 90 days the president's authority to use military forces, in the absence of further action of Congress, passed the House of Representatives but was not acted on in the Senate. Ibid., note 31.

chapter 8

Chief Diplomat

In a recent meeting with Republican members of Congress over Nicaraguan policy, President Reagan reportedly pounded the table as he declared: "We have got to get where we can run a foreign policy without a committee of 535 telling us what we can do."[1]

This presidential outburst reflects the continuing frustration that recent presidents have expressed over congressional "micromanaging" foreign policy. Mr. Reagan is not the first president to complain about foreign policy directives emanating from Capitol Hill. But since the Vietnam war-Watergate era, Washington observers have noted a growing trend on Capitol Hill of congressional determination to reshape and sometimes restrict American foreign policy.

Even a cursory reading of the Constitution would reveal that the president is the chief manager of foreign policy. "He shall have Power, by and with the Consent of the Senate, to make Treaties, provided two-thirds of the Senators present concur; and he shall nominate, by and with the Advice and Consent of the Senate, shall appoint Ambassadors, other Ministers and Consuls" (Article II, Section 2). While the Founding Fathers concluded that the president should share the treaty-making and appointment power with the Senate, they had little doubt that the president would be chiefly responsible for the day-to-day management of foreign affairs. Throughout most of our history, the president has been the "sole organ" of foreign relations, but in light of the Vietnam war and the Watergate scandals, increased congressional participation in foreign affairs is becoming the normal mode of foreign policymaking.

In this chapter we will trace the early development of the president's direction of American foreign policy, explore the constitutional sharing of power between the president and Congress on treaty making, the rapid increase in presidential use of executive agreements, comment on the extensive use of presidential special emissaries, discuss the shadowy role of the CIA, and assess Congress's growing role in foreign policy formation.

CONSTITUTIONAL BACKGROUND

If the Founding Fathers could have looked ahead two centuries, they would undoubtedly have derived the most satisfaction from their decisions to invest executive power in a single person—the president of the United States—and to empower him to handle foreign affairs. The Founding Fathers concluded that the best way for the young federal republic to avoid the same humiliating treatment from European diplomats experienced under the Articles of Confederation was to vest the management of foreign affairs in the hands of the president.

Without doubt, the Founding Fathers had profited considerably from the bitter experience of the Articles of Confederation that a government without an executive branch was impotent to deal with any serious foreign or domestic crisis. Under the Confederation, the determination of foreign policy and control of foreign relations lay with Congress, or more accurately after 1781, the Department of Foreign Affairs. But since no executive or council gave direction to the department, the results were chaotic. Indeed, the need for a single voice in negotiating with other countries had never been brought home more forcefully to the Framers than when the British foreign secretary disdainfully suggested to the American minister in London that if he sent one envoy to the Confederation, he would have to send thirteen.[2]

That the Framers vested the handling of foreign affairs in the hands of a president is not surprising, since their principal sources—Blackstone, Locke, and Montesquieu—were unanimous in contending that the power to conduct foreign relations must reside with the executive. Even so, under the Constitution the Framers granted the power to declare war to Congress, not the president. Under the Articles of Confederation, the power to declare war had also been vested in Congress. But the Framers required that treaties obtain the consent of the Senate, and by a two-thirds vote. The Senate's advice and consent was also required for the president's appointment of all ambassadors.

This shared constitutional power over foreign affairs, it could be predicted, made conflict between the two branches almost inevitable. Especially granting authority to Congress to approve appropriations, which can be essential to the development and execution of foreign policy decisions and to confirm all ambassadorial appointments, was in the words of one leading authority: "an invitation to struggle for the privilege of directing American foreign policy."[3] Still, the president holds most of the trump cards in directing foreign affairs.

George Washington firmly established the principle of executive authority over foreign affairs at the inception of his presidency. His proclamation of neutrality in 1793 to avoid taking sides in the European conflict, based upon his prerogative to determine foreign policy, aroused the ire of several factional groups. Those sympathetic to the French Revolution were incensed, as were the unreconstructed anti-Federalists who had all along distrusted the national government and its "elected king." Despite the vehemence of the attacks, Washington's view of presidential authority over foreign affairs prevailed and continues to the present to be the constitutional doctrine governing our relations with other nations.

Next to his duties as commander in chief and chief administrator, the role of chief diplomat is probably the third most important function performed by the president of the United States. In the past, however, the dominant voice in foreign policymaking has from time to time shifted between the Congress and the president. Clearly, the Spanish-American War was a congressionally sponsored war, heavily pushed by jingoist lawmakers and reluctantly acquiesced in by President William McKinley. Teddy Roosevelt, on the other hand, was an activist president determined to make the United States a first-class world power by his big stick diplomacy. To head off European intervention, Roosevelt moved American forces into Santo Domingo in 1904 to collect customs and duties for transmission to European creditors. A year later, Roosevelt agreed to offer his good offices and convene an international conference at Algeciras, a small seaport town in southern Spain near Gibraltar, to avert a major crisis between France and Germany over Morocco. Within a few months Roosevelt's diplomatic leadership in the Far East brought an end to the Russo-Japanese War in 1905. Woodrow Wilson also soon turned into a world statesman, but the Senate shattered his fondest dream —membership in the League of Nations—by rejecting the Versailles Treaty.

Throughout the period between the two world wars, isolationism dominated U.S. foreign policy. But Franklin Roosevelt's skilled diplomatic talents eventually enabled him to outmaneuver the isolationist-minded Congress and bring the United States to the aid of beleaguered Great Britain before America's entry into World War II.

Presidential domination of foreign policy continued after World War II, the Korean war, and through the early and middle period of the Vietnam war. But a congressional resurgence occurred with the passage of the War Powers Act in 1973. Since then, an uneasy power balance over foreign affairs has existed between the executive and legislative branches.

Despite frequent congressional involvement in foreign affairs, however, the president still remains the chief diplomat. There is no better recent example of this role than President Reagan's decision to hold a summit meeting in Geneva, Switzerland, with Soviet leader Mikhail Gorbachev in November 1985 to discuss nuclear disarmament. The president's power in foreign relations rests on both constitutional and international law, as well as his authority as commander in chief.

CONSTITUTIONAL PREROGATIVES

First of all, the president is the official channel for communications to and from other countries. The president appoints all ambassadors and consular officials and through the diplomatic corps maintains contact and receives reports from abroad through the State Department. He may appoint special envoys to work in some of the international trouble spots. All official negotiations with foreign countries are conducted under his overall direction, though usually through the State Department.

Second, the power of recognizing foreign governments derives from the presidential role in sending and receiving diplomatic representatives as well as international law. Early in our country's history, Washington set the precedent in 1793 when he received Citizen Gênet as the official representative of the French government and then some months later demanded his recall by France, without consulting Congress in either instance. Decisions on the timing and establishment of diplomatic relations, such as Franklin Roosevelt's decision to recognize the Soviet Union in 1933 and Nixon's decision to open a diplomatic dialogue with Communist China in 1972, after twenty-three years of nonrecognition following the takeover of mainland China in 1949, are two examples of the president's control over foreign policy that immediately come to mind.

Third, the president's constitutional authority as commander in chief gives him wide latitude in implementing his foreign policy. By use of the armed forces, the president can further his foreign policy goals and enforce American rights and interests abroad. In 1844, for example, President Tyler ordered American military forces into disputed territory near our southern border in order to protect Texas against Mexican reprisals while the pending treaty for annexation of Texas to the United States was under consideration.

Shortly after the turn of the century, Theodore Roosevelt moved American naval vessels near the Isthmus of Panama, then under the suzerainty of Colombia, to prevent the Colombian army from putting down the Panamanian insurrectionists. Within days Roosevelt recognized the insurgent government and quickly signed the Hay-Bunau-Varilla Treaty, which contained such advantageous terms as to make the newly founded Panamanian Republic a virtual military outpost of the United States.[4] Three years later, he sent the newly expanded U.S. fleet around the world to demonstrate American power and influence. In March 1917, while the United States sought to maintain neutrality, Woodrow Wilson ordered the arming of American merchant vessels, despite congressional opposition, as a move to counter unrestricted German submarine warfare. In 1958, Eisenhower sent 10,000 American troops to Lebanon to maintain an uneasy truce between warring Christian and Muslim factions. The mammoth American intervention in Vietnam, which in 1965 saw over 525,000 soldiers sent to help try to save South Vietnam from a North Vietnamese takeover, ended in failure a decade later. But Lyndon Johnson's actions, even though "legitimized" by a congressional resolution, underscored the broad authority that an American president can exercise to aid friendly countries. Indeed, the president can, by his management of foreign affairs and his use of American troops, so influence foreign policy and trigger events that Congress may have little choice but to support presidential actions, even to the extent of declaring war.

It is noteworthy that of all the wars in which the United States has been involved, only two—the War of 1812 and the Spanish-American War (1898–1899)—were clearly the result of congressional policy. Though congressional sentiment generally supported administration policies leading to the outbreak of hostilities, the development of these policies was basically a product of White House actions.

THE SUPREME COURT'S SUPPORT

Supreme Court decisions have repeatedly recognized the president's exclusive position as "the sole organ of the federal government in international relations." While this doctrine has long been accepted, the Supreme Court did not formally enunciate this position until 1936—almost 150 years after ratification of the U.S. Constitution—in *U.S.* v. *Curtiss-Wright Export Corporation.*[5]

This case involved a joint resolution passed by Congress in 1934 authorizing the president by a neutrality proclamation to prohibit the sale within the United States of military equipment destined for Bolivia or Paraguay, then locked in the protracted Gran Chaco War. Franklin D. Roosevelt promptly issued such a declaration. The Curtiss-Wright Aircraft Company, which had shipped 50 machine guns to Bolivia, was convicted of violating the presidential proclamation and joint resolution. But in court the aircraft company lawyers challenged the joint resolution on the grounds that the statute constituted an unlawful delegation of legislative authority to the president, because the action left "unfettered discretion" to the executive with no statutory guidelines to govern his decision. They felt confident that they would win their case, because the Supreme Court had recently invalidated three New Deal NRA (National Recovery Administration) cases as an unconstitutional delegation of congressional authority.

But in *Curtiss-Wright* Justice Sutherland differentiated this case from the three previous NRA cases by pointing out that the three cases had "related solely to internal affairs," whereas the "whole aim" of the neutrality resolution was "to affect a situation entirely external to the United States." In this latter area Justice Sutherland declared that the president possessed not only powers given to him by the statute, but also "the very delicate, plenary and exclusive power of the President as the sole organ of the federal government in the field of international relations." Justice Sutherland continued:

> It is quite evident that if, in the maintenance of our international relations, embarrassment . . . is to be avoided and success for our aims achieved, congressional legislation which is to be made effective through negotiation and inquiry within the international field must often accord to the President a degree of discretion and freedom from statutory restriction which would not be admissible were domestic affairs alone involved. Moreover, he, not Congress, has the better opportunity of knowing the conditions which prevail in foreign countries. . . . He has his confidential sources of information. He has his agents in the form of diplomatic, consular and other officials.[6]

This definitive ruling on the plenary power of the president in foreign affairs was not seriously questioned for almost half a century—until the aftermath of the Iranian hostage crisis in 1981. But a section of President Carter's executive agreement with Iran, which had canceled all attachments against Iranian assets in the United States and transferred from U.S. courts to an international tribunal all legal claims by American firms against Iran, was challenged by a number of American corporations that had done business with the former shah's government. The president's agreement was upheld by the Supreme Court in *Dames & Moore* v. *Regan* (1981).[7] The Court ruled that the 1977 Emergency Economic

Powers Act explicitly gave the president authority to void attachments against Iranian assets in the United States.

While the Court found no statutory authorization for the transfer of legal claims out of the United States, the Justices held that Congress had "implicitly" approved Carter's action by a long pattern of acquiescence in permitting the presidential settlement of claims disputes with other countries. Once again, the Iranian claims decision reaffirmed the Court's support of broad presidential authority to resolve thorny international problems, even though no specific grant of this power is found in the Constitution.

TREATY-MAKING AUTHORITY

The Founding Fathers envisaged treaty making as a joint presidential-congressional enterprise. But in practice the necessity of securing Senate consent by a two-thirds vote for the ratification of treaties has proved to be a sharp limitation on executive management of foreign policymaking. The men of 1787 thought the Senate would serve as a type of council with which the president would sit while treaties were being drafted and from which he would regularly obtain advice. As a matter of fact, Washington attempted to pursue this course of action, going directly in person to the Senate in August 1789 and presenting seven issues pertaining to a proposed treaty with the Southern Indians on which he sought "advice and consent." But the senators indicated that they wished to consult privately among themselves and then voted to refer the proposed treaty to a committee of five. Washington indicated his displeasure with the manner in which the Senate treated him as he left the chamber. Two days later, he returned to the Senate for an answer to his questions, but the entire episode proved so unproductive that no other president has repeated the experience.

When treaties are sent to the Senate in final form for ratification, their fate is often uncertain. Secretary of State John Hay, who served under Theodore Roosevelt, once wrote: "A treaty entering the Senate is like a bull going into the arena; no one can say just how or when the final blow will fall—but one thing is certain, it will never leave the arena alive."[8] While Hay's observation is, of course, exaggerated, treaties are frequently ruined by unacceptable amendments and reservations. Woodrow Wilson learned to his dismay that an intransigent minority in the U.S. Senate could scuttle a treaty no matter what the long-term consequences of the rejection might be. The Versailles Treaty, which would have provided for United States membership in the League of Nations, failed to receive the necessary two-thirds majority by a vote of 49 yeas and 34 nays.[9]

Because the two-thirds vote needed to ratify allows a determined minority to wreak havoc on the proposed treaties, some thoughtful commentators have advocated that consent to treaty ratification by a majority of both houses of Congress would be preferable to the existing constitutional requirement. Despite the president's wishes, the Senate can defeat a treaty entirely or consent to ratification with amendments. If the Senate tacks on amendments the president must, if he still favors the treaty, secure the acceptance of these amendments by the foreign power(s) involved before the treaty can be ratified. A recalcitrant

Senate may also attach reservations, which do not directly alter the content of the treaty, but which qualify or modify the obligations assumed by the United States under the treaty.

By its general lawmaking authority, Congress can also frustrate or limit presidential foreign policymaking. In 1924, for example, Congress passed the Japanese Exclusion Act over the protests of President Coolidge and Secretary of State Charles Evans Hughes, with damaging long-range consequences on the relations between the two countries. In the 1930s, President Franklin D. Roosevelt's reciprocal trade agreements, especially with Latin American countries, came under increasing congressional scrutiny, requiring legislative approval every two or three years. More recently, Congress has also resorted to statutory bans on trade or aid to countries in congressional disfavor. Legislative power can be used sometimes to fill the breach caused by the Senate's rejection of a treaty. Following the defeat of the Treaty of Versailles ending World War I, Congress resorted to a joint resolution to bring American participation in the war against the Central Powers (Germany and Austria) to a legal conclusion in 1921. It is also noteworthy that American membership in the United Nations was achieved not by treaty but by congressional statute, the United Nations Participation Act of 1945.

EXECUTIVE AGREEMENTS

Because the two-thirds vote requirement needed in the Senate for ratification of all treaties is such a formidable barrier, presidents have frequently made use of executive agreements to achieve foreign policy objectives. Since these international agreements are not treaties in name, they do not have to be submitted to the U.S. Senate for ratification. In the twentieth century, executive agreements have frequently been used to handle matters of major importance. Japanese immigration into the United States, a volatile subject early in the twentieth century, was governed for 17 years by the Gentlemen's Agreement of 1907.

One of the most famous executive agreements—the destroyers-bases deal—was concluded in 1940 between President Franklin D. Roosevelt and Prime Minister Winston Churchill. Under this pact, the United States agreed to transfer 50 over-age destroyers to the hard-pressed British to help their antisubmarine campaign against Nazi U-boats. The United States, in return, received 99-year leases on a string of British islands in the Caribbean to strengthen long-range defenses around the Panama Canal. Two other major World War II international agreements—the Yalta and Potsdam pacts—were in fact executive agreements.

While executive agreements are often based on acts of Congress, legislative approval is not needed to put them into effect. Indeed, the executive branch has claimed four sources of constitutional authority to make executive agreements: (1) the president's authority as commander in chief; (2) his duty as chief executive to conduct foreign policy; (3) his authority to receive ambassadors and other public ministers; and (4) his duty to "take care that the laws are faithfully executed." Attempts to distinguish the legal effects of executive agreements from treaties have generally failed. Nor has the contention that the force of an executive agreement terminates with the end of the administration which entered into it been upheld in the courts.

The contention that executive agreements, unlike treaties, are not the "law of the land" unless approved by Congress has no standing in the courts. In *United States* v. *Belmont* (1937),[10] the U.S. Supreme Court specifically rejected this contention, holding that the recognition of Soviet Russia in 1933 and the accompanying executive agreements constituted an international compact which the president was entitled to sign without consulting the Senate. This case developed after President Roosevelt had agreed with the Soviet authorities that title to all nationalized properties of the Soviet Union in this country would be handed over to the U.S. government. Under the Litvinov Assignment the United States would then decide which assets would be returned to the Soviet Union.

By way of background, the Communist government in 1918 had nationalized the Petrograd Metal Works and confiscated its assets, including those held in the New York bank of August Belmont and Company. In a lawsuit the Belmont Bank objected to Roosevelt's "executive agreement," claiming that it violated New York state law. But the U.S. Supreme Court ruled that executive agreements had the same force in law as treaties; furthermore, Justice Sutherland, in his opinion, held that these agreements superseded state law even though they had not been ratified by the Senate. Justice Sutherland also stated that the president's authority as "sole organ" in foreign relations permitted him to recognize foreign governments and negotiate executive agreements. Consequently the State of New York had no authority to interfere with the president's negotiation of international agreements.

Furthermore, the Court ruled in *United States* v. *Pink* (1942)[11] that executive agreements have the same effect as treaties in superseding conflicting state laws. In 1955, however, the Supreme Court in *United States* v. *Guy W. Capps, Inc.* struck down an executive agreement because it contravened an existing federal commercial statute with Canada.[12] Two years later, the Supreme Court in *Reid* v. *Covert* invalidated an executive agreement that permitted American military courts in Great Britain to rely on trial by court-martial for offenses committed by American military personnel or their dependents. The plaintiff's lawyer successfully argued for the constitutional right to a trial by jury.[13]

Continued unhappiness with the widespread use of executive agreements became a major issue in the United States Senate shortly after World War II. In the late 1940s and early 1950s, Senator John Bricker (R–Ohio) spearheaded a constitutional amendment drive to limit the scope of international treaties and to prevent the use of executive agreements to circumvent the role of the Senate in the treaty-making process. Supported heavily by isolationist Republicans from the Midwest—Bricker had been the vice-presidential running mate of New York's Thomas E. Dewey in the 1944 presidential race—and other senators opposed to strong presidential leadership in foreign affairs, the Bricker Amendment came within one vote of securing the necessary two-thirds majority in 1955.

Recent presidents have often used executive agreements to make end runs around the treaty process—sometimes without informing Congress of the content of those agreements. Although Congress passed legislation in 1950 requiring the secretary of state to publish annually all executive agreements concluded during the previous year, the executive branch in a number of instances withheld information on those agreements it considered sensitive to this country's national security.[14] News of these secret agreements did not come to light until the Vietnam war hearings. Members of Congress were told that America's commitment to the South Vietnamese grew in part out of executive agreements made between American presidents and the South Vietnamese government.[15] These startling revelations prompted Congress to establish a special committee to investigate the nature of American commitments abroad made via executive agreements. Congressional probers turned up a variety of important commitments that had never been revealed to the legislators. Included among these commitments were promises of American military support for the Ethiopian army, apparent or implied commitments for the defense of Thailand and the Philippines, and even a commitment to defend the far-right Franco regime in Spain against *internal* uprisings.[16]

Congressmen were even more alarmed when they discovered that the executive branch had secretly agreed to assist the Laotian government in fighting Communist insurgents in that country since 1964. This military assistance consisted mainly of training of Laotian soldiers by American advisers as well as bombing raids by American planes against Communist targets in Laos.

Executive agreements now clearly outnumber treaties. During the first half century under the Constitution, 60 of the 87 international agreements to which the United States was a signatory, and all the major agreements, were made in the form of treaties. In the next 50 years (1839–1889), the record shows that there were 215 treaties, again including the major pacts, and 238 executive agreements. In the third half-century, ending in 1939, the United States concluded 524 treaties and 917 executive agreements.[17] Since the onset of World War II, executive agreements have become the standard method, not the exception, for implementing foreign policy, as Table 8.1 indicates.

By the early 1970s members of Congress exhibited growing concern that the legislative branch had been excluded from participation in numerous major decisions affecting American commitments abroad. Many legislators felt, with considerable justification, that these secret agreements abridged Congress's foreign affairs power under the Constitution. To halt this erosion of authority and gain

Table 8.1 TREATIES AND EXECUTIVE AGREEMENTS

Period	Treaties	Executive agreements
1789–1839	60	27
1839–1889	215	238
1889–1939	524	917
1940–1970	310	5,653
1971–1977	110	2,062
1978–1980	62	1,052
Total	1,281	9,949

Sources: Louis Fisher, *President and Congress: Power and Policy.* Copyright © 1972 by The Free Press, a division of Macmillan, Inc., 45; figures for 1971–1980 provided by the Department of State, Washington, DC.

some control over these foreign commitments, Congress passed the Case Act. Signed into law in 1972 by President Nixon, the Case Act required that the president transmit all executive agreements to Congress within 60 days after they had been negotiated. The provisions of this act, named after its chief sponsor, Senator Clifford Case (R–N.J.), further required that Congress must be informed of all executive agreements in effect at the time this act was passed. But the Case Act required that only the House Foreign Affairs Committee and the Senate Foreign Relations Committee be informed of secret executive agreements.

Has the Case Act accomplished its objective? Recent history shows that the executive branch has informed Congress only of those pacts that fall under its own definition of executive agreements.[18] In fact, the Nixon administration failed to report a number of international agreements, notably several negotiated with the government of South Vietnam. Less than three years after passage of the Case Act, Congressman Les Aspin (D–Wis.) estimated that the United States had entered into between 400 and 600 agreements with foreign governments, none of which had been reported to Congress.[19]

One of the most dangerous secret pacts to surface was President Nixon's letter to President Thieu of South Vietnam, in which he stated that the United States would "respond with full force should the settlement (i.e., the Paris Peace Agreement) be violated by North Vietnam."[20] Senator Case, among others, contended that this secret commitment constituted an international accord that should have been transmitted to Congress for review. Nixon's original failure to abide by the Case Act ultimately provoked Congress to refuse to authorize additional military aid for the South Vietnamese government following North Vietnam's final invasion of the South in 1975. Among the more controversial executive agreements are military base agreements with Spain, Diego Garcia, and Bahrain.

Several bills have been introduced in Congress to correct the omissions or ambiguities in the Case Act. These proposals have sought to clarify what constitutes an executive agreement and also provide that Congress may, if it wishes, reject such agreements within 60 days after they have been signed. But these proposals have not generated strong support. Presidents have pointed out with some justification that they cannot be effective negotiators if their hands are tied while trying to make firm commitments with foreign governments. Further, presidents have persuasively argued that carefully negotiated compromises might come unraveled while waiting for Congress to make up its mind to approve or reject such agreements. Congress, however, has retained leverage over those executive agreements that clearly state the level of U.S. economic or military assistance to foreign governments and depend on annual authorizations and appropriations. This approach was used with Turkey in 1980 and Spain in 1982. Thus, Congress has discovered a weapon to narrow the president's freedom to enter into some executive agreements.[21]

While there is general agreement that treaty making is a shared power between president and Congress, the president appears to have the authority to terminate a treaty without Senate consent, although the Supreme Court has never ruled on the issue and the Constitution is silent on the point. At the time President

Carter moved to establish full diplomatic relations with the People's Republic of China, he announced his intention to terminate the American defense pact with Taiwan as of January 1, 1980. As justification for his action, Carter could point to a provision of the treaty permitting termination after one year's notice. Since no mention was made of Senate participation in the terminating action, the president felt that he was on solid ground in unilaterally nullifying the pact. Moreover, precedent for treaty termination could be found in several nineteenth- and twentieth-century diplomatic actions.

No sooner had the treaty abrogation been announced, however, than Senator Barry Goldwater and other critics declared that Senate consent was implied in the Constitution and in the treaty. He pointed out that the Senate had passed a resolution in 1978 requiring the president to engage in "prior consultation" before making any changes in American foreign policy toward Taiwan. Under Goldwater's leadership, a sense of the Senate resolution condemning the president's action was adopted by a vote of 59 to 35, but it had no legal effect on the executive branch's establishment of diplomatic relations with Communist China. Although the president carried the day in shifting diplomatic recognition to Communist China, it would no doubt have been prudent for him to consult with the Senate before announcing this major shift in foreign policy. In 1981, Senator Barry Goldwater introduced legislation to require a two-thirds affirmative vote in the Senate to terminate defense treaties. But Congress thus far has not acted on this bill or any other clarifying legislation.

Presidents, it might be noted, may sometimes withdraw treaties from the Senate before a final ratification vote is taken. If the Senate attaches too many conditions or reservations to a proposed treaty, the president may decide not to go through with the ratification process. In 1912, for example, President Taft dropped further ratification plans for arbitration treaties with Great Britain and France, even though the Senate had approved them by a vote of 76 to 3, after the Senate emasculated them by exempting from arbitration just about every question of importance that any other nation might want to arbitrate, including state debts and the Monroe Doctrine.[22] More recently, President Carter asked the U.S. Senate to drop further consideration of the Strategic Arms Limitation Treaty (SALT II) after the Soviet Union's invasion of Afghanistan in 1979 made defeat of the treaty almost a certainty. Carter, however, insisted that the pact, which included limitations on heavy bombers and ballistic missiles, was still in the national interest.

THE NATIONAL SECURITY COUNCIL

Foreign policy and national security considerations rarely fit neatly into separate compartments. Since the end of World War II the president has had an additional coordinating agency—the National Security Council—for handling the frequently overlapping and sometimes chaotic aspects of American foreign policy. The National Security Council, established in 1947, was created to help the president coordinate the far-flung activities of the foreign policy bureaucracy, the military establishment, and the intelligence community. Foisted upon President

Truman by a Republican-controlled Congress, despite his initial objections, the National Security Council has on more than one occasion been the de facto foreign policy agency for the president. Intended originally as a coordinating agency for the president, the National Security Council under some of its ambitious directors—McGeorge Bundy, Henry Kissinger, and Zbigniew Brzezinski— has often overshadowed the State Department in formulating foreign policy.

Founded partly as a congressional reaction to the freewheeling manner in which President Roosevelt and the military chiefs had dominated policymaking during World War II, the National Security Council (NSC) was a major segment of the National Security Act of 1947, which unified the Army, Navy, and Air Force (established in the act as a separate service) into a single new Department of Defense. The 1947 legislation also created the Central Intelligence Agency. Congress prescribed the NSC's chief function as "advising the President with respect to the integration of domestic, foreign and military policies relating to the national security."[23] Beyond the statutory listing of its members—the president, vice-president, and the secretaries of state and defense—the legislation did not prescribe duties for the council or delegate any powers. The act was also silent on how the council should operate, and staffing arrangements were left to the discretion of the president.

Though President Truman was initially suspicious of a legislatively mandated advisory body, he wasted no time in establishing his authority over the National Security Council by integrating it fully into the Executive Office of the President. Further, he determined that the NSC should be dominated by the Department of State, not the new Department of Defense, as sought by the first secretary of defense, James Forrestal. Following the outbreak of the Korean war, Truman used the NSC as an advisory forum to coordinate military and political responses to the Soviet-backed North Korean challenge.

Eisenhower continued the policy established by Truman to use the NSC as an advisory forum, strictly under the wing of Secretary of State John Foster Dulles. Eisenhower, however, enlarged the staff and assigned the council responsibility for reviewing and analyzing agency positions. Especially significant was Eisenhower's creation in 1953 of the position of special assistant for national security, which in subsequent administrations became a major factor in military and foreign policy development.

Kennedy seldom used the National Security Council as a forum for obtaining policy advice. But during the 1962 Cuban missile crisis, he established an ad hoc body of high-level officials called the Executive Committee of the National Security Council (Ex-Com) to serve as his personal advisers for drafting alternative responses to the Soviet attempt to place missiles in Cuba. Probably the most significant structural development within the NSC during the Kennedy administration was the enhancement of the role of the special assistant and the NSC staff. Under Special Assistant McGeorge Bundy, the National Security Council became the principal policy adviser to the president, with the responsibility of managing day-to-day national security affairs and meeting regularly with President Kennedy. Equally important, the position of the special assistant and the NSC staff gained major influence over foreign policy at the expense of the secretary of state and his department. This development did not entirely displease Kennedy; the young president frequently expressed displeasure in private with the State Department's ponderous handling of foreign policy matters.

Lyndon Johnson ignored the National Security Council as a major advisory council. Instead, he relied chiefly on the Tuesday lunch group—the secretaries of state and defense, the special assistant for national security affairs, the director of the CIA, and the chairman of the Joint Chiefs—for advice and counsel on foreign affairs and especially the conduct of the Vietnam war. Johnson, according to one source, "convened the full NSC primarily for 'educational, ratification, and ceremonial purposes.'"[24] But he depended heavily upon his Special Assistant for National Security Affairs McGeorge Bundy, a holdover from the Kennedy administration, until Bundy left government service in 1966. To demonstrate that as president he could manage national security affairs himself, Johnson denied the same title to Bundy's successor, Walt W. Rostow, calling him only a "special assistant."[25]

Nixon, with the guidance of his Special Assistant for National Security Affairs Henry Kissinger, developed a highly formal White House-centered system for management of national security policymaking and coordination. Kissinger, in effect, displaced Secretary of State William Rogers as the chief architect of American foreign policy. Kissinger's flamboyant "shuttle diplomacy" produced a flurry of activity and left Rogers shuffling papers in his Foggy Bottom office. Eventually Rogers resigned. Watson and Thomas have commented: "The result of the Nixon-Kissinger system was to convert what had originally been a staff position, the special assistant, into a main line operator. . . . Also, the NSC staff assumed many functions involving policy implementation and interagency coordination formerly performed by the State Department."[26]

When Kissinger became secretary of state in 1973 (while retaining the special assistant's portfolio), the controversy between a State Department-centered foreign policy and a White House-centered policy abated. But the rivalry resurfaced again during the Carter administration. Secretary of State Cyrus R. Vance and Zbigniew Brzezinski, the special assistant for national affairs, were publicly at odds, especially with respect to dealing with the Soviet Union. While Brzezinski did not eclipse Vance as the principal national security adviser to President Carter, he nevertheless enjoyed co-equal status with the secretary of state—a condition that sometimes created the impression of inept handling of national security policy within the administration.[27]

Reagan's announced commitment to cabinet government and major policy roles for the secretaries of state and defense suggested that the primary responsibility for foreign policy implementation would return to the State Department. And so it appeared when the strong-minded former White House aide, General Alexander M. Haig, was appointed secretary of state. But Haig's resignation two years later over policy differences with the White House staff once again opened the door for Special Assistant for National Security William Clark to move into the vacuum. Haig's replacement, former Secretary of the Treasury George Shultz, came into office with strong credentials as a problem-solving member in the Nixon and Ford cabinets. For a few months Shultz seemed to enjoy the undiluted confidence of President Reagan. But when Shultz's blueprint for Middle East peace initiatives fizzled, Special Assistant for National Security William P. Clark temporarily moved to the forefront of White House foreign policymaking. After the transfer of Clark to secretary of the interior in late 1983, Secretary of State Shultz appeared to regain the position of top foreign policy adviser to President Reagan.

THE SECRETARY OF STATE'S DECLINING ROLE

Traditional nineteenth-century doctrine had it that the secretary of state made foreign policy. But the emergence of the United States as a world power at the beginning of the twentieth century led several presidents to become their own secretaries of state. Theodore Roosevelt, though blessed with two strong secretaries, John Hay and Elihu Root, nevertheless ran the ship of state with gusto. Wilson, after his legislative successes in 1913–1914, increasingly turned his attention to foreign affairs. He became heavily involved in the growing crisis with Mexico and then sought to maintain American neutrality during World War I until unrestricted German submarine warfare led him to obtain from Congress a declaration of war against the Central Powers in April 1917. During this period one secretary of state, William Jennings Bryan, resigned, and his replacement Robert Lansing worked in the shadow of Wilson.

Franklin D. Roosevelt chose the respected Senator Cordell Hull of Tennessee to be his secretary of state, though he kept most of the foreign policy reins in his own hands. Harry Truman, in describing his duties to a group of White House visitors one afternoon, unabashedly announced: "I make foreign policy."[28] But this pattern of action flowed more from the conception of the office held by these presidents, rather than any structural changes in the management of foreign affairs.

John F. Kennedy chose to use his trusted White House staff and his Special Assistant for National Security McGeorge Bundy to maximize his own influence in foreign affairs. Johnson, as indicated earlier, retained Bundy as assistant for national security, and in the eyes of many observers, permitted Bundy to exercise authority equal to Secretary of State Rusk and Secretary of Defense Robert McNamara.

SPECIAL EMISSARIES

Throughout our history presidents have from time to time employed special emissaries to handle delicate missions that, for various reasons, they did not wish to entrust to regular ambassadors. Unlike ambassadors and ministers, the special emissaries are appointed solely by the president, without Senate approval. Although not mentioned specifically in the Constitution, their appointment may be implied from the treaty power and the all-purpose executive power clause.

Early in our history, George Washington sent John Jay to Great Britain to negotiate a special treaty relating to the settlement of claims arising from the

Revolutionary War and continued British occupation of frontier outposts. (These outposts had been officially ceded to the United States by the Treaty of 1783, but the British had refused to evacuate them.) A few years later, Thomas Jefferson sent future president James Monroe to the court of Napoleon Bonaparte to assist Robert Livingston with the crucially important Louisiana Purchase. In the twentieth century, Woodrow Wilson dispatched his special agent, Colonel Edward House, to Europe on a number of secret missions. During World War II, Franklin D. Roosevelt relied heavily on his personal confidant, Harry Hopkins, to conduct high-level negotiations with Prime Minister Winston Churchill and Soviet Dictator Josef Stalin.

Ronald Reagan, like many of his predecessors, has also displayed a penchant for special diplomatic representatives. In the fall of 1985, for example, he dispatched Senator Paul Laxalt (R–Nev.), his close personal friend and adviser, to the Philippines to urge President Ferdinand Marcos to undertake major domestic reforms to help quell a growing Communist insurgency. A few months later, during the 1986 Philippines election crisis and shortly before the fall of President Marcos, Mr. Reagan sent special envoy and veteran diplomatic troubleshooter Philip C. Habib twice to the Philippines. Upon returning from his first trip to the Far East, Habib told President Reagan that Marcos could not survive as president of the Philippines. Since Reagan trusted Habib's judgment far more than his diplomats at the U.S. embassy in Manila, the president reluctantly began backing away from his previous support of Marcos. It was shortly after Habib's second visit to the Philippines—and Marcos's trans-Pacific phone conversation with Senator Laxalt—that the Philippines president decided to step down and leave the country on a U.S. military aircraft.[29] No sooner had Habib returned to Washington than Mr. Reagan asked him to undertake another special assignment in Central America to find a "diplomatic solution" to the problems of the region, notably Nicaragua.[30]

To be sure, not all special envoys have succeeded in their tasks. Still, the publicity surrounding their mission often buys the president time to deal with political ramifications at home while the international crisis receives close attention from the president's hand-picked personal representative. Presidents also like to get fresh, first-hand reports from their emissaries, who have not been deeply involved in the internal politics of the host country and its neighbors. Heads of state and foreign ministers, in turn, like to deal with special envoys because they know their discussions will reach the president directly, not filtered through several layers of the State Department bureaucracy. Furthermore, they are confident that the president of the United States will honor any agreements made by his personal representative.

THE CIA AND FOREIGN POLICY

Presidents can also rely on covert operations conducted by the Central Intelligence Agency (CIA) to help achieve foreign policy objectives. Readers of *The New York Times* learned in early July 1983 that the CIA was funding a CIA-backed anti-Sandinista guerrilla force of several thousand in an attempt to overthrow the Marxist government of Nicaragua.[31] That CIA Director William Casey should now be in charge of a sizable combat army—the so-called Contras—did not raise many eyebrows in Washington. Indeed, it had been reported in the national press for several months that the Central Intelligence Agency had been actively involved in recruiting and training a band of mercenaries and anti-Sandinista exiles in Honduras. Nor was this the first instance since its founding in 1947 that the CIA had been heavily involved in paramilitary and counterrevolutionary operations.

Though the National Security Act of 1947, which authorized the establishment of the Central Intelligence Agency, says nothing about paramilitary operations, the CIA has been involved in this activity sporadically almost from the day of its founding. Soon after the China mainland fell to the Communists in 1949, the CIA started providing military and logistical support to the Chinese Nationalists on Taiwan for mounting raids against the offshore islands and the China coast. For a time the CIA also continued to support the remnants of the Chinese Nationalist army which had fled into northern Burma.

President Eisenhower had a reputation for straightforward diplomacy, but he frequently relied upon the CIA's undercover activity to attain some of his objectives. The CIA's most notable "successes" during the Eisenhower administration included aiding the overthrow of the left-wing Arbas regime in Guatemala (1954) and of the anti-American Mossadegh regime in Iran (1955). But the CIA was much less successful in its efforts to install a friendly government in Indonesia in 1954. Information also came to light from various sources that the CIA in the early 1970s sought to destabilize the Marxist-oriented government of Chilean President Salvadore Allende by supporting various right-wing opposition groups within the country.

Testimony had also appeared that the CIA may have engaged in assassination attempts on the heads of foreign states, including Fidel Castro of Cuba. Some sources have even hinted that as a result of this anti-Castro plot, the assassination of President John F. Kennedy may have had a "Cuban connection." In any case, it has only been in the last decade that American citizens have become more aware of how prominent a role the Central Intelligence Agency has played in presidential foreign policy.

Should the CIA engage in subversion of foreign governments by supporting insurgent forces or engaging in various "dirty tricks" to topple unfriendly governments? Does this type of activity abroad coincide with the democratic ideals or pretentions of the American system of government? Many citizens and legislators are deeply troubled by the contradictions generated by these practices as this country confronts totalitarian forces abroad.

In 1980, Congress passed the Accountability for Intelligence Activities Act, signed by President Carter shortly before the general election. In essence, this legislation stated that the president will normally be required to provide Congress with advance notification of any covert operations planned by the CIA. The 1980 act also reduced to two the number of committees that must be informed of covert operations and further stipulated that these committees must be kept "fully and currently informed of all U.S. intelligence activities." But the legislation stated that the two committees could not veto intelligence operations reported to its members.[32]

Whether the Intelligence Activities Act of 1980 will sufficiently rein in CIA activities and assure adequate congressional oversight remains an unanswered question. Ronald Reagan, soon after taking office, endorsed stepped-up CIA paramilitary activities in Central America. Congress, having been burned once in Southeast Asia less than two decades ago, has become increasingly nervous about the United States becoming involved in a Vietnam-type quagmire in Central America.

SHARED POLICYMAKING

Since World War II, the most successful collaborative foreign policy activity between the executive and legislative branches has occurred when the president has taken Congress into his confidence and consulted closely with the legislators.

President Truman, never known for his docility, established a hallmark for successful congressional consultation on foreign policy as he faced the enormous task of aiding the postwar economic reconstruction of Europe. Even though the 1946 election had seen the Republicans take over control of both houses of Congress, the president nevertheless obtained bipartisan congressional approval of the multibillion-dollar Marshall Plan for European reconstruction. Truman's secret weapon was his alliance with an old Senate colleague, Republican Senator Arthur Vandenberg, the influential chairman of the Senate Foreign Relations Committee and former isolationist turned internationalist.

To obtain Vandenberg's support and that of a number of other internationalist Republicans for the huge Marshall Plan, Truman permitted Vandenberg to name the administrator—Paul Hoffman, a leading industrialist—for the new program. Moreover, Truman agreed that the European Recovery Administration would be established as an independent agency rather than a bureau of the State Department, and further that "businessmen," rather than diplomats, would administer the program. Other presidents too, before and after Truman, have discovered that they cannot operate successfully in the field of foreign affairs without bipartisan support.

Most presidents, however, are tempted to rely on presidential prerogatives in conducting foreign policy because they frequently cannot count on support from their own party for their diplomatic initiatives. Theodore Roosevelt and William Howard Taft, for example, failed to obtain Senate approval for several Inter-American arbitration treaties. Coolidge and Hoover, even though their own party controlled both houses of Congress, could not turn around isolationist Republican opposition to United States membership in the World Court. More recently, Lyndon Johnson's most formidable critics of his Vietnam policies were Democrats. President Carter's plan to sell arms to Saudi Arabia was opposed by more than half of the Democrats in the Senate; only Republican votes "saved" the agreement.[33]

REASSERTION OF CONGRESSIONAL INFLUENCE

In the past two decades the increasing overlap between foreign and defense issues has produced a series of confrontations between the president and Congress. The legacy of the Vietnam war has encouraged Congress to take a more active role in monitoring foreign affairs. In contrast with the presidentially inspired post-World War II foreign policy initiatives—the Truman Doctrine, the Marshall Plan, American intervention in Korea and Vietnam, President Kennedy's limited nuclear test ban treaty and the opening of the door to China—the past dozen years have been marked by growing congressional resistance to presidential leadership. Since passage of the War Powers Act of 1973—the outgrowth of congressional disillusion with the Vietnam war—Congress has shied away from granting blank-check support of presidential leadership in foreign affairs, particularly if it appears that it may lead to hostilities and the sending of American troops abroad.[34]

As a result, the post-Vietnam, post-Watergate presidency has also witnessed more sharing of constitutional power between the executive and legislative branches than at any time in recent memory. Congressional participation (or intrusion) in foreign policy over the past decade has included the following: a limit on Soviet credits from the Export-Import Bank for as long as the Soviet Union curbed the emigration of Soviet Jews and other Soviet citizens; the banning of military aid to the Pinochet regime in Chile because of violations of human rights; severe restrictions on military aid to Turkey as a result of the Turkish invasion of Cyprus; the prohibition of aid of any kind to Angola (this so-called Clark Amendment has since been repealed); a rule that no more than 30 percent of American food aid could go to countries not in actual need, as determined by the United Nations. In early 1986 the House of Representatives twice voted to deny President Reagan's proposed military aid to the anti-Sandinista Contra rebels seeking to overthrow the leftist Nicaraguan government—another indication that the "post-Vietnam syndrome" is still very much alive on Capitol Hill.[35]

Many thoughtful leaders on both sides of the aisle in Congress, however, recognize that the present 535 members of Congress cannot hope to serve as an alternate secretary of state. Nor is the congressional role in foreign affairs enhanced by the fact that 14 of the 16 standing committees in the Senate and 17 of the standing committees in the House have some jurisdiction over at least some aspect of overseas activities. Finally, to a far greater extent than the president, Congress is susceptible to the persistent and unrelenting demands of various special interest groups—the Jewish and the Greek lobbies, the Farm Bureau, the AFL-CIO, major banking institutions with billions loaned to Latin American and Third World countries—indeed, the list of special interest groups with axes to grind abroad would fill volumes. Congress, it seems fair to say, does its best job in foreign affairs when it concentrates on oversight of policy, controls the military-foreign aid purse strings, and leaves the day-to-day policymaking duties to the president and the Department of State.

While increased congressional staffing in the past decade has enabled legislators to monitor foreign affairs more closely, committee activity on Capitol Hill indicated for a brief time that the legislators might be having second thoughts about the restrictions they had imposed on the president over the past decade. In September 1980, Congress passed legislation designed to allow the president and the CIA greater flexibility in the direction of covert activities abroad. Similarly, Congress decided to lift some of the restrictions placed on the president in the area of foreign aid. In the aftermath of the imperial presidency of Richard Nixon and the trauma of Watergate, leading members of Congress seemed more willing to give the president more latitude in foreign affairs. Continuing crisis in Lebanon, Iran, Afghanistan, Central America, Libya, and Chad; the rising tide of international terrorism; and the Soviet downing of a Korean Airlines 747 commercial airliner off the coast of Siberia in September 1983 have all contributed to the feeling that the president must have a freer hand in managing foreign affairs. Unlike the past, however, Congress can be expected to look frequently over the president's shoulder, checking to see if he may not be stretching the country's political and military commitments too far, possibly repeating a disastrous Vietnam type of intervention.

Does this latest round of presidential-congressional differences represent a swing of the pendulum back to the period in the nineteenth century when Congress was the leader and the president the follower in foreign policy formation? Probably not. While Arthur Schlesinger, Jr., has characterized presidential-congressional rivalry for control over foreign policy as a "guerrilla war" that has "dragged along through our history,"[36] twentieth-century presidents, with their instant sources of communication and intelligence throughout the world and their awesome nuclear weaponry, occupy a unique leadership position that Congress is unable to match. As one constitutional authority has put it: "The President has won most of the battles not because his constitutional arguments are necessarily stronger but because his temptations and opportunities are greater, because he has had all the advantages of 'sole organ,' and foreign policy is effectively what he communicates to other nations."[37] Still, the checks and balances mandated by the Founding Fathers have not left Congress entirely powerless.

The power of the purse can make the president sensitive to congressional concerns. While control of the purse enables Congress to resist a president only after the fact rather than to initiate foreign policy, this power is formidable. In 1974, for example, Congress cut off military aid to Turkey after its invasion of Cyprus, despite President Ford's objections. Two years later, Congress took similar action via the Clark Amendment to the defense budget to shut off CIA-directed military assistance to pro-Western factions fighting the Soviet and Cuban-based factions in Angola. Earlier, Congress finally cut off in 1973 funds to continue bombing in Cambodia and Laos after a protracted and bitter debate with President Nixon. Subsequently, Nixon blamed Congress for prematurely ending the war in Southeast Asia, commenting in his memoirs: ". . . [the] war and the peace in Indochina that America had won at such cost over twelve years of sacrifice and fighting were lost within a matter of months once Congress refused to fulfill our obligation. And it is Congress that must bear the responsibility for the tragic results."[38]

A "Sense of the Senate" (or House) resolution, passed by a bipartisan majority, can be a seriously inhibiting factor on the president's foreign policy actions. Though not binding on the chief executive, these resolutions can send a blunt message to the president to "go slow," or call upon the president to reverse a course of action.[39] Because these resolutions often reflect public opinion, they cannot be lightly disregarded. Nor should the congressional power of investigation be ignored. As explained by Louis Henkin: "Congressional committees and individual Congressmen have opportunities to inquire, cross-examine, expose, criticize, even harass and threaten officials engaged in the conduct of foreign policy, and the need to justify to Congressmen is a not insignificant influence on Executive policy."[40]

Equally important, informal extraconstitutional powers also give Congress —notably congressional leaders—formidable influence on a president's foreign policy. Chairmen of major committees in both houses, party leaders, and other key people must constantly be consulted and informed by the president if his foreign policy initiatives are to bear fruit. To assure friendly support from Congress, shrewd presidents have appointed congressional leaders to serve on delegations to international peace conferences and other major international meetings. Franklin Roosevelt, unlike Wilson, who failed to include any U.S. senators on the American delegation to the Versailles peace conference in 1919, in 1945 invited several influential opposition Republican leaders to the San Francisco conference which established the United Nations.

The investigative powers of Congress should not be discounted as a tool to influence foreign policy. In 1966, the Senate Foreign Relations Committee, chaired by Senator J. William Fulbright, conducted a full-blown, network-televised investigation of America's Vietnam policy. A year later, the Foreign Relations Committee adopted a Fulbright resolution asserting that "the executive and legislative branches of the United States Government have joint responsibility and authority to formulate the foreign policy of the United States" and further asserted that in the future American armed forces should not be committed to hostilities on foreign territory "without affirmative action by Congress specifically intended to give rise to such commitment."[41] Eventually, Congress resorted to its control over appropriations power to halt an escalating involvement in the Southeast Asian conflict. Though used belatedly, Congress's vote in 1973 to cut off support for American forces in Cambodia was decisive.

PRESIDENT REAGAN VERSUS CONGRESS

Almost two decades ago, Aaron Wildavsky developed the thesis of "the two presidencies," in which he showed by a long series of congressional votes that the president enjoyed far greater support in foreign policy and defense issues than domestic matters.[42] If Wildavsky were keeping score again during late 1983 and early 1984, he would have returned to the drawing board, for President Reagan encountered a series of foreign policy rebuffs.[43]

Congressional skepticism of presidential foreign policy motives resurfaced in the summer of 1983 as the American contingent of the international peacekeeping force in Lebanon came under insurgent artillery fire. The loss of 241 U.S.

Marines to a terrorist truck-bombing attack in late October 1983 triggered renewed congressional attacks on Reagan's Middle Eastern foreign policy. Congressional sniping on the retention of the U.S. Marines in Lebanon, even though the lawmakers had approved an 18-month troop extension, persisted throughout the late fall and winter. Finally, the President decided on February 7, 1984, to order the withdrawal of the U.S. contingent in Lebanon.[44] Subsequently, in a speech before the Georgetown Center for Strategic Studies, Reagan sought to pin a major share of the blame on Congress for America's diplomatic failure in Lebanon. Congress's constant "second guessing" of the administration's foreign policy, the president declared, was the major cause for the failure of the Lebanese mission and served to encourage Marxism in Central America.[45]

Less than two months later, President Reagan decided, in face of overwhelming congressional opposition, to withdraw the sale of advanced anti-aircraft Stinger missiles to Jordan and Saudi Arabia. Congressional ire had been raised by the publication in *The New York Times* of an interview with King Hussein of Jordan in which the Jordanian monarch rejected the idea of direct negotiations with Israel, called the United States unprincipled and too pro-Israel, and heaped criticism on supporters of Israel in Congress.[46] Confronted with the prospect of an amendment being introduced on the Senate floor to kill the sale of the Stinger missile, the Reagan administration decided to withdraw the proposal. Originally, the administration had hoped that in return for canceling the Stinger missile sale, Israel's supporters in Congress would agree to kill a pending bill that would require moving the U.S. embassy in Israel from Tel Aviv to Jerusalem. But this plan was dropped, too, after strong pro-Israel groups in the United States objected.

The string of administration foreign policy setbacks continued into April 1984, when the United States Senate passed by an 84 to 12 vote a nonbinding resolution condemning the CIA-directed mining of Nicaraguan harbors. Critics argued that the sowing of mines in territorial waters of a country that the United States was not at war with constituted a clear violation of international law.[47] The severity of the defeat was underscored by the fact that the policy was opposed by 42 Republicans, including Senator Howard H. Baker, Jr., of Tennessee, the majority leader, and Senator Paul Laxalt of Nevada, chairman of President Reagan's reelection campaign and general chairman of his Republican party.[48] To many Capitol Hill observers, the mass defection of Republicans signaled the end of congressional military funding for the anti-Sandinista Nicaraguan rebels through the Central Intelligence Agency. The overwhelming negative vote in the Senate even jeopardized economic and military aid for El Salvador.

By failing to consult adequately with key members of the Senate and House, especially the Senate Intelligence Committee, on the mining of the Nicaraguan ports, the Reagan administration managed to outrage many of its own party's strongest supporters. The most damaging blow came with the publication of a letter from Senator Barry Goldwater, chairman of the Senate Intelligence Committee, to Mr. William J. Casey, the CIA director, in which he responded to the president's earlier plea for a bipartisan foreign policy: "How can we back his foreign policy when we don't even know what the hell he is doing."[49]

The repeated confrontations between President Reagan and Congress, it should be noted, are not a recent phenomenon in the nation's capital. Difficulties over managing foreign policy, while seeking continuous approval from Congress, have plagued all modern presidents since Woodrow Wilson's failure to win Senate ratification of the Versailles Treaty after World War I.

In the ongoing debate over foreign policy, the Reagan administration hit another sensitive nerve when Robert C. McFarlane, the national security adviser, talked to reporters after Mr. Reagan's Georgetown University speech in 1984 and went even further than the president in suggesting that congressional criticism of the president's foreign policy was improper. Reagan's national security adviser told reporters that Congress "should be encouraged" to disagree with the president in the "formation" of policy. But, he added, "once the policy is formed, it can seriously undermine its hope of success if there is a continuing repetition of this earlier disagreement."[50] Adding to his remarks, the national security adviser said that once policy is formed, members of Congress who want to criticize it should do so in writing to the president, but not in public forums, at least in such situations as Lebanon, where American lives were at stake.[51]

Members of Congress were quick to point out that the national security adviser's reading of the Constitution was different from theirs. Though it has become increasingly difficult to separate foreign policy actions, which are a presidential prerogative, from actions that may lead to war, which would require a declaration of war by Congress, some congressional leaders appear to hold the view that within this "twilight zone" Congress can prescribe for future uses of force in situations that are tantamount to war.

One leading constitutional lawyer, in trying to delineate a line between the powers of the president and Congress, has said: "As regards hostilities 'short of war,' it may be that, although the President can use force if Congress is silent, Congress can forbid or regulate even such uses of force, if only on the grounds that they might lead to war."[52] But he quickly added: "Presidents, however, are likely to deny the control of Congress in such cases." Since passage of the War Powers Act of 1973, congressional opponents of the president have endeavored to deter presidential foreign policy adventurism by charging that the presence of American troops, especially training officers near the scene of hostilities, requires that the War Powers Act be invoked. This action, in turn, requires that the president inform Congress in writing within 48 hours of his military plans and, in effect, permits Congress to veto presidential warmaking after 60 days, unless the lawmakers grant an extension.

RECENT CONGRESSIONAL QUARTERBACKING

No president in memory—with the possible exception of President Nixon—has had to contend with more congressional quarterbacking of foreign policy than Ronald Reagan. Over an 18-month period in 1984–1985, the House or Senate, or both, voted more than a dozen times on the question of supplying some form of aid to the anti-Sandinista Contras opposing the leftist government in Nicaragua. In mid-June 1985, for example, the House reversed a negative vote on aid to the anti-Sandinista rebels taken in April; instead, it voted 248 to 184 to approve an amendment offered by House Republican Leader Robert Michel to authorize "non-lethal" aid to the rebels. Similarly, the House by a 232 to 196 vote refused to extend a ban on U.S. support for military or paramilitary action inside Nicaragua.[53] Previously, the House had voted several times to approve the restriction on U.S. involvement. What accounted for this congressional flip-flop? Most Washington observers attributed it to Nicaraguan President Daniel Ortega Saavadra's visit to the Soviet Union the day after Congress had voted in April 1985 to reject aid to the anti-Sandinista rebels.

"The primary concern," according to one anti-administration senator, "is that senators don't want the President to point an accusing finger at them and say, 'You lost Central America, you care more about a dictator in green fatigues [Ortega] than the freedom fighters (Contras).'" Thus, President Reagan could finally claim a limited legislative-foreign policy victory on Nicaragua after losing nearly a dozen votes on this issue over the previous 18 months. President Reagan's steady drumfire campaign against the leftist Nicaraguan government, discussed in two nationwide telecasts and pursued frequently on his weekly Saturday nationwide radio broadcasts, had finally paid off.

On another front, the Senate and House, in protest against the racial violence institutionalized fascism in South Africa, voted in July 1985 in favor of anti-Apartheid sanctions against the Union of South Africa. The proposed legislation—which the Reagan administration opposed—would prohibit bank loans to new businesses, ban the sale of materials used in nuclear production, block the shipment of scientific computer hardware to South Africa, and prohibit the sale of Krugerrands, the South African gold coins, in the United States. The administration, on the other hand, favored a policy of "constructive engagement" to pressure South Africa into modifying its Apartheid policy. But in the face of the threatened congressional action and widespread protests throughout the United States against the South African government's violent repression of anti-Apartheid demonstrators, the Reagan administration reluctantly imposed limited sanctions against the ruling white minority government in the fall of 1985.[54]

The resurgence of congressional involvement in foreign policy can be traced, in part, to the pervasive belief that President Johnson, more than two decades ago, had duped Congress into supporting his Vietnam policy. Lawmakers in both parties insist they want to avoid another Gulf of Tonkin Resolution, the act that Johnson frequently relied on to justify deepening involvement in Southeast Asia. Members of Congress, according to one ranking member, do not want to be embarrassed or "blindsided" later by votes cast in the dark.[55] Some members of Congress who were criticized for not playing a larger role in foreign policy then are not going to make the same mistake twice. According to one respected Western congressman: "The most important consideration in Congress is to limit Presidential authority out of fear that someone will abuse it the way that Nixon and Johnson did."[56]

Despite Congress's heightened role in foreign policymaking since the Vietnam war, it seems unlikely that the lawmakers will displace the president as chief policymaker. First of all, Congress lacks the capability to make quick decisions during crises. Unlike the single chief executive who can react and move at a moment's notice, a body that needs to deliberate before reaching a decision is not suited for fast-moving diplomatic events that may change or shift in the midst of negotiations. A legislative body simply cannot shift gears and reach or change decisions fast enough. Tatalovich and Daynes have reminded us about Congress's inability to legislate a foreign policy during the final days of the Vietnam war, after the collapse of the South Vietnam regime.

Because the Eagleton Amendment (banning funds for combat use in Indo-china) was still in force, President Ford was technically in violation of that law when he ordered U.S. helicopters to pluck American and Vietnamese staff members from the roof of the American embassy in Saigon. Throughout this final evacuation, Congress was still debating the merits of allowing the president to undertake this action, a circumstance that prompted the following exasperated commentary from Senator Barry Goldwater:

> When the North Vietnamese [get] within rocket range of Tonsonhut Air Base, there is not going to be any more evacuation unless we want to go to war. I think we are spinning our wheels. The President, and I am proud of him for having done this, has taken into his own hands the protection of Americans and American property and American freedoms, wherever they might be, around this world, regardless of the legislation that we, in my opinion, foolishly passed last year . . . I suggest that we're being a little foolish, a little redundant. We're not accomplishing anything. We may not pass this bill until the day after tomor-row, at which time, I think the whole action will be over and we will have again engaged ourselves in ridiculous debate. . .[57]

What was the final outcome of the congressional debate? Tatalovich and Daynes have pointed out that Congress never did agree on legislation authorizing the president to conduct the evacuation of Saigon.[58] No wonder strong defenders of the presidency insist that only the president is capable of decisive action in times of crisis.

In conducting foreign policy, presidents sometimes enjoy sudden surges of public support. John Mueller, in his seminal study, labeled these surges *rally events.* He defined a rally event as one that is international, directly involves the United States, particularly the president, and is dramatic and identifiable.[59] Rally events are salient to the public and generate public attention and interest. The inaugural period of a president's term is also included within his definition.

Mueller developed the theory that the public will increase its support of the president in times of crisis or during major international events, or at least in the short run because he is the symbol of the country and the center of attention at such times. Mueller also reasoned that people do not want to hurt the country's chances of success by denigrating the president. Further, the president has a prime opportunity to be a statesman and evoke a strong patriotic reaction from the people. To qualify as a rally event, the president has to gain an in-crease of 10 percentage points in public approval between two consecutive events.

Professor George Edwards III, in a study of presidential approval for the period 1953–1983, found 21 occasions when at least one of three party groups—Democrats, Republicans, and Independents—increased their public approval of the president 10 percentage points between two consecutive polls (see Table 8.2). Edwards' study, however, revealed mixed results in measuring the impact of rally events on presidential approval. The termination of U.S. involvement in Vietnam, for example, substantially increased the president's approval rating, but the ending of the Korean war did not. U.S. counteractions to the attempted Soviet intervention in Cuba (the Cuban missile crisis) and Communist Cambodia (the release of the U.S. freighter *Mayaguez*) raised the president's support level significantly. But U.S. military action against Cuba (Bay of Pigs), the Dominican Republic, and North Korea did not.

The capture of the American hostages in Teheran by Iranian revolutionaries produced the largest single increase in presidential approval in the history of the Gallup poll, but the capture of the U.S. naval communications ship *Pueblo* by the North Korean Communists did not have a serious impact on presidential approval. Significantly, President Eisenhower's 1959 goodwill trip to Europe and Asia boosted his public approval ratings, but all future presidential foreign tours

Table 8.2 **TEN-PERCENTAGE-POINT INCREASES IN PRESIDENTIAL APPROVAL, 1953–1983**

Date of poll	Party group	Rally event since preceding poll
December 11–16, 1953	D	Eisenhower UN Atoms for Peace speech
July 16, 21, 1954	D,I	None
December 2–7, 1954	D	None
November 17–22, 1955*	D	None
December 10–15, 1959	D,I	Eisenhower European-Asian "peace" trip
July 30–August 4, 1960	I	None
September 28–October 2, 1960	I	None
November 16–21, 1962	D,R	Cuban missile crisis
August 15–20, 1963	R	None
October 27–November 1, 1967	D	None
April 4–9, 1968	R	None
July 24–29, 1969	I	Moon landing
November 12–17, 1969	D,I	Nixon "Vietnamization" speech
January 15–20, 1970	R	None
January 26–29, 1973	D,I	Vietnam peace agreement
May 30–June 2, 1975	D,R	*Mayaguez* crisis
January 2–5, 1976	I	None
November 4–7, 1977	R	None
September 15–18, 1978	I	Camp David Accords
November 30–December 3, 1979	D,R,I	Iranian hostage crisis
September 12–15, 1980	D	None
October 7–10, 1983		Soviets shoot down KAL 747

*Two months since previous poll.
D = Democrat, R = Republican, I = Independent.
Source: From *The Public Presidency: The Pursuit of Popular Support,* by George C. Edwards III, 244. Copyright © 1983 by St. Martin's Press, Inc., and used with permission. Data derived from Gallup polls, 1983 data from *Gallup Report* 219 (December 1983), 23.

had much less impact. Eisenhower's atoms for peace proposal raised his support level, but Kennedy's limited nuclear test ban treaty in 1963—a far more significant event—had relatively little impact.

Strangely, many of the major events that might be expected to cause the public to rally behind the president have had little effect on presidential support (see Table 8.3). Edwards concludes:

> The impact of the rally phenomenon is difficult to isolate, but the preponderance of evidence indicates that it rarely appears and that the events that generate it are highly idiosyncratic and do not seem to significantly differ from other events that were not followed by significant surges in presidential approval. Moreover, the events that cause sudden increases in public support are not restricted to international affairs, and most international events that would seem to be potential rally events fail to generate much additional approval of the president.[60]

In light of this evidence, it would appear that "rally around the flag" events may be overrated as a means for presidents to revive their popularity.

Some recent evidence, however, suggests that the jury is still out on the question of the impact of rally events on presidential public support. President

Table 8.3 POTENTIAL RALLY EVENTS NOT FOLLOWED BY A SUBSTANTIAL INCREASE IN PRESIDENTIAL APPROVAL, 1953–1983

Event	Year
Korean truce	1953
Sputnik I launched	1957
U.S. troops sent to Lebanon	1958
U-2 shot down	1960
Bay of Pigs invasion	1961
Berlin crisis	1961
Test Ban Treaty signed	1963
Dominican Republic invasion	1965
Pueblo capture	1968
Tet offensive	1968
Cambodian invasion	1970
Mining Haiphong harbor	1972
Christmas bombing of North Vietnam	1972
Nixon trip to China	1972
Fall of Cambodia	1975
Fall of Vietnam	1975
Ford trip to China	1975
Soviet invasion of Afghanistan	1979
Summit meetings with Soviet leaders	1955, 1959, 1960, 1961, 1967, 1972, 1973, 1974
Beirut terrorist bomb kills 241 U.S. Marines	1983

Source: From *The Public Presidency: The Pursuit of Popular Support,* by George C. Edwards III, 247. Copyright © 1983 by St. Martin's Press, Inc., and used with permission. Data derived from Gallup polls, 1983 data from *Gallup Report* 219 (December 1983), 23.

Reagan's rating for handling foreign policy surged dramatically following the mid-April 1986 United States bombing of Libyan dictator Moammar Khadafy's headquarters and other Libyan bases thought to be havens for international terrorists. One week before the raid, the *New York Times*/CBS Poll showed 51 percent of the public approved the president's handling of foreign policy. The night after the U.S. planes returned to their bases, the new *Times*/CBS telephone survey of 708 respondents nationwide revealed that 76 percent approved President Reagan's handling of foreign policy—a 25 percent jump in one week.[61] His highest previous level rating was 56 percent just before the Reagan-Gorbachev Geneva summit meeting in November 1985.[62]

CONCLUSION

As we near the two-hundredth anniversary of our nation's founding, the wisdom of the Framers in dividing the power over foreign affairs between the executive and legislative branches seems as valid in this nuclear age as it did in Philadelphia in 1787.

Though crafted in an era of primitive communication, the shared power concept still offers a high degree of flexibility to the president in an age of instant communication and space travel. But it also imposes enough constraints upon the chief executive to keep him responsive to the concerns of Congress.

Put another way, under the American system of divided powers, the president is granted broad latitude to deal with foreign affairs and international emergencies, but the Constitution also grants to Congress, through its control over all appropriations and its power to declare war, the final word on whether the president's actions will be sustained over the long term.

Short of the constitutional amendment process, Congress retains several ways to impose constraints on a president. To head off another undeclared presidential war similar to the Vietnam conflict, Congress passed the War Powers Resolution of 1973. When it became known a year earlier that several presidents had made executive agreements with friendly governments that might involve the major commitment of American troops abroad to honor these presidential pledges, Congress passed the Case Act, which required that the Senate—the Foreign Relations Committee, in the case of secret agreements—be informed of all major executive agreements made by the president. Although the constitutional sharing of powers often creates a power struggle between the executive and legislative branches, this check and balance system operates exactly along the lines the Founding Fathers had in mind when they drafted the Constitution.

By and large, though, the president is in the foreign policy driver's seat, even though he knows that in the long run he must build a bridge of cooperation with Congress if his policies are to succeed. Louis Henkin's description of presidential-congressional relationships on foreign policy is perhaps closest to the mark: "In the end, while insisting on its constitutional autonomy, Congress has generally sensed that in the strange contraption which the Fathers created for conducting foreign policy, the Congress are the rear wheels, indispensable and usually obliged to follow, but not without substantial braking power."[63]

And in reviewing the balance sheet on foreign policy, C. Herman Pritchett, the constitutional lawyer, has put it well:

> Congress cannot run foreign policy, but it has the right and the obligation to use its appropriating and legislating power to fix outer limits for American foreign policy and military policy and to review and revise ongoing foreign and military commitments.[64]

While this system must seem cumbersome, indeed sometimes unworkable, to the foreign observer, the overall record of this shared arrangement seems to have found favor with most Americans over the years. Significantly, of the 16 amendments added to the Constitution since ratification of the Bill of Rights (the first 10 amendments) in 1791, none has involved the management or the distribution of power over foreign affairs.[65]

NOTES

1. Steven V. Roberts, *The New York Times,* May 29, 1985.
2. Thomas A. Bailey, *A Diplomatic History of the American People,* 10th ed. (Englewood Cliffs, NJ: Prentice Hall, 1980), 54.
3. Edward S. Corwin, *The President: Office and Powers 1787–1957,* 4th rev. ed. (New York: New York University Press, 1957), 171.
4. The treaty was ratified by the U.S. Senate after a bitter flurry of opposition on February 23, 1904—slightly more than two months after the Panamanian revolt. Bailey, *A Diplomatic History of the American People,* 491–496.
5. 299 U.S. 304 (1936).
6. Ibid.
7. *The New York Times,* July 3, 1981.
8. William R. Thayer, *The Life and Letters of John Hay* (Boston: Houghton Mifflin, 1915), vol. 2, 393.
9. Bailey, *A Diplomatic History of the American People,* 622.
10. 301 U.S. 324 (1937).
11. 315 U.S. 203 (1942).
12. 348 U.S. 296.
13. 354 U.S. 1 (1957). For a further discussion of these cases and others relating to executive agreements, see Louis Fisher, *Constitutional Conflicts Between Congress and the President* (Princeton, NJ: Princeton University Press, 1985), 272–283.
14. *Congressional Quarterly Weekly Report,* January 1, 1971, 24.
15. Arthur M. Schlesinger, Jr., *The Imperial Presidency* (Boston: Houghton Mifflin, 1973), 200–201.
16. *Congressional Quarterly Weekly Report,* January 1, 1971, 24.
17. Ibid., 87–88.
18. Robert E. DiClerico, *The American President,* 2nd ed. (Englewood Cliffs, NJ: Prentice Hall, 1983), 50–51.
19. *The New York Times,* April 17, 1975.
20. *Congressional Quarterly Weekly Report,* August 2, 1975, 1714.
21. Fisher, *Constitutional Conflicts Between Congress and the President,* 282–283.
22. Bailey, *A Diplomatic History of the American People,* 541.

23. P.L. 80–253, sec 101 (a).

24. Keith Clark and Lawrence Legere, *The President and the Management of National Security* (New York: Praeger, 1969), 37–54, as cited by Louis W. Koenig, *The Chief Executive,* 4th ed. (New York: Harcourt, Brace Jovanovich, 1981), 192.

25. I. M. Destler, "National Security II: The Rise of the Assistant (1961–1981)," in Hugh Heclo and Lester M. Salamon, eds., *The Illusion of Presidential Government* (Boulder, CO: Westview Press, 1981), 270.

26. Richard A. Watson and Norman C. Thomas, *The Politics of the Presidency* (New York: Wiley, 1983), 353.

27. Brzezinski, since leaving the White House staff, has argued that the primacy in the area of foreign affairs should not belong with the secretary of state. Instead, he recommends that the Office of Assistant to the President for National Security Affairs should be upgraded by designating it as the Office of the Director of National Security Affairs, comparable to the post of Director of the Office of Management and Budget. This reorganization would give the director and his staff the status and authority required for the coordination of national security recommendations as they emanate from the State and Defense Departments and the CIA. Brzezinski would also require that the Director of National Security Affairs be made subject to Senate confirmation. This would mean that the director would be expected to testify from time to time before congressional committees and not avoid the hearings, as Henry Kissinger did when he served as the national security adviser. See Zbigniew Brzezinski, "Deciding Who Makes Foreign Policy," *New York Times Magazine,* September 18, 1983, 62–74.

28. Clinton Rossiter, *The American Presidency,* rev. ed. (New York: Harcourt, Brace and Jovanovich, 1960), 10.

29. "Anatomy of a Revolution," *Time,* March 10, 1986, 28–34.

30. *The New York Times,* March 12, 1986.

31. Ibid., July 25, 1983.

32. DiClerico, *The American President,* 54.

33. Richard M. Pious, *The American Presidency* (New York: Basic Books, 1979), 356.

34. Daniel Yankelovitch, "Farewell to 'President Knows Best,'" *Foreign Affairs,* 57 (1979), 670–693.

35. In late June 1986, however, the House reversed itself, after President Reagan's heavy lobbying among conservative southern Democrats, and voted 221 to 209 to provide $100 million in military aid to the anti-Sandanista rebels. *The New York Times,* June 26, 1986.

36. Arthur Schlesinger, Jr., "Congress and the Making of Foreign Policy," in Thomas E. Cronin and Rexford Tugwell, eds., *The Presidency Reappraised* (New York: Praeger, 1972), 221.

37. Louis Henkin, *Foreign Affairs and the Constitution* (Mineola, NY: The Foundation Press, 1972), 122.

38. Richard M. Nixon, "RN: The Memoirs of Richard Nixon," *The New York Times,* May 3, 1978, 10.

39. Congressional resolutions sometimes become translated into national policy. Thus in 1912 the Lodge Resolution barring the Western Hemisphere to foreign powers for military and naval purposes, even when done through quasi-public corporations, became national policy. This action was directed against a reported attempt by a Japanese company to establish a coaling station in Mexico. S. Res. 371, 62nd Cong., 2d Sess., 48 *Cong. Record,* 100 46–47 (1912), as cited by Henkin, *Foreign Affairs and the Constitution,* 337, note 74.

40. Henkin, *Foreign Affairs and the Constitution,* 87.

41. As cited in C. Herman Pritchett, *The American Constitution* (New York: McGraw-Hill, 1968), 361.

42. Aaron Wildavsky, "The Two Presidencies," *Trans-Action, IV* (December 1966), reprinted in Aaron Wildavsky, ed. *Perspectives on the Presidency* (Boston: Little, Brown, 1975), 448–461.

43. As Bert Rockman commented recently, ". . . the so-called 'two-presidencies' thesis (deference to the president by Congress in foreign, but not domestic policy) is itself derived from measuring presidential success with Congress in foreign policy during a period of perceived intense threat. Easing of the latter weakened foreign policy consensus thereby reducing, for better or worse, presidential latitude. In recent times, it has been more difficult to arrive at an agreed upon definition of international peril. Not surprisingly, presidents of late have not fared well in regard to their foreign policy initiatives." Bert Rockman, *The Leadership Question: The Presidency and the American System* (New York: Praeger, 1984), 122.

44. *The New York Times,* February 8, 1984.

45. Ibid., April 7, 1984.

46. Ibid., March 21, 1984.

47. Subsequently, the Nicaraguan government took its dispute with the United States to the World Court in the Hague. Although the Reagan administration had announced that it would not recognize the jurisdiction of the World Court over any Central American dispute for two years, the World Court ruled unanimously that the United States should immediately halt any attempts to blockade or mine Nicaraguan ports. In granting the Nicaraguan request for a preliminary restraining order to protect its sovereign rights, the World Court also asserted by a 14 to 1 vote that Nicaraguan political independence "should not be jeopardized by any military or paramilitary activities." In issuing its decision the 15-member tribunal, known as the International Court of Justice, rejected the United States request that it dismiss the Nicaraguan application on jurisdictional grounds. The World Court's recommendation, it should be noted, is not binding. As the legal arm of the United Nations, the World Court advised the UN Security Council of its decisions. In theory, subsequent requests for enforcement may be made to the Security Council, but at no time since the founding of the United Nations has the Security Council taken any action to press a World Court ruling. *The New York Times,* May 12, 1984.

48. A nonbinding resolution vote should not be lightly dismissed. In May 1981, the Senate rejected the Reagan administration's proposal to reduce social security benefits and forced the White House to drop the plan entirely. For the next two years, this vote left the administration on the political defensive on this key domestic issue. *The New York Times,* April 12, 1984.

49. *The New York Times,* April 12, 1984.

50. *The New York Times,* April 7, 1984.

51. Ibid.

52. Henkin, *Foreign Affairs and the Constitution,* 103.

53. *The New York Times,* May 29, 1985.

54. Ibid., September 10, 1985.

55. Ibid., May 29, 1985.

56. Ibid.

57. *U.S. Senate Congressional Record* (April 23, 1975), S. 6611, as cited by Raymond Tatalovich and Byron W. Daynes, *Presidential Power in the United States* (Monterey, CA: Brooks/Cole, 1984), 280.

58. Ibid.

59. John E. Mueller, *War, Presidents and Public Opinion* (New York: Wiley, 1970), 208–213.

60. George C. Edwards, III, *The Public Presidency* (New York: St. Martin's Press, 1983), 246–247.

61. *The New York Times,* April 17, 1986.

62. *Ibid.,* The *Times*/CBS Poll, it should be noted, asks essentially the same questions as the Gallup poll does on the president's handling of foreign policy.

63. Henkin, *Foreign Affairs and the Constitution,* p. 123.

64. C. Herman Pritchett, "The President's Constitutional Position," in Thomas E. Cronin, ed., *Rethinking the Presidency* (Boston: Little, Brown, 1982), 136.

65. As mentioned earlier in the chapter, the closest that Congress has ever come to amending the President's constitutional control over foreign affairs occurred in 1954, when the Senate failed by only one vote, 60 to 31, to approve the so-called Bricker Amendment. Sponsored by John Bricker (R–Ohio), this proposed amendment would have required that all treaties and executive agreements not be self-executing—that is, they could not be implemented without congressional approval. For details surrounding debate over the Bricker Amendment, see Joseph E. Kallenbach, *The American Chief Executive* (New York: Harper & Row, 1966), 510–512; Pritchett, *The American Constitution,* 364–366.

chapter 9

Chief Administrator

If the head of a modern corporation were asked to perform the far-ranging administrative duties of the president of the United States, with its numerous constitutional constraints, shared powers, and inadequate authority to reorganize and consolidate various agencies in the executive branch, the corporate president would probably throw up his hands and resign in disgust over the incessant checks on his administrative authority. In terms of control and decision making, the administrative authority of the president of the United States is a far cry from that wielded by most corporate chief executives.

In this chapter we trace the president's role as chief administrator from the early days of the Republic to today. As we will explain, the Founding Fathers were in clear agreement on the need for centralized direction of the federal government and a single chief executive. But they were purposely vague on how the day-to-day activities were to be handled. We will discuss the growth and institutionalization of the White House executive office, especially in the twentieth century, as well as the problems that arise between the White House and the various executive departments within the executive branch. The eclipse of the cabinet and the centralization of the executive branch management in the White House since World War II will receive special attention. We will compare and contrast presidential management styles, and examine the emergence of the executive budget after World War I and the president's use of central clearance by the Bureau of the Budget (changed to the Office of Management and Budget in 1970) as a means of monitoring department budgets and reviewing proposed legislation originating in the executive branch. Congress's role in administrative reorganization and oversight will be evaluated in light of modern management theory. Finally, we will examine presidential efforts to reorganize the executive branch and the absence of long-range planning.

AMBIGUOUS GUIDELINES

Did the men of 1787 intend to invest the president with independent authority beyond the parameters of congressional control, or did they intend to let him function in this broad area as an agent of Congress? Nobody knows. Must the president execute laws that in his judgment violate his oath requiring him to "faithfully execute the office of President of the United States" and to "preserve, protect and defend the Constitution of the United States"? What about laws that in his judgment invade his own constitutional prerogatives as chief executive? The Constitution sheds no light on these questions.

The Framers, with their innate distrust of concentrated power, did not hesitate to divide responsibilities between president and Congress in some areas of administration. Thus, while the president's position of chief of administration is reinforced by a grant of broad appointive authority in the Constitution blanketing all the more important categories of executive and judicial officers, these appointments are nevertheless "subject to the advice and consent of the Senate" (Article II, Section 2). Further, the enumeration of the specific subjects on which Congress may legislate, in Article I, Section 8, supplemented by a grant of authority to "make all laws which shall be necessary and proper for carrying into execution . . . powers vested by this Constitution in the government of the United States or in any officer of department thereof" appears to be a distinct reservation of authority to Congress to regulate by law the manner in which the president should proceed in carrying out the duties placed in his hands by the Constitution. The requirement in the same article that no money may be withdrawn from the Treasury except "in consequence of appropriations made by law" is an additional reinforcement of congressional authority in the area of administration. This clause suggests that Congress may pass laws to implement and, incidentally, control and restrict the president's discretion in carrying out his responsibilities as chief of administration.

With the exception of the offices of president and vice-president in the executive branch, constitutional theory has held, since the founding of the Republic, that administrative offices are brought into existence normally by legislative act, not executive order. Indeed, the language of the "necessary and proper" clause indicates that Congress may by statute dictate the organizational structure of the executive branch.

Most presidents, however, have assumed that any power or responsibilities delegated by Congress to executive departments become a part of the president's authority, an integral part of his executive power, needed to carry out the president's duty of executing the laws faithfully. "Congressionalists" have taken the position that when the lawmakers delegate power directly to a government department or agency, the president is not to interfere with this delegation. The courts, seeking to achieve a balance, have come down on both sides of the issue, sometimes favoring the president and sometimes Congress. But in the final analysis, the courts have recognized, the same authority has commented, "two constitutionally established 'chains of command,' and the doctrine of coordinate powers makes it clear that neither Congress nor the president needs to subordinate its authority to the other branch."[1]

Which view of administrative authority did a majority of the Founding Fathers really favor? No one, of course, can say definitively. Louis Fisher's assessment comes down on the side of the president:

> The Framers shared a desire for greater efficiency and more reliable governmental machinery. Direct experience with state government and the Continental Congress convinced them of the need for a separate executive and interdepartmental checks. Chief among their concerns was the need to protect against legislative usurpations and to preserve the independence of the executive and judicial branches. Those were the dominant thoughts behind the separation of powers, not the doctrine of Montesquieu, fear of executive power, or a basic distrust of government. If the Framers had wanted weak government they could have had that with the Articles of Confederation.[2]

The American constitutional system, in fact, represents a blending and mingling of powers—a structure based on interdependence. Richard E. Neustadt has described it as "a government of separated institutions sharing powers."[3] Thus, while the president serves as the chief executive officer of the Republic, the power to organize and reorganize departments, including the Executive Office of the President, is assigned to Congress under the "necessary and proper" clause of Article I. Congress may exercise these powers, as it often does, or it may delegate them to the president through a law granting him authority to create or reorganize federal agencies. During wartime emergencies, Congress has readily passed broad statutes authorizing the president to create, reorganize, or even abolish agencies, subject to certain legislative restrictions.

The Constitution does not specifically grant the president the power to remove government officials, but the Supreme Court has held that Congress cannot interfere with the chief executive's right to fire officials he has appointed with the Senate's approval.[4] However, during President Franklin D. Roosevelt's first term, the Court ruled that the president did not have the right to remove officials serving in administratively independent "quasi-legislative, quasi-judicial" agencies, such as the Federal Trade Commission.[5]

EXECUTIVE DEPARTMENTS AND THE CABINET

The Executive Office of the President—the command center of the executive branch—is a creation of the twentieth century. The nation, however, has had executive departments in operation since the first administration of President Washington. Departments are established (or restructured or abolished) by Congress. The number has grown from 4 in 1789 to 13 in 1985. (The great bulk of the 2.9 million federal civilian employees are appointed by the department heads in the executive branch through the civil service system.) Though the Constitution alludes to executive departments, no specific clause directs that they be established. Nor is the term "president's cabinet" mentioned in the Constitution.

Over the years, new departments have been established as president and Congress have perceived a need for a new agency. During the Carter administration, two new departments—education and energy—were established. Less than a decade earlier, in 1970, Congress removed the Post Office from the list of regular departments and transformed it into a government corporation.

The president's cabinet is an extralegal advisory body to aid the chief executive in fulfilling his administrative responsibilities. Because the cabinet as an organization has no constitutional status—the Founding Fathers expressly rejected the idea of an executive council—its function within the executive branch depends upon the president. Washington's four-member cabinet would be clearly overshadowed by the size of the modern advisory body. Today the cabinet consists of the president, vice-president, the thirteen heads of the executive departments, the U.S. ambassador to the United Nations, and other top-level advisers that the president may wish to include.

Presidents are not required by law to form a cabinet, nor do chief executives have to take the advice of their cabinets. Unlike the British parliamentary system, votes are not taken; and even if they were, the president would not be obliged to follow their advice. As Lincoln said on one occasion when his entire cabinet opposed him: "Seven nays, one aye—the ayes have it." Most recent presidents have preferred smaller conferences with one or two cabinet members to discuss a major issue, instead of a full cabinet meeting. President Kennedy, for example, regarded full cabinet meetings as a waste of valuable time.

Most presidential scholars divide the executive branch into four categories according to proximity to the president and function in the government. They are: the White House staff, the Executive Office of the President, the cabinet, and the executive departments and agencies.

The White House Staff.   Until the 1930s, the executive branch consisted mainly of the president, the cabinet, and the employees who worked in the executive departments and agencies. But with the rise of the welfare state in the New Deal era, the need for additional White House staffing became obvious. The Committee on Administrative Management (the Brownlow Committee), appointed by Franklin D. Roosevelt, declared: "the President needs help."[6] Congress responded by creating the Executive Office of the President and authorized the appointment of six special assistants in 1939. This initial action heralded the formation of the modern White House staff, which now numbers roughly 500 persons.

Today the president meets regularly with his senior staff to discuss and decide on policy directions. Critics claim that this senior staff has preempted most of the decision making that formerly took place in departments and executive agencies. According to the critics, this aggrandizement of power both erodes the morale of the executive departments and raises serious questions about political accountability, since the presidential assistants—unlike executive department heads—are neither confirmed by or answerable to Congress. Thus, President

Johnson sought to run much of the federal establishment from the White House and largely ignored the executive departments. In a more extreme case, President Nixon relied almost exclusively on National Security Adviser Henry Kissinger to make foreign policy and cavalierly shunted aside Secretary of State William Rogers. This convenient arrangement permitted the president to keep the State Department in the dark on a number of policy initiatives (such as the reopening of the door to Communist China in 1972 after a 23-year hiatus) and prevent Congress from obtaining vital information on foreign policy needed by the lawmakers to perform their oversight function.

Another serious charge against the presidential staff is that it creates a "palace guard" around presidents, blocking out or denying them the benefits of diverse viewpoints. Because the White House senior staff invariably shares the president's world view, they tend to reinforce this view. Moreover, because they wish to retain the president's confidence and favor, they usually tell him what he wants to hear. President Johnson's one-time press secretary George Reedy has given us an insider's perspective on the White House courtiers who construct a nearly-impossible barrier to "presidential accessibility."[7]

Designed to help the president cope with the rising tide of paperwork and decisions, the White House staff operations have had a number of unintended consequences. The staff, established to help coordinate the federal bureaucracy, in the process has become another bureaucracy that often finds itself at odds with the heads of the executive departments.

Office of Management and Budget. Known as the Bureau of the Budget from its inception in 1921, this agency was renamed the Office of Management and Budget (OMB) in 1970. Created by Congress as a staff agency to assist presidents in formulating and presenting to Congress a comprehensive national budget proposal each year, the Bureau of the Budget was originally located in the Department of the Treasury. In 1939 it was moved into the new Executive Office of the President under the major reorganization plan approved by Congress. During the first Nixon administration it was renamed to reflect its expanded responsibilities for general management and oversight of the executive branch. Staffed by more than 500 employees, the Office of Management and Budget is now the largest single agency in the Executive Office.

National Security Council. Established by Congress in the aftermath of World War II (1947), the National Security Council (NSC) was created to provide presidents with advice in this crucial area and to facilitate coordination with all agencies and officials involved in national security decision making.[8] The council is headed by a national security adviser and a small staff of foreign policy and military affairs specialists. One reason Congress created the NSC was to formalize the decision-making process and thereby limit the flexibility of President Truman, whose experience in this field was considered marginal by a number of members of Congress. Truman, who had opposed the creation of the NSC, largely ignored the agency throughout his tenure in the White House, but Eisenhower met with the council on a regular basis. Though he never let the NSC interfere with his decisions, he used the NSC to legitimize his actions.

Clearly, presidents have not been constrained by the congressional attempt to reduce their prerogatives in this sensitive area. Since then, presidential use of the NSC and its staff has varied from administration to administration. Nixon relied heavily on his national security adviser, Henry Kissinger, and continued to do so when he appointed Kissinger secretary of state. More recently, Carter and Reagan have utilized the services of their national security adviser extensively.

Council of Economic Advisers.   For the first time in 1946, Congress assigned the president the responsibility of fostering and maintaining a healthy economy. The Employment Act of 1946 required the president to oversee the nation's economy and to make proposals to Congress that would "promote employment, production, and purchasing power." To aid the president in formulating economic programs, Congress created a Council of Economic Advisers (CEA), attached to the Executive Office. Under this legislation the president is empowered, with the advice and consent of the Senate, to appoint three members—usually nationally recognized economists—to advise him on the best means to keep the economy on an even keel or to revive a sagging economy. The CEA is supported by a small staff of approximately 25 professionals, mostly economists from the academic community. Generally, presidents appoint economists who are sympathetic to the chief executive's economic philosophy. (The role of the CEA is discussed more fully in Chapter 13.)

Domestic Policy Office.   First organized by Lyndon Johnson in 1965 to coordinate the Great Society programs, the domestic policy office developed a variety of policy initiatives for the president. These recommendations were then converted into a legislative package, executive orders, or departmental regulations.[9] Nixon created the Domestic Council in 1970 to "formulate and coordinate domestic policy recommendations to the president." Though the council included the heads of the 10 executive departments that deal with domestic policy matters —a kind of domestic cabinet—the Domestic Council soon began functioning as a staff organization under the direction of presidential adviser John Ehrlichman. All domestic policy documents to and from the Oval Office passed through his office.

Under a presidentially approved reorganization plan two years later, three cabinet secretaries were assigned additional responsibilities to cover three broad areas: human resources, natural resources, and community development. This "super cabinet" experiment was short-lived. When the Watergate scandal engulfed the White House, Ehrlichman was forced to resign, and before President Nixon stepped down, the super cabinet concept was dropped. Even if Nixon had stayed in office, it is doubtful that Congress would have formally approved such a heavy concentration of power in the White House inner circle.

President Carter disbanded the formal organization of the Domestic Council and replaced it with a Domestic Policy Staff, chaired by his assistant for domestic affairs, Stuart Eizenstat. Despite Carter's inability to get many proposals through Congress, his Domestic Policy Staff generally received good marks for its managerial competence and ability to resolve disputes between the White House and a number of federal agencies. Under President Reagan, the influence of the domestic policy staff declined. Instead, the Reagan White House *troika* of Chief of Staff James A. Baker III, Deputy Chief of Staff Michael Deaver, and Counselor Edwin Meese III, and the director of OMB David Stockman handled most top-priority domestic policy issues during his first term.

STAFFING THE EXECUTIVE BRANCH

Unlike a corporate president who has a free hand in the choice of his subordinates, the president of the United States must share this power with Congress. The Founding Fathers believed that the most effective way to check power was to share it. And in no area was this doctrine more evident than in the shared administrative power between the president and Congress.

While the president was granted authority to nominate the heads of the executive departments, the Founding Fathers required that these nominees be confirmed by the Senate. In short, the president of the United States must obtain the "advice and consent" of the Senate for all appointees to executive-level positions, except approximately 60 White House staff positions. Included in the executive-level category are 800 or more secretaries, undersecretaries, deputy secretaries, assistant secretaries of the executive departments, and administrators and deputy administrators for various independent agencies.[10]

In the final analysis, it is Congress that determines if a position requires confirmation by the Senate. Lawmakers determine which high-level positions will become political appointments and which will be career service appointments. Formerly, for example, the president's chief business manager—the director of the Bureau of the Budget—did not require Senate confirmation. But recently Congress amended the Budget and Accounting Act of 1974 to require that the Senate confirm both the director and the deputy director of the Office of Management and Budget.

Generally, the Senate follows a rule of comity in handling presidential nominees for executive-level positions. In other words, the president is allowed to select those he wants and whose views are compatible with his, even when an opposition party majority controls the Senate. Customarily, the chamber restricts itself to considering the "fitness" of the nominee rather than his politics. But the Senate, having been burned several times in recent years, has become more cautious in scrutinizing prospective appointees' credentials for possible conflicts of interest. The lawmakers may sometimes delay confirmation by holding extensive hearings to express concern about the policy implications of a particular nomination, especially if the prospective appointee espouses views strongly contrary to majority sentiment in the chamber.

The separation of powers doctrine, however, prevents the Senate from attaching formal conditions to the consent it gives to presidential nominations.

Nor may the chamber instruct the nominee, in his performance of his duties, if confirmation is granted. Thus, the power of advice and consent on appointments appears to differ from the apparently similar power of advice and consent of treaties. In contrast, the Senate may revise the draft of a treaty to which it grants consent through amendments. And on more than one occasion the Senate has attached reservations to its resolution interpreting the obligations of the United States.

Most executive-level nominations, it should be emphasized, are approved pro forma by the Senate. Ronald Reagan experienced little difficulty in obtaining congressional approval of his original cabinet. But when in 1984 he sought to replace Attorney General William French Smith with his White House counselor, Edwin Meese III, he encountered strong congressional headwinds. Several members of the domestic opposition raised questions about Meese's fitness for office, in light of disclosures that he had received an interest-free loan from an acquaintance while trying to sell his California residence after moving to the nation's capital. He was also criticized for helping to obtain a government position for the same acquaintance who had aided him with the interest-free loan. After protracted hearings, Meese was eventually confirmed by the Senate.

In the event that the president runs into a Senate roadblock on his nominees, he can exploit a loophole in the law that prohibits an official from serving more than 30 days in an executive-level position without obtaining the consent of the Senate by appointing the official as "acting" director of the unit for several months, especially until the end of the current session of the Senate. Recess appointments are also made for the period between congressional sessions.

INSTITUTIONALIZATION OF THE WHITE HOUSE STAFF

In the past three decades the White House staff, as indicated earlier, has displaced the cabinet as the most important decision-making body, next to the president, in the executive branch. This presidential bureaucracy has grown from a handful of employees to a huge cadre of approximately 1,400 special advisers, media specialists, overseers, and clerical staff. George Washington, by contrast, managed his office with only four employees, including his secretary. For the first century of the Republic, chief executives handled their White House duties with the aid of half a dozen secretaries, clerks, and aides, some of whom were borrowed from the regular departments. As late as the Grover Cleveland administration, the president's office staff consisted of 6 persons and operated on a budget of $13,800. By McKinley's time the staff had expanded to 27, maintained on a budget of $44,340. The continued growth of the Republic, and increased responsibilities of the federal government both at home and abroad, especially during World War I, led to further enlargement of the White House staff. By the Coolidge administration there were 46 persons on the staff of Silent Cal, with a budget of $93,500.[11]

Clearly, the New Deal administrations of Franklin D. Roosevelt mark a major dividing line between the traditional limited role of government and its active involvement throughout American society. With the rapidly expanding role of the federal government in combatting the Great Depression, the development of regulatory programs in agriculture, banking and securities, and communications, and government involvement in labor-management relations and numerous other aspects of the American economy, the need to expand the White House staff became obvious. The need for additional staffing help was underscored in the Report of the President's Committee on Administrative Management (the Brownlow Committee), issued in 1937. In a widely quoted passage, the report argued:

> The President needs help. His immediate staff assistance is entirely inadequate. He should be given a small number of executive assistants who would be his direct aides in dealing with the managerial agencies and administrative departments of government. These assistants would be in addition to his present aides who deal with the public, with the Congress, and with the press and radio. . . . They would remain in the background, issue no orders, make no decisions, emit no public statements. . . . They should be possessed of high competence, great physical vigor, and a passion for anonymity. They should be installed in the White House itself, directly accessible to the President.[12]

Impressed with the committee's work, Roosevelt submitted a reorganization plan to Congress based upon the report. The lawmakers also adopted another recommendation of the Brownlow Committee that led to the creation of a revamped Executive Office of the President. One immediate effect was the appointment of six senior aides to White House staff positions. Prior to the 1939 reorganization, there had been no formal office staff. FDR's brain trust, for example, consisted of a handful of administrators on loan to the White House. Thomas Corcoran, a brilliant attorney, was borrowed from the Reconstruction Finance Corporation; Raymond Moley and Adolf Berle, from the State Department, and Rexford Tugwell, from the Department of Agriculture.

Even after World War II, cabinet heads were still regarded as the major decision makers in the executive branch. Many of them were appointed because they had occupied high office—they were governors, senators, or previous cabinet members—or were leading members of financial institutions or clientele agencies. Presidents still looked to executive departments for important guidance and direction in policymaking. Chief executives also relied on cabinet heads for political advice and strategy. Seldom did presidents ignore the cabinet, and rarely did they preempt departmental decision making to handle a matter directly in the White House.

This traditional mode of administration began to change gradually in the years after World War II. The real growth and influence of the White House staff began in the 1960s. This staff expansion had a profound effect throughout the executive branch. Instead of most management decision making taking place within departments, more and more power was concentrated in the White House. Presidential assistants expanded their spheres of influence and tended to monopolize the president's attention. Institutionalization of policymaking functions in the White House became the trademark of the Kennedy and Johnson administrations. Senior presidential staff members became the president's principal policy advisers. These senior aides now had their own staffs in the Executive Office, and these staffs competed with those in the departments and other executive agencies for influence and power.

With the institutionalization of policy in the White House, several changes in presidential administrative style became evident. First, the president enjoyed more latitude in policy choices. Second, the president had more opportunity to formulate policies independent of the executive departments and agencies. Third, the growth of the White House staffs accelerated the shift in power from the executive departments and agencies to the White House.[13] Fourth, the shift helped focus nationwide media attention on the White House. Policy declarations and changes, announcements of nuclear disarmament meetings, and upbeat economic news all were now announced from the White House—and the president could claim the lion's share of the credit.

Nixon expanded the White House control over policymaking even further. Although Mr. Nixon announced at the outset of his first term that he planned a return to a cabinet form of government, with policymaking developed in the executive departments, he soon established the most centrally structured administration in the nation's history. Instead of a small staff of senior advisers as originally planned, he and his top aides established a large, specialized White House staff that reached 535 persons at its height. Clear lines of authority were established, and Nixon and his top policy managers called virtually all the signals.

Both Ford and Carter sought to cut down the highly centralized structure and fortress mentality of the Nixon White House. Both presidents also tried to build a White House staff structure similar to spokes on a wheel, with the president at the hub. Top aides were each assigned policy areas, but they were expected to operate collegially. Each was to have direct access to the president, and there was to be no chief of staff. On paper, the revamped White House administrative structure looked good. But in practice, turf wars soon developed between top aides and between them and the executive departments. Presidential advising also suffered. Both administrations experienced difficulty in setting priorities, even though the White House held the reins of power. Eventually, each administration managed to improve its policymaking procedures, especially after a chief of staff was appointed.

Reagan, who had made considerable political capital of Carter's inability to manage his White House staff effectively, endeavored to profit from his predecessor's mistakes. Even before he took the oath of office, Reagan and his top aides quickly concluded that the White House staff had grown too large and too specialized during the 1970s to operate effectively. The new president promised to clean house and to establish efficient operating procedures.

Despite his early announcement about reestablishing the cabinet as a major decision-making agency, President Reagan soon reverted to a highly centralized White House staff. To be sure, he avoided the idea of a super cabinet; instead, he implemented an administrative plan, developed by top assistant Edwin Meese III, to establish seven policy councils, each chaired by a cabinet head, to provide greater cabinet input and coordination. These seven councils—a plan similar to one proposed by Dr. Louis Brownlow in 1943—were tied to the White House through a secretariat staffed by presidential aides. Despite this functional differentiation of the Reagan White House from its predecessors, the White House Executive Office remained the command center of the federal government.

Reagan's cabinet council system not only reinforced central White House policy management, but also "helped insulate political executives from the permanent departmental bureaucracies and from the congressional committees by continually convening the executives in meetings under White House auspices."[14] Shortly after the start of his second term, however, President Reagan announced a major staff reorganization to streamline decision making in the executive branch. Under the reorganization plan developed by Chief of Staff Donald Regan, the seven White House cabinet councils, each managed by a cabinet officer in the first term, were consolidated into two super cabinet councils: an Economic Policy Council under Secretary of the Treasury James A. Baker III, and a Domestic Policy Council under Attorney General Edwin Meese III. Both report to the White House Chief of Staff Donald Regan, who emerged as the administration's most powerful official after the president.

The two new policy councils are composed of other cabinet members and administration officials. Vice-President Bush, an ex officio member, serves on both councils. Policy matters involving these officials and other White House aides flow through the new councils and then to Chief of Staff Regan. The new entities, according to President Reagan, will streamline policy development. "Together with the National Security Council, they will serve as the primary channels for advising me on policy matters," the president said.[15]

One of the key purposes of the latest reorganization, which further centralized power in the White House, was to cut down the number of cabinet council meetings. Formerly, the operation of the seven cabinet councils led to a proliferation of meetings for all cabinet members, because each cabinet officer sat on several councils. Cabinet members had originally been involved in the seven councils to avoid Nixon's error of neglecting cabinet officials.[16] Under the new structure, most members sit on just one or two. As a result, several cabinet members who formerly chaired a council lost a powerful tool of policymaking, the authority to prepare the agenda of issues to be resolved by the president. Sources close to the White House reported that the reorganization plan will enable Chief of Staff Regan to concentrate on overall management of the administration and leave the work on issues to Treasury Secretary Baker and Attorney General Meese. Most Washington observers concluded that the reorganization really did not change the basic operating style of the Reagan administration, but merely shifted two of Reagan's key advisers into new locations. Reagan's closest aides continued to be responsible for the operation of key areas in the administration.

By the fall of 1985, however, the dual policymaking councils had been superseded by a new Economic Policy Council. Patterned after the Economic Policy Council of the Ford administration, this new high-level group consists of Treasury Secretary James A. Baker III, Vice-President George Bush, the secretaries of state, commerce, labor, transportation, and agriculture, the chairman of the Council of Economic Advisers, and several other top White House staffers. But according to one reporter, most of the Reagan administration's economic policymaking is done by an informal group—the Big Six—consisting of Chief of Staff Donald Regan, Treasury Secretary Baker, Secretary of State George P. Shultz, Regan's top aide Alfred Kingon, Deputy Treasury Secretary Richard G. Darman, and surprisingly, the chairman of the Federal Reserve Board, Paul A. Volcker.[17]

One veteran public administration specialist, in assessing the Reagan system of administration, has observed: "The Reagan policy apparatus is structured and staffed around strictly partisan and personal presidential loyalty, largely excluding professional expertise. The gradual politicization and deinstitutionalization of the EOP since the late 1960's has culminated under Reagan in an unprecedented partisan presidential system that reaches from the White House deeply into agency operating levels."[18]

How successful has President Reagan's attempt to "presidentialize the federal bureaucracy" been? How effective have the Reagan White House's efforts to use ideologically committed appointees who share the president's vision to make the federal bureaucracy smaller and more cost-effective been? This is difficult to measure, and it is probably too early to assess its long-term effects. But the short-term results appear to have been mixed. President Reagan has learned once again that it is extremely difficult to make changes in our Madisonian governmental system, with its multiple checks and balances. Laurence E. Lynn Jr., author of one pilot study, concludes: "Although his appointees' performances were uneven, on balance all moved the government in directions consistent with his policies."[19] Richard P. Nathan, a leading authority in the field, is inclined to give the Reagan administration higher marks for its administrative strategy.[20]

ROLE OF THE CABINET

Members of the cabinet have dual functions: (1) They serve as heads of executive departments; (2) they serve as major advisers to the president. In the words of Richard F. Fenno, Jr., the leading authority on the cabinet, a cabinet member's "formal responsibilities extend both upward toward the President and downward toward his own department."[21]

Modern presidents have held diverse views toward the cabinet. Eisenhower relied heavily on his cabinet, meeting with this advisory council some 230 times during his eight years in the White House.[22] Johnson met regularly with the cabinet, but the conduct of the Vietnam war was normally discussed not in the cabinet meeting, but with his Tuesday luncheon group of top advisers. Nixon paid lip-service to the cabinet as an advisory body in his first term, but seldom convened this group during his abbreviated second term. Carter met with his cabinet frequently—more than any president since Eisenhower. But in one hectic week in July 1979, he fired or accepted the resignation of four cabinet members. These wholesale firings, as might be expected, badly eroded the confidence of the electorate in President Carter. Reagan during his 1980 electoral campaign, as indicated earlier, promised to institute a cabinet government. In practice, however, Reagan and his senior advisers usually made the final decisions. "Cabinet government is an illusion," one administration official conceded.[23]

The presidential chain of command often breaks down within the executive departments because the cabinet heads, strange as it may sound, frequently do not control their own departments. Several factors explain the inability of some cabinet heads to control their departments. Shortness of tenure undermines their ability to exert strong leadership. Most cabinet appointments are made for political reasons, not on the basis of the administrative talents of the nominees. Some secretaries provide geographical balance, such as a westerner being chosen for the Department of the Interior. Other secretaries may be selected on the basis of race, sex, religion, or ethnicity, to appease various interest group constituencies throughout the land, whether or not they have any talent for administration. Some cabinet members are chosen to serve as ambassadors to various constituencies, especially the secretaries of the treasury, commerce, agriculture, and labor.[24]

Unlike the past, when most cabinet members were often long-time acquaintances of the president, he may now meet some of them for the first time during the transition period between administrations. John F. Kennedy, for example, had not met his proposed Secretary of Defense Robert McNamara, president of a major auto company, before interviewing him for the job. In the years ahead the lack of acquaintance with future secretaries, undersecretaries, and assistant secretaries will probably be the rule, not the exception. Unlike the British parliamentary system, in which the prime minister fills his or her cabinet with members of the parliamentary party's front bench, all of whom he or she has worked with closely for years, the American presidential system relies upon new, frequently politically untested leaders to operate the government.

Below the cabinet level, the president and his advisers select approximately fifteen hundred political positions in the executive, noncareer, and noncompetitive category to operate the government bureaucracy. A wide variety of top jobs in regional offices, U.S. attorneys and U.S. marshals, are filled via senatorial courtesy appointments. A carryover from the nineteenth century, senatorial courtesy appointments consist of three main types: (1) The president clears his nominees for positions with senators of his own party from the state in which the appointment will be made. (2) If no U.S. senators belong to the president's party from the state concerned, the appointment will be cleared with national committee members. (3) This traditional method of appointment will in exceptional cases be extended to influential senators from the opposition party—for example, Presidents Kennedy and Johnson were unfailingly responsive to GOP Senate Minority Leader Everett McKinley Dirksen's patronage requests. Sometimes the president may extend some of this patronage to leaders in the House.

More often than not, the primary loyalties of these appointed officials in regional or local offices will rest with their congressional benefactors or state party leaders, not the national administration. Also, the president frequently nominates to top positions at the subcabinet level former lawmakers or lame duck congressmen and senators of his own party and even their senior staff assistants. Under these circumstances, team loyalty may be lacking.

Secretaries and top subcabinet officials have been depicted by one authority as "wasting assets whose value to the president depreciates during his administration."[25] While this is not always true, especially among cabinet members who are personal friends of the president, cabinet heads are frequently captured by the permanent bureaucracy on whom they depend for administering the department. For cabinet members who have not had previous experience in the federal bureaucracy, this process can occur rather quickly. Sometimes they "go native" by championing the interests of their bureaucratic and interest group constituencies.[26] If the cabinet member has been previously affiliated with these groups, this conversion may occur soon after he or she enters office.

The high turnover of cabinet members also limits their management effectiveness. In recent years their average tenure in office has been 40 months.[27] During the Nixon administration, it was only 18 months. In the first five years of the Nixon administration, the entire cabinet was replaced with a grand total of 30 appointees. Despite the high turnover, most cabinet resignations are not attempts to influence administrative policies, although Secretary of State Cyrus Vance resigned in protest against Carter's abortive Iranian rescue mission to obtain the release of the American hostages.

Because political executives rarely stay in office long enough to gain mastery of their departments, the incentive for career officials to make changes ordered by them is low. Frequently, bureau chiefs make end runs to Congress and their own constituencies to evade the presidential chain of command. While each side blames the other for conflict and delay, the business of the department goes on as usual. After all, presidents and cabinet heads come and go; career officials stay and stay until retirement. Cabinet officers have relatively few resources and lack the clout to control departmental bureaus. Except for the secretaries of defense, state, and treasury—the so-called Inner Cabinet—most cabinet heads do not have much access to or influence with the president. Sometimes members of the Outer Cabinet —those departments considered less crucial to the administration—do not meet with the president for weeks on end. Some of these departments have been depicted as little more than holding companies—a conglomeration of bureaus, agencies, and offices handling a wide variety of functions and responsibilities.[28]

THE ECLIPSE OF THE CABINET

Why has the White House staff come to overshadow the cabinet? Several reasons, or combinations of reasons, explain why the decision-making process has shifted to the White House staff. Close proximity of the White House aides to the president gives them a special advantage over cabinet members. Internal lines of communication, just as military theorists have always pointed out, are always an advantage in any major decision-making activity. In recent years the White House staff, rather than the Office of Management and Budget, has become the fulcrum or pivotal axis for coordination of all policy proposals affecting more than one department. And since very few major policy matters in our complex modern world are confined to a single federal department, this means that the White House staff becomes a massive switchboard for coordinating policy questions, especially in the areas of national security and foreign policy.

Recurring international crisis and nearly intractable domestic issues have produced further centralization of decision making in the White House. Presidents want immediate responses, and they wish to be kept fully informed on a daily or hourly basis. Executive departments generally move at a cumbersome pace, as policy options are weighed and reassessed. On many occasions the White House doesn't have the time to wait for a departmental response.

Power accrues to the White House staff at the expense of executive departments in other ways. The president's aides frequently operate as firefighters in crisis situations by assuming direct operational control of agencies. Indeed, in recent decades they have become, in effect, line officials themselves, especially in sensitive national security matters. To avoid a common administration problem of speaking with different voices in public, presidents now frequently ask White House aides to clear speeches to be made by cabinet members to ensure that the administration's policy line is followed. With this type of overseeing authority, it is little wonder that the White House staff has become a dominant force on the Washington scene, consistently overshadowing the cabinet.

Above all else, the power and influence of the White House staff has continued to grow because these presidential advisers are people he can trust. These staffers are mostly those who worked for the president throughout "the long march to the White House." As one veteran Washington insider has put it: "They bring to their jobs an understanding of the President, loyalty, and in some cases a set of skills that are transferable from the campaign—such as press relations and scheduling. Their primary interests, however, usually have been in the art of politics, not governance . . . often their chief qualification—and an important one in a campaign—was availability; their chief motivations may have been the expectation of excitement, an excess of zeal, or hero worship."[29]

The close advisers often share with the president a common background— Kennedy had his Bostonian Irish Mafia; Johnson, his Texans; Nixon, his advertising associates from California; Carter, his Georgians. Most recently, Reagan has relied heavily on devoted staffers who formerly served with him when he was governor of California. Possessing a similar background in education and occupational training to the president, they feel comfortable working together. The president knows that when he issues directives, these associates will carry out his orders without hesitation. The top layer or inner circle, while possessing no formal authority in their own right, know without asking what the president wants done and confidently carry out their duties, even if it sometimes means bypassing the cabinet member(s) most directly concerned.

The power and influence of the White House staff is also reinforced by presidents who come to view cabinet heads chiefly as advocates of their own department and their clientele, not the president's major policy goals or political objectives. More and more, presidents feel that they must depend upon their own top aides for sound advice. But this overreliance on staff aides has its dangers too. As one British writer has astutely noted: ". . . if a president needs to be protected by his White House staff against the departments, he also needs to be kept on guard by the department against the White House staff, who may all too easily begin to think only they know the purposes and needs and the mind of their president, until *he* becomes *their* creature and believes that his interests are safe with them."[30] Thomas E. Cronin, a former White House staffer who has conducted extensive research on the Executive Office of the President, has also pointed to some of the shortcomings of the president's staff:

> The presidency has become a large, complex bureaucracy itself, rapidly acquiring many dubious characteristics of large bureaucracies in the process: layering, overspecialization, communications gaps, interoffice rivalries, inadequate coordination, and an impulse to become consumed with short-term urgent operational concerns at the expense of thinking systematically about the consequences of varying sets of policies and about the important long-range problems.[31]

Presidential management of the federal bureaucracy is largely a matter of presidential style.

PRESIDENTIAL MANAGEMENT STYLES

Political scientist Richard T. Johnson, after analyzing the management styles of six presidents (Franklin Roosevelt through Nixon), concluded that they could be classified under three general approaches: competitive, formalistic, and collegial.[32] Johnson cautioned, however, that these descriptions oversimplify the complex reality of each chief executive's administrative style. Indeed, elements of two or three approaches may be present in different combinations at different times in each president. Still, these models help demonstrate the variations possible in managing the executive branch—and the costs and benefits of each. The three major models developed by Johnson and expanded upon by Alexander George are shown in Figure 9.1. Let's examine each of them briefly.

Competitive Model.   FDR's preferred management style rested on a competitive or dual principle of assigning two or more competing federal agencies to handle the same general management function. As described by historian Arthur M. Schlesinger, Jr.:

> His favorite technique was to keep grants of authority incomplete, jurisdictions uncertain, charters overlapping. The result of this competitive theory of administration was often confusion and exasperation on the operating level; but no other method could so reliably ensure that in a large bureaucracy filled with ambitious men eager for power, the decisions, and the powers to make them, would remain with the President.[33]

Thus, Roosevelt counterbalanced a Works Progress Administration (WPA) run by Harry Hopkins with a Public Works Administration (PWA) run by Harold Ickes, secretary of the interior. FDR parceled out electric power programs among agriculture, interior, and the newly established Tennessee Valley Authority

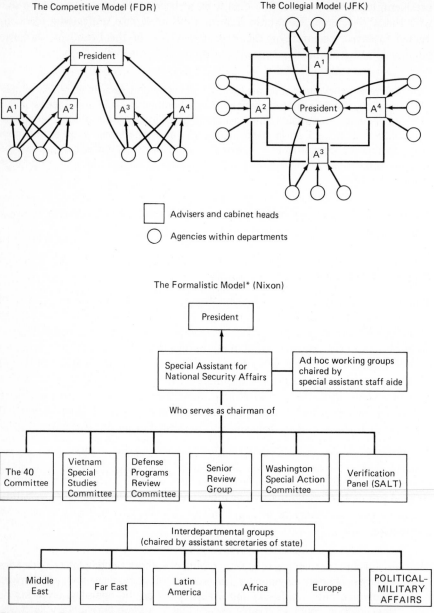

Figure 9.1 The Competitive, Formalistic, and Collegial Models of Presidential Administration (*Source:* Reprinted by permission of Westview Press from *Presidential Decision Making in Foreign Policy: The Effective Use of Information and Advice* by Alexander L. George, 150, 156, 158. Copyright © 1980 by Westview Press, Boulder, Colorado.)

(TVA), to mention only two examples of his unorthodox system of administration. That his subordinates might be at sword's point with one another did not bother FDR in the slightest. The administrative rivalry enabled Roosevelt to keep tight control of all final decision making in the Oval Office.

Formalistic Model.   President Truman used a more formalistic approach, delegating authority to cabinet heads and relying on the traditional bureaucracy to manage the government machinery. Presidents Eisenhower and Nixon generally adhered to the formalistic approach to managing the executive branch. Cabinet members were given broad latitude. Both Eisenhower and Nixon favored structured decision making and an extensive staff system. All interdepartmental planning was coordinated and funneled through a chief of staff who reported directly to the president. Before the recommendations reached the Oval Office, all the pros and cons were carefully examined. Ultimately, the president made his decisions on the merits of the evidence submitted. Under the formalistic approach, broad policy considerations are heavily weighted and political considerations deemphasized.

Collegial Model.   This pattern of management aims to build a team of colleagues who work together to generate solutions which, ideally, fuse divergent viewpoints. The collegial approach recognizes the existence—and in fact, the value—of conflict. Indeed, conflicting viewpoints are treated as a resource. The principal strength of this approach is its potential for forging solutions that are substantively sound and politically acceptable. Its chief limitation stems from its dependence on people working together. Richard T. Johnson terms the Kennedy approach "collegial."[34] Unlike Presidents Eisenhower and Nixon, Kennedy distrusted the federal bureaucracy and placed far more reliance on his New Frontiersmen, the White House staff.

   Lyndon B. Johnson's administrative style, though it tended toward the formalistic approach, might better be described as idiosyncratic. LBJ exhibited a preference for structured decision making, and he preferred to evaluate alternatives rather than participate in creating them. But more often than not he pressured his subordinates to follow his self-designed policies, no matter what the cost. Even within his inner circle, where differences and dissent should have been encouraged, "Johnson's demands for consensus quilted his advisers into patterns of static harmony."[35]

   Clearly, the competitive, formalistic, and collegial approaches to management oversimplify presidential modes of administration. But Richard T. Johnson's study demonstrates the usefulness of the three models. To the degree that a president follows one of these models, he can expect to incur the costs and reap the benefits that each approach generates. The cost and benefits are summarized in Table 9.1. As Johnson has explained, each president has used a different mixture of the formal and informal organizational approaches, and the result has been a corresponding set of strengths and weaknesses. Roosevelt's competitive management model generated a host of innovative policies, but created an immense amount of strife and tension within his administration. Eisenhower's formalistic mode of operation utilized bureaucratic resources, but at the cost of lost information and innovation. When Eisenhower decided on occasion to go outside of channels, his special staff came up with his imaginative "open skies" nuclear weapons inspection plan.[36] Kennedy's collegial approach retained flexibility and control, but sacrificed bureaucratic resources. In another instance, Kennedy's

Table 9.1   PRESIDENTIAL ADMINISTRATIVE MODELS

Benefits	Costs
Formalistic approach	
Orderly decision process enforces more thorough analysis.	The hierarchy which screens information may also distort it. Tendency of the screening process to wash out or distort political pressures and public sentiments.
Conserves the decision maker's time and attention for the big decision.	Tendency to respond slowly or inappropriately in crisis.
Emphasizes the optimal.	
Competitive approach	
Places the decision maker in the mainstream of the information network.	Places large demands on decision maker's time and attention.
Tends to generate solutions that are politically feasible and bureaucratically doable.	Exposes decision maker to partial or biased information. Decision process may overly sacrifice optimality for doability.
Generates creative ideas, partially as a result of the "stimulus" of competition, but also because this unstructured kind of information network is more open to ideas from the outside.	Tendency to aggravate staff competition with the risk that aides may pursue their own interests at the expense of the decision maker.
	Wear and tear on aides fosters attrition and high turnover.
Collegial approach	
Seeks to achieve both optimality and doability.	Places substantial demands on the decision maker's time and attention.
Involves the decision maker in the information network but somewhat eases the demands upon him by stressing teamwork over competition.	Requires unusual interpersonal skill in dealing with subordinates, mediating differences, and maintaining teamwork among colleagues.
	Risk that "teamwork" will degenerate into a closed system of mutual support.

Source: Richard T. Johnson, *Managing the White House* (New York: Harper & Row, 1974), p. 238.

delegation of authority to Secretary of Defense Robert McNamara showed that a formalistic approach served the young president well when he resorted to a different administrative pattern.

In the final analysis, executive administration is the product of both institutional and individual influence and tradeoffs. Policy outcomes are the result of both institutional constraints and individual administrative styles operating on a particular president at a particular time in history.

No matter what administrative style a president finds most comfortable, he has far fewer options when he faces the onerous task of managing the federal budget—our next topic.

THE EXECUTIVE BUDGET

The Constitution neither prescribes a budget process nor spells out a role in budgeting for the president. For more than 130 years Congress kept primary control over the entire budget process. Individual cabinet members went up to Capitol Hill, departmental budgets in hand, to testify before the House and Senate appropriations committees. After gathering the needed budget information from all the cabinet members and independent agency heads, the two congressional committees hammered out the entire federal budget, deciding which departments should have their budgets increased, decreased, or maintained at approximately the same level. Though responsible for administering the entire federal bureaucracy, the president of the United States had no final voice in the size of the federal budget.[37]

Before World War I this cumbersome system clanked along reasonably well, since the entire federal budget rarely exceeded $1 billion, and the size of the federal bureaucracy was only a fraction of its present level (see Table 9.2). President William Howard Taft was the first chief executive to raise serious questions about the inefficient federal budgetary process. He recommended in 1912 that an executive budget be established, one which the president—not Congress—would formulate and then send to Congress for action. Despite the soundness of the proposal, no action was taken on it until after World War I. Undoubtedly, the huge cost of the war and the resulting multibillion-dollar war debt—throughout most of the nineteenth century Uncle Sam usually ended the

Table 9.2 THE PRESIDENT'S CABINET

Cabinet office	Established	Number of paid civilian employees (1982)
State	1789	23,795
Treasury	1789	126,421
War	1789	See Defense
Navy	1798	See Defense
Interior	1849	73,825
Justice	1870	54,722
Post Office*	1872	663,876
Agriculture	1889	114,361
Commerce and Labor†	1903	
Commerce	1913	34,302
Labor	1913	18,975
Defense	1947	1,018,098
Health, Education and Welfare‡	1953	147,830
Housing and Urban Development	1965	14,921
Transportation	1966	60,946
Energy	1977	18,641
Education	1979	5,783

*An independent agency as of 1971.
†Split into two separate departments in 1913.
‡Now Health and Human Services.
Source: U. S. Bureau of the Census, *Statistical Abstract of the United States,* 1982–1983 (Washington, D.C., 103rd ed., 1982), 266.

fiscal year with a surplus—helped persuade Congress of the need for an executive budget.

Shortly after President Warren Harding took office, Congress passed the Budget and Accounting Act of 1921, requiring the president to establish a comprehensive budget. In the words of one commentator: "The Budget and Accounting Act of 1921, by which Congress delegated power over the budget to the President, was a historical watershed. Many believe that the modern presidency began with it."[38] Under the new legislation, Congress imposed upon the president the responsibility not only for proposed expenditures of the executive agencies, but also proposals for financing the executive agencies. To facilitate this task, Congress established a Bureau of the Budget, functioning under a director appointed by and accountable to the president. Placed originally in the Treasury Department, the Bureau of the Budget for the first time introduced into the federal government modern business management procedures.

The central purpose of the 1921 act was to place budgetary responsibility upon the president. But as Louis Fisher, among others, has noted: "The Budget and Accounting Act provided for an 'executive budget' only in the sense that the president initiated the budget and took responsibility for it."[39] The legislation still allowed members of Congress full freedom, either in committee or on the floor, to cut or increase the president's estimates.

In 1939, the Bureau of the Budget was transferred from the Treasury Department to the new Executive Office of the President, as recommended by the Brownlow Commission. Henceforth, the bureau was expected to become the president's management arm. In the meantime President Roosevelt also assigned the Bureau of the Budget the additional tasks of clearing and coordinating legislation for the president as well as monitoring the implementation of presidential programs in the interests of economy and efficiency.

Presidential control over the federal budget has given the president the upper hand in the management of the federal government. For the president, the budget is also a means to control administrators who may be working with interest groups and members of Congress to thwart his priorities.

More than anything else, the presidential budget message sets the legislative agenda for the year. Congress may whittle away at the president's proposals, shift some priorities, tack on additional appropriations for selective agencies, and refuse to fund some favorite presidential projects. But the legislative agenda is the president's, not that of Congress, as the Founding Fathers intended.

As chief administrator, the president must use the executive budget as a political weapon to demonstrate to the country his ability to manage the federal household. President Gerald Ford put it this way: "The budget is the president's blueprint for the operation of the Government in the year ahead."[40] To be successful, the president must package his multibillion-dollar budget in such a fashion as to convey his top priorities without splitting his own party or leaving himself vulnerable to heavy bombardment from the opposition party. To gain special political advantage, the president usually endeavors to project a frugal image. As explained by Richard M. Pious: "He underestimates revenues by projecting a booming economy. The purpose of these maneuvers is to lower the anticipated budget deficit. It also enables the president to blame Congress for 'irresponsible' spending proposals and for subsequent deficits."[41]

Ronald Reagan used this strategy against the Democratic members of Congress with stunning effect during the early days of his first term. One commentator depicted the Washington scene soon after Reagan's arrival in the nation's capital as follows: "Within forty-five days of his inauguration on January 20, 1981, he proposed the broadest, most radical, and most explicit agenda for economic and budgetary change that any president had ever presented to the American people."[42] To obtain the huge budget cuts he had promised during his presidential campaign, Reagan appointed a young, two-term congressman from Michigan, David Stockman, as director of the Office of Management and Budget and ordered him to slash the federal budget. Aided by GOP control of the Senate for the first time since 1954, and the defection of 40 or so southern House Democrats on key votes, Reagan strategists relied on an innovative parliamentary device—reconciliation—to short-circuit the cumbersome congressional budgetary process to achieve huge budget cuts. (*Reconciliation* is a procedure whereby Congress votes an overall appropriations ceiling and then orders its committees to tailor specific programs to conform to this ceiling.)

Plainly, the Reagan tax and budget policies represented a view of government radically different from that of any of his post-World War II predecessors. There was virtually nothing it left untouched in the domestic budget—there were wholesale reductions in government services, cancellation of programs, and elimination of departments.[43] Reagan's proposed tax cuts and budget reductions dominated the congressional agenda during the first six months of the new administration. By midsummer Congress had passed the Reagan program and put in place the basics of his entire tax-budget package. Congress and the American public were left in awe at the magic of Reagan's persuasive arguments in favor of "supply side" economics. One former OMB official noted: "When Ronald Reagan left Washington for his vacation in August 1981, he left behind a six-month record of political, legislative, and public achievement that few presidents have equalled."[44] Euphoria over the Reagan revolution was rather short-lived, however, and when record-breaking budget deficits began looming, Reagan was forced in late 1982 to accept a bipartisan tax increase of nearly $100 billion—the largest single peacetime tax increase in the nation's history.[45]

Under the Reagan administration, budget decision making has become more centralized, both in the Office of Management and Budget and the White House. In other words, top down budgeting has replaced bottom up or incremental budgeting. As a result, the role of cabinet secretaries and their departmental budget offices has been sharply curtailed. With the nation facing huge structural deficits year after year and the agenda dominated by spending retrenchment and possible tax increases, the White House's central role in national budget making vis-à-vis Congress will likely continue to be the order of the day.

While the president is still the chief budget maker, his influence over the total federal budget is probably less today than it was 25 years ago. In the early post-World War II period, most of the federal budget, as drafted by the Bureau of the Budget, was spent by federal agencies. But as Allen Schick has noted:

"Today, over three-quarters of the funds appropriated to agencies are passed through to outsiders who actually spend the funds provided by the government. Each year more than $100 billion is transferred to state and local governments, more than $100 billion to bondholders and tens of billions of dollars to contractors and other countries."[46] With the changing composition of the budget, more and more resources are allocated through legislative rather than budgetary decisions. Indeed, federal legislation has shaped the great entitlement programs (social security, agricultural subsidies) that now consume half the federal budget. Hundreds of grant programs have tripled the state-local share of federal outlays —from 5 percent in 1950 to 15 percent in 1975.[47]

Since 1974, the president and his OMB director have had to deal with new competition on Capitol Hill—the Congressional Budget Office (CBO) and its staff of experts. President Ford encountered this problem soon after he entered the White House. Indeed, as Allen Schick has pointed out: "The new Budget Committee quickly became the marshalling point for congressional opposition to President Gerald Ford's tax and expenditure policies."[48]

Even after President Reagan arrived on the scene, the federal budget continued to grow larger—though at a slower rate of increase—each year, and the president and his aides found they had influence over only one-quarter of the budget. To be sure, Reagan's spectacular cuts, approved by Congress in 1981, demonstrated that a president, intent upon scaling down the size of the federal government and with a fresh mandate from the electorate, could still play a key role.

BALANCING THE BOOKS

Presidents have, from time to time, used another budgetary spending restraint to help balance the books—impoundment of funds.

Impoundment of Funds.   From the time of George Washington, presidents have exercised some measure of spending control through the practice of impounding or returning appropriated but unspent funds to the U.S. Treasury. Presidents have routinely impounded funds to save money when appropriations have been insufficient to cover expenditures. They have withheld funds when authorized or directed to by Congress in order to establish contingency reserves or impose a ceiling on total spending. Since the New Deal era, presidents have also impounded some of the funds Congress has added, despite presidential objections, to both defense and domestic programs. Sometimes these impoundments provoked congressional criticism, but they did not lead to full-scale confrontations until President Nixon resorted to wholesale impoundments in the early 1970s. Nixon withheld huge sums (more than $18 billion) that Congress had already appropriated for regular programs in agriculture, housing, and water pollution control. Nor did he make any secret of the fact that he was using impoundment as a weapon in his battle with Congress over domestic spending priorities.

Congress, as expected, reacted to this flagrant use of the impoundment process, charging that the president was acting arbitrarily and illegally in substituting his spending priorities for those established by Congress. Instead of bargaining with Congress, as his predecessors had done, Nixon refused to compromise. His actions triggered a series of lawsuits to compel release of the impounded funds, which the president lost on statutory grounds.[49]

Congress also had the last word when it passed the Budget Control and Impoundment Act of 1974 to halt further massive impoundments. The new law limited impoundments to the establishment of contingency reserves and the saving of money that would otherwise be wasted. The legislation established procedures for congressional review and control of all future impoundments. Furthermore, the president was required to report all impoundments to Congress. Under the 1974 law, proposed recisions (returning appropriated funds permanently to the Treasury) must be approved by both chambers within 45 days. Proposals to defer spending until the next fiscal year could be rejected by either house.[50] While the statute is not a model of sound fiscal management, it has halted the unrestricted use of excessive impoundments as a political tool of the president against Congress. The law does not, it should be noted, block presidents from using impoundments to increase administrative efficiency. But it does put presidents on notice that they must act prudently and not flaunt congressional prerogatives.

Central Clearance.   Presidential assumption of chief responsibility for budgetary agenda setting could not have taken place without major organizational changes in the executive branch. With the passage of the Budget and Accounting Act of 1921, Congress gave the president a valuable management tool. The lawmakers, recognizing their own inability to keep track of the increasing number of budgetary requests arising throughout the growing federal structure, willingly vested in the president authority to formulate the federal budget and thereby put a price tag on his legislative proposals. Surprisingly, President Harding, who has generally been rated one of our weakest presidents, had the foresight to accept a suggestion made by the House Appropriations Committee to develop a central clearance system for all prospective budgetary proposals.

Under this new budget system, all agency proposals for legislation or plans on pending legislation that, if adopted, would carry a charge on the U.S. Treasury or commit the federal government to obligations which would later require funding first had to be submitted to the Bureau of the Budget for review before they could be sent to Congress.

When Roosevelt moved into the White House, central clearance was still viewed primarily as an adjunct to the budgetary control of the president. In order to keep pace with fast-moving events of the early New Deal, Roosevelt expanded central clearance procedures to include a review of all agency proposals affecting substantive policy. FDR also insisted that the Bureau of the Budget furnish him with recommendations as to whether he should sign or veto bills presented to him by Congress. Although many Washington observers may not have realized it at the time, Roosevelt's decision had far-reaching consequences, for it signaled his intention "to protect not just his budget, but his prerogatives, his freedom of action, and his choice of policies, in an era of fast-growing government and of determined presidential leadership."[51] Roosevelt, in short, converted the budget from a mere financial control mechanism into a policymaking tool.

As an indication of how vitally important the central clearance procedure had become to President Roosevelt, the Legislative Reference Division of the Bureau of the Budget reviewed and reported on 2,448 pending public bills during the course of only the first session of the 76th Congress.[52] It has been estimated that 50 to 80 percent of all legislation enacted by Congress originates in the executive branch and is filtered through the central clearance apparatus.[53]

During World War II, military planning priorities and the production of war material forced the suspension of central clearances procedures. But with the cessation of hostilities and the return to normal government operations, President Truman reestablished central clearance procedures to aid the development and measure the cost effectiveness of his legislative programs.

The adoption of the Employment Act of 1946 furnished an added incentive for a more closely coordinated system of central legislative clearance. Less than a year later, Truman assigned the Bureau of the Budget, working hand-in-hand with his own White House staff, the task of reviewing and coordinating into a comprehensive overall program all federal agency legislative and budgetary recommendations. As described by one commentator: "Formulation of a presidential legislative program thus became the end product of a careful audit of agency plans, reviewed and reduced into an integrated scheme conforming to the basic policy guidemarks set by the President himself."[54] Eisenhower's well-known predilection for a staff system and clear lines of authority made it easy for him to adopt the system of central clearance and program review of his legislative program, even though he initially offered only a relatively short list of legislative initiatives. Thus, by the mid-1950s it could be said that central clearance procedures had become an institutionalized part of the presidency.

Activist Presidents Kennedy and Johnson were less enamored by the Bureau of the Budget's domination of the legislative program. Both Kennedy and Johnson often preferred to obtain new ideas and proposals from special task forces chosen from the academic and business worlds. The reports of these task forces provided the basis for both Kennedy's New Frontier and Johnson's Great Society programs. So enthusiastic was Johnson about the task force concept early in his term that he had at least fifty task forces at work preparing reports on prospective legislation.[55] Johnson endeavored to have his White House staff coordinate the task force operations with the Bureau of the Budget in order to integrate all phases of the president's legislative programs. But as this president became ever more deeply mired in the Vietnam war, his domestic program agenda became shorter.

Nixon, who had served eight years as vice-president under Eisenhower, had his own ideas of government management. As part of his reorganization of the White House staff, Nixon established a Domestic Council and redesignated the Bureau of the Budget the Office of Management and Budget (OMB) in 1970. Nixon envisaged that the Domestic Council, composed of himself, the vice-president, eight cabinet members concerned mostly with domestic matters, and the two top officials in OMB, would serve as a top-level forum for discussing and hammering out public policy in a manner similar to the National Security Council.[56]

Reagan, who has made a political career out of arguing in favor of smaller, limited government, has shown no inclination toward decentralized control over domestic policymaking. His top-level White House strategy group and his director of Office of Management and Budget, as indicated earlier, make all the final decisions before sending proposed legislation to Capitol Hill.

ADMINISTRATIVE REORGANIZATION

Article I of the U.S. Constitution assigns to Congress, under the "necessary and proper" clause, the power to organize and reorganize departments, including the Executive Office of the President. Recent presidents, however, have all operated under the assumption that more administrative efficiency and greater presidential control of the bureaucracy can be achieved by executive reorganization.

Before the New Deal era, administrative reorganization was confined almost exclusively to Congress establishing new departments or dividing existing executive departments into new units. In 1939, following publication of the Brownlow Report, Congress authorized presidents to propose executive reorganization plans that would take effect after 60 days, unless disapproved by both houses.[57] Between 1939 and 1973, presidents submitted 105 reorganization plans to Congress; only 23 were disapproved. Truman won approval of 32 out of 48 such plans; Eisenhower, 14 of 17; Kennedy, 6 of 10; Johnson, 17 of 17; and Nixon, 8 of 8.[58] But in 1973 Congress, caught up in a continuing battle with Nixon over his efforts to centralize control in the executive branch, allowed this authority to elapse. Four years later, however, Carter requested from the Democratic-controlled Congress and received authority to reorganize executive branch agencies, subject to the veto of each house.

To achieve major organizational changes within the executive branch, the president generally asks Congress to pass reorganization acts. This legislation would normally provide that presidentially initiated reorganization plans will go into effect, if neither chamber disapproves by resolution within a specified period of time, usually 60 days. But the Supreme Court's invalidation of the legislative veto in 1983 will require that a new means be used to implement reorganization plans.[59]

Between 1789 and 1980, Congress approved the formation of 17 departments (see Table 9.2). As a result of department splits, mergers, and other administrative changes, the executive branch now consists of 13 departments. No attempt will be made here to survey all the administrative changes of independent agencies, corporations, and other nondepartmental agencies since the founding of the Republic. Indeed, the changes that have occurred within the Executive Office of the President for the period 1939–1979 constitute a formidable list (see Table 9.3). Thus, while the president has been able to effect some administrative reorganization of his White House staff on his own, he is not entirely the master of his own house.

If reorganization involves an executive department or major governmental

Table 9.3   THE EXECUTIVE OFFICE OF THE PRESIDENT, 1939–1979

Management agencies	
Council on Personnel Administration	1939–40
Office of Government Reports	1939–42
Liaison Office for Personnel Management	1939–43
National Resources Planning Board	1939–43
Permanent Advisory Committee on Government Organization	1953–61
Bureau of the Budget	1939–70
Federal Property Council	1973–77
Office of Management and Budget	1970–
Central Administrative Unit	1977–
Economic advisors and offices	
National Resources Planning Board	1939–43
Bureau of the Budget	1939–70
Council on International Economic Policy	1971–77
Council on Economic Policy	1973–74
Economic Policy Board	1974–77
Labor-Management Committee	1975–75
Cost of Living Council	1971–74
Council of Economic Advisors	1946–
Office of Special Representative for Trade Negotiations	1963–
Council on Wage and Price Stability	1974–
Policy advisors and offices	
National Aeronautics and Space Council	1958–73
Office of Science and Technology	1962–73
Economic Opportunity Council	1965–77
Office of Economic Opportunity	1964–75
National Council on Marine Resources and Engineering Development	1966–71
Council for Urban Affairs	1969–70
Domestic Council	1970–77
Office of Consumer Affairs	1971–73
Special Action Office for Drug Abuse Prevention	1971–75
Office of Telecommunications Policy	1970–77
Energy Policy Office	1973–74
Federal Energy Office	1974–75
Energy Resources Council	1975–77
Council on Environmental Quality	1969–
Domestic Policy Staff	1977–
Office of Science and Technology Policy	1975–
Office of Drug Abuse Policy	1975–

Table 9.3 (*Continued*)

National security advisors and offices	
Office of the Director of Mutual Security	1951–54
Board of Consultants on Foreign Intelligence Activities	1956–61
President's Foreign Intelligence Advisory Board	1961–77
National Security Council	1947–
Central Intelligence Agency	1947–
Director of Central Intelligence	1947–
Intelligence Oversight Board	1947–
Mobilization and preparedness agencies	
Office of Emergency Management	1940–54
Committee for Congested Production Areas	1943–44
Office of War Mobilization and Reconversion	1942–45
War Refugee Board	1944–45
National Security Resources Board	1947–53
Office of Defense Mobilization	1952–59
Office of Civil and Defense Mobilization	1958–62
Office of Emergency Planning	1962–69
Office of Emergency Preparedness	1965–73

Source: From *The American Presidency* by Richard M. Pious, 252–253. Copyright © 1979 by Richard M. Pious. Reprinted by permission of Basic Books, Inc., Publishers.

agency, Congress decides this matter. Indeed, several recent presidents have seen some of their reorganization plans flatly rejected by Congress. Truman's planned Department of Welfare was tabled on Capitol Hill, though Congress subsequently created a new conglomerate department—Health, Education, and Welfare (HEW)—during the Eisenhower administration. (The name was changed to Health and Human Services in 1980 when a separate Department of Education was established.) Kennedy's proposed Department of Urban Affairs, though initially turned down by Congress, was subsequently approved two years after his assassination as part of Lyndon Johnson's Great Society program. Jimmy Carter's plan for a Department of Energy was eventually approved, but not until after it was substantially modified by Congress.

The president is not, however, entirely at the mercy of Congress in running his shop. Some units of the Executive Office of the President have been created by executive order of the president based upon his executive power, and he can organize and reshuffle his White House office staff as he sees fit, since Congress has approved these reorganization plans as a matter of comity between branches.[60] Other presidential agencies in the Executive Office of the President have been created by statute, based upon the "necessary and proper" clause of Article I. Still others can be or have been set up (or abolished) by reorganization plans. From time to time, ad hoc agencies or presidential task forces have been created by executive order to deal with special problems as they arise—for example, the Rockefeller Commission on the Central Intelligence Agency, or President Reagan's special commissions on social security and Central America.

If major executive departments or agencies are involved, however, Congress calls the tune. The lawmakers may specify the authority of the departmental officials, and they may decide to grant some autonomy to bureaus. Also, Congress may specify the powers and duties of specific officials in the departments and bureaus. Congress, in its wisdom (or caprice), may decide to create independent agencies and commissions outside the departmental structure. Performing quasi-legislative and quasi-judicial functions, these bipartisan commissions and agencies enjoy autonomous status that puts them beyond reach of presidential supervision, although the president selects the members of these bipartisan commissions subject to Senate confirmation. To deal with complex administrative problems that cut across several departments, Congress may even decide to establish public corporations or quasi-public corporations with independent boards of directors, such as the Tennessee Valley Authority or the U.S. Postal Service.

While Congress has given presidents considerable latitude in reorganization of the executive branch, they have staked out firm outer limits. The lawmakers excluded independent regulatory commissions from 1939 to 1949. In 1977, the lawmakers prohibited the use of reorganization plans to eliminate enforcement of the statutory functions of a department or a federal agency. If a president wants to create a new department or eliminate or consolidate the functions of existing departments and independent agencies, he must persuade Congress to enact the proposal into law.

Despite presidential faith in the efficacy of governmental reorganization, recent history shows that reorganization does not necessarily result in greater effectiveness or clearer public accountability. Indeed, it would appear that there is no ideal form for a governmental agency, nor is there a set formula for structuring the executive branch. Herbert Kaufman is undoubtedly correct when he points out that the most far-reaching consequences of organizational change are not to be found in the "engineering realm of efficiency, simplicity, size, and cost of government," but rather occur in the areas of "political influence, policy emphasis, and communication of governmental intentions."[61]

LONG-RANGE PLANNING

Presidents seldom engage in long-range planning. As chief administrator of the government, presidents undoubtedly should put long-range planning near the top of their priority projects, but most chief executives soon become crisis managers after taking office and rarely give much thought to long-term goals.

Before the rise of the welfare state in the twentieth century and the development of nuclear weaponry, the need for long-range planning seemed less pressing. But the past half-century, which has seen a population explosion throughout the Third World, the depletion of critical natural resources, especially petroleum, and the splitting of the atom, has not resulted in any appreciable increase in presidential interest in national planning. In planning for the future, or at least anticipating some of the changes resulting from the powerful social, economic, and scientific forces at work in our society and abroad, recent American presidents have failed woefully. In retrospect, FDR's New Deal seems far more advanced in planning for the future than any subsequent administration.

The only major presidential experiment in long-range planning dates back to the National Resources Planning Board (NRPB), established by Franklin D. Roosevelt in 1939 as a unit within the White House Executive Office. Created to collect extensive data and develop long-range goals for the country—but purely on an advisory basis—the NRPB had barely assumed its mission before the outbreak of World War II. While Roosevelt strongly supported this governmental planning unit, he soon found that preparations for the defeat of Nazi Germany, Fascist Italy, and the Japanese military regime fully occupied his attention. Nevertheless, the National Resources Planning Board's comprehensive reports on anticipated postwar problems—full employment, social security, medical costs, and efficient use of land, water, mineral, and recreational resources—all received high marks from planning experts. Unfortunately, this New Deal planning agency did not have many friends in the nation's capital.

By 1943, bureaucratic opponents, especially the Army Corps of Engineers, persuaded Congress to abolish the NRPB. Furthermore, to make certain that it would hear no more of planning, Congress stipulated that the NRPB's functions should not be assigned to any other agency.[62] Since then, the presidency has never had a regular planning agency to anticipate future national consequences, with the possible exception of National Security Council plans and some units within the military complex. National planning, for the most part, has been left to chance. To be sure, national survival has dictated that foreign and defense policy planning be undertaken on a continuing basis. But domestic planning seems less compelling, even though—to cite one example—the rising demand for energy resources, especially oil, its spiraling costs in face of declining reserves, and the threatened interruption of oil shipments from the Middle East may pose a long-term, life-or-death threat to the national economy.

Planning has often been a dirty word for many Americans. It smacks of socialism, or even more extreme forms of statism. This bias has appeared again and again in the halls of Congress. While Americans were willing to forego necessities during World War II and accepted rationing of gasoline, tires, butter, and meat, they have displayed little patience with any national plans that would, for example, substitute mass public transportation for the private automobile. Consequently, American presidents have not attempted to push any systematic type of national planning. President Reagan, in his campaign to downsize the federal government, has displayed a strong penchant to cut government spending, but little enthusiasm for any long-range planning.

As far as long-term program development is concerned, Richard Pious is probably close to the mark in his observation that "when a new administration comes to power, it seems that it is constantly reinventing the wheel since it cannot draw on the experience of its predecessors."[63] Two White House study commissions—the Heineman task force (appointed by President Johnson) and the Ash task force (selected by President Nixon)— have both pointed out the need for long-term planning by the White House. They suggested the establishment of an office for management within the Executive Office of the President. But these proposals have been derailed by a combination of pressures from the Office of Management and Budget and the cabinet.[64]

In view of mounting problems involving nuclear weaponry; the exhaustion of critical natural resources, especially crude oil; population growth; and environmental pollution; to mention only a short list, the compelling need for an agency in the White House to address future problems is indisputable. But the short-run prospects for creation of a new presidential agency with management and planning functions remain dim.

CONCLUSION

Whether or not the president likes his role as chief administrator, he must share some managerial responsibility with a co-pilot—Congress. To be sure, the Founding Fathers' experience with the Articles of Confederation convinced them that the new nation needed a single chief executive to conduct the affairs of state; nevertheless, the president's role as chief administrator remained somewhat ambiguous. Consequently, the president and Congress have been involved in a periodic tug of war over the administrative direction of the nation. The Founding Fathers, with their innate distrust of concentrated power, did not hesitate to divide control over some areas of administration. Indeed, Richard Neustadt's description of the federal government as "a government of separated institutions sharing powers" was never truer than in the field of public administration.

To run the federal governmental machinery, the president relies heavily on the 13 executive departments and approximately 60 executive agencies. Since Washington's time, the heads of the executive departments have constituted the president's cabinet—an extralegal advisory body. For more than 150 years the president relied heavily on his cabinet for advice and important decision making. However, in the past quarter century the White House staff has gradually displaced the cabinet as the major influence in the executive branch. More and more, political power is becoming concentrated in the White House staff.

The Constitution neither prescribes a budget process, nor does it spell out the president's role as the nation's chief business manager. But since passage of the Budget and Accounting Act of 1921, Congress has empowered presidents to establish a comprehensive budget. One section of this legislation established a Bureau of the Budget (renamed the Office of Management and Budget in 1970) to oversee preparation of the federal budget. Franklin D. Roosevelt took another important step by ordering the Bureau of the Budget to review all legislative proposals originating in the executive branch to assess their feasibility, cost, and possible duplication with other proposals before recommending that the president transmit them to Capitol Hill for action. By use of this new central clearance procedure, FDR converted the budget from a mere financial mechanism into a presidential policy tool. Under Reagan, the Office of Management and Budget, first headed by David Stockman, has become the key agency in developing budget reduction and tax cut plans.

Though recent presidents have all had the benefit of large White House staffs, none since FDR has exhibited a serious interest in long-range planning. Despite the threat of nuclear warfare, of long-term energy shortages, of environmental pollution, and of the growth of the country's population, the executive branch—and Congress—continue to display an appalling lack of concern toward long-range planning for the nation's future.

NOTES

1. Richard M. Pious, *The American Presidency* (New York: Basic Books, 1979), 214.
2. Louis Fisher, *President and Congress* (New York: The Free Press, 1972), 26.
3. Richard E. Neustadt, *Presidential Power* (New York: Wiley, 1960), 9–10.
4. *Myers* v. *United States,* 272 U.S. 52 (1926).
5. *Humphrey's Executor* v. *United States,* 295 U.S. 602 (1935).
6. *Report of the President's Committee on Administrative Management,* 1937, 5.
7. George Reedy, *The Twilight of the Presidency* (New York: New American Library, 1970), especially Chapter 1.
8. P.L. 80–253.
9. George Edwards and Stephan J. Wayne, *Presidential Leadership* (New York: St. Martin's Press, 1985), 246.
10. Pious, *The American Presidency,* 218.
11. Joseph E. Kallenbach, *The American Chief Executive* (New York: Harper & Row, 1966), 440–441.
12. *Report of the President's Committee on Administration Management,* 1937, 5.
13. Edwards and Wayne, *Presidential Leadership,* 182–183.
14. Hugh Heclo, "One Executive Branch or Many," in Anthony King, ed., *Both Ends of the Avenue* (Washington, DC: American Enterprise Institute, 1983), 46–47.
15. *The New York Times,* April 17, 1985.
16. Chester A. Newland, "Executive Office Policy Apparatus: Enforcing the Reagan Agenda," in Lester M. Salamon and Michael S. Lund, eds., *The Reagan Presidency and the Governing of America* (Washington, DC: Urban Institute Press, 1984), 143.
17. Peter T. Kilborn, "How the Big Six Steer the Economy," *The New York Times,* November 17, 1985.
18. Newland, "Executive Office Policy Apparatus: Enforcing the Reagan Agenda," 167.
19. Laurence E. Lynn, Jr., "The Reagan Administration and the Penitent Bureaucracy," in Salamon and Lund, *The Reagan Presidency and Governing America,* 369.
20. Richard P. Nathan, "Comments," in Salamon and Lund, *The Reagan Presidency and the Governing of America,* 376.
21. Richard F. Fenno, Jr., *The President's Cabinet: An Analysis in the Period from Wilson to Eisenhower* (Cambridge, MA: Harvard University Press, 1959), 218.
22. Edwards and Wayne, *Presidential Leadership,* 173.
23. *Washington Post,* July 18, 1982.
24. Pious, *The American Presidency,* 236–241.
25. Ibid., 238.
26. Ibid.
27. Ibid.
28. Ibid., 239.
29. Stephen Hess, *Organizing the Presidency* (Washington, DC: The Brookings Institution, 1976), 16–17.
30. Henry Fairlie, *The Kennedy Promise* (Garden City, NY: Doubleday, 1973), 167–168.

31. Thomas E. Cronin, "The Swelling of the Presidency," *Saturday Review of Society,* 1 (February 1973), 30–36.

32. Richard T. Johnson, *Managing the White House* (New York: Harper & Row, 1974), 1–8.

33. Arthur M. Schlesinger, Jr., *The Coming of the New Deal* (Boston: Houghton Mifflin, 1958), 527–528.

34. Johnson, *Managing the White House,* 6–8.

35. Ibid., 197.

36. Ibid., 112–114.

37. Several nineteenth-century presidents—John Quincy Adams, Van Buren, Tyler, Polk, Buchanan, Grant, and Cleveland—did take a hand in revising budget estimates before they were sent to Capitol Hill. Also, after 1878, the Treasury Department began compiling the department requests into a single volume for submission to Congress. Fisher, *Presidential Spending Power* (Princeton, NJ: Princeton University Press, 1975), 10.

38. Howard E. Shuman, *Politics and the Budget: The Struggle Between the President and Congress* (Englewood Cliffs, NJ: Prentice-Hall, 1984), 23.

39. Louis Fisher, *The Constitution Between Friends* (New York: St. Martin's Press, 1978), 175.

40. Gerald Ford, "Budget Message of the President," *The Budget of the United States Government, Fiscal Year 1978* (Washington, DC: Government Printing Office, 1977), as quoted by Pious, *The American Presidency,* 256.

41. Ibid., 269.

42. W. Bowman Cutter, "The Presidency and Economic Policy," in Michael Nelson, ed., *The Presidency and the Political System* (Washington, DC: Congressional Quarterly Press, 1984), 483.

43. Ibid., 485.

44. Ibid., 487.

45. Catherine E. Rudder, "Fiscal Responsibility and the Revenue Committees," in Lawrence C. Dodd and Bruce I. Oppenheimer, eds., *Congress Reconsidered,* 3rd ed. (Washington, DC: Congressional Quarterly Press, 1985), 212.

46. Allen Schick, "The Budget as an Instrument of Presidential Policy," in Salamon and Lund, *The Reagan Presidency and the Governing of America,* 95.

47. Ibid., 96.

48. Ibid., 101.

49. Fisher, *Presidential Spending Power,* 189–192.

50. Ibid., pp. 198–201.

51. Richard E. Neustadt, "The Presidency and Legislation: The Growth of Central Clearance," *American Political Science Review,* 47 (September 1954), 643–644.

52. Ibid., 653.

53. John N. Pfiffner and Robert Presthus, *Public Administration,* 5th ed. (New York: Ronald Press, 1967), 5.

54. Kallenbach, *The American Chief Executive,* 342.

55. Johnson preferred the task force process because it sidestepped most of the departmental infighting and bargaining and because it largely avoided bureaucratic, congressional interest group pressures. Lyndon B. Johnson, *The Vantage Point* (New York: Holt, Rinehart, and Winston, 1971), 326.

56. Richard A. Watson and Norman C. Thomas, *The Politics of the Presidency* (New York: Wiley, 1983), 254.

57. Kallenbach, *The American Chief Executive,* 383.

58. Pious, *The American Presidency,* 214.
59. Louis Fisher, *Constitutional Conflicts Between Congress and the President* (Princeton, NJ: Princeton University Press, 1985), 178–183.
60. Pious, *The American Presidency,* 215.
61. Herbert Kaufman, "Reflections on Administrative Reorganization" in Joseph A. Peckman, ed., *Setting National Priorities: The 1978 Budget* (Washington, DC: The Brookings Institution, 1977), 403.
62. Watson and Thomas, *The Politics of the Presidency,* 324.
63. Pious, *The American Presidency,* 254.
64. Ibid.

chapter 10

Party Leader

The president of the United States is the only public officeholder, except for the vice-president, with a national constituency. Because the office enjoys far greater prestige and power than any other, and because partisan connections largely control which contenders will have a chance to be elected president, it is understandable that political partisans and the general public alike view the president as chief of the party. In the words of Woodrow Wilson:

> He can dominate his party by being a spokesman for the real sentiment and purpose of the country, by giving direction to opinion, by giving the country at once the information and the statements of policy which will enable it to form its judgments alike of parties and of men.[1]

In a real sense, the president *is* the national party, for most of the party effort at the national level is devoted to nominating and electing the president. Since no other officeholder represents nearly as broad a constituency, the president stands alone as the chief spokesperson of the party. Also, the president is the most visible representative of the party. By virtue of his party position, the president's programs become identified as his party's programs, his successes become the party's successes, and his failures are identified as his party's failures.

No matter what his party's congressional leadership may prefer, the president's symbolic leadership ties him inextricably to his party. Thus, just as Franklin D. Roosevelt's legislative successes have been viewed as Democratic successes and Ronald Reagan's budget reductions as Republican accomplishments, so too did Richard Nixon's Watergate illegal coverups become a Republican albatross and Jimmy Carter's leadership failures reflect unfavorably upon the Democratic party.

Since the age of Andrew Jackson, the presidency and the two-party system have complemented each other. Indeed, if the parties had not transformed the electoral vote system and if the national conventions had not emerged as the nominating agency for presidential candidates, the American party system would in all likelihood have faint resemblance to the present structure. Similarly, without the office of president as nationalizing force within our system, it seems unlikely that the federal system would have survived in its present form. Equally important, political parties have enabled presidents to overcome some of the limitations of our formal constitutional separation of powers to provide strong leadership in times of national crisis.

In this chapter the president's role as party leader, limited as it is by the separation of powers, will be explained and assessed. But we will also show that a president, if favored with effective working party majorities in Congress and if he understands how to operate the levers of power, can be a dynamic force within the American governmental system. All of the great presidents except Washington, who held office before the rise of parties, have been strong party leaders. We examine the influence of presidential coattails—the ability of the president as head of the party's slate to draw votes for other candidates on the same ballot —as well as the president's relationship with the national party committee. We also focus on the emergence of several factors that point to a declining influence of the president in party matters: the reformed nominating system, entrenched congressional incumbency, party decomposition, decline in partisan voting, decreased political patronage, and the uncertainty of renomination. Similarly, attention is focused on the lessening presidential dependence upon his party to achieve some of his major goals—the rise of instant communication between president and electorate via television, full federal government underwriting of the presidential election campaign, and the president's use of national interest groups to pressure Congress to support his legislative program.

THE CONSTITUTIONAL BACKGROUND

The constitutional job description for the president of the United States does not include the title "chief party leader"—the main reason being, of course, that political parties had not yet emerged when the Founding Fathers convened in Philadelphia. Even if the parties had existed then, it seems doubtful that the men of 1787 would have included the duties of party leader in the nation's fundamental document, for they regarded partisan groups as instruments of dissension and discord. John Adams, the second president, echoed George Washington's warning about the disruptiveness of parties by declaring: "Division of the republic into two great parties, each under its leader . . . is to be dreaded as the greatest evil under our Constitution."[2]

Despite the Framers' antipathy toward parties, the presidential election contest had, by 1800, become a battle between rival political leaders. But not until the rise of political parties in the Jacksonian era did presidential leadership have an opportunity to flourish. In James Sterling Young's words: "Converting the presidential office into a vehicle of leadership of Congress required basic changes in the style and structure of American national politics."[3]

THE NATIONAL CONVENTION AND THE PRESIDENT'S INDEPENDENT POWER BASE

The emergence of the national party convention as the nominating agency for presidential and vice-presidential candidates during the Jackson administration turned out to be a remarkable invention for facilitating party leadership by the chief executive. Instead of being politically indebted to the congressional caucus for the nomination, as was the case prior to the rise of the national convention, presidential candidates now owed their loyalty only to the convention delegates representing party membership in nearly all states of the Union. More than anything else, the national convention gave the presidential nominee an independent base of power separate from Congress and opened the door for the growth of executive leadership.

Andrew Jackson, the first chief executive to perceive the value of the national convention as a means of assimilating the party leadership function to the president's office, marshalled the power of the rapidly growing electorate into the Democratic party and used it as an instrument to reinforce his leadership. Indeed, the powerful backing of the Democratic voters liberated the presidency "from psychological bondage to anti-power attitudes and from institutional bondage to a kingmaking Congress." Moreover, the emergence of a popularly based political party gave President Jackson "a constituency and a role of citizen spokesmanship equal to that of Congress."[4] As party leader, Jackson could henceforth appeal over the heads of Congress to the electorate to have them pressure the lawmakers to follow the president's leadership.

From Jackson's time to the present day, the ability of the president to carry out his role as party leader has been the hallmark of effective government. Conversely, whenever presidents have failed to exert strong party leadership, the country has languished. The paucity of party leadership by the "postage stamp" presidents of the Gilded Age—Grant, Hayes, Garfield, Arthur, and Harrison— immediately comes to mind. Even President Grover Cleveland, who was viewed as one of the stronger presidents of the post-Civil War era, complained in late 1883 about Congress: "If a botch is made at the other end of the Avenue, I don't mean to be a party to it." On another occasion he insisted: "I did not come here to legislate."[5]

Cleveland's performance as party leader demonstrated another truism about presidential party leadership that led the late nineteenth-century scholar Henry Jones Ford to comment: "It is impossible for a party to carry out even a purely legislative programme unless it embodies a policy accepted by the President and sustained by the influence of his office."[6] Some years ago, another leading party scholar noted that presidents who tried to govern without the benefit of organized party support never succeeded well enough to inspire imitation.[7]

Political parties have enabled our presidents, especially Woodrow Wilson, Franklin D. Roosevelt, Lyndon Johnson, and Ronald Reagan, to overcome some of the limitations that the constitutional separation of powers has imposed on the American system of government and to provide powerful national leadership. Political parties, however, are two-way vehicles. While they have given the president the means to exercise broad power and influence over public policy, they have also served as a restraining force, keeping presidents responsive to the concerns of rank-and-file voters, especially if the president wishes to seek re-election.

LIMITED POWER AS PARTY LEADER

The president's influence over his party does not generally extend to state or local parties, or to congressional committees; his dominance is limited to the national committee. Although a strong president might campaign for party candidates and officeholders at the state or congressional level, presidents have usually learned that it is imprudent to intervene directly in party nominations or to become embroiled in state or local conflicts. Even Franklin D. Roosevelt, despite his great leadership skills and popularity, learned the hard way that intervention in state nominating politics is unwanted. In 1938, for example, FDR's efforts to purge a number of anti-New Deal Democratic senators and representatives in primary elections ended in almost total failure.

As party leader, the president often finds the political cards stacked against him. Unlike the British prime minister and his cabinet, who can count on party discipline to carry the vote in Parliament on all party programs, the president of the United States is in a sense an independent entrepreneur insofar as party leadership is concerned. Even party control of both the executive and legislative branches in the federal government does not operate in the same way as in the parliamentary system.

The American president has only limited means for imposing his will on members of his party in Congress. Why? First of all, the president and Congress answer to entirely different constituencies. Both houses of Congress function through their own party organizations. Some years ago, James MacGregor Burns suggested that the congressional party organizations and the party organizations headed by the president and the opposition party leader are so distinct that in this country we have, in effect, four rather than two national parties.[8] Nor does the president have any direct control over the selection of his party leaders in Congress. Indeed, as one historian has noted: "None of the framers' objectives were more explicit than to deny the head of government any influence over the selection, tenure, or career advancement of legislators."[9]

Party discipline in the United States is of limited utility to the president. As party leader, he lacks powerful sanctions or appealing rewards with which to influence the voting behavior of individual federal lawmakers. Patronage appointments, which had formerly served as bargaining chips to reward congressional party loyalty to the administration, have almost vanished as a result of repeated expansion of civil service job protection and greater emphasis on merit hiring in the federal service. Consequently, American presidents cannot rely on their party in Congress for consistent support, even when it is in the majority.

Most presidents soon learn the distinction between a paper or party majority in Congress and a working majority. John F. Kennedy, for example, had party majorities in both houses of Congress during his brief tenure, but the Southern Democrat–GOP coalition usually held a voting majority on most domestic issues. Like his predecessors, Franklin D. Roosevelt (after his first term) and Harry Truman, Kennedy often found his domestic proposals stalled or blocked by the Southern Democrat–GOP coalition.

Although it is a common practice to refer to the president as leader of his political party, the fact is that the president has no formal position in the party structure. Even though he may have been elected by a large majority, the president has little say or influence over the selection of his party's leaders in Congress. While a president or a president-elect may have expressed support for a congressional party leader whose position may be in some jeopardy, congressmen would strongly resent any presidential interference in their leadership affairs. Nor is there any record in the twentieth century of a president openly trying to get rid of a Speaker or floor leader.

One veteran presidential watcher has observed: "At most, the President can be only a quasi-party leader."[10] A combination of forces and pressures have dictated that the president be only a quasi-party leader. First of all, a president may face a Congress one or both of whose houses is controlled by the opposition party. During the period 1952–1986, for example, the president of the United States faced a Congress in which the opposition party controlled both houses for 14 years and 6 years in which the opposition party controlled one house—a total of 20 years of divided leadership out of 34 years. Congress was in the hands of the opposition party in all but two years of President Eisenhower's two terms and all eight years of the Nixon-Ford administrations. Reagan faced a Republican Senate and a Democratic House—Roger H. Davidson of the Library of Congress calls this division a "truncated majority"—throughout his first term and the first two years of his second term. Clearly, the American system of separation of powers and check and balances impedes majority rule.

Deprived of a strong party organization in the decentralized American party system, the president must depend heavily upon his personal magnetism and ability to work with congressional leaders if he is to carry the day. Still, he cannot expect to achieve much success with Congress without the support of his party. The president's ability to lead his party is aided by the fact that congressional leaders of his party have the same team loyalties and a similar stake in developing an attractive legislative program. As Austin Ranney has put it:

> Despite the often-mentioned weakness of their party ties, most congressmen still have some sense of belonging to one of two teams, and their team loyalty impels most of them to vote as a president of their party asks, except where such a vote would clearly go against what they perceive to be their constituents' interests or wishes.[11]

They want the president to succeed. Consequently, members of his party usually try to push the president's program through Congress. Failure of the president's congressional leaders to push his programs will, of course, signify serious trouble within the party and reflect unfavorably on both the lawmakers and the president.

Fortunately for the president, members of his party in Congress often find themselves in a mutually dependent relationship with the president. As Frank J. Sorauf has explained: "Members of the president's party know that if they make him look bad, to some extent they also make themselves and their party look bad."[12] Thus, members of his own party will, for example, vote to sustain his veto, even though their own legislative preferences may differ with their party leader.[13] The late GOP House Majority (and later Minority) Leader Charles A. Halleck, an arch-conservative Republican who often found himself in ideological disagreement with President Eisenhower, once summarized the party loyalist's view this way: "I do my arguing in the huddle, but when the signals are called, the argument ends. My only idea is to get the ball over the line."[14]

PRESIDENTIAL COATTAILS

Presidential party leadership has often been evaluated by its ability to affect other election outcomes. Although direct presidential intervention in other party contests has almost always been counterproductive, a presidential candidate or incumbent's electoral fortunes often correlate with those of other office seekers in his party. For many years "presidential coattails"—the ability of a presidential candidate to sweep into office, along with himself, many Senate and House members, governors, and elected state officials on the party ticket—provided an important incentive for lawmakers and state party leaders to work closely with the president. Since their fortunes were tied closely with those of the presidents, party leaders and elected officials at the national convention invariably sought to nominate a contender who would help the entire party ticket. The names of McKinley, Wilson, and both Roosevelts helped party candidates to ride into office on the president's coattails. But this phenomenon has declined in recent years (see Table 10.1).

Indeed, as Austin Ranney has commented: "A president running for reelection these days leads his party's ticket only in the sense that he is its best known candidate, not in the sense that the electoral fate of his party's congressional candidates depends heavily on how well or how badly he does."[15] The chief reason for the unraveling of the president's coattails is that incumbent members of Congress, especially in the House of Representatives, have become increasingly secure in their constituencies—over 90 percent of the incumbents in the House seeking reelection, no matter who is sitting in the White House, have consistently won in recent decades.[16] In 1984, for example, the return rate for GOP House members was just over 98 percent; for House Democrats, nearly 94 percent. The return rate for House incumbents has fallen below 90 percent only four times in the past 18 elections.[17]

The advantages of incumbency—great visibility, the ability to attract large amounts of political action committee (PAC) money for the reelection cam-

Table 10.1   PRESIDENTIAL COATTAILS (1932–1984)

Year	President	Party	Gains or losses of president's party	
			House	Senate
1932	Roosevelt	Dem.	+90	+9
1936	Roosevelt	Dem.	+12	+7
1940	Roosevelt	Dem.	+7	−3
1944	Roosevelt	Dem.	+24	−2
1948	Truman	Dem.	+75	+9
1952	Eisenhower	Rep.	+22	+1
1956	Eisenhower	Rep.	−3	−1
1960	Kennedy	Dem.	−20	+1
1964	Johnson	Dem.	+37	+1
1968	Nixon	Rep.	+5	+7
1972	Nixon	Rep.	+21	−2
1976	Carter	Dem.	+1	+1
1980	Reagan	Rep.	+33	+12
1984	Reagan	Rep.	+14	−2

Source: Updated from Congressional Quarterly, *Guide to U.S. Elections,* 928; and *Congress and the Nation,* IV (1973–1976), 28.

paign, the high cost of campaigning—have all sharply reduced the number of competitive congressional districts. As a result, members of Congress are less susceptible to the electoral influence of the president. Federal lawmakers no longer believe that their electoral fortunes are closely tied to the president's or even their own party. Whether or not they win reelection will depend largely on their own success in providing what Morris P. Fiorina calls "nonpartisan, non-programmatic constituency service," and much less on national trends.[18] Although the two-party vote for president seems to fluctuate widely from election to election, congressional elections (especially in the House) have become quite stable.

With the decline of party identification and the rise of a large bloc of independent voters, incumbency becomes a major factor in affecting congressional attitudes toward the president. The declining influence of presidential coattails is reflected in data which show that the percentage of congressional districts carried by a president from one party that elects a member of the opposite party to the House rose from 19.3 percent in 1952 to 44.1 percent in 1972.[19] Democratic presidential candidates often run behind congressional candidates and usually receive a lower percentage of the two-party vote. Few members of the Democratic congressional party regard the president as responsible for their own electoral victories.

As a matter of fact, when John F. Kennedy squeezed into the White House in the 1960 election, House Democrats lost 20 seats, and many of the defeated Democrats blamed the presidential campaign for their losses. Sixteen years later, Carter won the presidency with slightly over 50 percent of the vote, while 208 of 292 House Democrats received more than 60 percent of the total vote in the districts—a clear demonstration of greater enthusiasm for the legislative party.

This phenomenon prompted one British observer to remark: "If presidents no longer have coattails, there's no point in congressmen's clinging to them."[20] In some instances, it may be to a congressman's advantage to keep some distance from the president, as Republicans distanced themselves from Richard Nixon and Democrats from Jimmy Carter.

Republican coattails appear to be stronger than Democratic ones, but usually not strong enough to aid the party for any length of time. In 1952, General Eisenhower's coattails were long enough to enable the GOP to gain a narrow control of both the Senate and the House. But these wafer-thin majorities melted away two years later, and Eisenhower's coattails in 1956 were not long enough to enable the GOP to gain control of either house of Congress. In 1972, Nixon's landslide victory over George McGovern helped House Republicans gain 13 seats, though not enough to control the chamber.[21] Nixon's coattails also failed to help in GOP senatorial contests; the Republicans lost two seats.

Eight years later, Reagan's coattails helped the GOP win control of the U.S. Senate for the first time since 1954. The Republicans picked up 13 Senate seats for a five-vote margin. In the House the Republicans gained 33 seats, but not enough to overcome the almost 2 to 1 margin the Democrats enjoyed at that time. Thus, over the past 30 years the data show that Democratic congressional candidates do not need a strong presidential candidate, but the GOP can be helped to some extent by presidential coattails. Still, in 1984 Ronald Reagan's great popularity failed to prevent the net loss of two Senate Republican seats. Of the 17 GOP senators reelected, 11 won by margins greater than the president; 4 others had sizable winning margins ranging from 59 percent to 72 percent, indicating again the absence of presidential coattails (see Table 10.2).[22]

In off-year elections presidents are of little value in helping members of Congress retain marginal seats. With the exception of 1934, the party in the White House has always lost seats. Presidents Wilson, Roosevelt, Johnson, Nixon, Ford, and Reagan have all discovered that their White House occupancy does not translate into off-year congressional victories for their party. One longtime Capitol Hill observer has put it even more bluntly: "National trends don't affect congressional races anymore."[23]

PARTY REFORM AND PRESIDENTIAL PARTY LEADERSHIP

In the past two decades the role of the president as leader of his political party has been modified considerably by changes in the presidential nominating process, the financing of presidential nominating and election campaigns, and network television.

Prior to 1970, most presidents began to build their governing coalitions while in the process of winning the nomination. New York Governor Franklin D. Roosevelt and his advisers, for example, reached political "understandings" before and at the 1932 Democratic national convention with governors, U.S. senators, big-city mayors, state chairmen, and local party bosses. These party leaders controlled the selection of a majority of delegates to national conventions

Table 10.2   SENATE AND PRESIDENTIAL VICTORY MARGINS, 1984

State	Winning Party (Senate)	Percentage	Winning Party (Presidential)	Percentage
Alabama	Dem.	62%	Rep.	60%
Alaska	Rep.	71	Rep.	67
Arkansas	Dem.	58	Rep.	61
Colorado	Rep.	64	Rep.	63
Delaware	Dem.	60	Rep.	60
Georgia	Dem.	80	Rep.	60
Idaho	Rep.	72	Rep.	73
Illinois	Dem.	50	Rep.	57
Iowa	Dem.	56	Rep.	54
Kansas	Rep.	77	Rep.	67
Kentucky	Rep.	50	Rep.	60
Louisiana	Dem.	x	Rep.	61
Maine	Rep.	74	Rep.	61
Massachusetts	Dem.	55	Rep.	51
Michigan	Dem.	53	Rep.	59
Minnesota	Rep.	58	Dem.	51
Mississippi	Rep.	61	Rep.	62
Montana	Dem.	57	Rep.	60
Nebraska	Dem.	53	Rep.	71
New Hampshire	Rep.	59	Rep.	69
New Jersey	Dem.	65	Rep.	60
New Mexico	Rep.	72	Rep.	60
North Carolina	Rep.	52	Rep.	62
Oklahoma	Dem.	76	Rep.	68
Oregon	Rep.	66	Rep.	55
Rhode Island	Dem.	73	Rep.	62
South Carolina	Rep.	67	Rep.	64
South Dakota	Rep.	74	Rep.	63
Tennessee	Dem.	61	Rep.	63
Texas	Rep.	59	Rep.	64
Virginia	Rep.	70	Rep.	63
West Virginia	Dem.	52	Rep.	55
Wyoming	Rep.	78	Rep.	71

x = no opponent.
Source: Congressional Quarterly Weekly Report, 42 (November 10, 1984), 2923–31.

and could deliver their delegations during the convention balloting. FDR and his campaign manager even bartered away the vice-presidency (to John Nance Garner) in return for his delegates in Texas and California, in order to obtain the needed two-thirds majority to win the nomination.

In making deals with these party chieftains, presidential contenders had to make promises for cabinet posts, ambassadorships, and support for policies favorable to certain sections of the country in return for delegate support. "Favorite son" presidential contenders also had to be persuaded to give up their candidacies and their state delegates in return for future political favors. Always the chief purpose for cutting these deals was to collect delegate votes. But these "insider" negotiations also afforded opportunities for the presidential aspirant to become personally acquainted with public officeholders and party leaders who would be important to him if he reached the White House.

As late as 1960, John F. Kennedy and his lieutenants built these same alliances on his way to the White House. Governor David Lawrence of Pennsylvania and Mayor Richard J. Daley of Chicago, Kennedy's key preconvention supporters, would always find the door of the Oval Office open when they went to the nation's capital seeking federal help for their state or city. Furthermore, these powerful Democratic leaders could be counted on, in response to President Kennedy's requests, to exert pressure on their state's congressional delegation to support the president's legislative proposals. In short, the process of building nominating coalitions was an important foundation for the subsequent process by which the presidential nominee constructed his governing coalition.[24]

But the president's party leadership role, especially in the Democratic party, changed after the wholesale reforms in the nominating process by the McGovern–Fraser Commission in the early 1970s. Clearly, the reform rules aimed at taking the nominating process out of the smoke-filled rooms by stripping the party bosses and power brokers of their control over delegate selection, especially in the caucus-convention states.

To win the presidential nomination in the 1980s, a contender must tirelessly campaign personally for two years or more in many of the primary states as well as most of the remaining states that pick national convention delegates through the caucus-convention process. Especially in the early and large primary states, the candidate will also rely heavily on expensive media campaigns to reach prospective voters. Television enables the presidential contender to communicate directly with huge numbers of primary state voters without the need for any party organization workers.

Passage of the Federal Election Campaign Act of 1974 has virtually eliminated a nominee's financial dependence on his political party. The party nominee no longer has to turn to party sources to conduct the general election campaign, since the 1974 federal funding law now takes care of this $40.4 million bill. In short, the winner of the presidential election is no longer beholden to any party leaders or fat cats for financing and providing the party foot soldiers for his successful campaign.

Similarly, the party nominee can become the president-elect with relatively little or no contact with his party's leaders in Congress. The nominee owes these future working partners in Congress nothing, and they in turn have no obligation to him. The end result of these changes has been to separate the process of building the coalition needed to win the nomination from the process of building an effective coalition needed to govern. When a president takes office without any IOUs or political bills, and limited acquaintanceship with congressional leaders, he must build his governing coalition from ground zero. For he has reached the White House without creating any network of mutual obligations between himself and his party leaders in Congress and in the states. The nomination and election of political outsider Jimmy Carter in 1976 is, of course, the best-known example.

As presidents have lost their party leverage over Congress, they have come to rely more and more on the nonparty components of their leadership—popular nonpartisan appeals via national television, major out-of-town speeches, and closer ties to powerful interest groups. In the words of one commentator: "The nonpartisan direct television appeal has replaced the party rally."[25]

INTEREST GROUP SUPPORT

To counter an often uncooperative Congress, recent presidents have resorted each year to more out-of-town speeches before major national organizations and interest groups to get them to build political bonfires under Congress to generate support for the president's programs. As Samuel Kernell has noted: "Presidents Nixon and Carter averaged about seventy such appearances, and for Carter this figure excluded his numerous and lengthy 'town meetings.' Add to this an average of twenty-five Washington appearances and eleven days of foreign travel annually, and one has accounted for nearly a third of these presidents' time in office."[26] President Reagan, in his first term, matched Nixon and Carter virtually speech for speech.

As parties have become more fragmented, presidents and their White House staffs have steadily focused more attention on developing direct contacts with leading national interest groups to bolster White House influence and bargaining power with Congress. Presidents such as FDR and Truman dealt with interest groups through their allies in Congress and the party's national committee. But with the decline of political parties in recent decades, presidents have turned increasingly to dozens of major interest groups to help mobilize mass support for the chief executive's programs. More and more, presidents and their staffs have discovered that organized interest groups can exert needed legislative pressure on Congress that parties can no longer apply.

As one team of authors commented recently: "Except on brief and infrequent occasions, neither political party today can command a coalition with the potential to form an electoral or governing majority."[27] Consequently, presidents and their White House staffs now cultivate close relations with these interest groups "in order for the president to find a majority to support each of his policy goals, to win reelection, or simply to maintain the foundation of support necessary for managing conflict in the nation."[28] Interest groups, it seems, have filled the vacuum created by the decline of political parties.

The new political reality of the post-Watergate era reveals that presidents have relied less and less on their party leadership role; instead, they have sought to capitalize on their role as "president of all the people." This approach to presidential leadership has been especially widespread in years when a divided government (a Republican president and Democratic Congress, or a GOP Senate and Democrat-controlled House) has existed in the nation's capital. Indeed, divided government helps spawn the need for presidents to locate additional political support outside the party structure.

In recent years presidents have often preferred to rise above politics and avoid partisan rhetoric for another good reason. Aware that almost one-third of the American electorate now describe themselves as independent, recent presidents have been going public much more frequently, both on television and before live audiences, to push policies that appeal to these middle-of-the-road voters, who are often the key to electoral victory or defeat. Furthermore, this type of nonpartisan appeal seldom makes enemies, and it will also help create the impression that the president's actions are not simply done with an eye on the next election.

Bipartisanship is sometimes the only viable course of action to gain congressional acceptance of a presidential measure. Because on almost any major issue a president may lose the support of up to one-quarter of the votes from his own party, he must cultivate the support of some members of the opposition party to make up for these defections. This has been especially true for Republican presidents, for in the 24 years they have held the presidency from 1929 to 1984, they have had control of both houses of Congress for only 4 years (1929–1931 and 1953–1955).

Even strong presidents have recognized that they must pick up opposition party support on many major bills. Except for brief periods—the first terms of Woodrow Wilson, Franklin Roosevelt, and Lyndon Johnson—seldom have presidents had enough party support in Congress to affirm the principle of majority rule on a consistent basis. Generally, the president must negotiate, conciliate, cajole, and compromise almost every step of the way to pick up needed votes, including some from the opposition party, to win congressional approval of his priority measures. As Austin Ranney has commented: "No president has felt that he could afford to be so completely partisan in word and deed that he could offend all the members of the opposition party so much that they would never support him on anything."[29]

The author of one recent book on the presidency, deploring the weak control a president exercises over his party, has complained:

Our present decentralized and splintered party structures make it impossible for the president to command his fellow partisans. He must compromise with factions and even with partisan opponents to pass his programs. He must accommodate the interests of state and local leaders and elected officials by decentralizing programs rather than insisting on comprehensive national approaches to solve problems. The friction between president and Congress, and between national and state officials, slows down new initiatives and the small amount of party loyalty that exists provides precious little lubricant to prevent the clanking of gears in the machinery of government.[30]

From a formal standpoint, the accuracy of this statement is beyond dispute. But a formal assessment of the president's party scarcely explains how a string of great and near-great presidents have utilized their role as a party leader to achieve their goals and to move the country from a small fledgling republic to a world power in less than two centuries. Despite a system of limited government based upon divided powers and checks and balances, the party system has enabled the United States to overcome its constitutional impediments and meet its responsibilities to its own citizens as well as fulfill its obligations to the international community. More than a fraction of the credit belongs to those presidents who were strong party leaders as well as strong chief executives.

PARTY LEADERSHIP—THE HISTORICAL RECORD

Beyond doubt, the American national government functions most effectively when the president serves as a strong party leader. All great presidents after

George Washington—Jefferson, Jackson, Lincoln, Wilson, and Franklin D. Roosevelt—have been strong party leaders. But they became strong party leaders in spite of a decentralized, fragmented, confederate party structure and a separation of powers system established to hinder the exercise of power. Unlike the British prime minister or West German chancellor, who both serve dually as chief executives and party leader in Parliament and the Bundestag, the American president operates from a center of power outside the legislative branch. In point of fact, the president has no formal position in the party structure. Nevertheless, he is expected to serve as party leader, along with his other duties, such as chief executive, commander in chief, chief diplomat, and overseer of the economy.

If the foundation of the president's power base has been weak from the start, what reasons can be advanced to explain how Presidents Jefferson, Jackson, Theodore Roosevelt, Wilson, Franklin D. Roosevelt, and Ronald Reagan became such effective party leaders? Presidential success in party affairs has resulted from a combination of factors: personality, public popularity, ability to spell out goals clearly, and skill in developing political teamwork. Having effective working majorities in both houses of Congress also simplifies the president's party leadership tasks. Under these circumstances party discipline, limited though it may be, helps bridge the gap between the executive and legislative branches. But having working majorities, as explained earlier, is not of itself a guarantee of success, as Jimmy Carter demonstrated by his dismal inability to obtain strong party support in Congress during his four years in the White House, even though Democrats controlled the House of Representatives by nearly a 2 to 1 majority and the Senate by an almost 3 to 2 margin.

History shows, however, that party and legislative success have generally gone hand in hand. "Of all the Presidents," according to one leading authority, "Thomas Jefferson is unsurpassed as party leader and in the fealty he commanded from state and local party organizations."[31] Though parties were still in a formative stage when Jefferson first moved into the White House, he quickly displayed a firm grasp of the party reins. When the first Congress in Jefferson's administration convened, Jefferson and his advisers had already seen to it that not only the Speaker of the House but the chairman of every committee was a personal lieutenant of his. Jefferson and his cabinet members drafted a legislative agenda and then turned to members of his party in Congress to implement the program. Nor was Jefferson averse to using patronage to win legislative cooperation and ensure loyalty to his policies. According to one source, "Jefferson removed a larger percentage of civil servants for purposes of patronage than Andrew Jackson, who is the reputed founder of the spoils system in the federal government."[32]

Andrew Jackson also stands near the forefront of strong party leaders. Even before he occupied the White House, Jackson gathered about him a coterie of dedicated and accomplished politicians "who persistently sought the centripetal issues to hold intact the Democratic group coalition."[33] Though Jackson is best known for his frequent use of the veto to obtain his political ends, his adroit handling of Democratic party affairs kept the rival National Republicans and Whigs off balance throughout his two terms. Jackson's accomplishments as party leader transformed the office so extensively that he is often called the first modern president. As described by one commentator:

> The President became both the head of the executive branch and leader of the party. The first six presidents usually acted in a manner that accorded Congress an equality of power. However, starting with Andrew Jackson, the President began more and more to assert his role not simply as head of the executive branch but as leader of the government. By his skillful use of his position as head of the party he persuaded Congress to follow his lead thereby allowing him to assume greater control of the government and to direct and dominate public affairs.[34]

From the beginning of his presidency, Jackson held the House of Representatives in the hollow of his hand. Uncooperative senators on Jackson's "hit list" were picked off one by one as their terms expired, replaced by loyal Jacksonians. Before Jackson left the White House, the U.S. Senate was solidly dominated by Jacksonian Democrats. As he prepared to retire to Old Hermitage, he made his last great party leadership move—to pick his successor. Confronted with a party revolt against his plan to impose the nomination of his personal favorite, Vice-President Martin Van Buren, Old Hickory used the national convention to outmaneuver the managers of four leading presidential aspirants who were more widely regarded than Van Buren—Senators Thomas H. Benton and Henry Lawson White, Secretary of the Treasury Roger B. Taney, and House Speaker James K. Polk. Even the legislature of Jackson's home state of Tennessee nominated White for President and eventually cast its electoral votes for him. The party revolt spread to other states, but Jackson refused to yield on Van Buren.

In the end, the national convention not only nominated Van Buren for president, but also Richard M. Johnson as his running mate. To convention watchers of the period, the choice of Johnson was an almost incomprehensible act of defiance to the party insurgents, since Johnson openly acknowledged a black mistress and was alleged to have sought to have his two Paris-educated mixed-caste daughters introduced into Washington society. In the judgment of one leading presidential authority, Wilfred E. Binkley: "That Jackson could get away with the dictation of nominees for both offices by the Democratic convention in face of a determined opposition was a demonstration of presidential party chieftainship scarcely matched in the history of the presidency."[35]

While Abraham Lincoln is always remembered for having saved the Union during the nation's bloodiest conflict, his party leadership talents have often been overlooked. But as Wilfred Binkley has noted: "No president entered the great office more adept in the high art of party politics than Abraham Lincoln."[36] Lincoln's adroit handling of his cabinet appointments for the new administration has seldom been equaled. To many commentators, Lincoln's election to the White House was a political accident. Senator William H. Seward of New York, the early favorite to win the GOP nomination in 1860 until Lincoln elbowed him out, was viewed as the true leader of the new Republican party. Seward himself also seemed to feel that he, not Lincoln, should dictate the selection of the cabinet. Seward indicated to Lincoln that he would not serve in the cabinet if Salmon Chase were selected secretary of the treasury. Lincoln's counterproposal, to leave Seward out of the cabinet and make Chase as the head of the Treasury, soon brought Seward to heel. Lincoln demonstrated early in his administration that he alone was the party chieftain.

Soon after the outbreak of the Civil War, the composition of the Republican party began to change as more War Democrats came over to it. For the duration of the conflict, the Republicans and northern Democrats adopted the name the Union party. Lincoln had no hesitancy in using party patronage extensively to help cement ties with the Union party in states, cities, countries, and precincts. Post Office appointments were generously distributed to Union partisans, and when the supply ran low, Lincoln turned to the creation of captaincies, colonelcies, and brigadier generals to keep them out of the Democratic party. In Lincoln's mind, preservation of the Union justified his utilizing military patronage to achieve this supreme goal.

Even in the midst of the war, Lincoln managed to keep an eye on the 1864 election. He did not hesitate to ask generals in the field to furlough soldiers to go home to vote in close elections in those states that had not authorized their soldiers to cast ballots in the field. In a letter to General William T. Sherman, sent by a special messenger, Lincoln suggested: "Anything you can safely do to let [Indiana's] soldiers, or any part of them to go home and vote at the state election will be greatly in point. They need not remain for the presidential election, but may return to you at once."[37] Sherman obliged by not only granting wholesale furloughs to Indiana, but two of his generals, Blair and Logan, returned home and made campaign speeches. Union party victories in the October state elections heralded Lincoln's reelection in November.

In 1864 Lincoln also used party patronage blatantly to help secure ratification of the Thirteenth Amendment, which abolished slavery. Lacking one state to obtain the needed two-thirds vote, Lincoln sent Charles A. Dana on a special mission to win the support of two congressmen whose votes were necessary to get Nevada admitted to the Union—and to provide the extra votes required for ratification of the new amendment. As Dana recounted the event some years later, Lincoln declared: "Whatever promise you make to them I will do."[38] Subsequently, Nevada was admitted to the Union and the Thirteenth Amendment was ratified.

Not until the election of William McKinley in 1896 did the country see another consummate party chief in the White House. His successor, Theodore Roosevelt, was also a strong party leader. But the model party leader in the White House before the New Deal was Woodrow Wilson. Five years before his inauguration in 1913, Wilson the educator had noted the growing popular tendency to recognize the president "as the unifying force in our complex system, the leader both of his party and the nation."[39] A warm admirer of the British parliamentary system, Wilson had this advice for the White House occupant: "He must be the leader of his party. He is the party's choice and is responsible for carrying out the party platform. He therefore should have a large influence in determining legislation."[40] Furthermore, Wilson stated that the president "cannot escape being the leader of his party except by incapacity and lack of personal force because he is at once the choice of the party and nation."[41]

To be sure, Wilson's leadership task was simplified by a huge Democratic majority, consisting mostly of first-term congressmen who were especially responsive to party discipline. His handling of the Underwood Tariff Act was particularly noteworthy. At his urging, the Ways and Means Committee began working on the bill weeks before the inauguration. Within three weeks after moving into the White House, Wilson had a complete draft of the bill and announced his full support of the proposed legislation. He consulted with the Democratic caucus, and after a thorough study there, the membership took it to the floor of the House. Without even a motion to limit debate, the bill passed virtually intact by a large majority. Unlike his predecessors, Wilson then personally addressed the Senate, urging passage of the tariff bill.

Immediately after the address he appeared in the President's Room, just off the Senate chamber, to confer with the finance committee on the proposed legislation. Though the Democratic senators were far from united on the tariff question, the Senate Democratic Caucus declared the bill to be a party measure and urged all members to support it. The Underwood bill became law before the summer recess. In the words of one close observer: "President Wilson had quietly assumed leadership and secured a hold on his associates which astonished friend and enemy."[42]

In keeping with his views on party responsibility, Wilson reportedly twice considered resigning during his presidency, in the fashion of the British prime minister, if Congress rejected two major administrative measures—the repeal of the exemption of American vessels from Panama Canal tolls and the McLenmore Resolution warning American citizens against traveling on armed vessels of belligerents. But he was sustained in Congress both times.[43]

Wilson's party leadership skills, however, failed him in the closing days of World War I when he mounted his ill-fated appeal of October 1918 for the election of a Democratic Congress in the ensuing midterm election. This action was undoubtedly a consequence of his long-cherished theory of party responsibility. But it backfired. The Republicans won a sizable victory in the House, gaining 25 seats to outnumber the Democrats 237 to 190; the GOP also won the Senate by picking up 5 seats to control it by two votes.[44] Similarly, his request for a "solemn referendem" on the Covenant of the League of Nations in the presidential election of 1920 followed the same pattern. Wilson's experience as party leader underscores once again the evanescent nature of party leadership and the fragility of voting majorities. As party leaders, most presidents have enjoyed their greatest success during their first two years in office. (This subject is discussed further in Chapter 6 in connection with presidential legislative leadership.)

Twelve years later, Franklin D. Roosevelt entered the White House as the most adept politician of his time. Blessed with solid Democratic majorities in both houses of Congress, FDR mounted the famous Hundred Days legislative program in 1933, which produced more social and economic legislation than the country had ever seen. When bills dealing with the economic crisis were pending, congressmen came to the White House seeking patronage rewards—but FDR held them off with the coyly whispered information: "We haven't got to patronage yet."[45] FDR was not prepared to dispense jobs and federal contracts until the lawmakers had earned them with their pro-New Deal votes. Also, the Roosevelt party organization made clear that a congressman's sharing of patronage might depend upon his answer to the question, "What was your preconvention position on the Roosevelt candidacy?" Democratic National Chairman James A. Farley, Roosevelt's patronage manager, was also reported to have kept a private list of "eligible" job applicants, each bearing the cryptic initials FRBC (for Roosevelt before Chicago).

Roosevelt's party leadership became more systematic after the first Hundred Days, but by the time he was ready to announce his second-term reelection plans in 1936, his legislative accomplishments included the Social Security Act, the Wagner Act (authorizing collective bargaining), the Securities Exchange Act, the Federal Deposit Insurance Corporation, and a host of other New Deal measures. But as other chief executives before him have discovered, a president's party leadership influence seldom carries far into his second term.

Roosevelt's court packing plan, announced in 1937 after the Supreme Court had invalidated several of his pet New Deal measures, led to a rapid deterioration of his party influence on Capitol Hill. Many Democratic legislators, especially from the South, deserted the Roosevelt ranks. Indeed, the only major bill passed during Roosevelt's second term bearing FDR's special stamp of approval was the Fair Labor Standards Act of 1938 (which established a minimum federal wage and, in effect, abolished child labor). From that point on, Roosevelt shifted his major attention abroad to battle Nazism, Fascism, and the Japanese militarists.

Even so, FDR left a mark on the Democratic party that remained for nearly four decades. He had inherited a badly tattered minority Democratic party, consisting of big city bosses and southern and western farmers, held together by states' rights doctrine and periodic spurts of Progressivism. From this base he built an alliance of northern city machines, labor unions, blacks and other minority groups, intellectuals, and low-income farmers into a majority coalition that dominated the American scene, except for the Eisenhower interregnum, until the Vietnam war.

No president since FDR has been his equal as party leader. Lyndon Johnson for a brief shining period in 1964–65 almost matched Roosevelt in obtaining congressional support for a broad range of Great Society domestic programs and the two historic Civil Rights Acts of 1964 and 1965. But Johnson's rapid escalation of American involvement in Vietnam soon ended his string of legislative triumphs. By the 1966 midterm elections, Johnson's legislative magic had disappeared, and the Democratic party slipped forever from his grasp.

Nixon, Ford, and Carter never displayed firm mastery of party affairs, though Nixon and Ford were both veterans of Congress. Carter was the antithesis of a party leader. Upon reaching the White House, the former Georgia governor announced that he was beholden to no political or interest group, since he had won the party running as the anti-Washington candidate. And he was right. But Carter discovered over the course of his one-term presidency that his lack of strong ties with Democratic leaders on Capitol Hill undermined his ability to push through a comprehensive legislative program, especially in his favorite area of energy conservation. Carter's failure as party leader was a telltale omen that his entire presidency would also come to be viewed by many political professionals and a majority of the voting public as a failure too.

Ronald Reagan, though not generally concerned with the intricacies of day-to-day party management, has nevertheless displayed a firm grasp of party matters and legislative leadership. Although faced with a Democratically controlled House of Representatives, Reagan used his political skill and the GOP-controlled Senate to obtain passage of three high-priority agenda items—tax cuts, a reduced domestic budget, and increased military spending—during the first eight months of his administration.[46] Through support of the GOP National Committee and extensive use of sophisticated political technology—satellite broadcast hookups with congressional candidates across the land and computerized direct mail fundraising—Reagan, in the 1982 off-year election, lent a helping hand to the Republican party whenever needed. He did dozens of television and radio spots for congressional candidates, and he helped with party fundraising.

But in the aftermath of the 1984 presidential election, Republican House Minority Leader Robert Michel of Illinois complained to the press that President Reagan and his staff became so involved in winning a landslide—"running up the score" was the way one critic put it—that the president neglected to come to the aid of hard-pressed GOP candidates who might have won if Mr. Reagan had campaigned in their districts.[47] Still, a year later Reagan demonstrated his political clout by visiting Capitol Hill and persuading more than 50 additional GOP House members to switch their vote to bring a Democratic-sponsored tax reform bill (which, for tactical purposes, had Reagan's endorsement) to a final vote—and passage—shortly before the 1985 Christmas recess.[48] A few days earlier, only 14 GOP House members out of 182 Republicans in the chamber had supported a procedural vote on the tax reform bill that failed to pass the House.

CONTROL OF THE NATIONAL PARTY COMMITTEE

Presidential candidates become the titular leaders of their party as soon as they win nomination. Once elected, they assume undisputed leadership of the party for as long as they remain in the White House. This has not always been the case. In the nineteenth century, James MacGregor Burns reminds us, national conventions frequently refused to renominate incumbent presidents. Moreover, national party chairmen were independent of presidential control, and the national party apparatus was dominated by competing leaders or factions.[49] Twentieth-century presidents, however, have maintained tight control over the national party organization.

But most presidents soon become preoccupied with affairs of state and relegate management of national party affairs far down on their list of priorities. Indeed, several recent presidents—Johnson, Nixon, and Carter—permitted the national party committees, intentionally or not, to fall into a sad state of disrepair. Nixon, for example, followed the Johnson pattern to a remarkable degree—

concentrating political power in the White House staff, running campaigns totally divorced from the party, relying on personal loyalists to fill the top executive branch jobs, and virtually ignoring the national committee after his first year in the White House.

Ironically, national party committees are invariably stronger and exert more influence when the party is out of power. In the mid-1960s, for example, the Republican National Committee prospered under the leadership of Ray Bliss, the former Ohio state GOP chairman, while the Republicans were the opposition party during the Kennedy-Johnson years. Similarly, the Democratic National Committee under the stewardship of national chairman Robert A. Strauss, a Texas lawyer-radio magnate, staged a remarkable comeback from the 1972 McGovern fiasco to recapture the White House four years later. But soon after Carter moved into the White House and Robert Strauss left the national chairmanship to assume the post of U.S. trade ambassador, the Democratic National Committee began to fall into decline. And so the cycle of decline and party renewal in the Democratic party began all over again.

What is the explanation for the usual feast-and-famine cycle of national committees? If the president is the leader of his party and the national chairman is the hand-picked choice of the president, why does the national party committee lose its vigor just at the time it should be thriving on its most recent presidential victory? Several factors probably contribute to lassitude and ineffectiveness. First, the focus of partisan attention shifts from the national committee headquarters to the White House. Presidents and their staff do not look kindly toward a rival party agency setting the party agenda or grabbing national media attention. Few presidents, once they have assumed the reins of executive leadership, feel that they need the national committee or national chairman to conduct party business. Indeed, some recent presidents, such as Johnson and Nixon, have treated the committees and the chairman with outright disdain. As noted by Thomas E. Cronin: "National party chairpersons come and go with embarrassing regularity and regular embarrassment."[50] Between 1967 and 1978, for example, there were a total of eight Democratic and six Republican national chairpersons.

Few party chairpersons of the president's party have enjoyed much influence. As Robert Strauss, former Democratic national chairman, observed: "If you're Democratic party chairman when a Democrat is president, you're a goddamn clerk."[51] Another reason why the national committees of the president's party atrophy is that strong chairpersons resign to take other presidential assignments (because their main party task—getting the party nominee elected president—has been completed). Sometimes their services are terminated by a president who may doubt their loyalty to the White House. For example, GOP national chairman Ray Bliss, widely acknowledged as a brilliant organizational tactician, apparently was dumped in 1969 by President Nixon for this reason.

Lyndon Johnson treated the Democratic National Committee with equal contempt. At first, he placed Johnson loyalists (mostly Texans) in key positions on the national committee, but before long he began shifting committee operations to the White House. One White House staffer recalls: "Shortly after his 1964 election it became clear that Johnson regarded the Democratic National Commit-

tee as a debt ridden, presidentially irritating and irrelevant encumbrance."[52]
Columnist David Broder observed that Johnson often acted as if party obligations
and functions were the enemy, not the instruments, of responsible government:

> He [Johnson] did not see political parties as necessary vehicles for com-
> municating the often inchoate preferences of the voters to those in power. Nor
> did he see the parties as instruments for disciplining the whims of the elected
> leaders and holding them accountable for their actions. Instead he saw them
> as unwanted intruders on the process of consensus government.[53]

Joseph Califano, one of Johnson's close aides, also later recalled: "In my
years on Lyndon Johnson's White House staff never once did I hear him say that
he wanted to leave behind a strengthened Democratic Party."[54] In fact, Johnson
left the Democratic National Committee debt-ridden and in shambles long before
he departed the White House for retirement at his Texas ranch.

Jimmy Carter's view of the Democratic National Committee was not much
better. After his victory in 1976, Carter recommended to Democratic Party
National Chairman Robert Strauss that the size of the Democratic National
Committee staff be reduced by 70 percent. Shortly thereafter, the staff was cut
down to only 20 full-time employees.[55] Meanwhile, Carter campaign staffers held
the chief positions at the Democratic National Committee and the Carter White
House staff kept the entire national party apparatus on a short leash. In the 1980
presidential campaign Carter used virtually all the money assiduously raised by
the Democratic National Committee to underwrite his own reelection campaign,
leaving virtually nothing for financing congressional or senatorial races or as
"seed money" for future national party fundraising endeavors.

Reagan's adept handling of the Republican National Committee, however,
seems to have avoided the usual cycle. Though Mr. Reagan quietly jettisoned his
first GOP National Chairman Richard Richards after two years, reportedly for
management inefficiency, the president has used the Republican National Committee effectively in party fundraising and in strengthening the national party
organization. To oversee the Republican National Committee operations, however, Reagan installed his close personal friend, Senator Paul Laxalt of Nevada,
as "general" chairman of the GOP. In recognition of the need for a full-time
manager of the GOP National Committee, the White House appointed a close
Nevada associate of Senator Laxalt, Frank J. Fahrenkopf, as "regular" chairman.
Under this new dual arrangement, the GOP National Committee was positioned
to serve as part of the Reagan-Bush Committee in 1984. By installing his personal
friend and adviser as general chairman of the GOP, President Reagan removed
any threat of the national party committee becoming an independent power base
while he occupied the White House.

This control of the national committee was not unlike the method John F.
Kennedy used to run the Democratic National Committee in the early 1960s.
Kennedy installed his close associate and campaign adviser, John Bailey, the
Connecticut State Democratic chairman, as national chairman. Nor did he object
to Bailey retaining his Connecticut chairmanship while running the national

committee. Kennedy, however, did not use his national committee nearly as effectively as Reagan has done.

DECLINE OF PARTY INFLUENCE AT THE WHITE HOUSE

The traditional model of the presidency has generally held that the president should promote and fulfill the party platform, reward the party faithful, isolate the mavericks, carry the party banner on the campaign trail, respond to its interests, and solicit the advice of state party leaders. Above all, the president should be a party builder and expand the party ranks by communicating the party's message to the electorate. Presidents, in the words of one commentator, "should be as much the product of their parties as their leader."[56] Ideally, the relationship between the president and the party should be a two-way street, with the parties serving as a rein on the president to ensure presidential accountability; the president, in turn, would be expected to consult regularly with party leadership at the local, state, and national levels.

Presidential behavior today seldom matches this textbook model. One of the major paradoxes of the presidency is that a president is expected by many Americans to be a neutral public leader, the symbolic head of the country, and avoid political and party considerations. At the same time he is supposed to lead his party, help other party members get reelected, and build political coalitions to win passage of his legislative programs. However, with the multiplication of presidential responsibilities in recent decades—chief spokesman of the free world, national security manager, overseer of the economy—the president's schedule is usually devoured by pressing matters that will not go away. As a symbolic figure representing the entire nation, the president is expected to share the nation's concern over flood disasters, hurricane damage, and drought in the agricultural regions by visiting these areas. Foreign leaders arrive in the nation's capital on the average of one a week. These heads of state must be given the red carpet treatment, with formal dinners, guided tours, and high-level meetings.

Under these circumstances the party's business can wait—or, more likely, be put on the back burner until more time becomes available, which seldom happens. Nor do sitting presidents feel that they really need their party any longer. Since they have used their own independently organized campaign team, conducted most of their campaigns via television, and financed their general election race from the $40 million lump sum grant from the Federal Election Commission to reach the White House, most presidents do not feel that a political party has been a major factor in their successful election campaign. President Kennedy, according to one source, was "personally wary of working through party professionals, many of whom he viewed as collections of 'tired or tarnished holdovers from another era,'" and believed that "the Democratic party was something to win through, not govern through."[57]

Unlike presidents of yesteryear, the modern president has the advantage of instant communication with the American citizenry via nationwide television. Network cameras enable the president to bypass the party structure and Congress whenever he wishes to seek support for his policies from the American public.

Thus, one of the main functions of the party—serving as a source of information and communication between the citizens and their government—has been displaced by the electronic media.

The rise of special interest groups who build direct ties with the White House has further eroded party influence within the White House. These groups —labor unions, business groups, teachers, veterans—once worked through party groups. Now they are organized on a national scale, generally with headquarters and a staff of lobbyists in the nation's capital. High-level White House staffers work directly with these interest groups' leaders, listening to their problems, seeking solutions, perhaps arranging a special meeting with the president. According to Thomas E. Cronin, White House aides maintained contact in 1979 with an estimated 800 groups and organizations.[58] By working directly with these groups, the president and his staff have, deliberately or not, further short-circuited the party out of the decision-making process.

Although a partisan leader, the president is also expected to serve as the nonpartisan chief of state—the representative for all the American people. In a sense, the American president is asked to fill two essentially incompatible roles. He must serve as a chief spokesman for the "government party" as opposed to the loyal opposition party, similar to the way the British prime minister does. But at the same time he is also expected to perform as the ceremonial symbol of national unity and public authority, standing above the party, in the tradition of the British monarch. How the American chief executive serves as "President of all the people" and yet responds to the interests and demands of his own party remains a crowning paradox. But there is no indication that presidents object to this inconsistent, dual role; indeed, they frequently relish the practice of cloaking blatantly political goals in the magisterial robes of a chief of state.

RENOMINATION

The next election is never far from the minds of most first-term presidents and their inner circle. Consequently, nearly all their major decisions will be made with one eye on the election calendar. In the nineteenth century, sitting presidents, reflecting their limited role as party leader, were often rejected for renomination. Between 1840 and 1860, for example, no incumbent president was renominated. After the Civil War, GOP conventions failed to renominate Presidents Hayes and Arthur. During this period national party chairmen were usually independent of presidential control, and the national party organization, if it could be dignified with that title, was dominated by competing factional leaders. Since 1896, the most important change affecting the nominating process within the incumbent party, according to David, Goldman, and Bain, "has been the rising position of the Presidency and the increased recognition accorded the President as party leader."[59]

Since the turn of the century, most presidents could have renomination from their party merely for the asking. To be sure, William Howard Taft faced a tough fight in 1912 to win renomination before he beat down the challenge by former president Theodore Roosevelt. But he failed to win reelection in the three-way race among Wilson, Roosevelt (running as a third-party candidate), and himself. Even Hoover, running for reelection in 1932, with the country in the midst of the Great Depression, experienced no trouble in winning renomination. With the exception of the discredited Nixon, Hoover was probably the most unpopular president of the twentieth century; yet his party stood by him when he sought a second term. Presidential incumbents have usually had a special advantage over their intraparty challenges: Refusal to renominate a sitting president is tacit admission of the party's previous failure to choose a qualified leader; thus, the president's party can repudiate him only at the gravest risk of losing the ensuing general election.

In recent years no president has been unceremoniously dumped from the ticket when he sought renomination, but several have been seriously challenged by intraparty contenders. Harry Truman decided to bow out of his renomination drive in late March 1952 after suffering an upset loss to Senator Estes Kefauver in the New Hampshire primary. Sixteen years later, Lyndon Johnson was, in effect, driven from seeking reelection to a second full term in 1968 by militant antiwar activists and bitter primary challenges from Senators Eugene J. McCarthy and Robert F. Kennedy. In 1976 Gerald Ford, who had moved to the White House after Nixon's resignation, emerged as the GOP nominee by an eyelash, after a bitter, no-holds-barred challenge from former California governor Ronald Reagan. But the fratricidal conflict within the GOP helped contribute to Ford's loss at the hands of former Democratic Georgia governor Jimmy Carter in the general election.

Four years later, Jimmy Carter in turn had to fight back a furious intraparty challenge from Senator Edward M. Kennedy, the last surviving brother of the slain president. To achieve this goal, President Carter, in the words of one commentator, "exceeded all Presidents in his single-minded utilization of the resources of the Presidency to secure renomination."[60] Federal grants for transportation, water treatment plants, and pork barrel items were used to reinforce Carter's standing in key primary states. Florida, in the words of one reporter, "was drenched with federal money." Governors and big city mayors were invited to dinner at the White House, and their endorsement of the president was a high-priority item at the dinner. Cabinet members and White House staffers were sent out on the hustings while the president pursued his Rose Garden strategy of staying at the White House to monitor the Iranian hostage crisis. Though Carter successfully won the Democratic renomination in 1980, the bitter nominating fight helped sow the seeds of defeat for him in November.

With the decline in party loyalty, it would appear that we have reached a point where incumbent presidents can no longer be guaranteed renomination. Certainly, the resurgence of the presidential primary after World War II has provided ambitious incumbent party challengers with a potent weapon to attack a sitting president. With voters in 30-plus state primaries electing nearly three-quarters of all national convention delegates, an incumbent party challenger can have a field day attacking the president's first-term record. The primary campaign becomes, in effect, a referendum on the president's first-term performance. Aided by nationwide television and the 1974 Federal Election Campaign Act, which can provide a challenger with upward of $10 million in federal matching subsidies, rivals can mount an all-out attack upon the president.

Faced with this kind of opposition, few presidents can dismiss these challenges without launching an early renomination drive. This means establishing a full-scale campaign organization for the renomination race with all of the vital specialists—fundraisers, pollsters, media experts, schedulers, and accountants— that have become an integral part of preconvention campaigns. All this activity must be started well ahead of the primary season, usually at least a year before the national convention. Thus, if a president wishes renomination, he must plan to ignore the affairs of state frequently throughout this period. During a recent roundtable forum on the presidential nominating process, former President Gerald Ford estimated that he had to spend 20 percent of his time in 1976 seeking the GOP nomination.[61]

Unless the existing presidential nominating system is overhauled and shortened, future presidents can be expected to echo this complaint. Lyndon B. Johnson, in the early months of 1968 before he renounced seeking another term, bitterly observed: "The old belief that a President can carry out the responsibilities of his office and at the same time undergo the rigors of campaigning is, in my opinion, no longer valid."[62] Ronald Reagan's successful renomination drive in 1984, however, is a refutation of the Johnson thesis. But it seems fair to predict that other future sitting presidents, less fortunate than Mr. Reagan in managing the ship of state during their first term, can anticipate facing serious intraparty competition for renomination.

PATRONAGE

Since the founding of the Republic, rewards for dedicated service to the president have taken the form of jobs—cabinet posts, judgeships, regional directors of governmental agencies, ambassadorships. Thomas Jefferson and Andrew Jackson, as indicated earlier, always rewarded their key supporters with federal jobs. "To the victor belong the spoils" was long the rallying cry within the party occupying the White House. No president in the nineteenth century spent more time reviewing patronage requests and calculating how to distribute the "loaves and fishes" than Abraham Lincoln. A review of Lincoln's correspondence and official actions shows that the Civil War president spent a sizable share of each working day on patronage matters. Even the relentless demands of the war effort did not prevent him from dealing with political appointments.[63]

Early twentieth-century presidents were also not unmindful of the importance of patronage as political currency. The national party organizations were actively involved in the presidential appointment process. With strong party chairmen like Mark Hanna and James Farley, the president's party served as "the unofficial employment agency for filling certain jobs in the executive branch. . . ."[64] Farley, for example, despite the civil service protection afforded most federal workers in the 1930s, was able to distribute an estimated 75,000 political jobs during President Roosevelt's first two terms.[65]

By World War II, the steady "blanketing in" of most of the 3 million federal employees had left only a few thousand higher-level policymaking positions outside the classified civil service. Consequently, modern presidents no longer have the degree of political leverage their predecessors had in using patronage to reward party loyalists. Not all presidents have regretted the disappearance of the spoils system, for as President William Howard Taft observed many years ago, each time he made an appointment, he created "nine enemies and one ingrate."

Unlike earlier presidents, recent incumbents have selected most of their cabinet members and national security advisers not on the basis of their political affiliation, but on their professional competence and experience. President Kennedy, for example, relied on talent scouts to fill his top administrative posts, picking his New Frontiersmen from universities, the Eastern establishment, and the professions (see Table 10.3). Nor did he hesitate to appoint Republicans to high positions in the Defense Department. Nixon usually bypassed the GOP National Committee, selecting loyalists from law and public relations firms and from the ranks of management consultants. By the late 1960s, a nearly complete transfer of high-level appointment recommendations from the party national committee to the White House staff had occurred.[66]

While the number of political jobs has rapidly declined, the modern president nevertheless has another form of patronage—federal military or public works projects—that the White House can sometimes use to obtain its political goals. The placement of a new military base, a new veterans' hospital, a federal research facility, or a federal reclamation or flood control project in a favored senator or representative's state or congressional district can cement relationships and foster long-term loyalty to the president. And the financial windfall from these federal contracts on the economy of these areas will continue long after the president has left office.

Table 10.3 **DISTRIBUTION OF PARTY AFFILIATION AMONG MAJOR PRESIDENTIAL APPOINTEES, 1961–1984***

Administration	Number of appointees	Percent from president's party	Percent party affiliated	Percent unaffiliated
Kennedy	430	63%	73%	27%
Johnson	524	47	58	42
Nixon	737	65	73	27
Ford	293	56	64	36
Carter (1977–78)†	402	58	65	35
Reagan (1981–84)	524	82	85	15

*Major appointments as listed by the *Congressional Quarterly Almanac* include cabinet, subcabinet, and lower policy-level positions in the executive branch, including ambassadorships and positions on various boards and commissions. In the case of some positions, particularly those on independent regulatory commissions, the ratio of party affiliation among appointees is legislatively prescribed. Therefore, those cases were not included in the annual totals. The *CQ Almanac* indicates the party affiliation for every appointee for whom that information is available. When not listed or listed as "independent," the appointee's affiliation was included here as "unaffiliated."

†*CQ Almanac* lists of major presidential appointees confirmed during the years 1979 and 1980 contained a high proportion of names for whom no information on party affiliation was made available by the Carter administration. In 1979, out of a total of 256 appointees listed, only 48 were assigned a party affiliation. For 1980, only 22 of 148 listing included this information.

Sources: Compiled from the annual listings of confirmed presidential appointees in the *Congressional Quarterly Almanac* (Washington, DC: Congressional Quarterly, Inc., 1961–1985), vols. 17–39, by Roger G. Brown, "Party and Bureaucracy: From Kennedy to Reagan." Reprinted by permission from *Political Science Quarterly,* 97 (Summer 1982), 283. Data for 1981–84 have been supplied by Professor Brown. Letter to author, dated July 11, 1986.

FUNDRAISING ACTIVITY

Presidential fundraising appearances for senatorial and house candidates and state party organizations are another form of patronage dispensed by party-oriented presidents. As the highest-ranking party chieftain in the nation, the president of the United States is a stellar attraction at any national or state fundraising event. Indeed, a presidential appearance at a party function will almost automatically raise several hundred thousand dollars, and often the net proceeds will top a million. John F. Kennedy, for example, grossed over $1.3 million for Pennsylvania Democrats during the 1962 off-year election campaign at an outdoor fundraiser, attended by more than 13,000 contributors, near Harrisburg.[67]

More recently, Reagan has proved to be the biggest draw ever for the Republican party. In 1985, his appearance at a GOP fundraising dinner in the nation's capital helped the Republicans raise nearly $6 million—a new record.[68] In late May and early June 1985, President Reagan appeared at special fundraisers in Florida, Georgia, Alabama, and Oklahoma to aid four freshmen Republican senators facing reelection in 1986. His special foray into these four states netted the senators almost $2.5 million for their reelection drives. With 22 Republican senators and only 11 Democratic seats up for reelection in 1986, President Reagan was putting in a little extra political overtime to try and help preserve the 53 to 47 margin enjoyed by the GOP in the Senate.

With the House of Representatives heavily controlled by the Democrats, and with little real hope that the GOP could overturn this control in 1986, Reagan was especially anxious to maintain GOP control of the Senate in order to have a special bargaining chip in all legislative negotiations with Democratic House leaders. President Reagan's stopovers in these four southern states were also synchronized to help highlight a 100-day blitz—Operation Open Door—to persuade conservative Democrats to switch parties in these states before 1986.[69]

During August 1985, while he was recuperating from cancer surgery at his California ranch near Santa Barbara, President Reagan dropped in on a California GOP fundraising dinner in Los Angeles. This presidential appearance helped California Republicans collect more than $1 million from 1,000 dinner guests who paid $1,000 each to hear President Reagan.[70] Though there is no easy way to measure the impact presidential fundraising appearances have upon grateful senatorial and house candidates and state parties who are the beneficiaries, opposition party leaders can only look on with envy and pray for the day that an incumbent president of their party can make similar fundraising appearances on the campaign trail.

THE PRESIDENT'S NEED FOR PARTY SUPPORT

If a president has no control over the nomination of members of Congress over the 50 state parties, and if he lacks most of the nineteenth-century type of patronage, one might rightly ask, how can the president be the genuine leader of his party?

Though a number of factors—network television, independent campaign organizations, and government funding of presidential candidates—have all conspired to undermine the influence of political parties on American chief executives, party support still remains an essential ingredient in electoral success.

Presidents still must look to their partisans in Congress to carry the ball for the White House. Data collected for the period 1953–1978 show that each party's members in each chamber of Congress have supported the presidents of their own party approximately two-thirds of the time and the presidents of the opposing party less than half the time (see Table 10.4). These data alone, however, are not proof that members of Congress follow their president's lead most of the time, since the votes might indicate that the lawmakers are voting their own convictions, which frequently happen to coincide with the views of their parties' presidents. To overcome this methodological problem, several students of congressional voting behavior have sought to determine whether representatives' policy stands change perceptively when a president of the opposition party is replaced by one of their own party.

The evidence shows some degree of change. Data collected revealed that about one-fifth of the Republicans in both chambers who had been voting consistently against foreign aid bills proposed by Democratic presidents switched to support similar bills when they were proposed by Republican presidents. Approximately the same proportion of the Democrats in both chambers shifted their votes in the opposite direction. Another study showed that GOP lawmakers support activist federal domestic programs more often when they are proposed by Republican presidents than when they are proposed by Democratic chief executives, while Democratic lawmakers' support for such programs remained relatively the same, no matter whether a Democrat or Republican was in the White House.[71]

Additionally, the symbolic support the president draws from his party enables him to go forth to the country with his plans and programs, knowing that a formidable army of the party faithful are prepared to reaffirm and back up his demands for action at the next election. No president, it seems clear, can expect to achieve his goals or withstand the assaults from the opposition without broad

Table 10.4 AVERAGE PRESIDENTIAL SUPPORT SCORES BY PARTY, 1953–1978

Chamber	Democrats	Republicans
Percentage of roll-call votes supporting the president's position		
With Democratic presidents in office		
House	69%	40%
Senate	62	45
With Republican presidents in office		
House	46	64
Senate	44	66

Source: From *Presidential Influence in Congress* by George C. Edwards III. W. H. Freeman and Company. Copyright © 1980, 61–62.

party backing. As Gary Orren has commented: "A President who must depend overwhelmingly on his personal image to sustain himself, who cannot count on the obligations of party elites to support him, is an isolated and vulnerable leader."[72]

Reagan's 1984 personal campaign organization and the Republican party were, in the words of one commentator, "models of teamwork and cooperation."[73] Columnist David S. Broder reports that during 1983–1984 President Reagan made more than two dozen campaign and fundraising appearances for the party and its candidates, despite his own reelection campaign.[74] In one week during late October 1985, Reagan traveled 4,500 miles to Boise, Idaho, and Milwaukee, Wisconsin, to raise campaign funds for two GOP senators facing reelection in 1986; he also attended a fundraising dinner for the Republican Governors' Association to kick off a drive to improve GOP strength in the state capitals. And he held a special meeting with a former governor of Vermont to persuade him to run in 1986 for a U.S. Senate seat held by a Democrat.[75]

Unlike his recent predecessors who, in Broder's words, "used their parties when it suited their needs and stiff-armed them when they felt like it," President Reagan has toiled long and faithfully in the party vineyards.[76] If Reagan fails to achieve most of his program objectives during his eight years in the White House, it will not be because he shirked his party leadership responsibilities.

CONCLUSION

In reviewing the history of the American presidency, the record shows that the management of Uncle Sam's business "is considerably enhanced when the president commits time and resources to working closely with his party's establishment."[77]

Once in office, the president is the titular leader of his party. But this title is often misleading. Although the president controls the national party machinery and picks the national party chairperson, most presidents are distrustful of the national committee and prefer to direct party affairs from the White House. The president does not control his congressional party. Under the separation of powers, the leaders on Capitol Hill can establish their own agendas and their own financial and policy committees, that, in effect, duplicate those of the national committee.

Under our decentralized party system, the president has no control over state parties, each of which remains independent of the national party committee. Members of the Senate and House are nominated by the voters in direct primaries in virtually all states. In recent decades, the "blanketing in" of all but a few thousand federal jobs under the civil service has reduced the president's political patronage to a small trickle. To fill this void and to counter congressional independence of executive leadership, presidents have turned increasingly to national interest groups to pressure both parties in Congress to support legislative programs.

Nor have presidents in recent years had any special inducements to be good party team players. Presidents are no longer dependent upon state party leaders to win the nomination and the White House. Thanks to the rapid spread of presidential primaries, federal matching funds, and the formation of their own independent campaign organizations, candidates have been able to win the nomination without help from party chieftains. Federal funds ($40.4 million in 1984) can now be used to underwrite the general election campaign. Presidential candidates no longer need to rely upon the party to communicate the campaign message to the voters; the candidates now do it themselves via network television and 30-second spot TV ads. Still, President Reagan has demonstrated during his first term that if the president chooses to work closely with his party, this partnership can be mutually beneficial to both party and White House occupant. The truth of the matter is that both the president and his party need each other. The president needs the party's support in order to enact a legislative program; the party needs the president's leadership and the prestige of his office to achieve its goals.

NOTES

1. Woodrow Wilson, "The President's Role in American Government," in *The Power of the Presidency,* ed. Robert S. Hirschfield (Chicago: Atherton Press, 1968), 92.
2. Wilfred E. Binkley, *The Man in the White House,* rev. ed. (New York: Harper & Row, 1958), 95.
3. James Sterling Young, "The Presidency and the Hill," in Aaron Wildavsky, ed., *The Presidency* (Boston: Little, Brown, 1969), 430.
4. Ibid.
5. Richard Harmond, "The Presidency in the Gilded Age," in Philip C. Dolce and George H. Skau, eds., *Power and the Presidency* (New York: Scribner's, 1976), 58.
6. Henry Jones Ford, *Rise and Growth of American Politics* (New York: Macmillan, 1898), as quoted in Wildavsky, *The Presidency,* 433.
7. Arthur N. Holcombe, "Presidential Leadership and the Party System," *Yale Review,* 43 (1954), 321–335, as cited by John A. Crittenden, *Parties and Elections in the United States* (Englewood Cliffs, NJ: Prentice-Hall, 1982), 284.
8. James MacGregor Burns, *The Deadlock of Democracy* (Englewood Cliffs, NJ: Prentice-Hall, 1963).
9. Young, "The Presidency and the Hill," 411.
10. Louis W. Koenig, *The Chief Executive,* 4th ed. (New York: Harcourt Brace Jovanovich, 1981), 149.
11. Austin Ranney, "The President and His Party," in Anthony King, ed., *Both Ends of the Avenue* (Washington, DC: American Enterprise Institute, 1983), 146.
12. Frank J. Sorauf, *Party Politics in America,* 5th ed. (Boston: Little, Brown, 1984), 377.
13. Randall B. Ripley, in a study of Republican roll-call votes on nine bills vetoed by a GOP president in 1973 and 1976, found that GOP representatives and senators voted to sustain Presidents Nixon's and Ford's vetoes approximately 74 percent of the time. Randall B. Ripley, *Congress: Process and Policy,* 3rd ed. (New York: Norton, 1983), 210.
14. *The New York Times,* March 5, 1986.
15. Ranney, "The President and His Party," 140.
16. Thomas E. Mann, "Elections and Change in Congress," in Thomas E. Mann and Norman J. Ornstein, eds., *The New Congress* (Washington, DC: American Enterprise Institute, 1981), 34–35.

17. Charles O. Jones, "The Voters Say Yes," in Ellis Sandoz and Cecil V. Crabb, Jr., eds. *Election 84* (New York: New American Library, 1985), 95.

18. Morris P. Fiorina, *Congress: Keystone of the Washington Establishment* (New Haven, CT: Yale University Press, 1977), 37.

19. Walter Dean Burnham, *Critical Elections* (New York: Norton, 1970), 109. For data on ticket-splitting between 1920 and 1976, see *Congressional Weekly Report,* April 22, 1978, 972.

20. Anthony King, "A Mile and Half in a Long Way," in King, *Both Ends of the Avenue,* 249. For additional data on presidential coattails, see George Edwards III, *The Public Presidency* (New York: St. Martin's Press, 1983), 83–93.

21. Richard M. Pious, *The American Presidency* (New York: Basic Books, 1979), 134.

22. Charles E. Jacob, "The Congressional Elections," in Gerald Pomper, ed., *The Elections of 1984* (Chatham, NJ: Chatham House Publishers, 1985), 116–118.

23. Paul Pendergast, executive director of the Democratic Congressional Campaign Committee, as quoted in *Congressional Quarterly Weekly Report,* 35 (March 19, 1977), 489.

24. Ranney, "The President and His Party," 142–143.

25. Thomas E. Cronin, "Presidents and Political Parties," in Thomas E. Cronin, *Rethinking the Presidency* (Boston: Little, Brown, 1982), 291.

26. Samuel Kernell, "The Presidency and the People: The Modern Paradox," in Michael Nelson, ed., *The Presidency and the Political System* (Washington, DC: Congressional Quarterly Press, 1984), 243.

27. Martha Joynt Kumar and Michael Baruch Grossman, "The Presidency and Interest Groups," in Nelson, *The Presidency and the Political System,* 284.

28. Ibid.

29. Ranney, "The President and His Party," 150.

30. Pious, *The American Presidency,* 145.

31. Koenig, *The Chief Executive,* 135.

32. Binkley, *The Man in the White House,* 96–97.

33. Ibid., 97.

34. Robert V. Remini, "The Emergence of Political Parties and Their Effect on the Presidency," in Philip C. Dolce and George H. Skau, eds., *Power and the Presidency,* 32.

35. Binkley, *The Man in the White House,* 98.

36. Ibid., 100.

37. Ibid., 102.

38. Charles A. Dana, *Recollections of the Civil War* (New York: 1898), 174, as quoted by Wilfred E. Binkley, "The President as Chief Legislator," *Annals of the American Academy of Political and Social Science,* 307 (September 1956), 92–105.

39. Woodrow Wilson, *Constitutional Government in the United States* (1907), 54.

40. Ibid., 60–61.

41. Ibid., 67.

42. Quoted in H. J. Ford, *Woodrow Wilson: The Man and His Work,* as cited by Binkley, *The Man in the White House,* 108.

43. Binkley, *The Man in the White House,* 108.

44. Thomas A. Bailey, *Woodrow Wilson and the Lost Peace* (Chicago: Quadrangle Books, 1963), 61. This book was first published in 1944.

45. Binkley, *The Man in the White House,* 109.

46. See Barbara Kellerman, *The Political Presidency* (New York: Oxford University Press, 1984), chap. 11.

47. *The New York Times,* November 12, 1984.

48. Ibid., December 18, 1985.
49. James MacGregor Burns, *Presidential Government: The Crucible of Leadership* (Boston: Houghton Mifflin, 1965), 315.
50. Thomas E. Cronin, "The Presidency and the Parties," in Gerald M. Pomper, ed., *Party Renewal in America* (New York: Praeger, 1981), 176.
51. Joseph Califano, *A Presidential Nation* (New York: Norton, 1976), 153.
52. Ibid., 151.
53. David Broder, *The Party's Over* (New York: Harper & Row, 1977), 76–77.
54. Califano, *A Presidential Nation,* 159.
55. Pious, *The American Presidency,* 126.
56. Cronin, "The Presidency and the Parties," 178.
57. James MacGregor Burns, *The Deadlock of Democracy: Four-Party Politics in America,* 308–309.
58. Cronin, "The Presidency and the Parties," 182.
59. Paul T. David, Ralph M. Goldman, and Richard C. Bain, *The Politics of National Party Conventions* (Washington, DC: The Brookings Institution, 1960), 72.
60. Koenig, *The Chief Executive,* 130.
61. Jack L. Walker, "Reforming the Reforms," *Wilson Quarterly,* 5 (Autumn 1981), 98.
62. As quoted by Cyrus R. Vance, "Reforming the Electoral Reforms," *The New York Times Magazine,* February 21, 1981, 16.
63. Binkley, *The Man in the White House,* 101–102.
64. Cornelius P. Cotter and Bernard C. Hennessey, *Politics Without Power: The National Party Committee* (New York: Atherton Press, 1964), 138.
65. Ibid., 139.
66. Roger G. Brown, "Party and Bureaucracy: From Kennedy to Reagan," *Political Science Quarterly,* 97 (Summer 1982), 282.
67. *The New York Times,* September 21, 1962.
68. Source: Republican Senate Campaign Committee. In May 1986, President Reagan's appearance at the second Republican House and Senate Campaign Committees' jointly sponsored "President's Dinner" netted the GOP $6.5 million. *Ibid.*
69. See *The New York Times,* August 23, 1985.
70. Ibid., August 25, 1985.
71. Ranney, "The President and His Party," 144–145.
72. Gary Orren, "The Changing Styles of American Party Politics," in Joel L. Fleishman, ed., *The Future of American Parties: The Challenge of Governance* (Englewood Cliffs, NJ: Prentice-Hall, 1982), 41.
73. Walter Dean Burnham, "The Future of American Politics," in Ellis Sandoz and Cecil V. Crabb, Jr., eds., *Election 84,* 231.
74. David S. Broder, "Reagan: Life of the Party," *The Washington Post National Weekly Edition,* November 4, 1985, 4.
75. Ibid.
76. Ibid.
77. Roger G. Brown, "The Presidency and the Political Parties," in Michael Nelson, ed., *The Presidency and the Political System* (Washington, DC: Congressional Quarterly Press, 1984), 332.

The President and the Supreme Court

The Founding Fathers, as they groped toward constructing a constitutional framework that could protect the executive and judicial branches from a domineering Congress, were undecided about how much power should be given to the judiciary. For a time they considered joining the president and Supreme Court in a Council of Revision, with veto authority over legislation passed by Congress as well as state legislatures. Part of the Virginia Plan offered at Philadelphia, this idea was eventually rejected after being put to a vote three times, for fear it might lead the Supreme Court to follow too closely the views of the president.

In the end the Founders left open the basic question that from time to time has been a major source of potential conflict between the executive and the Supreme Court: Who has the final authority to interpret the Constitution? Chief Justice John Marshall may have thought he answered this question once and for all in favor of the Supreme Court in his famous *Marbury* v. *Madison* (1803) decision, which established the doctrine of judicial review. But as the dean of American scholars on the presidency, the late E. S. Corwin, reminded his readers: "Jefferson, invoking the principle of the Separation of Powers, denied that the President and Congress were bound by the view that the Supreme Court adopted by the Constitution any more than the Court was bound by their views."[1] Andrew Jackson held the same view.

Furthermore, Corwin writes: "Lincoln argued that to identify the Court's version of the Constitution, formulated perhaps for the purpose of deciding a single private lawsuit, with the Constitution itself was incompatible with the idea of popular government."[2] In retrospect, the tug-of-war between the president and the Supreme Court that sometimes emerges over the issue of final authority on interpreting the Constitution was probably what the Framers intended, since they viewed occasional conflict as an essential means of keeping the branches in their proper places.[3] Nevertheless, more often than not, the relations between the executive and judicial branches have been, in Robert Scigliano's words, "marked by broad and sympathetic cooperation."[4]

In this chapter our attention will be focused, first of all, on how the doctrine of judicial review has affected relationships between president and Supreme Court over the past two centuries. Throughout most of our history, the Supreme Court has done far more to expand than to restrain presidential power. Our discussion will indicate that the Court, when faced with a tough call on a borderline case, may call the issue a "political question"—a dispute beyond its competence. The Court's generally sympathetic views (since 1937) on congressional delegation of legislative power to the president in domestic and foreign affairs is examined in detail. We explore as well the Court's support of the president's powers as commander in chief, along with the justices' tendency to sidestep critical issues until after the crisis subsides.

But the Supreme Court, it will be pointed out, has not hesitated to blow the whistle on the president, if the justices believe he has exceeded his authority, as President Truman discovered when he took over the steel mills during the Korean war. And the Court has made it abundantly clear that no president is above the law, as Richard Nixon learned when he sought to withhold certain White House tapes needed in a criminal trial arising from the Watergate investigations. The nominees presidents select for the Supreme Court and whether they measure up to presidential expectations is also examined. Overall, we will show that the Supreme Court leans over backward to protect presidential prerogatives.

OVERVIEW: RELATIONS BETWEEN PRESIDENT AND SUPREME COURT

Taking American history as a whole, the Supreme Court has not been unduly harsh on the office of president. The record shows that during the period 1789–1977, the Supreme Court has decided against the president in only 61 cases in the domestic category and in only 8 foreign policy cases.[5] Especially noteworthy is the fact that during the last hundred years the Supreme Court has decided against the president in only two foreign policy cases. According to Michael A. Genovese, the Supreme Court has ruled against the president in 51 cases during normal times and against presidents 18 times during emergency periods (a total of 75 years out of the 188 years in Genovese's study).[6] Most of the emergency cases occurred during the Civil War and Great Depression years. As Table 11.1 shows, the Supreme Court decided against President Nixon in 25 cases (36 percent of all cases); Franklin D. Roosevelt is second with 8 cases, and Lincoln is third with 5.

Significantly, the president and the Supreme Court have been embroiled in only two grand confrontations in the twentieth century: the anti-New Deal decisions of the Hughes Court in the mid-thirties and the anti-Nixon rulings during the Watergate investigation of 1973–1974 by the Burger Court. Otherwise, the

**Table 11.1   SUPREME COURT RULINGS AGAINST
PRESIDENTS, 1789–1984**

President	Number of decisions
Jefferson	2
Madison	3
Monroe	1
Tyler	1
Fillmore	1
Lincoln	5
A. Johnson	2
Hayes	1
Garfield	0
Arthur	2
Cleveland	1
Wilson	2
Harding	2
Coolidge	3
Hoover	1
F. D. Roosevelt	8
Truman	3
Eisenhower	3
L. Johnson	2
Nixon	25
Ford	3
Carter	2
Reagan	0
	Total 73

Sources: Michael A. Genovese, *The Supreme Court, the Constitution, and Presidential Power* (Lanham, MD: University Press of America, 1980), 264. Data for Presidents Lyndon Johnson, Carter, and Reagan have been supplied by Professor Robert L. Dudley, Colorado State University. According to Dudley's data, the Supreme Court upheld President Reagan's position in all seven cases reaching the High Court during his first term. Though the final figures have not yet been compiled for the first two years of President Reagan's second term, the Supreme Court rebuffed the Reagan administration at least six times during the 1985–1986 court term. The cases involved affirmative action, abortion, voting rights, Social Security, disability benefits, and the treatment of handicapped infants. *The New York Times,* July 3, 1986.

president and the Supreme Court have generally seen eye to eye on the major social and economic policies of their era.

COURT SUPPORT OF PRESIDENTIAL ACTIONS

Since the founding of the Republic, the Supreme Court has done far more to expand than to restrain presidential power. In a number of instances, the Founding Fathers' lack of clarity in defining presidential authority has enabled the Supreme Court to interpret presidential power broadly. Respect for the president and a desire to avoid embarrassing clashes with executive authority have, for most of U.S. history, characterized the Supreme Court's behavior toward the nation's leader. Indeed, the Court has invalidated less than a dozen major presidential decisions in almost two centuries. As Edward S. Corwin observed some years ago: "While the Court has sometimes rebuffed presidential pretentions, it has more often labored to rationalize them; but most of all it has sought on one pretext or other to keep its sickle out of this 'dread field.' " Corwin also pointed out the tactical circumstances have been such that it has been more difficult for the Court to challenge the president than the Congress because "the Court can usually assert itself successfully against Congress by merely 'disallowing' its acts, [whereas] presidential exercises of power will generally have produced some change in the external world beyond ordinary judicial competence to effect."[7]

Chief Justice John Marshall was one of the first to recognize the judicial untouchability of the president operating in the sweeping field of executive action. Speaking of the president's "important political powers," Marshall said the principle is that "in their exercise he is to use his own discretion, and is accountable only to his country in his political character and to his own conscience."[8] The Supreme Court has deferred to presidential actions in several broad areas. Jefferson's Louisiana Purchase, a bold action of the type not mentioned in the Constitution, could have provided the Supreme Court with an opportunity to constrain presidential authority. Opposition Federalists viewed Jefferson's purchase of the vast Louisiana territory as an unconstitutional act. What happened? Nothing. The Court remained silent and, in effect, acquiesced to Jefferson's executive action. More than a half century later, the Court upheld Lincoln's imposition of a blockade of Confederate ports without congressional authorization during the Civil War.[9]

Less than four years later, the Supreme Court reaffirmed its recognition of the president's broad executive powers in two post-Civil War cases. In *Mississippi* v. *Johnson* (1867), the state of Mississippi sought to restrain President Andrew Johnson from enforcing certain Reconstruction acts on the grounds of their alleged unconstitutionality. Mississippi's lawyers sought to minimize the seriousness of the state's request to the Court by contending that President Johnson, in enforcing these laws, was performing a "mere ministerial duty" requiring no exercise of discretion. The Court rejected this line of argument and asserted that the president's duty to see that the laws were faithfully executed was "purely executive and political." In the words of the Court:

> An attempt on the part of the judicial department of the government to enforce the performance of such duties by the President might be justly characterized, in the language of Chief Justice Marshall, as "an absurd and excessive extravagance." It is true that in the instance before us the interposition of the court is not sought to enforce action by the Executive under constitutional legislation, but to restrain such action under legislation alleged to be unconstitutional. But we are unable to perceive that this circumstance takes the case out of the general principles which forbid judicial interference with the exercise of Executive discretion.[10]

A similar attempt by Georgia to enjoin the secretary of war and the generals commanding the Georgia military district from enforcing the Reconstruction acts was also thwarted by the Court, which ruled that the military officials represented the executive authority of the government.[11]

In several later cases the Court attributed powers to the president that were not specifically granted by statute or expressly stated in the Constitution. In the case of *In Re Neagle* (1890), the Court ruled the president had inherent power to defend the "peace of the United States." Neagle, a U.S. marshal, was assigned by the attorney general's office to protect a Supreme Court justice whose life had been threatened by a litigant. When the marshal killed the litigant after he attempted to attack the jurist, the marshal was arrested by state authorities. U.S. attorneys obtained a writ of habeas corpus ordering Neagle transferred from state to federal custody. Though this action was challenged by the state of California, the Supreme Court upheld the writ, stating that the president's duty was not limited "to the enforcement of the acts of Congress or of treaties of the United States according to their express terms," but also included "rights, duties, and obligations growing out of the Constitution itself, our international relations, and all the protection implied by the nature of the government under the Constitution."[12] In assessing this unique case, one constitutional authority has commented: "The compelling aspect of this case was the 'thesis' advanced by Justice Miller that there is a 'peace of the United States' and that it is the President who is to serve as the keeper of that peace. The Neagle case can serve as justification for almost any presidential act to halt domestic disorder."[13]

Five years later, the Supreme Court upheld the power of President Cleveland, acting through a U.S. attorney in Illinois, to obtain an injunction from a U.S. circuit court to keep the trains operating during the Pullman strike and to enjoin the strike led by Eugene Debs because the labor dispute threatened interference with interstate commerce and the transportation of the mail. In the case of *In Re Debs,* the Court sustained President Cleveland's action on the ground that although no statutory authorization for the injunction existed, the railroad strike affected the public at large, and the president, acting through the U.S. attorney, had inherent authority to seek a judicial remedy to correct the wrongdoing.[14] The late Clinton Rossiter, recognizing the far-ranging implications of these two decisions, wrote:

> In light of the Debs and Neagle cases, it might be easily argued that there are no judicial limits to the President's real or alleged "inherent power to protect the peace of the United States."[15]

More recently, the Court upheld President Truman's seizure of the coal mines to prevent a nationwide strike on the basis of the president's power to seize property in wartime (the Korean war).[16] In 1978, the Court approved President Carter's decision to terminate a United States defense treaty with Taiwan, despite objections from several U.S. senators.[17] Also, the Court upheld Carter's executive agreement with the revolutionary government of Iran, the regime that held 52 Americans hostage for more than a year, to establish an international commission to settle debts owed by the former regime to American businessmen.[18] Finally, throughout the Vietnam war the Court steadfastly refused to entertain suits that challenged the constitutionality of the United States' intervention in the Southeast Asian conflict.[19]

COURT REBUFFS

In assessing the power relationships between the Supreme Court and the president, one authority on the presidency, Robert J. Sickels, has observed:

> One reason the Court has kept its great power . . . is that it avoids serious clashes with the president. History suggests that presidents will retaliate if they are not treated with deference by the Court. Only when the president is out of office or merely hanging on is the Court likely to attack his programs and decisions.[20]

There is considerable validity to the assertion that the Court often sidesteps highly charged issues until the danger has passed, or the president has left office —or has died. The Supreme Court, for example, did not rule against Lincoln's suspension of the writ of habeas in areas where the civil courts were open during the Civil War *(Ex Parte Milligan)* until more than a year after Lincoln's assassination.

Franklin D. Roosevelt, however, found a conservative Supreme Court to be a major roadblock in his efforts to combat the Great Depression during his first term. By late 1936, the Supreme Court had declared unconstitutional 9 of the 16 laws which were at the heart of his New Deal program.[21] Included among the judicial casualties were the National Industrial Recovery Act, the Farm Mortgage Act, the Agricultural Adjustment Act, the Bituminous Coal Act, the Railroad Pension Act, and the Municipal Bankruptcy Act.

Deeply frustrated by the series of Supreme Court setbacks, FDR decided nevertheless that his landslide victory in the 1936 election gave him a mandate to take action. In early 1937, Roosevelt unveiled what was to become known as his court-packing plan. FDR's scheme aimed to force the Supreme Court majority to reverse its position on key New Deal legislation by enlarging the size of the Supreme Court. Roosevelt proposed that when any judge of any federal court who had been on the bench more than ten years failed to resign within six months after his seventieth birthday, the president would appoint an additional judge. But the number of judges of the Supreme Court could not be increased by more than six.

Roosevelt's plan stirred up a hornet's nest of opposition on the Court and in Congress. Public support was lukewarm. In the months that followed the surfacing of the plan, Congress refused to take action on it. But within three months the Court majority, notably Justice Owen Roberts, reversed its views. The Court upheld the Farm Mortgage Act of 1935, the amended Railway Labor Act of 1934, the National Labor Relations Act of 1935, a state minimum age law, and the Social Security Act of 1935. Pundits in the nation's capital and elsewhere concluded that although Roosevelt had lost the court-packing battle, he had won the legislative war. By 1941 the Supreme Court, with several new members selected by FDR, had done an almost complete reversal on New Deal legislation —a tacit recognition, some said, that the Court follows the election returns.

In a major post-World War II case, *Youngstown Sheet & Tube Co.* v. *Sawyer* (1952), the Court ruled, in a split 6 to 3 decision, that President Truman lacked the authority to take over the nation's steel mills to avert a nationwide steel strike during the Korean war.[22] While it is impossible to speculate at this late date on the various forces operating within the Court at the time, it is significant that Truman had announced two months earlier that he would not run for another term. (Truman was not prohibited from seeking another term under the newly adopted Twenty-second Amendment limiting a president's tenure to two terms.)

Although Justice Black's opinion recognized no inherent authority at all in the executive, the history of the presidency reveals that presidents have many times acted on their own with the blessing of the Court. Moreover, the weakness of Black's argument was further undermined by the fact that a majority of the justices (counting the separate opinions of six concurring and dissenting members) agreed that under some circumstances the president might exercise inherent or emergency powers. Chief Justice Fred Vinson, speaking for the three dissenters, argued that the constitutional grant of "executive power" to the president and his constitutional responsibility to execute the laws provided inherent power for his seizure of the steel companies. To underscore his argument, he cited a series of historical examples: Washington's vigorous suppression of the Whiskey Rebellion, Jefferson's initiative in negotiating the Louisiana Purchase, Lincoln's wholly unauthorized Emancipation Proclamation, and more recently, President Roosevelt's World War II nonstatutory seizures of aircraft and industrial plants.

Had the Court recognized that a full-scale national emergency existed— which it did not in this instance—and if President Truman had been in the first or second year of his first term and not hovering near an all-time low in the public opinion polls, one may wonder if the Court's view of his steel company seizure would have been different. As Michael A. Genovese has observed: "The Youngstown case is an example of the court restricting the power of one individual president and adding to the overall power of the President. In the long run, the power of one man may have been curtailed, but the power of the institution had, with the help of the judiciary grown."[23] Genovese continues:

> The main lesson that presidents have learned from the Youngstown case is that it will be a long time before any president will claim prerogative power or inherent power alone as a justification for action. Presidents will look for supporting statutes (as Truman could easily have done in the Youngstown case), for constitutional justification, or congressional support for their actions.[24]

President Nixon, though he appointed four members to the Supreme Court, suffered more serious judicial reversals (four major cases) than any president in American history. Nixon's first major setback came in the case *New York Times* v. *United States*[25] when the Court rejected the administration's argument that the executive had an inherent constitutional right "to protect the nation against publication of information whose disclosure would endanger the national security." The case grew out of the unauthorized publication by *The New York Times* and the *Washington Post* of the Pentagon Papers, an official documentary history of the Vietnam war. By a 6 to 3 vote, the Court rejected a presidential claim to inherent power that was unsupported by statutory authorization.

The second Nixon setback came a year later in *United States* v. *District Court,* [26] when the Supreme Court ruled that warrantless electronic surveillance in a domestic security case was unconstitutional because it impinged on First and Fourth Amendment values. By way of background, Congress stipulated in the Omnibus Crime Control and Safe Streets Act of 1968 that the federal government's use of wiretaps and electronic eavesdropping must be approved in advance by a judge, who is required to issue a warrant authorizing the electronic surveillance. The president's attorney general ordered, without obtaining a warrant, the electronic surveillance of an individual accused of bombing a CIA office in Ann Arbor, Michigan. The Nixon administration argued that this surveillance was a reasonable exercise of the president's power to protect national security. The Court disagreed, denying clearly and unequivocally the existence of any "inherent" independent presidential power in instances of suspected subversive domestic elements. Significantly, the majority opinion was written by Justice Lewis F. Powell, Jr.—a Nixon appointee.

Other than wait (in vain, as it turned out) until he could appoint a majority to the Court, Nixon could only fulminate against the liberal majority. Finally, with his back to the wall as he faced impeachment over his involvement in the Watergate scandals, Nixon claimed a right of executive privilege—as all presidents have—not only to withhold information from the press, but even from Congress and the Courts if, in the president's judgment, its release would jeopardize national security or interfere with the confidentiality of advice given to the chief executive. But in the celebrated case that led to Nixon's forced resignation, *United States* v. *Nixon* (1974), the Supreme Court held unanimously (Mr. Justice Rehnquist, a recent appointee and former Department of Justice staff member, did not participate in the case) that a president is subject to judicial subpoena for material relevant to a criminal prosecution. [27]

In this historic case, a unanimous Court ordered the president to turn over tapes of White House conversations with his advisers for use in a criminal case against several of his subordinates, despite his argument that executive privilege, considerations of national security, and presidential prerogative protected the confidentiality of these conversations. As the impeachment proceedings moved ever closer to a trial, Nixon may have hoped that the four justices he appointed would come to his rescue. As Robert J. Sickels has commented on this historic case:

> The opinion of the Court does not go into such "imperatives of events and contemporary impounderables," but it may be supposed that the justices were fully aware of the political and legal importance of their decisions. It is believed, in fact, that they drew together in unanimity out of concern that the president would refuse to obey a split decision. Afterward it was revealed that the president had been undecided about compliance until the last minute.[28]

Significantly, for the first time in the nation's history the Supreme Court decided a matter directly involving the president as a party to a case. Furthermore, executive privilege was a novel constitutional doctrine that had never previously been pled before or acknowledged by the High Court.[29]

While sanctioning executive privilege, the Supreme Court rejected the president's claim to *absolute* executive privilege and the idea that the president, rather than the judges, has the final word about what information to release and what to withhold. The justices held that neither the doctrine of separation of powers nor the alleged confidentiality of executive communications barred the federal courts from access to presidential tapes needed as evidence in a criminal trial of several Nixon subordinates. Commenting on the historic importance of this case, one team of legal scholars observed: "In constitutional theory and political consequences, *United States v. Nixon* is among the most remarkable decisions in the Court's history. Vindicated was the ideal 'government of laws and not of men.' "[30] Another legal scholar, Martin Shapiro, while conceding that the case drove the beleaguered president from the White House, suggests that "in the long run the case will be remembered as pro-presidency, the first that acknowledged the constitutional validity of the executive privilege doctrine."[31] In a sense, it was a case of the Court deciding against an individual president while adding to the power of the office. Subsequently, the Supreme Court, in *Nixon* v. *Fitzgerald* (1982), upheld the absolute immunity for the president in civil cases. The Court majority held the immunity "a functionally mandated incident of the president's unique office, rooted in the constitutional tradition of the separation of powers and supported by our history."[32] The justices also expressed concern about the "dangers of intrusion on the authority and functions of the Executive Branch."[33]

Nixon, however, lost another decision after he was driven from office. Less than a year after departing the White House, the Court ruled in *Train* v. *City of New York* that a president could not impound (refuse to spend) money duly appropriated by Congress for specific social programs.[34] In retrospect, Justice Robert Jackson was indeed close to the mark in his observation, made in a concurring opinion in the steel company seizure case, that presidential power was "at its lowest ebb" when the president "takes measures incompatible with the express or implied will of congress."[35]

POLITICAL QUESTIONS

Many presidential actions do not easily lend themselves to litigation, for they involve broad questions of leadership, foreign policy, or national security. Jefferson's decision to purchase the Louisiana territory, Roosevelt's decision to build the atomic bomb, and Reagan's decision to invade the Carribean island of Grenada are all cases in point. The Supreme Court will not review executive discretion; consequently, it will not intervene in presidential decisions of "political questions"—disputes beyond the competence of the Court. In one of the earliest cases, *Luther* v. *Borden* (1849), the Supreme Court refused to intervene in a case involving rival factions fighting for control of the government of Rhode Island.[36]

In 1841, Rhode Island, which still operated largely under a government established by charter under Charles II, faced a major crisis. Dissident groups, protesting against the limits of suffrage, called a popular convention to draft a new constitution. Elections were held and a new governor, Thomas Dorr, was elected. Meanwhile, the old charter government continued to operate and sought to quash what it regarded as a rebellion within its borders. When one of the agents of the charter government tried to arrest a Dorr supporter, he was sued for trespass.

One of the issues in the federal case was whether the charter government was "republican" under the terms of the Constitution. Chief Justice Roger Taney, speaking for the Court, denied the Court possessed either the machinery or equipment to conduct a plebiscite or to gather testimony from enough witnesses to determine which government had the support of a majority of the citizens. He held that this was purely a "political question" that would have to be decided by another branch of the government. The constitutional impasse ended when President John Tyler recognized the charter government governor as the legitimate executive authority of the state and announced that he had taken steps to "federalize" the state militia to support his authority should it be necessary.[37]

Since then, the Supreme Court has from time to time furnished operational definitions of what constitute political actions that are beyond the Court's review. Generally, these include the acquisition of foreign territory by presidential proclamation; the recognition of both foreign and our own state governments; the declaration on national emergencies; the declaration of marital law; "federalizing" the state militia (national guard); and the formal validity of legislative enactments and constitutional amendments. Similarly, the president's decision to carry out international obligations under an executive agreement or treaty has been treated as political to the extent that conflicting acts of a foreign government or individual states do not create a justifiable right in a federal court.

The fine line between a judicial issue and a political or policy issue is not always clear, but because the Court retains this option, it can make the distinction and thereby declare an issue to be a political question if it wishes to avoid ruling against a presidential or congressional action. During the Vietnam war, for example, a Federal Court of Appeals used this approach in a 1973 case *(Holtzman v. Schlesinger)* to avoid ruling on the constitutionality of the presidential war being waged in Cambodia.[38]

In recent years, however, the Supreme Court has taken a more assertive role when faced with questions involving another branch of government. As Robert Scigliano has noted: "The Supreme Court has discarded large parts of the doctrine of 'political questions' since the 1950's."[39] Still, it should be kept in mind, as Michael A. Genovese has cogently observed:

Political questions do provide the courts with a safe escape when they are asked to resolve conflicts which present a "no win" situation to the courts. There are political conflicts which might place the courts in the middle of the two branches. Alienating either the President or Congress could prove to be dangerous. The courts occasionally use the "political question" logic to bow out of the conflict and let the "political branches" fight it out.[40]

JURISDICTIONAL PARAMETERS

Can a president be subject to a civil suit because official actions damage someone's constitutional rights? In the case *Kissinger* v. *Halperin* (1981), former National Security staff member Morton Halperin charged that his home telephone had been wiretapped as the result of a presidential order issued by President Nixon. He sought damages from Nixon, his national security adviser, Henry A. Kissinger, and former attorney general John Mitchell. Reviewing a lower court ruling which upheld Nixon's liability to suit, the Supreme Court split 4 to 4. The tie vote left the lower court ruling in effect and thereby authorized the assessment of damages to be levied, but the Supreme Court left the issue of presidential liability unsettled.[41]

Robert Scigliano reminds us that Americans should take heart from the fact that "No president, so far as we know, has continued to enforce a law after the courts have definitively ruled it to be unconstitutional, nor has any president argued that he has such a right."[42] Have presidents ever refused to do as the courts have ordered? In a few cases, yes.

Thomas Jefferson refused to appear in person at the Aaron Burr conspiracy trial, furnish the requested documents, or even answer the court's subpoena. But Jefferson did forward some papers to the government attorney with permission to use them as he saw fit. In another instance, Jefferson ordered his attorney general to tell customs collectors to ignore Supreme Court Justice William Johnson's ruling that executive instructions to them violated the Embargo Act. Subsequently, Jefferson asked Congress to give him the authority he claimed he already possessed to issue them.[43]

Frustrated sometimes by the Supreme Court, several presidents have threatened to disregard judicial commands. In most instances they sought to anticipate confrontations that never happened.[44] It seems doubtful that Jefferson would have delivered a commission to William Marbury, one of the so-called midnight judges, if the Supreme Court had ordered it in the case of *Marbury* v. *Madison* (1803). But Chief Justice Marshall avoided this head-on collision by ruling that although Marbury was entitled to the commission, the writ of mandamus was issued by a court that lacked jurisdiction under the Judiciary Act of 1789.

Lincoln ignored several judicial decisions ordering him or his field commanders to release disloyal persons from military custody. In the most famous case, *Ex Parte Merryman,* Lincoln refused to order his field commander to turn over Merryman, who had been engaged in secessionist activities, to civil authorities. Though Merryman was subsequently indicted for treason, the case against him was eventually dropped. As Glendon Schubert has commented, this Civil War case makes it "abundantly clear" that "the civil courts have no power to interfere with or control the actions of the Commander in Chief if he wills otherwise."[45]

Lincoln informed Congress in 1863 that he would not "return to slavery any person who is free by the terms of [the Emancipation] Proclamation or by any of the acts of Congress." For the remainder of the Civil War no challenge was made against Lincoln's extraordinary action, even though it was not based on any statute or specified constitutional power.

Franklin D. Roosevelt reportedly threatened to disobey the Supreme Court on two separate occasions, but each time the Court's decision turned out to be acceptable to the president. The first instance occurred when the Court was considering cases that challenged Roosevelt's authority to take the country off the gold standard. But the Court's decision in *Norman* v. *Baltimore Railroad Company* (1935) upholding the president's action by a 5 to 4 vote averted a showdown. The second time occurred when the Court decided, much to Roosevelt's chagrin, to rule on whether he could appoint a special military tribunal to try eight Nazi saboteurs landed from submarines off the American east coast.[46] Since the Court upheld FDR's action, the threatened test of strength between the two branches never materialized.

More recently, Nixon hinted during the Watergate hearings that he might not turn over the White House tapes, no matter what the Supreme Court ruled. As he later stated in his *Memoirs,* Nixon realized that failure to turn over the tapes would bring about his impeachment; therefore, he considered "abiding" by an unfavorable ruling without actually "complying" with the Court's ruling— that is, furnishing only excerpts of the tapes held at the White House. But when the Court ruled against him unanimously, he concluded he had no choice but to comply.[47]

DELEGATION OF LEGISLATIVE AUTHORITY TO THE PRESIDENT

Since congressional legislation cannot always anticipate every contingency or action that may arise under a statute, the lawmakers often delegate authority to the executive to determine when a given statute shall be operative and spell out the rules and regulations needed to comply with the statute. Thus, although the separation of powers doctrine prohibits the delegation of legislative authority, Congress has recognized the impossibility of writing regulations and forms of procedure that cover every conceivable type of problem and contingency involved in the conduct of a governmental agency. Consequently, after passing a general statute, Congress assigns this task to the president or his subordinates. They must fill in the details with appropriate regulations. The courts have long recognized that administrative officers must be permitted some discretion in the enforcement of the law and carrying out congressional intent. In short, effective government often requires the exercise of legislative authority by the executive.

Even before the rise of the modern administrative state, the courts recognized the need for the delegation of legislative authority to the president. The Court, for example, sustained a flexible tariff act authorizing the president to raise or lower tariff rates by 50 percent to equalize the costs of production in the United States and competing foreign nations in *Hampton & Co.* v. *United States* (1928).[48]

In a unanimous opinion, Chief Justice Taft wrote:

> The field of Congress involves all and many varieties of legislative action and Congress has found it frequently necessary to use officers of the executive branch within defined limits to secure the exact effect intended by acts of legislation by vesting discretion in such offices to make public regulations interpreting a statute and directing the details of its execution, even to the extent of providing for penalizing a breach of such regulations.[49]

Prior to the New Deal, no federal statute had ever been declared invalid because of an unconstitutional delegation of legislative power to the president. In each case reviewed, the criteria set by Congress were held to be sufficiently definite, even though some rather vague standards were sustained. But in 1935 the Supreme Court invalidated two New Deal measures on the basis of unconstitutional delegation of legislative authority. In *Panama Refining Company* v. *Ryan* (the Hot Oil case), the Court ruled unconstitutional a provision of the National Industrial Recovery Act (NIRA) authorizing the president to ban the interstate shipment of oil produced or withdrawn in violation of state regulation. The Court ruled that an absolute and uncontrolled discretion had been vested in the president's hands, since the statute contained no policy and provided no criteria by which the validity of the president's action could be judged. The Court's majority saw no relationship between the broad generalities of the statute and the power given to the president. The opinion held that Congress had "left the matter to the president without standard or rule, to be dealt with as he pleased." But Justice Cardozo, dissenting, thought that the declaration of policy in the act's preamble contained a sufficiently definite standard. Cardozo concluded that he feared that the classical separation of powers had become "a doctrinaire concept to be made use of with pedantic rigor." "Discretion is not unconfined and vagrant," he continued. "It is canalized within banks that keep it from over-flowing."[50]

In the second case, *Schechter Poultry Corporation* v. *United States* (1935), decided shortly after the Hot Oil case, the Supreme Court ruled that the discretion of the president under the National Industrial Recovery Act was "virtually unfettered."[51] Justice Cardozo, in this case, joined the majority in condemning the attempted delegation to the president of code-approving authority. In his concurring opinion, Cardozo termed it "delegation run riot." Several New Deal supporters of the voided legislation attributed the judicial defeat to hasty and inefficient legislative draftsmanship.

Curiously, less than a year after the Supreme Court had declared the National Industrial Recovery Act unconstitutional, the Court decided that while the delegation of legislative power to the president was impermissible in domestic matters, no such constraints applied in foreign affairs. In *United States* v. *Curtiss-Wright Export Corp.* (1936), the Court sustained an embargo on arms to warring countries in South America (in this case, Bolivia and Paraguay) proclaimed by the president pursuant to a joint resolution of Congress authorizing the president to take such action if it "may contribute to the reestablishment of peace between those countries."[52] To reach this decision, the Court distinguished delegations of power over internal affairs and those over foreign relations. (This subject is covered in greater detail in Chapter 8.)

Less than 12 months after this historic foreign relations case, the Supreme Court—consisting of the same nine justices—experienced a change of heart and held that the Schechter case was "inapplicable" in a series of five cases, the most important being *National Labor Relations Board* v. *Jones and Laughlin Steel Corporation.* [53] Decided in the midst of President Roosevelt's abortive Supreme Court packing plan, the Court upheld the Wagner Act (which protected the right of labor unions to engage in collective bargaining) on a 5 to 4 vote as a justifiable regulation of interstate commerce. The favorable ruling on this key New Deal measure was made possible when Justice Owen Roberts abandoned his conservative brethren and voted with the four liberal justices.

With this evidence of a perceptive voting shift on the bench, Congress decided a year later to delegate authority to the president to regulate minimum wages and child labor. Twice in the previous two decades the Supreme Court had struck down congressional legislation to regulate child labor under the commerce clause and the federal government's taxing authority.[54] In the Fair Labor Standards Act of 1938, Congress added a rather detailed, though uninstructive, list of criteria to guide the administrators' judgment and specified reasonable limits within which administrative discretion was to be exercised. Three years later, in *Opp Cotton Mills* v. *Administrator,* [55] the Supreme Court unanimously sustained these regulations against the complaint that the statutory regulations were so vague and indefinite that the administrator was authorized to fix wages with practically no congressional guides or control. Chief Justice Harlan Stone, speaking for the Court, observed:

> In an increasingly complex society Congress obviously could not perform its function if it were obliged to find all the facts subsidiary to the conclusions which support the defined legislative policy in fixing, for example, a tariff rate, a railroad rate, or the rate of wages to be applied in particular industries by a minimum wage law. The Constitution viewed as a continually operative charter of government, is not to be interpreted as demanding the impossible or impracticable. The essentials of the legislative function are the determination of the legislative policy and its formulation as a rule of conduct. These essentials are preserved when Congress specifies the basic conclusions of fact upon ascertainment of which, from relevant data by a designated administrative agency, it ordains that its statutory command is to be effective.[56]

Two decades later, a leading constitutional authority, Glendon A. Schubert, Jr., observed that "The 'Hot Oil' and 'Sick Chicken' (Schechter) cases remain today isolated and unique as the only instances in which the Supreme Court has ever discovered an unconstitutional delegation of power—*legislative or otherwise*—to the President."[57] As we approach the half century mark since the Court's decision in these two historic cases, Schubert's verdict still stands.

Delegation of legislative authority to the executive reached its zenith during World War II. To aid President Roosevelt in mobilizing the full resources of the country, Congress delegated sweeping authority to the chief executive. Some critics felt that Congress had abdicated its lawmaking function in handing over virtually unlimited authority to the president, but the Supreme Court had no problem in sustaining these broad delegations of legislative authority. In *Yakus* v. *United States* (1944), the Court upheld the power of the Office of Price Administration (OPA), a special wartime agency established by President Roosevelt, to fight inflation and fix maximum prices for consumer goods under the Emergency Price Control Act of 1942. In a companion case, *Bowles* v. *Willingham* (1944), the Court also sustained the Office of Price Administration's authority to establish rent controls. Only Justice Roberts voted against permitting the OPA to set rent ceilings. These wartime delegations by Congress, as the late Edward S. Corwin commented, exceeded "any previous pattern of delegated legislation touching private rights directly."[58]

Since the end of World War II, the Court's attitude on peacetime delegations of authority by Congress to the president have continued to be extremely permissive. But the Court has indicated certain parameters that lawmakers must observe in drafting legislation: Congress must define the subject of the delegation and also provide a recognizable standard or criterion to guide the executive agent to whom legislative powers are delegated. The exercise of administrative discretion, however, is subject to judicial review, if an administrative regulation is involved, to determine whether it comes within the scope of the delegated authority. Also, if an administrative body is involved, the Courts will determine if that body is acting within its proper jurisdiction.[59]

PRESIDENTIAL NOMINEES TO THE SUPREME COURT

Presidents, especially if they serve two terms, can often exert a major influence over the direction of Court policy—and public policy—by their Supreme Court appointees. Franklin D. Roosevelt's appointment of Hugo Black, William O. Douglas, and Felix Frankfurter reinforced the Court's switch from opposition to endorsement of the New Deal's broad-scaled social welfare reforms. More recently, Richard Nixon's appointment of four conservative justices—Burger, Blackman, Rehnquist, and Powell—slowed down or reversed several Warren Court decisions affecting criminal procedures, school desegregation, and other minority rights.

We should not underestimate the impact of the president's appointment power on the judiciary. As Robert Dahl perceptibly noted some years ago, the appointment power helps insure that "the policy views dominant on the Court are never for long out of line with the policy views among the lawmaking majorities of the United States. Consequently, it would be unrealistic to suppose that the Court would, for more than a few years at most, stand against any major alternatives sought by the lawmaking majority."[60] Presidents invariably look to the Court, especially their own appointees, to legitimize the executive and legislative policies they have developed—though the record shows that the Court's decisions sometimes run counter to the president's preferences.

Since 1789, presidents have appointed 106 judges to the Supreme Court (see Table 11.2). Approximately 80 percent of the nominees formally sent by the

Table 11.2 NUMBER OF PRESIDENTIAL APPOINTMENTS OF U.S. SUPREME COURT JUSTICES WHO ACTUALLY SERVED ON THE COURT (ARRANGED CHRONOLOGICALLY)

President	Dates in office	Number of appointments
Washington	1789–1797	10
J. Adams	1797–1801	3
Jefferson	1801–1809	3
Madison	1809–1817	2
Monroe	1817–1825	1
J. Q. Adams	1825–1829	1
Jackson	1829–1837	6 (5)*
Van Buren	1837–1841	2 (3)*
W. H. Harrison	1841	0
Tyler	1841–1845	1
Polk	1845–1849	2
Taylor	1849–1850	0
Fillmore	1850–1853	1
Pierce	1853–1857	1
Buchanan	1857–1861	1
Lincoln	1861–1865	5
A. Johnson	1865–1869	0
Grant	1869–1877	4
Hayes	1877–1881	2
Garfield	1881	1
Arthur	1881–1885	2
Cleveland	1885–1889; 1893–1897	4†
B. Harrison	1889–1893	4
McKinley	1897–1901	1
T. Roosevelt	1901–1909	3
Taft	1909–1913	6
Wilson	1913–1921	3
Harding	1921–1923	4
Coolidge	1923–1929	1
Hoover	1929–1933	3
F. D. Roosevelt	1933–1945	9
Truman	1945–1953	4
Eisenhower	1953–1961	5
Kennedy	1961–1963	2
L. B. Johnson	1963–1969	2
Nixon	1969–1974	4
Ford	1974–1977	1
Carter	1977–1981	0
Reagan	1981–1986	2
		Total 106

*Jackson had nominated Catron, but the latter was not confirmed until Van Buren had taken over
†Two in each of his two terms, which split by Harrison's single term.
Source: From *The Judicial Process: An Introductory Analysis of the Courts of the United States, England, and France, fourth edition* by Henry J. Abraham, 55. Copyright © 1980 by Henry J. Abraham. Reprinted by permission of Oxford University Press, Inc.

president to the Senate have been confirmed.[61] But one out of five has been rejected. Most of these rejections, however, occurred in the nineteenth century. (One out of three nominees failed in the Senate.) Only four rejections—two were President Nixon's nominees—have taken place in the twentieth century. On average a Court vacancy has occurred about almost every 18 months since 1937 (approximately every 22 months since 1789). Thus, a two-term president can normally expect to appoint close to a majority of the justices before he leaves the White House.

The number of appointments, it seems, seldom rests on any actuarial tables. Taft, a one-term president, appointed six justices, but Woodrow Wilson appointed only three justices during his two full terms. Franklin D. Roosevelt, who served in the White House for slightly over three terms, holds the runner-up position to Washington, who selected the entire original Supreme Court, plus four replacements (ten in all). FDR appointed nine justices; Jimmy Carter, on the other hand, did not have the opportunity to appoint a single member to the Supreme Court—the first full-term president in history to be denied that chance.[62] Reagan appointed one justice—Sandra Day O'Connor—during his first term. Plainly, the appointment power gives most presidents the opportunity to exert a major influence on a co-equal branch of the federal government.

Who does the president appoint to the highest court in the country? Top-drawer legal minds are usually at the head of the list. The names of John Marshall, Joseph Story, Roger B. Taney, John M. Harlan, Oliver Wendell Holmes, Jr., Louis D. Brandeis, and Felix Frankfurter immediately come to mind. Political strategy sometimes dictates a judicial appointment. Franklin D. Roosevelt, probably one of the most partisan chief executives of the twentieth century, opted for statesmanship rather than partisanship when he elevated Associate Justice Harlan F. Stone to Chief Justice in 1941, six months before Pearl Harbor. Roosevelt picked Stone, a former Republican attorney general nominated to the Court by President Calvin Coolidge in 1923, over Democratic Attorney General Robert M. Jackson as a gesture toward national unity in face of a growing war crisis.

Retiring Chief Justice Charles Evans Hughes urged FDR to promote Associate Justice Stone (who had been one of Roosevelt's professors at Columbia Law School) on the basis of his record. Hughes also suggested that Roosevelt consult Mr. Justice Frankfurter, a Roosevelt appointee, regarding the chief justiceship. Frankfurter advised the president:

> . . . when war does come, the country should feel you are national, the Nation's President, and not a partisan President . . . [to bolster this assessment] you [should] name a Republican, who has the profession's confidence, as Chief Justice.[63]

Sometimes a president can score several points for statesmanship as well as political gain by an astute judicial appointment, such as Lincoln did with the selection of Stephen J. Field in 1863. Henry J. Abraham has summarized the background of this appointment as follows:

. . . Field, who was to serve longer than anyone but Douglas to date on the Court (thirty-four and three-quarters years), was chosen by Lincoln largely for three reasons: First, Field came from California, a part of the country not then represented on the Court—in fact, Congress created a tenth seat for that purpose —and even though he had been a Buchanan Democrat as late as 1861, Lincoln felt his nominee would help to "fuse" the Northern cause by preserving the loyalty of California and strengthening its political ties. Second, Field's many influential friends, including California Governor Leland Stanford, put considerable pressure on the President. Third, Field's brother, David Dudley Field, a bitter and vocal opponent of slavery, had played a considerable role both in the organization of the Republican party and in Lincoln's nomination as its standard-bearer in 1860.[64]

Personal friendship has sometimes been a significant factor, though obviously not the only consideration, in judicial appointments. William Howard Taft's appointment of Justice H. H. Lurton rested heavily on personal friendship. Both Taft and Lurton had served together for eight years on the U.S. Court of Appeals for the Sixth Circuit, where they became fast friends. Lurton, a Tennessee Democrat, had been elevated to Chief Judge when the future president went to the Philippines as governor-general. Later, President Taft called the nomination of his former colleague "the chief pleasure of my administration."[65]

President Truman's choice of Fred Vinson to be Chief Justice was based heavily on their long friendship. Vinson was serving in the cabinet as secretary of the treasury when Truman elevated him to the chief justiceship. And John F. Kennedy's choice of Byron F. (Whizzer) White, a former all-American football player and Rhodes scholar, probably was based as much on friendship as legal qualifications.

Geographical representation on the Court has in the past been a prominent factor in presidential choice, such as Lincoln's choice of a trans-Mississippi lawyer, Samuel F. Miller, to the bench during the Civil War, and the concern to have a southerner or westerner in one of the Court seats. President Harding's choice of Pierce Butler of Minnesota, a nominal Democrat, represented only the second justice born west of the Mississippi. President Nixon's choice of Lewis F. Powell, Jr., of Virginia, was, in current parlance, a "twofer"—he obtained at least two pluses from his appointee. Powell, a southern Democrat, was viewed by the president also as a strict constructionist.

More recently, ethnicity, religion, and gender have become more important factors than geography in making appointments. Legal scholars and politicians now commonly refer to a "Roman Catholic seat," a "Jewish seat," a "black seat," and, most recently, a "woman's seat" on the Court. Roger B. Taney's appointment in 1835 by Jackson marked the first Catholic appointment. Since the turn of the century, there has been a Roman Catholic sitting on the bench almost continuously. The first Jewish seat was filled in 1916 with Wilson's appointment of Louis D. Brandeis, followed by Benjamin N. Cardozo (Hoover, 1932), Felix Frankfurter (Roosevelt, 1938), Arthur Goldberg (Kennedy, 1963), and Abe Fortas (Johnson, 1965). But there have been no members of the Jewish faith on the Court since Fortas's resignation in 1969.

Two years earlier, President Johnson's Solicitor General, Thurgood Marshall, became the first black ever to be appointed to the Supreme Court, suggesting perhaps that there may come to be a reserved seat for a black jurist. Most recently, President Reagan's nomination of Sandra Day O'Connor, the first woman to sit on the Supreme Court, may lead to the establishment of a "woman's seat" on the bench. Perhaps in the future there may also come to be a "Hispanic seat." While it seems doubtful that the makeup of the Court will always reflect all these considerations, it is a virtual certainty that most of these constituencies will continue to be represented when the Court begins its annual session each October.

Despite the growing diversity on the Court, most members have been male Protestants of Anglo-Saxon heritage, upper-middle "establishment" background, who have held positions in the federal or state court systems and who previously were often involved politically. Significantly, approximately 85 percent of federal court appointees have come from the same political party as the president.[66] The last president to select a Supreme Court Justice from the opposition party was Richard Nixon, who appointed Lewis F. Powell, Jr., in 1971.

PRESIDENTIAL EXPECTATIONS

Do presidents get value received from the individuals they appoint to the Supreme Court? While it is impossible to measure with precision how every president has felt about every major issue decided by the courts, the record shows that presidents have obtained—approximately 75 percent of the time—what they wanted from their appointees.[67]

Despite a few well-publicized exceptions, presidents have generally not been disappointed with the voting records of the people they appoint. Evidence that a president usually gets what he wants from his appointees began showing up early in our constitutional history. President John Adams was not unhappy with John Marshall's strong national views and his defense of private property. As a matter of fact, both Washington and Adams restricted their court choices to persons who were firm adherents of Federalist doctrine—strong supporters of the broad exercise of power by the national government, especially relating to commerce and industry, and who would limit the power of states to interfere with these and other national goals. As Robert Scigliano has noted: "Their appointees hardly ever deviated from these policies, and two of them, John Marshall and Bushrod Washington, espoused them in careers of more than thirty years service on the Court."[68]

Indeed, the record shows that no Federalist justice dissent was ever recorded against landmark Federalist decisions of the first 40 years of the Republic.[69] Among the great decisions handed down were those which ruled that a treaty of the United States superseded state law (*Ware* v. *Hylton,* 1796); that the Supreme Court possessed the authority to invalidate legislation it judged to be unconstitutional (*Marbury* v. *Madison,* 1803); that legislative land grants and corporate charters were legal contracts that could not be impaired by subsequent state legislation (respectively, *Fletcher* v. *Peck,* 1810, and *Dartmouth College* v.

Woodward, 1819); that sustained the constitutionality of the United States Bank and voided a state tax on this federal instrumentality (*McCulloch* v. *Maryland,* 1819); and finally, the celebrated decision that construed the national power over commerce in broad terms while voiding a state law that infringed upon that power (*Gibbons* v. *Ogden,* 1824).[70]

Most of the justices appointed by Jackson, Van Buren, and Polk and other Democratic presidents of the pre-Civil War period were usually faithful to the states rights and anticorporation views of their appointees. Lincoln had no reason to be disappointed with the five justices he put on the Supreme Court. His first four appointees voted to uphold the Union blockade of southern ports, and at the same time withheld the status of belligerent power from the Confederacy (*The Prize Cases,* 1863). All of the Lincoln justices voted to invalidate a state bank tax that would have severely hindered the federal government's financing of the war effort (*Bank of Commerce* v. *New York,* 1863); moreover, they refused to take jurisdiction of cases challenging legal tender legislation (*Roosevelt* v. *Meyer,* 1863) and the military arrest and trial of southern sympathizers in areas outside the perimeter of war (*Ex parte Vallandingham,* 1864).[71]

Nor was President Ulysses Grant disappointed with his two appointees, who filled vacancies after the Court had originally denied Congress the power to issue paper money. Indeed, Grant's two appointees joined three of Lincoln's to promptly overturn this ruling—one of the key decisions of the post-Civil War era. Most post-Civil War presidents had their hands full finding appointees who would be acceptable to the Senate, which usually was opposition-controlled or closely divided. President Cleveland, for example, had his first two nominations to the Court rejected before Edward D. White received Senate approval.[72] Consequently, the presidents of this period had to be more concerned about geographical representation and general acceptability than ideological credentials.

Theodore Roosevelt, on more than one occasion, expressed his "bitter disappointment" over his appointment of Oliver Wendell Holmes, Jr., to the bench, but among his contemporaries it seems doubtful if Teddy would have been entirely satisfied with any justice, unless he were a clone. His distant cousin, Franklin D. Roosevelt, had no reason to be displeased with his judicial appointees (nine in all). As explained by Robert Scigliano: "Not one of Roosevelt's justices ever took the position in a case against the New Deal or against a state tax or business regulation on the grounds that the state enactment was not permitted by the due process clause of the Fourteenth Amendment."[73]

Until the Watergate hearings collapsed over Richard Nixon's head, the four justices he appointed all voted to cut back on criminal defense rights, the only Court issue, according to some observers, that seriously interested him.

Most recently, President Reagan has had every reason to be satisfied with his first Court appointee, Justice Sandra Day O'Connor, who has shown herself almost as conservative as Justice William Rehnquist, generally adjudged the most conservative member of the present Court. Dwight D. Eisenhower, on the other hand, was deeply disappointed with two of his appointees—Chief Justice Earl Warren and Justice William J. Brennan, Jr.—who turned out to be closet liberals. Asked if he had made any mistakes during his presidency, General Ike reportedly replied, "Yes, and they are both sitting on the Supreme Court."[74]

Generally, presidents who serve two full terms not only leave an indelible mark on the Supreme Court, since they may appoint a majority of justices, but also put a heavy imprint on the entire federal judicial system. In early 1985, for example, President Reagan had the opportunity to fill 114 federal district and appeals court judgeships—an extraordinary total that exceeds one-seventh of the seats on the entire federal bench.[75] Not since Franklin D. Roosevelt's administration has a president had such an open-ended opportunity to transform the federal judiciary. Nor are presidents unmindful of the importance of lower court appointments. Approximately 80,000 cases are decided in lower federal courts annually, compared with 150 or so that are decided by the Supreme Court. Because it is from the 12 courts of appeals and the 95 district courts that the Supreme Court gets most of its business, the president's ability to affect decisions of the lower courts by the appointment power can often affect the issues the Supreme Court decides to consider.[76]

By the end of his second term, President Reagan is likely to have named a majority of the nation's 744 federal trial and appellate judges, leaving a legacy that will far outlast his presidency. Of the 165 judges Reagan selected in his first term, approximately 98 percent have been white males and Republicans; only two blacks and thirteen women were appointed to the federal bench. This represented a sharp reduction from the forty women and thirty-seven blacks names to the federal bench by Jimmy Carter.[77] Table 11.3 shows the number of federal appointments made by the last nine presidents and the number of those serving in 1985. The table includes appointments to federal district courts, appeals courts, and the Supreme Court.

According to a study by Sheldon Goldman, one-quarter of Reagan's judicial

**Table 11.3 JUDICIAL APPOINTEES—
ROOSEVELT TO REAGAN,
1933–1985**

	Judges appointed*	Serving†
Roosevelt	194	7
Truman	136	26
Eisenhower	170	68
Kennedy	129	72
Johnson	156	124
Nixon	226	164
Ford	60	48
Carter	258	238
Reagan	201‡	175**

*Figures from *Judges of the United States,* 2nd ed., 1983, published by the Judicial Conference of the United States.

†Figures from the Administrative Office of the U.S. Courts. Only a judge's initial appointment to the federal bench is counted.

‡Appointments as of September 5, 1985.

**Does not include 11 Reagan appointees who were confirmed but not yet serving as of August 1, or 15 who were previously appointed to a lower court and subsequently elevated.

Source: Congressional Quarterly Weekly Report, 43 (September 7, 1985), 1760.

appointees during his first term have been millionaires. Their average age was fifty years. Approximately two-thirds had judicial experience, suggesting that the White House placed heavy emphasis on appointees with judicial track records.[78] In picking federal district judges, President Reagan has usually followed the long tradition of accepting candidates recommended by the home state senators of his party. However, administration sources report surprising numbers of unpublicized cases in which the White House has rejected a Republican senator's choice as too liberal or unqualified. Attorney General Edwin Meese III, a close confidant of President Reagan, has said that the administration will seek appointment of judges who believe in "the sanctity of human life." But Meese and White House counsel Fred F. Fielding have insisted that the administration has no "litmus test" and does not reject judges according to their stance on abortion or any other single issue.

Be that as it may, there can be little doubt that President Reagan has lived up to his campaign pledge to select judges who take a conservative view of law and order. "This administration," Goldman says, "is making a greater concerted effort to ideologically screen the people considered for the judiciary than at any time since Franklin D. Roosevelt's first term," 1933 to 1937.[79] As Goldman reminds us, "When we elect a president, we're electing a judiciary."[80] It therefore came as no surprise when President Reagan's Justice Department, early in the second term, submitted a brief to the Supreme Court urging the justices to reverse *Roe* v. *Wade,* the 1973 case upholding free choice on abortion. Some observers in the nation's capital felt that the brief was written more to demonstrate to the right-wing anti-abortionist adherents that the Reagan administration stood by its campaign promises than to persuade the Supreme Court justices to change their minds.

Once again, the separation of powers doctrine provides the president with plenty of opportunities to posture for political advantage without changing policy. In a later round of this attempt to influence the justices, the Supreme Court declined to let the Reagan administration participate in oral arguments involving abortion and affirmative action during the 1985–1986 term. The Court's action meant that it would not hear the Justice Department lawyers argue that the Court's 1973 decision legalizing abortion should be overruled. The Supreme Court justices did not reveal why they turned down the administration request.[81]

BEYOND THE COURTS

Judicial avoidance of political questions has left presidents with plenty of latitude to operate, especially in times of crisis. Does the Supreme Court or the president himself possess the right to decide whether his actions violate the Constitution? The Founders left this question unanswered. In fact, this question still remains open-ended. Sometimes the Court has extended the doctrine of judicial review to slap down a president who has exceeded his constitutional prerogatives. More frequently, however, the Supreme Court has been reluctant to intervene, especially in times of crisis, preferring instead to allow the president to exercise his executive power as he sees fit. Thus, during periods when presidents are likely to stretch their prerogatives to the limit, as during the Civil War and World Wars I and II, the Court has usually preferred to remain on the sidelines, even though the constitutional rights of American citizens were seriously undermined. Clearly, as two close students of the presidency have noted: "The Court considers the political costs of any decision it makes in terms of its own legitimacy and its power to enforce its decrees."[82]

In times of national emergency the president decides, in the words of one commentator, "when conditions warrant this exercise of the extraordinary Constitutional and statutory powers which then center around the person and office of our Commander in Chief."[83] Rarely does the Supreme Court attempt to stay the hand of the president under wartime conditions. If the Supreme Court chooses to intervene, it is usually to reaffirm the actions of the chief executive, as witness *The Prize Cases* (1863) during the Civil War or the Court's decisions in World War II upholding the president's authority to remove Japanese-Americans, clearly in violation of their constitutional rights, from the West Coast to relocation centers inland.[84]

Speaking of the president's proclamations, executive orders, and the broad statutory authority Congress has granted to the president, the late Clinton Rossiter concluded:

> Few were attacked; all were held Constitutional, often without as much as a word of opinion. . . . These few examples should be proof enough that in time of war Congress can pass just about any law it wants as a "necessary and proper" accessory to the delegated war powers; that the president can make just about any use of such law as he sees fit; and that the people with their overt or silent resistance, not the Court with its power of judicial review, will set the only practical limits to arrogance and abuse.[85]

To be sure, since World War II Presidents Truman and Nixon have been rebuffed by the Supreme Court in a handful of major cases, but the overall record shows that the justices have usually been solicitous in protecting executive prerogatives. Most recently, the Supreme Court struck down the legislative veto—a congressional weapon that has enabled lawmakers for a half century to delegate power to the executive branch and then take it away without having to secure presidential approval.[86] Since 1932, more than 210 pieces of legislation have contained some form of legislative veto. Almost half of these were enacted between 1972 and 1983.[87] Recent statutes containing legislative veto provisions included the Budget and Impoundment Act of 1974 and the Energy Policy and Conservation Act of 1975. Congress had contended all along that it may delegate authority to the executive on a conditional basis and that the legislative veto is necessary to control the vast bureaucracy in the executive branch. Despite the popularity of the legislative veto on Capitol Hill, many White House aides and supporters of the presidency have for years considered the legislative veto a violation of the doctrine of separation of powers. Since the New Deal era, presidents have criticized the legislative veto for bypassing their own power to veto measures and for interfering with their execution of the laws.

Finally, in 1983, the Supreme Court agreed with the president's supporters and ruled that the legislative veto violated the separation of powers.[88] In overturning the legislative veto, the Court declared that henceforth all exercises of legislative power must pass both houses of Congress and be submitted to the president.

Does the demise of the legislative veto mean that the president will hold all the trump cards in legislative confrontations with Congress? Not necessarily. In the long run, the presidency may be the real loser in the Court's ruling, since the lawmakers may now be encouraged to delineate more detailed and restrictive legislation, thereby curtailing the president's discretion. Congress may also turn to its power over the purse and use the appropriations process to checkmate the president.

With the exception of the legislative veto case, the Supreme Court has acted promptly in a number of recent cases to clarify the president's powers and duties, or limitations on his power. In *United States* v. *Nixon* (1974), concerning President Nixon's claimed executive privilege prerogative to withhold certain White House tapes from the Watergate Special Prosecutor, the Supreme Court agreed to bypass the U.S. Court of Appeals by issuing a writ of certiorari to hear the case directly from the U.S. District Court. The expedited time schedule read as follows: the District Court issued its decision on May 20, 1974; on June 6 the president's counsel filed a cross petition for writ of certiorari before judgment; the Supreme Court granted this cross petition on June 15 and agreed to hear the case on July 8; the Supreme Court handed down its decision in this precedent-shattering case on July 24, 1974—which, in effect, sealed the fate of President Nixon and led to his forced resignation less than two weeks later. To be sure, *United States* v. *Nixon* was a historic case, and the Supreme Court has always been sensitive to the need to move with dispatch in such cases. But the Court has moved with equal speed in other recent cases involving the president.

In *Goldwater* v. *Carter* (1979),[89] involving the issue of whether the president of the United States could unilaterally abrogate a U.S. mutual defense treaty with the Republic of China on Taiwan after agreeing to establish diplomatic relations with Communist China, Senator Barry Goldwater (Arizona) and several of his conservative colleagues in the U.S. Senate argued that President Carter had acted illegally by unilaterally cancelling the treaty. Once again, the case moved through the federal courts in double time. On October 17, 1979, the U.S. District Court judge ruled in favor of the Senate. On November 30, 1979, the U.S. Court of Appeals reversed, ruling in favor of the president. Less than two weeks later, the Supreme Court upheld the president's power to abrogate a treaty unilaterally.

The Supreme Court also reaffirmed its general policy to handle issues involving the president as expeditiously as possible in the recent Iranian–United States claims case. As part of the bargain to obtain the release of American hostages in Teheran in early 1981, the United States agreed to terminate all legal proceedings in the United States courts involving claims of United States nationals against Iran and to nullify all attachments and judgments against Iranian property. Under the joint agreement, all claims were to be terminated through binding arbitration in an Iranian–United States claims tribunal. In *Dames & Moore* v. *Regan,*[90] the American creditor filed action against the United States and Secretary of the Treasury Donald T. Regan seeking to prevent enforcement of the various executive orders previously issued by Jimmy Carter and later "ratified" by Reagan implementing the agreement with Iran.

Counsel for Dames & Moore argued that the actions went beyond the president's statutory and constitutional powers. The U.S. District Court dismissed the complaint for failure to state a claim upon which relief could be granted, but entered an injunction pending appeal to the U.S. Court of Appeals. Because of the need to settle the matter before July 19, 1981—the date agreed upon by both parties for the transfer of the Iranian assets—the Supreme Court granted certiorari before the U.S. Court of Appeals could decide the case. Oral arguments were held on June 24, 1981, and the Supreme Court announced its decision, just over a week later, upholding presidential authority once again to make executive agreements to settle international claims.[91] Thus, in each of these three cases, the Supreme Court moved with unusual swiftness to settle major issues involving presidential power.

CONCLUSION

A quick review of the nation's history shows that the Supreme Court generally gives great weight to the president's own interpretation and construction of the scope of his own powers. Indeed, the Supreme Court has seldom been a major barrier to the extension of presidential power. History also shows that for each case in which the Court has decided against the expansion of presidential power, we could list a dozen other cases where it has endorsed the extension of power by presidents. And in some instances when the Court has decided against the president, the effect of the decision, paradoxically, has been to add to the overall power of the office. The Supreme Court is more likely to overrule a president on domestic matters than in the field of foreign policy and much less likely to thwart a president in times of national emergency.

Since the fine line between a judicial issue and a political or policy issue is not always clear, the Supreme Court may exercise the option of declaring a sticky issue a "political" question and thereby avoid ruling against a presidential or congressional action. In recent years, however, the Court has not resorted to this option very often to evade key decisions affecting the executive and legislative branches. The recent action invalidating the legislative veto in 1983 is a case in point. The Court has also taken a permissive attitude toward the delegation of legislative authority to the president, though it has insisted that Congress establish a recognizable standard or criterion to guide the executive agent.

Presidents exert a major influence over the Supreme Court by their choice of nominees. Political affiliation (belonging to the president's party), ideological compatibility with the president's views, ethnicity, religion, and gender are all factors that presidents weigh before sending their nominees to the Senate. The historical record indicates that presidents have been pleased with their choices in about three-quarters of the cases.

If a president serves two full terms, the chances are better than even that he will have an opportunity to pick a majority of the justices in the federal judiciary—and thus leave a major imprint on the entire federal system. Ronald Reagan, now in his second term, is not likely to be an exception to this general observation.

NOTES

1. E. S. Corwin, *The President: Office and Powers, 1787–1984,* 5th rev. ed. by Randall W. Bland, Theodore T. Hindson, and Jack W. Peltason (New York: New York University Press, 1984), 329.
2. Ibid.
3. Robert Scigliano, *The Supreme Court and the President* (New York: Free Press, 1971), 15.
4. Ibid., 22.
5. Michael A. Genovese, *The Supreme Court, the Constitution, and Presidential Power* (Lanham, MD: University Press of America, 1980), 242.
6. Ibid. Political scientists Craig R. Ducat and Robert L. Dudley have found a high level of support for presidential power among votes cast by federal judges at all levels— federal district, court of appeals, and Supreme Court—in 531 cases decided between January 1949 and June 1984. "Of the 1337 votes cast, two-thirds (67 percent) favored the exercise of presidential power." Craig R. Ducat and Robert L. Dudley, "Federal Judges and Presidential Power: Truman to Reagan." Paper delivered at the Midwest Political Science Association annual meeting, Chicago, April 9–12, 1986, 7.
7. Corwin, *The President: Office and Powers,* 4th rev. ed. (New York: New York University Press, 1957), 16, 25.
8. Ibid., 25.
9. *The Prize Cases,* 2 Black 635 (1863).
10. 4 Wall. 475.
11. *Georgia* v. *Stanton,* 6 Wall. 50 (1868).
12. 135 U.S. 1 (1890).
13. Genovese, *The Supreme Court, the Constitution, and Presidential Power,* 153.
14. 158 U.S. 564 (1895).
15. Clinton Rossiter, *The Supreme Court and the Commander in Chief* (Ithaca, NY: Cornell University Press, 1976), 41.
16. *U.S.* v. *Pewee Coal Company,* 341 U.S. 114 (1951).
17. *Goldwater* v. *Carter,* 444 U.S. 996 (1979).
18. *Dames & Moore* v. *Regan* (1981). See also Chapter 8.
19. The Supreme Court denied certiorari in a number of cases, including *Mora* v. *McNamara* (1967), *Mitchell* v. *the United States* (1967), and *Sarnoff* v. *Shultz* (1972); see also *Massachusetts* v. *Laird* (1970) and *Holtzman* v. *Schlesinger* (1973), as cited by C. Herman Pritchett, "The President's Constitutional Position," in Thomas E. Cronin, ed., *Rethinking the Presidency* (Boston: Little, Brown, 1983), 138.
20. Robert J. Sickels, *The Presidency* (Englewood Cliffs, NJ: Prentice-Hall, 1980), 268.
21. Genovese, *The Supreme Court, The Constitution, and Presidential Power,* 169–170.
22. 343 U.S. 579.
23. Genovese, *The Supreme Court, the Constitution, and Presidential Power,* 175.
24. Ibid.
25. 403 U.S. 713 (1971).
26. 467 U.S. 297 (1972).
27. 418 U.S. 683 (1974).
28. Sickels, *The Presidency,* 265.

29. Martin Shapiro, "The Supreme Court: From Warren to Burger," in Anthony King, ed., *The New Political System* (Washington, DC: American Enterprise Institute, 1978), 184.

30. Alpheus Thomas Mason, William M. Beaney, and Donald Grier Stephenson, Jr., *American Constitutional Law,* 7th ed. (Englewood Cliffs, NJ: Prentice-Hall, 1983), 86.

31. Shapiro, "The Supreme Court," 184.

32. 457 U.S. 749, as cited by Louis Fisher, *Constitutional Conflicts Between Congress and the President* (Princeton, NJ: Princeton University Press, 1985), 327.

33. Ibid.

34. 420 U.S. 35.

35. 343 U.S. 579 (1952).

36. 7 Howard 1.

37. Pritchett, *The American Constitution,* 2nd ed. (New York: McGraw-Hill, 1968), 82–83.

38. Richard A. Watson and Norman C. Thomas, *The Politics of the Presidency* (New York: Wiley, 1983), 240.

39. Robert Scigliano, "The Presidency and the Judiciary," in Michael Nelson, ed., *The Presidency and the Political System* (Washington, DC: Congressional Quarterly Press, 1984), 414.

40. Genovese, *The Supreme Court, the Constitution, and Presidential Power,* 166.

41. Pritchett, "The President's Constitutional Position," 126–127.

42. Scigliano, "The Presidency and the Judiciary," 410–411.

43. Ibid.

44. Ibid.

45. Glendon Schubert, *The Presidency in the Courts* (Minneapolis: University of Minnesota, 1957), 185.

46. Scigliano, "The Presidency and the Judiciary," 411. See *Ex Parte Quirin,* 317 U.S. 1 (1942).

47. Ibid.

48. 276 U.S. 394.

49. Ibid.

50. 293 U.S. 388.

51. 295 U.S. 495.

52. 299 U.S. 304.

53. 301 U.S. 1.

54. *Hammer* v. *Dagenhart,* 247 U.S. 251 (1918); *Bailey* v. *Drexel Furniture Company,* 259 U.S. 20 (1922).

55. 312 U.S. 126 (1941).

56. Ibid.

57. Schubert, *The Presidency in the Courts,* 267.

58. Edward S. Corwin, *Total War and the Constitution* (New York: Knopf, 1947), 45.

59. Pritchett, *The American Constitution,* 202–203.

60. Robert A. Dahl, "Decision-Making in a Democracy: The Supreme Court as a National Policy-Maker," *Journal of Public Law,* 6, 1 (1958), 285.

61. Henry J. Abraham, *The Judicial Process,* 4th ed. (New York: Oxford University Press, 1980), 80.

62. For a list of appointments to the Supreme Court from 1789 to 1979, see Ibid., 56–58.

63. Ibid., 74.

64. Ibid., 70–71.

65. Silas Bent, *Justice Oliver Wendell Holmes* (New York: Garden City Publishing Company, 1932), 248, as cited by Abraham, *The Judicial Process,* 71.

66. The figure is even higher for appointees to the federal district and appellate courts—approximately 94 percent of the appointees have been of the same political persuasion as the president. Henry Abraham, *Justices and Presidents: A Political History of Appointments to the Supreme Court* (New York: Penguin Books, 1974), 59.

67. Scigliano, *The Supreme Court and the President*, 146. This section relies heavily upon this excellent text.

68. Ibid., 126.

69. Ibid.

70. Ibid., 125–126.

71. Ibid., 131.

72. Ibid., 158.

73. Ibid., 137.

74. Abraham, *Justices and Presidents*, 246.

75. Howard Kurtz, "The Ideology of Federal Judgeships," *The Washington Post Weekly Edition*, April 15, 1985. Reagan's opportunity to pick such a large number of appointees was due mainly to the 98th Congress's action in 1984 creating 85 additional district and appellate judgeships.

76. Robert H. Birkby, "The Courts: Forty More Years?" in Michael Nelson, ed., *The Elections of 1984* (Washington, DC: Congressional Quarterly Press, 1985), 250.

77. Kurtz, "The Ideology of Federal Judgeships," 9.

78. Ibid.

79. Ibid., 9.

80. Ibid., 10.

81. *Washington Post*, September 19, 1985.

82. Benjamin I. Page and Mark P. Petracca, *The American Presidency* (New York: McGraw-Hill, 1983), 294.

83. Schubert, *The Presidency in the Courts*, 258.

84. *Hirabayashi v. United States*, 320 U.S. 81 (1943); *Korematsu v. United States*, 323 U.S. 214 (1944).

85. Rossiter, *The Supreme Court and the Commander in Chief*, 99–100.

86. *The New York Times*, June 24, 1983.

87. James MacGregor Burns, J. W. Peltason, and Thomas E. Cronin, *Government by the People*, 12th ed. (Englewood Cliffs, NJ: Prentice-Hall, 1984), 366.

88. *Immigration and Naturalization Service v. Chadha*, 462 U.S. 919 (1983). This case involved a Kenyan citizen who sought to avoid deportation to his country. The U.S. attorney general had ruled that Chadha could remain in the United States and the House of Representatives, exercising the "one house veto" permitted by law in such cases, overruled him. But the Supreme Court sided with the president's chief legal officer.

89. 444 U.S. 996.

90. 453 U.S. 654.

91. The discussion in this section relies heavily on Sheldon Goldman, *Constitutional Law and Supreme Court Decision-Making* (New York: Harper & Row, 1982), 784–787.

chapter *12*

The Public Presidency

The twentieth century marks the rise of the "public" or rhetorical presidency. This political phenomenon has been described as follows:

> Popular or mass rhetoric which Presidents once employed only rarely, now serves as one of their principal tools in attempting to govern the nation. Whatever doubts Americans may now entertain about the limitations of presidential leadership, they do not consider it unfitting or inappropriate for presidents to attempt to "move" the public by programmatic speeches that exhort and set forth grand and ennobling views.[1]

Since the president is the chief policymaker in the nation, it is understandable why presidents devote so much time to rhetorical messages to win popular support for their programs. Indeed, if a time study were made of the chief executive's work schedule, it would soon be clear that next to national security, foreign policy, and ceremonial chief of state duties, a major segment of their time is spent speaking and lobbying to win public and congressional support for their programs.

In this chapter we will explore how the governing styles of presidents affect the style of presidential rhetoric. We will review how the nineteenth-century conception of the "head of state" presidency has been replaced by the "leader of the people" concept in the twentieth century. The president as the nation's agenda-setter plays a major role in molding public opinion. Special attention will be given to Ronald Reagan's effective use of rhetoric and his communications skills. Finally, a section will be devoted to the rise of the "plebiscitary president," described by one commentator as a president who endeavors to build "a direct, unmeditated relationship between himself and the American people" and who depends upon mass approval of his actions to maintain his standing as leader of the nation.[2] Spawned by the mass media and abetted by the decline of political parties in this country, the plebiscitary president may pose a more serious problem to democratic government than is presently realized. We will also look at the phenomenon of rising public expectations of the president, and the growing inability of recent chief executives, in the face of recognized national limitations and declining resources, to respond to these persistent demands.

Since the advent of television, Americans have become so accustomed to watching and listening to the president on the evening network television news programs that the president has become a part of our daily life. Seldom does a day pass that the president's activities or public pronouncements are not fully reported across the land. Clearly, the president's growing ability to reach mass constituencies and penetrate an individual's life space with his rhetoric has marked a new era of presidential leadership.

THE EARLY PERIOD

The public presidency, however, has not always dominated the American scene. Prior to this century, one team of political scientists has reminded us: "Popular leadership through rhetoric was suspect."[3] Presidents rarely spoke directly to the people, and even if they had wanted to, they lacked the magic of mass communication. But there is little evidence available to show that those earlier chief executives craved the opportunity to address the American people, or to go out frequently, in President Lyndon Johnson's words, "to press the flesh." Instead, they preferred written communication between the branches of government.

George Washington, who viewed his office as a "head of state" position, seldom delivered more than one major address per year and that one—the Annual Address (now called the State of the Union speech)—was virtually mandated by the Constitution. His audience was limited to the members of Congress and the handful of onlookers in the gallery. Thomas Jefferson, who conducted an "open" presidency compared to many of his successors, even ceased delivering the annual message in person—a precedent not broken until Woodrow Wilson decided to appear personally before Congress in 1913.[4] During this long hiatus the clerk of the House of Representatives read the speech to those lawmakers who chose to listen to him drone on. No TV cameras, no radios. "Media opportunities" had not yet entered the American vocabulary.

The Washington-Jefferson "head of state" model, characterized by few public speeches, continued throughout the nineteenth century. Unlike the numerous "policy speeches" of the modern era, the oratory of nineteenth-century chief executives consisted mainly of patriotic orations, discussion of a constitutional issue, and perhaps the conduct of war. Seldom did the president go to the people. In current parlance, the president maintained a low profile. In one conspicuous exception to this rule—President Andrew Johnson's speaking tour in the summer before the 1866 off-year congressional elections—the campaign "not only failed but was considered highly irregular."[5] Most other nineteenth-century presidents were content to perform the routine duties of the presidency and defer to Congress on major policy issues.

TWENTIETH-CENTURY DEVELOPMENTS

Significantly, the emergence of the public or rhetorical presidency at the turn of the century coincides with the rise of mass circulation daily newspapers and of the United States as a world power. Between 1875 and 1900 the daily circulation of newspapers throughout the country jumped from 2.6 to 15 million.[6] Undoubtedly the massive growth in population—from 4 million in 1790 to 76 million in 1900—convinced some leaders, such as Teddy Roosevelt and Woodrow Wilson, that the traditional methods of indirect political discourse were no longer adequate in the modern state.

Theodore Roosevelt's stewardship theory of leadership style personified the new public presidency. The first modern president to recognize the power of the media, Teddy Roosevelt called the presidency a "bully pulpit" and delighted in taking his messages "over the heads of Congress" directly to the people, who he said are "the masters of both Congress and the President."[7] Unlike his predecessors, Roosevelt cultivated the Washington press corps. The Rough Rider president clearly recognized that the press was the primary link between himself and the American people. The national press, in turn, found the colorful Roosevelt good copy and delighted in telling readers about Teddy and his exploits. Roosevelt's considerable oratorical talents and his gifted pen—he didn't need the stable of speech writers that recent presidents view as indispensable—exemplified the new rhetorical presidency.

But it was Woodrow Wilson who brought public oratory to the forefront of American politics with his dramatic appearances before Congress—shattering more than a century's precedent of presidential nonattendance. That President Wilson chose to move into the national spotlight as soon as he had taken the oath of office should have occasioned few surprises, for he had spelled out his concept of the public presidency in the Blumenthal Lectures he gave at Columbia University only a few years earlier:

> His is the only national voice in affairs. Let him once win the admiration and confidence of the country, and no other single force can withstand him, no combination of forces will easily overpower him. His position takes the imagination of the country. He is the representative of no constituence, but of the whole people.[8]

Better than anyone, Wilson understood that when it comes to telling the country what it needs to hear, no one is in a better position than the president of the United States. Wilson's concept of the public presidency, however, did not always achieve the ends he had in mind. His nationwide speaking tour to go over the heads of the Senate to win public support for United States membership in the League of Nations ended abruptly with his physical collapse in Colorado and the subsequent rejection by the Senate of the League of Nations Covenant (contained in the Treaty of Versailles) in 1919.[9] Still, as James W. Ceaser and his colleagues have pointed out: "Wilson articulated the doctrinal foundations of the rhetorical presidency and thereby provided an alternative theoretical model to that of the Founders. In Wilson's view the greatest power in modern democratic regimes lay potentially with the popular leader who could sway or—to use his word—'interpret' the wishes of the people."[10]

The Wilsonian concept of the rhetorical presidency consists of two major elements. One, the president should employ oratory to create an active public opinion that will pressure Congress into accepting his program. According to Wilson the scholar, the president has no means of compelling Congress to accept his views except through public opinion. To advance public policy, the president speaks to Congress not directly, but through his popular addresses.[11] Two, the President must tap the public's feelings and articulate its wishes if he hopes to advance his legislative program. Modern presidents understand that "rhetoric does not instill old and established principles as much as it seeks to infuse a sense of vision into the President's legislative program."[12]

Since the New Deal era, which also coincided with the golden age of radio, the presidency has become the most visible national office. FDR's twice-a-week press conferences altered the way the national media covered national politics. Henceforth the White House would become the center of the national political stage, and the president would always be in the news. And a permanent new role would be added to the president's job description: communicator in chief.[13] With this steady expansion in presidential visibility would come heightened expectations of presidential performance. Hand in hand with advances in communications have also come the steady proliferation of interest groups organized to promote the demands of their membership. These people expect the president to respond to their needs. In many instances, the president may, in turn, need the support of these organized groups outside government in order to generate support for his policies on Capitol Hill. Consequently, his rhetorical appeals to these groups have become an important aspect of presidential leadership. Presidents are, of course, importuned daily to speak to trade and professional associations, conventions, university commencements, veterans groups, trade union conclaves, and local government associations. Indeed, as Samuel Kernell points out: "The real explosion in presidential talk has occurred in the class of minor addresses. Presidents Nixon, Carter, and Reagan have surpassed their predecessors use of such rhetoric by nearly fivefold."[14]

Plainly, the continuing requirement of the president to win and maintain support for his policies has fostered an outpouring of presidential rhetoric that shows no signs of declining in length or volume. Indeed, in view of the steady growth of the president's responsibilities and the massive spread of televised and radio communication over the past half-century, it seems safe to predict that presidential rhetoric will never again decline to the level of the Harding-Coolidge era of the 1920s.

The rhetorical presidency and the rise of mass communications grew in tandem, especially after Franklin D. Roosevelt's arrival in the White House in

1933. Earlier, Theodore Roosevelt and Woodrow Wilson had used the presidential "bully pulpit" to influence public opinion. But to reach the public, their channel of communication was restricted to the mass circulation daily newspapers. Neither could hope to match the advantage FDR enjoyed with the newly expanded radio networks. Between 1928 and 1932, the number of radio sets doubled—from 9 to 18 million. By 1935, the number had jumped to 26 million sets.[15] For the first time in history, a president's voice was within reach of 50 to 60 million listeners. Moreover, the two major radio networks, NBC and CBS, had enough affiliates to blanket the entire country and give simultaneous coverage to a single speaker.[16]

Unlike metropolitan newspapers, which focused most of their news on local happenings, network radio served as a nationalizing force in the news. National stories, especially news of the president's programs and activities, enabled the president to exploit the new channel of radio communication and enlarge his potential audience throughout the United States. Instead of being one voice among many, the president's rhetoric became the dominant voice in the American political dialogue. Never again would the president have to operate in the shadow of the legislative branch, as was the case with most nineteenth-century presidents.

Only six days after his inauguration, for example, FDR made his first fireside chat to the nation to explain to the American public why he had closed all the banks, what he planned to do to restore their financial health, and what cooperation he expected from panicky depositors. Within the next 24 hours many banks reopened, large amounts of hoarded currency were redeposited, the banking crisis was halted, and Roosevelt in this swift action had established himself as a close friend and concerned leader to each of millions of apprehensive listeners.[17] Overnight, the president had exploited a new channel of communication, with its huge audience. As explained by Richard L. Rubin:

> Radio linked him personally and directly to the people. No interpretive screen mediated between Roosevelt and people receiving his voice, as it did with the print press. Radio gave Roosevelt the opportunity to present his program, his voice and his personality directly to his constituency. For Roosevelt, radio served as an effective communications alternative, a mechanism of person-to-person contact by which he could bypass a hostile commercial press. It was, in essence, an electronic adaptation of Bryan's national lecture program, and it enabled Roosevelt to react to his audience directly and instantaneously.[18]

To illustrate the impact of the growing influence of the rhetorical presidency, FDR's weekly mail from the American public ran an average of 35,000 to 55,000 pieces per week—ten times the amount of mail received by Herbert Hoover at the close of his term.[19] Beyond doubt, his fireside chats, frequent press conferences, and the steady stream of White House announcements had altered the relationship between the president and the rank-and-file voters. In the words of Richard L. Rubin: "By claiming and holding a newly-central position in mass communications, by orchestrating mass support for his public policies, and by symbolizing in his office the aspirations of political reform, Roosevelt effected a change in the relationship of the presidency, mass communications, and the public at large."[20]

More than any of his predecessors, "Roosevelt recognized the importance of the presidency not only as the center of government but also as the center of *political information.*"[21] Roosevelt's rhetorical presidency enabled him to communicate with the American public as no president had ever done, despite the overwhelming opposition of most newspaper publishers, especially the Hearst and Scripps chains. By 1935, for example, 63 companies controlled 328 newspapers, with 41 percent of all daily circulation and 52 percent of all Sunday distribution.[22] Although William Randolph Hearst had initially supported FDR in 1932, when the newspaper tycoon saw the direction of Roosevelt's New Deal programs, he switched his huge news chain to an all-out attack on the administration. With almost one-quarter of all Sunday and almost one out of eight daily newspaper readers, Hearst generated formidable opposition to the Roosevelt administration. The Scripps chain, one of the three largest in the nation, originally supported FDR too, but soon turned into a bitter New Deal enemy.

Despite this phalanx of newspaper opposition, Roosevelt used his rhetorical skills to make the White House the news center of the nation. His skillful exploitation of radio enabled FDR to restructure political communications and make radio a counterforce to newspaper influence over public opinion. As FDR used to say: "Just let me make the news on the front pages, and I don't care what they say on the editorial pages." Richard L. Rubin summed up FDR's rhetorical presidency as follows:

> He established a faster more centralized and more direct circuitry between the mass public and the presidency than possible before him and used the unique personal qualities of radio to deeply penetrate into a vast new listening audience.[23]

Franklin Delano Roosevelt, a Wilsonian in his own right, having served as assistant secretary of the navy in the two Wilson administrations, echoed his mentor's eloquent rhetoric. FDR's oratory surpassed Wilson's and moved the nation through its darkest days since the Civil War. Only a few of his bitterest critics challenged Roosevelt's claim that the presidency is "preeminently a place of moral leadership." Above all, the public president must inspire confidence in times of great adversity, as FDR did during the banking crisis of the Great Depression. His warm voice in all its resonant fullness came over the radio to say, "We have nothing to fear but fear itself," and a nation on the verge of panic moved forward in steadfastness and trust.

Clearly, a strong president has no choice but to use mass communication to sway public opinion. Every message to Congress, every speech made around the country, and even his veto messages must be gauged to influence people. No president excelled FDR in his skill in molding public opinion and in its use in achieving his goals. Despite a strong isolationist movement in the country, Roosevelt used his public addresses to alert the country to the growing menace of Nazi Germany even before Adolf Hitler swallowed up Austria and Czechoslovakia in

1938–39. But FDR had to move cautiously, even after the fall of France in May 1940, for fear of triggering further isolationist opposition to American involvement in the European conflict. FDR knew when to moderate his rhetoric in order to have the best chance of persuading the American public in the long run to come to the support of Great Britain and its allies in their gallant stand against Hitler.

To the post-World War II generation, Roosevelt's skillful molding of public opinion to oppose Nazi and Japanese totalitarianism before the United States entry into World War II might not seem a remarkable accomplishment, but merely a sensible response to imminent danger. But the reader should be reminded that so powerful was the America First isolationist movement in Congress and across the country in this era that only four months before Pearl Harbor the one-year extension of the first peacetime draft in history passed in August 1941 by a single vote—203–202![24] Without Roosevelt's public assurances of the overwhelming danger posed by the Nazi aggressors during the congressional debate on this measure, the United States would have been almost totally unprepared to wage war after the Japanese struck Pearl Harbor on December 7, 1941.

Truman proved to be an apt pupil of FDR in using masterful rhetoric to win over a doubting Congress. In one of the most influential presidential addresses delivered since World War II, Truman's March 21, 1947, Truman Doctrine speech in defense of aid to Greece and Turkey not only won support for that bill, but also opened the door for congressional acceptance of the Marshall Plan, which paved the way for the postwar economic reconstruction of Western Europe.[25]

Televised presidential addresses by Kennedy, Johnson, and Nixon, according to pollster Louis Harris, also produced positive responses in nearly every case.[26] Table 12.1 shows the results of Harris polls conducted before and after televised addresses by these presidents. It will be noted that in each case the percentages of the population favoring the president's policy or action increased,

Table 12.1 IMPACT OF TELEVISED PRESIDENTIAL SPEECHES

TV Appearance	Percent Favoring Policy	
	Before	After
JFK announces nuclear test ban treaty—July 26, 1963	73%	81%
JFK appeals for tax cuts—August 18, 1963	62	66
LBJ announces resumption of bombing of Vietnam —January 31, 1966	61	73
LBJ supports stronger gun control legislation—June 7, 1968	71	81
RMN announces phased withdrawal from Vietnam —May 14, 1969	49	67
RMN announces sending of U.S. troops to Cambodia—April 30, 1970	7	50

Source: "Equal Time for Congress: Congressional Hearings, 1970," in Robert O. Blanchard, ed., *Congress and the News Media* (New York: Hastings House, 1974), 106–113, as cited by George C. Edwards III, *The Public Presidency* (New York: St. Martin's Press, 1983), 43.

ranging from 4 percent for JFK's tax proposal to 43 percent for Nixon after he sent troops into Cambodia. More recently, Reagan's televised speeches in support of his tax and budget cuts in 1981 and the invasion of Grenada in 1983 orchestrated exactly the response he wanted from his audience—an overwhelmingly favorable reaction from the American public, coupled with thousands of phone calls and telegrams to the White House and a flood of letters to congressmen urging "Support the President." For the first time since early 1981, his Gallup poll approval rating rose above 50 percent.[27]

IMPACT OF THE MASS MEDIA

More than anything else, the rise of the mass media has changed the way presidents communicate with the American public. The televised picture and the radio transmission of the president's voice have replaced the written word. The old maxim that a picture is worth a thousand words explains better than anything why TV has drastically changed the president's relationship with the American people over the past three decades. In the age of television, the size of the president's audience averages 50 to 60 million viewers. Equally important, with vastly increased audiences the role of the speech itself has changed. Presidents have come to understand that it is the visual performance, not the tangible text, that creates the public image. With only slight exaggeration, James W. Ceaser and his associates note: "What is not seen or heard today does not exist."[28] No president has been more adept than Ronald Reagan before the cameras. His ability to clarify complex issues through a simple, straightforward, smoothly delivered message has made him the most effective national leader since Roosevelt.

Modern presidents feel the pressure to speak more frequently and to engage in a continuous campaign to keep their message before the public. The president's words, however, are more likely to have an ephemeral quality about them, and the more the president speaks, the less value can be put on any one speech he delivers.[29] Indeed, Ceaser and his colleagues are certainly correct in observing: "One of the great ironies of the modern presidency is that as the President relies more on rhetoric to govern, he finds it more difficult to deliver a truly important speech, one that will stand by itself and continue to shape events."[30] It taxes one's memory to recall a televised presidential speech that has had the long-term impact of Washington's Farewell Address, the Monroe Doctrine, or Lincoln's Emancipation Proclamation.

Presidential speeches today are not directed to the audiences they are personally addressing, but to millions of Americans viewing the speech on the TV set in their living rooms. It is therefore not surprising that present-day speeches "tend to be written so that any segment can be taken to stand by itself—as a self-contained lead. Argument gives way to aphorism."[31]

The roots of the rhetorical presidency can also be traced, in part, to the modern presidential nominating and election campaigns. Prior to 1912, parties conducted the bulk of these campaigns, and the candidates confined themselves almost exclusively to a few public statements on major issues and to written communications with state leaders. Before their nomination, presidential contenders conducted "front porch" campaigns, meaning that small batches of key delegates were invited to visit the candidate's home to bargain with him over future support and patronage—on his front porch, so to speak. William McKinley's highly successful 1896 nominating drive was a classic model of this old-fashioned nominating campaign, as he entertained visiting delegates at his Canton, Ohio, home. Even as late as 1932, Franklin D. Roosevelt never left Washington, DC, or his Hyde Park, New York, country estate to campaign in search of delegates. Instead, FDR and his predecessors left it to their political drummers to tour the country to round up delegate support.

Not until former Minnesota governor Harold Stassen and Tennessee Senator Estes Kefauver launched their personal hand-shaking tours and state-to-state campaigning for their party's nomination after World War II did the nominating race take on the character of today's contests. First of all, the candidates, unlike prior contenders, designated themselves to run. Presidential candidates mount highly personal appeals to differentiate their candidacies from those of their rivals. For the most part, they ignore state and local party leaders and seek their support directly from voters. Moreover, presidential candidates establish their own independent campaign organizations, equipped with their own fundraising experts, speechwriters, media specialists, advance men, and so on. These organizations operate entirely independent of the national and state parties.

Today, if a candidate is successful in winning the nomination and presidency, members of the campaign team are moved into the White House and executive agencies to staff the top positions. They owe their loyalty to no party, only to the president. Several commentators, including this writer, have spoken about the continuous or permanent nominating campaign.[32] Indeed, for a period of at least two years, presidential aspirants depend mostly on their television rhetoric and personal appearances to fill in the long months before the nominating race officially opens after New Year's Day of the presidential election year.

Governor Woodrow Wilson of New Jersey was the first victorious presidential candidate to undertake a full-scale speaking tour around the country during the fall campaign. To Wilson's way of thinking, despite his strong commitment to party rule, candidates should replace parties as the main rhetorical instrument for winning elections. "Indeed, with Wilson the distinction between campaigning and governing is blurred, as both involved the same essential function of persuading through popular oratory."[33] Partly a result of Wilson's influence, whistle-stopping and political barnstorming around the country became by FDR's time the standard operating procedure of presidential candidates during the general election campaign. Especially since the end of World War II, presidential campaigning had had an important impact on the process of governing. James W. Ceaser and his associates have summed it up this way: "So formative has the campaign become of our tastes for oratory and of our conception of leadership that presidential speech and governing have come more and more to imitate the model of the campaign. In a dramatic reversal, campaigns set the tone for governing rather than governing for campaigns."[34]

In the present era, rhetorical skills and a candidate's ability to perform well before the television camera have even become a significant factor in determining an aspirant's chances of winning the nomination and election. Candidates who are short on rhetorical skills and whose television performances are below standard face a serious risk of being passed over in the nominating sweepstakes. Even a modern-day Thomas Jefferson, despite his recognized rhetorical skills, could well be eliminated from serious consideration because his high-pitched, squeaky voice might annoy television viewers. Some commentators also doubt that Abraham Lincoln, somber and unphotogenic, would have done well in the age of television.

THE PRESIDENT AS AGENDA-SETTER

The rise of the rhetorical presidency has made the president the preeminent agenda-setter for the nation. Though the Founding Fathers may not have fully recognized how crucial the single chief executive could become in managing the federal government, they were aware of the need for unified action in times of crisis.

In the twentieth century the rise of the welfare state, the maintenance of a huge military establishment, and the United State's superpower role in the world have multiplied the responsibilities of the federal government. The chief manager of this gigantic enterprise is, of course, the president of the United States. He is expected to provide the leadership and energy to make the government function. No wonder the president's State of the Union message, the federal budget message, the Economic Report, and numerous special messages set the national agenda for the year. Beyond question, it is the president, not Congress, who dictates the issues that will occupy the nation's attention. Indeed, writes Bruce Miroff, "Press or partisan criticism may challenge a president on the form or details of his actions, but the outline of reality that he has sketched is usually left intact." Miroff continues, "His words and actions receive far more coverage from the mass media than the efforts of other political actors or institutions."[35]

By initiating action, the president can immediately occupy the center of the national stage. Presidential pronouncements will set the terms for political discussion and debate, whether the issue is a domestic problem or a foreign policy question. Thus, within hours after moving into the White House, Franklin D. Roosevelt began setting the nation's agenda—first, the national bank holiday, then the anti-Depression measures and regulatory reforms, to be followed within two years by the Social Security Act, collective bargaining legislation, and a host of other New Deal proposals. Similarly, Lyndon B. Johnson, capitalizing on his role as John F. Kennedy's successor, soon put Congress to work on some of JFK's top agenda proposals—civil rights legislation, federal aid to education—and a host of his own Great Society programs—Medicare, the Job Corps, urban mass transit.

Ronald Reagan's agenda-setting skills were never more evident than in his masterful timing to obtain continued funding of the controversial MX missile in the spring of 1985. Though Congress had in 1984 threatened to cut off further funding of the MX missile, President Reagan six months later won approval by close votes in both the Senate and House for another round of funding the controversial missile. By tying in the MX missile—dubbed the Peacekeeper by the media-minded president—with the Geneva arms control negotiations with the Soviet Union, Reagan mounted one of the most polished rhetorical campaigns seen in the nation's capital for many years. "The vote on the Peacekeeper is also a vote on Geneva," Reagan told a major business group. "Rejecting the Peacekeeper will knock the legs out from under the negotiating table," he continued.[36] As part of the highly professional lobbying campaign, Mr. Reagan spoke to 150 members of Congress in small groups at the White House, constantly emphasizing that the United States would lose leverage at the Geneva talks without the MX. Amplifying on this theme in his weekly radio broadcast, Reagan said that such a signal would tell the Soviet Union that "they can gain more through propaganda and stonewalling than through serious negotiations."[37]

Called "heavy-duty brainwashing" by one administration official, Reagan's rhetorical forays soon paid off in Congress. Although Democratic House leaders had confidently predicted two months earlier that they had enough votes to kill further funding of the MX, the anti-MX votes began melting away under the relentless pressure of the president's lobbying campaign. Two days before the scheduled vote in the House of Representatives, he recalled his chief arms negotiator in Geneva, Max M. Kampelman, to help twist legislative arms on Capitol Hill. Throughout this test of wills between the president and Congress, rarely did a day pass without the president "going public" to defend his MX funding proposal.[38]

To be sure, press or partisan criticism may challenge the details of presidential action, but the issues and the president's position will dominate the debate. Because the president sets the agenda, however, does not necessarily mean that the president's position will always prevail—indeed, on many domestic issues the president generally considers himself lucky if he can carry the day half of the time. Presidents have also come to recognize that generally they will experience a loss of popularity during the course of their terms (see Table 12.2). Especially if the public assesses the president's job performance negatively, the president will generally have a difficult time getting congressional attention for his top priority agenda items. His rhetoric will fall on deaf ears. For example, Carter's rhetorical campaign to obtain a major energy conservation measure failed miserably, despite four nationally televised addresses to the American people during his first 30 months in office.

His first speech, delivered less than a month after his inauguration, generated favorable media coverage. However, Carter's initial appearance before the cameras—he wore a cardigan sweater and spoke before a crackling fire—produced more commentary on the president's informality than the content of his message. Despite Carter's televised appeals to the American people on the energy crisis—he called it the "moral equivalent of war"—the Gallup poll reported one year later the exact same percentage of the public (41 percent) felt that the energy problem was "very serious" as before Carter's speeches.[39]

Similarly, Gerald Ford endeavored three years earlier to wage a major battle against inflation with his national WIN (Whip Inflation Now) campaign,

Table 12.2   **THE RECORD OF POSTWAR PRESIDENTS IN PUBLIC OPINION POLLS**

	Beginning of Term	Ending of Term*	Percentage Point Decline
Harry Truman	87	32	55%
Dwight Eisenhower	68	49	19
John Kennedy	72	58	14
Lyndon Johnson	78	40	38
Richard Nixon	59	24	35
Gerald Ford	71	45	26
Jimmy Carter	66	33	33
Ronald Reagan	51	55†	44

*For full terms as of July preceding the presidential elections.
†June 1984. A year earlier, however, before the nation's sharp economic recovery, Reagan's popular support stood at 41 percent.
Sources: Various issues of the *Gallup Opinion Index,* as compiled by Samuel Kernell, "The Presidency and the People: The Modern Paradox," in Michael Nelson, ed. *The Presidency and the Political System* (Washington, DC: Congressional Quarterly Press, 1984), 254; data for 1984 collected by author from *Gallup Report* 225, June 1984.

but within a matter of months the country suffered another recession and unemployment, not inflation, became the number one concern of millions of Americans. Most citizens refused to take the president's anti-inflation rhetoric seriously. Clearly, the president's message must closely reflect the concerns of the public if it is to have a positive impact.

For the public president to be a political success, he must create a sense of drama and mystique. Perhaps it is a reflection of the age of television, but the American public expects its presidents to be exciting and upbeat, and leave the distinct impression that they are in charge of the government. By and large, a president's impact on the American public seems to hinge less on his policies than his personal presence. Undoubtedly the Founding Fathers, if they ever returned to earth, would be shocked to learn that the mass media's general assessment of the public president can seemingly make or break his reelection prospects. No matter how forthright and courageous he may be, if he is viewed as clumsy or dull, his political future is likely to become cloudy. For example, Ford was portrayed in the media as clumsy because the TV cameras had shown him bumping his head on a helicopter door, or taking a tumble on the ski slopes at Vail, Colorado. In the same vein, Jimmy Carter came to be viewed as undramatic and dull.[40]

MOLDING PUBLIC OPINION

Strong presidents have never been content just to follow public opinion; rather, they have engaged in a variety of rhetorical approaches to lead the public. As Franklin D. Roosevelt, the master molder of public opinion in the twentieth century, put it: "All our great Presidents were leaders of thought at times when certain historic ideas in the life of the nation had to be clarified."[41] Sometimes the president's goals have been to gain long-term support for the administration's policies; at other times, he has been more interested in obtaining support for a specific program—the Marshall Plan, the Peace Corps, the Civil Rights Acts of 1964 and 1965, the SALT II treaty, the MX missile program. Often both the long- and short-term goals will persuade the president "to go public."

To influence and mold public opinion, modern presidents must, of course, become "great explainers."[42] Invariably they turn to national television, since no other medium routinely gives them instant access to such a huge audience. But no matter how effective a communicator the president is, he must contend with the general attitudes of his audience. As George C. Edwards III has noted: "The public's general lack of interest in politics constrains the president's leadership of public opinion in the long run as well as on a given day."[43] Indeed, the president has to wait until the issues he wants to discuss are on their minds, which generally occurs only when an issue in question is personally affecting their lives. Thus, although the president can use television to reach his multimillion-person audience, the president cannot turn to the American people every time an important issue crosses his mind. If he does, his televised rhetoric will become commonplace and lose its drama and impact.

Consequently, most presidents, following Roosevelt's tactics, will limit their appearances on prime time. Despite the fame and effectiveness of Roosevelt's fireside chats on radio, he made only 30 of them in 12 years.[44] FDR felt that he would "wear out his welcome" if he went to the airwaves too frequently. Reagan, on the other hand, believes that frequent TV appearances to argue his case are the more effective form of leadership.

How successful are these nationwide presidential appeals? Generally, presidents have had less success with domestic issues than foreign affairs. Are there any special explanations for these different attitudes? Foreign policy, for one thing, is more distant from the lives of most Americans. Generally, it is viewed as more complex and based on specialized knowledge. Consequently, the public tends to defer more to the president on these matters than on issues closer to home which they can relate to their own experience. Over and above these factors, Americans are basically individualistic and skeptical of authority, and therefore not especially favorable toward domestic policies that may intrude on their lives. While Americans have been prepared to sacrifice at great lengths during a period of national crisis, they do not like constraints on their lives in peacetime. If inflation is spiraling, Americans want prices controlled but not their incomes. If gasoline lines are growing and greater shortages of supply lie ahead, they still do not want to curtail their driving to save energy.

PRESIDENTIAL ORATORY

Most experts have rated only a handful of presidents as great orators—Lincoln, Wilson, Franklin D. Roosevelt, and John F. Kennedy. Just a shade below this foursome would be Ronald Reagan and Theodore Roosevelt.

Lincoln's place among the great orators is beyond challenge. Wilson's eloquence has also won him a high ranking among presidential orators, but his words failed him when he probably needed them the most—to win popular support for ratification of the Versailles Treaty and membership in the League of Nations. Franklin D. Roosevelt's memorable phrases, "We have nothing to fear but fear itself," "We have a rendezvous with destiny," and his ringing declaration, "A day that will live in infamy," which prefaced his request to Congress for a declaration of war against Japan in December 1941, have assured him a top rating among the all-time great presidential orators. These three presidential orators, it should be noted, all made their mark before the age of television, before the United States assumed its full responsibilities as a world power, and most important, before the nuclear age.

Of the post-World War II presidents whose oratory has exerted the most influence on world opinion, John F. Kennedy would most certainly rate at the top of the list. As the hero of the 1962 Cuban missile crisis, and newly recognized leader of the Western democratic alliance, Kennedy's powerful rhetoric never reached a higher point than during his famous visit to West Berlin—the western enclave a hundred miles behind the Iron Curtain—in July 1963, four months before his assassination. It was estimated that almost half of West Berlin's 2.3 million people turned out to greet the smiling young president. In the words of Herbert S. Parmet, his biographer: "No conquering hero ever received a more enthusiastic reception."[45] Kennedy's address in the Rudolph Wilde Platz outside West Berlin's city hall will long be remembered throughout the free world. Mixing defiance and appeal to pride, Kennedy told the huge crowd what they wanted to hear; indeed, it was almost as if he were campaigning for reelection.

"Two thousand years ago the proudest boast was *civis Romanus sum,*" he said right after his introductory remarks. "Today, in the world of freedom, the proudest boast is *Ich bin ein Berliner.*" Then came the rhetorical challenge: "There are some who say that communism is the wave of the future. Let them come to Berlin. And there are some who say in Europe and elsewhere we can work with the Communists. Let them come to Berlin." He went on to tell them that they lived "in a defended island of freedom, but your life is part of the main," and in conclusion declared: "All free men, wherever they may live, are citizens of Berlin, and, therefore, as a free man, I take pride in the words *Ich bin ein Berliner!*"[46] The ovation was deafening. No German crowd had ever responded as warmly and emotionally as they did to Kennedy, according to one official of the West German government—not even to Hitler at the height of his power.[47]

Several of Kennedy's aides felt that JFK's fiery rhetoric in West Berlin might have jeopardized the prospects for reaching final agreement with the Soviet Union on a limited nuclear weapons test ban treaty. But Kennedy had correctly gauged Soviet behavior, especially that of its leader, Nikita Khrushchev. Less than a month later, the final draft of the Limited Nuclear Test Ban Treaty was signed in Moscow. Unlike the failed ratification of the Versailles Treaty, the Limited Nuclear Test Ban Treaty between the Soviet Union and United States was ratified by the United States Senate in record time—exactly 50 days after the August 5, 1963, signing in the Kremlin—and by a decisive 80 to 19 vote margin, well above the required two-thirds majority.

Actually, the initial steps leading to the negotiations of the Limited Nuclear Test Ban Treaty were taken by Kennedy in his famous American University speech of June 10, 1963, described as a landmark in the history of post-World War II Soviet-American relations. Kennedy's American University address spelled out clearly JFK's views on the dangers of a nuclear holocaust and extended a friendly hand to Soviets, with an invitation to open discussions on nuclear disarmament. The highlights of the Kennedy message signaled an unmistakable desire to turn away from the Cold War. The Soviets, exhibiting a growing concern over the rising military power of Communist China, proved to be receptive to Kennedy's overture. Soon thereafter, Kennedy announced a significant breakthrough toward improvement of Soviet-American relations—the negotiation of a direct Washington-Moscow teletype line, the so-called hot line. Ten days after his American University speech, the two nations signed a memorandum of understanding to establish the hot line. This teletype link between the White House and the Kremlin became operational before the end of the summer of 1963.

Presidential rhetoric, as John F. Kennedy demonstrated, should never be discounted. The words of Kennedy, as much as those of any American president, have had a profound impact upon the long-term relations between the Soviet Union and the United States, underscoring, even two decades later, the continuing opportunities for avoidance of mutual nuclear destruction. The fact that the Limited Nuclear Test Ban Treaty remains in force, despite all the recriminations and rhetoric exchanged between the two superpowers before and since then, attests once again to Kennedy's diplomatic skills and the tremendous impact his rhetoric has had in shaping the course of events between East and West since his tragic death in November 1963.

Sometimes a president's rhetoric can produce remarkable results on the domestic front too. The power of the president's rhetoric was never more evident than in Kennedy's public tongue-lashing of Roger Blough, U.S. Steel Company chairman, following Big Steel's sudden announcement of a $6 per ton increase in April 1962, after seemingly having assured the president that no price increase would take place as part of the recent wage settlement between the steel companies and United Steel Workers. Few public figures have ever undergone the blistering verbal attack that JFK directed against the U.S. Steel chairman:

> The simultaneous and identical actions . . . constitute a wholly unjustifiable and irresponsible defiance of the public interest. In this serious hour in our nation's history, with grave crises in Berlin and Southeast Asia when . . . restraints and sacrifice are being asked of every citizen, the American people will find it hard, as I do, to accept a situation in which a tiny handful of steel executives, whose pursuit of private power and profit exceeds their sense of public responsibility, can show such utter contempt for the interest of 184 million Americans.[48]

What happened to the steel price increase? Two days after a series of behind-the-scenes meetings, in which Kennedy administration officials persuaded several small steel companies not to go along with Big Steel's price hike, and the president's brother, Attorney General Robert F. Kennedy, began looking into possible collusion and price-fixing between U.S. Steel and Bethlehem Steel, the second largest producer, U.S. Steel Chairman Blough backed down. Big Steel announced that the 3.5 percent price hike had been rescinded. The company spokesperson explained: "The price decision was made in light of the competitive developments today and all other current circumstances, including the removal of a serious obstacle to proper relations between government and business."[49]

This statement announcing Big Steel's cave-in to the president of the United States was, of course, a left-handed way of saying that it was under government pressure and had no alternative. Bethlehem Steel and the other big steel producers immediately fell in line and rescinded their price hikes too. And less than a week later Mr. Blough, at President Kennedy's invitation, returned to the White House for a private visit. Kennedy, who had castigated the tycoon only a few days earlier while the entire nation listened in, assured Blough that he held no grudges. The president reportedly said that he recognized the industry's need to modernize its old plant facilities, promised that the government would help in this process, and assured Blough that he would tell the nation so at his next press conference.[50] This magnanimous action by the popular young president reflected, most president watchers would agree, the most effective aspect of the rhetorical presidency.

Lyndon Johnson also made one of the most dramatic speeches of the twentieth century in March 1965 during the height of the civil rights protests. The nationally televised scenes of Reverend Martin Luther King, Jr., and his freedom marchers being brutally attacked by police and mounted state troopers at the outset of their planned, peaceful 50-mile march from Selma, Alabama, to Montgomery, the capital, in March 1965 horrified the nation and provoked President Johnson to demand prompt passage of federal voting rights legislation. So outraged was the American public at the scenes of Reverend King's peaceful marchers being bull-whipped and clubbed by local authorities that Johnson had no choice but to demand an immediate end to the brutal police action. No other American president introduced a civil rights bill—indeed, any domestic legislation—with such fanfare and rhetorical flourish.

Johnson had quickly sensed the mood of the public and Congress. But instead of immediately sending federal troops to Alabama and going on national television, he let the full impact of Bloody Sunday sink into the nation's conscience. In the midst of the turmoil, Governor George C. Wallace of Alabama asked for a meeting with Johnson, who granted the request. In the Oval Office they discussed, among other things, the question of federal troops. Two days later, Johnson "federalized" the Alabama National Guard as a necessary measure to halt further violence and to demonstrate that he was acting reluctantly but out of necessity.[51] Meanwhile, the Justice Department was putting together the final draft of the proposed Voting Rights Act.

Eight days after the brutal confrontation in Selma, Alabama, President Johnson addressed a joint session of Congress—and the American people. The three TV networks quickly acceded to his request for prime time coverage. All members of the cabinet were present for the address, as were members of the Supreme Court, leading members of the civil rights organizations, and other prominent citizens were in the House gallery.

"I speak tonight," Johnson began,

for the dignity of man and the destiny of democracy. . . . At times history and fate meet at a single time in a single place to shape a turning point in man's unending search for freedom. . . . So it was a century ago at Appomattox. So it was last week in Selma, Alabama. . . . There is no constitutional issue here. The command of the Constitution is plain. There is no moral issue. It is wrong . . . to deny any of your fellow Americans the right to vote. . . . This time, on this issue, there must be no delay, no hesitation, and no compromise with our purpose. . . . What happened in Selma is part of a far larger movement which reaches into every section and state of America. It is the effort of American negroes to secure for themselves the full blessing of American life. Their cause must be our cause too. Because it is not just negroes, but really it is all of us who must overcome the crippling legacy of bigotry and injustice.[52]

At this point Johnson stopped. He raised his long arms and repeated four words from an old Baptist hymn, now the marching song of the black civil rights movement: "And . . . we . . . shall . . . overcome." Suddenly, as one observer described it, "The whole chamber was on its feet. . . . In the galleries Negroes and whites, some in the rumpled sports shirt of bus rides from the demonstrations, others in trim professional suits, wept unabashedly."[53] All the emotional outpouring was picked up by the network cameras, and the national viewing audience had that rare opportunity to see and hear a presidential speech that would truly shape events for years to come.

Unlike the Civil Rights Act of 1964, which had been stalled by a Senate filibuster for nearly five months before final passage, the Voting Rights Act of 1965 (which banned literacy tests and provided for direct intervention by federal attorneys, if needed, in voter registration cases) passed both houses of Congress within a matter of weeks, reaching Johnson's desk less than two months after his address to Congress. Rarely have a president's words had such an immediate impact upon the conscience of Congress and the American people as President Johnson's rhetoric following the confrontation in Selma. And never again would the nation accord Mr. Johnson the same ringing endorsement they gave him in the days immediately following this nationwide telecast, for within five weeks he went back to Congress to obtain financial backing that would ultimately send 525,000 American troops to South Vietnam. From that day forward, Mr. Johnson's popularity began sagging, never to return to its former high mark. Even more serious, the credibility of President Johnson's rhetoric began to erode; indeed, his "credibility gap" continued to widen to a point that by early 1968 it became, in the eyes of many national observers, a significant factor in his decision not to seek another term in 1968.

PRESIDENT REAGAN'S RHETORIC

Not since John F. Kennedy's ringing addresses of the early 1960s would the nation be treated to such persuasive presidential rhetoric as when Ronald Reagan arrived in the White House in 1981. His first inaugural address signaled that the country had acquired a president who planned to lead the nation in a new direction:

> In the present crisis, government is not the solution to our problem; government is the problem. . . . It is my intention to curb the size and influence of the federal government. . . . It's not my intention to do away with government. It is rather to make it work—work with us, not over us; to stand by our side, not ride on our back. Government can and must provide opportunity, not smother it; foster productivity, not stifle it.[54]

What America heard in his inaugural speech was the same promise—the pro-free enterprise and anti-big government message—that he had been preaching for more than two decades. In his acceptance speech for renomination, in August 1984, Reagan gave the GOP convention and the national television audience another demonstration of the rhetoric that would soon carry him into a second term. He boasted: "Today, of all the major industrial nations of the world, America has the strongest economic growth; one of the lowest inflation rates; the fastest rate of job creation, six and-a-half million jobs in the last year-and-a-half, and the largest increase in real, after-tax personal income since World War II. We're enjoying the highest level of business investment in history."[55] This expansive optimism and pride, and the Reagan theme "America is back," served as the backdrop for launching his successful drive for a second term. Whether future accomplishments would match Reagan's campaign rhetoric still remains to be answered. But Reagan's rhetoric had served him well during his first four years, and he gave every indication that the nation would hear more of the same in his second term.

The central theme of his second inaugural address was a "new American Emancipation, a great national drive to tear down economic barriers and liberate the spirit of enterprise." Mr. Reagan warned:

> We must never again abuse the trust of working men and women by sending their earnings on a futile chase after the demands of a bloated federal establishment. You elected us in 1980 to end this prescription for disaster, and I don't believe you reelected us in 1984 to reverse course.[56]

The secret of Reagan's success, most pundits have agreed, has been to "concentrate on a few transcendent issues and let the details take care of themselves."[57] During his first term his close associates said that he had only three priorities, (1) economics, (2) economics, (3) economics.[58] His second-term agenda, his close associates said, would be largely confined to three main items: arms control, tax simplification, and the federal budget deficit. Reagan's rhetoric generally contained no surprises, no bold new programs, but rather the reassertion of the standard conservative principles—the need for a smaller federal government, lower taxes, and a strong national defense. One critic, in evaluating Reagan's first inaugural address, entitled it "Shadow or Substance?"[59] The same title might be given to most of Reagan's public addresses.

He has concentrated on the strength of America, its ability to meet any challenge; the president's rhetoric fosters an outpouring of pride and patriotism that leaves his audiences cheering. Even in small groups he has instilled the same sense of pride of accomplishment and challenge to the future. A pep talk to his top aides, delivered shortly after his second inaugural, contained the typical Reagan message: "There's an understandable tendency to think . . . that our great work is behind us," he told them. "Well, that's not true. . . . Our greatest battles lie ahead—all is newness now. We can change America forever."[60]

One veteran Washington commentator, Morton M. Kondracke, contrasted President Reagan's rhetorical style in his State of the Union Message with that of his predecessor, Jimmy Carter.

> If Jimmy Carter had sent Congress a budget as fraught with pain as Ronald Reagan's, his State of the Union Message would have brimmed over with—as one-time chief speechwriter James Fallows puts it—"stern talk about tightening our belts, sharing the sacrifice, taking our medicine and facing hard truths." It's all too possible, says Fallows, that Carter would have recited the list of impending budget cuts, pausing to lecture each interest group affected—farmers, small businessmen, college and recipients, Medicare beneficiaries—on why reduced funding was the only fair outcome.[61]

Unlike other presidents, Mr. Reagan did not even hint that some group might suffer under his budget. He announced: "We can help farmers best not by expanding federal payments, but by making fundamental reforms." The following week his Office of Management and Budget translated this rhetoric into drastic slashes in agricultural price supports. Nothing was said in the second inaugural address about his planned $50 billion cut in domestic spending, to be offered in his 1986 budget. Nor did he mention another of his special concerns—military aid for the anti-Sandinista Contras fighting to overthrow the Marxist government of Nicaragua.

According to White House officials, the avoidance of unpleasant specifics was part of a grand design to keep the message strictly upbeat. Reagan, unlike his predecessors, abandoned the traditional pattern of the State of the Union address and transformed it into a kind of second inaugural address directed to the American people rather than to the members of Congress in his listening audience. "The American people don't necessarily need a laundry list of legislation," reported one White House official. "They need more of 'What is the president thinking?'" The White House aide did not disguise the main purpose of the speech: "Uplift the American spirit, et cetera."[62]

What can be concluded from the Reagan rhetoric? Have we reached a point where, according to the late Marshall McLuhan, the Canadian high priest of communications, "the medium is the message?" Edward W. Chester concluded, after evaluating President Reagan's first inaugural address, that "In Ronald Reagan, the former motion picture and television star and present day conservative Republican ideologue, the style and content meet in harmonious whole."[63] In a prescient observation made in 1981 that has subsequently been confirmed by events, Chester commented:

> If Reagan does succeed as President, it will be due in large part to his skill in successfully communicating programs which run counter to the demands of numerous special interest groups, and to generate a climate of opinion through-

out America which will force a politically divided Congress to enact much, if not most of his proposals into law.[64]

Since then, Washington observers have continued to be amazed at Reagan's skill in winning legislative victories and popular support. Most agree that Reagan's training as an actor—his body language, his gestures, the way he modulates his voice, his sense of timing—all contribute to the calculated way he uses rhetoric.[65] "He plays the game very well—the game of changing rhetoric in response to specific needs and different situations," declared one political scientist. "But there's a key difference between Reagan and other Presidents. Reagan never changes his mind about the fundamentals, about what he wants to accomplish. He conveys a very consistent set of goals and does not lead people to think he's changing direction."[66]

Another feature of Ronald Reagan's rhetorical presidency has been his borrowing of a page from the playbook of leading football coaches: "A good offense is the best defense." Whenever an important aspect of the Reagan economic program has been attacked, the White House has resorted to an aggressive offense: blame the huge deficits on fifty years of profligate spending by past Democratic majorities in the House and Senate; blame Congress for its refusal to cut domestic spending by $50 billion; argue that projected deficits are less undesirable than raising taxes or cutting back on national security; or deny the accuracy of the Congressional Budget Office projections on taxes and revenue. Throughout his first term these tactics helped Reagan keep the political initiative and maintain the posture of a decisive chief executive. By occupying the nation's chief podium, he could mount almost daily verbal blasts at the "big spenders" on Capitol Hill.

He continued these rhetorical flourishes right into the second term. Typically, in one of his favorite weekend radio talks to the nation, he commented on "the political spectacle" of the House Budget Committee, with its Democratic majority, traveling the country and holding hearings, "inviting special interest groups to resist every proposal for budget savings."[67] Democratic Senate Minority Leader Robert Byrd summed up the Reagan phenomenon and his party's frustration in dealing with the popular president this way: "The president," he said, "takes credit for everything that is good, blames everything bad on the past, makes a whipping boy out of Congress, and delivers only good news. Others in the White House are messengers of bad news." Byrd added: "Thus, nobody blames Reagan for anything. He comes across as a likeable and charming person and we Democrats cannot compete with him on an equal footing." Throughout his first four years in the White House, the public's refusal to hold Reagan accountable for his actions continued to befuddle Democratic leaders and pollsters alike. The "teflon presidency" is the term Congresswoman Pat Schroeder (D–Colo.) has applied to President Reagan because, like a teflon-coated frying pan, "nothing sticks to him!"[68]

Given the fragmented nature of legislative decision making in this country, the president's use of the public forum of network television and radio gives him a special advantage in his battles with Congress. Throughout his first term,

President Reagan also kept the political initiative in his frequent public statements by focusing on a short list of priorities.

One of Reagan's most effective rhetorical weapons has been his weekly, nationwide, five-minute radio broadcasts on Saturday morning. Long before he was elected president, Ronald Reagan believed that radio was an extremely effective resource for communicating with the American public.[69] As a young radio sportscaster in Des Moines, Iowa, in the 1930s, Ronald Reagan developed a strong attachment to radio. Thirty years later, after leaving the California governorship in 1975, he agreed to broadcast a five-minute radio news commentary, sponsored by his conservative backers, over more than a hundred independent radio stations nationwide for several years. These short commentaries not only found a wide listening audience, especially among his future political supporters, but also provided an excellent source of income for the former movie-star politician. It was therefore not surprising when President Reagan decided early in 1982 to inaugurate a regular five-minute Saturday radio broadcast nationwide in an effort to shore up his sagging public support, which the Gallup poll showed at that time was below a 45 percent favorable rating.

This decision showed once again the president's keen appreciation of sound public relations and the importance of the rhetorical presidency. Generally, Saturday is a slow newsday in the nation's capital and elsewhere. Most Americans are home for the weekend, relaxing, working in the yard, shopping at the supermarket or the suburban mall, perhaps listening to the radio with one ear, or glancing at the TV set. If they don't hear the president's message directly, the chances are excellent that they will pick up the highlights on one of the radio network hourly, five-minute newscasts or watch the news clips during the evening television news.

Often the president's radio message receives front-page billing in the Sunday papers, the highest circulation day. Also, Mr. Reagan's radio topic frequently has spilled over to the TV networks' Sunday news interview shows, helping the White House to influence the coming week's agenda. Unlike President Franklin D. Roosevelt's sparing use of the fireside chat—he delivered only two or three per year—Reagan's radio chat on one of his top-agenda items generates a steady flow of news week after week. Not only have these broadcasts won a prominent place in the weekend news, but this continuous week-in and week-out radio talk is also consistent with modern advertising theory that repetition reinforces the strength of the delivered message. To be sure, the networks granted the opposition party equal time for a response, but invariably it was President Reagan's message and agenda that dominated the weekend dialogue.

Typical of the press coverage of President Reagan's weekend radio talk was the early March 1985 *New York Times* Sunday story reporting the president's sweeping attack on his critics. In his five-minute message delivered from the Oval Office, Mr. Reagan assailed Democrats, farm state legislators, business executives, educators, and mayors who were all critical of the administration's assault on domestic spending. With some of the harshest rhetoric heard since his second inaugural, Mr. Reagan capped his short message with a plea for Congress to exercise its political courage to cut $50 billion from the domestic budget by

Easter. And he added: "If there isn't enough courage to approve these cuts, then at least give me the authority to veto line items in the Federal budget. I'll take the political responsibility, I'll make the cuts and I'll take the heat." Mr. Reagan repeatedly pressed for the prerogative to reject individual items in appropriations bills passed by Congress.

To answer the president, the Democrats selected Speaker Thomas P. (Tip) O'Neill, who spoke caustically of the administration's planned cuts in its farm program. Though the Speaker holds the third highest office in the federal government, his five-minute, equal-time response was allocated 2 column inches. President Reagan's message received 18 column inches. In other words, the president's rhetoric commanded nine times the print coverage given the Speaker of the House.[70]

CEREMONIAL RHETORIC

Presidents have always been able to capitalize on the chief of state ceremonial rhetoric to strengthen their leadership role, while remaining above politics. Thus, President Eisenhower could officially greet the young Queen Elizabeth II at Washington National Airport in 1957, escort her down Constitution Avenue, and then preside over the formalities at the White House, all the while reaping the benefits that go with being a thoughtful host. While the national media cannot report every conversation or summarize every agreement reached, presidential hosting of foreign dignitaries offers a plenitude of opportunities for nonpartisan ceremonial rhetoric. In the same vein, scenes of the president greeting the astronauts by phone or in person, inviting the U.S. Olympic hockey team to the White House, pinning medals on national heroes have all attracted the nation's attention and generated a sense of pride throughout the country. The advent of television has multiplied the opportunities for the president to gain the general acclaim of the electorate, no matter what their brand of politics.

The president's use of ceremonial rhetoric has reached new highs during Reagan's White House tenure. Who can forget his official opening of the 1984 summer Olympics in Los Angeles? The public probably does not recall his exact words of greeting to all the participants and the throng of 80,000 watching the opening event, but no matter. The incumbent Republican president's direct involvement in the Olympic festivities in the midst of a presidential election year was considered a political bonanza by the White House. Since campaign managers regard televised coverage of candidates in a nonpolitical setting as far more effective than paid commercials, Reagan's ceremonial rhetoric, heard cost-free by millions of Americans watching the Olympics, underscored once again the political advantage the incumbent president usually holds over a challenger.

Similarly, Reagan became the special beneficiary of another major ceremonial national event when he was asked by the National Football Conference officials to flip the coin before the start of the Nineteenth Superbowl contest between the San Francisco Forty-Niners and Miami Dolphins in January 1985. Viewed by almost 90 million Americans, President Reagan once again occupied the center of the national television stage just before kickoff time. His brief remarks after the coin toss reinforced the sense of good sportsmanship most Americans revere. After the game, the ABC-TV network provided another opportunity for Reagan to deliver a congratulatory message to the winning San Francisco team, once again before a huge national television audience. In the course of this ceremony, the president did not miss the opportunity to remark jokingly that he could use the help of the victorious Forty-Niner squad on Capitol Hill to bring a recalcitrant Congress around to support major items of his legislative agenda.

Actually, this football scenario was President Reagan's third major appearance on national television on Superbowl Sunday, since it was also the official inauguration day for his second term. Although most inauguration ceremonies were postponed until Monday, January 21, the White House decided in accordance with long tradition to have a small official oath of office swearing in on January 20, 1985—once again covered by the four major network "pool" cameras.[71] Thus, within a period of eight hours, presidential rhetoric occupied the TV network airwaves on three separate occasions. No presidential media director could in his wildest dreams hope for more favorable exposure than President Reagan received on Superbowl Sunday 1985.

As one veteran reporter has summarized Reagan's effective use of ceremonial rhetoric: "Few Chief Executives have rivaled him as the White House 'master of ceremonies,' beaming like a game-show host and palming a small card of Oval Office announcement notes at each day's several minor ceremonies, all to help display the self-confidence that bolsters his approval rating in the polls."[72]

SLOGANS AND SYMBOLS

Political slogans and symbols can be an important aspect of presidential rhetoric and may be just the elements needed to launch a successful presidency. Indeed, as Edwards and Wayne have emphasized: "If presidents can get a substantial segment of the public to adopt symbols favorable to them, they will be in a position to influence public opinion."[73] Franklin D. Roosevelt quickly dubbed his administration the New Deal, and it will always be so remembered in the history books. Harry Truman, seeking to establish a special identity for his own administration, termed it the Fair Deal. Each slogan symbolized a multitude of programs, but they reflected action amid a sense of concern for rank-and-file Americans. Likewise, President Kennedy's New Frontier symbolized a sense of adventure and an innovative approach to national problems.

Presidents who fail to exploit slogans and symbols for their administrations can experience serious problems in relating to the public. In the case of the Carter administration, as Edwards and Wayne have pointed out: "Jimmy Carter faced a great deal of criticism for lacking a unifying theme and cohesion in the programs, for failing to inspire the public with a sense of purpose, and idea to follow. Instead of providing the country with a sense of his vision and priorities, he emphasized discrete problem solving."[74]

The administrations of Nixon, Ford, and Reagan have all lacked popular symbols and slogans. But in the case of the Reagan administration the absence of any catchy slogan or symbol has not diminished its general popularity. Perhaps the fact that Reagan was a former movie idol has filled this symbolic vacuum; also the overriding antigovernment theme of Reagan's rhetoric, repeated week-in and week-out, has come to symbolize the new direction of his administration.

SURROGATE OF THE PEOPLE

Presidential monopoly over public space sometimes has taken the form of the president proclaiming himself the chief surrogate for the mass public. This idea that the president is the sole representative of the national constituency goes back to Andrew Jackson, who portrayed himself as the sole protector of the people, who individually were unable to take action against the selfish, corrupt elites.[75] The Jacksonian image of the president serving as the surrogate for the American citizenry has, of course, recurred from time to time in American history. Teddy Roosevelt's campaign against the "great malefactors of wealth," FDR's rhetorical war of words against the "economic royalists" bent upon sabotaging the people's gains from the New Deal, and Ronald Reagan's relentless campaign against "big government" that suffocates individual initiative are the best-known examples. As depicted by Bruce Miroff: "Presidential action thus becomes—in a symbolic sense—our action, a scattered, divided, uncertain people are made one and exercise their popular power through their surrogate."[76]

Furthermore, as the national leader responsible for the nation's security and domestic well-being, "the president's singular national visibility, constitutional legitimacy, and acknowledged institutional expertise preserve for him a special place in public opinion. In judicial parlance, the president enjoys standing. Citizens take note of his appeals, whether they like him or not."[77] This unique position of the president has, since the age of mass communications, fostered the growth of a potentially alarming development that deserves special mention—the rise of the plebiscitary presidency.

THE PLEBISCITARY PRESIDENT

With the emergence of the rhetorical presidency, the marked decline of political parties, and domination of the mass media in presidential nominating and general elections over the past two decades, the country is moving in the direction, in the words of Theodore J. Lowi, of a "plebiscitary presidency."[78] Under these changed conditions the president increasingly maintains a direct personal relationship via television and radio with millions of American citizens. To most readers, the term *plebiscite* evokes images of Roman emperors and French Bonapartism, of rulers who governed on the basis of popular acclaim, with the masses giving their enthusiastic assent in the Coliseum or in a national referendum. While the term *plebiscitary* is an exaggeration, it is nonetheless not far from the mark in describing the American chief executive in the age of television.

Beginning with the nominating process, the presidential contenders independently seek mass support in the state primaries and seek to lay claim to enough personally loyal delegates who will work indefatigably to help them to capture the nomination. Over the past three decades the national nominating convention has become a ratification assembly, not a deliberative body, that anoints the winner of the primaries as the party nominee. The plebiscitary nature of the selection process is evident throughout both the primary and general election races. Presidential nominees run their own campaigns completely independent of all other contests, rather than building coalitions with state and local political organizations. Even the federal government's underwriting of the candidate's general election campaign expenses has reinforced the plebiscitary nature of the presidential selection process, for the $40.4 million in federal funds goes to the individual candidate, not his party, to spend as he sees fit—mostly for television advertising.

Throughout the entire selection process, the rhetoric and "image" of the winner and loser will be concentrated on building a personal constituency involving a direct and unmediated relationship between the candidate—or incumbent president—and the mass public. In the age of television, these ties between the leader and his followers become more evident once the country moves from the electing to governing process.

Clearly, the State of the Union address, the annual Economic Report, the budget message, while all delivered before Congress, are more pointedly directed at the American people. Nationally televised speeches to the American people reinforce this direct, personal relationship between the president and the mass electorate. As a result of these changes, the pressure and demands that the American public places on the president can be expected to increase. But it remains to be seen whether presidential rhetoric, the frequent personal appearances on national television and radio, will be sufficient to avoid electoral rejection after one term, or in the case of a two-term president, such as President Ronald Reagan, whether he can operate as an effective leader during his second term or become nothing more than a lame-duck president waiting out his days until retirement.

Throughout his reelection campaign, Ronald Reagan showed no indication that he found objectionable this plebiscitarian trend in the presidency. Time and again, Reagan's White House staff passed up opportunities to campaign on behalf of GOP senatorial and congressional candidates locked in tight races. Instead, Reagan concentrated his campaign on building up his own electoral majority. Indeed, as his Gallup poll lead widened over his challenger, Walter F. Mondale, during September and early October 1984, the president and his staff seemed far more intent on trying to sweep all 50 states than helping Republican congressional candidates involved in close races. After the election one of his staunchest supporters, House GOP Minority Leader Robert Michel, complained about the White House indifference to other 1984 GOP races and blamed Reagan's personal campaign for the Republicans' disappointing showing in the House elections. "He never really, in my opinion, joined that issue of what it really means to have the numbers in the House. . . . Here the son-of-a-buck ended up with 59 percent and you bring in [only] fifteen seats."[79] Plebiscitary presidents, with their direct and personal relationships with millions of voters, can easily overlook the critical needs of lesser party officeholders.

Another step toward further development of the plebiscitary president occurred early in 1985 shortly before President Reagan's second inaugural, when the White House launched its own "news service" to distribute presidential speeches and announcements. According to one White House official, President Reagan's top staff concluded that they can get the president's views across more effectively if those views are "unfiltered" by the independent media.[80]

The White House News Service offers subscribers, for a small fee, access to a computerized electronic mail network via telephone. With this new computer network, the White House hopes to establish a market for this service among radio stations and small newspapers around the country that cannot afford White House correspondents of their own. Although this electronic service is "still in its infancy," the network will not only provide official, unedited versions of the president's messages, but also news releases from the White House press office, the first lady's office, the vice-president's office, and the Office of Management and Budget.[81]

Armed with this type of news management, coupled with the president's arsenal of rhetorical weapons—televised press conferences, regular and special messages to Congress and the American people, the numerous "nonpolitical" speeches to various professional associations—the president would seem to have moved ever closer to a plebiscitary presidency.

What are some of the long-term prospects of the rhetorical presidency? One critic has put it this way:

> The presidency itself gained initially from the increased focus of both public demands and mass communications on the national government, being better equipped than other institutions to provide political and symbolic direction to the activation of the national government.[82]

Clearly, the president, as chief tribune of the American people, enjoys a preeminent position to articulate his programs to the American public. Except for wartime emergencies, the opportunities for the emergence of a plebiscitarian president are probably greater today than anytime in American history. However, the decomposition of American parties, the weakening of party loyalty among rank-and-file party members, and the president's lack of partisan tools to induce cohesion between the executive and legislative branches have all undermined his ability to provide national leadership, even though the quality of his rhetoric may be of the highest order. Richard L. Rubin has summarized the rhetorical president's dilemma:

> . . . the present environment of increasingly rapid, centrally focused mass communications, and the disjunction between the public's electoral demands on the president and his ability to develop and sustain cohesive public policy has now made the presidency the focus of unfulfilled expectations.[83]

The only politically responsible officeholder with the entire nation as a constituency, the president in recent decades has become the embodiment of government; millions of Americans concentrate their fears and hopes upon him. With this focusing of mass expectations upon the presidency, our national leader finds that he must constantly respond to ever higher demands of divergent constituencies and interest groups. And the harder presidents try to please the mass constituencies, the higher these groups make their expectations. In the words of Theodore J. Lowi: "As presidential success advances arithmetically, public expectations advance geometrically."[84] Lowi obviously overstates the point, but the list of public expectations of the president grows ever longer—rescue the hostages, cut the deficit, halt the nuclear arms race, protect American markets from foreign competition, halt rising medical costs. Because the American public sees the president on television almost every night, the electorate not only feels personally close to the national leader, but the voters come to expect him to respond promptly and effectively to every pressing national problem. Modern presidents can seldom put distance between themselves and these formidable problems. Consequently, they must constantly reassure the public via television and frequent personal appearances around the country that they are seeking solutions to seemingly endless and often intractable problems.

In a sense, the rhetorical president has become a victim of his own success. Proponents of the rhetorical model have created a dangerously inflated conception of the president as a persuader. They have promoted unrealistic expectations concerning the capacity of the president to fulfill promised goals, and when that president fails to "deliver" on his promises, his influence and authority become seriously undermined. To counter this pitfall, James W. Ceaser suggests that "the rhetorical strategy of any particular president should be designed to fit that president's own goals and purposes . . . presidents should attempt to set expectations at a realistic level and in line with what they can reasonably accomplish."[85] In the age of the mass media, this advice may be easier to give than to follow.

NOTES

1. James W. Ceaser, Glen E. Thurow, Jeffrey Tulis, and Joseph M. Bessette, "The Rise of the Rhetorical Presidency," *Presidential Studies Quarterly*, 11 (Spring 1981), 159.
2. Theodore J. Lowi, *The Personal President: Power Invested, Promise Unfulfilled* (Ithaca, NY: Cornell University Press, 1985).
3. Ceaser et al., "The Rhetorical Presidency," 159.
4. Jefferson, however, used his great rhetorical skill in his inaugural address in his attempt to reunify the country following the divisive campaign of 1800. See Dumas Malone, *Jefferson the President: First Term 1801–1805*, Vol. 4 (Boston: Little, Brown, 1970), 17–21.
5. Ibid. This discussion of Johnson's "swing around the circle" is based on Albert Castel, *The Presidency of Andrew Johnson* (Lawrence, KS: Regents Press, 1979), as cited by Ceaser et al., "The Rhetorical Presidency," 159.
6. Edwin Emery, *The Press and America: An Interpretative History of the Mass Media*, 3rd ed. (Englewood Cliffs, NJ: Prentice-Hall, 1972), 285.
7. As cited in Donald Bruce Johnson and Jack L. Walker, eds., *The Dynamics of the American Presidency* (New York: Wiley, 1964), 134–135.

8. Woodrow Wilson, *Constitutional Government in the United States* (New York: Columbia University Press, 1908), 68.

9. See Thomas A. Bailey, *Woodrow Wilson and the Lost Peace* (Chicago: Quadrangle Books, 1944).

10. Ceaser et al., "The Rise of the Rhetorical Presidency," 162–163.

11. Ibid., 163.

12. Ibid.

13. George C. Edwards III and Stephen J. Wayne, *Presidential Leadership* (New York: St. Martin's Press, 1985), 11.

14. Samuel Kernell, "The Presidency and the People," in Michael Nelson, ed., *The Presidency and the Political System* (Washington, DC: Congressional Quarterly Press, 1984), 241. Professor Kernell has also included several interesting tables listing the presidents' national televised addresses 1952–1980 and the total number of public appearances from Hoover to Reagan; Ibid., 238–245.

15. Richard L. Rubin, *Press, Party, and Presidency* (New York: Norton, 1981), 132.

16. Erik Barnouw, *Mass Communications: Television, Radio, Film, Press,* 2nd ed. (New York: Holt, Rinehart and Winston, 1960), 34. In 1943, the Justice Department ordered the National Broadcasting Company (NBC) to break up control of both its Red and Blue networks, or face an antitrust suit. Subsequently, NBC sold off its control of the NBC Blue Network, and it became the American Broadcasting Company (ABC). Listeners could also tune in on a fourth radio network—the Mutual Broadcasting System (MBS)—a network of nearly 500 stations.

17. Rubin, *Press, Party, and Presidency,* 133.

18. Ibid., 131–132.

19. Ibid., 133.

20. Ibid., 135.

21. Ibid., 125.

22. Emery, *The Press and America,* 629.

23. Rubin, *Press, Party, and Presidency,* 146.

24. *The New York Times,* August 13, 1941.

25. Samuel Kernell, "The Truman Doctrine Speech: A Case Study in the Dynamics of Opinion Leadership," *Social Science History* (Fall 1976), 20–45.

26. Robert O. Blanchard, ed., *Congress and the News Media* (New York: Hastings House, 1974), 106–113, as cited by George C. Edwards III, *The Public Presidency* (New York: St. Martin's Press, 1983), 43.

27. *Gallup Report,* December 1983, 18.

28. Ceaser et al., "The Rise of the Rhetorical Presidency," 164.

29. Ibid.

30. Ibid.

31. Ibid., 165.

32. Sidney Blumenthal, *The Permanent Campaign,* rev. ed. (New York: Simon and Schuster, 1980); see also James W. Davis, *National Conventions in an Age of Party Reform* (Westport, CT: Greenwood Press, 1983), 186.

33. Ceaser et al., "The Rise of the Rhetorical Presidency," 166.

34. Ibid., 167.

35. Bruce Miroff, "Monopolizing the Public Space: The President as a Problem for Democratic Politics," in Thomas E. Cronin, ed., *Rethinking the Presidency* (Boston: Little, Brown, 1982), 219.

36. "An Ambitious Arms Agenda," *Newsweek,* March 18, 1985, 19.

37. "Gearing Up in Geneva," *Time,* March 18, 1985, 22.

38. For a recent study of the phenomenon "going public," the presidential strategy of promoting himself and his policies by appealing directly to the American people for support, see Samuel Kernell, *Going Public* (Washington, DC: Congressional Quarterly Press, 1986). See also George C. Edwards III, *The Public Presidency,* especially Chapter 2.

39. Ibid., 42.

40. Bruce Miroff, to make this point, has cited columnist Russell Baker's satirical comment on President Carter. "If the Carter Administration were a television show, it would have been cancelled months ago. There are no chases, no shoot-outs, no jokes, no spectacles, no drama, no mystery, no comedy, and no star performer." Russell Baker, "The Jimmy Carter Show," *The New York Times Magazine,* December 18, 1977, as cited by Miroff, "Monopolizing the Public Space," 231, note 8.

41. Emmet John Hughes, "Presidency vs. Jimmy Carter," *Fortune,* December 4, 1978, 62, 64.

42. Michael Baruch Grossman and Martha Joynt Kumar, *Portraying the President* (Baltimore, MD: The Johns Hopkins University Press, 1981), 314–315.

43. George C. Edwards III, *The Public Presidency,* 41.

44. Arthur M. Schlesinger, Jr., *A Thousand Days: John F. Kennedy in the White House* (Boston: Houghton Mifflin, 1965), 715.

45. Herbert S. Parmet, *JFK: The Presidency of John F. Kennedy* (New York: Penguin, 1983), 322.

46. Ibid.

47. Ibid.

48. As cited in Hobart Rowan, "The Big Steel Crisis: Kennedy vs. Blough," in Earl Latham, ed., *J. F. Kennedy and Presidential Power* (Lexington, MA: D. C. Heath Company, 1972), 95.

49. Ibid., 110.

50. Ibid.

51. Doris Kearns, *Lyndon Johnson and the American Dream* (New York: Harper & Row, 1976), 228–230.

52. Lyndon Johnson, "The American Promise," March 15, 1965, *Public Papers,* 1965, 281.

53. Eric Goldman, *The Tragedy of Lyndon Johnson* (New York: Knopf, 1969), 322.

54. *The New York Times,* January 21, 1981.

55. Ibid., August 24, 1984.

56. Ibid., January 22, 1985.

57. "Four More Years," *Newsweek,* January 28, 1985, 19–21.

58. Hugh Heclo and Rudolph G. Penner, "Fiscal and Political Strategy in the Reagan Administration," in Fred I. Greenstein, ed., *The Reagan Presidency* (Baltimore, MD: The Johns Hopkins University Press, 1983), 39.

59. Edward W. Chester, "Shadow or Substance? Critiquing Reagan's Inaugural Address," *Presidential Studies Quarterly,* XI (Spring 1981), 172–176.

60. "Full Speed Ahead," *Newsweek,* February 4, 1985, 18.

61. Morton M. Kondracke, "More than Blind Luck," *Newsweek,* February 18, 1985, 22.

62. Ibid.

63. Chester, "Shadow or Substance?" 175–176.

64. Ibid, 176.

65. Bernard Weinraub, *The New York Times,* March 27, 1985.

66. Ibid.

67. Ibid., March 2, 1985.

68. The Byrd quote appears in Robert Thompson, *Seattle Post-Intelligencer,* March 11, 1985. Lou Cannon, "Reagan as the 'Teflon Presidency'," *The Washington Post National Weekly Edition,* April 30, 1984, 11.

69. For those who doubt the effectiveness of radio as a communication tool, the Electronic Industries Association, a national trade association, reported that 52 million radios were sold in the United States in 1983. Manufacturers report that in the past thirty-seven years, more than one billion sets have been sold. The Radio Advertising Bureau reports that 99 percent of American households have at least one radio set and that the average number is 5.5 sets per household. According to a leading trade publication magazine, there were 4,685 AM and 4,505 FM stations on the air in 1983. *The New York Times,* March 25, 1985.

70. Ibid., March 3, 1985.

71. Ibid., January 21, 1985.

72. Francis X. Clines, *The New York Times,* March 31, 1985.

73. Edwards and Wayne, *Presidential Leadership,* 125.

74. Ibid., 127.

75. Miroff, "Monopolizing the Public Space: The President as a Problem for Democratic Politics," 223.

76. Ibid.

77. Kernell, "The Presidency and the People," 249.

78. See Theodore J. Lowi, *The Personal President: Power Invested, Promise Unfulfilled,* 97–133.

79. *The New York Times,* November 12, 1984, as cited by Theodore J. Lowi, "An Aligning Election, A Presidential Plebiscite," in Michael Nelson, ed., *The Elections of 1984* (Washington, DC; Congressional Quarterly Press, 1985) 294. Michel made these comments before the election count disclosed that the GOP gained fourteen House seats, not fifteen.

80. Associated Press dispatch, *Seattle Post-Intelligencer,* January 7, 1985.

81. Ibid.

82. Rubin, *Press, Party, and Presidency,* 233.

83. Ibid.

84. Theodore J. Lowi, *The Personal President,* 20.

85. James W. Ceaser, "The Rhetorical Presidency Revisited," in Marc Landy, ed., *Modern Presidents and the Presidency* (Lexington, MA: D.C. Heath and Company, 1985), 31.

chapter 13

The President as Overseer of the Economy

Modern presidents, unlike their nineteenth- and early twentieth-century predecessors, are expected by the public not only to maintain the peace and security of the country, but also to maintain high employment and control inflation. If the economy turns sour, presidents are expected actively to fight the recession. Though the president's ability to manage the economy is minimal at best, the public nevertheless holds him personally accountable for the state of the economy. If he fails to maintain prosperity, they may turn against him at the next election. The same double standard that holds the president responsible for domestic and foreign policy decisions while excusing Congress also prevails for economic policy. Strangely, the lawmakers are not held individually accountable by the voters for poor economic conditions, though members of Congress clearly share a major responsibility for the economy. Congress as a body may be held responsible for economic policy decisions, but rarely are individual lawmakers singled out for blame so long as they are perceived as faithfully watching out for their constituents' interests. That over 90 percent of incumbent House members running for reelection are consistently returned to Congress is proof enough that the public is reasonably satisfied with their job performance.[1] Presidents, however, are judged less charitably by the voters.

To read the Constitution, one would not have the faintest idea that the president is the chief overseer of the economy. Indeed, as Richard M. Pious has noted: "The Constitution seems to make economic policymaking a congressional responsibility, since Article II provides no enumeration of economic powers, while Article I grants a considerable number of powers."[2] Nevertheless, since the early days of the Republic, presidents have used their executive powers to make

361

economic policy. President Andrew Jackson's decision to close down the Bank of the United States is a case in point.

In this chapter, after a brief historical review of the limited role presidents played in economic policymaking before the Great Depression, we will endeavor to show how presidents since the New Deal have sought to influence the general direction of economic policy through macroeconomic and microeconomic policymaking. The duties and influence of the president's economic team—the Council of Economic Advisers, the secretary of the treasury, and the Office of Management and Budget—are discussed. Special attention is focused on the autonomous Federal Reserve Board and its crucial influence on monetary policy and the general state of the economy. We examine the powerful impact of President Reagan's supply-side Reaganomics on the American economy, as well as the new direction in which this economic approach seems to be leading the country. Presidential alternatives to fiscal policy intervention are discussed and evaluated. Electoral economics—the president's efforts to stimulate the economy before elections—also receives detailed treatment, as does the role of the "pocketbook" issue in elections. Also included in this chapter is Congress's major, though less recognized, role in economic policymaking. Finally, we look at the so-called Reagan revolution—the president's remarkable success in winning congressional approval of his budget and tax reduction plans through the little-known, little-understood reconciliation budget process.

BACKGROUND

Until the Great Depression (1929–1933), presidents did not play a significant role in economic policymaking. As Pious bluntly put it: "There was no administration fiscal policy." Generally, presidents operated in the following fashion:

> In good times a president maintained the confidence of the business community by appointing financiers to the Treasury, by intervening on the side of management in strikes (if necessary with federal troops), and by keeping "hands off" the economy. In bad times presidents reassured the public that conditions would soon improve, maintained public order, and bailed out the banking system with the resources of the Treasury. The economy was supposed to be self-regulating.[3]

Nor did this lack of federal government involvement have the far-ranging consequences it has today. Even if the president had discovered fiscal theory as a tool to influence the economy, the low levels of federal spending—especially government spending and taxation in proportion to the gross national product—would have had virtually no serious impact on the nation's economy. Except for the wartime expenditures during the Civil War, the federal budget did not exceed $1 billion until the United States entered World War I in 1917.[4] (President Reagan's 1986 budget called for expenditures of $973.7 billion.)

Calvin Coolidge's banal observation in the 1920s that "the business of America is business" lost its meaning in the October 1929 stock market crash.

For the next three years the nation floundered helplessly while the Hoover administration (1929–1933) chose to remain on the sidelines, for the most part, and let market forces take their natural course. But this traditional "hands off" policy changed with the inauguration of Franklin D. Roosevelt in 1933.

President Roosevelt and his New Deal had as its central premise the responsibility of the federal government to halt depressions and restore prosperity. This commitment, formalized in the Employment Act of 1946, became a major source of presidential strength. Since the postwar economy kept expanding through the 1950s and 1960s, generating surpluses that paid for defense and expanded domestic programs, presidents were more than eager to claim credit for the booming economy. Administration economists in the 1960s were, for a time, speaking about putting an end to recessions. But this optimism came down to earth in the early 1970s. The United States—along with most other industrialized countries —moved into a period of declining growth and spiraling inflation (see Table 13.1). More and more, presidents found it increasingly difficult to find any prosperity to take credit for. Inflation became Public Enemy No. 1. Government spending came to be viewed as the chief agent of inflation. Thus, instead of gaining popularity and accolades by dispensing more federal benefits, a president had to put some distance between himself and the growing national deficit or risk being tarred as the culprit responsible for the nation's ills.

As Ben Heineman, Jr., a railroad executive and former official in the Carter administration, wrote after leaving government service:

> Fifteen years ago, the economy was a strong ally of Presidential power. It appeared to respond magically to executive will, providing on a lavish scale the resources needed for a long agenda of social reforms. Today, the economy is an adversary of Presidential power—perhaps the greatest adversary. It appears to mock all executive ministrations, provides insufficient resources for a host of government objectives and vexes Presidents with choices between politically unacceptable evils.[5]

Table 13.1   ECONOMIC CONDITIONS—KENNEDY-JOHNSON YEARS VERSUS CARTER YEARS (Average annual figures)

	1961–1965	1976–1980
Inflation	1.3%	8.8%
Unemployment	5.5%	6.7%
Productivity growth*	3.5%	0.7%
Trade balance	−$5.4 billion	−$27.1 billion
Oil import bill	$1.8 billion	$50.0 billion
Average federal tax rate on median-income family	10.2%	16.4%
Federal budget deficit	$4.6 billion	$50.0 billion
Federal budget deficit as percentage of GNP	0.8%	2.5%

*The growth of real GNP per hour of labor effort in the private, nonfarm business sector of the economy.

Source: Ben W. Heineman, Jr., and Curtis A. Hessler, *Memorandum for the President: A Strategic Approach to Domestic Affairs in the 1980s* (New York: Random House, 1980), 58.

Sudden increases in the price of steel or heavy wage increases for the steel or auto workers can seriously undermine presidential efforts to control inflation. World events, such as the 1973–74 Arab oil embargo, and the resultant shortages of gasoline and the skyrocketing price increases, are clearly beyond presidential control but can have a disastrous effect upon the domestic economy. Thus, the president can be blamed for the huge lines at the gas stations, but because the nation is heavily dependent on oil imports, he is virtually powerless to solve the country's short-term energy needs—that is, unless he wishes (with congressional approval in peacetime) to invoke rationing, a highly unpopular action. (President Reagan, it might be noted, was the beneficiary of declining world oil prices in 1983–84, which helped cool the inflation fires and contributed to his reelection victory in 1984.)

As the economic problems have multiplied, the public has demanded that the government—meaning the president—"do something." Yet while a president is expected to come up with solutions within his four-year term, most of the causes of economic distress usually require long-term corrective measures. To add to the president's woes, he must contend with an eroding global economic order that makes drastic economic policymaking hazardous and often impossible. Thus, the president must contend not only with unpredictable economic conditions at home, but with shifting tides abroad involving international exchange, debt-ridden Third World countries, and multinational corporations.

Recent presidents have done little to halt the "deindustrialization" of America—the shift of production operations overseas to take advantage of cheaper labor costs. American industrial leaders have opted for quick profits abroad instead of investing in plant expansion or rebuilding industries in the United States. American consumers have demonstrated relatively little concern over foreign competition. In 1981, for example, they purchased over $250 billion in imported goods—automobiles, TV sets, campers, motor scooters, textiles, shoes.[6] Since the late 1960s American productivity has declined while the productivity of its leading foreign competitor—Japan—has increased. During the last half of the 1970s, U. S. productivity rose only 1 percent. In the meantime, Japan's rate of productivity has increased four times faster.

The president lacks the power of an economic czar to block these major shifts in our industrial system, but the American chief executive, no matter which party he may belong to, will face severe criticism if the erosion of American production facilities is not halted in the immediate years ahead. Yet while the president is expected to maintain direction over the economy, the American chief executive has less control over the budget and monetary policy than the leader of any major Western democracy. Although the White House has the responsibility for preparing the budget, the final budget approved by Congress will be scarcely recognizable by its originators in the Office of Management and Budget. Congress has its own budgetary and fiscal powers and, more often than not, will have economic goals that differ considerably from those of the president. Both the House Ways and Means Committee and the Senate Finance Committee have long been noted for their independence and lack of interest in the executive agenda.

Furthermore, the structure of the budget permits far less flexibility to the president and Congress than would appear at first glance. "Uncontrollable" expenditures—approximately three-quarters of the federal budget—leave little maneuverability for either the president or Congress. Moreover, many uncontrollable programs are indexed to inflation and are thus subject to sizable and unpredictable increases almost every year. Roughly one-half of the federal budget is consumed by entitlements—social security, veteran's pensions and benefits, federal retirement pensions, Medicare, Medicaid, agricultural price supports, and unemployment compensation. More than one-quarter—approximately $287 billion in fiscal 1986—was devoted to national defense. Nearly 15 percent of the federal budget—approximately $142 billion—was earmarked in 1986 for interest on the national debt.[7]

If a president attempts a shift in priorities or sharply reduces budgets in any programs or agencies, it will trigger rapid counterattacks from members of Congress, organized interest groups, and the federal agencies affected. "Iron triangles" is the term coined to describe these powerful groups. Each of these so-called subgovernments will bitterly resist any budget or program changes unless they expand or enhance the constituencies affected.

The president has even less power over monetary policy. The responsibility for regulating the money supply, which most directly affects interest rates, production, and purchasing power, belongs not to the president, but to the Federal Reserve Board. To be sure, the president appoints, subject to Senate confirmation, members of the Federal Reserve Board whose seven governors serve 14-year terms; he also names the chairman and vice-chairman whose 4-year terms overlap the president's. But beyond this appointing power, the president has no formal role in the Federal Reserve Board's policymaking activities. Unlike the leaders of other Western democracies who can exert direct influence on their country's central bank policies, the president of the United States can only sit on the sidelines and comment on the Fed's decisions after the fact. No wonder incoming presidents privately shake their heads as they attempt to wrestle with the federal budget.

MACROECONOMIC POLICY FROM FDR TO REAGAN

The rise of Franklin D. Roosevelt's New Deal in 1933 marks the dividing line between traditional laissez-faire economic policy and the rise of macroeconomic policy—the name given to the general management of the economy by the government. Although macroeconomic policies were in operation before the 1930s, they took a great leap forward during the New Deal era, and they have continued to be a central feature of government policymaking since then. Macroeconomic policy has two broad purposes: first, to promote economic stability in place of widely fluctuating economic conditions, and second, to foster economic growth. President Roosevelt's emergence as the first public manager of the economy and his decision to use fiscal policy to correct imbalances within the economy came in the midst of the Great Depression. Actually, Roosevelt's discovery that government expenditures could have a major impact on the economy evolved more as a by-product of his emergency relief and spending programs than a planned effort on his part to turn the economy around. In the meantime, however, a leading British economist, John Maynard Keynes, whom FDR met in 1934, provided a theoretical framework for the phenomenon of economic response to fiscal stimuli.

Keynesian Theory.   According to Keynes, economic decline was caused by a drop in the demand for goods and services. During a depression, the accumulators of capital prefer to put their money into savings rather than investment. If total output is falling because of insufficient consumption or investment in the private sector, Keynes argued that the government could stimulate the economy by stepping up its own expenditures. Moreover, Keynes insisted, the temporary deficits created by the fiscal expenditures could be underwritten by government borrowing and repaid by higher tax rates during periods of growth in the economy.[8]

Traditional Economic Theory.   Keynes's theory flew in the face of traditional conservative economics, which viewed a balanced budget as the key to a sound economy. The conservative economists held that government deficits were dangerously inflationary and threatening to confidence in the monetary system. Faced with downturn in the economy, conservative economic theory required reduced government outlays to balance the budget. The government's demonstration of fiscal integrity would then lead to the restoration of economic confidence. Even during panics or depressions, the government was not required to act—nor did the people expect the government to get actively involved. To be sure, noninterference in the affairs of individuals and lack of action to change economic conditions sometimes came at a high cost, but according to the traditional economic theorists, prosperity would return as soon as the depressions were, to use President Herbert Hoover's phrase, "left to blow themselves out."[9]

Franklin Roosevelt, convinced that laissez-faire economics was not the answer to the Great Depression, found considerable merit in the innovative Keynesian theory. But he did not become a full convert until the 1937 recession, which followed his attempt to return the country to a balanced budget. When the recession wiped out almost half of the nation's hard-earned economic gains since the beginning of the New Deal—unemployment rose again to 19 percent in 1937 —FDR's reservations about Keynesian economics seemed to vanish. However, the American economy did not fully recover its vitality until total mobilization and the huge government outlays for armaments during World War II furnished empirical validation of Keynes's countercyclical pump-priming theory to many economists.[10] Thus, it is only since the New Deal that business cycles have been directly influenced through public policy.

Keynesianism continued to be the dominant macroeconomic policy until its limitations became evident during the rampant inflation of the early 1970s. The chief flaw in the Keynesian theory was more political than economic. Invariably, the president and Congress found it easier to increase spending and tax-cutting —Keynes's remedy for expanding the economy—since these policies would attract political support. But the policymakers bridled at Keynes's prescription for curbing inflation—cut spending and raise taxes. In other words, the president and Congress found only half of the Keynesian theory acceptable; they were unwilling to use the second half of the equation—raise taxes and cut government spending to cool down inflation—for fear of losing office. Furthermore, policymakers made little or no attempt to create a budget surplus during expansionary periods. Some commentators referred to this practice as "one-way" fiscal policy. As a result of this political defect, Keynesian lost some of its appeal to both policymakers and economists. Partly as a result of this disenchantment with Keynesianism, two other schools of macroeconomics—monetarism and supply-side economics— have emerged as possible alternative courses of action for government policy- makers.

Monetarism.   The first post-World War II challenge to Keynesianism came from the monetarists, sometimes called the Chicago School because the chief theorist, Nobel Laureate Milton Friedman, and his followers served on the fac- ulty at the University of Chicago. Monetarism is an economic theory which asserts that monetary policy or control of the money supply is the primary, if not sole, determinant of the nation's economy. The core element of monetarist theory is based on the proposition that prices, income, and economic stability are a function of growth in the money supply, not of the proportion of public expendi- tures paid for by borrowed funds. Monetarists hold that as long as the money supply grows at a constant rate commensurate with potential growth in gross national product, economic activity will expand without placing upward pressure on prices and wages. Management of the money supply to produce credit ease or restraint, monetarists claim, is the chief factor influencing inflation or deflation, recession or growth.

Monetarists dismiss fiscal policy (government spending and taxation) as ineffective in regulating economic activity. Since contraction of the money supply —the monetarist medicine for controlling inflation—results in higher interest rates and unemployment, monetarism has not been a popular economic policy at the White House or on Capitol Hill in recent years. By 1980, another theoretical approach to economic policy—supply-side economics—became popular among some conservative economists and especially some elected officials. The most prominent convert turned out to be none other than President Ronald Reagan.

Supply-Side Economics.   Combining features of both Keynesianism and monetarism, supply-side economics is based on the belief that economic expan- sion will come from lower tax rates. According to supply-side economists Arthur Laffer and George Gilder, a reduction in taxes will increase supply by encourag- ing production, providing greater incentives to work, and stimulating the savings and investment needed to support economic growth.[11] Furthermore, a greater supply of economic growth would produce a slowdown in inflation. Supply-siders insist that a tax cut will not, in the long run, reduce overall tax revenues because increased prosperity will offset the effects of lower tax rates. Members of the supply-side school of economics are not bothered by big budget deficits created by tax reductions. Supply-siders argue that the stimulative effect of tax cuts will create enough additional savings to finance the added deficits without an inflationary expansion of the money supply.[12] Eventually, according to the supply-siders, an expanded economy will produce enough added revenues at lower rates of taxation to balance the budget. In other words, the nation's prosperity will enable the country to "grow out" of its deficit.

Liberal critics of the supply-side school argue that it is simply a new version of the discredited "trickle down" theory in which tax breaks for the wealthy are justified on the basis that these advantages will encourage new investment and thus generate additional economic activity. The result: prosperity for everyone. Conservative critics, on the other hand, fear that the willingness of the supply-siders to incur huge deficits will produce excessive rates of inflation and loss of confidence in the monetary system. Liberal and conservative critics alike question the economic assumptions of the supply-siders.

Above all, they seriously doubt that the deficits produced by the supply-sider tax cuts will vanish; in fact, the critics believe the deficits, unless curbed, will produce even higher interest rates. To fund the deficit, the supply-side critics argue, it will be necessary for the federal government to gobble up most of the available credit funds just to refinance the government deficit, thus crowding out private sector investor opportunities. In short, excessive government borrowing tends to slow down private sector development. As the federal deficits grow, this adverse affect becomes even greater.[13]

ECONOMIC POLICYMAKING

Next to national security and foreign affairs, post-World War II presidents have spent more time wrestling with macroeconomic policy than any other governmental matter. Consequently, the two principal instruments of macroeconomic policy—fiscal policy and monetary policy—are never far from the top of the president's agenda.

Fiscal policy consists of the government's attempt to regulate the health of the nation's economic activity by shifting the level of taxes and spending in an effort to keep the economy on an even keel. Fiscal policy can be used in two ways: By increasing spending and reducing taxes, the economy can be expanded; conversely, it can be cooled off by increasing taxes and reducing spending. Budget deficits are expansionary and budget surpluses—a rarity these days—are deflationary. Fiscal policy, it should be noted, is made jointly by the president and Congress by budgeting and appropriating funds and through tax policy legislation.

Monetary policy consists of the government's attempt through its central bank (the Federal Reserve Bank in the United States) to regulate the supply of money. Established by Congress in 1913, the Federal Reserve Board uses three main devices to influence interest rates and to control the money supply: the rediscount rate, reserve requirements, and open-market operations.

The rediscount rate refers to the interest rate charged commercial banks to borrow from the Federal Reserve Bank, which in turn affects the availability of credit for business investment. By increasing the discount rate the Fed, as the central bank is popularly called, tightens the availability of credit to member banks because it forces banks to charge a higher rate of interest to borrowers. If the Fed permits a reduction in the member bank's reserve requirement, it increases the availability of credit to member banks who can then lend it to customers. Reserve requirements are the bank balances (usually 10 to 20 percent) that member banks must maintain on deposit at one of the regional banks in the Federal Reserve system.

To manage the money supply, the Fed uses open market operations— buying and selling commercial securities from commercial banks. If the Fed wants to expand the money supply, it orders its regional reserve banks to purchase government securities on the money market, paying for them by drawing from Uncle Sam's account. As soon as the checks are cashed by the Treasury at commercial banks, the Treasury's account balance at the commercial bank increases. The commercial member banks can then present the checks at the regional Federal Reserve bank for redemption. The regional Federal Reserve banks credit the checks to the reserve accounts of commercial bank members. With this increased balance, the commercial banks can then lend to more private borrowers. Generally, they can lend amounts to, say, ten times the amount of the government securities the member has put on deposit at the reserve bank.

Conversely, the Fed's sale of government securities in the open market reduces the money supply and thus the availability of credit. From time to time Congress has given the Fed temporary authority to fix terms of consumer credit. Federal Reserve banks also serve as depositories for government funds, clear millions of checks daily, and transfer funds among member banks. All of this activity, it should be noted, is conducted beyond the purview of the president and the White House staff.

While the Federal Reserve banking system generally works as its original sponsors planned, the President's Council of Economic Advisers and the Fed sometimes disagree on fiscal policy. In 1957 the Fed took action to moderate the expansionary course proposed by the President's Council of Economic Advisers, as it also did in 1966–1969 and 1974–1975.[14] Federal Reserve Chairman Arthur Burns in 1977 testified against the Carter administration's tax-cut proposals, again generating fears that the Fed might oppose administration policies. Clearly, the Federal Reserve's Board of Governors has the ability to counterbalance or aid attempts by a president or Congress to stimulate the economy.

From its inception, the Federal Reserve Board has intentionally been isolated from direct pressure from the president and Congress. Though it may have exceeded the expectations of its founders, the Fed has become a major economic policymaking institution that endeavors to provide national economic stability. Some observers, however, believe it is improper to delegate this major economic policymaking function to an agency so divorced from political accountability. The Fed's monetary policy, for example, can entail making a choice between fighting inflation, which may cause unemployment, or expanding credit, which may cause additional inflationary pressures, without the matter ever being put to a vote in Congress or reviewed by the president of the United States. Thus far, however, prevailing opinion in Congress and within the financial community has been to keep politics out of the Federal Reserve system.

Microeconomic Policy.   Macroeconomic policy is always the central concern of the president and his advisers. But from time to time they will also devote considerable attention to microeconomic policy—a term used to describe government regulation of specific economic activity and antitrust policy. Twentieth-century presidents, it should be noted, became involved in microeconomic policy long before they accepted the role of overall manager of the economy. Theodore Roosevelt and William Howard Taft pushed for vigorous enforcement of the Sherman Anti-Trust Act of 1890 in an attempt to preserve competition in the marketplace. Wilson, a Progressive Democrat, continued the Roosevelt-Taft tradition by obtaining congressional passage of the Clayton Anti-Trust Act of 1914 and the establishment of an independent regulatory agency, the Federal Trade Commission, to regulate and control unfair business practices. All three presidents believed the federal government had the responsibility and duty to prevent the excesses of trade restraints and unfair competition from suffocating the free market economy.

The collapse of the American economy in the Great Depression, however, persuaded Franklin D. Roosevelt that legislation was needed to bring the operation of the stock market, private utilities, communications, and airlines under the watchful eye of the government. Congress, at Roosevelt's urging, established a series of independent regulatory agencies—the Securities and Exchange Commission, the Federal Power Commission, the Federal Communications Commission, the National Labor Relations Board, and the Civil Aeronautics Board—to halt abusive business practices and to serve as a referee among competing companies. FDR also turned his antitrust lawyers in the Justice Department loose to pursue certain big businesses—"economic royalists"—whose anticompetitive practices, the president said, were impeding the nation's recovery. A pragmatist of the first order, Roosevelt used a variety of governmental actions in his efforts to improve the health of the economy, discarding those that proved unproductive.[15]

Post-World War II presidents—Truman, Eisenhower, Kennedy, and Johnson—pursued moderate microeconomic policies. Even Eisenhower, a moderately conservative Republican, chose not to dismantle the New Deal social reforms or disband New Deal regulatory agencies established to monitor various sectors of the economy. Antitrust activity continued, but it was more of a "shotgun behind the door" threat than a serious campaign against monopoly or unfair competition.

The late 1960s marked a new era of microeconomic policy. Instead of concern about restraint of trade, presidents echoed popular demands for a cleaner environment, safer automobiles, improved occupational safety, and higher health standards. The mounting costs of environmental protection and occupational safety, however, triggered a reaction from Presidents Nixon and Ford and their supporters in the business community. This reaction soon spawned a different crusade—deregulation. Between 1976 and 1982, microeconomic policies included deregulation (in varying degrees) of surface and air transportation, stock exchange brokerage operations, financial markets, and interstate communications. These microeconomic policies, both Carter and Reagan insisted, would have a stimulating effect on the economy by throwing open to competition markets that for decades had been subject to excessive governmental regulation.[16]

Clearly, over the past half-century presidential microeconomic policies have reflected the mood of the times—the Great Depression, the rapid post-World War II economic expansion, the environmental-conservationist movement of the 1960s, and the recently rediscovered popular appeal of open competition in the marketplace. Both macro- and microeconomic policies, it should be emphasized, are usually in operation at the same time and interact with each other. Indeed, they may sometimes be in conflict: A regulatory policy that emphasizes pollution control will tend to conflict with a macroeconomic growth policy. In any event, microeconomic policies have always been subordinate to macroeconomic policies. Despite their appeal, microeconomic policies cannot serve as a substitute for fiscal and monetary policies, which are the foundation of a president's program to achieve and maintain a healthy economy.

Until the end of World War II, White House economic policymaking was handled on an ad hoc basis. Franklin Roosevelt had no regular executive departments, other than the Treasury, involved in economic policymaking. Instead, he asked Congress to establish a variety of special agencies to help stimulate the economy and put people back to work—the Public Works Administration, the Works Progress Administration, the National Youth Administration, and until it was declared unconstitutional, the National Industrial Recovery Administration. However, once the United States entered World War II, FDR established a number of special agencies to provide overall direction of the economy—the War Production Board, the War Manpower Commission, the Defense Plant Corporation. When the war ended, Congress decided that the president needed a formal structure to oversee the economy, and it passed the Employment Act of 1946.

THE EMPLOYMENT ACT OF 1946

Although Truman did not request the legislation, Congress for the first time in the Employment Act of 1946 officially gave recognition to macroeconomic policy and made the president general overseer of the economy. As Samuel Kernell phrased it: "The Full Employment Act of 1946 may have acknowledged overall government responsibility for managing the economy, but public opinion makes the president personally responsible."[17] Passage of this legislation represented still another transfer of authority and responsibility from Congress to the president.

In this new legislation, Congress stipulated that the president must prepare an annual economic report for the lawmakers. The net effect of this action was to elevate the Economic Report of the President to the level of the State of the Union address and the budget message. Also, Congress voted to establish a Council of Economic Advisers to serve, in effect, as the president's in-house advisory board on economic matters. This legislation, which marked the acceptance of the Keynesian approach to management of the economy, set up the following machinery to carry out the government's responsibility:

1. *The Council of Economic Advisers.* This body, consisting of three members appointed by the president with the consent of the Senate, was placed in the Executive Office of the President. Its duties included forecasting economic trends, assessing the contribution of federal programs to maximum employment, and recommending to the president "national economic policies to foster and promote free competition, to avoid economic fluctuations or to diminish the effects thereof, and to maintain employment, production, and purchasing power."

2. *The Economic Report of the President.* Each January the president is required to submit to Congress an economic report based on the data and forecasts of the council. The report is expected to include a program for carrying out the policy of the act; it may also include recommendations for legislation.

3. *Joint Economic Committee (JEC).* Originally called the Congressional Joint Committee on the Economic Report, this committee of Congress, composed of eight senators and eight representatives, reports its findings and proposals in response to annual presidential recommendations. (Actually, the new Senate and House Budget Committee created in the mid-1970s has overshadowed the JEC in charting the federal budget and spending plans and conducting policy overview.)

The Employment Act of 1946 greatly enlarged the macroeconomic responsibilities of the federal government by requiring it "to promote maximum employment, production, and purchasing power." The word "maximum," it should be noted, was substituted for "full" employment. It should also be pointed out that the legislation did not specify the means or policies that should be used to meet these goals. Nor did the act, for example, mention price inflation, or any central planning. In other words, the Employment Act of 1946 did not define public policy, but rather confirmed the federal government's commitment to macroeconomic policymaking. As has often been the case with new legislation, the result was a compromise. However, the compromise has worked fairly well. As Hargrove and Nelson have noted: "Since 1946 liberals have been comfortable with the idea of selective government interventions in economic markets, and conservatives, while not rejecting that responsibility, have been more disposed to leave things alone in the belief that government intervention leads to market inefficiency, budget deficits, and inflation."[18]

THE PRESIDENT'S ECONOMIC TEAM

While many aspects of domestic policy can be delegated, the major questions of macroeconomics—employment, inflation, economic growth, participation in the international economy, and the interaction of fiscal and monetary policy—rest squarely on the president's shoulders. To handle this monumental and frequently frustrating task, all post-World War II presidents have relied on several agencies and advisers. The degree of influence wielded by these various members of the president's team, varies from administration to administration, but the president's macroeconomic policymaking depends heavily upon the following agencies.

Council of Economic Advisers (CEA).   Established by the Employment Act of 1946, the CEA has no line or operational responsibility; it serves exclusively as a staff arm to the president. This three-member team and small staff concentrate on gathering economic data, making forecasts, analyzing issues, and preparing the president's annual Economic Report to Congress. The relationship of the CEA chairman to the president will usually determine the degree of the CEA's influence in affecting national economic policy. Truman found little use for the first CEA chairman, Edwin Nourse, who often privately lectured the president on economics and yet was reluctant to defend the president in public.[19] His second chairman, Leon Keyserling, a New Deal activist, was much more to his liking because he vigorously defended Truman's policies before Congress. Kennedy made CEA Chairman Walter Heller the "point man" for his administration's economic policies. Kennedy, for example, relied on Heller to float trial balloons or to defend still-to-be-formulated administration policies, such as an innovative tax policy that the president for political reasons was not yet prepared to adopt publicly.[20] Later, Kennedy received widespread approval for the special tax cut and the rapid depreciation writeoffs, first advocated by Heller.

Reagan's CEA chairman, Marvin Feldstein, was recently put in the presidential doghouse because he continued to state publicly until the end of his term in June 1984 that the administration's record-breaking deficits, if not soon checked, contained the seeds of economic disaster for the nation. In recent years, it seems fair to say, the influence of the Council of Economic Advisers has declined as economic policy has become more political and the number of economic counselors to the president has grown.[21]

Treasury Department.   The role of the Treasury Department in economic policymaking should not be underestimated. Treasury has the main institutional authority and responsibility for income and corporate tax administration, currency control, public borrowing, and counseling the president on such questions as the price of gold, the balance of payments, the federal debt, monetary matters in general, and international trade. And there has been a blurring of the traditional distinction between domestic and foreign economic policy.[22] As a pivotal member of the cabinet, the secretary of the treasury will have important ties with the nation's financial community; indeed, he will usually have held a high position within that community before assuming his cabinet duties. Consequently, most presidents lean heavily on their secretary of the treasury for advice. Some presidents depend heavily on this secretary to sell the administration's fiscal program to Congress and to keep the president's critics at bay.

Truman often turned to his Treasury Secretary John Snyder, a midwestern banker, for support and advice. Eisenhower, whose respect for his Secretary of the Treasury George Humphrey, a former steel company executive, bordered on reverence, once described his trusted cabinet member this way: "In Cabinet meetings I always wait for George Humphrey to speak. I sit back and listen to the others talk while he doesn't say anything. But I know that when he speaks, he will say just what I was thinking."[23] Kennedy, on the other hand, preferred to receive economic advice from a variety of sources. He encouraged a debate between his advisers and set the CEA against the Treasury Department. This president, for example, created a Cabinet Committee on Economic Growth (chaired by the CEA) and matched this group in debate against a Cabinet Committee on the Balance of Payments (chaired by the Treasury) before making decisions.[24] Nixon, who preferred to concentrate on foreign policy and found economic matters boring, virtually handed over authority to Treasury Secretaries John Connally and George Shultz to make major decisions. Ford attempted to institutionalize his financial advisory system through creation of an Economic Policy Board. Consisting of all cabinet secretaries (except defense and the attorney general) the CEA, the Office of Management and Budget, and an international economic advisory group, the Ford administration's advisory structure resembled a "collective presidency."[25] But scant evidence has been uncovered to indicate that it operated any more effectively; in fact, many critics said it was less effective than the economic policymaking structures of other recent presidents.

Like Nixon, President Reagan during his first term gave almost free rein to Treasury Secretary Donald Regan in handling the president's economic responsibilities. So confident was Secretary Regan of the president's backing that he stunned members of the Senate Budget Committee in February 1984 by publicly trashing the annual report of the Chairman of the Council of Economic Advisers, Marvin Feldstein, which had warned of soaring deficits. Snapped Regan, "As far as I am concerned you can throw it away."[26]

The Office of Management and Budget.   Since President Nixon upgraded the Office of Management and Budget (formerly the Bureau of the Budget) in the early 1970s, this agency has moved into the inner circle of the president's economic policymakers. Though constituted originally to keep down the level of spending, the OMB has become the principal agency for shaping the spending component of fiscal policy. Presidents have differed in their level of confidence in the OMB, but Ford and Carter used it as a counterweight to the military budget prepared by the secretary of defense, and both upheld the OMB rather than the department on several crucial issues.[27]

Originally staffed with government careerists, the OMB since the Nixon years has become a political arm of the president. Top OMB officials have been recruited from outside the ranks of the civil service and now are clearly recognized as political assistants of the president. Furthermore, as one team of scholars has put it: "The budget has become as much a political weapon as a managerial tool or an instrument of fiscal policy."[28] If any Washington observers had cause to doubt the politicization of the OMB and the use of the budget as a major political weapon of the administration, these doubts were erased early in the first Reagan administration by the publication of former *Washington Post* reporter William Greider's article on OMB Director David Stockman's private views of the first Reagan budget. Stockman, in his candid discussions with Greider, conceded that the OMB's projection of a modest deficit in the fiscal 1982 budget had been grossly underestimated.[29] Stockman admitted that he had publicly defended the Reagan budget before congressional committees, while having deep private reservations about the Reagan economic plan—he called it a "Trojan horse."[30] The Stockman story produced, as expected, congressional demands for his resignation. But Stockman, after receiving a public reprimand from the president, continued as the OMB director. His encyclopedic knowledge of the budget and skill at preparing the president's chief economic document apparently convinced Reagan that he could ill afford to replace him. (Stockman continued as head of OMB until August 1985, when he resigned to take up duties with a big Wall Street investment house.)

The Federal Reserve Board.   Though an integral part of the economic subpresidency, the Federal Reserve Board is an independent agency charged with the responsibility for regulating the money supply and the banking system.[31] While the president appoints and the Senate confirms each of the seven members, neither the president or Congress can tell the Fed how to conduct monetary policy. But the president does have the authority to designate its chairman for a four-year term. The Fed, by its control of the money supply, affects monetary policy. With an expansionary monetary policy (pumping more money into the economy through the Federal Reserve system), the Fed can help stimulate economic activity and increase employment. If the Fed decides to impose a restrictive monetary policy on the economy, the result will be a slowdown in economic activity, tighter credit, and increased unemployment. The Fed's monetary policy also affects fiscal policy by making it easier or more difficult for the government to fund budget deficits and refinance government securities as they become due. Since high interest rates and tight money restrain deficit financing and make it more costly for the federal government to finance the national debt, the Fed by its actions often finds itself the target of critics in the White House and on Capitol Hill.

More than one Fed chairman has clashed with the White House over the impact of the central bank's actions on fiscal policy. Some observers, however, have concluded that the Fed's independent authority serves as a convenient scapegoat for president and Congress alike. In a political sense, the Fed is in a no win position, since its expansionary monetary policy can be attacked as inflationary and its restrictive policy can be said to contribute to recession and unemployment. In September 1980, the Federal Reserve drew loud complaints from President Carter after it raised its discount rate by a full point (from 11 to 12 percent) less than six weeks before the presidential election. Similarly, during the severe 1982 recession and the mounting deficits in fiscal year 1983, President Reagan and his Secretary of the Treasury Donald Regan could frequently be heard blaming the Federal Reserve Board monetary policy, not the administration's heavy defense spending and federal borrowing, for the record-breaking national deficits.

Fed Chairman Paul Volcker was often singled out as the chief culprit for causing high interest rates. But when Volcker's four-year term as Fed chairman came up for renewal in mid-1984—a presidential election year—President Reagan confounded his critics by reappointing him for another four years. Though Volcker had originally been appointed to this post by President Carter, Wall Street and the nation's banking community came to regard him as one of the strongest chairman in the history of the Federal Reserve. In any case, President Reagan decided to let well enough alone and reappointed the strong-minded Volcker. The decision was applauded by Republicans and Democrats alike. It also demonstrated once again Reagan's deft hand in major decisions.

FISCAL POLICY IN A DIVIDED GOVERNMENT

Presidential influence over fiscal policy is least effective during periods of split government, as former President Gerald Ford can readily attest. During his brief 30 months in the White House, Ford faced a Democratic-controlled Congress. For fiscal year 1977, which embraced part of a presidential election year, Ford submitted a restricted budget that emphasized basic stability rather than growth. Congress, however, under its new budget committee system, raised expenditures $17 billion higher in its first budget resolution than the totals proposed by Ford. Six months later, its revised resolution was still $13.1 billion higher than figures proposed by the White House. Ford also advocated a $10 billion cut in taxes if his budget were adopted in order to put the Democrats on the defensive in a presidential election year. He vetoed several appropriations bills in excess of his requests, and he submitted recision (or deferred) requests whenever the Democratic Congress appropriated funds in excess of the figures he requested.

But it was all to no avail. As Richard M. Pious summarized Ford's frustration: "The Democratic Congress denied these requests, shelved his proposed increase in payroll taxes, raised figures in appropriations, and prepared its own tax program. Ford eventually signed the tax bill."[32] Though Ford made his fiscal policy an issue in the election campaign, the voters obviously were not impressed with this complicated issue. His defeat was a further indication that Congress could, if the president's party did not control the legislative branch, retain the power to make the final decisions about fiscal policy.[33]

FISCAL POLICY: MYTHS AND REALITY

Most students of the federal government have long concluded that fiscal policy-making is truly an inexact science. In recent years the administration's calculations on expenditures, receipts, and the anticipated deficit have, more often than not, been grotesquely wrong. When Ronald Reagan presented his first budget for fiscal year 1982, the deficit was put at $24.1 billion. When the 1982 fiscal year ended, the official deficit stood at $110.6 billion—off the mark by 358.8 percent. And this was not an isolated case. Over the past sixteen years, in only five instances was the margin of error on the deficit less than 50 percent.[34] Why the gross miscalculations? In the case of fiscal year 1982, few economists foresaw the depth of the recession—the chief reason revenue fell $90.1 billion short of the initial forecast. While over the past sixteen years the average error for revenue has been 4.4 percent and for outlays 3 percent, even small errors in each of these categories can have a powerful effect on the deficit, especially when receipts and outlays move in opposite directions.

In assessing an administration's fiscal policy, outside observers should always remember that federal budgets are expressions of the president's political goals and hopes. Furthermore, the administration's budget is always biased on the side of optimism. According to one former congressional aide: "It has to be optimistic because it has to show things getting better because of what the President wants."[35]

Since 1974, the Congressional Budget Office (CBO) calculations on receipts, expenditures, and size of the deficit have injected more reality into the entire process. But even the CBO has had a tough time with its calculations because the inflation rate is so difficult to chart. Other factors—how many unemployed will be eligible for benefits or welfare? Will there be a drought or some other national disaster that will require increased payments to farmers?—also make precise calculations next to impossible. Briefly, then, nobody really knows what the economy will be doing the next year. Forecasters as a group have had a dismal record in recent years, but the recent introduction of computers has enabled them to make substantial gains in their econometric analysis. And despite all the flaws in economic forecasting, presidents will continue to paint a glowing picture of the future, telling the voters much of the time what they want to hear. Thus, even though OMB officials pointed out to President Reagan that the deficit would continue to remain above the $100 billion figure throughout his second term, the president continued for almost a year to argue in his televised speeches that with continuing prosperity the country can largely "grow" its way out of deficits.

Especially since the passage of the landmark Employment Act of 1946, the health of the nation's economy has been a major issue in presidential politics. Whether he wishes it or not, the president's political fortunes depend more on the state of the economy—the inflation rate, the prime interest rate, the rate of unemployment, and the consumer price index—than on whether the president understands the intricacies of the North Atlantic Treaty Organization or is on good terms with the party's national committee.

But as most post-World War II presidents have discovered, the labyrinth of the congressional committee structure, especially the massive growth of subcommittees since the mid-1970s, the proliferation of special interest groups that fight most reforms (except lower taxes) in economic policy, and the huge built-in entitlement costs for social security and Medicare all stand in the way of most presidential economic initiatives. Although the president is held fully accountable for managing the entire federal budget, his discretion now extends to less than 25 percent of the total outlays, since much of that budget has already been predetermined by decisions of his predecessors and earlier Congresses. With rare exceptions, presidents have formidable difficulties in getting Congress to pass their economic agenda or alter parts of their domestic programs. As Thomas E. Cronin has explained:

> Congressional barriers to Presidential initiatives are particularly apparent in the important areas of budget and tax policies, both of which must be approved by

Congress. Timely presidential fiscal initiatives, particularly countercyclical fiscal actions, become difficult to carry through because Congress generally resists any raising of taxes and, at the same time, any cutting of spending for federal programs. Even the threat of the latter brings an avalanche of protests from the interests groups inside and outside the government. Thus, for example, tax cuts passed in 1964, 1969, and 1971 were coupled with actual expansions of existing programs, which sharply reduced federal revenue receipts and strongly braked the ability of either the president or Congress to launch significant new social-action programs.[36]

In Chapter 6 we compared the track records of post-World War II presidents and the percentage of their domestic legislation and foreign policy initiatives passed. Presidents can consider themselves lucky if they obtain passage of 50 percent of their economic and other policy initiatives.[37] Therefore, if they wish to raise their economic batting average, they must constantly exhort, push, and prod Congress and frequently turn to national television and radio to sell their programs to the American people. Franklin D. Roosevelt, though he served before the age of television, keenly understood the value of constant communication with Congress and the American public to obtain support for his programs. Ronald Reagan has had an equally keen appreciation of the importance of mass communication in selling his economic and foreign policy initiatives to Congress and the American public. Indeed, throughout the transition period between his November election victory and his first inauguration, he seldom missed an opportunity to promote his proposed new tax reform plan to the American public— and to any congressman who might be listening—via radio and television.

REAGANOMICS

Unlike his Democratic predecessors, Reagan has had a long-term belief that prosperity required a far more limited role of government in the economic sphere, while the preservation of peace and traditional values required, in many cases, an expanded role. This philosophy, which combined a libertarian's distrust of government in the economic arena with the traditional conservative belief in moral absolutes, coupled with a fervent insistence on the need for a strong national defense against external foes, served as the driving force behind the rapid adoption of the Reaganomics economic package in 1981.[38] The clarity of the administration's top economic priorities enabled the Reagan team, aided by effective political liaison on Capitol Hill, to move its program through Congress before the opposition could organize. (The newly developed parliamentary tactic of bill reconciliation, used by Reagan's lieutenants on Capitol Hill to obtain speedy passage of the Reagan economic package, is discussed later in the chapter.)

Reagan's solution to the economic woes of the country was appealing: "Taxes would be reduced, defense spending accelerated, and the federal budget balanced. Inflation would be curbed without a rise in unemployment, and the solutions to the nation's economic ills would be equitable with no one group singled out to pay a higher price."[39]

John L. Palmer and Isabel V. Sawhill, in their systematic analysis of Reaganomics, summarized the administration's priorities as follows:

First, the tax cuts and the defense buildup took precedence over balancing the budget.

Second, reducing inflation took precedence over moderating the recession.

Third, it turned out that there was not enough fat in the domestic side of the federal budget to avoid reducing benefits and services. The deepest cuts were proposed for grants to state and local governments and for programs serving the poor. Little was done to reduce rapidly rising expenditures for Social Security, Medicare, government employee pensions, and other predominantly middle-class programs that have been the chief source of growth in the federal budget since the 1950's.

Fourth, the tax cuts were designed with economic growth, not equity, in mind. The fraction of each extra dollar of income earned that went to taxes had risen sharply since the mid-1960's, and the administration was determined to reduce the disincentives these high marginal rates implied for saving investment and work. Consequently, rates were cut across the board, providing the greatest benefits to higher-income families.

Fifth, the administration's regulatory policies emphasized productivity over the protection of health, safety, civil rights, and the environment. Productivity growth had slowed during the 1970's, in part, because of some of the actions taken to deal with these problems, and the administration's intent was to swing the pendulum back in the pro-growth direction.[40]

Commenting on the Reaganomics package sent to Capitol Hill, two veteran Washington observers noted: "It seems fair to say that no incoming administration had ever before staked so much on a specific, comprehensive economic program. In contrast, the administration of Franklin Roosevelt, with which Ronald Reagan and his supporters like to compare themselves, was a hodgepodge of political experience and unresolved economic theorizing."[41]

Once Congress had passed the administration's Economic Recovery Act of 1981, Reagan stood like a proud sea captain at the bridge, confident that the ship of state was right on course. To be sure, a few mid-ocean corrections might be needed, but with a high-quality gyrocompass and a dependable crew, Captain Reagan saw no reason to worry about the future. By 1983, the nation had emerged from a stormy recession that in mid-1982 saw unemployment exceed 10 percent. However, the recession bottomed out in January 1983, thanks chiefly to the Federal Reserve's belated easing of monetary policy but also to the tax cuts and defense buildup, which caused fiscal policy to turn sharply expansionary.[42] By 1984, a presidential election year, the American economy was moving ahead at full throttle. The favorable economic factors helped propel Reagan to a landslide reelection victory in 1984. On the day of his second inauguration, Reagan announced to the nation that national economic growth in 1984 was 6.4 percent—the highest recorded in 30 years.

In summarizing the economic policymaking endeavors of Ronald Reagan's first four years in the White House, Isabel V. Sawhill and Charles F. Stone of the Urban Institute commented:

> The administration's greatest success has been on the inflation front, but here it must share credit with the Federal Reserve. Moreover, it was a good time to be president: housing, oil, food, and import price movements all helped inflation fall, making policy look even more effective than it was.[43]

Clearly, supply-side economic policymaking has left a legacy that will continue to influence the nation's economy for years to come. Whether this unconventional approach to policymaking is the type of macroeconomic policy needed for the long term is a question that remains unanswered.

PRESIDENTIAL ALTERNATIVES TO
FISCAL POLICY INTERVENTION

Presidents are not limited to fiscal policy intervention to try and keep the economy healthy—and reelection prospects upbeat. To provide more jobs in both the private and the public sectors, he may propose various countercyclical employment and public works "pump priming" projects. Or he may prefer to push rapid tax depreciation write-offs, or to recommend tax credits to companies that employ the long-term unemployed, handicapped, unskilled, or those entering the job market for the first time. To control inflation, he may propose such microeconomic policies as deregulation of certain sectors of the economy, vigorous antitrust action in key industries, changes in tariff rates or special marketing agreements with friendly countries.[44]

To influence wage rates and prices, an activist president may resort to public appeal—"jawboning"—to persuade unions to moderate demands and convince management to keep down price increases. Second, the administration can establish guideposts—administration targets for wage settlements and price increases that unions and management may agree to consider in their negotiations. Third, the administration can resort to sector stabilization—that is, the establishment of labor-management committees to develop guidelines for settlements to keep price and wage increases at specified limits. Finally, if Congress agrees, the president can ask for standby wage-price controls. These are usually administered by a tripartite pay board (consisting of representatives from labor, management, and the public) and a price board consisting of members of the public.

By and large, these various ad hoc attempts to keep the economy healthy have seldom fulfilled the White House's expectations. President Kennedy's "jawboning" the steel industry to keep prices down made a good media story on the network evening news shows, but this confrontation with Big Steel eroded business confidence and sent the stock market plunging. Kennedy's wage guideposts were ineffective. Trade union leaders, who preferred to bargain without political interference, won concessions that clearly exceeded the administration guideline figures. Sector stabilization, labor-management committees to keep wage and price increases at specified limits were ineffective. More recently, "Carter's decision to establish a labor-management committee, instead of promoting sector stabilization, was taken as a signal that he would not impose controls."[45]

Nixon's dramatic announcement in summer 1971 that, as a result of skyrocketing inflation, he would impose the first peacetime wage and price controls in American history, stunned business leaders and labor union chieftains alike. Congress had originally passed, over Nixon's objections, standby wage-price control legislation in 1970 to put him on the spot politically, never dreaming that the conservative president would ever call their bluff. The net effect of the Nixon wage-price control program was to keep prices down until after he had successfully won reelection in 1972. Then the inflationary pressures began bursting the seams of the economy. By 1973, as the administration began relaxing controls, the inflation rate had climbed to 11.5 percent. By the time the last controls were removed and the standby wage-price control legislation expired in April 1974, inflation had soared to 12.2 percent. But by that time the nation's attention seemed to be focused more on the Watergate special prosecutor's efforts to obtain certain White House tapes and the House Judiciary Committee's impending impeachment hearings.

Generally, the president's task of trying to keep the nation's economy healthy requires that he should be a frequent oracle of good tidings. When the economy is booming, he should take the lion's share of the credit for the nation's prosperity; and when the economy is sliding badly, he should quickly find as many scapegoats as possible—the congressional budget process, the Fed, special interests, excessively high wage settlements, and Congress's refusal to give him the constitutional weapons needed to fight unbalanced budgets (the line item veto, a constitutional amendment requiring a balanced budget). How successfully the president performs this economic high-wire act largely determines whether the electorate will give him a second term. Unfortunately, most macroeconomic and microeconomic problems the president encounters have no easy solutions, but the American public's expectations of his solving these problems remain high.

ELECTORAL ECONOMICS

The relationship of macroeconomic policy and electoral politics has long been recognized, especially by national politicians and high-level economic advisers. They fervently believe that the economy affects the electoral fate of the incumbent party. Several articles of this faith have been summarized by political scientist Edward R. Tufte:

1. Economic movements in the months preceding an election can tip the balance and decide the outcome of the election.
2. The electorate rewards incumbents for prosperity and punishes them for recessions.
3. Short-run spurts in economic growth in the months preceding an election benefit incumbents.[46]

What truth is there to this political business cycle thesis? Do electoral cycles actually exist? Have presidents and congressional majorities successfully manipulated economic policy to improve their electoral standing with the voters? Tufte has argued that administrations will manipulate short-term economic conditions with expansionary fiscal policies, even if it generates more inflation or increased rates of unemployment after the election. In his studies Tufte has discerned a distinct improvement in the economy in presidential election years.

Tufte discovered two distinct electoral-economic cycles between 1948 and 1976, except during the Eisenhower administration.[47] The first two-year cycle, which meshed with congressional elections, showed that real disposable income per capita rises in even-numbered years and drops in the odd-numbered years. Tufte points out that stepped-up benefits in social security, farm programs, and other domestic programs as well as tax cuts have been used to boost income before elections. The second cycle, which occurs over a four-year period and synchronizes with presidential elections, involves a drop in unemployment in the months preceding the election and a rise in layoffs over the next 12 to 18 months.

Tufte has also concluded that *the greater the electoral stakes, the greater the economic improvement.*[48] Presidents often try to insure that the economy is booming with high employment and rising personal income in presidential election years.[49] According to Tufte: "Real disposable income increased an average of 3.4 percent in years when the incumbent president sought reelection, 2.6 percent in midterm election years, 2.0 percent in those years when the incumbent president did not seek reelection, and a dismal 1.5 percent in off-numbered years."[50] These findings held for the entire set of elections from 1946 to 1976, including the Eisenhower years. Throughout this three-decade period, the median rate of growth in real disposable income per capita was 3.3 percent in years when the incumbent president sought reelection and only 1.7 percent in all other years.[51]

ECONOMIC POLICYMAKING AND THE POCKETBOOK ISSUE

A conventional view in American politics is that ratings of the president are affected strongly by personal economic circumstances. According to this view, people "vote their pocketbook." What this maxim means is that the voters consider presidential elections to be referendums on the incumbent administration's management of the economy, and they are more likely to approve of the president if they feel they are prospering personally than if they feel they are not. Echoing this line of thinking, Lyndon Johnson, according to one of his aides, believed: "The family pocketbook was the root-and-branch crucial connection to all of his plans and hopes for the future."[52] Recently, however, some scholars have articulated a somewhat different perspective of presidential approval, insisting that citizens evaluate a president on the basis of broader views of the economy than merely their self-interests.[53] That is, rather than asking what the president has done for them lately, citizens ask what the president has done for the nation.[54]

George C. Edwards III, a close student of presidential popularity, has concluded: "There is substantial support for the assertion that general evaluations of the economy are more important influences on voting than are the narrow self-interests of the voters."[55] In other words: "Citizen's evaluations of the president's handling of unemployment, inflation, and the economy in general are related strongly to overall presidential approval. In sum, the public evaluates the president's role in the economy more on the basis of his performance than on its view of the state of the economy."[56] Brady and Sniderman have added support to the view that personal economic circumstances do not dominate personal assessments of the president. They have found that most people do not politicize their personal problems. Significantly, they report that most of those concerned about personal economic problems do not believe that the government should come to their aid.[57]

Additional support for the view that personal economic circumstances do not dominate evaluations of the president comes from a January 1981 Gallup poll, which found that although 81 percent of the public was dissatisfied with the way things were in the country, 83 percent were satisfied with the way things were going in their personal lives.[58] People, according to this theory, evaluate the president in terms of the state of the economy in broad terms rather than its effect on them personally. Furthermore, they may simply evaluate how well the president is handling overall economic policy, regardless of the short-term impact of his actions.[59]

If a president can point to his success in fulfilling these goals, especially in the third and fourth years of his first term, he will be well on his way to reelection, as Ronald Reagan clearly demonstrated in 1984. Failure to meet or approach these goals usually speeds electoral defeat, as several twentieth-century presidents can attest. President Hoover's failure to take strong governmental action during the Great Depression spelled electoral defeat for him in 1932, even though his opponent, New York Governor Franklin D. Roosevelt, campaigned on a policy of sharp cutbacks in government spending. Vice-President Richard M. Nixon narrowly lost his first bid for the presidency in 1960 against a young Democratic senator from Massachusetts, John F. Kennedy, partly because the American economy, facing the chill of its third recession of the decade, was slumping in the midst of the presidential campaign. Kennedy's earnest pledge "to get the country moving again" reflected more accurately the voter's mood.[60]

Gerald Ford, who assumed the presidency after Nixon's forced resignation in 1974, thought his chief economic problem was inflation. But within months, the economic winds shifted rapidly. The sudden downturn forced him into combatting a recession that persisted through the 1976 election and contributed to his defeat at the hands of former Georgia governor Jimmy Carter. But Carter proved no more adept at overseeing the economy: His antirecession program of increased federal spending and tax cuts to stimulate the economy worked almost too well. Carter, midway in his term, faced soaring double-digit inflation and interest rates that peaked near 20 percent in the midst of the 1980 presidential race.

GOP candidate Ronald Reagan's famous question, posed in his 1980 debate with President Carter, "Are you better off today than you were four years ago?" seemed to clinch the election, at least in the eyes of many pundits, since most

Americans answered that question in the negative.[61] Reagan also pledged to restore the economy the "old-fashioned" way, through major reductions in taxing and spending. Although Reagan encountered a rocky economic road midway in his first term as unemployment rates jumped to above 10 percent in 1982 (the highest since the Great Depression), the economy in early 1983 turned around sharply. In other words, the economy began rebounding at the right moment.

Throughout the 1984 presidential campaign, Reagan frequently pointed to the booming economy and declining unemployment, repeating to his friendly campaign audiences the old vaudeville line, "You ain't seen nothing yet." To reduce the high annual deficits created by Reagan's supply-side economics, his opponent, former Vice-President Walter F. Mondale, recommended a tax increase. The electorate was unimpressed with this proposal. Even though the federal debt was $1.6 trillion (not billion), and scheduled to rise, without major tax increases, to $3.1 trillion by 1989, the incumbent president swept 49 out of 50 states. President Reagan's ability to take the huge deficits in stride and to assure the voters that his policies, with the cooperation of Congress, would enable the country to "grow out" of the deficit problem in the years ahead made his reelection campaign task easy.

CONGRESS AND ECONOMIC POLICYMAKING

Despite the fact that the nation looks to the president to keep the nation's economy healthy, Congress plays a major role in formulating national macroeconomic and microeconomic policy. Over the years, Congress has assigned the president increased economic responsibilities through the Budget and Accounting Act of 1921, the Employment Act of 1946, and the Congressional Budget and Impoundment Control Act. But it has always retained its power over the purse.

Until passage of the Congressional Budget Office Act of 1974, however, the two chambers operated more as if they were overseeing the management of a department store, not an organizational structure with more than 3 million employees and a budget that exceeded $100 billion by 1968. Traditionally, Congress handled economic policy through separate consideration of tax legislation and annual appropriations. The House Ways and Means Committee and the Senate Finance Committee served as the two tax-writing committees on Capitol Hill, and each committee jealously guarded its prerogatives. Committee chairs, some of whom had seen several presidents come and go, did not take kindly to White House suggestions on tax reform. Nor was the full Congress receptive to White House proposals on tax legislation without major revisions. President Kennedy was unsuccessful, for example, in obtaining congressional approval of a White House request to make incremental adjustments in tax rates in response to shifting economic conditions. Like an old-fashioned board of directors, the tax-writing committees concentrated on annual incremental changes in the budget requests of the various departments and agencies. To these committees, the bottom line was the amount of annual increases of decreases in each agency's budget base.

Until recently, Congress seldom used its taxing or spending legislation to influence national fiscal policy. Instead, congressional decision making on taxing and spending reflected essentially the fragmented structure of the committee system, the absence of party discipline, and the special interest orientation of committee chairpersons and ranking minority members. As one authority put it: "In both houses the appropriations committees have become, in effect, holding companies for thirteen largely autonomous subcommittees, and in areas like health, public works and defense norms of fiscal austerity have tended to give way to those of client and constituent service."[62]

Not until passage of the Budget and Impoundment Control Act of 1974 could it be said that Congress had begun to put its own financial house in order. The 1974 legislation created, in Richard M. Pious's phrase, an "action-forcing process" for fiscal management. The lawmakers, in his words, "scrapped the ineffective system of expenditure resolutions and provided instead for passage of budget resolutions that would embody decisions about revenues and expenditures."[63] The legislation also created House and Senate Budget Committees with jurisdiction over the budget resolutions, and a Congressional Budget Office (CBO) to serve as a staff agency with a full complement of computer analysts, economists, and statisticians. No longer would Congress have to depend on the expertise of the executive branch for advice on anticipated tax revenues, projected deficits, interest on the national debt, and so on.

Paradoxically, it was President Nixon's unilateral impoundment of appropriations in 1972–73—his refusal to spend funds in excess of his own budget requests—that provoked Congress to pass the Budget and Impoundment Control Act of 1974. The lawmakers were so incensed by the president's action that they quickly pushed through legislation which placed limitations on the ability of the president to interdict the expenditure of appropriated funds. Also, the 1974 act permits greater control over all appropriations, budgetary priorities, and fiscal policy. Under the new budget process, Congress can impose a ceiling on estimates, outlays, and theoretically at least, clamp down on "backdoor spending."[64] Early in the session Congress develops a tentative first resolution budget setting targets for expenditures, receipts, and the size of the public debt. After the tax and appropriations committees have completed their work, Congress passes a second resolution that provides binding ceilings for major program categories and minimums for tax receipts, subject sometimes to later amendment. To meet final budget totals, this resolution must dictate any last-minute changes in expenditures and revenues.

How has the new system worked? The new process, which has meant more congressional participation in fiscal policymaking, permits Congress to consider taxing and spending as a whole package, rather than in bits and pieces.

Under the newly established budget committees, Congress can challenge the president's monopoly on fiscal policy proposals. However, the new process did not enable Congress to resolve the matter of uncontrollable spending arising from the costly entitlement programs and contracted obligations. To tackle this mounting cost, the Senate Budget Committee, chaired by Senator Edmund S. Muskie (D–Me.), developed in 1978 a technique called "reconciliation" to reduce expenditures.

Muskie's committee sent instructions in its second budget resolution to the Appropriations Committee and six legislative committees to prepare within ten days "reconciliation" measures that would reduce fiscal year 1980 expenditures by another $4.2 billion. Although the committee's attempt failed to produce the requested reductions, the House and Senate Budget Committees used it successfully the following year. Despite loud complaints and grumbling in both chambers, they achieved net budgetary savings of $8.3 billion. As Watson and Thomas assessed the budget process: "Through the reconciliation process Congress appeared to have acquired the self-discipline necessary to counteract its internal fragmentation and gain capacity for fiscal responsibility. This it accomplished at the expense of the power of its standing committees."[65] But President Reagan was soon to write another chapter to the budget-making process.

THE REAGAN REVOLUTION

Newly elected presidents soon discover how vitally important it is to have their fiscal policy plans—indeed, the major outlines of their full legislative program—etched out soon after they take the oath of office. For as Lyndon Johnson and Ronald Reagan wisely concluded, major legislation, whether it affects fiscal policy or not, must be passed by Congress in the first year or run the risk of becoming mired in the off-year congressional campaign, the third-year doldrums or in the next round of presidential combat.[66] Thus, within seven weeks of taking office in January 1981, President Reagan sent a full-blown budget to Capitol Hill containing his proposals for a reduction in personal and corporate taxes, a big cut in nondefense spending, and a huge increase in the defense budget. By adroit lobbying and two nationwide televised appeals for popular support of his program, Reagan managed to get the heart of his Reaganomics fiscal program passed before the August 1981 summer recess of Congress—less than seven months after arriving in the nation's capital.[67]

Ironically, the budget reconciliation technique developed by Senator Muskie's committee served as the key to the dramatic passage of the president's economic recovery package of tax cuts and budget reductions. As originally designed by the 1974 Budget Act, "reconciliation" was a procedure by which the House and Senate could instruct their committees at the end of the budget process to come up with spending cuts or tax increases to bring into balance (or to reconcile) what individual congressional committees proposed to spend on the one hand and the overall binding targets of the second resolution on the other. The Reagan strategists in the White House and on Capitol Hill now proposed that reconciliation be used at the beginning of the budget process as "a preemptive strike" by the House and Senate as a whole to overwhelm the individual committees and thus attain the Reagan goals. Clearly, in the words of one veteran of Capitol Hill politics: "It was a revolutionary method for achieving a revolutionary goal."[68] The story unfolded as follows.

By April 1981, the Reagan White House had persuaded the Senate to use the recently perfected reconciliation process to instruct its appropriations and tax-cutting committees to cut out $35.2 billion in the 1982 fiscal year budget sent to Capitol Hill by President Carter before he left office. Since the Republicans controlled the Senate by a 53 to 47 margin, they were able to draft a reconciliation measure without difficulty. The House, however, controlled by the opposition Democrats, moved more deliberately than the Senate. But when the House committee sent its budget resolution to the floor, a Republican–southern Democratic coalition offered a substitute bill—the Gramm-Latta resolution—supported by the Reagan White House. In the final showdown House vote on this substitute bill, the GOP–southern Democratic coalition carried the day by a vote of 232 to 193—a victory margin of 39. Some 47 Democrats had joined 185 Republicans to support the Reagan budget cuts of $37.7 billion.[69]

Under the newly discovered parliamentary process, the Reagan budget cuts were passed in a single vote in each chamber—89 to 11 in the Senate and 238 to 195 in the House.[70] To the amazement of many Capitol Hill watchers, Reagan's sweeping budget cuts were passed without any extensive committee hearings or major floor debate and without amendments. Frustrated Democratic opponents in the Senate could not even resort to the chamber's favorite delaying tactic— the filibuster—because the special rules under the Budget Act of 1974 limited debate on the First Concurrent Budget Resolution to 50 hours, on a reconciliation bill or resolution to 20 hours, on a second budget resolution to not more than 15 hours, and on a conference report to not more than 10 hours.[71]

Democratic critics charged that the Reagan administration had short-circuited the congressional committee process and denied Congress independent control of spending. As Watson and Thomas commented in reviewing Reagan's amazing success: "It is rather ironic that the reconciliation device, through which Congress acquired the self-discipline to gain parity with the president in making fiscal policy, so quickly became the instrument of presidential domination of congressional decision-making."[72] Howard E. Shuman has echoed this view, pointing out that "the president has used the institutions of the Budget Act, particularly reconciliation and the majority vote procedures, to enhance his power to initiate control and dominate budget procedures."[73]

It is noteworthy, however, that in 1982 the reconciliation procedure failed to produce a second budget victory for President Reagan. Indeed, throughout the remainder of his first term, he and Congress were stalemated over further budget cuts. In fact, Congress in 1982 pressured the president into deciding that the continually mounting deficit required not further tax cuts, but what President Reagan euphemistically called a "down payment on the deficit" in the form of a series of substantial tax increases—excise taxes on telephone calls, cigarettes, a five-cent-per-gallon tax on gasoline (to repair the federal interstate highway system), and airport and airline taxes.[74] Critics pointed out that the Reagan tax increases were in actual dollars (approximately $95 billion) the largest single tax increase in the nation's history.

Several economic storm clouds on the horizon in early 1985 suggested that Reagan might not have as smooth a journey during his second term as he had during his first four years in the White House. The continuing annual deficits (averaging slightly under $200 billion), the debate over the national debt that would grow to more than $2 trillion by late 1986, the rising protectionist demands from members of Congress from states adversely affected by huge foreign imports, and the persistent, costly agricultural support price program that has failed to solve the farm surplus problem all indicated that President Reagan had yet to find acceptable solutions, or at least palliatives, to reduce the damaging impact of these seemingly intractable economic problems. Failure to do so during the first half of his second term carried the risk for him of being consigned to the category of just another ineffective, lame duck president.

In late 1985 the Reagan revolution took a new turn, as the national debt approached $2 trillion. Congress, in an effort to half the skyrocketing federal deficits (which again exceeded $200 billion in fiscal 1985), passed the Gramm-Rudman-Hollings deficit reduction bill shortly before the Christmas holidays. The new law mandated a balanced budget in five years. President Reagan promptly fixed his signature to the bill, although at the time of the signing he said he doubted the constitutionality of key provisions of the automatic budget-cutting mechanism.

Named after Republican freshman Senators Phil Gramm of Texas and Warren B. Rudman of New Hampshire and Democratic Senator Ernest Hollings of South Carolina, the legislation establishes a rigid sequence of deficit goals beginning with a $180 billion deficit ceiling in fiscal 1986 and dropping by $36 billion each year until, theoretically at least, it reaches the magic number of zero by 1991. The new law dictates that half the cuts must come from military spending and half from nonmilitary outlays. Some portions of the budget, however, would be off-limits for reductions—social security, interest on the national debt, and existing contractual obligations. Under the new law every September 25, the Congressional Budget Office and the Office of Management and Budget would be required to forecast the deficit for the coming year. The deficit reduction law requires Congress to approve its budget plan by mid-April. If the deficit projections are not in compliance with Gramm-Rudman-Hollings, the law contains a budget-cutting mechanism empowering the comptroller general, with the advice of the Congressional Budget Office and the Office of Management and Budget, in effect to order the president to "sequester" or pull back as many billions in appropriated funds as needed to meet the Gramm-Rudman-Hollings targeted deficit ceiling.

The new law gives the president no power to determine spending cuts in any year and little power to make other cuts. Congress did not trust the president or his subordinates to put aside politics in making budget reductions. The mechanism to force "automatic" cuts was put into the law because Congress for years had been unwilling to vote and the president has been unwilling to propose the kinds of spending cuts both agree are necessary. For the past several years neither side has been willing to face the unpalatable choices—cutting popular domestic programs, slashing deeply into the president's expanded military budget, and raising taxes.[75]

No sooner had Gramm-Rudman-Hollings—known officially as the Balanced Budget and Emergency Deficit Control Act of 1985—been signed into law than a dozen lawmakers joined the National Public Citizen Litigation Group in asking the federal courts to declare the new law unconstitutional. The major question about the constitutionality of the budget-balancing law centered on the mechanism—the "trigger" or budget reduction procedure—that is supposed to make it work. This is the provision designed to insulate deficit reduction from electoral politics by forcing huge, unpopular budget cuts without requiring Congress to vote on them or the president to designate them.

Opponents of the law argued that the law is unconstitutional on its face because the mechanism violates the separation of powers by delegating to unelected officials, chiefly the independent comptroller general, authority to make huge cuts in congressional appropriations.

In early February 1986 a three-member Federal District Court panel in Washington, D.C., ruled that the provision granting the comptroller general power to make budget cuts violated the separation of powers.[76] The court held that Congress could delegate authority over the budget to the president or people answerable to him, but could not shift it to persons removable by Congress—in this case, the comptroller general—through legislation. The court noted under the new law that though the president appointed the comptroller general, this official could be removed by Congress—a constitutional violation of the separation of powers.

Without the budget-cutting mechanism, the new law loses the "club" its supporters thought necessary to get Congress and the White House to compromise on a budget plan. The Supreme Court, which quickly agreed to hear the case, ruled in early July 1986 that the section of the Gramm-Rudman-Hollings statute empowering the comptroller general to trigger automatic budget cuts was unconstitutional. By a 7 to 2 vote, the High Court ruled that the section of the statute that vested executive power in the comptroller general, an officer removable by Congress, violated the separation of powers.[77]

Looking ahead, some Washington observers noted that loss of the threat of automatic cuts might, in the long run, strengthen the hand of President Reagan over the budget issue and the economy by making it less risky for him to refuse to negotiate on tax increases or reductions in the military budget. Without the automatic budget-cutting mechanism hanging over his head, Reagan could afford to remain intransigent against any military cuts. Even if Congress votes to slash the military budget, the president could veto the bill.[78]

THE PRESIDENT AND THE ECONOMY: A RECAPITULATION

No area has a greater gap between presidential responsibilities and public expectations than the economic domain. Still, as Richard M. Pious has noted: "The public expects the president to provide full employment, stable prices, and a rising standard of living."[79] By and large, however, presidents face severe constraints in their attempts to manipulate the economy. Several reasons have been given why presidents cannot do this very effectively.

Presidents, first of all, can seldom act alone in any economic policy. Congress must approve the entire federal budget and all tax rates. John F. Kennedy, for example, asked Congress in 1962 for authority, if needed, to raise or lower taxes to "fine tune" the economy. Congressional leaders, appalled at the thought, rejected this proposal outright.[80] In recent years Congress has often been in the hands of the party that does not control the White House; consequently, cooperation between the two branches on economic (or any other) policy often becomes the victim of partisan politics. Why should a Democratic Congress, for example, enact policies that may help a GOP president win reelection? Even if the president's party controls Congress, this is not a guarantee that the lawmakers will automatically fall in line on policy matters. Special interest groups with close ties to leading factions within the majority party can often thwart presidential programs. Jimmy Carter's failure to obtain congressional approval of his comprehensive energy program immediately comes to mind.

Even when the president is on an economic course of action that seems to offer promising results, the clanking congressional machinery usually moves so slowly that by the time the president's program is enacted, most of the window of opportunity may be lost. For example, the tax cuts recommended by President Kennedy in late 1962 were not passed until sixteen months later—five months after he was assassinated. Before passage of this legislation and while Kennedy was still in the White House, southern Democrats were reportedly ready to stall the legislation to win concessions on civil rights from the president. But when Kennedy was slain and Lyndon B. Johnson was sworn in, talk of delaying action ceased, and under Johnson's heavy prodding the tax cuts were quickly passed.[81] In this instance, compensatory fiscal policy was delayed so long by Congress that its full impact was lost. Also, the president's budget is prepared so many months (upward of 16 months) in advance of its enactment into law that it is unclear what the state of the economy will be when it passes and what the impact of the budget will be upon it.

Second, with respect to fiscal policy the president must take a back seat to the Federal Reserve Board. The Fed has the authority to control the supply of money in the economy and thus affect the interest rates that corporations and individual firms must pay to invest in new enterprises. Among its other powers, the Fed establishes the reserve requirements of federally chartered banks (the amount of money they must keep in reserve at one of the Fed's regional banks and not lend). The Fed sets the discount rates at which banks may borrow from the central bank, and buys and sells government bonds to help keep the economy on an even keel. So important is the Federal Reserve Board to the economy that the interest rate banks charge their borrowers, the inflation rate, and the growth of the economy are all affected by the Fed's regulation of the money supply.

Though members of the Federal Reserve Board are appointed by the president, the length of their staggered terms (14 years) ensures that members will not be appointed by the same chief executive. Furthermore, since members cannot be removed except for cause (none have ever been removed), the president has minimal leverage over their actions. Much as the president may want to stimulate or deflate the economy, he can rely only on his persuasive powers and the Fed's willingness to cooperate.

Another constraint on the president's ability to manipulate the economy is the huge uncontrollable section of the federal budget, which constitutes approximately 75 percent of the total (and over 90 percent of the nondefense) budget in any given year. Federal entitlements—social security payments, Medicare, Medicaid, military pensions, veteran's compensation, and farm support subsidies—devour more than 50 percent of the budget. These entitlements, it should be remembered, are independent of specific appropriations by Congress.[82] Moreover, in 1974 Congress pegged social security benefits to the consumer price index (CPI), thus removing even retirement benefits from legislation decision making or executive management.

The vast majority of federal funding is either mandated under existing law or encumbered under previous law. Because the president cannot control these entitlements, his flexibility in dealing with federal expenditures is severely limited. Consequently, he is almost powerless by himself to lower the deficit or the percentage of the gross national product spent by the public sector. Even President Reagan's impressive budget cuts in 1981 were made mostly on the fringe of programs, and because they were accompanied by federal tax cuts, they had virtually no impact on the federal deficit.

The list of uncontrollable expenditures does not end here. Federal outlays for government contracts and obligations, interest on the national debt (the third highest item in the federal budgets, approximately $140 billion in 1985), general revenue sharing with states (to be terminated after 1987), payments for farm price support programs (over $22 billion in 1984), and deficits in the operation of the United States Postal Service all thwart efforts to reduce federal spending.

Over and above these unmanageable items, the president of the United States must contend with the unpredictable nature of the business cycle, the highly complex nature of our economic system, and decisions made by earlier administrations. The president also has relatively little control over the private sector of the economy, which far overshadows the public sector. The truth of the matter, in short, is that the president has only limited influence over economic policy. Yet the public expects him to be a miracle worker, especially in times of adversity.

NOTES

1. For figures on the high return rate of incumbents, see Norman J. Ornstein, Thomas E. Mann, Michael J. Malbin, Allen Schick, and John F. Bibby, *Vital Statistics on Congress, 1984–1985 Edition* (Washington, DC: American Enterprise Institute, 1984), 49–50.
2. Richard M. Pious, *The American Presidency* (New York: Basic Books, 1978), 293.
3. Ibid., 294–295.
4. *Historical Statistics of the United States 1789–1945, A Supplement to the Statistical Abstract of the United States* (Washington, DC: Government Printing Office, 1949), 299–300.
5. Ben W. Heineman, Jr., and Curtis A. Hessler, *Memorandum for the President: A Strategic Approach to Domestic Affairs in the 1980s* (New York: Random House, 1980), 56.
6. Harold M. Barger, *The Impossible Presidency* (Glenview, IL: Scott, Foresman, 1984), 327.
7. *The New York Times,* February 5, 1985.

8. John Maynard Keynes, *The General Theory of Employment, Interest and Money* (New York: Harcourt Brace, 1936).

9. As cited by Howard E. Shuman, *Politics and the Budget* (Englewood Cliffs, NJ: Prentice-Hall, 1984), 132.

10. The record shows that it took a mammoth eightfold increase in wartime spending from $9.1 billion in 1940 to $79.4 billion in 1943 to provide relatively full employment in the American economy and recovery from the Great Depression. *Supplement to Economic Indicators, Historical and Descriptive Background,* 90th Congress, 1st Session (Washington, DC: U.S. Government Printing Office, 1967), 35, 127, as cited by Shuman, *Politics and the Budget,* 139.

11. Generally, most of the dialogue on economic theory takes place within the academic community, but as noted by one team of Washington observers, "Supply-side economics was a peculiar addition to the economic scene of the 1970's in that it grew up outside mainstream economics and its propositions were debated in the popular press rather than in academic journals." Hugh Heclo and Rudolph G. Penner, "Fiscal and Political Strategy in the Reagan Administration," in Fred I. Greenstein, ed., *The Reagan Presidency* (Baltimore: The Johns Hopkins University Press, 1983), 26.

12. See Bruce Bartlett, *Reaganomics* (Westport, CT: Arlington House, 1981).

13. As one commentator put it, "President Reagan's contention that economic growth will eliminate the burden of the debt appears to put the cart before the horse by reversing the causality between public debt and economic growth. It neglects the damage that swelling public debt can do to long-term capital formation and economic growth." Leonard Silk, *The New York Times,* February 20, 1985.

14. Pious, *The American Presidency,* 313.

15. Arthur M. Schlesinger, Jr., *The Coming of the New Deal* (Boston: Houghton Mifflin, 1959).

16. See Alan Stone and Richard P. Barke, *Governing the American Republic* (New York: St. Martin's Press, 1985), 416–417; Perry D. Quick, "Businesses: Reagan's Industrial Policy," in John L. Palmer and Isabel V. Sawhill, eds., *The Reagan Record,* (Cambridge, MA: Ballinger, 1984), 304–312.

17. Samuel Kernell, "Explaining Presidential Popularity," *American Political Science Review,* 72 (June 1978), 520–521.

18. Erwin Hargrove and Michael Nelson, *Presidents, Politics, and Policy* (Baltimore: The Johns Hopkins University Press, 1984), 185.

19. Pious, *The American Presidency,* 307.

20. Ibid., 308.

21. Hargrove and Nelson, *Presidents, Politics, and Policy,* 186–189.

22. Roger B. Porter, "The President and Economic Policy: Problems, Patterns, and Alternatives," in Hugh Heclo and Lester M. Salamon, eds., *The Illusion of Presidential Government* (Boulder, CO: Westview Press, 1981), 206.

23. Richard H. Rovere, "Eisenhower: A Trial Balance," *The Reporter,* April 21, 1955, 19–20, as cited by Thomas E. Cronin, *The State of the Presidency,* 2nd ed. (Boston: Little, Brown and Company, 1980), 280.

24. Pious, *The American Presidency,* 308.

25. Ibid., 309.

26. "The Don and Marty Show," *Time,* February 13, 1984, 12.

27. Pious, *The American Presidency,* 267.

28. Richard A. Watson and Norman C. Thomas, *The Politics of the Presidency* (New York: Wiley, 1983), 380.

29. William Greider, "The Education of David Stockman," *The Atlantic,* December 1981, 27–54.

30. Ibid.
31. "Economic subpresidency" is a term coined by James E. Anderson; see Watson and Thomas, *The Politics of the Presidency,* 378.
32. Pious, *The American Presidency,* 325.
33. Ibid.
34. *The New York Times,* February 5, 1985.
35. Ibid.
36. Cronin, *The State of the Presidency,* 173.
37. See George C. Edwards III, *The Public Presidency* (New York: St. Martin's Press, 1983), 200–201.
38. John L. Palmer and Isabel V. Sawhill, "Overview," in Palmer and Sawhill, eds., *The Reagan Record,* 8.
39. Ibid., 3.
40. From Palmer and Sawhill's *The Reagan Record,* copyright 1984, The Urban Institute. Reprinted with permission from Ballinger Publishing Company.
41. Heclo and Penner, "Fiscal and Political Strategy in the Reagan Administration," 22.
42. Isabel V. Sawhill and Charles F. Stone, "The Economy: The Key to Success," in Palmer and Sawhill, *The Reagan Record,* 90.
43. Ibid., 104.
44. Pious, *The American Presidency,* 327.
45. Ibid., 328.
46. Edward R. Tufte, *Political Control of the Economy* (Princeton, NJ: Princeton University Press, 1978), 9.
47. Ibid., 22–27.
48. Ibid., 24. Two other authors, however, have cast serious doubt on the effectiveness of presidential attempts to manipulate economic policy to enhance their approval ratings. "The long and uncertain lags in the use of macro-economic policy, coupled with the political risks and liabilities of miscalculation, weaken the underlying logic of the political business cycle thesis." See David G. Golden and James M. Poterba, "The Price of Popularity: The Political Business Cycle Reexamined," *American Journal of Political Science,* 24 (November 1980), 696–714.
49. On the other side of the coin, one respected economist has even hypothesized that presidents try to cause recessions early in their terms so that the economy will be rebounding again at reelection time. William Nordhaus, "The Political Business Cycle," *Review of Economic Studies,* 41 (1975), 169–190, as cited by Paul J. Quirk, "The Economy, Economists, Electoral Politics, and Reagan Economics," in Michael Nelson, ed., *The Elections of 1984* (Washington, DC: Congressional Quarterly Press, 1985), 158.
50. Tufte, *Political Control of the Economy,* 24.
51. Ibid.
52. Jack Valenti, *A Very Human President* (New York: Norton, 1975), 151, as quoted by Edwards, *The Public Presidency,* 226.
53. See Donald R. Kinder, "Presidents, Prosperity, and Public Opinion," *Public Opinion Quarterly,* 43 (Spring 1981), 1–21.
54. Edwards, *The Public Presidency,* 227.
55. Ibid.
56. George C. Edwards III and Stephen J. Wayne, *Presidential Leadership* (New York: St. Martin's Press, 1985), 114.
57. Richard A. Brady and Paul Sniderman, "From Life Space to Polling Place," *British Journal of Political Science,* 7 (July 1977), 337–360, as cited by Edwards, *The Public Presidency,* 264.

58. Edwards, *The Public Presidency,* 227.

59. Ibid.

60. Afterward, Nixon wrote: "Unfortunately, Arthur Burns [the Council of Economic Advisers Chairman] turned out to be a good prophet. The bottom of the 1960 dip did come in October and the economy started to move up in November—after it was too late to affect the election returns. In October, usually a month of rising employment, the jobless rolls increased by 452,000. All the speeches, television broadcasts, and precinct work in the world could not counteract that one hard fact." Richard M. Nixon, *Six Crises* (Garden City, NY: Doubleday, 1962), 309.

61. Marilyn Moon and Isabel V. Sawhill, "Family Incomes: Gainers and Losers," in Palmer and Sawhill, eds. *The Reagan Record,* 317.

62. David E. Price, "Congressional Committees in the Policy Process," in Lawrence C. Dodd and Bruce I. Oppenheimer, eds., *Congress Reconsidered,* 3rd ed. (Washington, DC: Congressional Quarterly Press, 1985), 170–173.

63. Pious, *The American Presidency,* 322.

64. By 1974, it should be noted, only some 44 percent of the budget could be directly controlled by the appropriations committees on an annual basis. Price, "Congressional Committees in the Policy Process," 171.

65. Watson and Thomas, *The Politics of the Presidency,* 391.

66. Paul C. Light, *The President's Agenda* (Baltimore, MD: The Johns Hopkins University Press, 1982), esp. chaps. 1 and 2.

67. See Robert W. Hartman, "Congress and Budget-Making," *Political Science Quarterly,* 97 (Fall 1982), 381–402.

68. Shuman, *Politics and the Budget,* 254.

69. Ibid., 263.

70. For a play-by-play account of Reagan's spectacular 1981 budget victory, see Shuman, "The Reagan Budget Revolution," in his *Politics and the Budget,* 246–274.

71. Budget Act of 1974, Section 305 and 310, as cited by Shuman, p. 259.

72. Watson and Thomas, *The Politics of the Presidency,* 392.

73. Shuman, *Politics and the Budget,* 305.

74. Gregory B. Mills, "The Budget: A Failure of Discipline," in Palmer and Sawhill, eds., *The Reagan Record,* 119.

75. For a critical appraisal of the Gramm-Rudman-Hollings law, see Otto Friedrich, "A Bad Idea Whose Time Has Come," *Time,* February 3, 1986, 81–82.

76. *The New York Times,* February 8, 1986.

77. Ibid., July 8, 1986.

78. Ibid., February 8, 1986.

79. Pious, *The American Presidency,* 293.

80. Ibid., 296.

81. James L. Sundquist, *The Decline and Resurgence of Congress* (Washington, DC: The Brookings Institution, 1981), 80–81.

82. For an excellent discussion of uncontrollable expenditures, see Shuman, *Politics and the Budget,* chap. 4.

chapter 14

The Vice-Presidency

Somewhat surprisingly, the United States is the only major nation in the free world that has a designated officer—the vice-president—whose chief purpose is to be the ready successor to the chief executive in the event of a presidential vacancy. The other leading Western democracies either await a vacancy before designating a new leader or make some designated officer a caretaker pending the outcome of a special election.[1] When a British prime minister dies in office or resigns, the ruling party immediately chooses a successor. But in the United States the vice-president fills the remainder of the president's unexpired term. What is the reason for this unusual succession procedure? Was this constitutional arrangement just an afterthought of the Founding Fathers? Or was it a special insurance policy to protect the nation in the event of a sudden vacancy in the presidency?

Of greater importance have been recent institutional developments in the vice-presidency. In the past 15 years more institutional changes have occurred in the vice-presidency than in any single office in the federal government. As noted by Paul C. Light, in his recent study of the vice-presidency: "After two hundred years as errand-boys, political hitmen, professional mourners, and incidental White House commissioners, Vice Presidents can now lay claim to regular access to the President and the opportunity to give advice on major decisions."[2] For a position that has often been the butt of political jokes, what reasons can be ascribed to the rising importance of the nation's second-highest office?

No single explanation, it seems clear, can be given to account for the rapid growth of vice-presidential influence. But a number of factors have undoubtedly contributed to the rise of the modern vice-presidency; they will be discussed later in the chapter. Another goal will be to analyze the constitutional background and operation of the second highest office in the land. Shortcomings in the existing vice-presidential selection process will be discussed, and we will give special attention to the vice-president's role in case of presidential disability. Though the original flaws in the Constitution on this problem were thought to have been resolved, once and for all, by passage of the Twenty-fifth Amendment, recent experience during the Reagan administration indicates that loopholes still exist. Let's turn first to the establishment of the vice-presidency.

ESTABLISHING THE VICE-PRESIDENCY

The Founding Fathers, concerned with the problems of succession in the event of the death, removal, resignation, or inability of the president to perform his duties, decided that the runner-up in the presidential selection process should be designated vice-president. In their early discussions they had considered proposals that, in the event of a vacancy in the presidency, would shift power to the president of the Senate, the Chief Justice, or a presidential council. The men of 1787 first accepted the idea that the presiding officer of the Senate should be designated as the president's successor if the position should become vacant. Under an early convention plan to have the legislature pick the president, this plan seemed logical enough. But when the principle of legislative selection was dropped in favor of having a special body of electors, at least in the first stage, the Framers decided at a relatively late stage in the convention proceedings to have the vice-president selected in the same manner. This proposal was accepted with little objection, as was the proposal to have the vice-president serve ex officio as the presiding officer of the Senate.[3]

Just as the Framers followed most closely the model of the New York state constitution in drafting the office of president of the United States, they also chose to follow the New York document in drafting the office of vice-president of the United States. In the Empire State the lieutenant governor, who served ex officio as the presiding officer of the state senate, was elected by popular vote in the same manner as the governor. The terms describing the contingencies under which the powers of the president were to devolve on the vice-president also followed quite closely the terminology of the New York constitution.[4]

The Framers, reasonably satisfied with their craftsmanship, saw no reason to modify the role of the vice-president during Washington's two terms. John Adams, the first vice-president, however, wrote to his wife Abigail: "My country has in its wisdom contrived for me the most insignificant office that ever the invention of man contrived or his imagination conceived." Little did Adams realize that the vice-presidency was at the peak of influence during the period he served.[5] Prior to the passage of the Twelfth Amendment, the vice-president was the recipient of the second highest number of electoral votes and widely considered the logical heir apparent. Furthermore, as the dean of presidential scholars, Edward S. Corwin, points out: ". . . before the Twelfth Amendment the Vice President was in a sense—a fact not overlooked by Adams—'the constitutional equal of the President,' having been voted for by the Electors, not for 'Vice

President' but for 'President'."[6] It was therefore not surprising that the nation's first and second vice-presidents, Adams and Jefferson, became the second and third presidents. Also, because the Senate was still a small deliberative body and tie votes reasonably likely, Adams was able to cast a record 20 tie-breaking votes.[7]

In the pre-Twelfth Amendment era it was also possible for the vice-president to be a member of the opposition party (read faction), and that's exactly what happened in 1796 when Thomas Jefferson received 68 votes—3 less than President-elect Adams but 9 more votes than Adams's running mate, Thomas Pinckney of South Carolina.[8]

The real crisis in the vice-presidency came to a head in 1800 when the anti-Federalist Republican ticket of Jefferson and Aaron Burr received an equal number of votes in the Electoral College, but Aaron Burr refused to accept second place and acknowledge Jefferson as the president-elect. With a tie vote in the Electoral College, the presidential election, as required by the Constitution, moved into the House of Representatives, with each state casting one vote. For a time it appeared that the Federalists, to square old accounts with Jefferson, might shift their support to Aaron Burr and thus prevent Jefferson from moving into the White House. However, Jefferson's old cabinet adversary, Alexander Hamilton, concluded that Burr was far more unscrupulous than Jefferson and should be blocked from the presidency. Following a long series of inconclusive ballots, Hamilton finally prevailed upon a number of Federalist representatives to cast enough blank ballots so that Jefferson received a majority of votes—and the presidency—on the thirty-sixth ballot.[9]

THE IMPACT OF THE TWELFTH AMENDMENT

To avoid another constitutional crisis over tie voting in the Electoral College, Congress passed the Twelfth Amendment. Ratified by the required three-quarters of the states in 1804, the new amendment stipulated that Electoral College members cast a single ballot for a joint ticket of president and vice-president. During the debate over the proposed amendment, several members of Congress were unusually prescient in predicting the bad side effects the amendment would have on the vice-presidency. Because "the vice president will not stand on such high ground in the method proposed as he does in the present mode of a double ballot," Samuel Taggart forecast the nation could expect that "great care will not be taken in the selection of a character to fill the office." William Plumer admonished his colleagues that the chief concern in picking the vice-president would be "to procure votes for the president."[10]

For the next 150 years, the vice-presidency was viewed as a one-way ticket to political oblivion. Generally, vice-presidents were chosen to satisfy a constitutional requirement and to provide geographical or ideological balance to the ticket. Indeed, other than preside over the Senate for a few hours a day, the vice-presidents had little to do other than reflect on their idleness.

Thomas R. Marshall, the witty Hoosier who served under Woodrow Wilson, described his job in these words: "The Vice President is like a man in a cataleptic state. He cannot speak; he cannot move; he suffers no pain; and yet he

is perfectly conscious of everything going on around him, but has no part in it."
Marshall also liked to recite the story of the two brothers: "One ran away to sea;
the other was elected vice president. And nothing was heard of either of them
again." In 1924, Governor Frank O. Lowden of Illinois turned down second place
on President Coolidge's ticket, even though his nomination would have meant an
almost sure-fire certainty that he would become vice-president in the subsequent
Coolidge landslide.

Eight years later, John Nance Garner of Texas reluctantly gave up his
Speakership of the House of Representatives after one term to become the running mate of Governor Franklin D. Roosevelt of New York, apparently to his
everlasting regret. Some 28 years later, Senator Lyndon B. Johnson phoned the
crusty ninety-two-year-old Garner, living out his retirement in Uvalde, Texas,
and asked him if he (Johnson) should accept the vice-presidential nomination
offered by Democratic nominee John F. Kennedy. Garner replied that the office
"isn't worth a pitcher of warm spit."[11] Johnson, however, did not take Garner's
advice and accepted Kennedy's offer. According to most accounts, Kennedy
offered Johnson the nomination to help carry several southern states, especially
Johnson's home state of Texas. Kennedy's political strategy paid off handsomely
in November when the Kennedy-Johnson ticket collected 81 electoral votes in the
South, including 21 votes from Texas—enough to provide a 31-vote margin in his
cliff-hanging victory over former Vice-President Richard M. Nixon.

VICE-PRESIDENTIAL NOMINEES—
POLITICAL AFTERTHOUGHTS

Most vice-presidential nominees during the first 150 years of the Republic were
undistinguished political figures. Except for Martin Van Buren, Jackson's vice-
president, who succeeded him when "Old Hickory" retired in 1837, no vice-
president has succeeded to the presidency by election directly, and only one has
subsequently made it to the White House—Richard Nixon, who had to wait eight
years after his 1960 presidential defeat before winning election to the highest
office.

Despite the fairly good odds that the vice-president may become president
—13 out of our 40 presidents have reached the White House from the office of
vice-president—political parties and the party nominee over the years displayed
an extremely casual attitude toward picking candidates for the second highest
office in the land. Since both parties spent little time in screening their vice-
presidential nominees, there is little wonder they so consistently came up with
mediocrities. Most of these vice-presidents have long been forgotten—Daniel
Tompkins, George Dallas, Hannibal Hamlin, William Wheeler, Levi Morton,
and Garret Hobart, for example. All the nineteenth-century vice presidents who
succeeded to the presidency upon the death of the president were passed over for
their party's nomination at the next national convention. On more than one
occasion the parties have taken an almost cavalier attitude toward the vice-
presidential selection process. In 1904, for example, the Democrats selected
eighty-one-year-old Henry Gassaway as Alton Parker's running mate. In 1912,

the GOP convention renominated Vice-President James Sherman, even though the Republican leaders knew he was gravely ill—indeed, he died less than a week before the general election.[12]

Fortunately for the country, these weak people have been counterbalanced several times in the twentieth century by well-qualified candidates—Theodore Roosevelt, Harry Truman, Lyndon Johnson, Gerald Ford, Nelson Rockefeller, Walter Mondale, George Bush.

Until World War II, vice-presidential selection remained, for the most part, in the hands of state party leaders meeting at their respective national conventions. But in 1940, as the war clouds swept ever closer to the United States, President Franklin Roosevelt, who was seeking an unprecedented third term, insisted that he be allowed to pick his own running mate. Since FDR and Vice-President Garner had had a political falling out over Roosevelt's court packing plan and his attempt to purge conservative Democrats in the 1938 congressional election—in fact, Garner ran for president in the 1940 primaries on an anti-third term platform—Roosevelt decided that he wanted his Secretary of Agriculture, Henry A. Wallace, as his running mate.

When opposition to Wallace developed, Roosevelt informed Democratic convention officials that he would turn down his own renomination unless Wallace were on the ticket.[13] The convention acceded to Roosevelt's wishes. Since then, both parties have accorded their presidential nominees the prerogative of naming their running mates, if they wish, and conventions have routinely approved their choices. Except for 1956, when Democratic nominee Adlai E. Stevenson threw open the choice of the vice-presidential nominee to the convention, presidential nominees have personally picked their choice or asked their advisers to come up with a "short list" from which a vice-presidential nominee could be picked.

In recent years the spread of presidential primaries and the widespread use of pledged delegates has enabled the presidential nominee to play a decisive role in the choice of his running mate. Recent conventions consist of delegates whose chief loyalty lies not with state party leaders, but with the presidential nominee. Consequently, these delegates are willingly going to accede to the nominee's preference for a running mate without even bothering to check with their state delegation leaders.

With the onset of the nuclear age it would seem prudent for both parties to devote far more attention to selecting the nominee for the second highest job in the land, but the record of the two parties on this point has been uneven. In 1964, the Republicans chose Congressman William Miller of New York, at the request of the GOP nominee, Senator Barry Goldwater of Arizona, to give geographical balance, but also because, according to Goldwater: "He drives Johnson nuts."[14] Four years later, GOP nominee Richard Nixon decided that Governor Spiro Agnew of Maryland "would do the least harm to the ticket." Nixon's first preference, according to several sources, would have been to run without a vice-presidential candidate! Five years later, Vice-President Agnew resigned from office rather than face impeachment for tax evasion and involvement in financial kickbacks while he was a county executive and governor in Maryland.

In 1972, Democratic nominee George McGovern's original choice for running mate was Senator Thomas Eagleton of Missouri. But two weeks after his nomination, Eagleton was forced off the ticket when it was disclosed that he had been hospitalized several times and given electric shock treatment for mental depression.

FLAWS IN THE SELECTION PROCESS

Some critics say the existing vice-presidential selection process is undemocratic because it allows one person—the presidential nominee—to be the sole decision maker in picking the nominee. Other opponents of the existing system contend that the selection is based on purely political considerations, not the relative merits of the various contenders. Still other critics state that another flaw in the selection system arises from the haste with which the nominee must be picked. Under the existing rules of both major parties, the vice-presidential selection process must be undertaken less than 24 hours after the presidential nominee has been chosen. The selection process is further complicated by the fact that since the presidential nominee has often been so heavily involved in obtaining his nomination, he has scarcely had time to consider a running mate prior to the convention.

Not until the nominee has received the party nod can he and his staff seriously begin the frantic search for a running mate. But after three full days and nights of meeting most or all of the 50 state delegations, making prospective bargains with party or factional leaders, and rehearsing his acceptance speech for television, a presidential candidate will be physically and emotionally drained. Yet he must immediately begin screening prospective running mates. Although the 1952 Republican national convention is no longer typical, the Republican nominee, General Dwight D. Eisenhower, had only three hours between the balloting for president and vice-president. Eisenhower assembled his close circle of advisers and handed them a list of seven names from which to choose a nominee. His aides, worn out from the bitterly fought nomination battle against Senator Robert A. Taft of Ohio (Eisenhower won the first ballot count by less than fifteen votes), proceeded to cull the list. The first two names, Taft and Senator Everett McKinley Dirksen, were discarded. The next name on the list —Senator Richard M. Nixon of California—provoked no objection, and when several of those present spoke well of him, the group agreed without debate to go along with Nixon. They immediately called Eisenhower with their recommendation. Ike replied, "That's fine with me."[15]

Early in the 1952 fall campaign, Eisenhower must have regretted his haste in accepting Senator Nixon as his running mate when it was discovered that Nixon had been using a private $18,000 slush fund collected by wealthy California businessmen to underwrite his Senate office and mailing expenses. Amid the public furor created by this revelation, Nixon chose to defend himself by going on the newly established coast-to-coast TV networks to deliver his famous Checkers speech. So favorably received was this impassioned defense by the public that the skeptical Eisenhower decided to keep Nixon on the ticket; indeed, he pronounced Nixon "as clean as a hound's tooth."[16]

In 1960, Senator John F. Kennedy, expecting a hectic 24-hour search for an acceptable running mate, was surprised when his first choice, Senator Lyndon B. Johnson, his chief adversary in the fight for the nomination, unexpectedly accepted his offer for the number two spot on the ticket. But eight years later, GOP nominee Richard M. Nixon and his aides deliberated into the wee hours of the morning before agreeing to sleep on their decision for about four hours before announcing their choice—Governor Spiro Agnew of Maryland. If Nixon and his staff had had more time to review the background of Governor Agnew and his activities in Maryland, perhaps they might have uncovered some of the incriminating evidence that ultimately led to his hasty resignation five years later.

In 1972 the Democratic nominee, Senator George McGovern, received his party's nomination after midnight on the third night of the convention. He then commenced the search for a running mate. His staff, which had worked until dawn the first two nights during the bitter credentials fight and the protracted discussion on the platform—the convention recessed at 6:26 A.M. on the second night—began sifting through prospective nominees.[17] Earlier in the week, McGovern had informally offered the spot to Senators Edward Kennedy, Hubert Humphrey, and Edmund Muskie. They had all turned him down. McGovern and his staff finally came up with the name of Senator Thomas Eagleton of Missouri, a Roman Catholic with strong trade union ties, and a border state resident. With only a few hours to check his background, the staff failed to learn about Eagleton's past emotional problems, and since he did not volunteer the information, McGovern and his convention majority ratified Eagleton. When the medical information was uncovered by two probing national reporters two weeks later, McGovern was put in the embarrassing position of having to pressure Eagleton into resigning, although at first he had said he "was a thousand percent behind Eagleton." A month later the Democratic National Committee convened in Washington, DC, in a mini-convention to ratify R. Sargent Shriver, the late President Kennedy's brother-in-law, as Eagleton's replacement.

Nor was former California governor Ronald Reagan the model of a decisive nominee in picking his running mate at the 1980 Republican national convention in Detroit. Though Reagan had safely locked up the GOP nomination more than two months ahead of the convention, he failed to conduct an exhaustive search for a running mate. Some Reagan insiders had hoped to persuade former President Gerald Ford to team up with Reagan on a "dream ticket" to drive Carter out of the White House. Since public opinion polls prior to the convention showed Reagan and Carter running neck-and-neck, Reagan's inner circle felt that Ford would be a valuable asset in the general election campaign. But his proposed ticket fell apart in the closing hours before the presidential balloting was scheduled to get under way. According to several insiders, it collapsed when Ford insisted that former Secretary of State Henry Kissinger be reappointed to his old post in the new Reagan administration and that Ford's economic adviser be given the secretary of the treasury slot. This inflated asking price was, according to party insiders, too much for Reagan. The soon-to-be nominated Reagan was astounded to hear some of Ford's exorbitant demands publicly aired on television during a live televised interview between Ford and CBS anchorman Walter Cronkite in the network booth high above the convention arena.

By 9:00 P.M. Ford reportedly scaled down his demands, but his insistence on veto power over two cabinet appointments—state and defense—further soured Reagan's attitude toward the former president. Instead, two hours later, amid convention rumors that Ford would be Reagan's choice as vice-presidential nominee, Reagan abruptly selected George Bush—his chief rival during the hard-fought primary season.[18] In retrospect, Ronald Reagan apparently concluded that presidential power could not be shared, and he was not prepared to deal away the powers of the presidency to improve his chances of winning in November. By choosing Bush, Reagan scored points with the moderate wing of the GOP, especially in the East; he also added an experienced politician to the ticket. Bush had held five different national party and government posts over the previous ten years.

In the past decade, however, the hectic last-minute selection of a vice-presidential nominee has not always been the case. Jimmy Carter, who had safely locked up the 1976 Democratic nomination almost two months before the convention, devoted over four weeks to screening the backgrounds of a half-dozen prospective running mates. After carefully scrutinizing their records, he invited each of them to his home in Plains, Georgia, to discuss their conceptions of the office and possible future working relationships.[19] He renewed these discussions at the Democratic convention in New York City before announcing his choice—Senator Walter F. Mondale of Minnesota—on the morning after he had received the party nomination. Eight years later, Walter F. Mondale, who had the Democratic nomination safely in hand more than a month ahead of the San Francisco convention, followed the procedure used by Jimmy Carter. In this instance, however, Mondale announced his choice for running mate—Representative Geraldine Ferraro of New York—a week ahead of the convention.

The choice of Representative Ferraro—the first woman in history to be selected as a vice-presidential nominee—generated a huge wave of favorable national publicity. But Mondale's precedent-shattering move and his staff's careful scrutiny of each vice-presidential prospect revealed that even a lengthy search and careful review of prospective running mates is not foolproof. Less than two weeks after the Democrats had departed from San Francisco, reports began circulating in the press that Representative Ferraro had engaged in questionable financing of her first successful 1978 congressional race in her Queens, New York, district. While the Federal Election Commission had never ruled definitively on the matter of her selling a piece of property to a close friend of the family who then, in turn, resold it to her husband, the nature of this questionable transaction haunted the Mondale-Ferraro campaign during the early weeks of their presidential drive.[20] Over and above this issue, the unwillingness of Ferraro's husband to release his income tax returns (he subsequently relented) and unsubstantiated charges that he was a slumlord with possible connections to the Mafia hung like a huge cloud over the presidential campaign throughout the fall. Thus, even when the presidential nominee has the luxury of being able to shop around for a running mate, there is no guarantee that he can avoid all the potential political minefields involved in selecting a running mate.[21]

THE RISE OF THE MODERN VICE-PRESIDENCY

The vice-presidency is no longer regarded as a political dead end, as it once was. From the day of his election, the modern vice-president is considered a potential presidential nominee. Furthermore, an unanticipated consequence of the Twenty-second Amendment has also enhanced the stature of the vice-president. The amendment, though aimed at curbing the tenure of the president to two full terms, has focused the spotlight increasingly on the vice-president during a president's second term. The vice-president has become, in the minds of many citizens and politicos, the heir apparent. Actually, however, almost all vice-presidents who have become president owe their advance to succession rather than election.

In recent decades the growth in importance of the presidency has also helped elevate the stature of the vice-president. In Joel K. Goldstein's words, "The gravitational pull the strengthened presidency exerts has drawn the second officer into the executive orbit."[22] Both major party presidential nominees and the national convention delegates have come to recognize the necessity of nominating individuals of high caliber for the second spot. As a result, modern vice-presidents have generally been far more experienced, competent political figures—usually U.S. senators or former members of Congress—than their nineteenth-century counterparts. Many have been considered presidential timber before their nomination, and most have been so regarded after taking office.

Unlike their nineteenth-century predecessors, modern vice-presidents have been closely identified with the chief executive and his policies. Goldstein has also pointed out that, in light of the continuing expansion of presidential responsibilities, especially in foreign affairs, "The growth of the presidency creates an obligation to keep the second officer current."[23] Though the office of vice-president has often been downgraded, it is worth noting that almost one-third of our presidents were once vice-presidents, including four of our last eight chief executives.

THE INSTITUTIONALIZATION OF THE VICE-PRESIDENCY

For more than 150 years, vice-presidents performed essentially ceremonial roles —except when in time of emergency the nation called upon them to fill a vacancy in the White House. Generally, vice-presidents did little more than hold down duties as presiding officer of the U.S. Senate and make an occasional appearance at a federal dedication ceremony.

Franklin D. Roosevelt charted a new course for his second vice-president, Henry A. Wallace, by sending him to foreign lands as a goodwill ambassador. Presidents Eisenhower, Kennedy, and Johnson continued this practice, but there is no evidence that they gave serious consideration to assigning more substantive responsibilities to their second in command.

As Vice-President Gerald Ford wrote only weeks before Nixon's forced resignation:

> The Vice President is a Constitutional hybrid. Alone among federal officials he stands with one foot in the legislative branch and the other in the executive. The Vice President straddles the Constitutional chasm which circumscribes and checks all others. He belongs to both the President and Congress, even more so under the Twenty-fifth Amendment, yet he shares power with neither."[24]

Though assigned presiding duties in the Senate by the Constitution, the vice-president has been generally viewed by members of Congress as an interloper. It was not until President Kennedy made office space available for Vice-President Lyndon Johnson in the Executive Office Building, next to the White House, that the vice-president was accorded a direct symbolic connection with the executive branch. But the vice-president was still put on short rations. Unlike his former post as Senate majority leader with a full staff, Johnson had only a handful of staff members and a limited budget. Most of his former staffers chose to stay on Capitol Hill and retain their regular positions and salaries, rather than take up unspecified duties in the vice-president's office. In some instances, Johnson (and later Humphrey) managed to retain some veteran staffers by hiding them on the payrolls of several executive agencies. Until Gerald Ford became vice-president, occupants had been forced to rely completely on White House administrative support. Vice-President Humphrey, for example, had to have all his travel manifests and vouchers signed by the White House chief of staff.

Most of this second-class treatment has changed with the recent institutionalization of the vice-presidency. Since 1969, the vice-president's office has been given its own line in the annual budget—approximately $2 million. The executive budget allowed the vice-president's office to expand from 20 aides in 1960 to 70 people during Nelson Rockefeller's brief term. From scattered offices in several locations, the vice-president's staff is now consolidated in the Old Executive Office Building, with outposts on Capitol Hill and in the West Wing. With a regular budget and table of organization, vice-presidents are also now in a position to attract and retain high-quality staff. In fact, explains Paul C. Light: "The Vice President's office is now a replica of the President's office, with a national security adviser, press secretary, domestic issues staff, scheduling team, advance, appointments, administration, chief of staff, and counsel's office."[25] As a result of these recent institutional changes, Walter Mondale—unlike Lyndon Johnson—was able to bring virtually all his Senate staff with him to the vice-president's office.

In 1972, the *United States Government Manual* finally listed the vice-president's office as a distinct unit in the Executive Office of the President. This major sign of institutional identity was further acknowledgement that this hybrid office had become a part of the White House, not Congress.[26]

The institutionalization of the vice-president's office also makes the incumbent less vulnerable to changes in presidential moods or capricious presidential aides. Vice-presidents are now in a position to protect their staffs against arbitrary budgetary cuts. No longer do they have to beg for the use of White House jet aircraft, rely on presidential advance teams, or turn to White House speechwriters. To be sure, vice-presidents still clear all major speeches with the top White House staff, but they have their own speechwriters and foreign policy advisers, and their own Air Force Two jet. To monitor domestic matters more effectively, Vice-President Mondale also established his own domestic policy staff—a smaller version of President Carter's staff. Thus, the vice-president is now in a better position to offer independent advice to the president.

Symbolic of the growing stature of the vice-presidency was the purchase of a vice-presidential mansion—the Naval Observatory on Embassy Row—in the early 1970s. For the first time in history the vice-president was provided with an official residence. By contrast, Vice-President Agnew and his wife lived in a hotel during their five years in Washington. Clearly, establishment of an official residence enhanced the stature of the vice-president in the status-conscious Washington community.

With a staff of 70, the vice-president's office is now hierarchically organized, with chains of command and function. With specialized subdivisions to supply administrative, political, and policy support, the staff can now maintain ongoing operations, even when the vice-president is traveling. Inasmuch as the vice president may spend up to 30 percent of his official time on the road, a regular White House-based staff provides continuity to the management of his office. Formerly, most of the vice-president's aides traveled with him on his journeys.

Other benefits have accrued to the vice-president in recent years. As Paul C. Light has pointed out: "Part of the institutionalization of the Vice President's office involved regular access to presidential information—gaining a position in the White House paper loop."[27] Vice-presidents now receive most of the paper traffic and briefing papers that go across the president's desk. Although they lack decision-making authority to act on this information, they are nonetheless kept fully apprised of major domestic and international developments and, if asked, can give the president their best judgment on these matters. In short, the vice-president's office acts as a second source of information and a backup screening agency in the executive decision-making process.

Keeping the vice-president fully informed on national security matters should not be underestimated, especially in case of temporary presidential disability or the death of the chief executive. With the recent institutionalization, it is unlikely that any future vice-president will find himself or herself in the same position as Vice-President Truman at the time of President Roosevelt's death in 1945. Truman knew nothing about the development of the super-secret atomic bomb or the Allied war plans for the final offensives against Nazi Germany and Imperial Japan. According to Emmet John Hughes, Truman had only two appointments with Roosevelt during his 82 days in the vice-presidency before taking over the reins of government.[28]

Institutionalization is, of course, an ongoing process, with each new vice-president adding or subtracting some aspect of the second highest office in the land. But how does one explain the recent transformation of the office from an essentially benchwarmer position to a prominent advisory role to the president?

Undoubtedly, the lengthening presidential nominating race, the growing fragmentation in Congress, the decline of the national parties, and the rise of a new set of complex policy issues have all affected the growth of vice-presidential influence. The vice-president's campaign role in the midterm elections and renomination campaigns for the president has also contributed to the growing stature of the vice-presidency.

Surprisingly, the Watergate scandal of the early 1970s indirectly helped expand vice-presidential influence. Indeed, Watergate was probably the turning point in the evolution of the vice-presidency from a basically ceremonial office to a political and policy support agency.[29] President Nixon, in the face of a growing crisis, was forced to give prospective vice-president Gerald R. Ford more bargaining leverage for staff and access to presidential decision making than any predecessor. To obtain Ford's agreement to serve as vice-president after Spiro Agnew's hasty resignation, President Nixon readily agreed to give Ford an enlarged staff and expanded responsibilities. When Vice-President Ford moved into the White House after Nixon's forced resignation, he had to agree to a number of expanded vice-presidential duties before Governor Nelson Rockefeller was willing to come on board as number two man in the executive branch.

Beyond doubt, Watergate was the major catalyst in the growth of vice-presidential influence. As Paul C. Light has commented: "The rise of an independent vice presidential staff, the freedom to organize and reorganize the office, the arrival of greater administrative and political support, even the growth of an institutional identity, all coincided with Watergate."[30] Significantly, the greatest expansion of the size of the vice-presidential staff occurred in the crisis-filled years 1973 and 1974 at the height of the Watergate investigation.

Other factors also account for the growth of vice-presidential influence at the White House. The election of two *outsider* presidents—Carter and Reagan —coincided with the election of two *insider* vice-presidents, Mondale and Bush. As Paul C. Light has noted: "The President's inexperience creates vacuums for advice. Presidential outsiders—candidates with little Washington experience— have more use for active Vice Presidents than presidential insiders."[31] President Carter, a newcomer to the nation's capital, needed former Senator Mondale's advice and understanding of the legislative process to get his new administration off the ground. Equally important, President Reagan quickly utilized Vice-President Bush's executive and foreign policy experience, giving him two major assignments during the new administration's first year: (1) chairman of the president's Task Force on Regulatory Relief (established to review over 3,000 federal regulations for possible elimination or delay); and (2) responsibility for White House crisis management. By giving Bush this latter assignment—Bush had served as United Nations ambassador, CIA director, and U.S. envoy to Communist China —Reagan avoided having to make a choice between Secretary of State Alexander Haig and National Security Adviser Richard Allen to handle sensitive national security issues.

Expanded staffs have also increased vice-presidential influence. While the sheer number of staffers alone did not automatically translate into greater power for the vice-president, nonetheless the larger vice-presidential staff helped generate more information and provided greater staff expertise. As policymaking has become concentrated in the White House, and not in the executive departments, recent vice-presidents and their staffs have been brought into more and more White House senior staff meetings. In Paul C. Light's words: "As presidential doubts about executive branch loyalty grew, the Vice President's stock also increased."[32] Indeed, recent vice-presidents "have come to resemble senior members of the White House staff."[33]

To President Jimmy Carter belongs most of the credit for maximizing the influence of the vice-president. Carter deliberately aided the institutionalization of the vice-presidency by inviting Mondale to take a West Wing office. The acquisition of an office within the White House itself was probably the most important single factor in upgrading the vice-presidency, for it brought the number two constitutional officer within immediate proximity of the president and moved the vice-president into the center of the decision-making process. In the first year of the Carter administration, for example, Mondale met regularly with the president, averaging three to six hours a day in both public and private forums.[34]

But despite the expanded role of the vice-president over the past 15 years, the vice-presidential job description "remains highly dependent on the President." As Light emphasizes: "The Vice President's work is still largely whatever the President makes it."[35]

VICE-PRESIDENTIAL DUTIES

Five hundred and thirty-seven officials—the president, the vice-president, 100 U.S. senators, and 435 representatives—are sent to the nation's capital by American voters. Five hundred and thirty-six have a reasonably clear idea of their duties and responsibilities. But, as Thomas E. Cronin has explained, the vice-president is never sure, except for his constitutional duties as the presiding officer of the Senate and successor to the president, what responsibilities the president may from week to week assign him. In recent decades the number of tasks assigned to him has grown. On paper at least, they seem fairly formidable. Cronin has summarized them as follows:

1. President of the U.S. Senate
2. Member of the National Security Council
3. Chair of several national advisory councils
4. Diplomatic representative of president and U.S. abroad
5. Senior presidential adviser
6. Liaison with Congress
7. Crisis coordinator
8. Overseer of temporary coordinating councils
9. Presider over cabinet meetings in absence of president
10. Deputy leader of the party
11. Apprentice available to take over the job of the president, either on an acting or full-time basis
12. Future presidential candidate[36]

Although the Constitution assigns only three major responsibilities to the vice-president, recent presidents have delegated a variety of tasks to their second officer. They have appointed vice-presidents to head various commissions and task forces; vice-presidents have also been asked to serve as special emissaries abroad. The president, if he trusts the vice-president, will assign to him special legislative liaison work, lobbying special programs on Capitol Hill. In recent years vice-presidents have also become prominent administration spokesmen, especially during the off-year congressional elections and in the president's renomination campaign. During the presidential primary season, the vice-president may become the president's chief surrogate campaigner. Vice-Presidents serve as a leading salesman for the president, maintaining valuable contact with the party's state leaders and influential public figures. If necessary, the vice-president may become the president's hatchet man, chopping down the political reputation of the rival party's presidential nominee.

While modern vice-presidents are far busier than their nineteenth-century predecessors, their expanded duties are often tentative in nature. So long as a president lives, the vice-president has no authority to make policy. Additional assignments depend entirely upon the president. Job assignments, it should be noted, are not permanent. As the late Hubert H. Humphrey once put it, "He who giveth can taketh away and often does."[37] Humphrey had learned, as have other recent vice-presidents, that the constitutional position of the vice-president may constrain a president from assigning continuing responsibilities to the number two officeholder. The chief reason: The vice-president is the only major subordinate the president cannot remove. Understandably, the president may be reluctant to entrust duties to an official over whom he lacks this leverage.[38]

Congress has also granted the vice-president a few statutory responsibilities, but they can scarcely be described as major challenges. Congress, in an amendment to the National Security Act of 1947 two years later, made the vice president an ex officio member of the National Security Council. His other duties include affixing his signature to enrolled bills and joint resolutions before they are forwarded to the president, appointing a handful of members to the service academies, sitting on the Board of Regents of the Smithsonian Institution, and serving as chairman of the National Aeronautics and Space Council.

Goodwill Ambassador.   Richard Nixon, in his eight years as vice-president, visited 54 countries in Latin America, Africa, Western Europe, the Far East, and the Soviet Union. Nixon's most publicized foreign encounter was undoubtedly his "kitchen debate" with Soviet dictator Nikita Khrushchev over the relative merits of the American and Soviet systems.[39] As vice-president, Lyndon Johnson undertook more than 30 special overseas assignments for President Kennedy. Johnson visited Southeast Asia to consider the possibility of increasing military aid to the anti-Communist government of South Vietnam; he allayed the fears of the West German government after the Soviet Union's erection of the Berlin Wall in 1961; and he also informed the governments of Greece, Turkey, Cyprus, and Iran of impending reductions of foreign aid.[40]

Both of the most recent vice-presidents—Walter F. Mondale and George

Bush—have handled a variety of foreign assignments in Canada, Latin America, and Western Europe. Mondale logged over 600,000 miles during his vice-presidency. In early 1983, Vice-President Bush traveled to the Soviet Union to represent the United States at the funeral of Soviet leader Yuri Andropov. By early March 1985, Bush had logged 610,000 miles on official government business. When news suddenly reached Washington that Soviet leader Constantin Chernenko had died, President Reagan asked Bush, who was visiting the starving refugees in Ethiopia, to attend the Soviet leader's funeral—the third funeral of a Soviet head of state that Bush had attended since assuming the vice-presidency in 1981. The frequency with which U.S. vice-presidents attend state funerals led columnist William Safire to quip, "You die, I fly."

On his return trip home, Bush made a side trip to Brazil for the inauguration of a new civilian government. By the time Bush reached Washington, D.C., again, he had traveled more than 29,600 miles. While in the Soviet Union Bush also had the opportunity to meet the new Soviet leader, Mikhail S. Gorbachev. Most Washington observers, with one eye on the 1988 Republican presidential nominating race, concluded that Bush had comported himself nearly flawlessly on this long pilgrimage. As a result, he had strengthened his early frontrunner position to succeed President Reagan, who is ineligible to run for another term.

As diplomatic representatives and troubleshooters, vice-presidents can serve as presidential surrogates whenever the president, for reasons of state, time constraints, or whatever, prefers to remain in the nation's capital.

Legislative Liaison. Despite his constitutional role as president of the Senate, the major activity of the vice-president on Capitol Hill is not his official capacity as presiding officer of the Senate, but his informal role as administration lobbyist.[41] Because the Constitution places the vice-president with one foot in the executive branch and the other in a legislative chamber, he would seem to be ideally suited to serve as the president's lobbyist on Capitol Hill. But this does not necessarily follow. A few twentieth-century vice-presidents—John Nance Garner, Hubert H. Humphrey, and Walter F. Mondale—have performed these duties in an effective manner; the others less so. Harry Truman, who served as vice-president for only 82 days, later made the following observation about this position: "The Vice President's influence on legislation depends on his personality and his ability, and especially the respect which he commands from the senators. Here is one instance in which it is the man who makes the office, not the office the man."[42]

Vice-presidential involvement in legislative activity dates only from the New Deal era, for only since this period has the president assumed the responsibility for presenting Congress with a comprehensive legislative program. The record of effective vice-presidential lobbying over the past half-century should be higher than most critics rate it, for since 1933, nine of the twelve vice-presidents served previously in one or both Houses of Congress.[43]

Vice-President Garner, a former Speaker of the House, performed yeoman service on Capitol Hill during President Roosevelt's first term. Though a southern conservative Democrat, Garner is generally credited with playing a major role in pushing New Deal measures through Congress. Shortly after Roosevelt's reelection in 1936, he and Garner had a falling out over FDR's court packing plan. Garner also became disenchanted with the growing national deficit and made no secret of his displeasure in the halls of Congress. By 1940, the break between FDR and his vice-president had become irreparable. Garner announced that he would seek the presidency even before Roosevelt made his own intentions about a third term known. When Garner failed to win several presidential primaries against favorite son and Roosevelt stand-in candidates, however, he bowed out of the race and retired to his Texas ranch.

Vice-President Richard Nixon, though a relative newcomer to Capitol Hill, served as a go-between for the White House and Senator Joseph McCarthy, the professional anti-Communist crusader of the 1950s. He persuaded McCarthy to drop his plans to investigate the CIA and also his drive to block several Eisenhower nominations. Along with other Eisenhower staffers, Nixon negotiated with Senator John Bricker over changes in his proposed constitutional amendment to curb presidential executive agreements and treaty-making power.

Vice-President Humphrey, before he was consigned to the presidential doghouse for his opposition in a cabinet meeting to President Johnson's policy of bombing North Vietnam, was one of the more active vice-presidential lobbyists on Capitol Hill; he helped push through a number of Johnson's Great Society programs during 1965. Vice-President Walter Mondale was particularly valuable to President Carter and his staff because, as new arrivals in the nation's capital, they had so little experience in dealing with members of Congress. But the overall record of vice-presidential lobbying, according to Larry O'Brien, Kennedy's congressional liaison chief, is not impressive.[44] As explained by Joel K. Goldstein:

> Vice presidential lobbying is necessarily limited. To begin with, Congress is not a malleable institution. On most issues, relatively few legislators are susceptible to executive influence. Not only the Vice President but the President is unable to engineer many shifts. Benefits of incumbency have produced a proliferation of safe seats. Electoral security has further insulated Congressmen from presidential persuasion. Presidents and their legislative staffs must work hard to achieve even marginal gains in legislative votes.[45]

In many other ways, the vice-president is operating against great odds. His legislative role offers him no bargaining power, for as Vice-President Theodore Roosevelt noted many years ago, he has few favors to trade. Even though he is the presiding officer of the Senate, the vice-president must be sensitive to senatorial prerogatives. His relationship with the Senate can become especially precarious if he lobbies too vigorously at the wrong time. As Goldstein has noted: "The Vice President may offend Congressional leaders if he appears to compete with their operations. Humphrey's efforts apparently upset Senate Majority Leader Mike Mansfield."[46]

Party Worker.   Vice-President Nixon set a record of party service in the 1954 off-year election that has seldom been equaled. His 48-day campaign schedule included visits to 95 cities in 31 states, 204 speeches, and more than 100 press conferences.[47] Vice-President Spiro Agnew, who resigned in 1973, was one of the more politically active vice-presidents. In the 1970 off-year elections, Agnew campaigned for GOP candidates throughout the land and in the process raised $3.5 million on their behalf.[48] His withering attacks on members of the Democratic opposition and national media—"the nattering nabobs of negativism"— may, however, have been counterproductive in the long run.

Walter F. Mondale, in the first three years of his vice-presidency (1977– 1981), visited 48 of the 50 states, frequently to help fellow Democrats win public office.[49] By campaigning on behalf of various candidates, Mondale crated a number of valuable IOUs redeemable later, and he also gained widespread visibility on local television stations across the country. Undoubtedly, his work in the political vineyards for President Carter was a major factor subsequently in helping him win the Democratic presidential nomination in 1984.

Vice-President George Bush has been equally active in party circles. For example, in December 1984, shortly after the Reagan-Bush team had won reelection, Bush visited the Republican Governors' Conference in Des Moines, Iowa, warning the GOP state leaders that the United States must face up to "tough" budget cuts. He also described President Reagan as "determined to control the federal budget and get this deficit under control." Afterwards, he held a closed-door session with the GOP governors and governors-elect.[50]

While the vice-president is serving as the president's surrogate, he is also reaping some benefits for himself. His public appearances bring the vice-president into contact with numerous groups and acquaint him with a wide variety of regional and local issues. Additionally, he is gaining media exposure for a future run for the top spot on the ticket.

Another prominent role of the vice-president is to promote the president's renomination. Two recent vice-presidents—Mondale and Bush—worked indefatigably for their presidents, Carter and Reagan, especially during the presidential primary season. Looking to the future, vice-presidents can be expected to perform a wide variety of political chores for the president—some of which may have long-term benefits for the vice-president, too.

SOME RECOMMENDATIONS

Despite the wide variety of presidential assignments given to vice-presidents, however, many presidential scholars have until recently considered the vice-president one of the most underutilized officials in the executive branch. Although presidents have delegated special assignments to their vice-presidents—attending the funerals of foreign dignitaries, conducting goodwill trips abroad, speaking at fundraising dinners, and so on—presidents have, over the years, relied most on their trusted aides for most top-level duties. The special assignments given to Harry Hopkins, Clark Clifford, Joseph Califano, Jr., and H. R. Haldemann completely overshadowed the ceremonial functions performed by the vice-presidents during the White House years of FDR, Truman, Lyndon B. Johnson, and Nixon. However, as a result of the recent institutionalization of the vice-presidency, and especially the establishment of a vice-presidential office in the West Wing, the two most recent vice-presidents—Mondale and Bush—have become major policy advisers to the president.

Vice-presidential involvement in the activities of the various executive departments, however, has seldom been productive. As Thomas E. Cronin has observed: "The departmental secretaries preside over congressionally authorized departments; hence a vice president is very much an intruder, unless a problem arises which is definitely interdepartmental."[51]

Some reformers have recommended that vice-presidents be given cabinet portfolios, such as secretary of defense or attorney general, but no president has opted for this suggestion. Nor is it likely that cabinet members would look with favor on this recommendation. As Cronin has pointed out: "Critics of this suggestion say existing cabinet members are already tough to make responsive to the White House. As an elected departmental official, a vice president who served also as a cabinet secretary/departmental head would be even tougher to get around or to 'fire'."[52]

Aware from firsthand experience of the need for more executive help, Presidents Hoover and Eisenhower recommended the creation of an additional appointed vice-presidential post. Hoover urged the appointment of an administrative vice-president; Eisenhower, a "first secretary of government" for foreign affairs. Neither proposal generated much support in Congress. More recently, Milton Eisenhower, the late president's brother, advocated the creation of two executive vice-presidents, to be appointed by the president. One would handle domestic policy, the other international affairs, but both would work "in close collaboration with the President."[53] A skilled administrator in his own right, Milton Eisenhower argued that the elected vice-president could not hope to achieve what appointed vice-presidents could, chiefly because the elected vice-president is not a full-fledged member of the executive branch.

Far more important, however, than finding additional jobs for the vice-president to perform is the task of delineating the precise role the vice-president must perform in the event the president suffers a major physical or mental disability.

THE ISSUE OF PRESIDENTIAL DISABILITY

For some unexplained reason, the Founding Fathers never addressed the problem of presidential disability and the vice-president's stand-in role during such a period. Did the vice-president become "acting" president? Or did the vice-president become merely a substitute for the chief executive? Nor did the Founders spell out the powers of the vice-president if he succeeded a president who had died or resigned. Did only the "powers and duties" shift to the president? Or did the office transfer to a new president?

The question of transfer of the office was actually resolved first, though the initial test did not come until the death of President William Henry Harrison in 1841—only one month after his inauguration. His successor, Vice-President John

Tyler, insisted that he became president and not "acting president." Although opinion on the point was divided at the time, all seven other accidental vice-presidents who have succeeded to presidency have made the same claim as Tyler —and it has been sustained. As a result, when Presidents Garfield, Wilson, and Eisenhower suffered from clear disabilities, their vice-presidents refused to assume presidential responsibilities. They feared that any action would make them appear to be usurpers of the office. The country therefore drifted in a state of semi-paralysis during periods that sometimes extended over several weeks. Nothing was done about this dangerous gap in the constitutional system until President Eisenhower's second term.

In 1957, President Eisenhower proposed a constitutional amendment that would permit the vice-president, with the advice of the cabinet, to decide when a stricken president was unable to carry out his duties, provided the president was unable to make the decision himself. Congress failed to act on Eisenhower's proposal.[54] The following year, however, President Eisenhower, after recuperating from three serious illnesses, which included a heart attack and a mild stroke, decided to formulate a set of extralegal guidelines. Eisenhower and Vice-President Nixon agreed that the president would inform the vice-president of his disability, if possible, at which point the vice-president would act as president. If such communication were impossible, the vice-president "after such consultation as it seems to him appropriate under the circumstances" would decide whether to act as chief executive.[55] In any event, the president would decide when he was capable of resuming his duties. Significantly, this type of agreement was subsequently adopted by Kennedy and Johnson and Humphrey.[56]

While this type of pact was a distinct improvement over the previous ambiguous condition, it was nevertheless an inadequate stop-gap measure in a crisis-ridden modern world. Furthermore, it lacked legal sanctions so that the right of the vice-president to sign laws, appoint and dismiss officials in the executive branch, or act as commander in chief was not beyond constitutional challenge.[57] Additionally, the informal arrangement required a close relationship between the two highest officers. Equally important, the Eisenhower-Nixon agreement depended solely on the president's judgment that he could function.[58] No wonder that as late as 1964 Professor Clinton Rossiter could still describe the problem of presidential disability as "a situation that has no easy solution, perhaps no solution at all, except patience, prayer, and improvisation."[59]

In the same year, Richard M. Nixon, who had served eight years as vice-president, called the clause in Article II on presidential disability, "this one great defect in an otherwise remarkable document."[60] A combination of circumstances —Eisenhower's three major illnesses, the death of President John F. Kennedy, concern over the state of President Lyndon Johnson's health (he had suffered a heart attack in 1955), and the long-recognized constitutional hiatus on presidential disability—all prompted Senator Birch Bayh (D–Ind.) and some of his colleagues to draft the proposed Twenty-fifth Amendment to the Constitution to deal with the issues of presidential disability and vacancies in the office of vice-president.[61]

THE TWENTY-FIFTH AMENDMENT

Ratified in 1967 by three-quarters of the states, the Twenty-fifth Amendment specifically provides that either the president himself or the vice-president and a majority of his cabinet (or some other body designated by Congress) can declare that the president is unable to discharge the powers and duties of his office, in which case the vice-president becomes *acting* president (not president).[62] The president is also authorized to declare when his disability is over and to resume the powers and duties of the office. However, if the vice-president and cabinet (or some other body designated by Congress) disagree with the president's decision, Congress is designated to decide the issue. Thus, the amendment deals directly with the issues of (1) who precisely determines whether presidential disability exists; (2) what responsibilities does the vice-president succeed to—the powers and duties of the office, or the office itself; and (3) who decides if and when the president has recovered from his disability, and if there is a disagreement on this point, how it is resolved.

The amendment also resolves the problem of a vacancy in the vice-presidency. Interestingly, the United States has always had provisions to assure presidential succession, but until 1967 it did not have any constitutional means to fill a vice-presidential vacancy. Throughout the nation's history, Congress had designated some federal official to be first in line of succession—the president pro tempore of the Senate, 1792–1886; the secretary of state, 1886–1947; the Speaker of the House (1947 onward).[63] Seven vice-presidents have died in office; two have resigned; and nine others have succeeded to the presidency, leaving the vice-presidency vacant for a total period of nearly 38 years—roughly 20 percent of the nation's existence (see Table 14.1).[64] The absence of any constitutional arrangement for more than 175 years suggests how much importance the Founding Fathers attached to the second office. But this indifference would have had untold consequences if something had happened to the new president during this interim, for the country would have had a double vacancy in the top two leadership posts. The Twenty-fifth Amendment removes this gap in the constitutional machinery. If the vice-presidency is vacant under the new amendment, the president nominates a successor, who may be confirmed by a majority in each chamber of Congress.

Since adoption of the Twenty-fifth Amendment in 1967, two vacancies in the vice-presidency have already occurred. After Spiro Agnew resigned, President Nixon nominated Representative Gerald Ford, the House GOP minority leader, to the vice-presidency. Less than a year later, President Nixon resigned rather than face an impeachment trial, and when Ford moved into the White House, he nominated New York Governor Nelson Rockefeller as the new vice-president. Thus, for the first time in the nation's history, neither the president nor vice-president had been elected to these positions.

PRESIDENTIAL DISABILITY: STILL AN ISSUE

Loopholes still remain in the Twenty-fifth Amendment, especially concerning the determination of presidential disability. As Goldstein has pointed out: "A Chief

Table 14.1 VICE-PRESIDENTIAL VACANCIES

Vice-President	Reason for Termination	Length of Vacancy		
		Years	Months	Days
George Clinton	Death		10	12
Elbridge Gerry	Death	2	3	9
John C. Calhoun	Resignation		2	4
John Tyler	Succession	3	11	0
Millard Fillmore	Succession	2	7	23
William R. King	Death	3	10	14
Andrew Johnson	Succession	3	10	17
Henry Wilson	Death	1	3	10
Chester A. Arthur	Succession	3	5	13
Thomas A. Hendricks	Death	3	3	7
Garret A. Hobart	Death	1	3	11
Theodore Roosevelt	Succession	3	5	18
James S. Sherman	Death		4	5
Calvin Coolidge	Succession	1	7	2
Harry S. Truman	Succession	3	9	8
Lyndon B. Johnson	Succession	1	1	29
Spiro T. Agnew	Resignation		1	26
Gerald R. Ford	Succession		4	10
Total		37	9	1

Source: Reprinted in abridged form by permission of the publisher from John D. Feerick, *The Twenty-Fifth Amendment* (New York: Fordham University Press, 1976), Appendix D 2, p.255.

Executive may clearly be incapable of performing his duties, but if both he and the cabinet refuse to acknowledge his inability, the Vice President cannot act."[65] Nor does the Twenty-fifth Amendment deal easily with the determination of presidential disability, if the president is gravely injured in an accident or badly wounded in an assassination attempt.

Fortunately, no major constitutional crisis occurred in the hours immediately after the attempt on President Reagan's life in March 1981. Although he was unconscious for more than two hours while in surgery, he recovered quickly. Indeed, the next day he was able to meet with his top advisers at his bedside and sign a bill concerned with dairy price support subsidies.

But in connection with the attempt on President Reagan's life, columnist William Safire and others have called attention to a critical problem about presidential disability that may arise under Section 4 of the Twenty-fifth Amendment when the "president's men"—the White House staff—refuse to alert the cabinet about the seriousness of a president's disability.[66] The problem actually arose in the hours immediately following the attempted assassination of President Ronald Reagan on March 30, 1981. While President Reagan was undergoing surgery to remove a bullet from his lung at George Washington Hospital and Vice-President George Bush was en route to Washington by jet from Texas, four top-level White House staffers—the counsel to the president, Fred Fielding, Secretary of State Alexander Haig, Jr., Admiral Dan Murphy, the vice-president's chief of staff, and Richard Darman, deputy to White House chief of staff James Baker—were in the White House Situation Room reviewing the documents needed to put into effect

Section 4 of the Twenty-fifth Amendment. This section of the amendment, theoretically at least, ensured a rapid shift of executive authority when the cabinet decides the president is unable to discharge his duties: A majority of the cabinet now has the power to appoint the vice-president to be president until such time as "no inability exists."

Instead of calling the cabinet together to consider invoking Section 4, however, Darman persuaded the White House officials that he should lock up the vital documents in his safe and not convene a cabinet meeting. The public's attention over the failure to invoke Section 4 was unintentionally diverted by Secretary of State Alexander Haig's unfortunate effort to calm the nation with his flamboyant assertion "I am in control here . . . pending return of the Vice President." Events moved swiftly over the next 24 hours, but according to a White House correspondent for *Time* magazine, Laurence Barrett, a single White House staff member, in effect, made the decision to ignore the Twenty-fifth Amendment because (1) the truth about the precarious medical condition of the president might have seriously disturbed the citizenry, and (2) the cabinet might have voted to strip the president of his powers temporarily.[67]

In retrospect, White House aides could say that there was no reason to panic, for no international crisis was brewing and Reagan was soon on the road to recovery. But four days later the president was running an unexplained fever, and his doctors recommended a bronchoscope examination, which ordinarily required sedation. In the meantime, the CIA reported its concern about a possible Soviet invasion of Poland to quash an antigovernment protest movement. Reagan's top advisers, according to Barrett, secretly considered the wisdom of invoking the Twenty-fifth Amendment, but then decided "to do so would cause confusion . . . and would offset their effort to assure the country and the world that Ronald Reagan was on the mend."[68] Thus, in the midst of a potential international crisis, White House insiders kept the decision making on presidential disability in their own hands, rather than follow the constitutional procedure outlined in the Twenty-fifth Amendment.

Did this White House staff decision on presidential disability have any serious impact on the government and the public? Probably not. Maybe the cabinet and the vice-president could have done nothing better but wait for further reports on the president's condition. But someday, if another president is stricken, it would seem prudent to follow the constitutional procedure set down in Section 4 of the Twenty-fifth Amendment, and not leave the matter of presidential disability in the hands of the president's palace guard.

President Reagan's second encounter with the Twenty-fifth Amendment occurred in July 1985 when he underwent colon cancer surgery. Before Mr. Reagan entered the operating room he signed a letter transferring his powers to Vice-President George Bush. However, Mr. Reagan chose not to invoke the Twenty-fifth Amendment, even though he followed the procedures spelled out in it. In his letter to Vice-President George Bush, President Reagan said he was mindful of the provisions of the amendment, but pointedly added:

> I do not believe that the drafters of this amendment intended its applications to situations such as the instant one. Nevertheless, consistent with my long-

> standing arrangement with Vice President George Bush, and not intending to set a precedent binding anyone privileged to hold this office in the future, I have determined and it is my intention and direction that Vice President George Bush shall discharge those powers and duties in my stead, commencing with the administration of anesthesia to me in this instance.[69]

Despite President Reagan's disclaimer, several legal authorities, including former Senator Birch Bayh (D–Ind.), one-time chairman of the Senate Judiciary Committee and the chief drafter of the amendment, and Dean John Feerick, Fordham University Law School, said the president had indeed invoked the Twenty-fifth Amendment. "To suggest they didn't use the power of the Twenty-fifth Amendment—there isn't any other place to get the power," said former Senator Bayh. "The president (alone) doesn't have the power to give up his office and then reclaim it." Dean Feerick agreed: "I don't see any basis (for the transfer) without the Twenty-fifth Amendment." Both men were interviewed on ABC-TV's "This Week with David Brinkley."[70]

Nor did the temporary transfer of power from Reagan to Bush come off exactly in the clockwork fashion that the White House Staff portrayed it. For some unexplained reason, Vice-President Bush, who was on his way back to Washington from his summer home in Maine, was not notified of the temporary transfer of power for 22 minutes after President Reagan went under anesthesia.[71]

Overall, the Twenty-fifth Amendment clarifies the status of a vice-president who takes over in case of presidential disability—the vice-president succeeds only to the powers and duties of the office, not the office itself. Moreover, as Donald Young has observed: "An ailing President may now safely relinquish his duties secure in the knowledge that he can resume his duties upon conclusion of his disability."[72] Almost as important, the amendment offers an effective mechanism for filling the vice-presidency when it is vacant.

John Adams, the nation's first vice-president, once declared: "In this I am nothing, but I may be everything."[73] Significantly, nine vice-presidents have succeeded directly to the White House through the death or resignation of the president—five of them thus far in the twentieth century.

Vice-presidents, however, do not have any of the tools of power. They cannot issue executive orders; they cannot command the White House resources to push for special programs; they cannot order military forces to take appropriate action in an international crisis. In short, they possess no decision-making authority; instead, they can only serve as troubleshooters or advisers to the president. In the case of presidential disability, the Twenty-fifth Amendment now stipulates that the vice-president serves as acting president during the period of the president's disability. However, the machinery for determination of presidential disability still has not functioned as the amendment's sponsors envisaged.

CONCLUSION

Except for his presiding officer duties in the Senate, the vice-president's work is still largely whatever the president makes it. For the first 150 years, vice-presidents were selected chiefly to "balance the ticket" to add geographic or some other strength to the campaign. If elected, they confined themselves to purely ceremonial duties. Once out of office, they were quickly forgotten.

Over the past quarter-century, however, especially since Watergate, vice-presidents have been chosen more on the basis of their political experience and qualifications. In office they have become increasingly influential as presidential advisers. The real breakthrough occurred when President Carter invited Vice-President Mondale to occupy an office in the West Wing of the White House. Instead of being confined to an ornate office in the Executive Office Building across the White House grounds and out of the mainstream of executive decision making, the vice-president now occupies a strategic spot down the corridor from the Oval Office with ready access to the president.

It is noteworthy that President Reagan has seen fit to continue this precedent with his vice-president, George Bush. Since proximity can easily be translated into access and potential influence, Vice-Presidents Mondale and Bush—unlike their predecessors—have been able to assume roles as major advisers to the president. More and more, as vice-presidents have moved beyond ceremonial duties into the political and policy areas, they have come to resemble senior members of the White House staff. Whether future presidents will continue to maintain this type of official contact with their vice-presidents cannot, of course, be determined. But unless an unforeseen series of events occurs, it seems unlikely that this practice will be discontinued and the vice-president once again relegated to an office in the Executive Office Building.

Clearly, the recent institutional changes—the executive budget, the expanded support staff, the move to the West Wing of the White House, the establishment of a special residence for the vice-president, and the integration of the vice-president's staff into the White House policy process—have all contributed to the growing stature of the vice-presidential office.

NOTES

1. Joel K. Goldstein, *The Modern American Vice Presidency* (Princeton, NJ: Princeton University Press, 1982), 207.
2. Paul C. Light, *Vice Presidential Power: Advice and Influence in the White House* (Baltimore, MD: Johns Hopkins University Press, 1984), 1.
3. Joseph E. Kallenbach, *The American Chief Executive* (New York: Harper & Row, 1966), 200.
4. Ibid.
5. Erwin C. Hargrove and Michael Nelson, *Presidents, Politics, and Policy* (Baltimore, MD: Johns Hopkins University Press, 1984), 29.
6. Edward S. Corwin, *The President: Office and Powers,* 5th rev. ed. by Randall W. Bland, Theodore T. Hindson, and Jack W. Peltason (New York: New York University Press, 1984), 67.
7. Corwin, *The President: Office and Powers,* 67. Twentieth-century vice-presidents, however, have cast tie-breaking votes on the average of only one every two years— chiefly because the growth of the Senate from the original 26 members to the present 100 lessens the chances of tie votes.
8. Kallenbach, *The American Chief Executive,* 77–78.

9. Ibid., 78.

10. Goldstein, *The Modern American Vice Presidency,* 6.

11. Michael Dorman, *The Second Man* (New York: Dell, 1968), 6.

12. Ibid., 98.

13. Donald Young, *American Roulette: The History and Dilemma of the Vice Presidency* (New York: Viking Press, 1974), 181–182.

14. Goldstein, *The Modern American Vice Presidency,* 81.

15. Herbert Eaton, *Presidential Timber: A History of Nominating Conventions, 1868–1960* (London: Free Press, 1964), 451–453.

16. For more details of this controversial episode, see Young, *American Roulette*, 256–259.

17. James W. Davis, *National Conventions: Nominations Under the Big Top* (Woodbury, NY: Barrons, 1972), 106–108.

18. James W. Davis, *National Conventions in an Age of Party Reform* (Westport, CT: Greenwood Press, 1983), 149.

19. Goldstein, *The Modern American Vice Presidency,* 61.

20. "Furor over Ferraro Finances," *Newsweek,* August 27, 1984, 20–22.

21. For a discussion of several proposals to eliminate the game of "vice presidential roulette," see Goldstein, *The Modern American Vice Presidency,* 271–299; see also Davis, *National Conventions in an Age of Party Reform,* 144–150.

22. Goldstein, *The Modern American Vice Presidency,* 306.

23. Ibid., 308.

24. Gerald R. Ford, "On the Threshold of the White House," *Atlantic Monthly,* 1974, 63–65, as cited by Light, *Vice Presidential Power,* 7–8.

25. Light, *Vice Presidential Power,* 63. The discussion in this section relies heavily on this excellent study.

26. Ibid.

27. Ibid., 66.

28. During this fateful period Roosevelt was in the nation's capital less than a month. Truman later estimated that he saw FDR only eight times in the twelve months before Roosevelt's death—and this time span included the entire 1944 presidential campaign. Emmet John Hughes, *The Living Presidency* (New York: Coward, McGann, and Geohegan, 1972), 123.

29. Light, *Vice Presidential Power,* 100.

30. Ibid, 61.

31. Ibid., 138.

32. Ibid., 134–135.

33. Ibid., 238.

34. Paul C. Light, "The Institutional Vice Presidency," *Presidential Studies Quarterly,* 13 (Spring 1983), 207.

35. Light, *Vice Presidential Power,* 131.

36. Thomas E. Cronin, "Rethinking the Vice Presidency," in Thomas E. Cronin, ed., *Rethinking the Presidency* (Boston: Little, Brown, 1982), 326–327.

37. As cited in Goldstein, *The Modern American Vice Presidency,* 309.

38. Ibid.

39. Young, *American Roulette,* 276–278.

40. Paul David, "The Vice Presidency: Its Institutional Evolution and Contemporary Status," *Journal of Politics,* 29 (November 1967), 737–738.

41. Actually, he chairs the Senate only 30 minutes or so a day. Usually he turns the gavel over to a junior senator each day—unless an important vote is coming. It was a tragic

irony that the young thirty-two-year-old Senator Edward M. Kennedy was in the chair when word reached the Senate that President Kennedy had been shot in Dallas. Young, *American Roulette,* 378.

42. As quoted by Young, *American Roulette,* 380.
43. Goldstein, *The Modern American Vice Presidency,* 178.
44. As cited by Goldstein, 181.
45. Ibid., 182.
46. Ibid., 183.
47. R. J. Donovan, *Eisenhower: The Inside Story* (New York: Harper & Row, 1956), 280, as cited in Goldstein, 185.
48. Jules Witcover, *White Knight: The Rise of Spiro Agnew* (New York: Random House, 1972), 393.
49. Goldstein, *The Modern American Vice Presidency,* 189.
50. *The New York Times,* December 3, 1984.
51. Cronin, "Rethinking the Vice Presidency," 332.
52. Ibid.
53. Ibid.
54. Dorman, *The Second Man,* 235.
55. Ibid., 238.
56. Young, *American Roulette,* 392.
57. Ibid.
58. Ibid.; see also Stephen W. Stathis, "Presidential Disability Agreements Prior to the 25th Amendment," *Presidential Studies Quarterly,* 12 (Spring 1982), 208–215.
59. As cited by Young, *American Roulette,* 390.
60. Ibid.
61. The Senate passed its version of the Twenty-fifth Amendment on February 19, 1965, by a vote of 72 to 0. The House acted favorably on its version in April 1965 by a vote of 368 to 29. The report of the conference committee was approved in the House by a voice vote on June 30, 1965. Six days later the Senate approved it by a vote of 68 to 5. Goldstein, *The Modern American Vice Presidency,* 232.
62. Twenty-fifth Amendment, Sections 2 and 3.
63. Goldstein, *The Modern American Vice Presidency,* 229–230.
64. Ibid.
65. Ibid., 223.
66. William Safire, *The New York Times,* June 6, 1983.
67. Laurence I. Barrett, *Gambling with History: Reagan in the White House* (Garden City, NY: Doubleday, 1983), 120–122.
68. Ibid.
69. *Seattle Post-Intelligencer,* July 15, 1985.
70. Ibid.
71. Ibid. Some Washington insiders reported that the White House staff's failure to notify Bush of the transfer of power immediately was not an oversight, but reflected a power struggle going on between Bush and White House Chief of Staff Donald Regan, who saw no need for Bush to return to Washington. Bush, however, according to the same sources, insisted that he be on hand in the nation's capital during the president's hospitalization.
72. Young, *American Roulette,* 393.
73. Ibid., 10.

chapter 15

Proposed Reforms of the Presidency

Proposals to reform the presidency are nearly as old as the Constitution itself. That proposed presidential reforms have appeared frequently throughout our history should occasion no surprise, since the Founding Fathers deliberated longer and debated more vigorously over the power and structure of the presidency—as well as the selection process—than any other part of the nation's fundamental document.

Though proposals to reform the presidency number in the hundreds, it is noteworthy that only four constitutional changes affecting the presidency—the Twelfth, Twentieth, Twenty-second, and Twenty-fifth amendments—have been approved since the Bill of Rights was added to the Constitution in 1791. Significantly, all four of these amendments have dealt with mechanical problems—a joint presidential–vice-presidential ticket, a shift in the date of the presidential inauguration, the two-term limitation, and presidential disability as well as vice-presidential vacancies. But none of the amendments has altered the formal structure or power of the executive branch.

In this chapter we examine and evaluate a wide variety of institutional reforms that have been proposed over the years—parliamentary government, the plural executive, the no-confidence vote in the president amendment, the six-year nonrenewable term plan, the direct election of the president, and modification of the Electoral College system—and then assesses the prospects and desirability of presidential reform.

BACKGROUND

Early critics of the presidency usually sought to impose restraints on the chief executive. Prior to the Civil War, for example, several constitutional lawyers and powerful leaders in Congress, such as Daniel Webster and Henry Clay, seriously disturbed about Jackson's strong presidency, argued that the chief executive was the major flaw in the American system and should be checked by Congress or a council of state. During the fateful years leading up to the Civil War, several proposed amendments were also introduced in Congress that would have provided for two or three presidents, chosen on a sectional basis and serving as co-equals in power.[1] Few observers at the time realized, however, that the real threat to the Union would lie in a succession of weak incumbents incapable or unwilling to use the executive power to halt the fragmenting forces within the young Republic.

In the aftermath of the Lincoln presidency and the Reconstruction years, one leading scholar concluded that only by replacing the president with an executive council, patterned after the Swiss model, could American liberty be preserved.[2]

Toward the end of the nineteenth century, public law scholars, undoubtedly influenced by a series of weak, passive incumbents in the post-Civil War era, thought the presidency was evolving into a ceremonial office. The leading scholar (and future president), Woodrow Wilson, suggested that a parliamentary system might be preferable, though shortly after the turn of the century he became convinced, after watching Theodore Roosevelt in action, that the presidential system offered far more opportunity for executive leadership.

To make presidential candidates more responsive to the popular will, leaders of the Progressive movement, the major reformers of the early twentieth century, concluded that the machinery for selecting presidents—the national convention—should be overhauled, especially the delegate selection process, and if possible be replaced by a national direct primary. Even Woodrow Wilson, in his first message to Congress in 1913, urged passage of a constitutional amendment to establish a national presidential primary. But this proposal was soon forgotten as Wilson pushed ahead with his banking and tariff reforms. In recent years, however, this proposal has been revived by a number of members of Congress.

In the half-century spanning the decades between World War I and United States involvement in the Vietnam war, a variety of presidential reforms—most of them favoring some form of the British parliamentary system—were advanced by a number of American scholars.[3] But the proposals failed to attract any serious public or congressional support.

During this era the only proposed reform to capture the fancy of Congress, state lawmakers, and the country at large was the Twenty-second Amendment, ratified in 1951, to limit a president to two terms. From time to time critics of this constitutional restriction on presidential tenure have urged repeal of the amendment, but not until Representative Guy Vander Jagt (R–Mich.), Chairman of the House Republican Campaign Committee, urged repeal of the Twenty-second Amendment in late spring 1986, in the hope that President Reagan might be persuaded to seek a third term, has the proposed repeal of this amendment attracted national attention. Congressional inaction on this issue in recent years, however, should not be construed as a complete absence of interest in presidential reform in the halls of Congress or in academic circles. Indeed, various proposals to improve the effectiveness of the chief executive or to constrain the powers of the president have surfaced periodically over the past quarter-century, especially during the Watergate era. Thus, it seems appropriate at this point to analyze and assess some of the more widely publicized proposals before making a final judgment on their potential suitability and, equally important, their prospects for adoption.

PARLIAMENTARY GOVERNMENT

One of the oldest reforms proposed for the presidency is the substitution of parliamentary government for the separation of powers and balanced constitution —a tried and tested system that has been in operation for nearly two centuries. Proponents of the parliamentary system (which fuses executive and legislative powers under the leadership of a prime minister and cabinet) claim that an American parliamentary system would achieve democratic responsibility and accountability and improve the link between public opinion and public policy. Clearly, a parliamentary system would reduce the direct accountability of the president and the executive branch to the national electorate and virtually eliminate constitutional checks and balances.

Critics of the existing system argue that the separation of powers prevents the development of responsible party government; in other words, voters have no assurance when they elect a president that he can implement a specific legislative program, since the legislative branch may be controlled by the opposition party, or control of the two houses of Congress may be divided between the two major parties. Under these circumstances the president finds himself, in effect, a prisoner of the separation of powers and nearly powerless to act. Even if the president's party controls both houses of Congress, opponents of the presidential system point out that members of his party may defy party discipline and vote with impunity against the president's legislative program.

PARTY GOVERNMENT

One interesting variation of the parliamentary system is the plan for party government developed by Professor Charles Hardin more than a decade ago. According to Hardin: "The foremost requirement of a great power is strong executive leadership."[4] But this executive must not be allowed to escape the political controls needed to maintain constitutional—that is, limited—government. The problem is further complicated by the danger that restraints may seriously weaken the effectiveness of the president.

Hardin's solution is "presidential leadership and party government." To achieve this goal, Hardin proposes a fundamental constitutional change in the American separation of powers system. This is how his new plan would be established:

1. Presidents, senators, and congressmen would all be elected for four-year terms. The election date would be fixed at four years from the date of the last inauguration of the last government, but a provision would allow the government to change the date and call a special election.
2. The House of Representatives would continue to be elected from single-member districts, but an additional 150 members would be elected at large. To assure a majority in the House, each party would nominate 100 candidates; the party winning the presidency would elect its entire slate. The losing party would elect a maximum of at-large candidates, diminished by whatever number would be required to give the winning party a majority of five in the House. At-large candidates would be nominated by committees of 41 in each party. The winning party's committee would be composed of the President, the ten cabinet members, and 30 congressmen for single-member districts. The opposition party's nominating committee would be composed of the opposition party leader, the "shadow" cabinet (the opposition party leadership), and 30 congressmen. In both parties the 41-member nominating committee would have the right to reject local nominees if they had refused to accept party discipline.
3. Presidential candidates would be nominated by party committees composed of all house members from single-member districts as well as all candidates for election in such districts. In the event of either physical or political presidential disability, the nominating committee of his party would be empowered to suspend him temporarily or to remove him, but in any case it would be required to replace him. The office of Vice President would be abolished.
4. The Senate would be deprived of its power to approve treaties and presidential nominations. Bills would continue to be considered in the Senate but if the Senate rejected a bill that had passed the House twice in the same form (60 days would have to elapse between the first and second passage), the bill would go to the President.
5. The presidential veto would be retained but it could be overridden by an adverse majority vote in the House. The Senate could require the House to reconsider but it could be overridden by the House after 60 days.
6. Article I. Second 6, Clause 2 of the Constitution, which prevents members of Congress from serving in other offices of the United States, would be repealed, but the similar office-holding ban for the judiciary would be retained.
7. The loser in the presidential election would be designated the leader of the opposition and given a seat in the House with privileged membership on all committees and privileged access to the floor. The opposition leader would have an official residence and adequate funds for office staff, travel, and other items essential for the vigorous operation of his office. Like the president, the opposition leader could be removed by his party's presidential nominating committee.
8. Presidential elections would be by national ticket. The winning party would be required to secure a national plurality of votes.
9. All parts of the Constitution which are presently in conflict with the foregoing proposals would be repealed or modified to conform to them.

The 22nd Amendment (which limits the President to two terms) would also be repealed.[5]

To the critics' charge that his plan is unrealistic and unworkable, Hardin's reply is that the existing system cannot cope with a politically disabled president who operates under a system of fixed calendar elections. To those opponents apprehensive of change, Hardin points out that all major Western democracies have undergone constitutional change in the past century. He reminds us: "Only the United States persists with constitutional forms essentially as they were devised nearly two hundred years ago."[6] Hardin argues that the party government system, which could provide party accountability and a smooth transition of presidential leadership, is preferable to the crippled system we now have.

The case against parliamentary government for America, however, seems stronger. Hardin's party government would reduce the direct accountability of the president and the executive branch to the national electorate and substantially undermine constitutional checks and balances. The merger of executive and legislative leadership does not guarantee governmental effectiveness. As Norman C. Thomas has commented: "In all probability . . . an American parliamentary system would be characterized by a multiplicity of political parties, given our social pluralism, and hence it might encourage chronic instability like that of the French Fourth Republic or the current Italian Republic."[7]

PRESIDENTIAL-CONGRESSIONAL
CONSTITUTIONAL RELATIONSHIPS

Several reformers of the national government have proposed other presidential-congressional constitutional arrangements. Generally, these reforms aim to strengthen the capacity of the presidency for leadership not through the selection of strong, competent leaders, but through revisions in the rules of government so that the lawmakers on Capitol Hill will have more inducements to cooperate with the chief executive.

Lloyd N. Cutler, a White House adviser in the Carter administration, for example, has recommended adoption of Congressman Jonathan Bingham's plan, which would require in presidential election years that voters in each congressional district vote for a trio of candidates as a team—president, vice-president, and a House of Representatives member. Under this plan the political fortunes of the party's presidential and congressional candidates would be tied to one another and provide some incentive for sticking together after they are elected. Furthermore, Cutler and Bingham would extend the term of House members to four years to foster greater teamwork and, hopefully, to provide House members with greater protection against the pressures of single interest groups. Actually, Cutler would prefer to move a step further and elect two senators to four-year terms, along with the candidates for president, vice-president, and the House of Representatives.[8] Thus, members of Congress would come into office as part of a presidential team.

Another proposal Cutler has put on the counter for consideration would permit or require the president to select 50 percent of his cabinet from among the members of his party in the Senate and House; they would retain their seats while serving in the cabinet. This plan, which helps bridge the separation of powers, would require a change in Article I, Section 6, which provides that "no person holding any office under the United States shall be a member of either house during his continuance in office."[9]

Still another proposal that Cutler has offered for consideration would provide the president with the power, to be exercised not more than once in a term, to dissolve Congress and call for new congressional elections. Cutler believes this plan would provide the opportunity that does not now exist to break an executive-legislative deadlock and permit the public to decide whether it wants to elect senators and members of Congress who support the president's legislative program. This plan, Cutler admits, would require a number of constitutional changes relating to the timing and conduct of the election and the staggering of senatorial terms, but Cutler believes his reform "would significantly enhance the president's power to form a Government."[10] Experience over the past several decades suggests, however, that a new election would be no guarantee that the president would gain more legislative support; in fact, loss of congressional seats in the president's party has been the normal pattern.

Cutler has also suggested another variant of his special election plan: Empower a majority or two-thirds of both Houses to call for new presidential elections. This plan too would require amending the Constitution.

Cutler's proposals, which are reactions against the weaknesses of the Carter presidency, aim to reinforce the hand of a beleaguered president. Unfortunately, as Erwin Hargrove and Michael Nelson have cogently noted: "Reforms of this kind would not strengthen such presidents because they seek to substitute rules for politics, and this cannot be done effectively."[11] The reason is simple: "New rules will not cause legislators to follow presidents."[12]

PLURAL EXECUTIVE

Some reformers believe that the job of president has become too big to be entrusted to one person. Even the Founding Fathers were concerned about this problem; in fact, they considered and then dropped the idea of a plural executive. As the complexities and demands of the presidency have multiplied in the twentieth century, the concept of the plural executive has received renewed attention. Several variations of the plural executive have been suggested. Some students of the presidency have advocated the election of two or three presidents, dividing domestic and foreign responsibilities, or splitting up the policy formulation and implementation tasks of the presidency.

Tugwell's Plan.   Some years ago, Rexford Tugwell, a member of FDR's original brain trust, proposed a new constitution that provided for two vice-presidents to be elected with the president. One would be designated as first successor should the president die or become incapacitated. The job of these two officials would be to relieve the president of the managerial, regulatory, and custodial duties that he presumably can no longer perform effectively. The chancellors of foreign, financial, military, and legal affairs would be responsible to the vice-president for general affairs. Chancellors of other departments would report to the vice-president of internal affairs at the president's discretion. The president, freed of many administrative responsibilities, would be able to function full time as a policymaker in the critical area of government. Under this system, Tugwell argued, responsibility would be easy to pinpoint.[13]

Among the other collective leadership plans to surface in the 1970s Barbara Tuchman, the noted historian, suggested a six-person directorate elected on a party ticket for a period of six years. Each member would serve one year as a chairperson. The chairperson's vote would carry the weight of two members to avoid a tie. In Tuchman's view: "Personal government can get beyond control in the U.S. because the President is subject to no advisers who hold office independently of him." According to the distinguished historian, "Spreading the executive power among six eliminates dangerous challenges to the ego." Each of the six executives would be designated from the time of nomination as secretary of a specific department of government affairs: foreign (including military), financial, judicial, business, physical resources, and human affairs.[14]

The Finer Plan. A far more radical departure—indeed almost a revolutionary proposal—is Professor Herman Finer's plan to elect a president and eleven vice-presidents together for a four-year term to serve as a kind of ministry through which the executive functions of government would be discharged. All twelve would be nominated together by national party conventions and elected for four years. Congress would be elected at the same time for a four-year term. Under the Finer plan, the president would preside over his cabinet or vice-presidents, assign them their respective jobs, dismiss any of them if he wished, and appoint others to their positions. Only persons who had served in Congress for at least four years would be eligible to run for the presidency or vice-presidencies. The president-elect and his cabinet or vice-presidents would be given seats in Congress and the duty of leading the "loyal opposition." If there were a vote of no confidence, the president could (with the concurrence of a majority of his cabinet or vice-presidents) force the resignation of the entire team and thereby cause Congress to be dissolved. New elections would then be held for all seats in Congress as well as for the president–vice-president "cabinet."[15] Thus, the Finer plan would connect the executive and legislative branches through standard terms of office for Congress and cabinet.

Corwin's Legislative Cabinet. Almost three decades ago a leading authority on the presidency, Edward S. Corwin, suggested that more harmonious relations would develop between president and Congress if the president would choose part of his cabinet from leading members of Congress. The restructured cabinet would be selected by the president from both houses of Congress. Added to this group would be as many executive department heads as were required by the nature of the activity.[16]

Corwin's proposal of a legislative cabinet to replace the presidential cabinet, however, takes little account of the political facts of life governing the American separation of powers system. The legislative cabinet idea is an attempt to change the recognized ineffective advisory role of the cabinet as it is presently constituted. But the possibility of developing a viable advisory relationship between a president and cabinet composed of independently elected senators and representatives who are firmly entrenched in a seniority system is extremely remote. Not only would this proposal weaken congressional political leadership, it would also undercut the president's independent sources of political authority.

As the chief magistrate, the president can go over the heads of Congress and appeal directly to the people for support of his programs. By adroitly playing competing interest groups against each other and by appealing to the "national interest," the president has frequently achieved his goals despite congressional foot-dragging. To force the president to surrender his initiative in both domestic and foreign affairs and to limit his goals to what he can sell to a legislative cabinet of senior members of the two houses would leave him at the mercy of a congressional cabal. In addition, the legislative cabinet idea gives the president no more support or clout than he can secure at present by direct negotiation with party leaders on Capitol Hill.[17]

The Cohen Plan.   A less ambitious proposal, offered by former FDR adviser Benjamin Cohen, calls for the establishment of a small executive council of not less than five nor more than eight distinguished citizens who would be consulted by the chief executive prior to major policy decisions.[18] The Cohen plan aims to realize some of the aims of a plural presidency while leaving our present single chief executive virtually intact. His small super-cabinet members would be nominated by the president, but subject to Senate confirmation. Membership on this executive committee would be full-time. Presidents would be expected to consult with this group of experienced professionals *before* acting on critical national security matters. The ultimate power of decision, however, would rest with the president.

Cohen's proposal for this executive council seeks to guard against the dangers of solitary presidential leadership. Recognizing that presidents can have bad days, suffer from special anxieties, or barely tolerate certain foreign leaders, Cohen viewed his super-cabinet as a special guardian shield. In his words: "Quiet consultation by our Presidents before they make their momentous decisions with a small Council of wise and respected persons may protect our presidents, our nation, and our world from much of the hazards of fateful decisions which ultimately must be made by one man."[19]

The Cohen executive council proposal, it should be noted, is one of the few plural executive plans that could be implemented simply by legislation rather than through the laborious constitutional amending process.

Executive-Legislative Council.   Another suggestion from academe is Professor Charles S. Hyneman's proposal to establish a central council to serve the president as an official advisory body. Members would be selected from the congressional leadership, the president's own administrative staff, and individuals outside the government in whose judgment the president has confidence.[20] Several states have established joint executive-legislative councils of the same general structure as those proposed by Corwin and Hyneman. Wisconsin, the originator of this idea, ended its experiment after a brief trial. But Virginia has had greater success with its joint executive-legislative council.[21]

Senator Mark Hatfield (R–Ore.) has recommended that our federal executive have an elected vice-president, an elected attorney general, and elected heads of the major domestic departments. Hatfield's plan is based upon the plural executive used in most states.[22]

Shortcomings of the Plural Executive.   The flaws of most plural executive plans are not hard to find: competition and disputes within the executive, a splintering and confusion of responsibilities, and further growth of the executive branch. One of the great virtues of the single executive is the ability to reach a quick decision, if needed, and to move with dispatch. But could a collective presidency reach a unified agreement in times of crisis? Would the public have confidence in, say, split decisions within the executive branch? Also, it seems doubtful if this federal bureaucracy would operate as effectively under a divided executive council. And, as Thomas E. Cronin warns: "Might not a collectivized presidency court paralysis or indecision, or both in a nuclear attack or in an international monetary crisis, when swiftness and decisiveness are often most needed?"[23]

Other defects of the plural executive are evident. The plural executive would probably compound the problems of an already top-heavy executive establishment. Undoubtedly each president and each vice-president would want his or her own staff, his or her own legislative liaison team, public relations staff, and press secretary. Presidential bureaucratization would reach new highs. Nor is it difficult to visualize each of the executives engaged in headline-hunting and credit-taking for every accomplishment within the executive branch.

Clearly, a plural executive could be expected to suffer from executive internal competition. Might not an intra-executive veto process emerge that could hamstring or undercut executive unity and dispatch? Cronin reminds us that our existing system of checks and balances and limited government already seems, according to many people, designed more for paralysis than leadership. The plural executive would just accentuate this shortcoming.[24]

To leading critics, the most serious objection to the plural executive concept is that it would be exceedingly difficult to assign accountability. The finger-pointing would probably never end. As Alexander Hamilton argued two centuries ago, the restraints of public opinion on the president would lose their efficacy if there were several executives rather than one president. Who should the people blame for disastrous policies? Which set of executives should ultimately face impeachment? Hamilton wisely concluded that it would be far easier for the people to oversee a single chief executive.[25]

Beyond question, proposals for institutionalizing more assistance for overburdened presidents, such as strengthening presidential planning and evaluation staff services, by legislation or grafting onto the Constitution proposals for a plural executive should be scrutinized with extreme caution. As Norman C.

Thomas has noted: "Present structural arrangements result in a form of collective leadership, and a President can achieve many of its alleged advantages through use of his high-level assistants."[26]

All strong presidents of the twentieth century—Teddy Roosevelt, Wilson, Franklin D. Roosevelt, Truman, Kennedy, Johnson, and Reagan—have always been able to attract capable staffers to handle the heavy load of White House business. Co-chief executives or additional vice-presidents have been neither needed nor wanted.

THE NO CONFIDENCE VOTE

The Constitution, critics have reminded us, does not cover the question of what to do about a failed president who, although not physically or morally disabled, has lost the capacity to lead the country, but is not removable under the disability provisions of the Twenty-fifth Amendment or the impeachment clauses of the nation's basic charter. In the midst of Watergate and before President Nixon's forced resignation, Representative Henry Reuss (D–Wis.) proposed a constitutional amendment that would permit the ouster of a president by a no confidence vote. Borrowed from the parliamentary government system, the no confidence vote is a means of presidential removal on policy or performance grounds, without the complicated procedural arrangements of impeachment, coupled with a provision for the dissolution of Congress and the call for a special presidential election.[27] Ruess's no confidence proposal was one of the more drastic responses to the widespread belief that the presidency in modern times has become too powerful in times of crisis, especially in foreign affairs. Supporters of the no confidence proposal hold the view that presidential power has grown beyond the level where checks and balances can be used effectively to constrain the president.

How would the no confidence amendment operate? According to the Reuss plan, the House and Senate could vote no confidence in the chief executive by an extraordinary three-fifths (60 percent) majority of members present and voting. If called for, the no confidence resolution would take priority over any other pending issue before Congress. If adopted, the president would step aside at once. He would then be succeeded by the vice-president—a member of his own party. The new president would serve until a special presidential election could be held. Meanwhile, Congress would fix a date between 90 and 110 days for a special election for president and vice-president as well as for members of Congress.

Representative Reuss's plan allows considerable flexibility on the time for the special election. If the no confidence vote came during the last year of a president's term, Congress could decide against a special election. If the vote occurred in a year of midterm elections (for example, 1986 or 1990), the presidential election would simply be added to the congressional races. The president elected in this manner would assume office the following January and serve four years. If the special election occurred at any other time, Congress would specify when the new term would start, but it could not be less than 60 or more than 75 days following the election. The Reuss plan also contains a unique provision: An ousted president would be able to run again. The theory is that a defeated president should be given the opportunity to win vindication.[28] The two-term limitation of the Twenty-second Amendment would also be rescinded.

James L. Sundquist, a senior Fellow at the Brookings Institution, has also proposed introducing an element of collective judgment into the exercise of executive power through a parliamentary vote of no confidence, which could be implemented by a simple constitutional amendment. According to Sundquist: "The direct effect would be to make possible the removal of a President who, though not guilty of provable 'high crimes and misdemeanors' that are the basis for impeachment, has lost the capacity to lead and inspire and unify the country —in short the capacity to govern."[29] In the past, Sundquist points out, an incompetent president, surrounded by subordinates guilty of gross negligence, egregious mismanagement, or crimes and misdemeanors, but who have acted in his name, "has remained in office until the end of his allotted four years—and nothing could be done about it." In Sundquist's view, "No other democratic government leaves itself so vulnerable."[30]

In short, supporters of the no confidence vote have concluded that impeachment is an inefficient check, since it only protects the country against criminal violations of the public trust, but not against presidential incompetence. Advocates of the no confidence proposal have reminded the country that incompetence is not an indictable offense.[31] The no confidence vote, its supporters point out, does not take power away from the president; instead, it makes him more accountable for how he uses his powers. Indeed, it would aid in preventing a president from operating entirely above politics and isolating himself from criticism.[32] The merit of the parliamentary no confidence vote, Sundquist argues, would be that:

> A President who was forced, under the Constitution, to maintain the confidence of the country and of the Congress would find it necessary to consult with congressional leaders in the exercise of his executive powers. He would not dare to do otherwise; it would be dangerous to flout them and risky to keep secrets from them. To retain their confidence, he would have to take them into his.[33]

Sundquist believes that if Congress were granted the no confidence vote and the president were not given the power to dissolve the legislature, which the British cabinet has, the overall effect—contrary to its critics—would exert a restraining influence on the presidency and restore a needed balance of power between the branches.[34]

Sundquist is also certainly on sound ground when he observes:

> An institutional principle applied almost universally in the English-speaking world is that major decisions should be made not by one man acting alone, but by a collective body of some kind.[35]

Beyond question, the no confidence vote would require more presidential-congressional cooperation, and it would provide a method of ending deadlocked or leaderless government such as occurred in 1919–20, 1931–32, and 1973–74.[36]

Plainly, the no confidence plan, if adopted, would tilt the constitutional balance away from the president and toward Congress.

THE CASE AGAINST THE NO CONFIDENCE AMENDMENT

Critics of the Reuss and Sundquist proposals argue that "the cure is worse than the occasional ailment."[37] They remind enthusiasts that Congress is not without resources to hold a president in check, short of impeachment—the War Powers Act, the Case Act (requiring presidential notification of executive agreements), the Budget and Impoundment Control Act of 1974, the National Emergencies Act of 1976, and the power of the purse.

As Thomas E. Cronin has observed: "In certain situations it would seem that the vote of no confidence would give Congress the power to continually frustrate a president with whom it disagreed."[38] The alternative would seem to be a government of continuous presidential elections, not unlike the revolving governments of postwar Italy, and "overall paralysis or a government in which the president and Congress are so close as to defeat the basic concept of the separation of powers so fundamental to our system."[39] The resulting instability would make the development and implementation of long-term programs very uncertain. Cronin also notes: "A vote of no confidence arrangement might lead presidents to avoid making significant changes in policy that would antagonize Congress."[40] Imaginative leadership might also be cast aside in favor of policies rated highly popular in the opinion polls, whether sound or not.

The danger of a plebiscitarian type of democracy emerging from the no confidence proposal should not be entirely dismissed. Cronin has pointed out that "a vote of no confidence could actually be used to strengthen the hand of an already strong leader, much as Hitler and DeGaulle used plebiscites to weaken their oppositions."[41] National leaders have rarely, if ever, lost plebiscite votes. Indeed, these leaders can time and word their plebiscites in such a fashion that they automatically guarantee a favorable vote. As Cronin has commented: "One imagines, for example, Lyndon Johnson could have won a vote of no confidence on his Vietnam policy in 1966. Or, Richard Nixon might have won a vote of no confidence during the early stages, say the spring or summer of 1973, of his Watergate crisis."[42]

Clearly, the no confidence proposal offers no guarantees of higher quality leadership or greater presidential accountability. Indeed, the measure might make the president too dependent upon Congress. And it might produce presidents who would tilt at every shift in public opinion. Furthermore, as Thomas has noted: "The potential for both Congressional and presidential manipulation of the procedure for short-run political advantage makes it unduly risky."[43] It is difficult to disagree with Cronin's final assessment of the no confidence vote proposal:

> This measure might at some future time give us an endless line of unsuccessful short-term presidents and as a result a paralyzed nation. We risk the unwise weakening of the presidency by such an amendment. Abuses of presidential

power do need to be curbed, but this proposal is not the way to do it. We need better leadership, not a weakened presidency.[44]

Opponents also insist that the no confidence dissolution reform is unnecessary, because impeachment and other available checks and balances can and have worked effectively. For proof, they point to the forced resignation of President Nixon as a recent example.

THE MANDATORY QUESTION PERIOD

In 1864, Representative George Pendleton (R–Ohio), who is better remembered for his civil service reform bill, proposed that cabinet members be given seats in the House of Representatives, with the privilege of entering debate and being present a certain number of days each month to answer questions. Almost a century later, Senator Estes Kefauver (D–Tenn.) revised this plan for a question-and-answer period for department heads on the floor of either house. More recently, former Vice-President Walter F. Mondale, when he was a member of the Senate, offered the same proposal again.

Over the years, however, the proposal for mandatory questioning of the present and principal department and agency heads has not generated much public support. Gerald Ford's voluntary appearance before the House Judiciary Committee in late 1974 to explain his pardon of former President Nixon undoubtedly further deflated support for the mandatory question period proposal. Nevertheless, Philippa Strum and others have argued that the proposal deserves serious consideration because of the excessive claims of executive privilege and the executive department's heavy preoccupation with secrecy, especially the Johnson and Nixon administrations.[45] Also, Strum insists the mandatory question period would be the proper antidote to the frequent reluctance of top-level officials, such as President Nixon's Secretary of State Henry Kissinger, to testify before congressional committees and especially their insistence on delineating the topics and areas to be discussed in the hearings.

Designed in part as a symbolic attack on the imperial presidency, the mandatory question period would, its supporters insist, help achieve two reform goals: restoration of constitutional balance and greater presidential accountability. Professor Strum argues that the proposal would not require amending the Constitution, since Article II, Section 3, can be interpreted as providing a basis for a statute mandating a question period. Opponents of this plan doubt whether a mandatory question period is worth the price in terms of policy effectiveness and the possibility that the proposed reform might foster renewed secrecy by the White House. Critics have also made a case that constant questioning of the president and top-level members of the executive branch might seriously stifle presidential initiative and contribute to a further undermining of legitimacy in the American governmental system. Critics also insist that most objectives of the mandatory question period could probably be achieved by legislation spelling out the scope of executive privilege and the conditions under which it could be invoked. Furthermore, as James L. Sundquist has wisely observed: "To require officials to appear for questioning in the Senate or the House against their will would not contribute to harmonious relationships nor add significantly to the store of knowledge available to legislators."[46]

THE SIX-YEAR NONRENEWABLE TERM PROPOSAL

From time to time reformers of the presidency have proposed that the office be limited to a single six-year nonrenewable term. This is not exactly a new idea. Originally proposed in Congress in 1826, the single six-year term proposal has been reintroduced more than 150 times since then. In 1830, Andrew Jackson recommended a single term, stating the office of the president should "be placed beyond the reach of any improper influences." At least nine other presidents, including Lyndon Johnson, Nixon, and Carter have also endorsed the proposal. According to the Gallup poll organization, less than one-third of those polled in 1981 favored changing to a six-year term (see Table 15.1).[47] Republican presidential candidate John B. Connally included this six-year presidential term as part of the cornerstone of his unsuccessful 1980 presidential drive. To achieve a six-year presidential term, it would be necessary, of course, to amend the Constitution.

Proponents of the single six-year term—or the "term and a half," as it is sometimes called—have argued that it has many advantages over the existing four-year, renewable term. First of all, it would enable the president to devote his full time and attention to the job. No time would have to be devoted to seeking renomination and reelection. Under the existing system the president must set aside the fourth year (and sometimes more time) of his first term to running for

Table 15.1 SIX-YEAR PRESIDENTIAL TERM

	Yes, Favor	No, Oppose	No Opinion
1983 (Feb.)	31%	61%	8%
1981 (Jan.)[a]	30	63	7
1979	30	62	8
1973	28	64	8
1971	20	73	7
1969	18	75	7
1945[b]	25	68	7
1943[c]	29	59	12
1938	21	67	12
1936	26	74	—*

*"Don't know" figures, which were allocated between favor and oppose, are not available.

Question variations:

[a]"Would you favor changing the term of the president of the United States to one six-year term with no reelection?"

[b]"Would you favor changing the term of office of the president of the United States in the future to one six-year term with no reelection?"

[c]"Would you favor changing the term of office of the President hereafter to one six-year term with no reelection?"

Source: *Gallup Report* No. 209, February 1983, 12.

reelection. The six-year single term, its supporters argue, would remove this political pressure and give the president an additional two years to carry out his long-term plans. As Tom Wicker commented recently: "The argument that running for reelection takes too much of a President's time may be the strongest for the single six-year term."[48] Former Secretary of State Cyrus Vance has made the point in stronger language: "Every President needs eight or nine months to learn his job. Then he has about one and one-half years to feel comfortable in a job he knows. Then he's running again for twelve to eighteen months."[49] Also, not to be forgotten, there is a midterm congressional election that no president can afford to neglect.

Furthermore, six-year term advocates insist that the current four-year term is too short for the president to achieve the goals he has set during his successful drive for the White House. The nature of the budget process, for example, is such that he is well into his second year before the impact of his program can be felt. Supporters of the six-year term argue that the proposal permits long-term study, planning, and implementation of a president's program, without wasting the fourth year in reelection campaigning.

One of the strongest arguments in favor of a single six-year term is that it would "liberate a president from the pressures of special-interest groups and party-line politics, allowing him to exercise greater independence of judgment and nonpartisan leadership."[50] Advocates of the single six-year term want "to take the politics out of the presidency, to deemphasize the divisive aspects of electoral and partisan politics, to elevate the presidency above selfish or factional ambitions."[51] Some advocates also see the single six-year term as a means of making certain that no president succeeds himself. The concept of the citizen politician serving a single term, they say, should be recognized as the maximum demand to be placed on any single individual. A few proponents argue that a single-term chief executive would find his hand strengthened in recruiting top managers for the executive departments.[52]

Other supporters of the one-term presidency have also argued that it would permit a president to make decisions free from the temptation of political expediency. Former President Carter has reported that near the end of a first term, when a president opens a reelection campaign, there is a "driving pressure" on his challengers to "dispute or contradict the President on the issues for strictly political reasons."[53] Carter also recalled how Gerald Ford, seeking renomination in 1976, had to back off from strategic arms agreements reached with the Soviet Union at the Vladivostok summit and from trying to obtain ratification of the Panama Canal treaties when both projects came under heavy fire from his intraparty challenger, Ronald Reagan.[54]

Nor was President Carter immune from such pressures; he withdrew SALT II from Senate consideration early in 1980 after the Soviet Union's invasion of Afghanistan. His former Secretary of State Cyrus Vance believes "it would have been different" in a nonelection year. "It's inevitable," he reports, that a president will "draw back or not take political risks" when facing reelection, and the consequences can be ominous. Cyrus Vance, whose long term of public service in foreign affairs for three presidents qualifies him as an experienced observer, argues that the single six-year term would provide "more stability for a period within which predictability would be possible," thus quieting the anxieties of many foreign officials over shifting American policies, such as nuclear arms control.[55]

Advocates of good government insist that a single six-year term would relieve a president of political considerations in his decision making and permit him to act as a statesman in the national interest. The six-year term would, of course, also remove the advantages of incumbency from presidential election campaigns.

THE CASE AGAINST THE SIX-YEAR TERM

Deceptively appealing at first glance, the single six-year term would probably create more problems than it would solve. First of all, as several critics have pointed out, the president would be a lame duck from the moment of his election. The one-term president would still have to engage in political bargaining in order to win congressional support, but his political firepower would be considerably less than if he could stand for reelection.[56] Eligibility for reelection, Alexander Hamilton argued two centuries ago, is necessary "to enable the people, when they see reason to approve of his conduct, to continue him in his station, in order to prolong the utility of his talents and virtues."[57]

Clearly, the required reelection of a chief executive after four years is one of the most democratic features of the presidency. The need to seek reelection enhances the likelihood that a president will carefully weigh his policy options and their possible effect on his reelection chances before moving ahead. Presidential accountability is best maintained when the president must answer again to the electorate. Furthermore, as Thomas E. Cronin reminds us: ". . . a political party should retain the threat of dumping a president as a check upon the incumbent and the office, especially upon a president who refuses to honor his party's pledges."[58] But this party threat to deny an incumbent reelection is probably only an empty threat in the twentieth century. Indeed, in 1912 Woodrow Wilson had been elected on a Democratic platform calling for a single six-year term, but less than four months later—probably with an early eye on his reelection prospects—he asked A. Mitchell Palmer, a leading member of Congress and later Wilson's attorney general, to stonewall a proposed constitutional amendment for a six-year term after the U.S. Senate had approved the amendment by a 48 to 23 margin on February 13, 1913.[59]

In his letter to Representative Palmer, President-elect Wilson (before passage of the Twentieth Amendment in 1933, presidents were not inaugurated until the fourth of March) wrote that a four-year term was "too long for a President who is not the true spokesman of the people, who is imposed upon and does not lead. It is too short a term for a President who is doing or attempting a great work of reform and who has not had time to finish it." Switching to six years, he insisted, "would increase the likelihood of its being too long, without any assurance that it would, in happy cases, be long enough. A fixed Constitutional limitation to a single term of office is highly arbitrary and unsatisfactory from any point of view."[60]

Cronin's telling argument against a single six-year term is equally persuasive: "The president who cannot be reelected after four years is unlikely to accomplish anything of value if he is given a free ride for another two."[61] Likewise, a president who shirks his political responsibilities and refuses to face reelection is not likely to accomplish much in the way of program development and substantive policy. As Cronin has aptly put it: "Reeligibility, used or not, is a potentially significant political resource in the hands of a president; and denying that resource, even in the more limited way that the Twenty-second Amendment has done, will diminish the leadership discretion of future presidents who desire to be activist initiators of policy." Harry Truman made the point well after his retirement: "You do not have to be very smart to know that an officeholder who is not eligible for reelection loses a lot of influence. . . . It makes no sense to treat a president this way—no matter who he is—Republican or Democrat. He is still President of the whole country and all of us are dependent on him; and we ought to give him the tools to do his job."[62]

George Reedy, who served as secretary to Lyndon B. Johnson and later wrote one of the more thoughtful studies on the presidency, has argued that single-term proposals are "based on the belief that a President's authority is somehow separable from his political leadership. . . . The reality is quite different. A president whose political leadership has suffered from erosion is virtually helpless." Separating the president from the pressures of the public, Reedy observed, would only "tend to make him an ineffective voice issuing orders and decrees. . . ."[63]

Clark Clifford, adviser to several presidents and a prominent Washington lawyer, once said that he found "the notion that a president should be above politics inconsistent with our system of government, just as I find the prospect of a presidential dictator to be inconceivable under the same system. . . . Politics, in the final analysis, is an essential part of democracy. A president above politics is a president remote from the processes of government and removed from the thoughts and aspirations of his people."[64] Clearly, the single six-year term would make presidential accountability and executive branch responsiveness more difficult to achieve than under the present two-term system.[65]

Nor should the possibility be ignored that the single six-year term, with reelection precluded, would intensify the presidential selection process. Thomas E. Cronin has warned: "Certainly in a winner-take-more situation, there is the likelihood that ideological competition would be more aggressive and perhaps more bitter than at present. Conflict would assuredly be heightened."[66] More than 75 years ago, Senator John Sharp Williams of Mississippi put his finger on another significant reason for rejecting the six-year term. A single six-year term, Williams argued, would extend periods of divided government, such as existed in 1910–1912 (and more recently for 14 years out of 18 between 1968 and 1986) for two additional years, thus "emphasizing rather than diminishing the defect of our system as it is."[67]

What are the prospects for the proposed amendment to limit the president to one six-year term? While one hesitates to rely on the crystal ball, it would appear that, despite the support of several former presidents and a number of prominent national leaders, the prospects are not bright. The formidable obstacles of the amending process itself—approval of a two-thirds vote in each house of Congress and ratification by three-fourths of the states—makes any basic change in the Constitution unlikely. Only 16 amendments have been added to the nation's basic document since the Bill of Rights was attached to the Constitution in 1791, and two of these—the Eighteenth and Twenty-first—in effect canceled each other on the prohibition issue. And as the supporters of the original equal rights amendment and District of Columbia statehood question have painfully learned, it is almost impossible to amend the Constitution without massive public support.

Furthermore, many supporters of the single six-year presidential term amendment also favor term limitations on members of Congress—12 years for members of each house. It seems rather unlikely that present members of Congress would support the single six-year presidential term if it meant that they would soon be pressured into supporting an amendment to shorten their own political lives.

REPEAL OF THE TWENTY-SECOND AMENDMENT

Whether advocating repeal of an amendment previously added to the Constitution less than four decades ago constitutes reforming the presidency may be debatable. But it is the author's view that the Twenty-second Amendment two-term limitation on presidents should be repealed, chiefly because it makes a chief executive a lame duck the day after he is reelected. The Founding Fathers provided indefinite eligibility for presidents; the four-year term represented a compromise between those who favored the president serving during "good behavior," meaning indefinitely so long as he comported himself within constitutional guidelines, and those who favored a seven-year term. Some Framers thought a second term should be banned. Jefferson and Monroe, although neither attended the convention, favored periodic rotation in office.

Long after the Founding Fathers left Philadelphia, the length of presidential service continued to occupy national attention. Between 1789 and 1947, Thomas E. Cronin reminds us, "No less than 270 resolutions to limit eligibility for reelection were introduced in Congress."[68] Why did the Twenty-second Amendment win favorable approval after World War II, despite many previous rejections? The explanation can be traced to the special political conditions existing after World War II. During the 80th Congress (1946–1948), Republicans dominated both houses of Congress, and they were determined not to see a repeat performance of four successive presidential victories by another FDR-type candidate.

To push the proposed amendment through Congress, GOP lawmakers were joined by some conservative Democrats, chiefly from the South, who had soured on the New Deal and Roosevelt. In less than four years, Republican-dominated chambers in most of the states helped speed ratification of the two-term limitation. Proponents made a strong case that there is no indispensable man in a democracy; extended incumbency might lead to entrenched power and inflexibility. As one observer phrased it, the "Twenty-second Amendment protects us from periodic hardening of the governmental arteries!"[69]

Ironically, the Twenty-second Amendment, ratified in 1951, first applied to Republican President Dwight D. Eisenhower, who was barred from running in 1960. If Eisenhower had been eligible to run and wished to seek a third term, most political pundits agreed that he would have easily won renomination and reelection.

This amendment is, according to some critics, antidemocratic, for it limits the national leadership choice of party and electorate alike. Furthermore, if the nation were in the midst of a major war or domestic crisis, it compels a rotation in office just when the electorate may wish to see an experienced president continued. Passed more as a result of political spite than adherence to sound democratic doctrine, the Twenty-second Amendment turns a reelected president into a lame duck from the moment he is declared the winner.

Though we have the experience of observing only Presidents Eisenhower and Reagan in their second terms, most political experts seem agreed that the long-term effects of the amendment will undermine the effectiveness of most second-term presidents. Harry Truman, although not prohibited by the amendment from seeking another term, testified that any officer who is ineligible for reelection loses a lot of political clout. In the words of the plain-spoken man from Independence, the American people put the president "in the hardest job in the world, and send him out to fight our battles in a life and death struggle—and you have sent him out to fight with one hand tied behind his back because everyone knows he cannot run for reelection."[70] Truman added: "If he is not a good President, and you do not want to keep him, you do not have to reelect him. There is a way to get rid of him and it does not require a constitutional amendment to do it."[71] The late Clinton Rossiter, a leading authority on the presidency, predicted almost thirty years ago that the Twenty-second Amendment would prove to have permanently weakened the presidency. "Everything in our history tells us," he wrote, "that a President who does not or cannot seek reelection loses much of his grip in his last couple of years, and we no longer can afford Presidents who lose their grip."[72]

What does the future hold for the Twenty-second Amendment? While most citizens support the two-term tradition, they sometimes view it as too restrictive to be cemented into the Constitution. However, there has been no groundswell to repeal the limitation. Possibly an emergency near the end of a popular president's second term might trigger a major repeal drive. But it seems doubtful if enough time could be found to repeal it before election, even discounting the additional obstacles that might arise if it became a partisan issue, as seems likely. Nor should the possibility be dismissed that the repeal drive might run head on into an equally strong constitutional amendment drive to adopt the widely publicized single six-year presidential term.

DIRECT ELECTION OF THE PRESIDENT

Direct popular election of the president is a reform proposal that would probably have the most far-reaching impact—and undoubtedly a number of unanticipated consequences—on the presidency and the American party system. Andrew Jackson, a losing candidate in the 1824 electoral college deadlock, four years later in his first annual message advocated that the electoral college be abolished and the president chosen by popular vote, with a runoff election between the two high candidates if one received a majority in the initial ballot.[73] More recently advocated by Senator Birch Bayh (D–Ind.), the main sponsor of the Twenty-fifth Amendment on presidential disability, the Bayh plan would have presidents elected directly by the voters just as governors are. Additionally, the Bayh version also contained a provision that called for a national runoff election between the two top vote-getters in the event that no candidate received 40 percent of all votes cast.[74] The proposed direct vote amendment, after more than a decade of debate and parliamentary skirmishing, was finally put to a vote in the U.S. Senate in July 1979. With 99 senators voting, the proposal received 51 votes—15 votes short of the 66 needed for a proposed constitutional amendment.[75] Failure on this vote ended further attempts in Congress to win approval of the direct vote amendment.

By far the most democratic electoral proposal, the direct popular vote amendment is deceptively appealing. This plan would give every voter the same weight in the presidential balloting, in accordance with the one person, one vote doctrine. On paper, at least, the winner would gain more legitimacy as a result of a clear-cut popular triumph. Furthermore, the shortcomings of the present system, especially the constitutional requirement that presidential choice will be made by the House of Representatives if no candidate receives a majority of the electoral votes, would be replaced by a simple, direct, and decisive method.

The direct election plan, however, is fraught with numerous potential boobytraps. Critics suspect that the new rules would change electoral behavior. The runoff proposal, for example, might encourage third-party, independent, or "spoiler" candidacies and seriously undermine the two-party system. The possibility that a defeated candidate from a national convention might obtain a ballot listing as a new party or an independent candidate cannot be easily dismissed.

Arthur M. Schlesinger, Jr., has expressed the fear that minor parties or single-cause candidates could magnify their strength under the direct vote plan. "Anti-abortion parties, Black Power parties, anti-busing parties, anti-gun control parties, pro-homosexual rights parties—for that matter, Communist or Fascist parties—have a dim future in the Electoral College. In direct elections they could drain away enough votes, cumulative from state to state, to prevent the formation of a national majority—and to give themselves strong bargaining positions in case of a run-off."[76]

Cronin also raises another direct election specter: "The direct vote method could easily produce a series of 41 percent presidents."[77] Though we have elected 15 minority presidents (that is, candidates elected by less than 50 percent of the popular vote), the present Electoral College system—a two-stage process in which popular votes are transformed into electoral votes—magnifies the popular vote margin of the winner. Thus, even though there have been a number of cliff-hanger presidential election contests—Kennedy-Nixon in 1960, Nixon-Humphrey in 1968, and Carter-Ford in 1976—only once in the past century has a president failed to receive 55 percent of the Electoral College vote.

Direct popular vote, if it were extremely close—say, within a few thousand votes nationwide—might easily lead to interminable recounts and challenges, leave open the possibility of electoral fraud in some states, and raise serious questions over the legitimacy of choice. Opponents insist that it would encourage unrestrained majority rule and probably political extremism. Lawyer Charles Black, a scholar not often given to exaggeration, has stated that direct election would be the most deeply radical amendment ever to enter the Constitution.[78] The present Electoral College process, which rests on a federal system of choice, dampens electoral tensions, and for a century has produced, without fail, a popular vote winner.

Opponents of the direct system also point out that the small states would be submerged and lose some of the power they presently enjoy in the federal system. Furthermore, the direct popular vote plan, among other things, necessitates some form of national administration of presidential elections, upsetting the present decentralized and economical state management of elections. Direct popular election would probably trigger demands for a uniform ballot in all states and uniform voter qualifications. Moreover, as Thomas E. Cronin cautions: "Once members of Congress attack details of this nature, they are also likely to regulate further the presidential primary process, the methods of voting, and hence, at least indirectly, to influence the national conventions."[79]

Some critics fear that the direct election plan would make the candidates more remote from the voters by transforming the campaigns into national telethons, since the sole object would be to reach as many potential voters in the large populous states in the most efficient manner possible. The late Theodore H. White, chronicler of presidential elections, considered the direct election plan a revolutionary measure that would transform the entire system of elections and upset two centuries of American political history. Media professionals, White believed, would become the new political bosses, and state boundaries, which give us a sense of place in presidential politics, would give way to maps of major media markets:

> This plebiscite proposal will withdraw from us a large and throbbing memory of our history—all those lovely maps of elections which tell school children as well as grownups how the country has swung section by section from mood to mood. Instead, we will have this boiling pot of 75 million votes stirred by mixmaster, manipulators, and television—understandable only by statisticians and social scientists.[80]

State electoral victories would not be important, only the single national mandate would count. In defending the present system, columnist George Will observed some years ago: "The electoral college promotes unity and legitimacy by helping to generate majorities that are not narrow, geographically or ideologically, and by magnifying (as in 1960, 1968, 1976) narrow margins of victories in the popular vote."[81]

Defenders of the direct vote plan point out that three times in the nation's history (1824, 1876, and 1888) the Electoral College has failed to give the popular vote winner a victory. Nor do they believe that the direct vote plan will undermine the federal system in any way. "The vitality of federalism," columnist Neal Peirce writes, "rests chiefly on the constitutionally mandated system of congressional representation and the will and capacity of state and local governments to address compelling problems, not on the hocus-pocus of the eighteenth-century vote count system."[82]

Jimmy Carter, in his first year of office, recommended that Congress adopt a constitutional amendment to provide for direct popular election of the president. In July 1979, the Senate voted 51 to 48 in support of Senator Bayh's direct election proposal—a simple majority but far short of the needed two-thirds majority for constitutional amendments. Opponents of the amendment consisted of an alliance of southern conservatives and northern liberals. They were responding to black and Jewish groups who feared they might lose their "swing" vote power under the existing system.[83] Several senators from the small states, worried about possible diminution of their voting strength, also cast votes against the proposed constitutional amendment. Until a major electoral college crisis occurs in a close election—if a candidate won the popular vote and yet lost in the Electoral College, or if a third-party candidate should garner enough electoral votes to force the presidential choice into the House of Representatives and the lawmakers remained deadlocked on their choice—the prospects for the direct election amendment do not seem bright.

OTHER PROCEDURAL REFORMS

Dissatisfaction with the Electoral College over the years has produced several other proposals to modify its operation. But support for these plans has been so splintered that they have failed to stimulate much public support. Each of these plans, however, deserves brief mention.

The first, called the *automatic plan,* would result in the least change to the existing system, and it would remove the possibility of faithless electors—those who refuse to support the electoral winner in their home state. Under the automatic plan the presidential electors would be abolished, and the state's electoral vote would be automatically cast for the popular vote winner in that state. If no candidate won a majority of electoral votes nationwide, a joint session of Congress would select the president, with each representative and senator having one vote.

Under the second proposal—the *district plan*—the nation would return to the method used in the states early in our history (and recently readopted in Maine). In the district plan the presidential candidate who wins a plurality vote in each congressional district receives its electoral vote, with the remaining two electoral votes (derived from the two U.S. Senate seats) going to the statewide popular vote winner. If no presidential candidate receives a majority of the electoral votes, senators and representatives, meeting jointly and voting individually, would select the president from the three candidates having the highest number of electoral votes. By and large, most of the support for the district plan has come from members of Congress and interest groups based in the rural areas.

The third proposal, called the *proportional plan,* would split each state's electoral vote in proportion to the division of the popular vote. Thus, a candidate receiving 60 percent of the popular vote in the state would collect 60 percent of its electoral vote. In 1950 such a proposal, the so-called Lodge-Gossett plan, named after its two leading sponsors—Republican Henry Cabot Lodge, Jr., of Massachusetts and Democratic Representative Ed Gossett of Texas—passed the Senate but failed to survive in the House. This plan, which would reduce the advantage of the large states by preventing them from giving all their votes to one candidate, has usually been opposed by lawmakers from the populous states. Critics of the plan have also argued that the proportional division of the electoral votes would usually be fairly evenly split between the two major-party contenders, thus denying either candidate a majority of the electoral votes. Under this plan there would be frequent likelihood of presidential elections being thrown into the House of Representatives.

The fourth proposal, developed by members of the Twentieth Century Fund task force, is known as the *national bonus plan.* [84] If adopted, the national bonus plan would retain the Electoral College, but it would be heavily weighted toward the popular vote winner. Under the plan a pool of 102 electoral votes (two for each state and the District of Columbia) would automatically be awarded to the candidate who won the popular vote, to be added to the candidate's electoral vote. In all, there would be a combined total of 640 national electoral votes (538 Electoral College votes, plus 102 national bonus votes). If a candidate collected a majority in the Electoral College (321 votes), he or she would be declared elected. If not, a runoff would be held within 30 days between the two candidates winning the most popular votes.

Advocates contend the plan would ensure that the popular vote winner would usually be the electoral vote winner and thus make it unlikely that the popular vote winner would lose the election, as happened in 1888 and could have occurred in 1960 and 1976. Furthermore, proponents insist the plan would reduce the chances of electoral deadlock, encourage two-party competition in one-party states, and eliminate the faithless elector who votes against the popular choice in his or her own state.

Critics of the bonus plan contend that, among other things, the plan would discourage minor parties and independent candidates. Small states, it has been noted, might lose some of their influence in a diluted electoral vote and control over state election law. One respected political scientist, Allan P. Sindler, has expressed concern that the national bonus plan might also allow a plurality leader with a highly sectional base of voting support to collect the 102 bonus votes and thereby capture the presidency. [85] The national bonus plan would, of course, require a constitutional amendment.

Several other procedural institutional reforms with considerable potential value have also been offered by Joseph A. Califano, Jr., President Lyndon Johnson's principal domestic policy aide. Califano has called for (1) a Presidential

Powers Impact Statement Act, which would require an analysis by the executive and legislative branches of the "impact of each significant new legislative program on the powers of the Presidency"; (2) legislation requiring that "certain specific reports" relating to such matters as social programs and national security policy accompany the annual State of the Union message; and (3) a presidentially prepared annual National Posture Statement that compares executive branch performance with defined statutory goals and presidential achievement claims for these programs.[86]

Impact statements, which have become an essential tool for state and local governments in their efforts to anticipate future problems, especially in environmental matters and land planning, might result in more careful delegations of legislative authority to the president and help curb aggrandizement of executive power. Moreover, as Norman C. Thomas has noted: "Requiring the President, in effect, to document and substantiate the State of the Union message and annually to measure program performance against congressional presidential objectives and promises could substantially reduce the dangers to governmental legitimacy caused by unmet expectations of the masses resulting from exaggerated promises by their leaders."[87] These reforms, which aim to restore governmental legitimacy, constitutional balance, and increased presidential accountability, would not require a constitutional amendment, but could be accomplished through legislation.

PROSPECTS FOR INSTITUTIONAL REFORM

Although the public continues to expect the president to perform more duties and solve more problems each year, the prospects for institutional reform of the presidency are not promising. The obstacles to major change appear almost insurmountable in the United States. History shows that radical reform of the presidency or other political institutions has never attracted much popular support. Most of the proposals that would come closest to meeting the goals outlined by the reformers involve structural changes in the presidency and the party system. To establish a parliamentary system in the United States, for example, or even a single six-year presidential term, would require a constitutional amendment. Yet, pushing aside the merits of each reform proposal for the moment, the prospects for reforming the presidency by constitutional amendment in the immediate years ahead are almost nil.

The diversity of American society, and the countervailing pressures from numerous single interest groups, constitute a major barrier to the formation of the majority coalitions needed to achieve reform. The Founding Fathers devised a series of checks and balances that make it extremely difficult to amend the constitution. Furthermore, as Neal Peirce and others have observed: "No constitutional amendment has much of a chance of ratification without the support or at least the acquiescence of all the major political forces in the country—the controlling groups in each major political party, spokesmen of each section, state and national party leaders."[88] Unless a near tidal wave of public support develops for a constitutional amendment, such as when the right of eighteen-year-olds to vote gained widespread national favor during the Vietnam war, the proposed change inevitably ends up in the legislative boneyard.

In spite of widespread distrust of government and a latent fear about the reappearance of the imperial presidency, a strong popular demand for radical reform of the presidency, or other parts of the federal system, has yet to appear on the horizon. Unless another major domestic crisis occurs rivaling the size of the Watergate scandals in the early 1970s, the country is not likely to hear many serious demands for reform of the presidency—except possibly the single six-year presidential term—from leaders in Congress, the public, or academia.

Patchwork reforms of the presidency, such as greater accountability to Congress for presidential actions at home and abroad, improved liaison between president and Congress, reorganization of the Executive Office, and so on, seem to be preferred to a major overhaul of the system. Thus, during the Vietnam war and the Watergate era, the imperial presidency was reined in by what President Nixon's onetime Secretary of State William Rogers termed a "straitjacket of legislation"—a series of congressional statutes and resolutions passed in the 1970s narrowing the president's power to wage war, to conduct intelligence operations, to sell war planes and sophisticated military hardware abroad, and to enter into executive agreements with foreign governments.[89] But no major reform of the presidency was seriously considered.

CONCLUSION

Although the numerous proposals for reforming the presidency outlined in the chapter may possess some merit, they are by no means a panacea. Breaking down the barriers between the president and Congress by including members of Congress in the cabinet, for example, may merely result in shifting the location of conflict, not removing it. James L. Sundquist has cogently noted: "When executives and legislators are disposed to cooperate, ample means for cooperation exist and additional formal mechanisms are scarcely needed."[90] Similarly, the six-year term may give the president ample time to learn the job—but what if he opts for one ill-advised policy after another? The country would be saddled with an incompetent chief executive for an additional two years. In the case of the no confidence vote, the so-called cure (greater presidential-congressional cooperation) might well be worse than the ailment. The no confidence vote, in all likelihood, would give Congress the opportunity continually to frustrate the president. More than likely, it would lead to a government of continuous presidential elections. Government instability would probably be the chief result of this "reform." Clearly, institutional reform offers only the possibility, not the certainty, of improvement.

The most important lesson to be drawn from proposed reforms of the presidency is that for each remedy there are as many problems as solutions. No single, all-purpose reform exists to help the president cope with the unrelenting demands placed on him. Indeed, a careful analysis of the various reform proposals suggests that most of the remedies merely exchange one set of difficulties for another—or, worse yet, undermine the existing effectiveness of the American chief executive.

As indicated in the opening chapter, the office of the president is basically sound. But the presidency in recent years has been seriously undermined by the excessive expectations the American public has placed upon the White House occupant. Indeed, in the words of one presidential scholar: "The failures of the presidency in recent years are less the fault of individual presidents than the result of excessively unrealistic expectations."[91]

What is needed for the remaining years of the twentieth century is "a revolution in lower expectations" for the presidency. Thomas E. Cronin has urged that we ". . . deflate the notion that presidents can provide all or even the major amount of national leadership. We could achieve this in part by strengthening local, state, and regional government to address problems that should be solved at those levels."[92] In Cronin's words: "We must refine our expectations of the president and raise our expectations of ourselves."[93]

Still, the record of the twentieth century shows that the nation has surged ahead most dramatically under the strong leadership of three presidents—Wilson, Franklin D. Roosevelt, and Lyndon Johnson—who had the wholehearted support of their party majorities in Congress. When the president and his party majority in Congress can work closely together, presidents have far more opportunities to move the country ahead and attain higher levels of social progress and reform. There is, of course, no foolproof method of guaranteeing that the electorate will choose wisely in picking a president and congressional majority that will see eye to eye on public policy and act accordingly. But parties can serve as vehicles for mobilizing support for presidential programs in Congress. By the same token, the separation of powers system can continue to serve as a restraint on presidents who in their zeal to achieve their political goals may choose to ignore constitutional constraints and the rights of the minority opposition.

In conclusion, no major overhaul of the presidency, it would seem, is needed at the present time. However, we should be mindful that an institution almost two hundred years old may from time to time need some fine tuning. Past experience suggests that "the presidency will be revived not by a few grand strokes of constitutional change, but by the accumulation of small improvements at the right points in the system."[94] In the meantime, we should turn down the thermostat on presidential expectations and rely more heavily on the judgment of the American electorate to choose presidents who can meet the challenges of the 1980s and 1990s and yet operate within the constitutional framework of the American shared powers system.

NOTES

1. Joseph E. Kallenbach, *The American Chief Executive* (New York: Harper & Row, 1966), 571.
2. Henry C. Lockwood, *The Abolition of the Presidency (1884),* as cited by Edward S. Corwin, *The President: Office and Powers,* 5th rev. ed. by Randall W. Bland, Theodore T. Hindson, and Jack W. Peltason (New York: New York University Press, 1984), 25.

3. See, for example, William Y. Elliott, *The Need for Constitutional Reform: A Program for National Security* (New York: McGraw-Hill, 1935); Henry Hazlitt, *A New Constitution Now* (New York: McGraw-Hill, 1942); Thomas K. Finletter, *Can Representative Government Do the Job?* (New York: Reynal & Hitchcock, 1945); and C. Perry Patterson, *Presidential Government in the United States: The Unwritten Constitution* (Chapel Hill: University of North Carolina Press, 1947).

4. Charles M. Hardin, *Presidential Power and Accountability: Toward a New Constitution* (Chicago: University of Chicago Press, 1974).

5. Ibid.

6. Ibid., 183.

7. Norman C. Thomas, "Reforming the Presidency: Problems and Prospects," in Thomas E. Cronin and Rexford G. Tugwell, eds., *The Presidency Reappraised,* 2nd ed. (New York: Praeger, 1977), 329.

8. Lloyd N. Cutler, "To Form a Government—on the Defects of Separation of Powers," *Foreign Affairs,* 59 (Fall 1980), 126–143.

9. Ibid.

10. Ibid., 173.

11. Erwin C. Hargrove and Michael Nelson, *Presidents, Politics, and Policy* (Baltimore, MD: The Johns Hopkins University Press, 1984), 270.

12. Ibid.

13. Rexford Tugwell, "Constitution for a United Republics of America," Version XXXVII, *The Center Magazine,* 3 (September–October 1970), 31–32.

14. Barbara Tuchman, "Should We Abolish the Presidency?" *The New York Times,* February 13, 1973.

15. Herman Finer, *The Presidency: Crisis and Regeneration* (Chicago: University of Chicago Press, 1950), chap. 7.

16. Edward S. Corwin, *The President: Office and Powers,* 4th ed. (New York: New York University, 1957), 297–299.

17. Rowland Egger, *The President of the United States* (New York: McGraw-Hill, 1967), 151–152.

18. Benjamin V. Cohen, "Presidential Responsibility and American Democracy" (1974 Royer Lecture, University of California, Berkeley, May 23, 1974), as cited by Thomas E. Cronin, *The State of the Presidency,* 2nd ed. (Boston: Little, Brown, 1980), 361–362.

19. Ibid.

20. Charles S. Hyneman, *Bureaucracy in a Democracy* (New York: Harper & Row, 1950), Chap. 25.

21. Kallenbach, *The American Chief Executive,* 575.

22. Mark O. Hatfield, "Resurrecting Political Life in America . . . ," *Congressional Record,* 93rd Cong., 1st Sess. 12 Oct. 1973, No. 153, S. 19104–19107, as cited by Cronin, *The State of the Presidency,* 369, note 45.

23. Cronin, *The State of the Presidency,* 363.

24. Ibid.

25. *The Federalist,* No. 70 (Modern Library, 1937), 460–467.

26. Thomas, "Reforming the Presidency: Problems and Prospects," 338.

27. H.D. Res. 903 (93rd Congress, 2nd Session) February 14, 1974, copy supplied by Representative Reuss. For a more detailed discussion of the Reuss plan, see Henry S. Reuss, "A No-Confidence Amendment," *Commonweal,* C (April 12, 1974), 127–129.

28. Two other no confidence proposals for removing a failed president, offered by Reps. Jonathan B. Bingham (D–N.Y.) and Edith Green (D–Ore.) during the Watergate era, are discussed in James L. Sundquist, *Constitutional Reform and Effective Government* (Washington, DC: Brookings, 1986), 65–66.

29. James L. Sundquist, "Needed: A Workable Check on the President," *The Brookings Bulletin,* 10 (Fall 1973), 11.
30. Ibid.
31. Cronin, *The State of the Presidency,* 345.
32. Ibid., 346.
33. Sundquist, "Needed: A Workable Check on the President," 11.
34. James L. Sundquist, "Parliamentary Government and Ours," *New Republic,* October 26, 1974, 10–12.
35. Sundquist, "Needed: A Workable Check on the President," 11.
36. Thomas, "Reforming the Presidency: Problems and Prospects," 330.
37. Cronin, *The State of the Presidency,* 348.
38. Ibid., 347.
39. Ibid.
40. Ibid.
41. Ibid.
42. Ibid.
43. Thomas, "Reforming the Presidency: Problems and Prospects," 330.
44. Cronin, *The State of the Presidency,* 348.
45. See Philippa Strum, "A Symbolic Attack on the Imperial Presidency: An American 'Question Time'," in Cronin and Tugwell, *The Presidency Reappraised,* 248–264.
46. Thomas, "Reforming the Presidency: Problems and Prospects," 330–331. Sundquist, *Constitutional Reform and Effective Government,* 177.
47. Tom Wicker, "Six Years for the Presidency?" *New York Times Magazine,* June 26, 1983, 18.
48. Ibid.
49. Ibid.
50. Cronin, *The State of the Presidency,* 356.
51. Ibid., 354.
52. Ibid.
53. As cited by Wicker, "Six Years for the Presidency?" 19.
54. Ibid.
55. Ibid., 19.
56. See Thomas, "Reforming the Presidency: Problems and Prospects," 334.
57. *The Federalist,* No. 72.
58. Cronin, *The State of the Presidency,* 356.
59. Wicker, "Six Years for the Presidency?" 18.
60. Woodrow Wilson letter placed in the *Congressional Record,* 64th Cong., 2nd Sess., 15 August 1916, 53, pt. 13: 12620, as cited in Cronin, *The State of the Presidency,* 368, note 38.
61. Ibid., 359.
62. Harry S Truman, testimony before the Subcommittee on Constitutional Amendments of the U.S. Senate, Committee on the Judiciary Hearings on S.D. Resolution II: Presidential Term of Office, 86th Cong., 1st sess., 1959, Part I, p. 7, as cited by Cronin, *The State of the Presidency,* 360.
63. George Reedy, *The Twilight of the Presidency* (New York: New American Library, 1970), 138–139.
64. As cited by Wicker, "Six Years for the Presidency?" 57.
65. Thomas, "Reforming the Presidency: Problems and Prospects," 334.
66. Cronin, *The State of the Presidency,* 366, note 40.
67. *Congressional Record,* January 30, 1913, 2265–2266, as cited by Sundquist, *Constitutional Reform and Effective Government,* 45.

68. Cronin, *The State of the Presidency,* 47.

69. Reo M. Christenson, as cited by Cronin, *The State of the Presidency,* 72, note 26.

70. Harry S Truman, *Senate Judiciary Hearings,* 86th Cong., 1st session, 4 May 1959, p. 7, as cited by Cronin, 72, footnote 28.

71. Ibid.

72. Letter to Representative Stewart L. Udall (D–Ariz.), *Congressional Record* (March 25, 1957), as cited by James L. Sundquist, *Constitutional Reform and Effective Government,* 48.

73. Ibid., 42.

74. 96th Congress, 1st Sess., S.J. Res. 28.

75. Neal R. Peirce and Lawrence D. Longley, *The People's President,* rev. ed. (New Haven, CT: Yale University Press, 1981), 205.

76. As cited by Cronin, *The State of the Presidency,* 61–62.

77. Ibid., 65.

78. *Direct Election of the President* (Washington, DC: American Enterprise Institute, 1977), citing Black's testimony before the Senate Judiciary Committee in 1970, 392.

79. Cronin, *The State of the Presidency,* 64.

80. *Hearings Before the Subcommittee on the Constitution of the Committee on the Judiciary United States Senate,* 96th Cong., 1st Sess. (Washington, DC: Government Printing Office, 1979), 345.

81. George Will, "Don't Fool With the Electoral College," *Newsweek,* April 4, 1977, 96.

82. As cited by Cronin, *The State of the Presidency,* 65.

83. Stephan J. Wayne, *The Road to the White House* (New York: St. Martin's Press, 1980), 21.

84. For a more detailed discussion of the plan, see *Winner Take All,* Report of the Twentieth Century Fund Task Force on Reform of the Presidential Election Process (New York: Holmes Meier, 1978); Thomas E. Cronin, "Choosing a President," *The Center Magazine* 11 (September–October 1978), 5–15.

85. As cited by Cronin, *The State of the Presidency,* 69–70.

86. Thomas, "Reforming the Presidency: Problems and Prospects," 339.

87. Ibid.

88. Neal R. Peirce, *The People's President* (New York: Simon and Schuster, 1968), 198. Significantly, only three amendments (the Eleventh, Sixteenth, and Twenty-second) have needed more than three years to obtain ratification by the constitutionally required three-quarters of the states. Most amendments have needed less than two years. Only four months were needed to ratify the Twenty-sixth Amendment (the 18-year-old vote). James MacGregor Burns, Jack W. Peltason, and Thomas E. Cronin, *Government by the People,* 11th ed. (Englewood Cliffs, NJ: Prentice-Hall, 1981), 43.

89. "The Presidency: Can Anyone Do the Job?" *Newsweek,* January 26, 1981, 37.

90. Sundquist, *Constitutional Reform and Effective Government,* 205.

91. Harold M. Barger, *The Impossible Presidency* (Glenview, IL: Scott, Foresman, and Company, 1984), 10.

92. Cronin, *The State of the Presidency,* 379.

93. Ibid.

94. Godfrey Hodgson, *All Things to All Men* (New York: Simon and Schuster, 1980), 259.

chapter 16

Presidential Power and Popular Support

Throughout this text, the general theme has been that there is a widening gap between high public expectations of the presidency and the seeming inability of recent chief executives to measure up to these public expectations in solving pressing domestic problems and mounting international threats to the United States and its free world allies. Terms such as the "no win" presidency, the "impossible" presidency, the "throwaway" or disposable presidency have been used increasingly to characterize the American presidency in the past decade. Demands placed on the presidency, according to several scholars, exceed the ability of any single chief executive to satisfy them. As a result, the president's power and influence has been badly eroded and the nation has seen a rapid succession of presidents—six chief executives between 1963 and 1980. Some writers predict that the country may continue to see a series of one-term presidents until the end of the century—and possibly longer. However, Ronald Reagan's overwhelming reelection victory in 1984, and his continued high popularity ratings (68 percent favorable, according to the late April 1986 Gallup poll) suggest that a reassessment of the revolving door presidency may be in order.

IMPORTANCE OF PRESIDENTIAL RATINGS IN THE POLLS

Over two decades ago, presidential scholar Richard Neustadt, in his brilliant treatise *Presidential Power,* argued that the key to presidential effectiveness can be measured most directly by the chief executive's standing with the public and the president's ability to persuade Congress to support his programs.[1] In other words, the level of presidential support is both a result and a determinant of the president's choices. Recently, several political scientists have echoed Neustadt's reciprocal relationship thesis. As put by one team of scholars: "The president's standing in the polls has become the most important determinant of his power to persuade. In fact, presidential politics has become a kind of perpetual election with the public assessing the president's performance each month and the politicians watching the results."[2]

Political scientists Ostrom and Simon, in their study of the Gallup monthly poll on the president's overall performance, have pointed out the average number of these presidential performance polls has grown from 12 per year during the Eisenhower administration to roughly 24 per year during the Carter administration. Significantly, since the election of Eisenhower, occupants of the Oval Office have been subject to almost continuous evaluation via the Gallup opinion poll. Between 1953 and 1980, for example, the Gallup organization has posed the following general performance question to cross sections of the American public 538 times: "Do you approve or disapprove of the way [names of the incumbent] is handling his job as president?"[3] This Gallup poll question, in effect, serves as a relatively continuous referendum on the president and heavily influences his current power situation. Throughout the past 30 years the Gallup poll data show that three issues—peace, prosperity, and domestic tranquility—have dominated the public's agenda. It is on these three issues that presidential performance is most closely judged.

Recent studies show that presidents have been most effective when their standing with the public has been above 55 percent in the Gallup poll. For example, President Reagan, his popularity riding above 55 percent, was able to push his tax reform, budget cuts, and military buildup program through Congress with ease during his first year in the White House. Most post-Roosevelt presidents have experienced similar legislative success when their popularity ratings were above 55 percent, even if—as in the case of Eisenhower—the opposition party controlled both houses of Congress for six years. President Johnson was able to move his ambitious Great Society program through Congress during his first 18 months in the White House, partly because he was the beneficiary of a huge outpouring of goodwill and public support that followed the Kennedy assassination (see Table 16.1). But his legislative program came to a near standstill after mid-1965 when his policy of escalating United States involvement in the Vietnam war drove his popularity ratings down to 50 percent and below. Low levels of public support have a way of immobilizing a chief executive. Furthermore, declining public approval generally translates into a declining probability of success for subsequent decisions and actions.[4]

President Carter saw his popularity ratings plummet to 38 percent in the second year after he failed to obtain congressional passage of his comprehensive energy program. Not until he successfully negotiated the Camp David accord between Israel and Egypt in September 1978, which generated a surge of popular support, did Carter obtain congressional approval of his energy package. But then Carter's ratings began to slide again, and even after the Iranian hostage crisis temporarily boosted his ratings, his last two years in the White House were widely regarded as a period of presidential ineffectiveness. In each instance, when a

**Table 16.1 PUBLIC SUPPORT FOR MODERN PRESIDENTS:
A SUMMARY**

Administration	Average Approval Rating			
	Year 1	Year 2	Year 3	Year 4
Truman 1949–1952	58.5	41.0	28.3	29.6
Eisenhower 1953–1956	69.3	65.4	71.3	73.3
Eisenhower 1957–1960	65.0	54.6	63.3	61.1
Kennedy 1961–1963	76.0	71.6	63.5	—
Johnson 1964–1968	66.4	51.2	44.0	41.5
Nixon 1969–1972	61.4	56.9	49.9	56.4
Nixon 1973–1974	41.8	25.9	—	—
Ford 1974–1976	—	53.9	43.1	48.1
Carter 1977–1980	62.4	45.5	38.1	39.5
Reagan 1981–1984	57.0	43.7	44.6	54.3

Source: Gallup Report, No. 182, October–November 1980; *Gallup Report,* No. 219, December 1983; *Gallup Report,* No. 225, June 1984. Reprinted from John H. Aldrich, Gary J. Miller, Charles W. Ostrom, Jr., and David W. Rohde, *American Government: People, Institutions, and Policies* (Boston: Houghton Mifflin, 1986), 490.

president has kept his popularity rating high, he has been able to translate this popularity into political power and win most of his legislative battles with Congress. As one team of scholars has recently noted: "Presidential power is an ephemeral commodity. It cannot be stored in a bank like money, and it cannot be withdrawn when needed. It depends on the president's popularity."[5]

PRESIDENTIAL POPULARITY AND PUBLIC CONFIDENCE

Several recent studies suggest that the impact of public support of the president extends far beyond specific policy issues. The electorate's confidence in the president and their trust in government rises when a president's popularity is high. Indeed, the importance of public support to the president is nowhere more evident than in its impact on reelection prospects. As Table 16.2 shows, the four post-

**Table 16.2 PRESIDENTIAL POPULARITY AND PRESIDENTIAL
ELECTIONS**

Year	Popularity in June	Election Result
1952	32%	Truman declines to run.
1956	69	Eisenhower is reelected.
1960	57	Eisenhower is not eligible.
1964	74	Johnson is elected.
1968	40	Johnson declines to seek reelection.
1972	55	Nixon is reelected.
1976	45	Ford is defeated.
1980	31	Carter is defeated.
1984	55	Reagan is reelected.

Source: Gallup Report, No. 182, October–November 1980; *Gallup Report,* No. 219, December 1983; *Gallup Report,* No. 225, June 1984. Reprinted from John H. Aldrich, Gary J. Miller, Charles W. Ostrom, Jr., and David W. Rohde, *American Government: People, Institutions, and Policies* (Boston: Houghton Mifflin, 1986), 487.

Truman presidents whose popularity ratings were 55 percent or above in the last year of their first term—Eisenhower, Johnson, Nixon, and Reagan—easily won reelection. On the other hand, no president whose standing in the Gallup poll for June of each year in which incumbent presidents were eligible for reelection was below 55 percent has been reelected. Presidents Truman and Johnson, influenced in part by their low standing in the Gallup polls, declined to seek another term. Presidents Ford and Carter tried for another term—and failed.

Recent research has confirmed the conventional view that the president's legislative performance and his actions toward the Soviet Union operate as important determinants of public support. Public support for the president appears to rise whenever the United States becomes involved in a diplomatic confrontation with the USSR.[6] Also, presidential handling of the economy weighs heavily in the public's assessment of the White House occupant. A president's public support will usually be above 50 percent if the nation's "misery index" (the combined rate of inflation and unemployment) is low.[7] Conversely, when the misery index rises over a period of months, presidential popularity will drop noticeably.

In the wake of 10 percent unemployment in 1982, President Reagan's popularity level had dropped to 36 percent in January 1983—its previous all-time high had been 68 percent in May 1981, shortly after the near-fatal attempt on his life. But by December 1983, his rating had rebounded to 55 percent. Three major factors seemed to account for President Reagan's resurging popularity. First, between March and December 1983 the misery index declined from 15.4 in June to 11.8 in December. Second, the adverse impact of the economy was not only neutralized by declining unemployment and inflation rates, but there was a marked shift of public attention away from domestic matters. Between March and December 1983, the percentage of the public citing inflation and unemployment as "the most important problem" the country faced dropped from 79 to 43 percent, whereas the percentage of the public identifying foreign affairs as the nation's number one problem rose from 6 to 37 percent. Third, the Soviet downing of the Korean Air Lines 747 with the loss of 263 lives, including 69 Americans; the terrorist bombing of the U.S. Marine barracks at the Beirut airport that killed 241 American troops; and the U.S. military action in the Caribbean island of Grenada triggered a rapid upswing in public support of President Reagan.

This favorable reversal of public opinion was noteworthy for two reasons: First, no post-Eisenhower president had earned a higher approval rating after three years in office (President Kennedy had a higher rating but served less than three years). Second, President Reagan was the first chief executive in the history of the Gallup poll to drop below 40 percent and then rebound to sustain a 50 percent-plus level.[8] Since then, President Reagan's approval ratings have continued to climb gradually—they reached 64 percent in January 1986. Indeed, his popularity ratings are more reminiscent of the Eisenhower-Kennedy years than the revolving door presidencies era of the late 1960s and 1970s.

Foreign policy issues dominated the Eisenhower-Kennedy years. Both these presidents benefitted from approval-enhancing events—summit meetings, the Formosa Straits resolution of 1955 directed against Communist China, General Eisenhower's open skies nuclear test inspection proposal, the Cuban missile crisis, the Kennedy-sponsored limited test ban treaty signed in record time in 1963, and the Washington-Moscow hot line. These events, it should be noted, were not only beneficial to the Eisenhower-Kennedy popularity ratings but also diverted attention from the economy and divisive domestic problems. By contrast, the 1964–1980 period was marked by a prolonged, unpopular war, the Watergate scandal, and a period of spiraling inflation, escalating unemployment, and skyrocketing oil prices. As a result, public attention shifted from consensual issues to a set of divisive issues. Dissatisfaction and cynicism replaced public approbation of national leadership. Presidents failed to live up to public expectations. White House occupants seemed unable to extricate themselves from a vicious spiral of high public expectations and low job performance ratings.

President Reagan's remarkable ability to reverse his poor popularity ratings of 1982 and regain widespread public support in subsequent years leads to our final conclusion: The throwaway or no win presidency need not be an inevitable feature of late twentieth-century American government.

NOTES

1. Richard Neustadt, *Presidential Power* (New York: Wiley, 1960).
2. John H. Aldrich, Gary J. Miller, Charles W. Ostrom, Jr., and David W. Rohde, *American Government: People, Institutions, and Policies* (Boston: Houghton Mifflin, 1986), 486.
3. Charles W. Ostrom, Jr., and Dennis M. Simon, "Promise and Performance: A Dynamic Model of Presidential Popularity," *American Political Science Review,* 79 (June 1985), 334.
4. Charles W. Ostrom, Jr., and Dennis M. Simon, "Managing Popular Support: The Presidential Dilemma," *Policy Studies Journal,* 12 (1984), 677–690.
5. Aldrich, Miller, Ostrom, and Rohde, *American Government,* 487.
6. Ostrom and Simon, "Promise and Performance: A Dynamic Model of Presidential Popularity," 355–356.
7. See D. A. Hibbs, Jr., "On the Demand for Economic Outcomes: Macroeconomic Performances and Mass Political Support in the United States," *Journal of Politics,* 44 (May 1982), 426–462.
8. Ostrom and Simon, "Promise and Performance," 354.

The Constitution: Provisions on the Presidency

ARTICLE I

Section 3

(6) The Senate shall have the sole power to try all impeachments. When sitting for that purpose, they shall be on oath or affirmation. When the President of the United States is tried, the Chief Justice shall preside; and no person shall be convicted without the concurrence of two-thirds of the members present.

(7) Judgment in cases of impeachment shall not extend further than to removal from office, and disqualification to hold and enjoy any office of honor, trust, or profit under the United States; but the party convicted shall, nevertheless, be liable and subject to indictment, trial, judgment, and punishment, according to law.

Section 7

(2) Every bill which shall have passed the House of Representatives and the Senate shall, before it becomes a law, be presented to the President of the United States; if he approves he shall sign it, but if not he shall return it, with his objections, to that house in which it shall have originated, who shall enter the objections at large on their journal and proceed to reconsider it. If after such reconsideration two-thirds of that house shall agree to pass the bill, it shall be sent together with the objections, to the other house, by which it shall likewise be reconsidered, and if approved by two-thirds of that house it shall become a law. But in all such cases the votes of both houses shall be determined by yeas and nays, and the names of the persons voting for and against the bill shall be entered on the journal of each house respectively. If any bill shall not be returned by the President within ten days (Sundays excepted) after it shall have been presented to him, the same shall be a law, in

like manner as if he had signed it, unless the Congress by their adjournment prevent its return, in which case it shall not be a law.

(3) Every order, resolution, or vote to which the concurrence of the Senate and the House of Representatives may be necessary (except on a question of adjournment) shall be presented to the President of the United States; and before the same shall take effect, shall be approved by him, or being disapproved by him shall be repassed by two-thirds of the Senate and House of Representatives, according to the rules and limitations prescribed in the case of a bill.

ARTICLE II

Section 1

(1) The executive power shall be vested in a President of the United States of America. He shall hold his office during the term of four years, and, together with the Vice President, chosen for the same term, be elected as follows:

(2) Each state shall appoint, in such manner as the legislature thereof may direct, a number of electors, equal to the whole number of Senators and Representatives to which the State may be entitled in the Congress; but no Senator or Representative, or person holding an office of trust or profit under the United States shall be appointed an elector.

(3) The electors shall meet in their respective states and vote by ballot for two persons, of whom one at least shall not be an inhabitant of the same state with themselves. And they shall make a list of all the persons voted for, and of the number of votes for each; which list they shall sign and certify and transmit to the seat of the government of the United States, directed to the President of the Senate. The President of the Senate shall, in the presence of the Senate and House of Representatives, open all the certificates, and the votes shall then be counted. The person having the greatest number of votes shall be the President, if such a number be a majority of the whole number of electors appointed; and if there be more than one who have such a majority, and have an equal number of votes, then the House of Representatives shall immediately choose by ballot one of them for President; and if no person have a majority, then from the five highest on the list the said House shall in like manner choose the President. But in choosing the President the votes shall be taken by states, the representation from each state having one vote; a quorum for this purpose shall consist of a member or members from two-thirds of the states, and a majority of all the states shall be necessary to a choice. In every case, after the choice of the President, the person having the greatest number of votes of the electors shall be the Vice President. But if there should remain two or more who have equal votes, the Senate shall choose from them by ballot the Vice President. [Superseded by the Twelfth Amendment.]

(4) The Congress may determine the time of choosing the electors and the day on which they shall give their votes, which day shall be the same throughout the United States.

(5) No person except a natural born citizen, or a citizen of the United States at the time of the adoption of this Constitution, shall be eligible to the office of President; neither shall any person be eligible to that office who shall not have attained to the age of thirty-five years, and been fourteen years a resident within the United States.

(6) In case of the removal of the President from office, or of his death, resignation, or inability to discharge the powers and duties of the said office, the same shall devolve

on the Vice President, and the Congress may by law provide for the case of removal, death, resignation, or inability, both of the President and Vice President, declaring what officer shall then act as President, and such officer shall act accordingly until the disability be removed or a President shall be elected. [Modified by the Twenty-fifth Amendment.]

(7) The President shall, at stated times, receive for his services a compensation, which shall neither be increased nor diminished during the period for which he shall have been elected, and he shall not receive within that period any other emolument from the United States or any of them.

(8) Before he enter on the execution of his office he shall take the following oath or affirmation:

"I do solemnly swear (or affirm) that I will faithfully execute the office of President of the United States, and will to the best of my ability preserve, protect, and defend the Constitution of the United States."

Section 2

(1) The President shall be Commander in Chief of the Army and Navy of the United States, and of the militia of the several states when called into the actual service of the United States; he may require the opinion, in writing, of the principal officer in each of the executive departments, upon any subject relating to the duties of their respective offices, and he shall have power to grant reprieves and pardons for offenses against the United States, except in cases of impeachment.

(2) He shall have power, by and with the advice and consent of the Senate, to make treaties, provided two-thirds of the Senators present concur; and he shall nominate, and by and with the advice and consent of the Senate, shall appoint ambassadors, other public ministers and consuls, judges of the Supreme Court, and all other officers of the United States, whose appointments are not herein otherwise provided for, and which shall be established by law; but the Congress may by law vest the appointment of such inferior officers, as they think proper, in the President alone, in the courts of law, or in the heads of departments.

(3) The President shall have the power to fill up all vacancies that may happen during the recess of the Senate, by granting commissions which shall expire at the end of their next session.

Section 3

He shall from time to time give to the Congress information of the state of the union, and recommend to their consideration such measures as he shall judge necessary and expedient; he may, on extraordinary occasions, convene both houses, or either of them, and in case of disagreement between them with respect to the time of adjournment, he may adjourn them to such time as he shall think proper; he shall receive ambassadors and other public ministers; he shall take care that the laws be faithfully executed, and shall commission all the officers of the United States.

Section 4

The President, Vice President, and all civil officers of the United States shall be removed from office on impeachment for and conviction of treason, bribery, or other high crimes and misdemeanors.

AMENDMENT XII (RATIFIED 1804)

The electors shall meet in their respective states and vote by ballot for President and Vice President, one of whom, at least, shall not be an inhabitant of the same state with themselves; they shall name in their ballots the person voted for as President, and in distinct ballots the person voted for as Vice President, and they shall make distinct lists of all persons voted for as President, and of all persons voted for as Vice President, and of the number of votes for each, which lists they shall sign and certify, and transmit sealed to the seat of the government of the United States, directed to the President of the Senate. The President of the Senate shall, in the presence of the Senate and House of Representatives, open all the certificates and the votes shall then be counted. The person having the greatest number of votes for President shall be the President, if such number be a majority of the whole number of electors appointed; and if no person have such majority, then from the persons having the highest numbers not exceeding three on the list of those voted for as President, the House of Representatives shall choose immediately, by ballot, the President. But in choosing the President the votes shall be taken by states, the representation from each state having one vote; a quorum for this purpose shall consist of a member or members from two-thirds of the states, and a majority of all states shall be necessary to a choice. And if the House of Representatives shall not choose a President whenever the right of choice shall devolve upon them, before the fourth day of March next following, then the Vice President shall act as President, as in the case of the death or other constitutional disability of the President. The person having the greatest number of votes as Vice President shall be the Vice President, if such number be a majority of the whole number of electors appointed, and if no person have a majority, then from the two highest numbers on the list the Senate shall choose the Vice President; a quorum for the purpose shall consist of two-thirds of the whole number of Senators, and a majority of the whole number shall be necessary to a choice. But no person constitutionally ineligible to the office of President shall be eligible to that of Vice President of the United States.

AMENDMENT XX (RATIFIED 1933)

Section 1

The terms of the President and Vice President shall end at noon on the 20th day of January, and the terms of Senators and Representatives at noon on the 3rd day of January, of the years in which such terms would have ended if this article had not been ratified; and the terms of their successors shall then begin.

Section 2

The Congress shall assemble at least once in every year, and such meeting shall begin at noon on the 3rd day of January, unless they shall by law appoint a different day.

Section 3

If, at the time fixed for the beginning of the term of the President, the President elect shall have died, the Vice President elect shall become President. If a President shall not have been chosen before the time fixed for the beginning of his term, or if the President elect shall have failed to qualify, then the Vice President elect shall act as President until a President shall have qualified; and the Congress may by law provide for the case wherein neither a President elect nor a Vice President elect shall have qualified, declaring who shall then act as President, or the manner in which one who is to act shall be selected, and such person shall act accordingly until a President or Vice President shall have qualified.

Section 4

The Congress may by law provide for the case of the death of any of the persons from whom the House of Representatives may choose a President whenever the right of choice shall have devolved upon them, and for the case of the death of any of the persons from whom the Senate may choose a Vice President whenever the right of choice shall have devolved upon them.

AMENDMENT XXII (RATIFIED 1951)

Section 1

No person shall be elected to the office of the President more than twice, and no person who has held the office of President, or acted as President, for more than two years of a term to which some other person was elected President shall be elected to the office of President more than once. But this article shall not apply to any person holding the office of the President when this article was proposed by the Congress, and shall not prevent any person who may be holding the office of President, or acting as President, during the term within which this article becomes operative from holding the office of President or acting as President during the remainder of such term.

AMENDMENT XXIII (RATIFIED 1961)

Section 1

The District constituting the seat of Government of the United States shall appoint in such manner as the Congress may direct:

A number of electors of President and Vice President equal to the whole number of Senators and Representatives in Congress to which the District would be entitled if it were a State, but in no event more than the least populous State, they shall be in addition to those appointed by the States but they shall be considered, for the purposes of the election of President and Vice President, to be electors appointed by a State; and they shall meet in the District and perform such duties as provided by the twelfth article of amendment.

Section 2

The Congress shall have power to enforce this article by appropriate legislation.

AMENDMENT XXIV (RATIFIED 1964)

Section 1

The right of citizens of the United States to vote in any primary or other election for President or Vice President, or for Senator or Representative in Congress, shall not be denied or abridged by the United States or any State by reason of failure to pay any poll tax or other tax.

Section 2

The Congress shall have the power to enforce this article by appropriate legislation.

AMENDMENT XXV (RATIFIED 1967)

Section 1

In case of a removal of the President from office or of his death or resignation, the Vice President shall become President.

Section 2

Whenever there is a vacancy in the office of the Vice President, the President shall nominate a Vice President who shall take office upon confirmation by a majority vote of both Houses of Congress.

Section 3

Whenever the President transmits to the President pro tempore of the Senate and the Speaker of the House of Representatives his written declaration that he is unable to discharge the powers and duties of his office, and until he transmits to them a written declaration to the contrary, such powers and duties shall be discharged by the Vice President as Acting President.

Section 4

Whenever the Vice President and a majority of either the principal officers of the executive department or of such other body as Congress may by law provide, transmit to the President pro tempore of the Senate and the Speaker of the House of Representatives their written declaration that the President is unable to discharge the powers and duties of his office, the Vice President shall immediately assume the powers and duties of the office as Acting President.

Thereafter, when the President transmits to the President pro tempore of the Senate and the Speaker of the House of Representatives his written declaration that no inability exists, he shall resume the powers and duties of his office unless the Vice President and a majority of either the principal officers of the executive department or of such other body as Congress may by law provide, transmit within four days to the President pro tempore of the Senate and the Speaker of the House of Representatives their written declaration that the President is unable to discharge the power and duties of his office. Thereupon Congress shall decide the issue, assembling within forty-eight hours for that purpose if not in session. If the Congress, within twenty-one days after receipt of the latter written declaration, or, if Congress is not in session, within twenty-one days after Congress is required to assemble, determines by two-thirds vote of both Houses that the President is unable to discharge the powers and duties of his office, the Vice President shall continue to discharge the same as Acting President; otherwise, the President shall resume the powers and duties of his office.

Selected Bibliography

GENERAL WORKS ON THE PRESIDENCY

Barger, Harold M., *The Impossible Presidency* (Glenview, IL: Scott, Foresman, 1984).

Corwin, E. S., *The President: Office and Powers, 1787–1984,* 5th ed., eds. Randall W. Bland, Theodore H. Hindson, and Jack W. Peltason (New York: New York University Press, 1985).

Cronin, Thomas E., *The State of the Presidency,* 2nd ed. (Boston: Little, Brown, 1980).

DiClerico, Robert C., *The American President,* 2nd ed. (Englewood Cliffs, NJ: Prentice-Hall, 1983).

Funderburk, Charles, *Presidents and Politics: The Limits of Power* (Monterey, CA: Brooks/Cole, 1982).

Griffith, Ernest S., *The American Presidency: The Dilemmas of Shared Power and Divided Government* (New York: New York University Press, 1976).

Hargrove, Erwin, *The Power of the Modern Presidency* (New York: Knopf, 1974).

Hoxie, R. Gordon, *The Presidency of the 1970's* (New York: Center for the Study of the Presidency, 1973).

Hughes, Emmet John, *The Living Presidency* (Baltimore: Penguin, 1974).

Hyman, Sidney, *The American President* (New York: Harper & Row, 1954).

James, Dorothy, *The Contemporary Presidency* (New York: Pegasus, 1974).

Kallenbach, Joseph E., *The American Chief Executive* (New York: Harper & Row, 1966).

Koenig, Louis W., *The Chief Executive,* 4th ed. (New York: Harcourt Brace Jovanovich, 1981).

Laski, Harold J., *The American Presidency* (New York: Harper Brothers, 1940).

McConnell, Grant, *The Modern Presidency,* 2nd ed. (New York: St. Martin's, 1976).

Mullen, William F., *Presidential Power and Politics* (New York: St. Martin's, 1976).

Page, Benjamin I., and Petracca, Mark P., *The American Presidency* (New York: McGraw-Hill, 1983).

Pious, Richard M., *The American Presidency* (New York: Basic Books, 1979).

Reedy, George, *The Twilight of the Presidency* (New York: New American Library, 1970).

Rossiter, Clinton, *The American Presidency,* rev. ed. (New York: Mentor Books, 1960).

Sickels, Robert J., *The Presidency* (Englewood Cliffs, NJ: Prentice-Hall, 1980).

Strum, Philippa, *Presidential Power and American Democracy,* 2nd ed. (Pacific Palisades, CA: Goodyear, 1979).

Tatalovich, Raymond, and Daynes, Byron W., *Presidential Power in the United States* (Monterey, CA: Brooks/Cole, 1984).

Thach, C. C., Jr., *The Creation of the Presidency, 1775–1789: A Study in Constitutional History* (Baltimore: Johns Hopkins University Press, 1922).

Watson, Richard A., and Thomas, Norman C., *The Politics of the Presidency* (New York: Wiley, 1983).

Wayne, Stephen, and Edwards, George C., III, *Presidential Leadership* (New York: St. Martin's, 1985).

ANTHOLOGIES ON THE PRESIDENCY

Bach, Stanley, and Sulzer, George T., eds., *Perspectives on the Presidency* (Lexington, MA: Heath, 1974).

Barber, James David, ed., *Choosing the President* (Englewood Cliffs, NJ: Prentice-Hall, 1974).

———, ed., *Race for the Presidency: The Media and the Nominating Process* (Englewood Cliffs, NJ: Prentice-Hall, 1978).

Bessette, Joseph M., and Tulis, Jeffrey, eds., *The Presidency in the Constitution* (Baton Rouge: Louisiana State University Press, 1981).

Caraley, Demetrios, *The Presidential War Powers* (New York: Academy of Political Science, 1984).

Cronin, Thomas E., ed., *Rethinking the Presidency* (Boston: Little, Brown, 1982).

Cronin, Thomas E., and Tugwell, Rexford G., eds., *The Presidency Reappraised,* 2nd ed. (New York: Praeger, 1977).

Dolce, Philip C., and Skau, George H., eds., *Power and the Presidency* (New York: Scribner's, 1976).

Franck, Thomas M., ed., *The Tethered Presidency* (New York: New York University Press, 1981).

Greenstein, Fred I., ed., *The Reagan Presidency* (Baltimore: Johns Hopkins University Press, 1983).

Harmel, Robert, ed., *Presidents and Their Parties: Leadership or Neglect* (New York: Praeger, 1984).

Heclo, Hugh, and Salomon, Lester M., eds., *The Illusion of Presidential Government* (Boulder, CO: Westview, 1981).

Hirschfield, Robert R., ed., *The Power of the Presidency,* 3rd ed. (New York: Aldine, 1982).

King, Anthony, ed., *Both Ends of the Avenue* (Washington, DC: American Enterprise Institute, 1983).

————, ed., *The New American Political System* (Washington, DC: American Enterprise Institute, 1978).

Latham, Earl, ed., *J. F. Kennedy and Presidential Power* (Lexington, MA: Heath, 1972).

Lengle, James I., and Shafer, Bryon E., eds., *Presidential Politics: Readings on Nominations and Elections,* 2nd ed. (New York: St. Martin's, 1983).

Malbin, Michael J., ed., *Money and Politics in the United States* (Washington, DC: American Enterprise Institute, 1984).

Mann, Thomas, and Ornstein, Norman, eds., *The New Congress* (Washington, DC: American Enterprise Institute, 1981).

Mansfield, Harvey C., Sr., ed., *Congress Against the President* (New York: Harper & Row, 1975).

Ornstein, Norman J., ed., *President and Congress: Assessing Reagan's First Year* (Washington, DC: American Enterprise Institute, 1982).

Palmer, John L., and Sawhill, Isabel V., eds., *The Reagan Record* (Cambridge, MA: Ballinger, 1984).

Polsby, Nelson, ed., *The Modern Presidency* (New York: Random House, 1973).

Ranney, Austin, ed., *The Past and Future of Presidential Debates* (Washington, DC: American Enterprise Institute, 1979).

Roberts, Charles, ed., *Has the President Too Much Power?* (New York: Harper & Row, 1974).

Salomon, Lester M., and Lund, Michael S., eds., *The Reagan Presidency and the Governing of America* (Washington, DC: Urban Institute Press, 1984).

Thomas, Norman C., ed., *The Presidency in Contemporary Context* (New York: Dodd, Mead, 1975).

Thomas, Norman C., and Baade, Hans W., eds., *The Institutionalized Presidency* (Dobbs Ferry, NY: Oceana, 1972).

Wilcox, Francis, and Franck, Richard, eds., *The Constitution and the Conduct of Foreign Policy* (New York: Praeger, 1976).

Wildavsky, Aaron, ed., *The Presidency* (Boston: Little, Brown, 1969).

————, ed., *Perspectives on the Presidency* (Boston: Little, Brown, 1975).

CAMPAIGNS, ELECTIONS, PARTIES, AND THE ELECTORAL COLLEGE

Abrahamson, Paul R., Aldrich, John, and Rohde, David W., *Change and Continuity in the 1980 Elections* (Washington, DC: Congressional Quarterly Press, 1982).

Aldrich, John H., *Before the Convention* (Chicago: University of Chicago Press, 1980).

Alexander, Herbert E., *Financing Politics: Money, Elections and Political Reform* (Washington, DC: Congressional Quarterly Press, 1980).

Asher, Herbert, *Presidential Elections and American Politics,* 3rd ed. (Homewood, IL: Dorsey, 1984).

Best, Judith, *The Case Against the Direct Election of the President: A Defense of the Electoral College* (Ithaca, NY: Cornell University Press, 1975).

Bickel, Alexander, *The New Age of Political Reform: The Electoral College, the Convention, and the Party System* (New York: Harper & Row, 1968).

Bishop, George F., et al., *The Presidential Debates: Media, Electoral and Policy Perspectives* (New York: Harper & Row, 1978).

Brams, Steven, *The Presidential Election Game* (New Haven, CT: Yale University Press, 1978).

Broder, David S., *The Party's Over* (New York: Harper & Row, 1971).

Burns, James Macgregor, *The Deadlock of Democracy: Four-Party Politics in America* (Englewood Cliffs, NJ: Prentice-Hall, 1963).

Ceaser, James W., *Presidential Selection: Theory and Development* (Princeton, NJ: Princeton University Press, 1979).

———, *Reforming the Reforms* (Cambridge, MA: Ballinger, 1982).

Chester, Lewis, Hodgson, Godfrey, and Page, Bruce, *An American Melodrama: The Presidential Campaign of 1968* (New York: Viking, 1969).

Crotty, William, and Jackson, John S., III, *Presidential Primaries and Nominations* (Washington, DC: Congressional Quarterly Press, 1985).

David, Paul T., Goldman, Ralph M., and Bain, Richard C., *The Politics of National Party Conventions* (Washington, DC: The Brookings Institution, 1960).

Davis, James W., *National Conventions in an Age of Party Reform* (Westport, CT: Greenwood, 1983).

———, *Presidential Primaries: Road to the White House,* 2nd ed. (Westport, CT: Greenwood, 1980).

DiClerico, Robert C., and Uslaner, Eric M., *Few Are Chosen: Problems of Presidential Selection* (New York: McGraw-Hill, 1984).

Germond, Jack W., and Witcover, Jules, *Blue Smoke and Mirrors: How Reagan Won and How Carter Lost the Election of 1980* (New York: Viking, 1981).

Goldman, Peter, and Fuller, Tony, *The Quest for the Presidency, 1984* (New York: Bantam, 1985).

Keech, William B., and Matthews, Donald B., *The Party's Choice* (Washington, DC: The Brookings Institution, 1976).

Lammers, William W., *Presidential Politics: Patterns and Prospects* (New York: Harper & Row, 1976).

Longley, Lawrence, and Braun, Allen, *The Politics of Electoral College Reform* (New York: Yale University Press, 1972).

Marshall, Thomas R., *Presidential Nominations in a Reform Age* (New York: Praeger, 1981).

Nelson, Michael, ed., *The Elections of 1984* (Washington, DC: Congressional Quarterly Press, 1985).

Novak, Michael, *Choosing Our King* (New York: Macmillan, 1974).

Page, Benjamin I., *Choices and Echoes in Presidential Candidates* (Chicago: University of Chicago Press, 1978).

Peirce, Neal R., and Longley, Lawrence D., *The People's President: The Electoral College in American History and the Direct Vote Alternative,* rev. ed. (New Haven, CT: Yale University Press, 1981).

Polsby, Nelson W., *Consequences of Party Reform* (New York: Oxford University Press, 1983).

Polsby, Nelson, and Wildavsky, Aaron, *Presidential Elections: Strategies of American Electoral Politics,* 6th ed. (New York: Scribner, 1984).

Pomper, Gerald, ed., *The Election of 1980: Reports and Interpretations* (Chatham, NJ: Chatham House, 1981).

———, ed., *The Election of 1984* (Chatham, NJ: Chatham House, 1985).

Ranney, Austin, *Curing the Mischiefs of Faction* (Berkeley: The University of California Press, 1975).

Roseboom, Eugene H., *A History of Presidential Elections* (New York: Macmillan, 1964).

Sayre, Wallace S., and Parris, Judith H., *Voting for President* (Washington, DC: The Brookings Institution, 1970).

Schram, Martin, *Running for President, 1976: The Carter Campaign* (New York: Stein & Day, 1977).

Watson, Richard, *The Presidential Contest,* 2nd ed. (New York: Wiley, 1984).

Wayne, Stephen, *The Road to the White House,* 2nd ed. (New York: St. Martin's, 1984).

White, Theodore H., *The Making of the President: 1960, 1964, 1968, and 1972* (New York: Atheneum, 1961, 1965, 1969, and 1973).

Witcover, Jules, *Marathon: Pursuit of the Presidency* (New York: Viking, 1977).

PRESIDENTIAL LEADERSHIP

Bailey, Thomas, *Presidential Greatness* (Englewood Cliffs, NJ: Prentice-Hall, 1966).

Barrett, Laurence I., *Gambling with History: Reagan in the White House* (New York: Doubleday, 1983).

Buchanan, Bruce, *The Presidential Experience: What the Office Does to the Man* (Englewood Cliffs, NJ: Prentice-Hall, 1978).

Burns, James Macgregor, *Presidential Government: The Crucible of Leadership* (New York: Avon Books, 1967).

Califano, Joseph A., Jr., *A Presidential Nation* (New York: Norton, 1976).

Donovan, Robert J., *Tumultuous Years: The Presidency of Harry S Truman, 1949–1953* (New York: Norton, 1982).

Fishel, Jeff, *Presidents and Promises* (Washington, DC: Congressional Quarterly Press, 1985).

Halberstam, David, *The Best and the Brightest* (New York: Random House, 1972).

Hargrove, Erwin C., and Nelson, Michael, *Presidents, Politics, and Policy* (Baltimore: Johns Hopkins University Press, 1984).

Jordan, Hamilton, *Crisis: The Last Year of the Carter Presidency* (New York: Putnam's, 1982).

Leuchtenberg, William E., *Franklin D. Roosevelt and the New Deal* (New York: Harper & Row, 1963).

———, *In the Shadow of FDR: From Harry Truman to Ronald Reagan* (Ithaca, NY: Cornell University Press, 1983).

Neustadt, Richard E., *Presidential Power: The Politics of Leadership from FDR to Carter* (New York: Wiley, 1980).

O'Brien, Laurence, *No Final Victories: From John F. Kennedy to Watergate* (Garden City, NY: Doubleday, 1974).

Rockman, Bert, *The Leadership Question: The Presidency and the American System* (New York: Praeger, 1984).

Safire, William, *Before the Fall: An Inside View of the Pre-Watergate White House* (Garden City, NY: Doubleday, 1975).

Schlesinger, Arthur M., Jr., *The Coming of the New Deal* (Boston: Houghton Mifflin, 1958).

Sorenson, Theodore C., *Watchman in the Night: Presidential Accountability and Watergate* (Cambridge, MA: MIT Press, 1975).

Woodward, Robert, and Bernstein, Carl, *All the President's Men* (New York: Simon & Schuster, 1974).

THE PUBLIC PRESIDENCY

Cornwell, Elmer E., Jr., *Presidential Leadership of Public Opinion* (Bloomington: Indiana University Press, 1965).

Edwards, George C., III, *The Public Presidency* (New York: St. Martin's, 1983).

Edwards, George C., III, Shull, Steven A., and Thomas, Norman C., eds., *The Presidency and Public Policy Making* (Pittsburgh: University of Pittsburgh Press, 1985).

Graber, Doris A., *Mass Media and American Politics* (Washington, DC: Congressional Quarterly Press, 1980).

Grossman, Michael Baruch, and Kumar, Martha Joynt, *Portraying the President* (Baltimore: Johns Hopkins University Press, 1981).

Hodgson, Godfrey, *All Things to All Men* (New York: Simon & Schuster, 1980).

Kellerman, Barbara, *The Political Presidency* (New York: Oxford University Press, 1984).

Kernell, Samuel, *Going Public* (Washington, DC: Congressional Quarterly Press, 1986).

Lowi, Theodore J., *The Personal Presidency* (Ithaca, NY: Cornell University Press, 1985).

McGinniss, Joe, *The Selling of the President, 1968* (New York: Pocket Books, 1969).

Minow, Newton N., Martin, John Bartlow, and Mitchell, Lee M., *Presidential Television* (New York: Basic Books, 1973).

Miroff, Bruce, *Pragmatic Illusions: The Presidential Politics of John F. Kennedy* (New York: McKay, 1976).

Paletz, David L., and Entman, Robert M., *Media Power Politics* (New York: Free Press, 1981).

Patterson, Thomas E., *The Mass Media Election: How Americans Choose Their President* (New York: Praeger, 1980).

Patterson, Thomas E., and McClure, Robert, *The Unseeing Eye: The Myth of Television Power in National Elections* (New York: Putnam's, 1976).

Ranney, Austin, *Channels of Power* (Washington, DC: American Enterprise Institute, 1984).

Robinson, Michael J., and Sheehan, Margaret A., *Over the Wire and on T.V. CBS and UPI in Campaign '80* (New York: Sage, 1983).

Rubin, Richard L., *Press, Party, and Presidency* (New York: Norton, 1981).

Saldich, Anne Rowley, *Electronic Democracy* (New York: Praeger, 1979).

Spear, Joseph C., *Presidents and the Press* (Cambridge, MA: MIT Press, 1986).

Spragens, William C., *The Presidency and the Mass Media in the Age of Television* (Washington, DC: University Press of America, 1978).

THE PRESIDENT AND CONGRESS

Binkley, Wilfred E., *The President and Congress,* 3rd ed. (New York: Vintage, 1962).

Davidson, Roger H., and Oleszek, Walter J., *Congress and Its Members,* 2nd ed. (Washington, DC: Congressional Quarterly Press, 1985).

Edwards, George C., III, *Presidential Influence in Congress* (San Francisco: Freeman, 1980).

Fisher, Louis, *Constitutional Conflicts Between Congress and the President* (Princeton, NJ: Princeton University Press, 1985).

———, *President and Congress* (New York: Free Press, 1972).

Moe, Ronald, ed., *Congress and the President: Allies and Adversaries* (Pacific Palisades, CA: Goodyear, 1971).

Shull, Steven A., *Domestic Policy Formation: Presidential-Congressional Partnership?* (Westport, CT: Greenwood, 1983).

Shuman, Howard E., *Politics and the Budget: The Struggle Between the President and Congress* (Englewood Cliffs, NJ: Prentice-Hall, 1984).

Sundquist, James L., *The Decline and Resurgence of Congress* (Washington, DC: The Brookings Institution, 1981).

Wayne, Stephen J., *The Legislative Presidency* (New York: Harper & Row, 1978).

Wilson, Woodrow, *Congressional Government (1885),* 2 vols. (New York: Meridian Edition, 1918).

PRESIDENTIAL WARMAKING

Corwin, Edward, *Total War and the Constitution* (Westminster, MD: Knopf, 1947).

Eagleton, Thomas, *War and Presidential Power* (New York: Liveright, 1974).

Hassler, W. W., Jr., *The President as Commander in Chief* (Reading, MA: Addison-Wesley, 1971).

Holt, Pat M., *The War Powers Resolution* (Washington, DC: American Enterprise Institute, 1978).

Javits, Jacob, *Who Makes War?* (New York: Morrow, 1973).

Mueller, John, *War, Presidents and Public Opinion* (New York: Wiley, 1973).

Pusey, Merlo, *The Way We Go to War* (Boston: Houghton Mifflin, 1969).

Rossiter, Clinton, *Constitutional Dictatorship* (Princeton, NJ: Princeton University Press, 1948).

NATIONAL SECURITY AND FOREIGN POLICY

Barilleaux, Ryan J., *The President and Foreign Affairs: Evaluation, Performance, and Power* (New York: Praeger, 1985).

Crabb, Cecil V., Jr., and Holt, Pat, *Invitation to Struggle: Congress, the President and Foreign Policy* (Washington, DC: Congressional Quarterly Press, 1980).

Destler, I. M., *Presidents, Bureaucrats, and Foreign Policy* (Princeton, NJ: Princeton University Press, 1972).

George, Alexander L., *Presidential Decision-Making in Foreign Policy: The Effective Use of Information and Advice* (Boulder: CO: Westview, 1980).

Henkin, Louis, *Foreign Affairs and the Constitution* (New York: Norton, 1975).

Hunter, Robert E., *Presidential Control of Foreign Policy* (New York: Praeger, 1982).

Kolko, Gabriel, *The Roots of American Foreign Policy* (Boston: Beacon, 1969).

Neuchterlein, Donald E., *National Interests and Presidential Leadership: The Setting of Priorities* (Boulder, CO: Westview, 1978).

Plischke, Elmer, *Diplomat in Chief* (Westport, CT: Greenwood, 1986).

ADMINISTRATIVE LEADERSHIP AND MANAGING THE WHITE HOUSE

Anderson, Patrick, *The President's Men* (Garden City, NY: Doubleday, 1968).

Berman, Larry, *The Office of Management and Budget and the Presidency, 1921–1979* (Princeton, NJ: Princeton University Press, 1979).

Fenno, Richard T., Jr., *The President's Cabinet* (Cambridge, MA: Harvard University Press, 1959).

Fisher, Louis, *Presidential Spending Power* (Princeton NJ: Princeton University Press, 1975).

Heineman, Ben W., Jr., and Hessler, Curtis A., *Memorandum for the President* (New York: Random House, 1980).

Hess, Stephen, *Organizing the Presidency* (Washington, DC: The Brookings Institution, 1976).

Johnson, Richard T., *Managing the White House* (New York: Harper & Row, 1974).

Light, Paul C., *The President's Agenda* (Baltimore: Johns Hopkins University Press, 1982).

Nathan, Richard P., *The Administrative Presidency* (New York: Wiley, 1983).

———, *The Plot that Failed: Nixon's Administrative Presidency* (New York: Wiley, 1975).

Pfiffner, James P., *The President, the Budget and Congress: Impoundment and the 1974 Budget Act* (Boulder, CO: Westview, 1979).

Tufte, Edward R., *Political Control of the Economy* (Princeton, NJ: Princeton University Press, 1978).

PRESIDENTS, THE SUPREME COURT, AND THE CONSTITUTION

Abraham, Henry J., *The Judicial Process,* 4th ed. (New York: Oxford University Press, 1980).

———, *Justices and the President: A Political History of Appointments to the Supreme Court* (New York: Penguin, 1974).

Berger, Raoul, *Impeachment: The Constitutional Problems* (Cambridge, MA: Harvard University Press, 1973).

Bowen, Catherine Drinker, *Miracle at Philadelphia* (Boston: Atlantic-Little, Brown, 1966, 1986).

Fisher, Louis, *The Constitution Between Friends* (New York: St. Martin's, 1978).

Genovese, Michael A. *The Supreme Court, the Constitution and Presidential Power* (Lanham, MD: University Press of America, 1980).

Jensen, Merrill, *The Articles of Confederation* (Madison: The University of Wisconsin Press, 1940).

Pritchett, C. Herman, *The American Constitution,* 2nd ed. (New York: McGraw-Hill, 1968).

Rossiter, Clinton, *The American Presidency,* rev. ed. (New York: Mentor, 1960).

Schlesinger, Arthur M., Jr., *The Imperial Presidency* (Boston: Houghton Mifflin, 1973).

Schubert, Glendon, *The Presidency in the Courts* (Minneapolis: University of Minnesota Press, 1957).

Scigliano, Robert, *The Supreme Court and the President* (New York: Free Press, 1971).

THE VICE-PRESIDENCY

Bayh, Birch, *One Heartbeat Away: Presidential Disability and Succession* (Indianapolis: Bobbs-Merrill, 1968).

Dorman, Michael, *The Second Man* (New York: Dell, 1968).

Feerick, John D., *The Twenty-Fifth Amendment* (New York: Fordham University Press, 1976).

Goldstein, Joel K., *The Modern Vice Presidency* (Princeton, NJ: Princeton University Press, 1982).

Light, Paul C., *Vice Presidential Power* (Baltimore: Johns Hopkins University Press, 1984).

Natoli, Marie D., *American Prince, American Pauper: Contemporary Vice Presidency in Perspective* (Westport, CT: Greenwood, 1985).

Sindler, Allan P., *Unchosen Presidents* (Berkeley: University of California Press, 1976).

Young, Donald, *American Roulette: The History and Dilemma of the Vice Presidency* (New York: Viking, 1974).

REMAKING THE PRESIDENCY

Finer, Herman, *The Presidency: Crisis and Regeneration* (Chicago: University of Chicago Press, 1960).

Hardin, Charles M., *Presidential Power and Accountability: Toward a New Constitution* (Chicago: University of Chicago Press, 1974).

Mondale, Walter F., *The Accountability of Power: Toward a Responsible Presidency* (New York: McKay, 1975).

Rose, Richard, and Suleiman, Ezra, *Presidents and Prime Ministers* (Washington, DC: American Enterprise Institute, 1980).

Shogan, Robert, *None of the Above* (New York: New American Library, 1982).

Sorenson, Theodore C., *A Different Kind of President* (New York: Harper & Row, 1984).

Sundquist, James L., *Constitutional Reform and Effective Government* (Washington, DC: The Brookings Institution, 1986).

Tugwell, Rexford, *The Enlargement of the Presidency* (New York: Doubleday, 1960).

BIOGRAPHIES, AUTOBIOGRAPHIES, AND PSYCHOLOGICAL STUDIES

Ambrose, Stephen E., *Eisenhower the President,* vol. 2 of *Eisenhower* (New York: Simon & Schuster, 1984).

Bailey, Thomas A., *Presidential Greatness: The Image and the Man from George Washington to the Present* (New York: Appleton-Century-Crofts, 1972).

Barber, James David, *The Presidential Character,* 3rd ed. (Englewood Cliffs, NJ: Prentice-Hall, 1985).

Boyarsky, Bill, *Ronald Reagan: His Life and Rise to the Presidency* (New York: Random House, 1981).

Cannon, Lou, *Reagan* (New York: Putnam, 1982).

Donovan, Robert J., *Eisenhower: The Inside Story* (New York: Harper & Row, 1956).

Evans, Rowland, and Novak, Robert, *Lyndon Johnson: The Exercise of Power* (New York: New American Library, 1966).

Fairlie, Henry, *The Kennedy Promise* (Garden City, NY: Doubleday, 1973).

Ford, Gerald, *A Time to Heal: The Autobiography of Gerald R. Ford* (New York: Harper & Row, 1979).

Freidel, Frank, *Franklin D. Roosevelt,* 4 vols. (Boston: Little, Brown, 1952–1973).

Glad, Betty, *Jimmy Carter: In Search of the Great White House* (New York: Norton, 1980).

Goldman, Eric, *The Tragedy of Lyndon Johnson* (New York: Knopf, 1969).

Greenstein, Fred I., *The Hidden Hand Presidency* (New York: Basic Books, 1982).

Hargrove, Erwin C., *Presidential Leadership: Personality and Political Style* (New York: Macmillan, 1966).

Johnson, Lyndon B., *The Vantage Point: Perspectives of the Presidency* (New York: Holt, Rinehart and Winston, 1971).

Kearns, Doris, *Lyndon Johnson and the American Dream* (New York: Harper & Row, 1976).

Link, Arthur, *Woodrow Wilson,* 5 vols. (Princeton, NJ: Princeton University Press, 1917–1955).

Nixon, Richard M., *Six Crises* (Garden City, NY: Doubleday, 1962).

Parmet, Herbert S., *Eisenhower and the American Crusades* (New York: Macmillan, 1972).

———, *JFK: The Presidency of John F. Kennedy* (New York: Penguin, 1984).

Philips, Cabell, *The Truman Presidency* (New York: Macmillan, 1966).

Schlesinger, Arthur M., Jr., *A Thousand Days* (Boston: Houghton Mifflin, 1965).

Sorenson, Theodore C., *Kennedy* (New York: Bantam, 1966).

Index